BEING "DUTCH" IN THE INDIES

BEING "DUTCH" IN THE INDIES

A History of Creolisation and Empire, 1500–1920

Ulbe Bosma and Remco Raben

Translated by
Wendie Shaffer

NUS PRESS
SINGAPORE

OHIO UNIVERSITY
RESEARCH IN INTERNATIONAL STUDIES
SOUTHEAST ASIA SERIES NO. 116

OHIO UNIVERSITY PRESS
ATHENS

First published by:

NUS Press
National University of Singapore
AS3-01-02, 3 Arts Link
Singapore 117569

Fax: (65) 6774-0652
E-mail: nusbooks@nus.edu.sg
Website: http://www.nus.edu.sg/npu

ISBN 978-9971-69-373-2 (Paper)

Published for distribution in the United States by:

Ohio University Press
Ohio University Research in International Studies
Southeast Asia Series
Athens, OH 45701, USA

Executive editor: Gillian Berchowitz
Area consultant: William H. Frederick

Website: http://www.ohioswallow.com

ISBN-10   0-89680-261-2
ISBN-13 978-0-89680-261-2

National Library Board Singapore Cataloguing in Publication Data

Bosma, Ulbe, 1962–
    Being "Dutch" in the Indies: a history of creolisation and empire, 1500–1920
    / Ulbe Bosma and Remco Raben; translated by Wendie Shaffer. – Singapore:
    NUS Press, c2008.
    p. cm.
    Includes bibliographical references and index.
    ISBN-13 : 978-9971-69-373-2 (pbk.)

    1. Dutch – Asia – History. 2. Indonesia – History – 1478–1798. 3. Indonesia
    – History – 1798–1942. I. Raben, R. (Remco). II. Shaffer, Wendie. III. Title.

DS643
959.802 – dc22   SLS2007016887

Printed in Singapore

Contents

List of Illustrations   viii

Abbreviations   x

Acknowledgements   xi

Prologue   xiii

Chapter 1   **Separation and Fusion**   1
             Crossroad of peoples   1
             Europeans   8
             Colonies and classifications   14
             Racism and mestisation   21

Chapter 2   **The Baggage of Colonialism**   26
             Christian discipline   26
             Marriage and citizenship   33
             Mixtures in Ceylon   38
             Javanese circuit   42
             Slave children   46
             Asian Burghers   51
             Career in the Dutch East Indies   54
             Demarcation lines   59

Chapter 3   Contraction   66
             The shrinking world of the Indies   66
             Malaccan diaspora   72
             Citizens of Ceylon   76
             New masters, old patterns   83
             In the service of England   89
             Landed gentry and powerful merchants   94

Chapter 4   Lordly Traditions and Plantation Industrialism   104
The Principalities   106
Two contrasting worlds: Surakarta and Yogyakarta   112
The economic cycle of Central Java   119
Landholders in the Sunda   124
Dissolving views   128
Ups and downs of life in the Principalities   134
The noble landlord   137

Chapter 5   Mixed Worlds in the Eastern Archipelago   143
Makassar   144
Wide is the sea and Banda small   150
Variations of mestisation   159
Ternate: economic stagnation and social mobility   161
Ambon: citizens, civil servants and migrants   166
Soldiers and teachers   173
Civil servants of Makassar   176

Chapter 6   Rank and Status   184
Newcomers   184
Competition   188
Anxious fathers and voices of rancour   194
A distinctly "Indische" voice   201
Schooling   206
Opportunities   211
Race and status in the world of the East Indies   215

Chapter 7   The Underclass   219
Upstairs, downstairs   219
Civic registry   223
The discovery of pauperism   228
Living on charity   236
Life in the barracks   244
Propagating the artisan   250

Chapter 8   Crisis and Change in the Indische World   258
Family firms in an age of economic consolidation   262
Aftermath of the agricultural crisis   266
Survival strategies   269
Cris de coeur of early nationalism   276

Recognition for Jong Indië 280
Two newspapers: *De Oosterling* and *De Telefoon* 284

Chapter 9 **"Indische": Defined and Identified** 293
Indische grievances and the prejudices of
the motherland 297
The Indische Bond, the union for
Indo-Europeans 305
The Indo-pauper revisited 309
Discrimination and education 313
The Indische Party 320
The Dutch East Indies: old and new 328
A fork in the road 334

Epilogue: End of an Old World 339

Glossary 344

Notes 348

Bibliography 392

Index 421

List of Illustrations

1.   Map of Asia   2

2.   Europeans and their slaves in Ceylon, 1660s   30

3.   Children in the Batavia orphanage, 1682   33

4.   The Resident's office in Surakarta, *ca.* 1822   45

5.   The "Portuguese" church in Batavia, *ca.* 1775   48

6.   A "Portuguese" woman and two Sinhalese butter-traders,
     Ceylon, 1785   54

7.   A tea visit in Batavia, 1780s   65

8.   Slave market in Batavia, mid-19th century   71

9.   Portrait of Pieter Philip Juriaan Quint Ondaatje   79

10. Houses in Colombo Fort, 1888   83

11. Portrait of Catharina Rica Cranssen   89

12. The estate of Campea, West Java, 1833   96

13. Portrait of Andries de Wilde   99

14. A general store in Batavia, mid-19th century   101

15. Portrait of Johannes Augustinus Dezentjé   108

16. Portrait of George Weijnschenk   111

17. Portrait of Carl Friedrich Winter   117

18. Portrait of Georgius Leonardus Dorrepaal   119

19. Portrait of Ludovica Manuel   122

20. The crown prince of Surakarta visiting the
     Dezentjé family at Ampel, *ca.* 1900   129

21. Portrait of Geertruida-Louisa Dom   132

22. David Birnie with wife and son in an automobile, 1905   140

23. Map of the Indonesian archipelago 142

24. The estate of Maros in southern Sulawesi, *ca.* 1824 147

25. Banda Neira, 1868 151

26. The Matalengko Estate on Banda, 1920s 153

27. A soirée in the palace of the sultan of Ternate, *ca.* 1840 165

28. Johannes Willem Mesman and his family, Cirebon, *ca.* 1905 182

29. The society *De Harmonie* and the tailor's shop of Oger Frères in Batavia, 1870s 196

30. The Willem III School in Batavia, *ca.* 1890 210

31. Photograph of Gottlieb Neumann, *ca.* 1890 213

32. Resident of Yogyakarta, Jan Abraham Ament and his family, *ca.* 1898 216

33. Buitenwachtstraat, Makassar, 1846 230

34. An African soldier of the Dutch Indies' Army with his children, mid-19th century 238

35. Parapattan orphanage, Batavia, 1880s 241

36. Military drill at the Army Training School in Gombong, 1898 248

37. Military orphans in the boys' home of Johannes van der Steur in Magelang, *ca.* 1897 251

38. The sugar factory Pangka on Java's north coast, 1872 260

39. Photograph of Carel van Stralendorff, *ca.* 1900 264

40. Visiting card of Johannes Augustinus Dezentjé, *ca.* 1900 266

41. Indische man posing with guitar, *ca.* 1915 274

42. The bookstore of G. Kolff & Co. in Batavia, *ca.* 1870 278

43. Staff at the Bantool sugar factory near Yogyakarta, *ca.* 1898 298

44. The editorial staff of the *Bataviaasch Nieuwsblad*, *ca.* 1909 316

45. Leaders of the Indische Party in the Netherlands, 1913 327

46. Demonstration in Batavia's Decca Park, 1916 330

47. Braga Street in Bandung, *ca.* 1920 340

Abbreviations

ANRI	Arsip Nasional Republik Indonesia, Jakarta
CBG	Centraal Bureau voor Genealogie, The Hague
GB	Gouvernementsbesluit (Governmental Decree)
Hisdoc	Afdeling Historische Documentatie
HTK	Handelingen der Tweede Kamer (Proceedings of the Lower House of the Dutch Parliament)
KB	Koninklijk Besluit (Royal Decree)
KoBib	Koninklijke Bibliotheek (Royal Library), The Hague
KITLV	Koninklijk Instituut voor Taal-, Land- en Volkenkunde (Royal Netherlands Institute of Southeast Asian and Caribbean Studies), Leiden
KV	Koloniaal Verslag (Annual report on the state of the colonies)
MvK I	Nationaal Archief, The Hague, Archief van het Ministerie van Koloniën 1814–1849
MvK II	Nationaal Archief, The Hague, Archief van het Ministerie van Koloniën 1850–1900
NA	Nationaal Archief, The Hague
NHM	Nationaal Archief, The Hague, Archief van de Nederlandsche Handel-Maatschappij (Netherlands Trading Company)
SLNA	Sri Lanka National Archives, Colombo
UBL	Universiteitsbibliotheek (University Library), Leiden
VOC	Nationaal Archief, The Hague, Archief van de Verenigde Oostindische Compagnie (Dutch East India Company)

Acknowledgements

In the book *Being "Dutch" in the Indies*, we have tried to chart new terrain — at least, terrain that was new to us. This meant hacking away a narrow path through a jungle of assumptions and *idées reçues*. A great many people have assisted us in our research, in preparing the book in Dutch, with the translation, and eventually in seeing it through the press.

First and foremost, we thank our wonderful, scholarly and creative translator Wendie Shaffer. As almost every word in this book is hers, this is in the first place *her* book.

The people at NUS Press have been extremely kind and trusting. We thank Paul Kratoska for taking us on, Sunandini Lal for her meticulous editing, Lena Qua for carefully preparing the manuscript and Winnifred Wong for doing much of the rest and for making the book available to see a wider public.

We thank Esther Tak and Maaike Mintjes for helping us in exploring archives and newspapers; Elsbeth Locher-Scholten for her kind comments; and Cees Fasseur, Jur van Goor and Jan Lucassen for their useful guidance. We are very grateful to the staff of the Arsip Nasional in Jakarta, the National Archives in Colombo, the Genealogical Bureau in The Hague (above all Peter Christiaans), the National Archives in The Hague, the Royal Netherlands Institute of Southeast Asian and Caribbean Studies in Leiden and the International Institute of Social History in Amsterdam for their unstinting help in providing the stuff of which this book is made.

We leave unmentioned the many friends and colleagues at home and abroad who have provided comments, criticism and hospitality at conferences, in workshops, and in private discussions during our research. Books carry few names but have many authors.

We thank our employers and colleagues at our home institutes, the International Institute of Social History and the Netherlands Institute for War Documentation, both in Amsterdam, for maintaining our jobs whilst we were involved in this project.

During our preparation and writing of the book we received financial assistance from the Netherlands Organisation for Scientific Research, which also financed the larger part of the translation. We thank them for their generous support.

Ulbe Bosma and Remco Raben
Utrecht and Amsterdam
July 2007

Prologue

This book discusses one aspect of the history of the old world of the Dutch East Indies. It recounts the fortunes of the "Indische" people, whose lives were inextricably interwoven with the East Indies but who to some extent considered themselves different from the indigenous people. The East Indies that we speak of does not comprise a single clear geographical entity, nor is it inhabited by a single well-defined community. Rather than zooming in on a clear cultural or racial category, we have tried to analyse the flux and fluidity of the Indische world. The essence of what we mean by "Indische" can be illustrated by some biographical facts about one woman.

Around 1870 the young Emilie Mesman sailed into the harbour of Surabaya. She was following her husband, Wilhelmus Henricus (Hein) Neijs, a lieutenant in the Netherlands-Indies army, to his home town on the island of Java. Emilie had come from Makassar, a busy port on the southern tip of Sulawesi — and for her, Java was utterly foreign. Her husband had many relatives in town, whom Emilie considered "thoroughly Javanese", reporting that they were "brown-skinned" and spoke Dutch with a heavy accent. The world in which Emilie had grown up was one of wealth and privilege. Her father owned vast plantations and operated several schooners that plied the Indonesian seas as far eastward as New Guinea (sometimes with his wife and children). Emilie's life was full of adventure: she encountered pirates on the neighbouring seas, she was brought up by friendly slaves, she went with her father on wild deer hunts. She attended soirées in the Dutch club in Makassar but was no stranger at the royal court of Tanete, a neighbouring principality. In Java, Emilie encountered a strange and incomprehensible world. Nevertheless, both her birthplace, Makassar, and Hein's native Surabaya belonged to the same geographical category: the old world of the Dutch East Indies, the Indische world. Emilie and Hein had Dutch names and were classified by the Dutch Registry Office as "Europeans", just like their parents. And, like their parents and grandparents before them, they had close ties with the Dutch colonial authority. The Neijs and Mesman families were not Javanese or Makassarese — they were Indische.

What defined the Indische world was that its members had grown up in the Dutch colonies, first under the Dutch East India Company (Verenigde Oostindische Compagnie, or VOC) and later under the government of the Netherlands Indies. Had there not been a colonial government in the East Indies, the Indische community would slowly have dissolved, as indeed it did when colonial rule ended. To speak of one unified Indische world would be far from accurate. This world resembled a string of loosely threaded beads; each place had its own culture, family networks, and social and ethnic fabric. However, despite local idiosyncrasies, the Indische communities were linked to one another and to the Dutch colonial government in countless ways. The government was the largest employer and determined the career opportunities of many. Far more than in the Dutch motherland, the government regulated economic life and intervened in social relationships. The unique nature of the Indische community was the product of continual migration of Europeans to the East Indies — and vice versa — together with the presence of the Dutch government administration controlling the colony's major economic activities and bestowing a distinctive status upon a group of the population of (partial) European ancestry. It also decreed by statutory regulation who belonged to which population group. Colonial authorities found it essential from their earliest days to stipulate boundaries: where did their domain end, and the realms of the indigenous begin?

The word "Indische" generally has two meanings: it can be used to imply "colonial", or it can signify "Mestizo", that is, of mixed racial origin. So, broadly speaking, we can say that Indische refers either to a power relationship or to racial mixture. But neither of these definitions is wholly satisfactory. For a start, we cannot argue that the Indische world was entirely a colonial construct, even though it could only have emerged because of colonialism. The dynamics of the life of local-born "Europeans" included religion, patterns of migration and economic opportunities. Furthermore, the colonial presence varied greatly from region to region.

If the "colonial" definition fails to satisfy, the same goes for the racial perspective. In those regions where population groups from differing cultures came together, a process took place that is widely known as mestisation or hybridisation — terms that imply mixing and cross-fertilisation in both the biological and the cultural sense.[1] There is something spurious about this notion of miscegenation; it cannot exist without the *idée fixe* of racial or cultural purity — an idea redolent with the preconceptions carried by the colonial newcomers. Furthermore, the concept of "mixing" is an administrative description and as such represents the expression of a certain bureaucratic mentality. Its descriptive value is limited. A "mixed" marriage between a European and a native was given this name only because the colonial government had seen fit to define these legal-ethnic categories. It ignores the fact that for the people in question — even when their choice of partner involved not only love but also convenience — the matter of "legal status" was surely only one of several considerations. Moreover, descriptions such as Mestizo and "mixed culture" presuppose a static notion of culture and identity, whereas creolisation is a process of ongoing change and renewal of social and cultural patterns. When the hybrid is the norm, it ceases to be a hybrid.[2]

Colonial historiography, also in its more critical forms, is based upon sources that are chiefly shaped by newcomers and figures in authority. It often adopts the social blueprints that tend rather to support the system of colonial categorisation than to question or contextualise it. Having mixed Asian and European ancestry is then seen as the ultimate deciding factor in determining a person's future, character and social position. This results in an excessive emphasis on racial characteristics, which come to be seen as the key criteria of distinction in colonial society, while other factors, such as class, gender, education, culture and local conditions — arguably equally significant — are neglected or ignored.

Another all-too-common feature of colonial studies is the emphasis on the Mestizos' marginal situation.[3] A more positive approach, but similarly drawing upon the mixed and thus intermediate character of the Mestizos, pictures them as go-betweens, linking European and Asian aspects of the community.[4] But whatever the terminology and qualifications, these images remain burdened by an unjustifiable dose of essentialism and an outsider's perspective. Even the idea of mixing is a false one: Whereas Mestizos or Indo-Europeans are generally depicted as a blend or mixture of a European and an Asian, most of the Indische people had a family history spanning several generations of Europeans in the East Indies. The topography of the East Indies determined their world view, and they made use of family networks that had profound local roots. We should therefore distinguish between terms such as "Mestizo" and "Indo-European", with their overriding racial connotations, and "Indies-born Europeans", a social category that refers to creolised Europeans who might or might not have mixed parentage.

The vast majority of the European population living in the Dutch East Indies were Indische — they were born and raised in the East Indies, where they enjoyed their earliest experiences, the colours, smells and stories of the land, and formed their world views. Following the arrival of the first generation of colonists from Europe, new communities soon arose. Although often closely connected with colonial authorities and values, they developed a local approach in their contacts and strategies. The Indische world thus formed a chain of strongly localised European communities, in which newcomers from Europe sometimes played a powerful part but were never unequivocally dominant.

To understand the considerable differences between (Indische) communities living in the widely scattered regions of the East Indies, we must be prepared to use an approach that accounts for the fact that after one or two generations, European settlements become *local* Indische communities. A city of civil servants would have seemed quite different from a garrison settlement, a bustling port or a plantation community. Each was affected by the colonial regulations in a different manner. Until well into the 19th century and perhaps even later, the port of Batavia was the only place that could boast a substantial proportion of newcomers; here the expatriate culture developed most strongly. This culture also existed outside Batavia, but to a far lesser extent. In places with a large community of indigenous Christians who could function as potential marriage partners, the boundaries between European and indigenous remained somewhat loosely defined. Economic opportunity also determined the nature of the world of the East Indies: where Indies-born European citizens had sources of income outside the colonial government they were more likely to shake off the straitjacket of colonial social stratification.

In writing this book we were convinced of the need to describe the Indische world "from the inside" — thereby avoiding the prescriptive and often cliché-ridden viewpoint of colonial governments, of travel accounts by Europeans who ventured to the East (and returned) or of novels with a colonial setting (generally written by Europeans). Of necessity, however, we have made use of such sources from time to time. But it is the outlook of the people who were born in the Indies, and based on that built their perspectives and expectations, that forms the mainstream of our narrative. Thus, we have tried to analyse the different types of social engagement between people, families and ethnic groups in the world of the East Indies, which were determined by financial circumstances, ancestry, official category, profession — and skin colour. This book describes how the internal boundaries in the society of the Indies were defined and experienced. Nothing illustrates this better than the ups and downs of some families living in the Indies, revealing patterns of birth, marriage, careers and mobility. This book concentrates on people and families for whom the Dutch East Indies was home. Other inhabitants of these islands appear in the wings — Indonesians, of course, as well as Chinese, slaves and European newcomers.

In this way the Indische world transcends the schematic interpretations that view the former Dutch colony as a strictly racially stratified society. We hope to dismiss once and for all the notion that Indische families formed a racially, culturally and socially homogenous community between the Totoks (European newcomers) and the indigenous population, as well as the cliché that, as a group, they were a kind of marginalised Europeans.

The Indische world will be studied through several crucial issues and mechanisms that regulated the lives of the people of the Indies. First, there was the presence of the colonial government. Even though neither its presence and policies, nor its views on colonial society, were hegemonic, there cannot be the slightest doubt that the Indische world sprouted from colonial expansion and its ensuing power relations. One of the most consequential decisions taken in the colonial Dutch East Indies was to accept children of mixed parentage as Europeans — provided that the child was legally acknowledged or adopted by the European father. Through their legal status, Indische children became the object of a policy of "Europeanisation". This did not aim to provide everyone who had European civil status with an equal opportunity to prosper in society; but it implied the cultivation of loyal citizens who would support and defend the prestige of the colonial authority.

A crucial instrument in the process of Europeanisation was European education. Apart from being a tool of the government, it was a means whereby the Indies-born European could move ahead in society. Until the late 19th century, the major form of employment for Europeans was government service. With the professionalisation of the civil service after the 1820s, new demands were made on the educational standards of civil servants. This put pressure on children from Indische families to attend European schools in order to attain the necessary qualifications. But such schools were expensive, and a good education became closely tied in with income and class. At the same time, a European education

— especially secondary or higher — was the perfect vehicle for escaping a poor social milieu. Until the 1860s, higher education could be acquired only in Europe and remained primarily a function of income.

Family background and social networks were just as important as the regulations of the colonial government and an appropriate education. In many parts of the Dutch East Indies there was a tightly woven web of families controlling most of the key positions in government and ruling certain branches of local business life. For such dynasties, the newcomers from Europe were no more than curious birds of passage. Naturally, army officers and high-ranking civil servants were often welcomed as marriage candidates for the Indische daughters. These sons-in-law from Europe were then received into the local clans and became in turn part of the family networks.

Economic opportunity, or the lack of it, had an enormous influence on the fate and fortunes of the Indische population. In many places the inhabitants of the Indies remained dependent upon the colonial government for employment. Elsewhere, Indische families found alternative sources of income and prosperity, for instance in the privately owned estates in West Java, the plantations on long-term lease in the semi-colonised Javanese Principalities, or the nutmeg groves of the tiny Banda islands in the Moluccas. In those places autonomy was maintained in the face of the colonial authorities. Towards the close of the 19th century the economy of the Netherlands Indies began to diversify while the public sector expanded; this gave a boost to employment and encouraged greater social mobility.

Another recurring topic in this narrative concerns the articulation of interests and grievances of the Indies-based people and the way in which they organised themselves. These movements followed trends set in Europe and other parts of the world. During the 19th century the political voice of Indies-born Europeans grew ever louder. It is scarcely coincidental that this political awareness ran parallel with the rise of an independent press in the Dutch East Indies and a growing concern with the lot of the poorer classes — that is to say, the poorer Europeans. From the time of the first petition to the Dutch government in 1648, on through the welfare organisations of the second half of the 19th century, and up to the emergence of the first nationalist party in 1912, the inhabitants of the old world of the East Indies sought methods of furthering their civil rights.

Finally, there is the theme of migration. The world of the East Indies was one of constant flux. It was peopled by civil servants and soldiers

— such as the above-mentioned Emilie Mesman's husband, Wilhelmus Henricus (Hein) Neijs — who were regularly transferred to new posts, in this way getting to see many nooks and crannies of the Indonesian archipelago. This helped to cultivate a sense of unity in the Indische world, without ever severing the links with the motherland and Europe, which were essential to this community. A European education was the gateway to a successful career in the Indies. Thus, the Indische world existed thanks to two-way traffic: Europeans came to live and work there, while people from the Indies went to live and study in Europe (and returned). This migration circuit gave rise in the 19th century to two concepts: the people who stayed (*blijvers*) and those who came for a limited period, so-called sojourners (*trekkers*). Those who managed to climb the social ladder became sojourners and would return or travel to the motherland; those with lower incomes simply stayed put.

The Indische world of this book is indeed an old world, and it has gone forever. It was marked by considerable local variation as well as local autonomy; levels of wealth and the boundaries between the European and the indigenous population became more rigid in the late colonial period. In that old world, for instance, Emilie's father followed the local traditions and at the end of a deer hunt would drink the warm blood of the slain animal. Emilie and her sisters were considered members of the princely dynasty of Tanete. The Dutch dynastic families who lived in Java's Principalities certainly thought of themselves as European — but they had an independent economic and social network.

By the early 20th century this world had undergone a rapid transformation. European life in the Indonesian archipelago became increasingly homogenous and was consolidated by the spread of Dutch education, increasing government intervention, and the rise of the (local) press. With the advent of mass organisations and nationalist sentiments, public life became politicised, with significant consequences for the lives and outlook of the European classes. Large groups of the population were mobilised into social and political organisations such as labour unions, welfare organisations and political parties; this sharpened the distinction between those who were considered Netherlanders and those who were considered Indonesians. The large-scale technological advances and innovations of the 20th century, with the consequent widening disparity in peoples' standards of welfare, as well as the vast numbers of Netherlanders arriving in the colony, only served to widen the split between the modern European section of the population and the poorer masses. The late colonial period, which brought many new ideas and "modern" institutions and bristled with political tension, meant the end of the old Indische world. That world would live on in the memory of many as *tempo doeloe*, the days of yesteryear. But this was not the end of the Indische world: Another, no less Indische, community lived on, finding new forms and customs.

CHAPTER 1

Separation and Fusion

Crossroad of peoples

Colonial rulers are noted for their attempts at racial and ethnic engineering. In the European colonies worldwide, governments classified and segregated groups into watertight compartments, each having its own function within society. The world of the East Indies was undeniably shaped by colonial powers and indisputably the product of racial and ethnic stratification. But that is only part of the story. After all, wherever groups of people from differing backgrounds live together, there is both mingling and exclusion. Colonial societies were no exception to the rule. The misconception concerning the colonial "plural society" is twofold. First, the boundaries between the various groups in colonial societies remained porous, however the fictions composed by colonial population statistics and legislation may plead to the contrary. Furthermore, it was not colonial rulers who invented the plural society; it goes back farther than that — it was an offshoot from an earlier world with its own patterns and mechanisms of separation and fusion. Before moving on to examine the peculiarities of colonial society, we should first consider that entity named Asia where, from the late 15th century, Europeans had been putting down roots.

Since time immemorial the coasts of Asia have been a meeting place for merchants, explorers, fortune-seekers, missionaries, diplomats and conquerors. The sea passage between the Middle East and China was among the most ancient and oft-plied routes transporting people and cargo — not to mention ideas — across great distances to the east and west. The trade routes in early modern Asia embraced every coast of the known and navigable seas, from Japan to East Africa, from the Persian Gulf to the islands of the eastern Indonesian archipelago. At the beginning of the 15th century, Chinese vessels reached the coasts of India, Persians made contacts with the Japanese, Maldive merchants explored the coasts

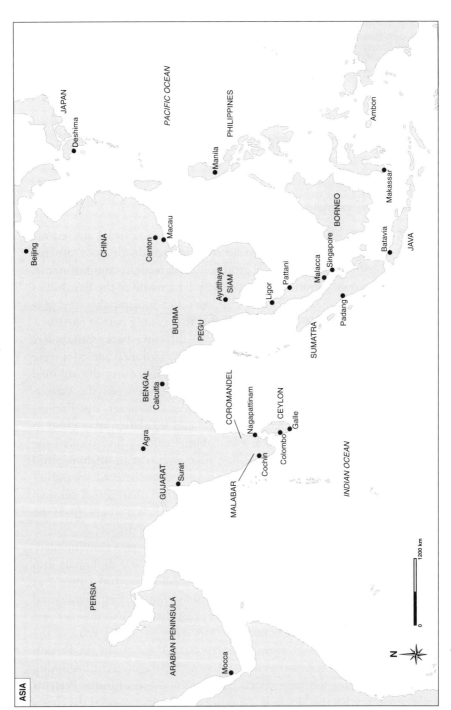

Illustration 1 Map of Asia showing the major Dutch East India Company settlements

of North Sumatra and East Africa, while Arabs ventured as far east as the Indonesian archipelago. Wherever travellers set foot on shore, they encountered other merchants: Armenians, Persians, Arabs, Gujaratis, Tamils, Bengalis, Acehnese, Malays, Javanese, Luzonese, Chinese and Ryukyuans and, a little later, Portuguese, English, Dutch and other Europeans.

Few eyewitness accounts of travels through pre-colonial Asia have survived, but one exception is that of Abu Abdullah Muhammad Ibn Battuta. Born to a family of lawyers dwelling in the North African port of Tangier, he set out in 1325 and travelled for many years through the Middle East and Asia. His journeys were to continue until 1349. His primary destination was — not surprisingly for a good Muslim — Mecca, after which he continued farther eastwards to Persia, India, the Maldives, Ceylon (today's Sri Lanka), Sumatra, and as far as China. He noted when he was in the Indian port of Cambay (today's Khambhat) that most of the population were from other countries, chiefly Persia, Arabia and Turkey. He also reported that the harbour of Calicut (today's Kozhikode) in southwest India was one of the largest in the world — and Ibn Battuta certainly knew what he was talking about. "Merchants from every corner of the world gather here," he observed. There he saw travellers from Java, Ceylon, the Maldives, Persia and Yemen, and even met Chinese who were waiting for the southwesterly monsoon before returning eastward.[1] During the centuries that followed, traffic in the Indian Ocean only increased. Although the Chinese almost totally ceased their overseas activities in the 15th and 16th centuries, other seafaring nations expanded their long-distance commerce to embrace every corner of the old world. The large trading centres saw the number of foreigners and their descendants increase steadily, often rising into the thousands. When Persian envoys arrived in Ayutthaya, the capital of Siam (today's Thailand) in 1685, they discovered a considerable number of their fellow countrymen — not only traders recently arrived to do business there, but also families who had been living in Siam for several generations and had close ties with the Siamese court.[2] In this way the coastlands of South and Southeast Asia became strewn with hundreds of communities where Chinese, Gujaratis, Tamils, Javanese and many other ethnic groups became embedded in the local societies.

Foreigners were not immediately and completely assimilated into their host societies. The differences in cultural background, religion and language were obvious and remained a source of differentiation. But of greater importance was the fact that the traders, as foreigners, were not

incorporated into the local system of servitude and tributary obligations. Since many merchants stayed in a city for only a short time, and
because their numbers fluctuated considerably, local rulers were obliged
to regulate the relations between the various communities. The groups
of foreigners living in Asian cities were often housed in separate quarters
and were allowed to follow different legal systems. It was not unusual
to have separate districts housing different groups — after all, African
and European cities too had distinct commercial districts where foreign
traders were concentrated along lines of origin or commodity; but in the
towns and cities of Asia such segregation went even farther. Generally,
the foreign communities would have a headman responsible for maintaining law and order among his people and for promoting their interests
with the local ruler.

Segregation and extra-territoriality — the principle that foreign
merchants were subject to their own laws — had many advantages. The
local ruler had to negotiate with only a few representatives rather than
each individual trader. Maintaining law and order — especially when it
had to do with family and inheritance law — could be left to the internal
authority of the immigrant community. And the advantages were all too
clear for the foreign merchants: they were able to continue living under
their own laws. "Legal pluralism" — that is, different groups falling
under different legal systems and authorities — was characteristic of the
fragmented power relations in the cities and states of South and Southeast
Asia. The highest authority was the king, but he was not all-powerful.
He had to deal with courtiers, regional governors, religious leaders and
the representatives of foreign merchants. Each one of these had their own
followers, their own servants and their own slaves who remained outside
the reach of the central ruler.

The distribution of political power was reflected in urban space. In
Ayutthaya large communities of foreign merchants lived in *ban* (villages
or districts) situated just outside the city walls. At the close of the 17th
century we find mention of communities from Gujarat (Hindustanis),
Coromandel (Moors), Pegu, Malacca (Malays), Makassar, Cochin-China
(Vietnamese), China, Japan, Portugal, France and the Netherlands.[3]
Each of these communities had its own headman; the large Chinese
community even had two. However, although in theory the ethnic
groups seemed juridically and spatially segregated, daily reality was
somewhat more complicated than the above might suggest. Foreigners
and their descendants were not prevented from gaining access to the
Siamese community. The extensive "Portuguese" settlement — outside

the city walls and facing the Dutch trading post — was peopled by "a Portuguese race descended from black women"; in other words, Mestizos, children with a Portuguese father and a Siamese mother.[4] In other communities, too, there was considerable mixing between travellers from abroad and local women, again resulting in children of mixed parentage.

The mixing went beyond family relations; some foreigners even attained high-ranking posts at court. At the end of the 17th century, for instance, the royal guard of Ayutthaya was composed of a couple of hundred Persians, while for three successive generations the chief minister (*chaopraya*) came from a Persian family, only to be followed by a Greek. Other first ministers were of Indian, Chinese and Mon descent. The king of Siam also employed Englishmen — for instance, as harbour master.[5] Evidently, the king preferred to employ foreigners in key positions, since they did not command a large band of followers who might pose a threat to the throne. But their difference stopped there. Nowhere do we find the suggestion that these families behaved as foreigners. On the contrary, it seems that they adapted themselves to the culture and customs of the Ayutthaya court. They married into Siamese families and ultimately became totally assimilated.[6]

Along the coast of the Malay peninsula and in the Indonesian archipelago, the pattern of segregation and mediation was essentially no different from that in Siam. The city of Malacca, which during the 15th century thrived on the expanding international trade and attracted many foreigners, appointed four *syahbandar* (harbour masters) to maintain contacts between the local government and various trading communities, and also to administer justice and act as military commanders in times of war. The syahbandar appointed from the Gujaratis of northwest India was described by the Portuguese traveller Tomé Pires as "the most important of them all". Then there was a syahbandar for the merchants from Coromandel, Bengal, Pegu and Pasai (in north Sumatra); one for the foreigners from Java, the Moluccas, Banda, Palembang, Borneo and Luzon; and, finally, one for the Chinese and other traders from the East.[7]

In the 16th and 17th centuries, Ayutthaya and Malacca were among the largest cities in Southeast Asia. Travellers from Europe estimated the population of these places to be as large as 200,000 — although in reality the number would have been closer to 10,000.[8] But whatever the actual figure, there is no doubt that these were bustling emporiums, where a foreigner was not an uncommon sight. There was a prevailing pattern of segregation, but we cannot say with any accuracy how strictly this was applied. Primarily, there was formal, juridical separation, particularly for

the trading communities. Even in a comparatively small city such as
Pattani — on the east coast of the Malay peninsula — there were
segregated kampongs for merchants from Java, Gujarat and Pasai and,
beginning in the early 17th century, also for those of Dutch and English
descent; sizeable communities of Chinese and Portuguese also found
residence in the trading districts.[9] But not every group was supplied with
its own settlement area. Smaller communities of foreign traders apparently
clustered around the group that appeared to be the most familiar or
advantageous. Arriving in a city, foreigners tried to attach themselves to
a group with whom they felt the greatest affinity — and from whom
they could expect the most support. Usually this was a community from
the same region, or at least with the same religion.[10]

Generally speaking, cultural and ethnic plurality presented few
problems. The borderlines between the many nationalities were porous,
despite the suggestion by the (chiefly Western) sources that there was
considerable regimentation and segregation. In daily practice, life tended
to be far less ethnically compartmentalised. Indeed, there was no rigid
administrative structuring of ethnic differences and boundaries. This
appears from the welcoming attitude adopted by local potentates towards
foreigners, and the way in which many visitors from distant countries
integrated apparently painlessly into Asian communities. Many traders
and travellers stayed for a period in the guest country and would often
take a local woman as partner and start a family — even though this
might last only for the duration of their stay. These women were also
instrumental in the trading process — they functioned as go-betweens,
or middlewomen, and were frequently active traders themselves.[11]

Mixing and integration were encouraged by the absence of a strong
sense of national identity. Since polities and identities were fairly fluid
in maritime Southeast Asia, a person's country of origin was not considered the major factor in defining his identity. On the whole, loyalty
was a personal choice rather than based upon ethnicity. The sense of
nationality was most developed in those countries with a history of
strong centralisation, countries possessing their own written language
and a consciousness of long cultural traditions, such as Persia, China and
Japan, and the states of the Southeast Asian mainland. However, even
for merchants coming from these countries, their sense of belonging was
somewhat ambiguous. For instance, a Persian's identity would be overshadowed by his awareness of being part of the world of Islam.[12]

Hybridity was part and parcel of Asian society, particularly in the
many towns and cities of the coastal regions. Although there were few

bureaucratic barriers to assimilation and integration, forms of prejudice certainly existed, and strangers and their customs were sometimes greeted with intolerance. One Chinese source records that Chinese in Malacca were viewed with outrage by the Muslim Malays because they ate pork.[13] And in Mocca, in Yemen, at the far west of the Indian Ocean, the authorities had great difficulty dealing with the Indian Hindu custom of cremating their dead.[14] However, all in all there appears to have been very little pressure from the state to enforce ethnic segregation. The institution of separate trading communities was essential to regulate international commerce, but once traders were settled in a place the ties with their home community soon slackened. In the case of marriage and religious conversion, integration was usually a swift process. Once religious barriers were overcome, there was little to stand in the way of integration. In Malacca, for instance, marriages between Muslims from very different geographical backgrounds was commonplace.[15] Indeed, this was so for the entire Islamic world. Through the centuries, there are countless cases of Arab, Persian and Indian Muslims settling in Southeast Asia, marrying local women and becoming indigenous.

We lack statistical information concerning pre-colonial towns and cities, but it is evident from the early history of colonial cities such as Malacca, Makassar, Batavia and Penang that large numbers of immigrants settled there and soon integrated with the local population. Most of the people in these cities were either newcomers or the offspring of immigrants.[16] It also appears that slaves made a major contribution to the growth of urban populations and added to the rapid process of hybridisation and integration by becoming partners for the immigrants, with whom they started families.

The story of the Chinese in Southeast Asia is an interesting one, since they had no language, script or religion in common with the local peoples and thus were truly outsiders. But despite this apparently high hurdle they, too, quickly integrated. We find in the 14th and 15th centuries that shipping along the north coast of Java was to a large extent controlled by captains and shipowners of (partly) Chinese descent. Their forefathers had settled in Java and had become subsumed into court circles or married into the local communities.[17] The cities of the North Java coast were dynamic trading centres with a heterogeneous mixture of Javanese and Indian Hindus, Arab and Indian Muslims, and Buddhist and Confucian Chinese. Our scanty sources do not recount how the amalgamation took shape, but the close commercial ties between kings and merchants and between the traders themselves were presumably strengthened by marriage bonds.[18]

The Chinese — who in the 19th and 20th centuries would become viewed in colonial policies as a quintessentially separate community — were far more integrated into Javanese life three or four centuries earlier. Even though at this time separate Chinese neighbourhoods, or *pacinan*, existed in the ports, intermarriage and religious conversion were commonplace. The ensuing assimilation was made easier by the hierarchical structure of Javanese society in which ties of personal loyalty held more sway than did one's origin. The severance of ties between China and Southeast Asia in the 15th century encouraged the blending of the Chinese with other groups living in Java.[19] Later, too, relations between the Javanese and Chinese were characterised by a high degree of harmony, cooperation and intermingling. Just as in Ayutthaya, the descendants of Chinese immigrants occupied many top positions, including not only that of harbour master or syahbandar, a function often held by foreigners, but also that of provincial governor.[20] Among the nobility, mixed marriages were not uncommon, and it is to be supposed that they also took place regularly in less elevated circles.[21]

Newcomers from China looked askance on phenomena such as conversion and intermarriage. At the end of the 18th century the Chinese traveller Ong Tae Hae (Wang Dahai) observed in reference to the Chinese he encountered in Java, "When the Chinese live abroad for several generations, without returning to their motherland, they frequently cut themselves off from the teachings of the sages."[22] This traveller saw his fellow countrymen diluting their beliefs and their culture, and watering down their race; all commonplace in the cosmopolitan societies of Asian harbour towns. Under European colonial rule, however, the fluid and flexible character of ethnic categories altered. Ong noted that the group of Javanese Chinese known as Peranakan were officially distinguished, under colonial rule, not only from the Chinese newcomers but also from the Javanese, and that they even appointed their own headman. Something similar took place in both the Spanish Philippines and the British settlements on the Malay peninsula.[23] Colonial rulers introduced far more stringent ethnic distinctions than had been the case in pre-colonial times.

Europeans

Initially, the arrival of Europeans in Asia produced little apparent change in the patterns of pluralism, mixing and integration. The Europeans, after all, were only one group among many to settle in the Asian ports and cities. Their arrival merely added to the cultural diversity in the harbour towns, and their exotic appearance failed to cause any shock. Indeed, in many places Europeans were welcome guests, bringing commercial advantages to the Asian rulers.[24] The system of extra-territorial concessions simplified matters for the European merchants. In many cases they were simply treated like any other foreign traders: they were given a separate plot of land in the city and were permitted to trade according to specific regulations. But the difference with the Asian traders was that the Europeans did not represent the interests of a private financial backer or a shipowner but those of a mercantile company or even a monarch. They presented themselves as the ambassadors of a sovereign state or organised company, and often their arrival in a city would go hand in hand with the presentation of letters of recommendation from their monarch, followed by negotiations about their trading privileges.[25]

European trading communities sprang up all over Asia alongside those of the Chinese, the Javanese, Tamils, Gujaratis, Armenians and others. Adapting quickly, the Europeans learned the commercial lingua franca of the area and mastered the rules of the local market. They entered into (temporary) relations with local women, and many trading posts were soon peppered with their offspring. Most of these children remained in the country of their birth and were subsumed into the local community or else entered the service of European merchants and companies. The Dutch East India Company (VOC), for instance, made good use of such people, born and brought up locally. They could speak the language of their birth country and understood its conventions, and they proved excellent middlemen for the Europeans. For the same reason, these Eurasians were extremely useful to Asian rulers.

Siam is a good example of an Asian country where the Dutch forged themselves a position among other foreign merchants. In 1608, 12 years after the first Dutch ships reached Asia, the VOC established a trading post in Ayutthaya. It was moved in 1636 to a location outside the city walls, a little south of the city, on the Chao Phraya River, which linked Ayutthaya with the sea. Other trading communities such as the Japanese and the Portuguese also had their settlements in this neighbourhood. The VOC post consisted of some 30 to 40 men, lodged only temporarily in Siam, who would leave when their period of employment ended. All the men, irrespective of rank, maintained a concubine, whom they supported financially and provided with a house.[26] Although some of these women were Siamese, most of them came from the Mon, a people originally from Pegu on the Bay of Bengal. There were laws forbidding Siamese and even Mon and Lao women from having intercourse with European men, but these rules and regulations had little effect.[27] Thus, in the shadow of the sober VOC buildings, there arose a community of potential concubines. The company employees were lodged in premises on the VOC site, and their women had houses nearby. There the men of the VOC sought their partners, and the children who happened to be born out of these relations would also grow up in this satellite community. When a VOC employee left, his partner would often attach herself to another company employee.

Some Europeans and their descendants occupied important positions in Siamese society and even achieved high posts at court. Most noteworthy of these was the Greek Constantine Phaulkon, who arrived in Asia as a cabin boy with the British East India Company and, while in the employ of an English captain, ended up in Ayutthaya. There, in 1680, he bought himself a job in the department of the *phrakhlang*, the minister of trade and foreign affairs. Phaulkon proved himself a faithful servant of Siamese interests and climbed to the very top of the court ladder, attaining the rank of deputy phrakhlang; he was even appointed governor of the coastal provinces. Eventually, however, he became so involved in internal politics that he met his death in a typically Siamese manner. In 1688, in a dispute over the royal succession, he supported one of the claimants to the throne, the adopted son of the ailing King Narai. He gambled and lost. Their party was defeated, and Phaulkon met with a sticky end.[28]

Less well known is the De Brochebourde family, who served the kings of Siam for three generations and whose story has been unearthed by the Thai historian Dhiravat na Pombejra. The founder of this dynasty was Daniel de Brochebourde, a surgeon from the north of France, who in 1659 was stationed with the Dutch East India Company in the southern Siamese town of Ligor (Nakhon Si Thammarat). Here he married a local woman. In 1669 he was transferred to the VOC station in Ayutthaya, where, at the request of King Narai, he was appointed to the royal household in 1672 as the monarch's personal physician. Thanks to his marriage, De Brochebourde spoke Thai, and he evidently felt a strong bond with the country. He had already demonstrated his medical skills by curing several courtiers of their maladies. The VOC was happy to oblige the king and even continued to pay De Brochebourde's wages. Clearly, this was to prove most advantageous to them, since during the

25 years that De Brochebourde served as the king's physician he also acted as an interpreter and middleman for the Dutch in negotiations with court officials — a delicate business at the best of times — and as an informant for the Dutch.

De Brochebourde had four children. His oldest son, Moses, showed a good command of both Dutch and Thai and evidently acquired considerable knowledge of the surgeon's profession from his father. He was appointed to the same positions as his father — court physician as well as interpreter. He married a Mon woman in Ayutthaya. His younger brother Paulus, who began as a "native employee" in a low rank of the VOC, soon left service to become a ship's captain in the service of the Siamese king. It would seem that he broke all ties with the Dutch community, for nothing more is heard of him. Interestingly, Moses de Brochebourde had apparently also intimated that he would be happy to be employed entirely by Siamese authorities — but the Dutch East India Company needed his services as a translator and would not dismiss him. When the VOC head threatened to send Moses to Batavia, the latter protested via the minister of trade and foreign affairs, the *phrakhlang*. The minister reminded the VOC that the children of Siamese women were not allowed to leave the country and that Moses, as court physician, was not only a subject of the Siamese king but in fact held an official rank at court. Moses remained in Ayutthaya and was paid wages by the company until his death in 1724.

The third generation of De Brochebourdes was the last to figure in the archives of the company. One of the sons of Moses, named Jeremias — it would seem that the family continued to think of themselves as Christians — followed in his father's footsteps. He married a Mon woman. It is believed that Jeremias spoke Thai, Mon, Portuguese and Dutch, which made him valuable to both the VOC and the Siamese court. However, it would seem that the family's knowledge of Western medicine got watered down with successive generations. When King Thaisa was being treated for terminal cancer of the throat in 1732, Jeremias appears to have been considered in the same category as native doctors. With the following generations, the De Brochebourdes disappear from the company records.[29]

There appear to have been quite a few VOC employees who spent most of their working lives in Siam. One of them was Nicolaas Bang, who came from the neighbourhood of Zaandam, just north of Amsterdam. He arrived in Ayutthaya in 1723 as a trumpeter, and there he remained — apart from a brief intermezzo in Batavia — for the rest of his life.

He perished in 1760 during the attack on the city by the Burmese army. He lived with a Siamese or Mon woman named Meutha just north of the lodge belonging to the Dutch East India Company. Four of their children were born in Siam. At least one of them, his son Michiel, joined the company at the age of 13 or 14.[30] After the lodge was disbanded in 1765, Michiel set sail with the last VOC ship for Batavia — but the other members of the Bang family fade from the records.[31]

Many children of mixed Siamese and European parentage were to be seen in Ayutthaya. In 1689 there were at least 17 children who had local mothers and whose fathers were employees of the VOC.[32] Most children got swallowed up into the Siamese community and left no trace in the company archives. When writing their wills, men from the VOC would often provide for the upkeep of their concubines and children. For instance, in 1739 the merchant Willem de Ghij bequeathed a house to each of his two concubines, Meu Nooy and Meuka; the houses lay close to the VOC lodge. In addition, he gave them each a sum of money, some silver objects, textiles and several slaves. De Ghij had fathered five children with the two women, and he hoped they would be allowed to travel out of Siam to Batavia.[33] We do not know whether his wish was fulfilled. Without permission from the court, neither the children of Siamese mothers, nor the women themselves, were allowed to leave the country. This law had arisen because of a labour shortage in Siam.

Officials of the Dutch East India Company, along with the many fathers, were distressed to see these children growing up as paupers and without any knowledge of the Christian faith. There were bitter struggles with the Siamese court over the fate of such children.[34] In some cases the VOC managed to win the case, and the children were shipped to Batavia to join their fathers or to be brought up in an orphanage. But most boys and girls remained in Siam after the departure or death of their father. In the mid-17th century many Eurasian children were being looked after by one Tomas de Fransman (Thomas the Frenchman), who had the status of *vrijburger*, that is, a free citizen not employed by the VOC. He had found his way to Ayutthaya and ran a tavern not far from the company's lodge — possibly not the most favourable of environments for children.[35] Not surprisingly, the girls grew up to be concubines for the following generation of VOC employees stationed in Siam. Thus Pieter de Brochebourde, brother of the above-mentioned Moses, was engaged to the Mestizo daughter of a Swede in the company's employ. Very few of the Mestizo boys who remained in Siam were able to join the Dutch East India Company like their fathers — and if they did, it was generally in a low rank.[36]

There are many other countries where the picture resembles that of Siam, with local variations, depending on the character of the government and the variety of ethnic and religious groups. For instance, the major trading centre of Surat in northwest India harboured a large Armenian Christian community. The European employees of the VOC there preferred to choose their wives from among the daughters of the Armenians. There was a clear preference for European, Mestizo and Christian women as marriage partners, although VOC men would also marry slave women — after they had been set free and converted to Christianity.[37] But most often there was no flourishing Christian community producing nubile daughters. Thus, the majority of European men chose to have a concubine rather than wed a local woman, since the latter would usually mean that the man was bound for the rest of his life to remain in Asia. At the beginning of the 18th century Jacobus Canter Visscher, a minister in Cochin, southern India, and later in Batavia, bewailed the lack of Christian morality in these cities: "The manner in which Europeans live there is in general so lecherous and lawless, and whoredom is so widespread, that it exceeds all measures, and it may well be for this reason that no ministers are sent to this place."[38] The whoredom, the term by which the reverend minister referred to the various forms of unmarried sexual relationships such as concubinage, was widespread in the smaller stations of the Dutch East India Company — indeed, it was the norm. Few of the men brought their European wives with them. Frank Lequin calculated that in the VOC settlements in 18th-century Bengal, as few as 47 of the 115 members of the local governing council — in other words, the highest-ranking officials — were registered as being married. In 28 of these cases the wives were European.[39] The majority of company employees in Bengal remained unmarried — which presumably explains the zealous but naïve clergyman Canter Visscher's diatribes concerning licentious living.

Throughout Asia, tiny communities of Europeans arose and — through their wives and concubines — became embedded in their new country. An extensive Mestizo culture developed in the cities of Asia, not only in company towns, but also at the Asian courts. Asian rulers were glad to use the services of Europeans and other foreigners, employing them for their military know-how, their international contacts or their language skills. Frequently, such people would be deserters from the trading companies — especially in tense times of conflict and war. For instance, the Indian mughals of Agra and Delhi often employed European deserters, who were welcomed as artillerymen.[40] In other cases the men might be merchants or fortune-hunters, such as the above-mentioned Phaulkon. The Asian coastal cities sheltered large numbers of these Asian Europeans, who formed — along with the Arab, Gujarati, Tamil or Malay merchants — a highly flexible and diverse community. They followed the lure of freedom and financial or social gain, or in some cases they remained because of family ties.[41] These Europeans have been relegated to the margins of our history books. Forming a small but essential element in the urban centres of Asia, they are nevertheless a confusing phenomenon: they do not fit neatly into the polarised picture of colonial history. But in light of the long history in Asia of ethnic, cultural and legal pluralism, we may conclude that a flexible integration of European immigrants was the norm rather than the exception. Indeed, contacts between ethnic groups along the Asian coastlands would appear to have been more widespread and varied, with greater moral elasticity, than was the case in the large colonial possessions of the European trading companies.

Colonies and classifications

Small company stations such as in Ayutthaya formed only small pockets of European traders, soldiers and clerks. In those centres of independent Asian empires, European merchants formed clusters of expatriates. Cut off from the cultural, juridical and administrative bodies operating in their home countries, they were forced to adapt to the social and moral order of their host land. But all too often, the Europeans would not accept their powerless position. When extensive commercial or political goals were at stake, the Europeans would capture a strategic trading post, sometimes even a whole city. As time went by, complex communities grew up in the shadow of the vigilant fortresses, and the colonial government had to take on the task of maintaining law and order. Many settlements developed a hybrid character, Asian institutions existing side by side with political structures imported from Europe. In this way the plural structure of pre-colonial society was retained in areas under European rule. When the Portuguese captured Malacca in 1511 and occupied this highly strategic city, they took over the existing model of pluralism, with separate suburbs for immigrant groups, that had prevailed in the days of the sultanate.[42] Malacca continued to have separate kampongs (wards) while the Portuguese were in power, retaining the same ethnic distinctions as under the sultans: Javanese, Chinese, Tamil and Gujarati.[43] Things were scarcely different in the settlements founded by the Dutch East India Company. Portuguese, VOC and other colonial powers followed a similar pattern of (spatial) segregation, group representation and legal administration within their own circle. But in fact there *was* a difference. The separation of different ethnic groups gained a highly bureaucratic and legal nature under colonial rule. The pluralist structure of such societies was not only imposed by existing circumstances, it was also sustained by the considerable advantages it offered to colonial governments. It relieved them of intensive, expensive and risky interference in the affairs of the local communities.

In early modern times, the European presence in most colonial stations consisted of concentrations numbering from a few dozen up to several hundred persons. Even in the largest European settlements there were rarely more than a few thousand European inhabitants; most of them were local-born. The statistics for Portuguese migration to Asia and the numbers living there in Portuguese settlements are scarce and far from reliable. Some estimates reckon that during the 16th century there was an annual migration from Portugal to Asia of 2,000 men at most. But few of them remained in Asia. During the 17th century the pace of emigration slackened sharply.[44] In 1635 the Portuguese António Bocarro provided an overview of the Portuguese colonists in Asia, estimating the total to be about 6,700 *casados brancos* (white colonists) — almost a quarter of whom were in holy orders — and at least 7,500 *casados pretos* (black colonists). The capital of the *Estado da India*, Goa, sheltered 800 white and 2,200 black colonists, little more than the population of a provincial town.[45] However, the numbers may have been slightly higher, since it is not clear whether they included the military and civil servants. By 1800 there were no more than 1,851 Europeans and their descendants living in Goa.[46]

Information concerning the Dutch settlements is more extensive. In the early years, in the settlements in Asia, there were approximately the same number of people from the Dutch Republic and Portugal. Each year a few thousand undertook the voyage to Asia — and most of them, provided they survived, returned to Europe within a few years. But during the 17th century the movement of shipping, and with it the transport of company employees, steadily increased. In Batavia, for instance, in 1632 there were at least 8,000 people, of whom 2,368 were VOC employees and European citizens.[47] Their numbers peaked in about 1700, when around 3,400 Europeans and Mestizos were living in Batavia, plus an extra 3,000 or so soldiers in the fortresses and guardrooms.[48] After a low point in the early 19th century, numbers only reached their former level around 1870, when the civil population totalled 6,386 (of whom 4,043 were born in the East Indies).[49]

The number of Europeans living in Batavia was far higher than that in other VOC settlements. In 1694, Colombo (in Ceylon), the second major city of the Dutch East India Company, was home to about 2,200 Europeans and Mestizos, of whom more than 1,600 were company employees.[50] In 1678 Malacca had 145 *vrijburgers* (free European citizens), 666 company employees and their families, and 1,489 Mestizos and "Portuguese", while in 1694 the town of Ambon had 257 European civilian families and 409 VOC employees.[51] During most of the 18th century there were about 20,000 European VOC employees throughout Asia. The majority of the newcomers would only be stationed there temporarily, alongside a more settled European population numbering several thousand.[52] Hardly a huge number, but then Batavia — and with it all the other colonial cities in Asia — was not a settlement colony similar to those in North America. Nevertheless, for the early modern period, these migration figures were considered most impressive in both European and Asian terms. The numbers of Europeans were appreciably smaller in the colonial settlements of other powers, among whom, moreover, there was scarcely a European woman to be found. For instance, in 1756 there were only 671 European men and 80 European women in British Calcutta (today's Kolkata, in India).[53] And in around 1810 there were only 250 European women and 4,000 European men in Bengal, the heart of British India.[54]

Until the late 19th century most colonial migrants were soldiers. In the 18th century 57 per cent of the Dutch East India Company personnel consisted of soldiers, while in 1860 the military made up 32 per cent of the entire European population in the Dutch East Indies.[55] Until 1895, soldiers accounted for the majority of the male European newcomers.[56] In British India the story was much the same, although the numbers there were considerably higher. In 1861, for instance, a census in British India registered a count of 70,962 European soldiers — including their families — and 40,379 civilians.[57] The predominantly military nature of the European presence in the East Indies made an indelible impression on colonial life there. Although the world of the barracks stood remote from civilian life, the military left a deep imprint on East Indies society. Until well into the 20th century the soldiers' barracks contributed to the burgeoning of concubinage and prostitution, and the colonial army was largely to blame for the widespread problem of pauperism among Europeans in the Indies.

A widely held picture of colonial migration is that there was a gradual acceleration over the centuries, but in reality growth was far more erratic. Towards the close of the 18th century the large-scale shipment of Dutch East India Company employees to Asia more or less died down. Numbers would not return to their former level for almost the whole of the 19th century. The upshot was that locally rooted or creolised Europeans became more prominent than ever before — or after. We may therefore consider the 19th century to be the most Indische period in colonial history — when localised Europeans dominated most. Indeed, not until the final years of the 19th century did emigration once more begin to pick up, both in British India and in the Dutch East Indies, and this time it included more women than ever before. These European women are generally seen as having introduced many far-reaching changes into colonial society. Without a doubt, their arrival meant that the administrative and economic elite became more intensely oriented towards their own group. But interestingly, the number of mixed marriages in the Dutch East Indies did not decrease. Even more than the arrival of women from Europe, the sharp rise in the number of Europeans as a whole led to a noticeable assertion of European social and cultural life within this community. Besides, the greatly reduced travel time between the motherland and the colonies consolidated the European orientation of colonial society. Finally, new patterns of consumerism developed with the introduction of, for instance, gas-lights, automobiles and refrigerators. This increased the gap between the rich European elite and the poorer families who could not afford such luxuries.

The shifting patterns of migration and technological innovations deeply affected colonial society. But they changed nothing. Indeed, they only served to strengthen the two essential characteristics of the colonial situation: most top-ranking administrators were foreign to the land and its society, and their primary attachment and loyalty were to the culture and authorities in Europe. Their motherland required them to be loyal and responsible servants, which greatly affected the shaping of colonial society. The colonial governments had to "invent" colonial society, which in turn had to be adapted to the local traditions as well as to the administrative traditions of the motherland, and the economic and political goals of colonial rule. The administration of the Dutch East India Company in Asia was partly modelled on institutions in the

Dutch Republic, but there were significant differences. Colonial rule combined a strong autocratic tendency with a predilection for indirect rule, so the company retained as much power as possible in its own hands. For instance, the VOC did not set up independent town councils, because these might endanger the company's commercial interests. The emphasis of the colonial state lay on preserving law and order, and on financial management. But since the Dutch East India Company was unfamiliar with the traditions and legal practices of the various states and communities it had to deal with, it limited itself to a rudimentary administration of criminal justice for the Asian population, leaving the complicated matters of family law and inheritance law to the individual groups. Thus, as early as 1619, the Chinese community in Batavia had their own "captain" who served as intermediary between his group and the colonial authority and had the task of arbitrating disputes between the Chinese inhabitants.[58] Gradually the Chinese community developed their own infrastructure, the axis being the Chinese council, or Kong-kuan. Later on, other groups were also given their own official leaders, but the institutionalisation of communal authority was far less than in the case of the Chinese.

In other colonial towns, too, comparable forms of indirect administration along ethnic lines appeared. It would be inaccurate to speak of a total split between communities along juridical, administrative and ethnic lines, but the colonial system certainly stimulated the crystallisation of distinctions between the various population groups. This distinction was two-pronged: first, between the Europeans — who followed the Roman-Dutch Law system — and second, between the various Asian groups. People were being defined and registered, far more intensively than in pre-colonial times, according to their ancestry. In countless ways the racial, religious and linguistic differences between people became bureaucratically and legally recorded. Already in the 18th century the Dutch East India Company attempted to codify the laws governing some of the communities under its rule, such as the Tamils in northern Ceylon (in 1707) and the "Mohammedans" and Chinese in Batavia (in 1760 and 1761).[59] The VOC attempted to impose the Islamic law of Batavia upon the Muslims of Ceylon — a powerful example of the rigid categorical thinking of VOC administrators.[60] The results of the registration and codification were twofold: group boundaries sharpened increasingly, while variety within the groups diminished because the laws and regulations about their internal governing structure were made uniform.

It goes without saying that there were marked differences between the various colonial states in the aims and methods with which social interventions were implemented. Unlike the Portuguese Estado da India, the Dutch East India Company was characterised by a passion for registration and accounting, possibly a reflection of the commercial and calculating nature of the Dutch expansion. The frequent population censuses bear evidence of this tendency. Interestingly, these censuses only began to be held with greater regularity in the 17th century, when the VOC settlements were gaining an ever-more-varied population and the notion of establishing predominantly European settlements became untenable. The censuses defined precise categories, based on religion, language and place of origin. The differences between the Portuguese and the Dutch East India Company became visible not only in the passion for quantifying. They also appeared when the Dutch captured cities previously occupied by the Portuguese — such as Malacca and Colombo. The Portuguese fortresses may have been enclosed by a city wall, but inside they were a tangled skein of streets and buildings. The Dutch took over, straightened the streets, reduced the city's area and built new fortifications. Municipal quarters and houses were numbered and assigned to certain groups.[61] Such extensive restructuring was not only the product of a strong architectural tradition in the Dutch Republic, but it also reflected a powerful need for ordering and rationalisation in colonial society.

The VOC settlements gradually took on a shape of their own. Elsewhere, segregation and pluralism were pragmatic and flexible concepts, but under the VOC they became far more rigid and formal. It is noteworthy that most of the population categories were defined by specific obligations — people might have to pay taxes, perform military service, or carry out corvée labour. Thus, the censuses not only fulfilled a bureaucratic need, they also determined to which group a family belonged and what its social obligations were. Since the VOC depended on local labour, definitions and distinctions were drawn up in such a way that as much of the local workforce as possible was available for the company, with the help of native authority structures. In Ambon, for instance, a distinction was made between *burgers* (citizens) and *negorijlieden* (villagers). The latter, who had to carry out compulsory labour, were under the authority of their village headmen, who organised the corvée for the VOC.[62] The citizens, most of whom lived in the city of Ambon, were exempt from the compulsory delivery of cloves and other forms of corvée. In Southwest Ceylon the VOC distinguished three groups: the Sinhalese, who remained subject to the system of servitude to the lord of the land, with tasks being defined along caste lines; the "foreigners", mainly Hindu or Muslim Tamils, who had to pay taxes and perform certain services; and the *burgers* (citizens), a group exempt from the obligations of the caste system, enjoying certain other privileges and coming under the legal jurisdiction of the VOC.

Benedict Anderson once referred to the enormous and far-reaching effect of the colonial passion for classification.[63] Although Europeans did not invent pluralistic juridical and administrative structures, they certainly adopted them and gave the system more formal weight. The census was both a reflection and an instrument expressing the deep desire of colonial government to compartmentalise various aspects of life in the Indies. The aim of the census was not simply to establish statistics — to count the number of inhabitants, able-bodied males or taxpayers — but it clearly had strong social implications. Every individual was made part of a labelled community that determined his or her place of residence, amount of tax paid, and such rights and obligations. It does not take much to realise that in actuality this was considerably more complicated than the clerk with his lists and numbers would have us believe, and the consequences were significant.

According to Anderson, the process of categorisation increased in the late 19th century, thanks to the expansion of the colonial state. But even much earlier, the administrators of the Dutch East India Company, more than their contemporaries, were displaying strong symptoms of a desire to classify and regulate, as demonstrated by the regular censuses, the codification of local laws and the issue of identity papers — all of which were based upon a detailed grid of ethnic distinctions. The colonial states soon developed into what Theo Goldberg has termed a "racial state", in which racial classifications become an essential instrument of government and social policy. The primary concern of colonial governments was the management of heterogeneity.[64] One of the mechanisms used was to emphasise the homogeneity and exclusivity of one's own colonial community. One effect of colonial government was that status hierarchies were separated according to population categories; for instance, someone of Chinese descent could never attain the rank of *bupati* (regent, or district head) in the Dutch East Indies, as had been the case under pre-colonial and early colonial rule.[65] The colonial categorisation of groups according to their nature and function in society also promoted greater competition among the groups, both Asian and European.[66]

The colonial authorities regarded interracial mingling with suspicion and dismay. After all, the blurring of ethnic distinctions would open the door for people to move out from their villages or assigned neighbourhoods into the cities and evade compulsory labour. This would threaten not only the internal order but also the colony's commerce and prosperity. To prevent this, the VOC authorities in Batavia repeatedly issued orders forbidding mixed marriages, thereby revealing the basic characteristics of a colonial regime trying to formalise social distinctions and controlling many aspects of public and private life with its web of laws and regulations.

Racism and mestisation

The colonial classifications were something new in the history of Asia, but in day-to-day reality they had less impact than we are led to believe from reading the colonial reports. Even in colonial towns and cities where European governments attempted to introduce a functional distinction between various ethnic groups, the boundaries between communities remained porous. Since the colonial administrative archives are almost the only sources available for the early colonial period, it is difficult to find evidence of the mixing and mingling of groups and races, of what one might term "creolisation" or "mestization". But if we delve into the scattered information about marriages among the Asian population in Batavia, we find that unions between people of different ethnic origin were commonplace. When it came to the marriages of Europeans, however, things were somewhat different, because the colonial regime kept a firm hold on the reins; it maintained a far closer watch over the European community than it did over other racial groups. After all, it was in the interests of the colonial authorities to guard the nature and boundaries of their community. Not only did they wish to protect their religion and culture and thereby the group's cohesion, but they also wanted to safeguard their prestige with the peoples they had colonised. As a consequence, the (sexual) contact between Europeans and members of other communities often took place in a twilight zone, not dignified by formal marriage, frequently appearing as concubinage. This was a general pattern. In all the colonies, such relations led to heated discussion and attempts to regulate and restrict inter-ethnic marriages.

There is considerable mystification about the various European communities in Asia and in particular about the frequency of — and attitude towards — sexual contact between European men and Asian or

Eurasian women. For instance, it is often claimed that the Mestizos in
the Portuguese Estado da India were more numerous than under other
colonial powers and that the Portuguese were less inclined to racism
than the British or the Dutch.[67] And indeed, other Europeans in Asia
refer to the large number of Mestizos and "black" Portuguese in the
towns of Asia where the Portuguese held sway. In fact, for a short time
the Portuguese were taken as a model in VOC discussions about the
colonisation of their settlements with Mestizo citizens.[68] One often-
heard argument was that the Portuguese rulers actually encouraged
mestization in order to populate their colonies and create a military and
labour reserve out of their local-born descendants.[69] This is a reference
to the decision taken by the Portuguese conqueror and governor of Goa
Afonso de Albuquerque (1509–1515) to encourage his soldiers to marry
local women.

In sharp contrast to this sanction of interracial communion — still
according to the widely accepted view — was the attitude prevalent in
Dutch and especially British colonies; here, mixed marriages were, at
best, tolerated. There is, however, nothing to suggest that there was less
ethnic mixing taking place among the Dutch and English in Asia than
among the Portuguese. In Ceylon, for instance, within 30 years of the
arrival of the VOC, the majority of the population in the company
settlement was Mestizo, that is, having at least one Asian or Eurasian
parent.[70] In the 19th century about 80 per cent of the Europeans in the
Dutch East Indies were local-born, and most of them had one or more
local-born ancestors. In British India, at least half the adult Europeans
were labelled "Eurasian" in the 1901 census.[71]

None of this in any way denies the existence of racist attitudes in
colonial circles. It is not difficult to assemble a long list of invectives and
prejudices against Mestizos and other non-whites or non-European-
born, by fishing in the waters of the European colonial sources flowing
from Asia. In India, where in the 17th century the British East India
Company had actually encouraged marriage between soldiers (except
those of higher rank) and "native women", by the end of the 18th
century Eurasians were being quietly manoeuvred out of the company.
And the 19th century saw a growing resistance among the British
ruling classes to mixed marriages.[72] Similar sentiments may be detected
in the Dutch East Indies. In 1650, discussions were held in Batavia as
to how best the colony could be populated. Gerard Demmer, a member
of the Council of the Indies, based in Batavia, went so far as to state that
the children of mixed marriages inherited the nature and primitive

characteristics of the mother and led "a filthy and debauched" life.[73] In the Dutch East Indies, like in British India, measures were taken to ensure that Mestizos did not gain positions within the company, and there was considerable opposition to marriage with local women, although objections usually failed to obtain official sanction. Nor was Portuguese colonialism devoid of racial prejudice. António Bocarro, as we have seen, drew a clear distinction between white and black colonists — presumably he thought this relevant. The British historian Charles Boxer has shown clearly that the Portuguese empire was riddled with racism. Within Portuguese circles there was profound resistance to mixed marriages. The *reinols*, that is, the Portuguese from Europe, looked down upon the local Mestizos, while the authorities continually issued directives discouraging and indeed preventing the appointment of *Mestiços*.[74]

Thus, colonial authorities attempted to preserve the exclusiveness of their own community. The presence in the colonies of mixed-race locals with European ancestry often caused great embarrassment; these locals frequently became the target of exclusionary mechanisms. This became even clearer when one colonial regime succeeded another. With a change of regime, it could happen that population categories were redefined; new variations would be created in the complex definition of Mestizo and other groups. For at least a century before the Dutch and British arrived in Asia, the Portuguese had been mixing with the local populations. A large diaspora of (Mestizo) Portuguese had spread throughout the ports and cities of the Indian Ocean. So wherever the Dutch or British East India Companies arrived in Asia, they found Portuguese and their descendants — who were, however, often indistinguishable from Lusified converts to Christianity. They left an indelible mark on the ports and places that were later captured from the Portuguese — such as Colombo, Cochin and Malacca. The women of this community became the first wives of VOC soldiers and clerks, since they were more familiar to the European newcomers than were the native women. The same goes for the choice of Portuguese brides in the settlements of the British East India Company.[75] Until well into the 20th century the term "Portuguese" was used for the descendants of Portuguese and also of Christian converts who had been given a Portuguese name at baptism. It should be borne in mind that few of these people had, in fact, any ancestor from the land of Portugal, but this was generally ignored. Thus, for instance, the dark skin colour of the Malaccan "Portuguese" has nothing to do with the gradual dilution of the genetic inheritance of their Portuguese name-givers with those of locals — rather, it is because they are descended from South Indian slaves who converted to Christianity and in so doing acquired Portuguese names. On the island of Ceylon, too, there were "Portuguese", who were called *Tupass* or *Mechanics* and who were said to have Portuguese ancestry, although in many cases they were the descendants of converted slaves from the days of the VOC.[76] During the British colonial period, after 1796, subtle distinctions developed in Ceylon between the terms British, (British-Sinhalese) Mestizos, Dutch Burghers and Portuguese.[77] This brief selection serves to show the complexity of social distinctions in colonial society and how the process of classification was used in order to create and maintain divisions of class and status.

The colonial inclination to guard European exclusiveness and to compartmentalise the various other population groups should be seen against the backdrop of European perceptions of the non-European. This perception was dominated by a deeply entrenched racial-biblical way of thinking, which traced its roots back to pre-colonial Europe. It is often said that racism only assumed its modern, scientifically based shape with the Enlightenment movement.[78] Indeed, the taxonomic pre-occupation of 18th-century scholarly study undoubtedly had a strong influence on notions concerning variations within the human species and its link to other primates. Writings of the 18th century recorded the distinctive characteristics of different races and recounted the differences between humans and monkeys.[79] But even before this, racist (or biological) explanations about the human species had been propagated — sometimes influenced by biblical stories of the offspring of Noah's son Ham who had gone astray — but undoubtedly largely shaped by colonial experiences.[80]

Although racial thinking clearly affected the structure of colonial society, a concept such as "race" does not exist in isolation. It is part of a wider perspective on the non-European world. It would seem that in the world of the East Indies, race — or, rather, skin colour — was the dominant criterion in determining one's status. In reality, and certainly in everyday reality, other criteria were equally important — such as the economic structure, the balance of various religious groups, and the number of European newcomers entering the community. Class, profession, geographic origin, religion, education as well as skin colour contributed to the placing of an individual within the social hierarchy. Many high-ranking Dutch civil servants were prejudiced against people with a different skin colour, an alternative way of dress, or other modes of behaviour. But if we examine the world of the East Indies more closely, we discover how far the colonial rhetoric was removed from the reality. The prejudices harboured by the colonial elites against people of mixed race failed to lessen the urge to mix and intermarry. Indeed, there were extensive regions in the world of the East Indies where racial demarcations counted for far less than they did on the sun-bleached verandas of the Dutch colonial administrators.

The colonial prescriptions were important, but not overriding, in shaping the world of the East Indies. The very fact that the majority of the population were "Europeans" who had been born and bred in the East, and that there were countless local variations in the level of prosperity, in social status and in the intensity of colonial authority, meant that social hierarchies tended to differ widely between places in the Indies.[81] Demarcation lines within the European community were many and varied, determined by rank, origin and, of course, connections. Undoubtedly, in the centres of administration the hierarchical nature of the Dutch East India Company and later the Dutch government, with its obsessive bureaucratic ranking order, stamped its mark all too firmly on the communities of the East Indies. But there were other worlds in the East Indies where the codes of colonial bureaucracy were less pervasive; entrepreneurs, merchants, artisans and shopkeepers adopted world views different from those of colonial bureaucracy. Thus, the story of the world of the East Indies includes more than government bureaucrats, white-skinned governors, Mestizo clerks and native coolies. It also records the success of local-born — often Mestizo — entrepreneurs and the vivid life in ports and cities where newcomers from Europe were an exotic sight; and it recounts the migration circuits between the Indies and Europe that were to involve many born in the East. Finally, it is the story of how Dutch East Indies citizenship was defined, a story in which the determining factor was not so much race as orientation and place of birth.

CHAPTER **2**

The Baggage of Colonialism

Christian discipline

The story of colonial trading settlements in Asia is generally told from the point of view of the newcomers, that is, the colonisers. The towns and forts are viewed primarily as Dutch graftings upon foreign stock. But besides colonial policy and the culture of the Netherlands, countless other factors influenced the social structure of the settlements in the East Indies — for instance, economic conditions, patterns of migration and the presence of slaves. In and around the trading posts and towns of the Dutch East India Company lived Asian people of all descriptions — chiefly slaves, but also merchants, street-traders, shopkeepers, artisans, small farmers and labourers. The Asian population provided the workforce, the goods and, to a large extent, the money in these colonial towns. Undeniably, colonial government contri-buted a specific twang of its own, a somewhat bizarre blossom produced by grafting a European system of government upon an Asian society.

One thing was of supreme importance: the creation of urban Christian communities controlled by the colonial administration and thus impressed by the morals and bourgeois values of a European elite. Christian morality was propagated by the Dutch Reformed Church and staunchly supported by the governors of the VOC. And although church and government were not always of one mind, the Dutch East India Company defined itself as a Christian ruler.[1] The Christian religion provided the basis for marriage laws, was the underlying principle in the care of the poor, and occupied a central position in urban life both physically — with the presence of church buildings — and in ceremonial matters, such as church services and public days of prayer. The church paid much attention to matters concerning marriage and sexual inter-course and in this way exerted a powerful influence over society. For instance, the prohibition against marriage between Christians and non-Christians had far-reaching effects upon the demarcation of the European community in the East Indies, as well as upon relations between the sexes and among the various population groups. The colonial government also took upon itself the regulation of such matters as concubinage, adultery and prostitution. However, the Asian community was far from being a mass of dough that could be kneaded by the colonial government into the requisite racial and sexual shape.[2] Each place had its local customs and traditions concerning marriage, choice of partner, and interracial relations.

As soon as the Dutch East India Company established itself in a new location and set up a garrison and offices, it began to regulate sexual and social behaviour. The VOC, an organisation that was primarily established and equipped for trade and warfare, found itself forced to regulate relationships between the inhabitants of its settlements and to guarantee a stable community, since sexual contact between local women and company employees could injure the interests of the company — and it troubled the Christian consciences of the VOC authorities. Concubinage and the illegitimate infants thereby produced caused much soul-searching, especially when such children were not brought up in the Christian faith. Thus, in every VOC settlement, measures were enacted to guard against Christians straying from the flock and to strengthen the fabric of Christian life. This became necessary almost from the moment the Dutch set foot on Asian soil, as illustrated by the case of Ambon. Shortly after the VOC established a settlement on the island in 1605, it was decided not to ban sexual contact between the soldiers and local women, but to offer them the opportunity to marry.[3]

From 1615 onwards, Protestant ministers from the Netherlands arrived in the Indies. This helped to regulate the patterns of sexual life. Only after Jakarta was captured in 1619 and renamed Batavia did the company begin to develop a system of church government. The first church council met towards the end of 1620. In a joint effort to curb the excesses of Batavian life, the church and company authorities drew up regulations disciplining marital and sexual behaviour in the city. Governor-General Jan Pieterszoon Coen (1587–1629), who showed a conscientious and god-fearing concern in such matters, wished to combat the debauchery and concubinage and to avoid, as expressed in 17th-century Dutch, *dat deen bysit door fenijn ende vergift den anderen soeckt te vermorden* (that one concubine seeks to murder the other with venom and poison).[4] Strong pressure was placed upon company employees either to marry or not to engage in concubinage (at least in public) —

but this failed to eradicate the evil. A few years later, Coen was forced to re-enact the prohibition and impose severe punishments.[5]

The same story can be told of Ceylon, where in 1640 the Dutch East India Company captured the citadel of Galle from the Portuguese. Initially, the Dutch soldiers and sailors there led a licentious life. They gambled away their weapons and clothing, extorted money from local merchants and sank into drunken debauchery (even when they were on guard duty). Before long, proclamations were issued censoring the "foul and filthy indecency", a phrase that implied "public whoredom and concubinage". The soldiers were living together with local women "as if they were legally married". The authorities felt that such behaviour demonstrated a great contempt for true Christianity, damaged the reputation of the Dutch nation, and called down the wrath of God upon the perpetrators. Although the VOC issued stern prohibitions against such behaviour, it offered leeway to those who "did not possess the faculty of abstinence": they were permitted to marry local women.[6] Concubinage and adultery, as defined by the worldly and church authorities, were a problem not only among the loose-living VOC soldiers; they were a common phenomenon among the Sinhalese people and prompted the VOC to order that all Christian marriages be registered. Furthermore, as was the habit in the Netherlands, the marriage banns were to be read out on three successive Sundays. Stern punishments were imposed for adultery and concubinage, including fines, forced labour, having one's ears cut off, and even more severe measures for repeated offences.[7] The history of the town of Galle was repeated in Colombo, on Ceylon's west coast, where the fortress was captured from the Portuguese in 1656. Sexual immorality was promptly suppressed.[8] Yet however fierce the measures and punishments, there was little that could curb or control sexual promiscuity. It would seem that the European soldiers were not always inspired by the ideal of a Christian marriage and certainly did not attract the most noble and pure-minded of the female sex. When a European man wished to marry a local woman, he had to appear before two members of the local government and give evidence concerning the good conduct of the wife-to-be. Only then were they granted permission to marry.[9]

Most of the VOC establishments in Asia were wrested from the Portuguese; consequently, company authorities everywhere had to deal with the residual Portuguese population who had chosen to stay on after the Dutch takeover. For instance, after the capture of Ambon — a small Portuguese settlement with at most a couple of thousand inhabitants —

the Portuguese garrison was allowed to sail unhampered to Malacca, followed a year later by about 250 Portuguese inhabitants from Ambon, whom the Dutch shipped off to the Philippines. In the end only 46 families of Portuguese origin — supposedly consisting of Mestizos and former slaves — decided to stay, and they swore an oath of allegiance to the Dutch East India Company.[10] In Colombo the only Portuguese who remained after the city was captured were "widows and daughters", 142 in total.[11] Probably most of them were not of Portuguese descent but were manumitted female slaves and their children. Whatever the precise case, they felt too strongly attached to the place to depart along with the disbanded Portuguese garrison. Out of necessity, these women soon turned to the new male arrivals in the VOC garrison, who would be able to provide them with food and shelter. In Batavia, a city lacking a history of Christianisation, the female partners tended to be non-Christian slaves. The strategy was to baptise the women before marrying them. But a Christian marriage did not prove the panacea for which the VOC had hoped. The number of married couples remained a minority, while marriage itself created new problems, such as adultery, double-dealing, blackmail and violence. Thus, in any of the places where it founded a settlement, the company failed to maintain its policy of encouraging marriage; indeed, after the early years, the lower ranks were even discouraged from marrying.

It is a truism that harbour cities and garrison towns are cesspits of vice. Batavia was not only a garrison town, it was also a port, and this was all too evident. The majority of the Europeans stationed there were either soldiers or office clerks. In 1632, 13 years after the Dutch East India Company had captured the citadel of Batavia, its population included 1,560 employees of the company and 229 *vrijburgers* (Burghers, former employees of the VOC who had been granted a resident's permit when their contract expired). The men far outnumbered the women — there were only 366 females on the lists, of whom 106 were registered as wives of company employees. Batavia could thus be described as a male enclave. No Chinese women lived there and very few European women. In 1632 women comprised no more than 22 per cent of the free inhabitants. For the exiled European men, outings to taverns and brothels were about the only available form of light relief in their monotonous life of copying records and marching on guard duty in the tropical heat.

Prostitution, adultery and other forms of unruly behaviour created a huge problem for the Dutch rulers. The VOC employees were

Illustration 2   Most of the Dutch community living in Ceylon in the 17th century were soldiers. Only high-ranking officials in the Dutch East India Company were permitted to bring along their wives from Europe. Esaias Boursse arrived in Ceylon in 1662 or 1663, a few years after the city of Colombo had been captured from the Portuguese, and made this sketch of a group of officials with their wives and a female slave.
[Drawing, Rijksmuseum, Amsterdam.]

continually running up debts, contracting venereal diseases, or becoming embroiled in conflicts of one kind or another. The widespread presence of slaves made sexual exploitation a simple matter. After all, slaves were the property of their owners; provided no actual mistreatment or real violence arose, slave owners were free to behave as they chose. It was quite normal for an owner to send his male and female slaves out to earn their own coolie wages. At regular intervals, the slaves would deliver their profits to their masters. Some owners would allow their slaves to keep part of the wages for themselves; after a time they would thus be able to buy their freedom. The slave-owners were not always particularly interested in the way in which their slaves earned their money. There were evidently many slaves and former slaves working in the organised prostitution industry for which Batavia was famous.

Many female slaves, having gained their freedom, soon fell prey to poverty, and prostitution was for them an obvious way to earn a living. More than a few VOC soldiers, having ended their contracts with the company, would try their fortune running a tavern or brothel (the two were often synonymous). A good many women — often former slaves — were active in this branch of business. We hear in 1651 of the "free" woman Datangh — the adjective "free" generally meant that a person had been something different (a slave) in the past — who was sentenced for "pairing off" slaves (using them for prostitution) and for encouraging whoring.[12] The streets running through the northern part of Batavia, close to the shipyards and fort where many soldiers and sailors were to be found, teemed with taverns and brothels. However, most of the brothels lay outside the city walls, where the grip of the authorities and social control was weaker. To the south of the city an entertainment district developed — here female slaves would sell liquor while a *Liebhaber des Frauenzimmers* (a fancier of women's chambers), as a German soldier once described it, could enjoy himself for the small price of two stivers.[13]

Every VOC settlement had a shadow side, just like Batavia. The German Johann Wolfgang Heydt, who served in the company between 1734 and 1737 in Ceylon, observed that even in the provincial town of Galle, on the island's south coast, there was no shortage of bordellos. The Dutch authorities opposed the growth of an extensive sex industry but were chary of systematic actions against it, despite repeated exhortations from the church councils. The government would, however, intervene if peace and quiet were disrupted. Company employees could enjoy a more-or-less regular sexual partner not by visiting prostitutes, but by maintaining one or more fixed partners for a longer stretch of time or even the length of their stay in Asia. Heydt also noted that the European soldiers managed quite well on their modest wages. They were paid three times a year and from this could enjoy a fairly comfortable life, keeping a "black" housekeeper who also served as a sexual partner.[14] Or they maintained women outside their homes. Precise statistics are not known, but we come across many examples of women who were supported by a soldier or a company employee. These women had no income of their own, and they often lived in narrow side streets in the city, close to the city walls, or just outside the fortifications in lower-class neighbourhoods.

The church councils and the *schepenen* (bailiffs) who formed the city's judicial council had their hands full with cases of prostitution, adultery and fornication, particularly among slaves and Mardijkers (former slaves, now baptised, and their descendants) — and the chief offenders were women. The church, however, was not all-powerful and had limited means of exerting pressure. Only those who were actually church members were subject to reprimands and punishments such as visits from elders, exhortations (to behave piously) and, as a last resort, exclusion from the Lord's Supper. In most places in the Indies, however, only a minority of the Christian residents were members of the Dutch Reformed Church. All others fell outside the authority of the Dutch church.[15] The VOC also attempted, by posting up edicts and administering the law, to counteract loose living. One of the VOC registers, dating from 1632 and 1633 and containing the records of the examination of witnesses who appeared before the bench of bailiffs, indicates that it was chiefly female ex-slaves who appeared in court for sexual offences.[16] During the 17th century, however, the civil authorities withdrew more and more from the realm of moral jurisdiction. It appears that the bailiffs increasingly left such matters to the church council. In cases concerning adultery, bailiffs would regularly pronounce judgment, but cases dealing with premarital sexual relations or sexual contact between Christians and non-Christians are rarely reported after 1650.[17] Even the Dutch Reformed Church eventually gave up its stern public condemnation of Europeans who visited prostitutes or lived with women outside wedlock. During the period 1677 to 1691, 90 per cent of the church's sentences in cases of sexual offence and concubinage were connected with violations by Mardijkers, often women. It seems as if a form of class-, race- and sex-related justice was being applied. The many cases of adoption of illegitimate children suggest that there was no shortage of unlawful sexual contact by European men.

Several employees of the VOC chose either not to marry, or to postpone wedlock. For the civil servants in Batavia, concubinage was banished indoors and the authorities turned a blind eye. Undoubtedly the most frequent form of sexual contact among the European men was with a slave, since this could take place behind closed doors. It goes without saying that such liaisons often produced children. Many of these children — the numbers are not known — disappeared into the community of slaves and Mardijkers, but often a father would adopt his child. It became customary in the 17th century — as prescribed by the Dutch Reformed Church — to adopt the child by notarial deed, prior to having it baptised. In the 15 years between 1683 and 1698 there were at least 299 such adoptions according to notarial deed.[18] In most cases the mothers of the children were slaves. This practice became widely accepted within a few generations. Indeed, it formed part of the established

Illustration 3　Most of the children in the Batavia orphanage were fathered by a European working for the Dutch East India Company; their mothers were generally slaves or concubines. Some children were found living in Asian neighbourhoods and were placed in the orphanage so they could be brought up as Christians.
[Engraving in: Joan Nieuhof, *Gedenkwaerdige zee en lantreize* (1682) (detail).]

social pattern in colonial towns and settlements, where deviation from Christian morality was made good by adoption.

Marriage and citizenship

The account of the VOC's struggle against lax morality may have created the impression that the Indische community, that is, Europeans born in the East Indies, was founded upon fornication; but the very opposite is true. Stern discipline and the propagation of Christian standards formed the cornerstone of these communities. The early years of VOC rule in Asia were evidently somewhat chaotic, but before long, Christian bourgeois norms became firmly entrenched. This did not happen simply because of pressure from above. The marriage tie was seen as a means to further one's career, to gain a certain position. Furthermore, within a few decades there was a generation of men and women who had been born in Asia or had lived there a considerable time, and who benefited from a well-regulated marriage system. Although in the first instance marriage was intended to curb lechery and mitigate conflicts, the governors of the Dutch East India Company realised that in promoting marriage they were also encouraging colonisation. After all, it was in the company's interests to create a loyal following within its forts and towns. Early experiments had been unsuccessful: it proved impossible to ship over young women from the Netherlands and to transform Dutch Burghers into colonial settlers. As an alternative, almost all VOC settlements experienced a short-lived period when company authorities actively encouraged their employees to marry. The upshot of the marriage policies was the birth of a new community — composed of European men and their local wives, the children bearing the father's name and thus, for all intents and purposes, being classed as European.

The effects of this marriage policy could be seen immediately in the VOC establishments. In Batavia the number of marriages rose immediately after the church council issued its edict forbidding men from having concubines. Between October 1621 and January 1623, 175 couples were wedded by the ministers of Batavia.[19] Of the grooms, 63 were company employees, 17 were Burghers, and 95 were Asian. The Asian men were usually Mardijkers. During these years most of the (European) men married Asian women, generally slaves. The registries of baptism also bear witness to the many mixed marriages. For instance, 44 children are recorded as having been baptised during these years; 30 had a European father, and only three had a European mother.[20] Indeed, there were scarcely any European women in Asia in the early years of the VOC. This changed somewhat in 1622, when the Dutch East India Company began shipping — at its own expense — orphan girls from the Netherlands to Batavia as prospective wives for VOC employees. Between 1622 and 1631, 379 European women were married in Batavia, accounting for just over 41 per cent of all the Christian marriages solemnised there in those years. The choice of partner reveals an emerging pattern of social stratification. Of the first shipload to Batavia, comprising 29 Dutch women, 26 were married to employees of the Dutch East India Company, generally men holding a high rank in the company. On the other hand, women of Asian descent who married European men generally married company employees from the lower ranks.

The practice of shipping out orphan girls from the Netherlands lasted for ten years before it was terminated. It proved too expensive, and many of the girls pined for their homeland and soon returned to Holland; in this respect, the colonisation of Asia by the Dutch never really took off.[21] Indeed, the entire colonisation scheme ground to a halt. In 1632 the VOC government even decided to restrain its employees from marrying and decreed that they could marry only with the permission of the governor-general.[22] The number of marriages declined drastically; while before 1634 there had been roughly 70 per year, in the years that followed the number fell to less than half of that.[23] However, although the company ended its attempts at colonisation, it did not ban the emigration of European women. Women from the Netherlands continued to travel to the East, and this source never entirely dried up. So a trend that had begun in the 1620s continued at a low level. Since higher-ranking company employees tended to prefer European women, while men from the lower echelons often married women of Asian descent, class differences became reflected to quite an extent in skin colour. The children from a marriage between a European man and an Asian woman were called Mestizos. However, the word "Mestizo" came to mean not only of mixed blood, but also of lower class. Thus, the Christian community split into various classes, the distinctions being strengthened by marriage patterns.

With the passage of time, a community developed in Batavia consisting of Europeans and Mestizos who were deeply attached to the place where they lived. This Indische generation attained adulthood in the 1640s and 1650s and in those years began to make its mark on the city scene. Up until then, Batavia had been dominated by newcomers, even in the circles of the Burghers, who were mostly former employees of the VOC. The development of the Burgher community never made significant headway, as Burghers were not given much economic latitude. The Dutch East India Company dominated international trade and monopolised dealings in the most lucrative goods. Equally discouraging for the economic chances of the Burghers was the practice whereby employees of the company set up their own trading businesses, on which the VOC tended to turn a blind eye. In the early years the Burghers had a certain amount of freedom to engage in maritime trade, but from 1632 on their sphere of activity became increasingly limited — they could only trade along the coasts between Bengal, in Northeast India, and Cochin China (today part of Vietnam), and within the waters of the Indonesian archipelago with the (then still independent) ports of

Makassar (Sulawesi) and Solor. The lucrative trade with the Moluccas, India, China and Japan was closed to them. Goods such as textiles, diamonds and spices were solely in the hands of the VOC.[24] Many Burghers in Batavia gave up the unequal struggle. Their numbers shrank, from 229 in 1632 to 170 four years later.[25] The disappointed entrepreneurs returned to the Netherlands or rejoined the Dutch East India Company.

The Burghers' opportunities for setting up their own businesses in trade and commerce received their death-blow in around 1649. That year the VOC High Government in Batavia and its directors in the Dutch Republic became embroiled in a fierce debate. The question at issue was whether the East Indies should offer the opportunity to build a firmly rooted colony of Burghers who would to some extent be composed of Dutch colonists or their descendants, who would feel their home to be the East Indies.[26] If the VOC wanted to encourage colonies of citizens in its settlements, then these people should be allowed a share in the lucrative trade presently monopolised by the company. The Burghers of Batavia joined in the debate. Their protests against trade restrictions were in fact the first sounds of what would grow into the East Indies particularism and blossom into full flower in the 19th century. Back in 1648, a group of 58 Burghers presented a petition to the governor-general.[27] We may assume that all citizens who had some interest in maritime trade had signed it. Almost all of them were *Totoks*, that is, newcomers, born in Europe.

The petition proved to be a dead duck. The directors of the VOC in the Netherlands, fearing the growth of a dynamic group of tradesmen, effectively axed the colonisation plans in 1649. This was to have a profound effect on the world of the East Indies. The margins within which the Burghers could act became so narrow that most of them withdrew from the shipping business. A list drawn up in 1674 noting all the Burghers and their professions shows that the vast majority of them earned their living as shopkeepers or artisans. No more than 16 described themselves as "free merchants", and there were six skippers who sailed to nearby Banten and four to Macau.[28] Although throughout the entire VOC period there were employees who, when their contract with the company expired, applied to be a Burgher, during the 17th and 18th centuries their number remained more or less stable, at around 300. The wealthiest citizens had made their fortune in the company's service. Most of the others were dependent upon small businesses and earned their living as smiths, jewellers, bakers, tailors, shoemakers and glassblowers or by renting out carts and carriages.[29] A few Burghers made a fortune moneylending and dealing in real estate, but this market was also served by company employees — who were often more successful agents than the local-born.[30] Landed property was an investment reserved for the upper classes. Many of the Mardijkers also owned land, but usually this would be only a few hectares; those in the upper echelons, in contrast, might own, or rent, hundreds of hectares.[31] The very first grants of land were given free; only when property was transferred or bequeathed, did payment have to be made. Consequently, land was gradually concentrated in the hands of the wealthy, while the middle classes got pushed into the margins.

In the mid-17th century other developments took place that drastically changed the character of the city. During the first decades the European military dominated the city, but by the 1650s changes began to appear due to the explosive growth of the community of freed slaves, or Mardijkers, and other ethnic groups. Immigrants from China, Java and other parts of the Indonesian archipelago increased by leaps and bounds, soon outnumbering the Christian inhabitants. The VOC government gave up not only the plan of converting Batavia into a settlement colony, but also the idea that it should become a Christian town. New distinctions arose, not only between Christians and non-Christians, but also within the Christian community. Racial and social differences became sharper.

In the middle decades of the 17th century a process of restratification took place whereby the nature of the Batavian community changed radically. The colony acquired the characteristics of an administrative plutocracy with a powerful elite firmly distinguishing itself from other groups in the community, including the Asians, the poorer Europeans and the Eurasians. Marriages (recorded in the Dutch marriage registers) from around 1650 offer clear evidence of this emerging social pattern.[32] The number of mixed marriages, frequent in the early years of the VOC, declined sharply. In 1650, out of 46 marriages, only 19 were between a European man and an Asian woman; all the other women were from Europe. Former slave women, and women born in Batavia, tended to marry men from the lower ranks, such as soldiers, sergeants, artisans, an assistant, a quartermaster, two surgeons, and Burghers, who evidently did not enjoy much social standing.

One remarkable statistic is the large number of women from the Netherlands recorded as marrying in the years around 1650. We read that at least half the brides of European men in Batavia came from Europe. Many of these women were widows, already previously married in the Indies, but almost half of them were single women from the Netherlands marrying for the first time. Clearly, there were still considerable numbers of women sailing eastwards to the Indies. The ships' passenger lists from the 17th century also evidence this. Not until later in the 17th century did the numbers of passengers to Asia drop drastically. This deeply affected the whole pattern of marriage and choice of partner.[33] In the years around 1720, about six women born in Europe are annually recorded as marrying in Batavia; of these almost half were widows. Gradually the number decreased, so that later in the century the average number of women from the Netherlands marrying was a mere four or five annually.[34]

Epidemics of malaria, which ravaged Batavia from 1733 onwards, affected many newcomers, and it is probable that this put off many women from travelling to Asia. Because of this, the number of Dutch women in Batavia decreased. All in all, the ratio of men to women among the Europeans (excluding the garrison population) went from 3:2 in 1689 to 7:2 100 years later, and if the Mestizos are included the figure doubled from 1:1 to 2:1.[35] Reports concerning concubinage and adoption of illegitimate children became more numerous, and more white men tended to marry an Asian bride, even if she were not a Mestizo. At the ceremonial inauguration of Petrus Albertus van der Parra as governor-general in 1763, of the 60 Batavian notables present only nine married (sooner or later) a Dutch woman, while eight remained unmarried. The remaining 43 had wives who were born in Asia.[36] In this sense, the East Indies was far more Indische in the 18th century than in the previous century.

Mixtures in Ceylon

Batavia was by far the largest Dutch colonial settlement. The East Indies of the VOC consisted of considerable numbers of fortresses and settlements grouped around Batavia like a ring of planets, with several having satellites of their own. These societies should not be seen as mini-reproductions of the mighty Batavia. They developed their own patterns of mixing and mingling, and their own variations of distributing power and wealth. European circles in Batavia were dominated by the newcomers from Europe. Most of the Totok women remained in that city. Most important functions were held by Totoks. In Batavia the number of local-born people employed by the company ranged from approximately 250 to 450, which was seldom more than 10 per cent of the total employees. This low percentage may partly be explained by the large number of soldiers in Batavia, almost all of them newcomers. The number of Totoks in the company's personnel decreased in the 18th century; this was most noticeable in civil functions. A peak year such as 1779 saw 303 out of the 513 civil company employees in Batavia being local; in other words, 59 per cent were Asian-born.[37]

Other parts of the East Indies world had a stronger Indische character than Batavia. In Colombo, for instance, the second largest settlement of the Dutch East India Company in Asia, in 1749 almost 32 per cent of the 1,648 VOC employees were born in Asia. The majority of the functionaries working in the offices and warehouses there were local-born: in 1749 they numbered almost 169 of the 219 members of staff, in other words, more than 77 per cent. And 40 years later this number had climbed to 84 per cent; entire offices, including the merchant at the top, were manned by people who had spent their entire lives in Ceylon.[38] Likewise, in the city of Cochin in southern India, 80 per cent of the civilian personnel in 1788 were Asian-born, most in Cochin itself.[39] In many of what were known as the "outlying provinces", established families ruled the roost, and Totoks only occupied certain posts and functions, such as governor and soldier.

An overview of the population of Colombo in 1684, showing the European, Mestizo and local (native) components, reveals the patterns that had emerged in the fewer than 30 years since the city had been captured from the Portuguese.[40] In that year, it is recorded that the city housed 393 European, Mestizo and local company employees and Burghers. Of this number, 276 were married men; the rest were widows, widowers or unmarried. Of the wives, only 37 were from Europe. Of these, 34 were married to company employees, most of them men in higher functions, while three were married to Dutch Burghers. Far and away the largest number of wives of Europeans were Mestizo or Asian (in the census they were labelled "native", "Portuguese" or "black"). This indicates how swiftly the process of mestization had occurred. The story is continued in their children. In 1684 there were 678 children of Christian inhabitants living in Colombo, of whom only 83 (that is, approximately 12 per cent) had two European parents. Approximately 63 per cent had a European father and a Mestizo or Asian mother, while about 24 per cent had two Mestizo or Asian parents.[41] In the city of Galle, in southern Ceylon, which was smaller than Colombo, the same story could be told. Here only 31 of the 228 registered children had two European parents. The number of illegitimate children from European fathers was small — in Colombo only 19, and in Galle 18. The statistics on this point are somewhat unreliable, since there might well have been unlisted children in the families of slaves or others. Despite this, the concept of Christian marriage had clearly acquired a central place within the community. In the space of one generation a layered society was emerging, buttressed by a strong body of local families who intermarried with the European newcomers and the descendants of former slaves.

For Burghers in such places as Galle and Colombo, opportunities for economic advancement were even more limited than in Batavia. A few tradesmen were Burghers, but most of the Europeans born in Ceylon entered the service of the Dutch East India Company at an early age. In Colombo, trade with India, on the other side of the water, was jealously guarded, and the company held a monopoly on the most important goods. A small number of Burghers traded between Ceylon and ports in India, in particular Nagapattinam, Cochin and Bengal. They dealt largely in rice, as well as textiles and saltpetre (potassium nitrate).[42] They gradually lost this trade to the Chettiyars and Moors (Hindu and Muslim Tamils), who, especially after 1700, arrived in large numbers. Chettiyars and Moors also took over the tax farms and other farmed-out privileges.[43] The textile trade became concentrated in the hands of one agent, who distributed the cotton goods to the stall-holders. No single Burgher managed to get together sufficient capital to compete with this.[44] Ceylon had very few prosperous Burghers. Most of them lived off their land or ran a tavern, the two often being complementary: their palm trees produced the toddy and arrack that they served their clients.[45]

The Burghers frequently colluded in their attempts to prise greater privileges out of the governor. The officers of the militia, who evidently enjoyed great respect in the community, acted as spokesmen. The first petition was drawn up in 1678, and many were to follow. At the time of the first petition there were more than 100 Burghers living in Colombo who, according to the wording of their requests, found themselves "in a wretched state".[46] It is not surprising that the Burghers were desperate. Initially, the Dutch East India Company had encouraged retired employees and independent colonists to establish businesses, in the hope of defeating any trading attempts of the locals. But despite this, the Asian merchants — whom the Burghers denounced as rabble — had managed to gain a secure footing in the city and indeed had wrested lucrative trade from the Burghers. Time and again the Burghers claimed that because they were descended from employees of the VOC they were entitled to preferential treatment — a plaint that was to echo through into the 20th century. But the governor and his councillors seldom acquiesced to the Burghers' demands. They did attempt to involve them in agricultural activities, granting plots of land in the vicinity of Colombo, but to little avail.[47] The small estates produced only coconuts, betel nuts or palm wine, and none of these crops was going to make a Burgher very rich. To make matters worse, the growth of free landownership was soon curbed, because the cinnamon trees, yielding their valuable spice, grew in the wild. The Dutch East India Company could not permit them to fall into the hands of private landowners, and it stopped the expansion of private estates.

Initially, Colombo had a large population of Burghers, encouraged by the active colonisation policy of the early governors. But when it appeared that there were few fortunes to be made, many disappointed men returned to their former jobs with the Dutch East India Company.[48] In the 60 years between 1736 and 1796, of all the 4,257 Christian marriages registered in Colombo, including both "European" and "Native" marriages, only 313 of the grooms are stated to have been Burghers or freemen (a term used for Asian Burghers). About five times as many were company employees.[49] Just as in Batavia, most Burghers married Mestizo or Asian women, which indicates that most of these men were from the lower income bracket and suggests that Burghers stood fairly low on the social ladder. In Malacca, records tell us that even the most prosperous Burghers married "free black" women or Mestizos.[50] Insofar as there were European women living in the outlying provinces, they had usually arrived in Asia as married women — they had simply followed their husbands eastwards. This was permitted only among the higher ranks. Thus, we observe that the creation of a white upper class was implicit in the regulations concerning migration. This tendency was reinforced by the fact that Totok women who married in Asia — they were generally widows — usually chose high-ranking VOC officials as spouses. In the period 1736 to 1796 — the years for which we have an extant marriage register — the records show that in Colombo only 23 women from Europe were married. Their husbands were, in the main, employees of the VOC, in high- or middle-ranking positions.[51] Nevertheless, cities like Colombo or Malacca were not simply Mestizo communities, because there was a continuous influx of newcomers from Europe — mainly soldiers and, to a lesser extent, high-ranking company officials. Depending on their position, these newcomers would select their wives

from the women in the local European community and, to a lesser
extent, from among the Portuguese who were the Christian descendants
of freed slaves and other converts to Christianity.

Javanese circuit

The Dutch East India Company's settlements on the north coast of
Java formed, just as in Ceylon, a separate network of local families and
(Dutch) company employees. During the 17th and 18th centuries the
VOC established settlements in such places as Jepara, Rembang and
later Semarang, Pasuruan and Surabaya. They remained small coastal
trading posts, with the exception of Semarang, which grew into a centre
of trade during the 18th century thanks to its favourable position as the
major port for the Central Javanese hinterland. In around 1710 there
were no more than 25 "freemen" living in Semarang, most of them
Mardijkers, and three or four Netherlanders.[52] The majority of European
Burghers in Semarang were garrison soldiers who had remained when
their contract with the VOC expired — often because they had formed
family ties. In 1767 there were 2,011 people living in the European part
of the city. At least half this number were slaves and *pandelingen*, a kind
of debt-bondsmen. They were usually local men and women who had
accumulated debts and were obliged to work for their creditor for a
certain length of time — sometimes the length of time was not stated
— until they had worked off their debts. The creditor, in turn, was
obliged to feed and protect the debtors. One remarkable statistic from
Semarang is the excessive number of unmarried men — 238 men
and only 35 unmarried women — although this is partly balanced by
the category headed "free women", which numbers 137.[53] These latter
women are presumably the concubines of unmarried men in the city.
This suggests that in Semarang concubinage was far more prevalent than
in the VOC settlements in Ceylon.

During the 18th century Semarang grew into the second-most
important port in Java, with a trading network extending along the
whole north Java coast and farther westwards to Palembang (southern
Sumatra) and the Straits of Malacca.[54] Overseas trade was dominated by
the Chinese and Javanese. Only the most audacious Europeans dared
to venture into this sea trade. Around 1775 scarcely 3 per cent of the
skippers listed are European, compared with 26 per cent Chinese and
41 per cent Javanese.[55] Most Europeans remained dependent on the
VOC for their living, or they set up businesses as shopkeepers or artisans.

Although Semarang, like Batavia, was plagued by malaria, it was apparently a place where VOC employees were happy to retire. In around 1812, no fewer than 1,077 Europeans had made their home in the city.[56]

Colonial officials looked to the slave women for company — but more often, it seems, they looked to the female debtors (pandelingen) of the Javanese regents. A lively trade in pandelingen arose in the northern Javanese settlements. Javanese regents (district heads) would hand over female debtor-slaves to Dutch soldiers and Burghers, who would pay for them or, in some cases, discharge their debts.[57] Many European newcomers seemed to have preferred a non-committal relationship with a pandeling or slave woman, rather than marriage, since the latter would bring with it great responsibility and also tie them to the East. There was no question of furtive behaviour or the need for secrecy. Women from the Netherlands scarcely ever came to the outlying regions, and church control was loose — ministers of the Dutch Reformed Church at the end of the 18th century were stationed only in Semarang and Surabaya. Furthermore, in Javanese tradition cohabitation was quite customary, something that made its mark on the lifestyle of the Europeans.

Many women and children were left abandoned by the European partner when he took up a post elsewhere, repatriated or died. Usually the children remained with their mother and grew up in the Javanese quarters or villages. Some stayed wandering around close to the garrison and would be looked after by the soldiers. And sometimes illegitimate children who were found in Java's coastal towns were sent to the orphanage in Batavia. In 1709, for instance, 23 children were brought to Batavia; all of them had a European father and a Javanese mother — whose names, interestingly, were recorded.[58] In 1716 it was noted that there were 70 illegitimate children in Semarang, but on this occasion the governor-general decreed that they must be looked after locally, not sent to Batavia. It is not known what happened to them. Clearly, the VOC felt a certain responsibility towards these children; this reflected itself in the founding of an orphanage in Semarang in 1769. But for one reason or another, the government took no steps to regulate the "dissolute life of the local officials with the Javanese whores".[59]

A circuit developed in Central and East Java consisting of civil servants, soldiers and Burghers who journeyed between the various European settlements. Many of the employees of the Dutch East India Company were recruited locally — although less than in Ceylon. Both among the local recruits and among the newcomers there was great mobility between the various (VOC) posts on Java.[60] The VOC garrisons in the semi-independent Central Javanese kingdom of Kartasura also formed part of this circuit, as did the garrisons stationed in Yogyakarta and Surakarta after the kingdom was split in 1755. The garrisons were small, consisting of a few hundred men, but their presence was to be of huge significance in the history of Central Java. They spawned the fore-fathers of a European community that would settle in Java's Principalities and remain there for generations. Before long, there were reports of contacts between VOC soldiers and Javanese women and the children born from these unions. In about 1720 a "free" Javanese woman named Santiap gave her daughters Maria and Cecilia, who had been "fathered by certain Europeans in Kartasura", into the care of Sgt. Vincent Piquerie, who promised to look after them and give them a Christian upbringing.[61] There were many children like these two little girls. We do not know whether they had been baptised, but their father had certainly given them Christian names. Many fathers wanted their children, legally acknowledged or not, to be given a Christian upbringing. Later in the 18th century it became quite common for Javanese mothers to disclaim their children; this would be done by notarial deed, whereby the mothers relinquished all rights to their children. In the year 1780 at least 29 children, varying in age from a few months to a few years, were ceded in this way.[62] A European male guaranteed that the child would be raised in "the true Christian Protestant religion". The man would certainly not always be the child's biological father. An intricate pattern of adoption developed, making family connections within the Principalities extremely complicated. There would frequently be legitimate, illegitimate and adopted children within one family.

By the second half of the 18th century, European communities had developed in Yogyakarta and Surakarta that had close ties with their Javanese surroundings while retaining their own identity; this was partly determined by the fact that they were employees of the Dutch East India Company and were Christians. Of 166 adult European males registered in Yogyakarta in 1804, five were Burghers and almost all the rest soldiers and dragoons. Just 126 came from Europe. Many of those born in the Indies — almost always in Yogyakarta or Surakarta — were to be found holding civilian posts or among the dragoons. The soldiers in the artillery and infantry generally came from Europe. Of the 166 men mentioned, 32 were married.[63] There were 66 men who fathered children — a total of 129 children, of whom at least half were illegitimate. Nearly all the men with illegitimate children were unmarried. This state of affairs was completely accepted. There was no Dutch Reformed minister in

Illustration 4 In Surakarta (Central Java), a small community of European soldiers and officials emerged in the late 18th century. Many descendants were also employed by the Dutch East India Company and later the colonial government, most as dragoons in the guard of the *susuhunan*. Resident's office in Surakarta.
[Pen drawing by Hubert J.J.L. de Stuers, *ca.* 1822, Royal Tropical Institute, Amsterdam.]

Yogyakarta, and the church was far away; indeed, of all the men there, only five were active church members.

These statistics alone indicate how widespread concubinage was in Java and how great the number of children born out of wedlock. The lifestyle in the Principalities was very different from that in colonial urban centres such as Batavia. In Yogyakarta, too, the VOC was the major employer of Europeans, but its control over local society was limited. After all, the Principalities did not form part of the company's territories, and the dragoons, trumpeters and coachmen of the company were part of the local sultan's retinue. Until well into the 20th century the cities of the Principalities remained known for their high rate of concubinage, even among high-ranking officials and the military.[64] For instance, in the 1770s a resident of Surakarta, Friedrich Christoph van Stralendorff, fathered eight children with two concubines. With permission from the High Government in Batavia, he had them declared legitimate. He had had relationships with the two women for many years. His first concubine was the Javanese Sintes, while the second was named Margaretha Juliana Abrahams and was a "European". Because she had died, it was no longer possible for the ageing resident to legitimate the children by marriage; thus, in 1779 he had to apply to the government in Batavia to legitimate their births.[65] The Van Stralendorffs would continue into the 20th century as one of the prominent families in Yogyakarta, running plantations and trading in sugar. Other well-known dynasties from the Principalities, such as the Burgemeestre, Deux and Dezentjé families, sprang from the officials and dragoons of the Dutch East India Company and their Javanese partners. Where a firm marriage regime was absent, legitimisation and adoption were crucial in the formation of a European identity and community, which was primarily based not on skin colour, but on Christian baptism and naming.

Slave children

While Mestizo communities were growing rapidly in the colonies in South Asia, Java and the Moluccas, things were looking very different in Batavia. Here the social spectrum was, in a manner of speaking, weighed down under the burden of two opposing immigrant streams. On the one hand were the large numbers of newcomers from Europe. They continued to occupy the upper ranks in the Dutch East India Company, fashioning their world with their conventions and status norms. Among the newcomers were thousands of soldiers living in the garrisons who were not permitted to marry. On the other hand, the city swarmed with slaves who had been brought there from neighbouring regions and who, after manumission, filled the ranks of the urban proletariat. During the 17th and 18th centuries between 200,000 and 300,000 slaves were transported to Batavia. Indeed, the majority of those living in Batavia had a background of slavery. Inside the city walls, where about 20,000 people lived, at least half the population were slaves and 10 per cent were Mardijkers. Most of the extramural communities also consisted of former slaves and their children. The demographic effects of the slave trade were enormous: when slavery was abolished in 1813, population growth ceased for a long time.[66]

The Europeans were the largest group of slave owners. There are no statistics recording how many slaves there were per household in Batavia, but figures from other comparable cities can offer some idea. In Colombo in 1694, 70 per cent of the slaves were owned by Europeans, with an average of almost 11 slaves per household; on Ambon these figures were respectively 59 per cent and almost five.[67] In Batavia the Mardijker community fluctuated with the number of Europeans in the city, which suggests a close correlation between the number of Europeans and the emancipation of Christian slaves.[68] There appears to have been an almost insatiable demand for slaves. The whole of Batavia — from the company's dockyards to household personnel, from orchestras to agriculture — depended on slave labour. The ubiquitous slaves also provided easy sexual contacts for their owner. Presumably, sexual relations between masters and their slaves were so common, and so much a matter of course, that they were seldom given special mention.

Slavery left other traces on the pattern of urban life. It was customary for Europeans to baptise their slaves. This practice took off after 1648, when baptised slaves were admitted to the religious celebration of the Lord's Supper in the Dutch Reformed Church.[69] In Protestant churches it was not the sacrament of baptism but that of the Lord's Supper (Eucharist or Holy Communion) that admitted a person into the community of Christian believers. Furthermore, many Batavian Europeans took pride in emancipating their baptised slaves. They would usually do this in their wills. Some of the emancipated slaves would, not surprisingly, be the natural children of slave women and European fathers.[70] Once they had been baptised and emancipated, these former slaves merged into the Mardijker community. The Mardijkers were a flock of varied plumage. Initially, most of the slaves in Batavia came from India and Bali. This changed between 1660 and 1670, when the VOC halted its slave trade from India and Pegu (southern Burma) and, after the capture of the southern Sulawesi kingdom of Goa, channelled the extensive slave-trade network from Makassar to Batavia.[71] The slaves of Indian origin living in Batavia quickly became a minority group. After some decades, this shift in slave supply areas resulted in the establishment of a Malay-speaking church in Batavia. The slaves from India tended to speak Portuguese, and the lingua franca in most households with slaves would probably also have been Portuguese. Thus, after their emancipation, slaves from India as well as the East Indies joined the Portuguese-speaking community. Between October 1688 and February 1708 there were 4,426 people accepted into the Portuguese-speaking church, while in the Malay-speaking church the number is no more than 306.[72] With time, the Portuguese language began to fade out of use, and so during the 18th century the balance shifted. In the 1780s each year saw about 30 people joining the Portuguese congregation, while 31 were accepted into the Malay church.[73]

Illustration 5 The main church of the "Portuguese" community in Batavia stood just outside the city walls, to the east, where most of the Mardijkers lived. The church was built in 1695, when the Mardijker community was rapidly expanding.
[Drawing with brush and ink by Johannes Rach, *ca.* 1775, Perpustakaan Nasional Indonesia, Jakarta.]

The Mardijker community in Batavia died a quiet death. During the 18th century the stream of slaves from India slowed to a trickle and dried up; more and more slaves were brought from the Indonesian archipelago, eroding the culture of the Portuguese-speaking Mardijkers of Indian ancestry. Furthermore, the number of Europeans coming to Batavia fell during the 18th century; consequently, the number of Christian slaves declined, together with the number of baptised slaves who were given their freedom. Another factor was the high death rate among the local-born, which, together with the epidemics that ravaged the city after 1733, caused a drastic fall in the number of children.[74] So if the number of Mardijkers were to increase, it would have to be through emancipated slaves of Europeans and other Christians. A further possibility is that the habit of baptising household slaves fell into decline. We know, for instance, that even the Lutheran minister Jan Brandes, who was living in Batavia between 1779 and 1785, did not baptise his own slaves.[75]

Within the Christian community of Batavia, the Mardijkers formed a separate group. A crucial criterion for determining someone's status in society was whether they had slave ancestry or not. If someone had Portuguese forefathers, that meant a slave ancestry — even when the slaves were many generations in the past. A similar stigma, hard to stamp out, was attached to the Portuguese in Colombo. Until well into the 19th century they were looked down on because of their low status.[76] The same tendency could be seen in British India, where the Anglo-Indians of the northern cities looked down on the "half-castes" in the southern city of Madras (today's Chennai) who were more imbued with Portuguese influences.[77] The latter people, whose skin was a darker brown, who spoke a different language (Portuguese), and who were often poorly off, were burdened with the baggage of their former slavery — although this was rarely explicitly referred to.

Although distinguished from the European community, the Christian former slaves could certainly appeal to the church's charity. And many did. Reading the petitions for alimony made to the *diakonie* (church welfare board), we are able to sketch the outlines of Batavian poverty. Most of the requests came from Mardijkers, although Burghers, Mestizos and ex-VOC employees also knocked at the church's door. The latters' numbers were small, because a European or Mestizo who found himself out of money and employment could re-enlist with the Dutch East India Company — which probably explains why there were relatively few Europeans and Mestizos dependent on charity. For instance, in December 1728 it is recorded that 136 Mardijkers were being sheltered in Batavia's poorhouse, whereas there were no more than six Mestizos and 25 Europeans.[78] Only those who were too old or infirm to care for themselves could reckon on assistance. One such man was the former barber Christiaan Kittelman, who in around 1700 hired himself out to take the place of other citizens in the militia, for a small sum, until he grew too old even to fulfil this task. Then he had to resort to poor relief. Another case concerned a Mardijker widow, Anna de Zoza, who had taken her grandchildren into her home when their mother, her daughter, died; their Mestizo father, De Zoza wrote to the church welfare board, was a write-off, and she begged for poor relief.[79] Most of the applicants for assistance were widows, invalids and children, all unable to support themselves independently. If someone was simply poor, they had no choice but to make do with whatever kind of employment was at hand.

With more and more slaves being set free, more and more Mardijkers applied for poor relief.[80] The Dutch East India Company attempted to reduce the burden by decreeing that slaves could only be set free when *schepenen* (bailiffs) had confirmed that they were able to support themselves; furthermore, freed slaves might only ask for church poor relief after six years. But despite all these efforts, the numbers on the church assistance lists remained high — though no higher than in the Netherlands. Out of a population of around 7,500 Mardijkers, there were, on average, 1,000 (13 per cent) receiving welfare at the end of the 17th century; in the Dutch city of Haarlem, percentages of families living on church welfare were as high.[81] Poverty remained a grave problem throughout the 18th century, even if the number of families on welfare appears to have fallen after the 1730s.[82] This did not mean that life improved for the Mardijkers; over those years their total number gradually decreased.

Although the church was expected to assist all its members, in the poorhouse a clear distinction was made between Europeans, Mestizos and Asian Christians. For instance, Europeans generally received four rix-dollars (9.60 guilders) a month, with some receiving six or more; Mestizos were given something between half a rix-dollar and three; and Asians (called *inlanders,* or natives, in the books) were usually given just one. Most of the poor living outside the poorhouse would get something like one rix-dollar or less, though certain families received far more. The differences — however arbitrary — were very significant for the people in question, and they were monitored carefully. Quite often, descendants of Europeans would be discovered among the natives. Immediately, their welfare would be increased. In 1769–1770 four Mestizos were found to be listed among the Mardijker recipients of charity. One of them was named Jan van Batavia and was presumably a former slave.[83] A person's family background would be translated not only in terms of money but also in terms of clothing. European and Mestizo men received trousers, stockings and a hat; European women received a dress; and Mestizo women had a *kebaya,* a light cotton blouse to be worn over a sarong or wraparound skirt — they did not receive any Dutch-style clothing.[84]

The orphanage was another hive of poverty. Here, not surprisingly, we find more Mestizos than in the poorhouse. Many of the orphaned offspring of Batavia were the fruit of a union between a European man and an Asian woman, be it slave, concubine or spouse. The number of Mestizo children in the orphanage varied between 30 and 50, in addition to which there were between 10 and 20 European children. The orphanage was also home to slave children.[85] Many orphans did not remain for long within the walls of the orphanage but would go to live with foster families and were often adopted, although not in every case. For instance, a widow named Maria Simons van der Heijden took under her wing the little Magdalena, a natural child begotten by either Van der Heijden's brother or her father in Jepara (northern Java). Initially the little girl had lived with Van der Heijden's mother, but when the latter died, Van der Heijden took on the responsibility. It is hardly surprising to learn that Magdalena, who had been passed from pillar to post, was a child with behavioural difficulties. So in 1702 the despairing Van der Heijden asked the church welfare board whether it would take over the care of the girl.[86] To balance such a story, there were many people who took orphans out of the poorhouse — especially artisans, who used the boys as apprentices and taught them a craft.

Asian Burghers

Seldom could Mardijkers achieve fame and fortune. Very few of them possessed any capital. If they were lucky enough to learn to write, they might perhaps gain employment in one of the Dutch East India Company's offices; but not many did so. Mardijkers rarely cut free from the entanglements of their social background, that of the proletariat and petty middle classes; they were forced to earn their living by selling their agricultural produce, pen-pushing for a private individual, or signing up as soldiers in the VOC. In the latter position they were — unlike the European soldiers — recruited for only one particular campaign. On their return to Batavia they would be demobilised. In the second half of the 17th century several hundred Mardijker soldiers fought for the VOC.[87] After 1700 the enthusiasm apparently waned somewhat, although we do find Mardijkers forming companies for the civic guards until well into the 19th century. Not only was this a compulsory service, it also provided both status and income.

In the lower reaches of Christian Batavian society, boundaries between the various groups tended to be fluid. Nonetheless, the Mardijkers formed a distinct community. An illustration of the social horizons of the Mardijkers may be found in the writings of a certain Isaac Jansz, who is probably the only Mardijker from such circles to have left extensive autobiographical notes.[88] His grandfather had been brought as a slave from the island of Bali to Batavia. There, he landed up in a Christian household and was baptised. As was customary, at his baptism he assumed a Christian name: Jan Thomaszoon — the patronymic presumably referring to his owner. He married one Anna Cardoso, whose Portuguese name suggests she was a slave of Indian origin. We know neither why they got married, nor how they experienced their diverse cultural backgrounds. Possibly they both enjoyed a Hindu upbringing, which would have meant they had something in common; and they were both Christian converts. Whatever the story, they presumably both spoke Portuguese, attended the same church, and were part of the same community of Mardijkers.

Jansz was born in about 1679 in Batavia and lived there his entire life. He must have been well educated, for he wrote good Dutch. He earned his living as a scribe and secretary to several notables of Batavia. Indeed, one may almost speak of a career, for his patrons become evermore-prominent figures and his earnings correspondingly higher — although they remained on the modest side. Jansz did not seek his fortune with the Dutch East India Company but operated as a freelance clerk. Undoubtedly, he was proud of the modest career he made for himself and recorded it in detail. He began as an office boy when he was aged 18, penning for the civic notary David Reguleth. The latter found a young man such as Jansz, with his good command of Dutch, Portuguese and probably also Malay, a useful asset. Jansz earned two rix-dollars (4.8 guilders) a month. By way of comparison, a European soldier earned nine guilders. In 1699 Jansz's income doubled when he went to work as a clerk for the bailiff Cornelis van Outhoorn. He also worked for the Court of Marital Affairs and Petty Claims, but he clearly reached the peak of his career when from 1705 to 1709 he was clerk to Laurens Pijl, a member of the Council of the Indies and a former governor of Ceylon. In this position Jansz earned eight rix-dollars a month. Important as this was to him, he probably earned far more from his incidental services for other urban residents. All this combined to give him an income above that of the average soldier or artisan working for the Dutch East India Company. Furthermore, he earned between three and four rix-dollars monthly as an officer in the Mardijkers' militia. All in all, he did rather well for himself. In 1707 he bought a house within the city, for the not-paltry sum of 2,200 rix-dollars; this he then rented out for between six and ten rix-dollars a month to Chinese and European ship captains and VOC employees who wanted a temporary lodging in the city.

Jansz kept a careful record of all his affairs, both public and private. A baptismal ceremony was a major event in the life of Batavian Christians and a moment when social ties were strengthened. Jansz stood godfather at the baptism of at least 28 children and adults. Indeed, he was proud of the number of baptisms in which he had taken part. All those baptised were slaves, former slaves or Mardijkers, as may be seen from their (Portuguese) names and patronymics. Jansz was evidently held in considerable regard by his patrons and employers, but there was no great intimacy. It always remained a relationship of patron to client, permitting little familiarity. His business relations often brought him into contact with Chinese and other cultural groups; but for real friendship and closeness he sought his own kind. This would be a group of Mardijkers and Mestizos, local-born, for whom Batavia was home. For such people, it was unthinkable that they might gain a post within the VOC apart from that of clerk; thus, they earned their living through agriculture, artisanal work, minor speculation and, in a few cases — such as Jansz — as a scribe. All in all, Jansz was a respectable citizen and seems to have kept himself aloof from the riff-raff and the shadier sides of the Batavian economy.

The Mardijkers were a pot-pourri sprouted from the descendants of widely disparate cultures blown from many corners of Asia. It was impossible to be more of an ethnic mix than a Mardijker. Some of them were descendants of Europeans — children born of slave mothers, neither recognised nor adopted by their fathers. Presumably, the genetic background of these children must have been obvious, but they are seldom officially listed or even mentioned. After all, they stood far removed from the high-placed VOC officials and educated European travel writers. The distinction between the Mardijkers and the Mestizos was fuzzy and in a way chiefly an administrative construct only partly based on reality. Indeed, for newcomers from Europe the difference was often far from clear.[89] Nevertheless, at certain moments the distinction was an important one — for instance, when determining the amount of poor relief to be paid by the church.

The military made their own idiosyncratic contribution to the world of the urban poor. Inevitably, they met others in the intimacy of taverns and brothels, but for many soldiers that was perhaps as far as it went. Some soldiers had dealings with Mardijkers, of a business, social or sexual nature. But we regularly hear of tension between the Mardijkers and the European soldiers. These outbursts would be accompanied by streams of abusive language, marked by pejorative descriptions of the other's ancestry and faith. "Son of a nigger bitch" was a favourite epithet to fling. Interestingly, the European soldiers always liked to pair it with words referring to skin colour. The soldiers, in search of booze and pleasure, terrorised the streets and posed a constant threat. In 1655 two

Illustration 6 Most of the "Portuguese" in Ceylon were descended from freed slaves. They peopled the streets and byways of company settlements in places such as Colombo and Galle. In 1785 Jan Brandes spent several months in Ceylon and made this drawing of a Portuguese woman buying butter from two Sinhalese street-traders.
[Watercolour drawing, Rijksmuseum, Amsterdam.]

German soldiers were hauled before the Court of Justice. They had been on the rampage and had knocked at a Mardijker's house, ordering some arrack to drink. Failing to get what they wanted, they flew into a fury, cursing the man and his wife, calling him a "filthy pig" and her a "dirty black bitch", and even drawing their swords and wounding the innocent man.[90] By Batavian standards it was a minor incident, but it reveals some of the feelings rife in the city, where questions of race and social status were always smouldering just beneath the surface.

Career in the Dutch East Indies

In a city such as Batavia, few roads led to riches. The fastest way was to vault to a high position in the Dutch East India Company. Certain posts were known to confer abundant emoluments and indeed paved the path to fortune, if not fame. Some powerful and wealthy men emerged from the European ranks of the VOC. One much-coveted post was that of Commissioner of Native Affairs, which involved control over the lands surrounding the city of Batavia. Here the commissioner ruled like a prince and in no time at all would be able to rake in a fortune selling various licences and purveyances. Another highly desirable position was that of administrator of the island of Onrust (lying off Batavia), who was in charge of the richest warehouses of the city and who earned thousands of guilders a year from bribes and contraband.[91] Generally the most important and best-paid functions were given to Totoks, those recently arrived from Europe. Very few Europeans who had grown up in Asia, whether Mestizo or not, managed to penetrate the upper echelons of the Dutch East India Company. The deep-rooted system of patronage in the Dutch colony was the pivot of career-making. Under company rule, life in the East Indies was not yet in the thrall of the passion for diplomas and certificates that would later dig its claws into every social class. Instead of diplomas, a letter of recommendation sufficed. Of course, a certain amount of good luck also helped: it was useful if the person to whom the letter was addressed was still alive — and occupying an influential position — when the bearer arrived in Batavia.

Another good strategy was to make a useful marriage — preferably with a daughter of one of the high officials. In her penetrating study of life in Indonesia, Jean Gelman Taylor has pointed out the importance of a politic marriage for the ambitious European.[92] One such European was Reynier Bernardus Hoynck van Papendrecht, who arrived in Batavia in 1778 and, on the demise of his Dutch wife, married a wealthy widow. When she in turn expired, Hoynck van Papendrecht inherited a huge sum, with which he established an extensive trading and shipping empire on the coast of Malacca. He married for a third time, this time a Malaccan woman. The nouveau-riche shipping magnate had outspoken views of the Indies world. Thus he wished only for daughters, as he deemed nothing worse for European fathers than to beget sons. Irrespective of the amount of energy invested in their education, boys would grow up in the wrong spirit, and besides, they had little hope of making a good career. Hoynck van Papendrecht was determined, like many a father in his situation, to send any son of his back to Europe when he reached the age of three. However, all his wives died with remarkable rapidity shortly after marriage and he himself died without issue in 1788.[93]

Hoynck van Papendrecht was quite right. Children born in Asia had a poor outlook. Education in the settlements of the Dutch East India Company was inadequate, while the career path upward was long and arduous. Indeed, in 1727 the government in Batavia announced explicitly that "Indische children", that is, Europeans born and educated in the Indies, could be accepted into government service only in situations of extreme emergency.[94] Although the shortage of staff was too great for this to be taken seriously, nevertheless it remained a hard struggle to reach the upper ranks. So if they could, Europeans sent their sons at an early age to Europe for their education. In 1773 Pieter Sluijsken, the captain of cinnamon culture — the official supervising the collection and delivery of cinnamon bark — in Colombo sent his son Gerrit Hendrick to the Netherlands because it was "not possible to provide a child with a decent education here; and still less to have a child learn those skills and manners with which a well-bred young man would be able to earn his daily bread …". Thus, every VOC ship returning to the Netherlands bore several small boys being sent far from home to board with friends or family across the seas. The boys would often be entrusted to the care of a colleague or acquaintance who was repatriating and who would keep an eye on them during the long journey. Once in the Netherlands, he would hand them over to the foster family.[95] An education in Europe was a costly enterprise: we know that Sluijsken gave his son 600 rix-dollars per year.[96] But despite the expense, it was general practice among the higher-ranking Europeans in Asia.

Thus, place of birth did not form the most relevant distinction between children born in Asia and newcomers. It mattered far more where someone was educated. If a father pursued a successful career in Asia and remained there for some time, the sons — having completed their education in the Netherlands — would join him in the East. There, with their father's assistance, using his network and influence, they would take steps to acquire a good position themselves. There were many families whose children were born in Asia and lived there generation after generation. Take, for example, the Van Angelbeek family. The first Van Angelbeek to arrive in Asia was Johann Gerhard (1727–1799), the son of a cleric from Wittmund, in Germany. He surmounted almost every hurdle in the Dutch East India Company, rising to the heights of governor of Ceylon — incidentally, as successor to his son-in-law, Willem Jacob van de Graaff. Three generations of Van Angelbeeks were to follow, all of whom were sent to the Netherlands at a tender age. The first was Johann Gerhard's son Christiaan, who studied law in Utrecht and married a younger sister of Van de Graaff. In 1780 Christiaan returned to Asia, where he made a career as a public prosecutor in Colombo. His son Johan Gerard had been born in Utrecht and arrived in Ceylon with his father in 1780; he left for Europe in February 1786 to pursue his studies. Six sons were born to Johan Gerard — four in the Netherlands — and all of them returned to live and work in Asia. Succeeding generations of the Van Angelbeeks remained in the East Indies.[97]

The circular migration between the Indies and the Netherlands was an accepted part of the lives of wealthier Europeans. It has often been suggested that the sons quit Asia while the daughters formed the social cement for the upper classes, but this is only partly true.[98] Many sons, after an education in the Netherlands, returned to Asia. They too cemented the ties between the governing class in the Dutch Republic and that in the East Indies, and spurned an interest among the colonials for life back home in Holland. The magnetic pull of the Netherlands upon the male scions of the company's upper echelons in the Indies had an immense effect on life in the East. Unlike what happened in, for instance, South American colonies, where a sizeable local elite developed, increasingly identifying itself with the colony, the major colonial families in the East Indies during the 17th and 18th centuries remained dependent for employment on the Dutch East India Company. Their sights were set towards Europe. Those who wanted to make a career, and who could afford the journey, would first travel to Europe.

Meanwhile, those born in Asia and not sent home to Holland for their upbringing and education would need to have money, good connections and a long life if they were to reach the heights. One such man was Pieter Gerardus de Bruyn. Born in Colombo in 1732, he entered the service of the Dutch East India Company at the age of 14, like many of his contemporaries born in the Indies. He started off as a petty clerk and slowly worked his way up to a post in the civil departments in Batavia. In 1776 — he was by then 44 — he was appointed governor of Malacca, where he served until 1788.[99] The fact that he was born in the Indies continued to be a source of contempt for some; the above-mentioned Reynier Bernardus Hoynck van Papendrecht, harbour master of Malacca, scathingly referred to him as "a Ceylonese, only capable of penpushing".[100]

De Bruyn's career path was exceptional, but it was not unique. In 1763, at the inauguration of Governor-General Petrus Albertus van der Parra in Batavia, 60 notables were present, of whom 10 were born in the Indies (the origins of 16 of them are not given). Van der Parra himself was born in Colombo. The other notables came from the top ranks and comprised former governors, members of the Council of the Indies and senior officials.[101] In the VOC establishments outside the Indonesian archipelago, about 5 per cent of governors and directors had been born in Asia, and more than half of them had spent some time in Europe.[102] In Ceylon, for instance, several of the governors were Indies-born: Johan Paul Schagen (1725–1726) was a son of Malacca, and his successor, Pieter Vuyst (1726–1729) was born in Batavia. Later in the 18th century Ceylon had a governor who was one of its own sons: Iman Willem Falck (1765–1785). His father was public prosecutor in Colombo and his mother, Adriana Gobius, came from Semarang, on Java.[103] But all of them spent a considerable time in Europe before returning to Asia.

Until the end of the colonial era, an education in the Netherlands would remain a major asset when ascending the social and professional ladder in the East Indies. Most people depended on the Dutch East India Company, which opened the gateway to success and prosperity. Apart from a well-paid job with the company, there were only two ways to get wealthy: shipping and landowning. One of the successful Burghers from the early 18th century was Frederik Ribalt, son of the chief surgeon at the Batavian lepers' home, named François Ribalt, who came from the French Alps. Frederik followed in his father's footsteps and became an assistant surgeon, apparently without having received any medical training in Europe. However, before long he had had enough of the Dutch East India Company and set himself up as an independent merchant and landowner in Batavia. For those who persevered, there was always some hope of becoming successful in the private sector. Frederik's ships sailed as far as China. In 1718 he owned five sugar mills — undoubtedly hired out to and exploited by Chinese. He inherited a large sum from the bailiff Hendrik van der Stel, and with this he purchased the sizeable estate of Soetendaal to the west of Batavia.[104]

There were other sons of European fathers who made a success of life outside the Dutch East India Company (although in the company's protective shadow). One such man was Andries Teisseire (1746 or 1747–1800), who at the close of the 18th century was one of the mightiest landowners of Batavia. Born in Ligor (Siam), he was the son of Guillaume Teisseire and the "freeborn woman" Helena Damsi.[105] He arrived in Batavia with his father and at a young age — about 14 or 15 years old — he joined the company as an assistant-surveyor, which was quite a common function for an Indies-born boy. He probably realised that he would not get very far working for the VOC, and he

gave it up in 1769 and registered as a Burgher. It seems as if his work
as a surveyor had provided the opportunity to buy large estates. He
devoted himself to the business of landowning, carrying out many
agricultural experiments. In 1793 he tried producing pepper on a vast
scale on his estate in Tangerang — without great success. He married
four times, each of his wives being Indies-born.[106]

Despite the resounding success of the lucky few, Batavia offered
scant opportunities to an independent local-born elite. Even a successful
Burgher such as Andries Teisseire sent his son Guillaume Elie (1769–
1845) to the Netherlands, with the express permission of the governor-
general. Guillaume was not to return for 14 years. Then within a year
he married Maria Clara du Chêne de Vienne, sister of the wife of Jacobus
Martinus Baljé, former chief surgeon and one of the most powerful
citizens and landowners in the city. Guillaume stayed out of the company's
service, although he did hold various functions on church and urban
committees. Not until 1806 did he take up an official appointment as
the first commissioner for sugar culture, and in 1810 he accepted the
post of administrator, functions that developed logically from his position as landowner. Thus he followed the opposite path from that of
his father.[107]

Demarcation lines

The old world of the Dutch East Indies was criss-crossed by legal,
cultural and class barriers. In their legal pluralism the towns of the
Dutch East Indies strongly resembled Asian cities. What was different
about the Dutch settlements was, apart from the introduction of
(Protestant) Christian moral discipline, the development of a European
upper class completely dominated by the bureaucratic hierarchy of the
Dutch East India Company. A person's social status was measured
primarily in terms of his rank within the VOC. The upper echelons in
the colony consolidated their positions through prudent marriages and
patronage, and they jealously guarded a European lifestyle, particularly
in the official domain and among males. The status hierarchy was
completely dominated by the company; only as the 19th century ran its
course would this begin to loosen up. Then alternative ways of gaining
wealth and prestige started to appear.

It is inaccurate to speak as if there were one homogenous European
group living in the old world of the East Indies. Undoubtedly there was
an idea of a European community, and one's membership was deduced

from having a European name (from which one's cultural background was assumed). Apart from that, there was little unity, the community being split into subgroups consisting of the elite, the soldiers and the urban poor. It is difficult to shake off the image of colonial society as one governed by rigid racial hierarchy, with the European newcomer as lord and master, and the native toiling in the paddy field. And between the European and the native we find the Mestizos, the half-castes — or, at least, that is the common picture. It is attractively simple, but it is false.

It appears from marriage documents that after the first turbulent years in the East Indies, a form of restratification took place, which determined the future shape of the bureaucratic-social European elite. In every VOC settlement — especially outside Batavia — there were leading families with a racially mixed background and deeply rooted in their locales. Most high positions circulated among these families. The local elite distanced itself from all matters to do with soldiers, Mardijkers and the indigenous population. Marriage was one key to establishing status. Newcomers could sidle into these circles via strategic marriages.

In Batavia, where most newcomers arrived, the centrality of these clans was much weaker. Despite what Jean Gelman Taylor suggests, these Batavian clans never completely dominated Batavia society. Taylor argues, "One is hard put to discover a prominent Dutchman not tied to his colleagues by marriage".[108] But simple observation reveals that the reality was less concise. Many high-placed Totoks had wives who had come from Europe or another part of Asia; or they remained unmarried. The prospect of marriage with a woman from Batavia was, for many European men, far from appealing. It meant an expensive life, and a return to the Netherlands became less certain. Reynier Bernardus Hoynck van Papendrecht, whom we have already encountered, stated, "No one could be more poorly educated than the women of these parts'. And the Lutheran minister Jan Brandes, who in the same period alighted in Batavia with his wife, was not greatly attracted to Batavian women. When his wife died within a year of their arrival, and he was considering his options, he shrank from marriage, saying: "If I had so sought it, I might well have remarried here, having the choice of rich and poor, white and black women and also those who possessed at least 80,000 rix-dollars; but I am all too well acquainted with these mares, and a man may break his neck riding them. Thus I prefer to go on foot and remain alive and healthy so that I may perchance once more see the snow softly falling on Holland's fields".[109] In the meantime Brandes was in close contact with the widow of Governor-General Van der Parra, née Adriana Johanna Bake, whom, without the slightest irony or superiority because of her Indische background and lifestyle, he named his "patroness". Like most newcomers there, Brandes did not intend to make the East Indies his permanent residence. He was there to make money and to leave as soon as he had accomplished his end. He hated Batavia, where he found life barren and infertile, with the exception of the "wickedness, which flourished on every side".[110]

We should not ignore the fact that many prominent unmarried European men in the colonies sought the hand of a wealthy widow with good connections, or of the daughter of a high-ranking company official. Undoubtedly, local-born European women were significant pawns in the marriage game, both in Batavia and elsewhere. Indeed, in the Dutch Republic the same was true, as it was for Javanese princes and other members of the ruling aristocracy. Nor was intermarriage between major dynasties a phenomenon peculiar to the late 18th century. From the very start of the European presence in Asia, numerous marriages are recorded in VOC documents, unions that were clearly intended as career promotion. Take the Pit clan, which was well represented in the VOC of 17th-century Asia. Laurens Pit, who came from the German port of Bremen, joined the Dutch East India Company as a young man. In 1632, while still holding a minor position, he married Elisabeth Vogels, who was born on the island of Ternate, in the Moluccas. He spent some time as a Burgher in Batavia and on the island of Banda (in the Moluccas), and following a brief stay in the Netherlands he returned to the East in the service of the VOC, where he climbed to the rank of governor of Coromandel, in southeastern India. His children fanned out through the East Indies, gaining high positions in the colonial hierarchy and marrying into the upper circles. His oldest son, Laurens, who was born in India, became, like his father, governor of Coromandel. Laurens Pit Jr. married Maria Hustaert, daughter of the governor of Ceylon. Maarten Pit became a councillor of the Indies and married Elisabeth van Riebeeck. Johan Pit succeeded in becoming *secunde* or second-in-command of the company posts in Bengal. The daughters of Laurens Pit married senior officials in the Dutch East India Company: Elisabeth married a senior merchant, Rijckloff de Bitter, and Maria married Willem Hartsinck, who later became the governor of Makassar (Sulawesi).[111]

This is just one of numerous examples. There were many families in the Dutch East Indies who, spanning several generations, held important positions, made strategic marriages, and sometimes spent several years gaining a European education before returning to Asia. In a society that was rigidly hierarchical, where success depended on the right connections, where the upper class of Europeans formed a tiny group, and where there were many single folk, widows and widowers, marriage played a major role in welding alliances and fostering careers. One thing, however, is clear from the records we have about marriages: they do not support the idea that Mestizo daughters were the main means of gluing together Batavian society.

Although Mestizos are essentially a product of colonial society, at the same time they seem to disappear out of accounts and records, slippery as mercury. The label of "Mestizo" is a complicated affair. We may assume that the term was used only for children who had one Asian parent, and less easily for more diluted combinations. Many children in the elite families were not the offspring of a first-generation mixed marriage but had one or two Indies-born parents from families who had intermarried in the Indies for several generations. The elites came from families that one would scarcely describe as Mestizo and which indeed were not given that appellation. There are many indications that the upper classes of Batavia tended to marry as "white" as possible. At the other end of the spectrum, most mixed relations between Asians and Europeans were to be found in poorer social milieus or were illegitimate. The children of these unions carried the stigma of their cultural mix, and their chances of making it in society were slight. The label "Mestizo" was not only applied to indicate mixed racial origin; it was also a social category. Those who came from the upper ranks of the company's European employees rarely ran the risk of being labelled Mestizo.

But the Mestizo label not only betrays dominant class considerations, it is also gender-specific. It is most remarkable that accounts of the Indies seem only to refer to Mestizo women. Seldom do we find a reference to a Mestizo man — although they evidently filled the offices of the VOC. Most Indies-born men performed menial functions in the VOC offices or warehouses, although we also find them in higher positions. Another interesting point is that male employees of the VOC in high positions were expected to conform to the bureaucratic mores, and this was regarded as more important than skin colour. Indies-born men — especially if they had been educated in the Dutch Republic — could not easily be distinguished, as far as their behaviour was concerned, from newcomers to Asia. It was a different matter for women. Their role in society was specifically linked to the bearing and raising of children; not surprisingly, this is where they received greatest criticism. They were also blamed for their over-familiarity with household slaves. As for the men's familiarity with the slaves — a veil of deep silence was drawn over this.

In the company establishments outside Batavia, the number of European newcomers was comparatively small — that is, disregarding the military. The communities were limited, the atmosphere parochial. The high-ranking company officials, often merely a handful, would see each other every day and were dependent on each other for their leisure entertainment. They would meet at the governor's banquets and at ceremonial receptions for ambassadors. They marched according to rank in funeral processions, they sat cheek by jowl in the church's front pews, and they held dinners and dance parties. Indeed, the VOC settlements in Asia had little to offer in the way of entertainment apart from receptions and banquets and, towards the close of the 18th century, the Freemasonry.

In every colonial Asian city an upper crust of locals had developed, which absorbed the newcomers. The local-born Europeans retained strong ties with European culture — not least because the male scions would be sent, finances permitting, to be educated in Europe. Those who had a European cultural background were seen as socially superior, although this was not always true. For instance, Malacca-born Catharina Johanna Koek, who in 1785 married the Dutch governor Abraham Couperus, remained faithful to the lifestyle she had become accustomed to as a girl. She dressed and behaved according to the local tradition. This was quite horrifyingly inappropriate for certain visitors from outside, for instance when in January 1796 the English fleet cast anchor off Malacca, and Governor Abraham Couperus invited the British admiral and his companions to join them for dinner. In his memoirs, Capt. Walter Caulfield Lennon recalled the following about this occasion:

> Madam Couperus was dressed in the most unbecoming manner possible, a mixture between the Malay and the Portuguese, her outward garment being made exactly like a shift, she looked as if she reversed the order of her dress altogether. Her hair was drawn so tight to the crown of her head, and the skin of her forehead so stretched, that she could scarce wink her eyelids; she seemed however very affable and well bred for a person never out of Malacca.[112]

Presumably Catharina was wearing a long kebaya, possibly trimmed with lace, which to the Englishman would have resembled an undergarment. Such a dress was not typically Malaccan. The sarong and kebaya were customary dress in all the VOC settlements, although of course European garments were frequently worn. Distinctions were not rock-hard, as European and Indische clothing were adapted according to the climate. For instance, in addition to the formal dress and the kebaya, there was a garment called a *saya*, a wide skirt made of Indian chintz, ironed in broad pleats and held up with a large belt. It is quite clear that Abraham Couperus did not force his Malaccan wife into a European straitjacket. It seems most probable that Abraham — a Frisian by birth — adapted his own lifestyle to the local pattern. The codes provided for a certain separation between the Dutch East India Company and home life. As governor, Couperus would naturally conform to the prescripts of his Dutch employers and wear the company uniform; when off-duty he doubtless strolled the streets dressed like a dapper Malaccan gentleman.

It was above all the upper class who, apparently without difficulty, managed to combine different cultural elements — often to the horror or disgust of visitors from Europe. Eight years before the above-mentioned Englishman Lennon, John Pope visited Malacca and witnessed an evening of feast and dance in one of the local inns. As Pope describes it, the daughters of the Dutch men were all "chichis", a common English term for Eurasians. They were "all dressed *à la costume du pays* [of the country] and chewing beetle [betel]". The evening began with the dancing of minuets in a most respectable German style, but this soon gave way to much wilder variations, until an old Portuguese man and the drunken wife of the local watchmaker performed a fandango (an old Spanish courtship dance) — at least, that's what Pope took it to be — after which the entire assembly burst into song, performing Dutch and Malay melodies until the wee hours, when people began to straggle homewards, their clothes dishevelled and their hair tousled. The next day Pope met the whole group again, this time in church, where, he reports, the women were "well dressed with a profusion of gold and diamonds" and all attended by a female slave carrying the betel box.[113] The fine folk of Malacca had a good life and liked to show it.

For newcomers, the customs in Malacca were disturbing; they appeared to be an aberration of European mores or, at best, bizarre. But for those who remained in the East Indies, or had grown up there, it was perfectly normal. Indeed, after a short time in Asia, newcomers usually adapted to its ways. We have an account from the German Lt. Heinrich Ludwig Morgenstern telling of how he was introduced to the sarong, a garment worn both around the house and to sleep in. He recalls: "To begin with I wouldn't wear it. I found it embarrassing, but now I think it's a most comfortable garment for indoors."[114] How quickly one adapted to the new world bore a close correlation to the presence or absence of sizeable groups of newcomers. In Malacca the local culture would have been more strongly Indische than it was in Batavia, a city with more newcomers and bearing the marked stamp of the European upper classes. Yet there too the different lifestyles met and mingled. In around 1780 the Lutheran minister Jan Brandes made a drawing of an afternoon visit from a woman dressed in full European feather; she is seen conversing animatedly with another woman — obviously a Mestizo — clothed in a local saya. Evidently, the hostess was permitted to wear less formal clothing than her tea-time guest.[115] The old world of the East Indies was highly fragmented, but it also produced a vibrant mixture of peoples, customs and styles that seemed normal to those born and raised in the Indies but often caused considerable consternation to outsiders.

Illustration 7   A tea visit in Batavia, 1780s. The watercolour drawing by Rev. Jan Brandes shows the variety of women's dresses and the intimate, if always hierarchical, relationship with the personal slaves.
[Watercolour drawing, Rijksmuseum, Amsterdam.]

CHAPTER 3

Contraction

The shrinking world of the Indies

Between 1780 and 1820 the old world of the Dutch East Indies changed drastically. To begin with, there was war with Britain (1780–1784), which cut off the Dutch colonies from their mother country. Similar spells of isolation arose during the period of the Batavian Republic in the Netherlands (1795–1806) and the Napoleonic years (1806–1813). Although the isolation was never complete, these periods still made a deep impact upon life in the East Indies. Equally drastic was the rapid shrinking of the company's trading empire. During those years the VOC lost almost all its possessions outside the Indonesian archipelago. This resulted in a flux of emigrants leaving the former colonies for Batavia, on Java's northern coast; there, the officials from the lost company establishments around Asia gathered to lick their wounds. And finally, the colonies in the Indies were sucked into the political quarrels, wars, ideological conflicts and changes that were taking place in the Netherlands and other parts of Europe.

During the 18th century, Batavia had become an increasingly dismal place. There were recurrent epidemics of malaria, starting in 1733, which took their toll of lives — particularly those of newcomers. So serious was this plague that during dire epidemics most new arrivals would be dead within a year of their arrival in the Indies.[1] At the same time, as if to compensate for the depletion of the Dutch population in the city, more and more Chinese traders and journeymen arrived in their junks, as did merchants from India and the Arab countries. Those Europeans who could afford to, settled on estates around the city, at a safe distance from the malaria-ridden swamps and fishponds on the coastal edges.[2] In other parts of northern Java people were equally affected by the raging fever of malaria. Here the death rate among employees of the Dutch East India Company was almost as high as in

Batavia. In the administrative year 1768–1769, 33 per cent of the VOC personnel in Batavia died of malaria, while in settlements on Java's north coast the figure was 27 per cent; in comparison, the mortality rate on Ambon and in Malacca was only 6 per cent, while in Makassar and Ceylon it was as low as 4 per cent.[3]

The epidemics did not affect just the newcomers: local-born people were also afflicted, with drastic demographical consequences. Altogether, this presented the Dutch East India Company with a huge shortage of personnel, further exacerbated by the periodic interruptions in communications with Europe. December 1780 saw the outbreak of the Fourth Anglo-Dutch War, with ramifications as far as Asia. The British occupied the VOC settlements in India — Coromandel, Bengal and Surat — and captured any VOC ships they happened to encounter. For two years, shipping connections with Europe were obstructed. Although after the war the damage was soon repaired, there was now a painful personnel shortage in the Dutch East Indies, which only became worse after 1790, when the recruitment of employees in the Netherlands limped to far below its former levels.

To make matters worse, in 1795 shipping links between the East Indies and Europe once again came under pressure. The French invaded the Dutch Republic, and a pro-French government came to power. This prompted the (anti-French) British to declare war on the Dutch. It looked like an exact repetition of what had happened 14 years previously. Again, shipping links between Europe and Asia were jeopardised, and again the supply of European emigrants to Asia diminished. In Batavia, living conditions deteriorated. The Christian church's poor relief faltered, and the schools that taught European children the rudiments of reading, writing and arithmetic (as well as geography and Dutch) closed one by one for lack of pupils. In 1797 there were only 41 European children living in Batavia, as well as 109 Asian Christian and 71 Mestizo children.[4] About 100 years earlier, the numbers had been 704, 1,164 and 211 respectively.[5]

By the 1790s, with growing isolation, the threat of war, financial and commercial complications and the ever-present dead and dying, life in Batavia had become a bitter struggle. A senior official in the Dutch East India Company, Isaac Titsingh, returning to the city from Bengal in 1792 after 12 years' absence, recorded with dismay the cheerless atmosphere in the decaying and depleted town:

> [...] an impoverished and exhausted colony, suffering more than ever before from the fatal effects of its infected air [...] there are scarcely

four citizens to be found worthy of the name of merchant; compared
with former years the colony is bereft of its European population and
because all is so depressed the few capitalists here are reluctant to do
business; this adds to the general misery and everything falls to rack
and ruin.[6]

Isolated and malaria-infested, the city acquired a petty, parochial
atmosphere. Newcomers were horrified by the rampant nepotism and
the bitter infighting, but in most cases they had no choice but to take
part. The discontent took on a political tint in December 1795, when
83 prominent Batavian citizens drew up a petition in reaction to events
in the Netherlands, where, in the wake of the French army, the anti-
Orangist Patriots had gained power and established the Batavian Republic.
The petition was directed against the un-Patriotic administration in the
Indies. It requested a public celebration of the turn of events in the
Dutch, or "Batavian", Republic, as well as the abolition of the rigidly
hierarchical regulations controlling the display of wealth and position in
the East Indies. It also demanded that a suitable plan be drawn up for
the defence of the city of Batavia, now that the British had declared war
on the Batavian Republic since it had become a satellite of France.[7]

This petition had little to do with an assertion of an Indische
identity — at any rate, far less than the protests of 1648, when the
Burghers rose up in anger against the restrictions placed upon their
trading rights; and also far less than the demonstrations of 1848, when
the civil servants would complain about the poor educational opportunities
for their children and demand better pension rights. The protest
movement of 1795 was a typically 18th-century power struggle between
two ruling factions.[8] There was not the slightest suggestion of a dawning
Indies particularism, as opposed to metropolitan interests, nor of the
colony's longing for political emancipation. Only ten of the 83 signatories
had been born in the Indies; similarly, of the 76 petitioners who, a few
days after the first request, presented a counter-petition in support of
the government, only 15 were Indies-born. Most of the signatories of
the first petition were high-placed officials in the VOC. The ten Burghers
were also almost all prominent members of the European community
who occupied key positions in the urban government and had formerly
held high ranks in the VOC.

There is a striking absence of family connections among the signatories of the two petitions.[9] Likewise, of the 47 members of the Council
of the Indies who held office between 1795 and 1811, only three were
born in Asia. Moreover, Batavian politics were less influenced by ties of

marriage and clan-forming than has been suggested. It was by no means a hard-and-fast rule that most newcomers from Europe should marry a "daughter of Batavia". If we glance at the marriage records of councillors' families from the years between 1795 and 1811, we find less than half of them marrying women from Batavia.[10] A system of patronage cemented the Batavian world but was not necessarily tied in with marriage. The shrinking numbers of Europeans in Batavia and the city's isolation did not lead to a process of creolisation whereby the elite became more Indische (that is, with an increasing presence of Indies-born men who were keenly loyal to local interests).

After 1780 the trickle of white women sailing to Asia virtually dried up. The marriage registers for Batavia after the Fourth Anglo-Dutch War (which ended in 1784) record scarcely any Dutch-born women — whether young daughters or eligible widows.[11] That they were present in the city is clear — but it was in ever-decreasing numbers. Men from the higher ranks adapted to the situation; they would take an Asian woman — often a slave — as a concubine or have sexual partners of a more temporary nature. Isaac Titsingh, who lived in Asia for 30 years, never married; but for the rest, his activities knew few restraints other than those of taste. To a friend he wrote: "As I never married while living in the Indies, I settled for the general custom and begot a son upon one of my damsels in 1790".[12] In both Deshima (Japan) and Chinsura (Bengal) — he served the company as director in the two places for a total of 12 years — he had long-term and intimate relations with local women, first the Japanese Ukine and later the Bengali Amaril. The latter was the mother of Titsingh's son William, whom he had legitimised by the (VOC) High Government.[13]

The government in Batavia sanctioned extra-marital children by loosening up the rules regarding legitimisation. In 1808 Governor-General Herman Willem Daendels received a request from the chief administrator of the forestry in Java to legitimise his ten children, born to five different Malay women. Of these women, three had died and the other two had got married; thus, the usual method of legitimisation — marriage — was impossible. The forestry administrator's prolific and eclectic procreation was by no means unique in the East Indies. Daendels acknowledged that at the time the number of illegitimate children was rising sharply, which he attributed to the decreasing number of European women coming to Asia.[14] The government in the Indies approved the legitimising of children, partly with the idea that this "charitable deed would bind them all the more strongly to the government" and turn them into "useful members of society". There were also considerations of decency — the illegitimate girls might later on make suitable spouses for officials arriving from the Netherlands; but a smear on their birth would naturally blot the escutcheon of the European men. The legitimisation thus served the highly practical purpose of producing a supply of acceptable Indies brides of untarnished reputation. One hundred and fifty years earlier things had been quite different: then the VOC High Government had tried to banish concubinage on grounds of Christian morality.

High-placed functionaries on the north coast of Java could allow themselves far more leeway than the inhabitants of Batavia, where the church council actively guarded and governed public mores. In Semarang, Surabaya and the smaller company posts it was not unusual to find households with harems. Indeed, Dutch newcomer Dirk van Hogendorp was deeply shocked by the "scandalous behaviour" of his superior Johan Frederik van Reede tot de Parkeler, who was appointed governor of Java's north coast in 1796. To Van Hogendorp's horror his superior was to be seen "reading the Bible and praying in the midst of a dozen Makassarese and Javanese harlots, who encouraged his lechery".[15] It should be added that Van Hogendorp had good reason to speak ill of his former boss, who had stymied his career in the East Indies; but other sources also provide a picture of Van Reede lording it over his household like a Javanese prince.[16]

Shortly after his arrival in Batavia from the Netherlands, Van Reede had married Ida Petronella Jacoba Vos, daughter of a former governor of Java's north coast, Johannes Vos, and his wife, Ida Wilhelmina Bake. Following his wife's death, Van Reede preferred to live in bachelor style, with slave women to keep him company. By 1798 he certainly had three natural children. He wrote somewhat shamefacedly to his aged father, "I had more children than this — but they have all died".[17] The governor of Java had considerable freedom and could keep a large number of male and female slaves, with whom he could virtually do what he liked. Others — perhaps not so highly placed — had to content themselves with less. Undoubtedly, concubinage came in many different forms and guises. A governor or high-ranking official living on the north coast of Java might prefer concubinage out of convenience and love of freedom, while soldiers in Yogyakarta engaged in it out of necessity, since they were not allowed to marry. In the lower classes of local-born men and women, the only things that prevented marrying were a lack of income and an emulation of Javanese marriage practices.

The flow of women from the Netherlands may have almost petered out, but the influence of Europe on Asian life seems to have become all the stronger during these years. There was still enough wealth in the colonies to pay for the import of European luxury products. Even when communication was disrupted during the war years, the supply of luxury goods and delicious frivolities from the Netherlands continued. Thus we find a delicatessen shop run by a certain Mr H. Schulz on one of the prominent canals in Batavia, placing an advertisement in January 1811 for such thoroughly Dutch commodities as sauerkraut, haricot beans in vinegar, salt bacon and sides of meat. In the same month, a short distance outside the old city, Huibrecht Senn van Basel, a former company official turned retailer, was selling "genuine Macuba snuff", cognac and chocolate.[18] These articles, like most luxury items in those days, were imported by American cargo vessels sailing under a neutral ensign, which could reach the East Indies unhindered. Much had changed since the first European residents in Batavia filled their homes with locally made

Illustration 8   Until the early 19th century the street scene in Batavia was dominated by the presence of slaves. Then their numbers swiftly declined. This lithograph showing a slave market, made in the mid-19th century, dates from a time when there were scarcely 1,000 slaves remaining in Batavia. Ten years after it was made, slavery was abolished.
[Lithograph by E. Spanier in: *Tijdschrift voor Nederlandsch Indië* (1853).]

furniture and Chinese paintings. European luxury goods were chiefly destined for the well-to-do, who also saw the ornamental knick-knacks and edible delicacies as status-enhancing. Powerful as the influence of the Asian environment may have been, political, cultural and personal ties with the Netherlands were evidently essential elements of life in the upper echelons. Indeed, the elite emphasised their European background in many ways — through the people they mixed with, their dress, what they ate, the education of their children in Europe. Asia did indeed imprint itself deeply on the colonists' daily lives, but for those who were dependent on European circles, accommodation had its limits.

Most European consumer goods exported for the colonial elite were out of the range of small shop owners, small farmers and minor civil servants; they would have had a monthly income of between 10 and 20 guilders plus any other small sums they could scrape together. For many of them Europe was a dim and distant model, chiefly important because it confirmed their European status. In this sense, the colonial elite exercised a strong influence on the lower classes. As time went by, this only grew stronger, especially when governments started more energetically to propagate and support the European way of life — for instance, by expanding European educational systems. But at the close of the 18th century things had not yet reached that stage.

Malaccan diaspora

After the French had invaded the Dutch Republic and Britain declared war on her in 1795, the British captured most of the Dutch East India Company fortresses outside the island of Java. In July 1795 the British seized the VOC settlements in India — in Surat, Bengal and Coromandel. This was followed in August by the surrender of Malacca, and in the succeeding months the VOC fortresses in Ceylon were delivered into the hands of the British. In early 1796 the islands of Banda and Ambon in the Moluccas were taken by the British. When it became clear that most of these captured settlements would not soon revert to Dutch control, a stream of VOC employees and Burgher families began to flow from the outlying provinces towards the Indonesian archipelago. Evidently, they preferred to live under the Dutch government in Java than under the British in the land where they had been born or had made their careers. It was largely the elite families who set off for Java. Generally, their ties with the Netherlands and the company were stronger than those of the lower classes, and their ambitions and mobility were greater.

Among the emigrants who left Malacca after its capture by the British was the Couperus family.[19] Abraham Couperus had left the Netherlands in 1775. When he arrived in Asia, he first worked as a junior merchant. He then edged his way up until, after 13 years, he had attained the rank of governor of Malacca. Meanwhile, he had married a Malaccan woman named Catharina Johanna Koek. They had six children, including a son, Petrus Theodorus or Piet. Abraham had already decided, when Piet was still a toddler, to send him to the Netherlands to be educated. And so it was.[20] Like most employees of the VOC, Abraham invested considerable sums in various enterprises. He was, for instance, joint owner of at least two ships. And with his brother-in-law, the tax collector Jacob van Kal, he set up a business enterprise in Malacca.[21]

It was Abraham's bitter lot to surrender Malacca in 1795 to the British. Together with other company employees he was transferred to Tranquebar, a Danish stronghold on the east coast of India, which the British had occupied. His future son-in-law Johan Hendrik Meijer was also sent here. Meijer had set out from the German port of Hamburg as a young man and in 1780, in the employ of the Dutch East India Company, arrived in Malacca, where he was appointed boatswain, responsible for the maintenance of ships and their equipment. Here he married and later became a widower. In 1801 or early 1802, in Tranquebar, he married again — this time, Abraham's daughter Gesina.[22] Gesina, then aged 17, was 22 years younger than her husband and one-and-a-half years younger than Hendrina, Johan's daughter from his first marriage.[23] Shortly after the wedding, the Meijer couple set off for Batavia, where they were welcomed by Governor-General Johannes Siberg and his wife, Pieternella Gerhardina Alting. Although Johan had lost all his possessions in Malacca, he was soon able to obtain credit in Batavia — where there was never a shortage of capital — and start up business once more.[24] But he never enjoyed the fruits of his new enterprise, for he died in June 1809.

Johan's widow, Gesina née Couperus, shortly afterwards remarried. Her new husband was the widower of her above-mentioned stepdaughter, Hendrina Meijer. Her second husband, Jan Samuel Timmerman Thijssen, born in the Dutch port town of Hoorn, had also served the VOC in Malacca and had come to Batavia in 1810. The Meijer-Timmerman Thijssen couple were the sole heirs to the fortune built up by Johan Meijer. This enabled them to buy a "garden" and an extensive property, Kampong Malayo, far to the south of Batavia, for 22,000 rix-dollars.

The estate had been created by the former Governor-General Willem Arnold Alting, and in the opinion of its new owners it was one of the most attractive properties on Java.[25] Jan founded a business in Batavia that was soon flourishing. It was a sign of the times that he earned his fortune from trade outside employment with the government. Under the British, who occupied Java in 1811, citizens had greater opportunity than before to make a fortune in independent trading. True, Jan held the post of second magistrate, a prestigious position — but it earned him only 200 Spanish dollars a month; in contrast, his brig the *Gesina* would, with her cargo, bring in a profit worth ten times that amount. Without a doubt, Jan's business was impressive. He was part-owner of at least four ships, one of which even plied the long route to London. He also ran a mercantile firm with the Dane Bernt Wilhelm Westermann, which operated as the agency for Palmer & Co., the major trading establishment in Calcutta.[26]

It was not many years before Jan was a rich man. When he lost one of his ships in 1814, his brother-in-law Piet Couperus dryly commented that after all, he had already made his pile, so the loss was no big disaster.[27] Perhaps the methods used by Jan differed from those of colonists in bygone years — but the goal was still the same: to get rich and go home to Europe. With that aim in sight, in 1815 he started to wind up a lot of his businesses. He sold his estates (at a profit) and closed down his firm with Westermann.[28] Even Gesina Timmerman Thijssen, born and bred in Malacca, wanted to go to the Netherlands.[29] In fact, her children Henry (from her marriage to Johan Meijer) and Olivia had already preceded her to Europe. Clearly, despite their roots in the Indies, the wealthy Batavian families felt strongly oriented towards the chilly north.

On the estate of Kampong Malayo, life was far from dull, for there lived mother Couperus, well into her seventies but still singing and dancing like a young girl, as well as Gesina Timmerman Thijssen's two sisters, Jacobina and Elise, and their husbands.[30] In 1809 Gesina's brother Piet returned to Asia. He had been sent to the Netherlands in 1795, just prior to the fall of Malacca. Now, at the age of 22, he arrived in Batavia.[31] After the British marched into Batavia in August 1811 and occupied it, Piet immediately entered their service and became one of the most loyal henchmen of the government of the British lieutenant governor, Thomas Stamford Raffles. Piet lived in Raffles's residence in Buitenzorg (Bogor), far up-country from Batavia, and had a son by one of the slaves there.

"In the Indies this does not cause such a scandal as in Europe," wrote Gesina and Jan Samuel Timmerman Thijssen, to an aunt living in Holland.[32] Indeed, it was perfectly normal.

In Batavia the lines of the old world of the East Indies met and came together. In 1807 Abraham Couperus reached Batavia from Tranquebar. He had first wanted to exonerate himself of any discredit that might be attached to his surrender of Malacca, before he made his appearance in Batavia. On his arrival in the city he was appointed president of the board of *schepenen* (bailiffs), and not long after that he was appointed a member of the Council of the Indies. Two years later, in 1809, his wife and the remaining children followed him to Batavia; the four younger sisters of Gesina were now of marriageable age. However, it was son Piet who made the most advantageous marriage, in 1812, to the daughter of Willem Jacob Cranssen. "A splendid alliance," wrote his brother-in-law in a letter to the Netherlands, and the remark was amply justified, for Cranssen was as rich as Croesus, having made a fortune as governor of the spice islands of Ternate and Ambon.[33] This marriage forged a firm tie between the two most Anglophile clans of Batavia — those of Couperus-Timmerman Thijssen and Cranssen.

Understandably, it was the top-ranking functionaries of Malacca who ended up in Batavia. Some chose to remain in Malacca, so attached had they become to the city — or possibly because they had major business interests there. There were quite a few Burghers who operated as shipowners, but chiefly they were landowners of some substance.[34] At best, we can only surmise how hard the decision to leave must have been, certainly for those who were born in Malacca and had lived there most of their lives. Indeed, most chose to stay back and watch how things turned out. Their businesses did not appear to have suffered from the British presence. There was a secret hope that when hostilities were over, Malacca would revert to the Dutch. Unlike the Cape of Good Hope and Ceylon, Malacca had not been formally annexed by the British in 1802 under the Peace of Amiens. And indeed, between 1818 and 1825 it did return to Dutch hands and several members of the Couperus family went back for a while. In 1818 Jan Adriaan Steijn Parvé, husband of Antje Couperus, was appointed receiver of import and export taxes in Malacca; but he returned to Batavia in 1819.[35] And in 1818 Jan Samuel Timmerman Thijssen took up the post of high commissioner for the takeover of Malacca. He later became governor of the port, and he died there five years later, in 1823.

Citizens of Ceylon

For those who remained in Ceylon, the outlook was not so rosy. Here the entrepreneurial world had never quite managed to take off, and most people had to survive on the profits from their smallholdings. When Ceylon was lost to the VOC, a modest flow of emigrants started to trickle towards Batavia, especially in 1807 and 1808. Late in 1807 the British ship *Coromandel* left Ceylon, carrying 65 former employees of the Dutch East India Company from Cochin and Ceylon; the ship reached Batavia in early February 1808.[36] Probably the *Coromandel* was the last vessel to transport VOC employees and their families, who had been left stranded in Ceylon after the arrival of the British. At least two other ships had performed a similar service earlier in 1807. It would seem that the deaths from malaria of many who made the journey to Batavia acted as a considerable deterrent to others.

There were various routes leading from Ceylon to Batavia. Another was the much-used migration circuit between colonial possessions in Asia and the mother country. It was following this route that a scion from a Ceylonese family, one Adriaan Marius Elaarst Ondaatje, arrived in the Dutch East Indies. He came from a remarkable family whose origins remain a little obscure.[37] The family tradition records that the Ondaatjes came from Arcot in southern India and served as court physicians to the king of Thanjavur (Tanjore). In the 17th century one of the VOC governors of Ceylon sent for Michael Jurie Ondaatchi — his first names were presumably given when he was baptised — to attend to and cure his sick wife. Ondaatchi stayed on in Colombo as a city surgeon and converted to Christianity. There he married first the Portuguese Magdalene de Croos and then, after her death, a native woman, according to family legend.[38] Archival sources are unable to confirm this story of the family's roots. There is a record that in 1686 a local doctor named Michiel Jurjansz alias Ondaatie acquired a plot of land east of Colombo; 22 years later he appears still to be holding the function of a doctor.[39]

The Ondaatjes were one of the families, which included both Tamils and Sinhalese, who studied at the seminary in Colombo and thereafter gained prominent positions as schoolmasters, interpreters and (aspirant) clergymen. A college was founded in 1690 in Nallur, close to Jaffnapatnam in the north of Ceylon, and a second one in Colombo in 1696. The aim was to create a loyal, well-educated Protestant elite among the Tamil and Sinhalese peoples. Later, the college trained aspirant (Protestant) ministers.[40] A few students from the college were able to continue their education at universities in the Netherlands and later became clergymen in Ceylon. Some of them were Mestizos, for instance, the future ministers in Colombo Siebert Abrahamszen Bronsveld and Johannes Jacobus Meijer; but there were also Tamils such as Petrus de Silva, Philip de Melho and Manuel Moergappa, and Sinhalese such as Hendrik Philipsz, Daniel Rodrigo and Gerardus Philipsz, who became ministers in Colombo, Galle and even Batavia.[41] The Tamil and Sinhalese students traced their Portuguese or Dutch names back to their ancestors who had converted to Christianity; but according to the laws of the Dutch East India Company, they remained Tamil (then usually called "Malabar") or Sinhalese.

It is not easy to place the Ondaatjes in one specific colonial category — something that only serves to emphasise how profession, religion, marriage and place of residence all determined a person's position on the ethnic spectrum, as formalised by the colonial government. In the 20th century the branch of the Ondaatjes who had remained in Ceylon labelled themselves Tamils, but in the 18th and 19th centuries many Ondaatjes referred to themselves as Colombo Chetties (Chettiyar), which was a mixed group descended from southern Indian traders and the children of manumitted slaves. Most Ondaatjes were to be found among the Christian Chettiyar elite of Ceylon and married into other prominent families such as the De Melhos, De Silvas, Moergappas and Aserappas, who also populated the world of preachers and schoolteachers. But there were also Ondaatjes who classified themselves as Burghers of Colombo (which was the name given under the British to descendants of Dutch East India Company employees).[42]

The best route to becoming a European citizen in the Indies was via Europe, and this also applied to the Ondaatjes. Willem Juriaan Ondaatje, grandson of the above-mentioned doctor, attended the seminary in Colombo and in the 1750s went to the Dutch Republic, where he continued studying theology in Utrecht. There he encountered Iman Willem Falck, who like him was born in Ceylon and was to become governor of his native island in 1765. In the Netherlands Willem found himself a bride, Hermina Quint from Amsterdam. Three things — his studies in the Netherlands, his Dutch wife and his friendship with Falck — would serve to raise Willem Juriaan Ondaatje far above the social class into which he had been born. After his return to Ceylon he served for 12 years as a Protestant minister for the Dutch Malabar (Tamil) and Portuguese church in Colombo and Jaffnapatnam. In 1769 he was

appointed director of the training college.[43] Willem adopted the habit
of high-ranking VOC officials of sending their sons to Europe. In 1773
off went the 15-year-old Pieter Philip Juriaan Ondaatje, who would
later add his mother's family name of Quint to his own — to complete
his education in the Dutch Republic. Initially he stayed in Amsterdam
with grandfather Quint, attending the Latin and Greek School for about
four years. Then he went to study at the University of Utrecht, where
he earned a doctorate in philosophy. He was even granted citizenship,
achieving a status that was unthinkable for his family in Ceylon. Like
his father he found his bride — Christina Hoevenaar — in the
Netherlands. In 1787 he earned his doctorate in law from the University
of Leiden. He was never to return to Ceylon. He emerged as a fervent
member of the Dutch Patriot party and, like many of his political
persuasion in the years following the Prussian invasion of the Netherlands in 1787, wandered through Europe in exile. He returned to the
Netherlands after the Batavian takeover and held high positions in the
government, including membership of the Committee for East Indies
Affairs. With the reinstatement of the House of Orange in the Netherlands
in 1813 he no longer felt at ease, and he applied for a post in the Dutch
East Indies.[44] In 1816 he set off for Batavia, where he was appointed a
member of the Council of Justice.

Pieter Philip Juriaan Ondaatje died within two years, in 1818,
followed a few months later by his wife. They left two sons, Adriaan
Marius Elaarst and Pieter Philip Christiaan, and two daughters. Adriaan
and Pieter were 15 and 14 respectively and had not studied in the
Netherlands. They stayed on in the Dutch East Indies, and although
they could no longer profit directly from their father's protective presence,
they were ensured a good start by their name, their European upbringing
and, presumably, the circles of their father's friends. Adriaan began as
a secretary in Palembang, southern Sumatra, and quickly made a career
for himself. He climbed to the position of resident in Banjarmasin (on
the south coast of Borneo) in 1836. He married when he was 20. He
kept a record of eligible young ladies, noting their physical attractions,
fortune and family connections. In Adriaan's list of candidates, the
weightiest considerations were status, capital and family background.
Whether he took all this into account when making his final choice, we
cannot know. What is apparent is that for a young man with considerable
prospects, he made a very modest marriage. In 1823 he wedded Geertruida
Carolina Frederica Carels, the illegitimate daughter of the former slave
Rosie van Bima. Geertruida was adopted — and presumably also fathered

J.A.BOLAND SC.

Illustration 9   Pieter Philip Juriaan Quint Ondaatje (1758–1818) has gone down in history as the first Asian to play a significant role in European politics; he was a prominent figure in an uprising of the Netherlands' Patriot party. He was descended from a doctor who came from southern India and emigrated to Ceylon in the 17th century. His father was a clergyman in Ceylon, while his mother came from Utrecht, in the Netherlands.
[Anonymous lithograph in: C.M. Davies, *Memorial and times of Peter Philip Juriaan Quint Ondaatje* (1870).]

— by an employee of the Dutch East India Company, Jan Frederik Carels.[45] Adriaan never ceased to feel the pull of the Netherlands, and upon retirement he returned to Europe.

   Adriaan's brother, Pieter, also fared well — although an early death, at 37, cut short his promising career. Unlike his brother, he chose to follow a military path. He qualified in military engineering and made a name as a designer of defence works in various places in the Dutch East Indies. His greatest achievement was the construction of the fortress of Surabaya. Although famous in its day as an example of modern defence architecture, the huge citadel was in fact never completed and was gradually demolished during the 19th century.[46] Little is known about Pieter Philip Christiaan's wife — Charlotte Elizabeth van Ginkel — although it would appear that like his brother he too did not marry "upwards". The children of the two Ondaatje brothers followed more modest paths than had their fathers: one of Adriaan Marius Elaarst's sons became an inspector and another a clerk, while Pieter Philip Christiaan's two sons attained the ranks of sergeant, and clerk to the Orphans' Chamber in Batavia.[47]

In as many patterns as there were families, the threads stretched out from the Dutch East Indies and were spun around the world. Sometimes forced by circumstance and sometimes attracted by the hope of making a career, men sailed to and fro between the Netherlands and Asia, possibly taking their families with them, and ending up in the Indonesian archipelago. As the East Indian trading empire contracted, so the world of the Indies became more concentrated. The links between the Indonesian archipelago and the settlements in Malacca, India, Ceylon and the Cape of Good Hope were severed. The British takeover of these places brought on a sudden change in the social status of the local families, which had for so long profited from their connections to the colonial power. In Ceylon, the local European community, which had existed during the rule of the VOC in a fairly symbiotic relationship with the newcomers, suddenly lost its moorings. It was not connected to the new rulers. The British looked askance upon the large group of Burghers whom they encountered in Ceylon. Around 1800, a newcomer visiting Ceylon lumped all the subtly different groups together in one:

> Under the denomination of Burghers are comprehended Europeans, and descendants of Europeans, not being Englishmen [...]; descendants of Europeans and native women; children of Singhalese or Malabars, who have become Christians, and [...] have changed their dress, and assumed that of Europeans; (these are not distinguished from those who are called Portuguese;) and, lastly, descendants of slaves made free by their masters.[48]

It is very likely that the distinctions were not particularly relevant for the new managers in Ceylon, but it was a very different story for those who had been born in Ceylon and expected to live and die there.

With the contraction of the world of the East Indies, the Indische communities set out on different paths. Soldiers serving the Dutch East India Company were press-ganged or voluntarily joined the British forces. Officials who felt strongly attached to the Netherlands or the government in Batavia (at the most a couple of hundred people) went to the island of Java; those who felt strong ties to a local place remained there. During the first decades of their rule, the British community, forming a bureaucratic and military elite, was very small. In Colombo in around 1800 there were no more than 100 "gentlemen" and 20 "ladies". Soldiers were not included in the counts. From the European families of VOC extraction who remained after the British takeover, there were 300 people in Colombo and a further 600 elsewhere on the island.[49] In addition there were about 5,000 Portuguese, according to one English observer, "completely degenerated" and with a darker skin than the locals. In fact, these people were probably the descendants of freed slaves, and not of European origin; most of them would have come from South India, which explains their dark complexion.[50] As they were Christians, wore European clothes and had been categorised as (native) citizens by VOC statistical lists, the confusion is understandable.

The British and Dutch Burgher communities lived — quite literally — separate lives. The British settled inside the walled fortress of Colombo, while the Burghers lived in the city. An eyewitness describes an atmosphere of cool friendliness: "They meet seldom, unless on public occasions, when they are mutually friendly and agreeable to one another. Intercourse of this nature does not occur sufficiently often to breed intimate acquaintance, or lasting attachments."[51] Yet as early as 27 August 1796, a short six months after the British occupation of the city, the first marriage was celebrated between a young woman from a Burgher family and an Englishman. And more were to follow.[52] In addition, little by little the British fluttered forth from their entrenched position and started to rent houses in the city and surrounding districts from the impoverished Burghers.

Although we have little information about the material circumstances of Burghers in the 18th century, it is evident that after the British occupation many fell upon hard times. Before February 1796, most of the Europeans had been working for the Dutch East India Company; now they had to make ends meet in some other way. Anyone who owned land would try to manage by selling coconuts, areca nuts and palm wine, and by renting out houses to the English.[53] Burghers gradually gained modest positions in the government, since they were very useful to the British, providing a cheap source of labour and being well acquainted with the island. The Burghers, who lived mainly in the colonial centres and traditionally worked for the government, continued to be a community of civil servants. Several prominent clergymen and lawyers emerged from their midst, but on the whole they held posts in the lower ranks of the law courts and various administrative government departments.

With the arrival of the new authority in Ceylon, the social position of the Burghers changed. Just as, 150 years earlier, high-ranking officials in the Dutch East India Company had looked down upon the Portuguese, so after 1796 the "Dutch Burghers" were dismissed by the British as a "mixed-race breed" with extraordinary habits. Only very gradually did a mixed British-Ceylonese community develop; hence, for a long time the local Mestizo community remained synonymous with the term "Burgher". Their sense of unity was strengthened by their loss of status and the arrogant attitude of their new masters. Already under the Dutch East India Company the Burghers had regularly approached the government as a group, demanding certain rights and privileges. They continued to do so under the British. They were concerned about the erosion of their social standing, as exemplified by their (privileged) custom of keeping slaves, their educational privileges, and their job opportunities, which were being threatened by the emerging class of well-educated Sinhalese and Tamils. However, they seem to have lacked a strong sense of Dutch identity. When in the mid-19th century the Burghers began to voice their own political and cultural agenda in the press, it was not to Dutch examples that they turned, but rather to British models, and they found inspiration in antiquity and the rise of nationalism in Europe. It was chiefly Burghers who supported the founding of the newspaper *Young Ceylon* in 1850. Inspired by Giuseppe Mazzini's Young Italy movement for the unification of Italy, *Young Ceylon* voiced the thoughts of a rising elite of Burghers and cautiously promulgated the sentiments of Ceylonese patriotism.[54] It was an expression of the intellectual ambitions of a young generation imbued with Western culture yet maintaining a markedly Ceylonese perspective. Like the newspaper's founders, Charles Ambrose Lorenz and the brothers Frederick and Louis Nell, most of those working on the newspaper were descended from Dutch East India Company employees, although there were also a few Sinhalese involved. Not until the close of the 19th century did a movement arise in Ceylon that rediscovered the Dutch roots of the Burgher community and made these into the core of their individual identity — interestingly, the movement developed more or less simultaneously with the first Indo-European organisations in the Dutch East Indies.

Burghers from the British colonies made their own tracks throughout the world. Some Burgher families from Ceylon, such as the Eberts, the Van Geyzels, the Leembruggens and the Van Cuylenburgs, left for Singapore (which had been founded in 1819) during the 19th century.

Illustration 10   Colombo retained its "Indische" character into the 20th century. The houses within the fort, which were largely the homes of government personnel, were constructed in a typical "Dutch style" with verandas, sturdy Doric columns and only a single storey.
[Watercolour by John Leonard Kalenberg van Dort, 1888, KITLV, Leiden.]

There they encountered emigrants from another former Dutch colony, Malacca, in the shape of the Westerhout, Cornelius, Desker and Hendricks families.[55] This serves to illustrate the convoluted patterns of the Indische delta. In Malacca, too, the descendants of the Dutch and employees of the Dutch East India Company retained a sense of their own history, in which the European (more specifically, Dutch) component played the major role, dominating the Malay and other ancestral input. In the Dutch East Indies, the shaping of people's identity would take place in another manner. The local-born Europeans had no need to define themselves culturally, since they were supposed to belong to the same cultural community as the newcomers from the Netherlands. This explains why political activities among the Europeans in the Dutch East Indies concentrated more on socioeconomic emancipation than on ethnic or cultural orientation.

New masters, old patterns

With the 19th century came even more changes in the world of the East Indies. Governor-General Herman Willem Daendels, who arrived in Java on 1 January 1808, was to shake the dignitaries in the Indies out of their parochial slumber. Here was a man who was not recruited out of the world of the Indies and who was not to be swayed by the factions in Batavia or seduced by the Batavian daughters. (In fact, it was the daughter of the sultan of Banten who, after Daendels's military intervention in 1808, followed the general to Buitenzorg as "lady-in-waiting".)[56] Daendels attempted, in soldierly fashion, to revive and reform the languishing colony. But he could not solve the fundamental problems. Thus, for instance, the number of Europeans in Batavia continued to steadily decrease. Fewer and fewer ships managed to get through to Java since England and France — and therefore also the Netherlands, then a kingdom under Napoleonic control — were once more at war. When the British arrived in 1811 there were no more than 376 European men in Batavia — excluding soldiers — and 176 women. Apart from them, there were 706 men and 779 women who were classified as descendants of Europeans. In his description of Batavia, Piet Couperus records almost identical figures. Interestingly, Couperus in his account names the descendants of Europeans "native Christians", a description that well illustrates the distance between the upper and lower classes within the city. Altogether there were fewer than 2,000 Europeans, the majority of whom were born in Asia and were probably Mardijkers.[57] To this number should be added the European soldiers. Sickness, epidemics and reduced contact with the Netherlands had considerably shrunk the numbers in the European community. The colony of the Dutch East Indies had almost ceased to exist.

The English period is often depicted as one of rapid decline for the Indische way of life. Indeed, the historian Jean Gelman Taylor even referred to an "assault" on the Indische culture.[58] As is often the case, the perspective here is that of the British elite who certainly — although on a limited scale — concerned themselves with the lifestyle of the European community in the Indies. However, seen from the viewpoint of the Indies inhabitants, the five years of British rule were a continuation of old patterns, if under slightly different conditions. The notables tried to make the best of the situation and to occupy the few important positions, while the Europeans holding lower posts simply continued to do the office work. The picture of an assault on the Indische culture is nurtured by the spicy judgments of some English observers of life in the East Indies, of the marriages between European men and native or Mestizo women, of the lack of European culture, and the general lifestyle in the Indies. For instance, it was observed that there was a great scarcity of European-born women in the Indies. "Of pure Dutch there are few here," wrote the secretary of Raffles, "and the language universally talked among the Yafraus [*juffrouwen*, Dutch for "Misses"] is Malay; and indeed many of them understand no other. Dutch is almost as foreign as English."[59]

Only an estimate can be made of the number of British who lived in the Indonesian archipelago during the years 1811 to 1816; most of them were soldiers. The invasion of August 1811 was carried out by a considerable force of 12,000 men, which included 5,344 Europeans.[60] After a swift conquest, most of them had departed by October. The occupying forces consisted of a small number of officials and, of course, the military garrisons. The arrival of this British elite created a new class distinction in Java. High-ranking officers, in particular, held a snobbish outlook on the colonial world, and they felt superior to the Dutch "colonists", as they termed them. Remarkably, their criticism, aired particularly in the official newspaper, the *Java Government Gazette*, was directed not so much against the specifically Indische nature of the community as against the curious customs of the Dutch colonists, which included keeping windows and doors closed, smoking excessively, starting the working day at a late hour, and other perceived or imagined habits and characteristics such as maltreatment of slaves.[61] Undoubtedly there was a fine collection of chauvinistic snobs among the British, who looked down on everything that was Dutch (and Indische). A writer in the *Gazette*, calling himself "Anglicus", described the colonists as "a set of illiberal, narrow-minded, ignorant and unfeeling wretches".[62] Further grounds for ridicule were the separation of the worlds of the two sexes, which had become customary under the VOC, and the general attire of the Batavian women:

> The candid and good-natured Englishman endeavours to improve the fair-sex, wishing to promote a higher degree of civilization amongst them; he requests them to banish for ever from their social parties the Pawn, the Beetle-nut [betel], Sierie-boxes [sirih], the Saya and Cabaya [skirts], with many other elegant appendages of Java luxury.[63]

The key word here was "civilization": This was reflected in garb and plumage but extended beyond mere appearance. With the growing emphasis on the importance of upbringing and education, the quality of mothering and the mother's caring role became very important. Thus, a letter sent to the *Gazette* expressed concern about the passion for gambling among the women of the Indies: "Maternal affection and connubial bliss cannot live paramount in that bosom which is enflamed with the itch of gaming." Furthermore, playing cards led to a public show of emotions that was far from seemly. "Of all enemies to a beautiful face there is nothing so detrimental as a gaming table," was the writer's opinion.[64]

The letter produced violent reactions. One correspondent leapt to the defence not so much of women, as of card playing. Another was incensed at this attempt to poke fun at Batavian women and brown people. He composed the following ditty:

> Although my skin is brown and yours is white
> Though you are Europe's son, and so can write,
> Here pens an Indian some words (rhymes too!)
> Just to present another point of view:
> Never scoff at man or woman of any sort
> We let you enjoy your roast-beef and your port,
> We do not jeer at you for swilling beer
> Which, truth to tell, appears your chief pleasiere![65]

This is quite likely the earliest expression of colour awareness written by a citizen of the Indies — at least, the earliest published. In turn, an Englishman calling himself Dick taunted this "brown son of Apollo" for the colour of his skin, his jingling verse and his poetic pretensions.[66] Another man who supported the women of Batavia was Piet Couperus, himself born in Malacca and married to the Batavian Catharina Rica Cranssen. He argued that Batavian women were in no way inferior to women in any colony throughout the world. "Indische women with European parents are morally superior to European women who have sailed here across the seas; the women of Batavia have more natural commonsense, are better housekeepers and are better mothers." Couperus did not use the term "Mestizo" or "mixed-blood" because in his view these labels were probably not relevant. The Indische women were in a different category altogether from the women of lower classes. He stated: "The black women's moral make-up has always been the same; however, I think it true to say that they resemble warm wax ready to be imprinted with a stamp; they can be shaped to good or evil, and it all depends on the people with whom they live and associate." Here Couperus suggests the fundamental difference between Indische women and black women; it is both a colour difference and a distinction of class and culture. Furthermore, Couperus repudiated the suggestion of a depraved colony: "Morality here is no more lax than in other colonies [...]

Although much strong drink is consumed, there is respect for the marriage vows. Only those who are unmarried use their freedom to have concubines, who are generally female slaves."[67] Here Couperus was drawing on his personal experience.

The British tried to establish their own mores among the upper classes of Batavian society, and with some success. Couperus, an Anglophile, observed some changes in the Batavian way of life: "The showiness in such material things as carriages, clothing and household furnishings has noticeably diminished over the past few years. Generally there is less emphasis on outward display than there used to be. People seem to have adopted a more English taste." The British introduced a greater degree of sobriety but also a new fashion — which, recounts Couperus, was followed by many Batavian women. "Over the past few years the clothes of European women here have changed remarkably, greatly influenced by the example of the first lady of the colony."[68] This was Marianne Olivia, Raffles's first wife, a woman whose edifying influence in Batavia is often mentioned. Indeed, the *Java Government Gazette* was able to report in 1812 that at official receptions and parties the kebaya had yielded place to English gowns, with the sugary footnote: "We congratulate our friends on the amelioration of the public taste."[69] Couperus himself was a faithful follower of the British civilising mission to the Indies. In June 1814 the *Java Government Gazette* announced that a new form of entertainment had been introduced: Couperus had organised a concert followed by a ball and buffet in his house.[70]

The *Java Government Gazette* and Couperus, however, could hardly be described as neutral observers. Not only did Couperus have a measure of self-interest in buttering up the British, he spoke on behalf of the best circles of Batavian society — an upper echelon consisting of a few dozen families. Only this elite class of civil servants and well-to-do citizens came under the influence of the British presence. That too, only to a limited extent. Insofar as it is possible to reconstruct the situation, we see a very mixed picture. The influence of English taste was as visible as it was superficial, and the attempt to instil the beauties of British civilisation would seem to have been chiefly rhetorical. Discussions in the newspapers were often passionate, and the exasperation felt by the British missionaries was probably quite justified; but old habits were deep-rooted. Where there was a dominant British presence, the Batavians probably adapted their lifestyle, traditionally sensitive to changes of fashion. But Johannes Siberg, a former governor-general, celebrated his 75th birthday on 14 October 1815 in the old style. The women sat separately, in the back rooms of the house, while the men, complete with pipe and playing cards, relaxed in the front rooms. Only during the meal did the sexes mingle. The women's attire — traditionally a source of astonishment and amused gibes from European visitors — was also little changed in those sunset days of the British occupation. Joseph Arnold, one of the four English people invited to attend Siberg's festivities, commented: "The Dutch ladies have a peculiar way of dressing, generally a white bedgown, such as nurses wear in England." The women had their hair in a kind of plaited bun at the back of the head, and they were richly adorned with jewellery. Mrs Siberg, the second daughter of ex-Governor-General Alting, may well have appeared from a distance like an English nurse, wearing her kebaya, but she was dripping with diamonds worth about 5,000 or 6,000 pounds, declared the astonished Arnold.[71]

Although according to Couperus the show of luxury in Batavia became more restrained, it would seem that in their own circles the Batavian notables continued their extravagant ways. Many were out of work and lived on their estates, which they made ever more splendid as the years passed. Large landholders such as Nicolaus Engelhard, Willem Jacob Cranssen and Rijck van Prehn built new houses on their estates, which compared favourably with the grandest buildings in and around the city. Nor was there the slightest attempt at economy when Cranssen organised a banquet to celebrate the victory over Napoleon and peace in Europe. On 24 July 1814, the birthday of the Dutch Prince of Orange, 500 guests assembled in Cranssen's house for a lavish celebration: "The banquet combined delicacy, profusion and luxury. The wines were excellent and due justice was paid to the sparkling champagne in particular." And as if this were not enough, Cranssen repeated the festivities two days later.[72]

Thus, the impact of the English cultural offensive was tempered by the tough adhesion to tradition among the settled population and the brevity of the British presence — as well as by the fact that the British themselves adapted to their new surroundings. Not surprisingly, the luxurious lifestyle of the Batavian notables jarred with the English administrators. Dr Arnold, arriving in Java in September 1815, was shocked by what he beheld: "It is truly disgusting to see the expensive manner the Government officers live in here."[73]

Some Englishmen married into established Batavian families, following the tradition established in the previous centuries. The first such marriage between an Englishman and a Batavian bride was that of the assistant-accountant and friend of Raffles, William Barrett, who married

Illustration 11   Catharina Rica Cranssen (1795–1845) was the daughter of the governor of Ambon, Willem Jacob Cranssen. In 1812 she married Petrus Theodorus Couperus, thereby uniting two prominent families of the Dutch East Indies. They gained great wealth and prestige under the British colonial government.
[Oil painting, n.d., Iconografisch Bureau, The Hague.]

Jacoba Maria Goldman on 17 April 1812.[74] She was a daughter of the Batavian notable Johan Christiaan Goldman, who had been a senior merchant under Daendels. Many such marriages were to follow. Clearly, the Batavian daughters held some charm for the critical English, who in their daily lives managed to overcome without too much difficulty their prejudices against the Batavian ways of life. During the ball held to celebrate the birthday of King George III of Britain on 4 June 1813, one of the many toasts was to "the ladies of Batavia", accompanied by the ditty "Off she goes".[75] This seems to have become the accepted completion of the round of toasts made at formal balls and banquets.[76]

In the service of England

In Batavia the reaction of the settled population to the English administrators probably differed from class to class and from district to district. Many Batavian notables supported the Dutch House of Orange and were pro-English. Orange stadholder William V fled to England during the French invasion of 1795, and from there he issued an order to hand over the Dutch colonies into British custody. Out of conviction or opportunity, some Batavians embraced the new British regime as if that were exactly what they had been waiting for. Others seemed less enthusiastic. Apparently, there was not such a strong affinity with the Dutch administrators. The national character of the Dutch East India Company had always been somewhat ambivalent, partly because many of its employees were of foreign extraction. On 4 June 1812 the Batavian community celebrated the birthday of George III, in the absence of the British colonial administrator, Lt. Gov. Sir Thomas Stamford Raffles.[77] According to reports, the celebration on the part of the Batavians was massive and enthusiastic. Yet the old guard had little cause to rejoice. Very few Batavian notables received important appointments under the British administration. The exceptions were Willem Jacob Cranssen, Piet Couperus, Wouter Hendrik van IJsseldijk, Nicolaus Engelhard and J.A. van Braam — all of whom had worked their way up to high positions before 1811 and now chose to cooperate closely with the British. Cranssen's motives were patently clear. Several years previously, he had been removed from his post as governor of the Moluccas by Daendels, charged with neglect of duty.[78] His resentment against Daendels, together with his antipathy towards the French, made him a suitable candidate for a post in Raffles's administration. He became a member of the Council of the Indies and held the position of chairman of the Bench of Magistrates, together with other functions. Like his son-in-law Couperus, he was favourably disposed to the new administrators, so much so that in 1813 he expressed a wish to acquire British nationality. When the Dutch returned to power in 1816 he found himself in the bad books of the new administration, who — not surprisingly — regarded him as unpatriotic. Until his death in 1821 he remained without office, though he led a far-from-miserable life on his estate of Pondok Gedeh.[79]

Couperus made his Anglophile feelings clear by baptising his son Willem Jacob Thomas Raffles Couperus.[80] Clearly, the whole family felt a great affection for the British. Couperus's brother-in-law, Jan Samuel Timmerman Thijssen, a wealthy merchant, renamed one of his ships the *Governor Raffles*. On the evening after the ship had been (re)named, Timmerman Thijssen hosted a grand ball in his house, at which Raffles was a guest of honour.[81] The Batavians had not forgotten how to hold splendid parties. The firstborn daughter of Timmerman Thijssen and

Gesina née Couperus was named Olivia, after Raffles's wife, and the lieutenant governor and his wife were godparents for the little girl. At about the same time, Gesina's younger sister, Jacobina Maria, who was married to John Tulloch, gave birth to a son, who was baptised Stamford William Raffles. The Raffleses were his godparents too. Following the baptismal service, a grand ball and buffet was held for around 100 guests. The estate of Kampong Malayo was illuminated with 3,000 lamps. Some of the guests, it was reported, departed only at five in the morning.[82]

Although at the top level the consequences of the British takeover were quite far-reaching, in the lower circles little changed: many civil servants simply retained their jobs. And in the regions outside Java, the old pattern continued. The newcomers (now the British) occupied the highest positions, while the office work and more menial tasks were carried out by the local-born Dutch. Generally, a British resident was appointed head of a province and a British garrison was stationed there. For some local-born Europeans, the British period offered new opportunities. The new administrators lacked the necessary knowledge about the country and were more dependent on the local officials than their predecessors had been. One of the civil servants who was able to spread his wings under the British was Jacobus Arnoldus Hazaart.[83] Under Daendels he had been *drost* (bailiff) of Timor, and in June 1810 he had repulsed the British from the coast. Only when news reached him of the Dutch capitulation in distant Java did he, too, surrender. He retired from government administration and immersed himself in trade. But then the British resident, Burn, a hardened alcoholic, died, and his deputy expired too; so the notables of Kupang and the regents of the district begged for the return of the competent Hazaart. After 1816 he remained as resident.[84]

Another example of a local-born civil servant who survived the changes of government and was appreciated by successive regimes for his outstanding qualities was Johannes Alexander Neijs (1775–1835). Born in 1775 in Sumenep, on Madura, he began his career at the age of nine as a pupil in the Surabaya office and worked for many years on Ambon, where he got into a bit of career rut. However, with the arrival of the British his opportunities expanded, and he served as resident in various places in the Moluccas and Manado (northern Sulawesi). In 1817, when the Moluccas were once again taken over by the Dutch, Neijs was appointed resident of Ternate — he was also offered the more prestigious position as resident of Ambon, but he turned that down. After his retirement in 1829, he and his family remained in Ternate. There his two daughters got married, one to a marine commander, and the other to a Dutch assistant-resident.[85] One son became a horse captain. Neijs Sr. was a well-educated man. On his visit to the Moluccas in 1824, the Dutch Governor-General Godert Alexander Gerard Philip baron van der Capellen stayed at the Neijs home; he admired the collection of books and the resident's literary knowledge.[86] And the painter Antoine Payen, who visited Ternate in the same year in the train of the Natural Historical Commission led by Caspar Georg Carl Reinwardt, described Neijs as "*un homme instruit*", a cultivated man.[87]

Thus, it would appear that in many ways the British presence in the East Indies did not create a drastic break with the past. At the end of May 1814 it became known that the Netherlands and Britain were allies once more. Straight away, some of the Dutch citizens in Batavia composed a congratulatory address to the Prince of Orange, which they presented to Raffles during the celebrations in honour of the British King George III's birthday, on 4 June. On that day the grand house of Cranssen flaunted the words "Orange Restored by British Assistance".[88] It was not until 19 August 1816 that the East Indies returned to Dutch administration; in the two or more years between the announcement of peace and the restoration of Dutch authority, it seems that friction between the Dutch and British in the Indies increased, at least if the discussions in the *Gazette* are anything to go by. Their tone grew steadily more aggressive, and the mutual taunts and jeers became more frequent. Relations between the two groups certainly did not improve.

The English period left only superficial traces in the Indies, even though the British did their best to spread notions of European civilisation among Indische circles. They had introduced horse racing and theatrical performances, forms of entertainment unknown to the Batavians under the Dutch East India Company. Plays — such as *Mahomet the Imposter* — were provided by the Military Bachelors Theatre, founded by army officers. The theatrical performances were evidently also intended for the lower classes in the city (but surely not for the Muslims), since tickets could be paid for in kind, with candles, bacon, butter, soap and the like. Members of the audience had to wear shoes and stockings.[89] All the plays were performed in English, so for the benefit of the audience a short Dutch-language summary of the plot was printed in the *Gazette* in advance.[90] The British presence produced several other entities, such as the Java Benevolent Society, or *Javaans Menschlievend Genootschap*, which busied itself with the abolition of the slave trade; and the Java Bible Fellowship, *Javaansch Medewerkend Bijbelgenootschap*. The English also published a newspaper that gave a prominent position to European items as well as government decrees. Much of this did not survive the departure of the British.

But not all novelties disappeared when the British left. For instance, the theatre remained, together with the dress code for the audiences. Most changes affected outward appearance. The deputy quartermaster Jan Baptist Jozef van Doren described the theatre audience in Batavia in around 1827. His report reveals that in some respects little had changed since the end of the 18th century. There were very few women from Europe; most of the women in the audience were local-born. And to his astonishment, Van Doren found he could hardly understand a word they said. They were dressed in the European fashion — white gowns with short puff sleeves, their hair adorned with pearls and flowers.[91] Elsewhere in the East Indies, theatre also appeared, for instance in Semarang, where the *Liefhebberij Toneel* (Amateur Theatre) was founded in 1817, performing in an abandoned warehouse made available by the government.[92]

Probably the greatest change introduced by the British concerned slavery. Already towards the end of the 18th century the import of slaves into Batavia had decreased, but when the British arrived slavery became illegal and the slave trade more or less ceased. In February 1813, after the English takeover, the slave trade was officially banned, as it had been since 1807 in British colonies.[93] When the Dutch returned in 1816, the prohibition remained in force. The results were immediately apparent. In 1789 there had been 36,942 registered slaves in and around Batavia; under Raffles the number dropped to 23,239. In 1828 the figure had become 6,170, and in 1844 it was a mere 1,365.[94] Thus, by 1860, when it was officially banned by the Dutch, slavery was hardly a significant part of city life. Gone were the large trains of slaves accompanying the ladies on their Sunday church visit. More significant — although more gradual and possibly not immediately discernible — was the disappearance of the Mardijker community. By the close of the 18th century, the group of Mardijkers (they were increasingly known as "native Christians") had decreased considerably, and this trend continued. Although we still find members of this group until the mid-19th century, their numbers became negligible.

With the end of the slave trade came the end of the influx of people to Batavia from the far corners of the archipelago. If we consider that in 1779 at least 70 per cent of the population of the inner city of Batavia consisted of slaves and Mardijkers (this does not include the freed slaves who were not Christians), it becomes clear that the cultural diversity in the city must have been enormous. Even in the 19th century Batavia remained a city of migrants, though by then its newcomers were chiefly from Java and China. Indeed, the ethnic range in Batavia, as in other Javanese cities, narrowed down to four groups: Javanese, Chinese, Dutch, and the group of former slaves who came to develop a distinct "Betawi" culture. With the disappearance of slavery, the nature of concubinage also changed, especially in Batavia, where it was largely female slaves and ex-slaves who had been the (temporary) partners for European men. Now the housekeeper made her appearance. Probably this changed very little in the frequency of concubinage, for the differences in prosperity and power encouraged extramarital relationships.

The greatest social shift was to take place only after the return of the Dutch administrators. The new civil servants who arrived in 1816 disseminated a national sentiment that was a continuation of the spirit of Daendels. Little by little, the Dutch East Indies would gain an ever-stronger Netherlandish identity — even though this remained largely a matter for the newcomers and the elite who participated in the circulation between Europe and Asia. Thus, in 1816 a foundation was established to support the victims of the Battle of Waterloo. A similar charity had already been set up in London, but the Dutch did not want to be bettered by the British and tried to make Waterloo their victory too. Dutch subscribers to the fund could sign in at the customs house headed by Piet Couperus. A total of 90,804 Dutch guilders was collected.[95]

The newcomers who arrived in the Indies, sent out under the new Dutch King Willem I, wanted to draw a line under old quarrels and differences and introduce a more efficient style of administration.[96] However, the effects of this would be seen only later.

Landed gentry and powerful merchants

The story of the Couperus-Timmerman Thijssen clan has already shown that the period of French and English dominance opened up new opportunities for private entrepreneurship in the Indies; possibilities arose to achieve wealth and status outside government employment, via private trading ventures and through landownership. In the 17th and 18th centuries there was little scope for private trading ventures (unless they involved smuggling practices, which became the hallmark of VOC employees), and ownership of land was also closely bound to holding high office in the VOC.

The phenomenon of a landed gentry in the Dutch East Indies dates from the 17th century, when the countryside around Batavia was reclaimed. Already in the early days most of the land was held by just a few Europeans, all of them high-ranking officials in the Dutch East India Company.[97] Many Batavians had a small plot of land close to the city. Owning land provided an opportunity for earning money — not just for the wealthy civil servants but also for the poorer urbanites. Land was cheap. A small plot with a hut (*petak*) built of brick or bamboo outside the city walls cost a mere 15 to 20 rix-dollars. It is worth noting that those who invested in land were chiefly VOC employees, Burghers and Mardijkers; very few Chinese became landowners.[98]

During the 18th century vast estates were created, at an increasing distance from Batavia and in the hilly country around Buitenzorg (Bogor). Not only were these estates different in size from the plots close to Batavia, but the local people were obliged to give one-tenth of their produce to the landowner and to perform corvée labour on the estates. Although in the first 150 years after the land reclamation the acreage had greatly increased, little had changed in the social composition of the landholders. A study of the 91 major properties at the close of the 18th century reveals that by far the majority were owned by high-ranking VOC employees, most of them born in Europe.[99] The property was primarily an investment and thus frequently changed owner. It was usual to sell one's property on returning to the Netherlands or if one went to another part of the Dutch East Indies. Almost every European who stayed for any length of time in Batavia bought property there, which he then rented out or put to agricultural use.

The small estates around Batavia were tilled by slaves; but for the vast stretches in the Batavian hinterland the owners used the Javanese inhabitants. Only part of the estates was farmed directly by the owners; it was far more profitable to have the land farmed by local people who then had to give one-tenth of the crop to the landowner. The powerful position of these big landowners was underlined in 1752 when the rank of *hoofdingelanden* was created. *Hoofdingelanden* (chief landowners) were those who owned land with a value above 20,000 rix-dollars; they had to be of European ancestry.[100] In December 1803, when the Mardijker Pieter Michielsz, owner of the estates of Cipaminkis and Kelapanunggal, requested that he might receive the title of *hoofdingeland*, he was refused.[101] Many owners held positions in the administration of these landed districts or the "upper lands" (the districts in the heights of Java's western Priangan or Preanger), as Commissioner of Native Affairs or Inspector

Illustration 12   During the 18th century vast estates were created in the regions surrounding Batavia. The landholders lived from the tithes and corvée labour performed by the Javanese and Sundanese peasants. Initially, the estates were viewed as investments and frequently changed hands. After 1800 they tended to be passed down from generation to generation within one family, for example, the huge estate of Campea, belonging to the Van Riemsdijks.
[Oil painting by Antoine Payen, 1833 (detail), Rijksmuseum voor Volkenkunde, Leiden.]

of Agriculture. It was necessary to acquire substantial credit if one were to buy vast lands — and this was usually easier if one held a high rank in the Dutch East India Company.

After 1800 a remarkable change occurred in the management of estates. The close connection between the company and landowners became diluted, because many families were made non-active by Daendels and later Raffles. It also became more difficult to travel back to the Netherlands, and many company employees chose, on retirement, to remain in the Indies. This led to the development of a group of landowners who retained the estates in the family; a hereditary class of landed gentry came into being. The estates became more than a mere investment as more and more landowners became increasingly active in developing their property. At the same time, the estates became concentrated in the hands of a few families, such as the Cranssens, Engelhards, Van Riemsdijks and Michielses.[102]

The large plantation estates near Buitenzorg concentrated on the cultivation of rice, but nearer Batavia the cultivation of indigo dye proved highly successful. The pioneer of indigo production was Louis Petel, who carried out experiments on his estate of Bergzicht. He later settled in Pekalongan in north Central Java, where he established another indigo production plant.[103] However, such an entrepreneurial spirit remained exceptional. Most landowners lived off the profits of their rice production, thanks to their Javanese farmers. Another major source of income was cattle rearing. In 1818 the Van Riemsdijk family owned about 6,000 heads of cattle on their vast estate at Tandjong-Oost (East Tanjung).[104] The landed gentry scarcely suffered during the English rule, for many of them built new houses and beautified their property. Well-managed, the large estates proved an excellent investment even though in the Batavian districts few crops were produced for export.

Under Daendels and Raffles large sales of land took place. In 1810 Daendels sold the extensive estate of Buitenzorg, which was then divided into smaller parcels. The British went much farther. Besides the need for ready cash, the British had a vision of a desirable management and exploitation system for the colony. The British viceroy in Calcutta and conqueror of Java, Lord Minto, was an outspoken opponent of the system in the Dutch East Indies, with its forced production of crops and their delivery to the government. He proposed introducing a scheme of ground rent like the one used by the British in Bengal. Raffles even toyed with the idea of selling all the land to Javanese regents and to colonists.[105] This plan did not materialise, but in the neighbourhood of Batavia, Semarang and Surabaya there was large-scale auctioning of government lands. All land was described as "uncultivated ground". The auction in Batavia in January 1813 was badly organised and took place in a somewhat dubious manner, with certain investors being given preferential treatment. Also, the lots were all very large, making it difficult for small buyers to get a foot in the door.[106] Once again, large landownership was favoured.

At the auction, Raffles himself bought four large estates in the Priangan (Preanger) area of Cianjur, between Bogor and Bandung — later named Sukabumi — as a partner in a group of four investors.[107] He invested half the cost, amounting to 58,000 Spanish dollars. The three other investors were well acquainted with the Priangan district of Java: Nicolaus Engelhard, Thomas Macquoid and Andries de Wilde. With the exception of Raffles, the quartet represented a well-known phenomenon in East Indies society: high-ranking officials would become landowners of large estates in the area over which they governed. Engelhard had for many years been the Commissioner of Native Affairs. Macquoid was an old friend of Raffles from their Penang days and was one of his protégés. He was the superintendent of coffee cultivation and bailiff of Buitenzorg, and in November 1812 he was appointed resident for the Priangan and Karawang districts and chairman of the committee in charge of the sale of land in those parts.[108] Thus, he was able to wangle his own purchase.

De Wilde was born in Amsterdam. In 1803 he arrived in Batavia, where he became an army surgeon in the artillery. Later he held the post of inspector of the coffee plantations, and in May 1815 he was appointed the superintendent of vaccination. Already under Daendels he had attempted to acquire land in the Priangan district, but he only succeeded under Raffles. When in 1814 Raffles was charged with corruption — for, among other things, his share in the buying of Cianjur — he sold his share to De Wilde and Engelhard. De Wilde became the administrator. He had previously bought the estate of Ujungbrung, near Bandung in West Java, and now he became one of the greatest landowners in Priangan. De Wilde proved very successful. During his first years, coffee production shot up. According to the English doctor Joseph Arnold, who visited him in November 1815, his coffee plantation in Sukabumi extended over 40 kilometres. Furthermore, De Wilde introduced new vegetables and fruits from Europe. He also set up a stud farm. When the Dutch authorities returned to power, De Wilde became embroiled in a conflict with the authorities in Batavia in connection with his estates in Sukabumi. Governor-General Van der Capellen attempted to set the clock back with respect to the sale of land in Priangan because he thought that private ownership of land was detrimental to government interests, as it would harm the extraction of produce by the state. In 1819 De Wilde sold Ujungbrung, and four years later he sold Sukabumi.[109] Unable to found a dynasty, in 1823 he departed for Europe a disillusioned man, and he continued his feudal ambitions on an estate in the Netherlands, near Utrecht.

The English land-hawking did not restrict itself to Priangan. Enormous as the new estates in Priangan were, they were outdazzled by the sale, also in 1813, of the extensive properties of the Pamanukan and Ciasem lands, which lay midway between Batavia and Cirebon. The first buyers were British: James Shrapnell and Philip Skelton, representing the Bombay merchant Charles Forbes. Even after 1816 the estates remained in British hands, until in 1840 they were acquired by Pieter Hofland,

Illustration 13   Andries de Wilde (1781–1865) arrived in the Indies in 1803 and became an inspector for coffee plantations. Under the British colonial government he was appointed superintendent of vaccination. He was familiar with the Priangan region of Java and had good connections with the British, which helped him in 1813 to acquire large tracts of land in the region. He became the pioneer of the Priangan plantation agriculture.
[Lithograph in: Cora Westland, *De levensroman van Andries de Wilde*, (n.d.).]

with financial backing from the Netherlands.[110] Parcels of land were also auctioned around Semarang and Surabaya, and in a few isolated instances along the north coast of Java. These lay closer to towns and were smaller than the vast estates in West Java; furthermore the buyers were — apart from the commissioners who had organised the deals — local citizens.[111]

In South Sulawesi, close to Makassar, private ownership of land also increased. Following the British war against the raja of Bone, the lands belonging to the royal court of Bone were divided among those who had made themselves of service (to the British) during the war.[112] Not surprisingly, some of these fortunates were British, but there was also the captain of the Malays and the community of Peranakan (local-born) Chinese. Furthermore, certain prominent citizens of Makassar, such as the interpreter Jacob Trouerbach and the resident Johannes Mesman, were given a parcel of land, which meant that local families could make the leap to become landowners. In 1830 there were 29 registered estates in the Makassar region.

Ultimately, it was a matter of a mere handful of huge estates owned by an equally small number of families. It is noteworthy that particularly in Central and East Java and in Sulawesi, local families found it possible to acquire land. Owning land created a firm financial basis for these families who were thereby able to solidify their position and act more independently *vis-à-vis* the colonial government in Batavia.

Elsewhere in Java, too, in the territories of the rulers of Yogyakarta and Surakarta (Solo), a particular system of landownership developed. It was quite different from that in West Java and on the north coast. In the Principalities it was not the British who took the initiative to sell uncultivated land, but the apanage holders at the royal courts, who rented out their holdings. Although the beginnings of the system are shrouded in mystery, the practice of Javanese courtiers renting out their lands to private parties, especially Chinese and Europeans, appears to have begun during the final decades of the 18th century.[113] A peculiar feature of the land-rental system was that the colonial authorities in Batavia had little control over it and thus were unable to give undue preference to their favourites. Most of those renting land were born into the European communities that had developed around the royal courts since about 1755 — offspring of the garrison troops and their children. The old, deep-rooted ties between the courts and the European-Javanese families were a great advantage to the leaseholders. In 1837 no fewer than 29 of the 44 land tenants in Surakarta were designated "local-born", in contrast to Netherlanders and "foreigners".[114] One of these local-born tenants was Johannes Augustinus Dezentjé. He was a son of Surakarta, his father a French lieutenant and his mother Javanese. Initially he followed in his father's footsteps and became a lieutenant in the detachment of the colonial army in Surakarta, presumably a position of some responsibility.[115] When the British were in power he resigned his position and tried his luck as an indigo planter; as we shall see, this enterprise met with considerable success. Pieter Henry Meijer Timmerman Thijssen, stepson of the previously mentioned Jan Samuel Timmerman Thijssen, was another man who made the most of the new possibilities. He had inherited the entrepreneurial spirit of his father and stepfather. Although he is listed in the register of leaseholders as "local-born", he attended school in Delft, in the Netherlands, and did not return to the Indies

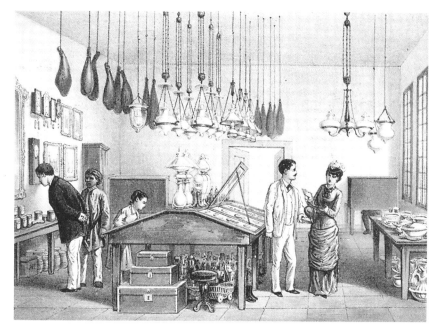

Illustration 14   Towards the close of the 18th century people began moving out of the old city centre of Batavia. However, the offices and stores remained. A wide variety of imported and local goods could be bought in these stores — ranging from jewellery to paintings, clocks, paraffin lamps and joints of ham.
[Lithograph after a drawing by J.C. Rappard in: M.T.H. Perelaer, *Het kamerlid Van Berkenstein in Nederlandsch-Indië* (1888).]

until 1825. There he worked for several years for the Nederlandsche Handel-Maatschappij (NHM, or Netherlands Trading Company) before starting up on his own, with the firm of Meijer & Co. In 1832 Henry branched out in Surakarta, leasing a parcel of land and setting up a coffee plantation.[116]

The enormous estates could only be bought or developed by taking out a loan. Credit was provided by the many trading houses that sprang up after about 1800. The (modest) flourishing of private trading businesses was connected with the disappearance of the Dutch East India Company and its monopolies. The first trading houses in the Indies date from around 1800, but both their number and their sphere of influence increased noticeably under the British. The newspaper *Bataviasche Courant* shows how at the beginning of the 19th century there were various trading houses. Their advertisements make it clear that they initially concentrated their business on the import and sale of luxury articles from Europe. The trading houses also sold locally made goods, such as furniture, textiles and ceramics, while at the same time introducing Chinese and Japanese products to the Batavian market, such as flour from Amoy and soya beans from Japan.[117]

Under the British, increasing numbers of citizens turned to trading. The second husband of Gesina née Couperus, Jan Samuel Timmerman Thijssen, was one of them. In 1812 or early 1813, together with his Danish partner Bernt W. Westermann, he founded a trading house in downtown Batavia dealing in porcelain and textiles, among other commodities.[118] Even though the days of the VOC's monopoly were numbered, it still did not hurt to have good connections with the lieutenant governor. Indeed, Raffles assisted Timmerman Thijssen with favourable contracts and by giving him interest-free credit.[119] The majority of trading houses were in Batavia, but some also arose in Semarang and, to a lesser extent, in Surabaya and Makassar. In Semarang, for instance, Robert Scott, born in Penang but educated in Scotland, set up his firm. After the British took over Java, he founded the firm of Deans, Scott & Co. Not only was his business active in trade, it also supplied credit to entrepreneurs in Central Java, especially those in the growing number of leased lands in Yogyakarta and Surakarta. He assisted, among others, his compatriot Harvey Thomson in setting up indigo plantations in Yogyakarta, for which he had been granted permission in 1817.[120] This was the beginning of a pattern that was to last into the 20th century: the marriage of money from Semarang with entrepreneurs from the Principalities.

Several dozen British traders tried their luck in Java under Raffles. Many merchants came from Calcutta and Penang, where they had had great success in the "country trade". Their experience and background gave them a great advantage over the Netherlanders in the Dutch East Indies. Members of the army that accompanied Lord Minto also established trading houses. For instance, Harvey Thomson began his career in the Indies as an assistant-surgeon in the British invasion force. And there were many others, lured by the riches of Java, who set up firms. Many trading houses were short lived. After Napoleon's defeat, some of the trading firms withdrew from the Indies to set up shop elsewhere. But others remained, continuing to do business even after the East Indies was handed back to the Netherlands in August 1816.

The British trading houses were far more energetic than their Dutch predecessors had been. They had the advantage of an established network stretching as far as the Indian city of Calcutta. This also explains why the British trading houses were able to survive the return of the Dutch government to the East Indies. According to the Dutch East Indies Almanac, in 1817 there were 11 trading houses in Batavia, of which five were still British-owned. Eleven years later the number of trading firms had more than doubled, reaching 27, and there was still a strong non-Dutch presence. In Semarang and Surabaya, too, there were many non-Dutch trading houses actively trading.[121]

Dutch, English or Scottish they might be, but most of the trading houses, however small, were run by men from Europe. In most cases the tradesmen were small-time adventurers trying their luck — and usually faltering or failing.[122] Not many trading houses survived more than a few years. In a very few instances an Indische trading house was a branch of a firm based in the Netherlands — one example of this being the firm of Reynst & Vinju, a famous Batavian trading house established in 1836. This firm survived until the end of the colonial period, because it was able to operate using the financial reserves of the Rotterdam shipowner Anthony van Hoboken. In fact, economic possibilities for trading houses were always strained, particularly with the introduction of the so-called Cultivation System. Under this system, government products for export from the East Indies — this constituted most crops — were entirely controlled by the NHM (Netherlands Trading Company). Trading houses had to be content with local business, rather than the export trade. Not until 1855 would this system become less restrictive.[123] The spirit of the Dutch East India Company had a long lease of life.

Opportunities for local European entrepreneurs to stretch their wings and search for success beyond the shadow of government control remained limited. In many ways the established patterns of life in the East Indies stayed in force. For most of the European population, there were few new openings. It was a small group of newcomers and the local ruling families who saw chances for expansion. That was how it had been under the Dutch East India Company, and that was how it would continue after 1816. Significantly, it was outside the circles of bureaucracy and government that local families would find possibilities to forge ahead and acquire wealth. This happened not through a career in government or a tactical marriage, but by acquiring land. For a few Indische families, landownership in West Java and especially the Principalities, which were not formally colonial territory, provided a gateway to prosperity and greatness — and sometimes a slippery slope towards decline and fall.

CHAPTER **4**

Lordly Traditions and Plantation Industrialism

V ast plantations, princely lifestyles and a patriarchal hierarchy — these are the associations we have with the burgeoning class of landowners and leaseholders in the Indies. The massive land purchase during the British interregnum in the East Indies only served to strengthen the image of feudal lords ruling over a local population of many thousands. They certainly formed a colourful collection, those wealthy landowners with their spacious, hospitable homes, their extravagant hunting parties and their undeniable conceit, which frequently brought them into conflict with the equally arrogant representatives of the colonial government of the time.

After the short period of British rule a new type of landholder appeared; these men were planters cultivating cash crops for export. They often required credit on a large scale. Most of the planters lived in a state of constant debt — to support their enterprises they took out one loan after another. Despite this, they somehow managed to maintain a princely existence full of pomp and ceremony. Their royal lifestyle was also expedient, since it helped maintain their authority over the *desa* (village) population on the estates, who grew their products for the world market. Furthermore, to recruit labour from the villages, employers had to speak their language and understand their social structure. Indeed, certain planters became famous for their knowledge of the local language and culture. Others are known for their technological innovation, having introduced machines and expertise from Europe. The landholder was initially a kind of noble lord governing his extensive estates, like the famous and fabulously rich Mardijker Augustijn Michielsz, also known as Major Jantji, who created his own world of splendour. Then, during the 19th century, the gentleman-landholder evolved into an agricultural industrialist, aiming to produce the maximum profit by exploiting the people living in his domain.

The government in Batavia played a major part in this process of changeover from feudal landlord to planter. In 1823 Governor-General Godert Alexander Gerard Philip baron van der Capellen declared quite accurately that the landed gentry of the day were like a "parasite plant" wriggling themselves into a position between the Javanese peasantry and the government, and thus accumulating wealth at the expense of the local people and the Netherlands Exchequer.[1] Considerations of this nature persuaded the government to take the production of cash crops for the world market into its own hands, and in 1830 it introduced the Cultivation System. The local population were forced to cultivate products to be sold on the European market and were paid a fixed, low "plant wage". The Cultivation System, however, also stipulated an important role for private entrepreneurs. They were responsible for the sugar production, later also for tea. Under the agreement, they were obliged to supply the government with a share of the final products at a pre-arranged price. The Nederlandsche Handel-Maatschappij (NHM, Netherlands Trading Company) then arranged for export to the Netherlands.[2]

The production of sugar from cane required an expensive factory, so the government advanced loans — amounting to as much as half a million guilders — to the contracting parties. The sugar contracts were extremely lucrative for entrepreneurs. Many contractors became fabulously wealthy, whereas the colonial government itself began to make a profit only when sugar prices started to rise after 1845.[3] Meanwhile, the government did succeed in its aim of placing the sugar production in Dutch hands. In 1833 the Chinese made up three-quarters of the sugar-contracting parties (175 to 180 contracts), but in 1837 the East Indies government declared that when new contracts were issued, European candidates should receive preferential treatment.[4] The government assisted by enforcing a low wage for planting and providing extensive advance loans. The air was full of accusations — the criticisms, of course, coming from people who been passed over. And it was certainly true that a connection with the minister of the colonies, or the Dutch king, would often be sufficient to procure a contract.[5]

This did not mean that the contractors should be seen as a kind of rentier class who could comfortably live off the income from their property without lifting a finger. Far from it — if only because the government obliged them to introduce new technologies. Some sugar contractors, such as Theodoor Lucassen and Otto C. Holmberg de Beckfelt, took their assignment very seriously. They made an expedition to northern France, where they studied the sugar-beet industry and hired technical experts.[6] They left their mark on history as the founders of successful Indies family firms. Partly thanks to their pioneering spirit, under the Cultivation System the average production of sugar steadily increased from 20 to 23 *pikols* (1 pikol = 61.8 kg) of sugar per *bouw* (approximately 0.71 of a hectare) in 1834 to at least three times as much 40 years later. In the 1880s, Java was second only to Cuba as the greatest cane sugar producer in the world. This remained true until the 1930s.[7]

The Principalities

The sugar contractors were especially active along the north coast of Central Java in Cirebon and Pekalongan, and in East Java in Surabaya, Besuki and Pasuruan. The contractors came from the immediate circle of the governor-general, the minister of the colonies or the king of the Netherlands; they were almost always European newcomers. In the semi-independent Principalities, a network dominated by Indies-born planters developed outside the Cultivation System. The Principalities were residencies ruled by the sultan of Yogyakarta and the *susuhunan* of Surakarta. The planters there managed, without advance loans from the government, to develop a sugar industry that by the early 1880s was producing as much as 17 per cent of Java's sugar.

Most of the leaseholders in the Principalities came from the small European communities living there, which in around 1815 consisted of no more than 113 adult European men and at most 77 families. The men often came from local garrisons.[8] Among the 113 adult European men, there were, for instance, retired army officers, a trumpeter and a coachman from the retinue of the sultan and the susuhunan. Others made a living in a great variety of ways: there were merchants and shopkeepers, clerks, a schoolteacher, a musician, a smith, a barber, a botanist, someone who rented out carts and coaches, a carpenter and a surgeon. Among these officers, clerks and small businessmen were to be found the progenitors of famous dynasties of planters and linguists.

During the time that Huibert Gerard Nahuys van Burgst was resident of Yogyakarta (1816–1822) and Surakarta (1827–1830), the lives of this small European community were to alter drastically. Within a few decades they were enjoying enormous prosperity and prestige. Nahuys van Burgst used his position to arrange land-rental contracts with Javanese princes and their apanage holders for his favourites, including some Chinese. He also contrived to have advances of capital from British trading houses in Semarang and the occasional one in Batavia; thanks to the opium trade there was no shortage of funds.[9]

Van der Capellen's snide remark, describing this new class of European and Chinese entrepreneurs as a parasitic plant, seems highly apposite. The governor-general perceived a grave danger in these entrepreneurs, often Eurasian, and most of them of non-Dutch origin. Furthermore, it was with the backing of British trading houses that they had wormed their way into the entourage of the Javanese rulers, with whom the colonial government had relations of an extremely intricate nature.[10] Van der Capellen wished to put an end to the large-scale land rental and in 1823 ordered the leaseholders to return their estates in exchange for compensation from the Javanese apanage holders.[11] In issuing this decree the governor-general could reckon on the support of the princes Diponegoro and Mangkubumi, who were the guardians of the underage sultan of Yogyakarta, and who were greatly distressed by the growing influence of Chinese and Europeans in their territories. However, their approbation quickly turned to fury when they realised that they were expected to compensate the leaseholders — and pay them a pretty penny too.[12] Van der Capellen's decision — prompted by his concern about the political risks involved in an uncontrolled planters' industry — would, ironically, prove to be one of the sparks that ignited the rebellion of Diponegoro, which came to be called the Java War (1825–1830). The war brought the Dutch colonial government to the very edge of the abyss.

The war also provided a new start for the leaseholders, and it engendered a legendary planters' tale. Van der Capellen's measures against the leaseholders of the Principalities were retracted. In 1827 it became once more possible to rent land — provided the renters were Dutch; henceforth, Chinese people were excluded from that possibility.[13] The most prominent leaseholder at this time became the landlord of Ampel in Surakarta, one Johannes Augustinus Dezentjé (1797–1839). He was the son of a European officer enlisted in the susuhunan's guard, and a Javanese mother. When he was 23 he had begun as a small-time planter, but within three years Van der Capellen had nullified his rental contract. During the Java War, Dezentjé created his own corps of *prajurit*, Javanese soldiers, with whom in 1828, at the request of the resident, Nahuys van Burgst, he contrived to capture a number of conspirators. Although the resident claimed all the glory for this successful operation, Dezentjé had no need to complain: Nahuys van Burgst repaid him with important land-rental contracts.[14]

Illustration 15   Of all the coffee planters of the Principalities, the most magnificent
was Johannes Augustinus Dezentjé (1797–1839). His lifestyle rivalled that of a local
prince. Although his enterprise experienced financial difficulties, it was saved thanks
to other entrepreneurs and remained in the Dezentjé family until the 20th century.
[Oil painting by B.L. Hendriks, *ca.* 1870, after a painting by J.C. Muller Kruseman,
ca. 1835, Bronbeek Museum, Arnhem.]

The number of contracts needed for Dezentjé's extensive coffee
plantations amounted to about 200. He produced roughly one-third of
the total coffee crop from the Principalities. In 1835 Dezentjé married
a Javanese princess named Raden Ayu Condro Kusumo, from the court
of the susuhunan. At their marriage she was given the baptismal name
of Sara Helena. Dezentjé earned great respect for his expert knowledge
of the local people and their language, and he gradually adopted the role
of a Javanese nobleman.[15] He converted his house on the Ampel Estate
into a *dalem* (palace court) in the style of the local nobility and maintained
a large *gamelan*, or percussion orchestra. He had his own private guard
to ensure the security of his walled palace.[16] Very much in the style

of Major Jantji in the Batavian countryside, Dezentjé never left home without an equestrian escort and a retinue of servants.

During the 1830s Dezentjé shifted his interests and took up sugar cultivation. His financier and business representative, Gillian Maclaine, the Scot who founded the Batavian trading house of Maclaine, Watson & Co., concluded a three-year contract with the NHM to this effect. Dezentjé received an advance loan of 1,181,000 guilders, the greater part of which — 840,000 guilders — was earmarked for sugar deliveries.[17] Despite the immense loan, Dezentjé was soon in huge financial trouble. Indeed, finance was not his strongest point, but in this case that was not the cause of the problem, because Maclaine had already been in charge of the financial affairs. He had, in fact, written to his brother in Scotland in 1837, saying, "Dezentjé is an extensive coffee and sugar planter, with a gross income of upwards of 30,000 [pounds sterling] a year, and yet I cannot keep him out of debt. His failing is an all-too-common one to require any particular description. I have, however, put him on an allowance, and he has given me carte blanche to do as I think fit."[18] It would seem, therefore, that Dezentjé's financial woes were caused by the fact that for both coffee and sugar production, there had to be a huge outlay before there could be any profits. When the NHM representative came to investigate the situation, he found Dezentjé in a situation of "pressing financial embarrassment" and gave him the benefit of the doubt.[19]

In 1839 Dezentjé's enterprise was poised on the verge of disaster, as a result of sharp competition from Brazilian coffee on the world market and the threatened collapse of the Indies' currency circulation as a result of the primitive monetary system in the colony. In this hour of crisis, with his empire crumbling on all sides, Dezentjé died. The NHM attempted until 1841 to keep his business going by advancing credit, although they would have preferred to liquidate their interests in his estate straight away, as they had done with other coffee planters who had fallen victim to the crisis.[20] But in Dezentjé's case there was not only an extremely large amount of money in question, there was also scarcely any collateral. The contracts in the name of the deceased did not represent "right in rem", that is, connection with property — which meant that they could not be transferred to a third party. The most the NHM could do was administer the property themselves.[21] For eight years the affair dragged on, until finally the creditor was content to auction the movable property and the growing crops. However, friends of the family had agreed not to outbid one another. So instead of fetching its market value of around 500,000 guilders, the auctioned property brought in only 12,000 guilders.[22] Family friends returned the effects, and the Dezentjés remained one of the most important planter dynasties of the Principalities until into the 20th century.

The continuity of the Indische family businesses as seen in the Principalities was surpassed elsewhere in the East Indies only by the *perkeniers* (owners of the nutmeg groves) in the small Banda archipelago in the southern Moluccas. The strong position of the planters in Central Java was the result of government policy aimed at maintaining a firm footing in the Principalities by means of the leaseholders. The lesson of the Java War had been learned. In line with the new approach, Chinese and Europeans who were not of Dutch origin were excluded. Dutch fortune-hunters who wanted to establish an agricultural business were also ruled out.[23] In principle, leasing land in the Principalities was permitted only for the cultivation of cash crops by planters with sound financial warrants. There were also, however, planters who were not so wealthy. They were often descendants of Europeans who had fallen on hard times but, being born in the Principalities, were able to settle there; others were newcomers living like gentlemen-farmers from the corvée labour of the local residents. Although the government of the Indies strove to implement a Western type of business management, at the same time it stipulated through its land-leasing regulations that the leaseholders should behave like Javanese noblemen. Most of them found it took little effort to comply with this condition.[24]

The fusion of these two elements — an aristocratic lifestyle resembling that of the indigenous nobility, and the management of a business aimed at the export market — could be clearly seen in Yogyakarta, where a small coterie of Yogyakartan Europeans held the reins. Of the 53 enterprises there in 1865, 35 were owned by old families from the Principalities — that is, families who had been there during the English period. Another business was owned by the Timmerman Thijssen family from Malacca, who had settled in the Principalities in about 1830. Seven other businesses were owned by entrepreneurs who had "married in". These included three officers, a doctor, a man born in the Indies named Louis Frederik Berretty, a Protestant minister and his son. Altogether there were only 11 firms owned by people from outside this close-knit network of local-born entrepreneurs. The undisputed heads of the established Principalities' families were George Weijnschenk and his brother George Lodewijk Weijnschenk. Through their marriages and

Illustration 16 The leader of the network of Yogyakartan planters in the mid-19th century was George Weijnschenk (1811–1878). He was said to be a friendly but autocratic ruler over those dwelling on his estates.
[Photograph, n.d., Iconografisch Bureau, The Hague.]

those of their sisters, they were in-laws of the Baumgarten, Dom, Raaff and Van Stralendorff families, all of whom were living in the Principalities before 1830.[25] That the Weijnschenk brothers were key figures in this society also appears from their initiative in establishing the Freemasons' lodge "Mataram" in Yogyakarta in 1870; this became a meeting place for the most prominent leaseholders.[26] Incidentally, the Freemasons' lodge met in the sultan's palace, which tells much about the cordial relations between the court and the leaseholders.

The court in Surakarta was considerably less accessible, although the financial support the susuhunan gave to the construction of the theatre in Surakarta may certainly be taken as a sign that he was well disposed towards the leaseholders. As we have seen, there were also close ties between the Dezentjé family and the royal court, as a photograph attests, showing the crown prince with his retinue on the veranda of the Dezentjé home.[27] Nevertheless, the Surakarta leaseholders were not as warmly accepted as part of the susuhunan's entourage as were their colleagues in Yogyakarta by the sultan. In Yogyakarta, according to a family legend, in about 1850 the leaseholder's son, Frederik Wilhelm Wieseman, paid a visit to the sultan to tell him about his intention to marry Geertruida Louisa Dom — a woman who, because of her great beauty, was known as the Rose of Yogya. Apparently His Royal Highness reacted with the spontaneous gift of a gold fob watch.[28]

Throughout the succeeding generations, the warm ties between court and leaseholders were maintained. Wieseman's sons-in-law, Jacobus Marinus Pijnacker Hordijk and Wolter Broese van Groenou, would form part of the gathering — together with other leaseholders — on such important occasions as the *garebeg puasa* (the end of Ramadan), coronation day, and the birthdays of the sultan and crown princes. The leaseholders were included in the court protocol that determined the course of such important occasions; there would first be a ceremonial procession through Yogyakarta, with the resident and the sultan at the head, followed by his elephant, then the highest nobility and European officials, and finally the leaseholders. The royal court, which had lost much of its splendour after the British interregnum and the Java War, gained renewed prestige with the flowering of the economy. The ceremonial procession was intended to impress the local people. An essential part of the day's celebrations would be a game of cards, in which the sultan and chief nobility were joined by leading Europeans and leaseholders. But this was no informal get-together; the card games were strictly organised and regulated. The stakes were also strictly limited. The resident could wager 25 guilders, and when after several hours he retired, the sultan and leaseholders would continue to play for a while, the stake being raised to 100 guilders.[29]

Two contrasting worlds: Surakarta and Yogyakarta

Despite their acceptance within the royal entourage, the leaseholders maintained their orientation towards Europe; and this only increased in the 19th century as they grew more wealthy. In this process the planters' daughters played an even more important part than the planters' sons. Some, such as the above-mentioned Rose of Yogya, married the son of another leaseholder. Her well-dowered cousins, however, proved a particularly attractive prospect for newcomers who arrived with little

fortune but with an acceptable position in society. As elsewhere in the
Indies, the garrisons of Yogyakarta and Surakarta provided many dashing
young military officers for the marriage market. This increased the
competition among planters' sons, who had no supply of suitable ladies
arriving from Europe. Many of them took a Javanese wife, in some
instances a Chinese one, often only marrying them after they had sired
several children.[30] Marriage ceremonies were a costly affair, with all the
formalities they entailed; in fact, it is safe to say that marriage was
reserved for the rich.[31] So, not surprisingly, in the second half of the 19th
century it was the wealthy Yogyakartan planters who would wed Javanese
women. Among these 12 planters were George Weijnschenk and his son
George Lodewijk, the most important planter of the second generation
of Weijnschenks.[32]

George Weijnschenk's attitude towards marriage — he was to wed
three times — says much about the politics of marriage in the Principalities. His first wife was Maria Dorothea Baumgarten. His marriage
to her in 1836 created an alliance between the two major Yogyakartan
planters' families. Because his brother and sisters also made excellent
marriages, it looks very much as if these unions were arranged by the
parents. Within a year, however, George Weijnschenk was a childless
widower. He then fathered three children with the Javanese Ramag, or
Busug, whom he later married, in 1850. He proved a good father, and
by legitimising his children he ensured that his inheritance remained
within the family.[33] When Ramag died, he married again, this time his
brother's widow, Wilhelmina Krämer. Although this union produced a
son, it would seem that it was chiefly a marriage of convenience, and
it ended after a few years in a legal separation.

Many leaseholders were not strictly monogamous. They would
often keep concubines, which was perfectly acceptable in Java. The
children born from such unions would frequently be accepted within a
family hierarchy, although on the lower rungs. In George Weijnschenk's
will it appears that he had adopted two children of his brother-in-law
Christoffel Willem Baumgarten; he himself had also had four of his
children adopted by his other brother-in-law, Pieter Dom. The children
were given the names of both their adoptive father and their natural
father; they were thus recognised as members of the clan but could not
make any claims to the family inheritance of either the Doms or the
Weijnschenks. George Weijnschenk bequeathed to each of his four
"Weijnschenk-Dom" children a house and 100,000 guilders.[34] George's
ten children by Ramag and his son by Wilhelmina Krämer received

even more, since they inherited the rest of the estate in equal portions. When George Weijnschenk died in 1879 his total legacy must have been somewhere between three million and four million guilders.[35] Polygamy may have been more or less socially acceptable in the Indies, but European family law did not acknowledge it, which resulted in complicated notarial constructions.

The majority of Yogyakartan leaseholders had either a mother or grandmother(s) who was Javanese. However, the reports made by the residents of Yogyakarta in the 1850s and 1860s list only one leaseholder as "coloured/Mestizo", while those of Surakarta actually emphasise the Mestizo nature of the group of European planters in their residency.[36] Clearly, the contrast did not lie in the differing ethnic background of the established planters' families — for the families from Yogyakarta and Surakarta were branches of the same tree, closely connected by many a marriage. The explanation must be sought in the fact that in the Dutch East Indies, notables, despite their Javanese grandmothers or even mothers, were registered as "Creoles" — that is, local-born but having two European parents. The distinction between Creole and Mestizo then becomes not biological, but largely socioeconomic. Yogyakarta, certainly after 1850, had a small, virtually closed circle of wealthy leaseholders; in Surakarta, by way of contrast, there were many small leaseholders who sometimes survived on meagre profits.

The distinction between Mestizo and Creole in the local resident's reports was based entirely upon the way in which the *Binnenlands Bestuur* (Interior Administration) decreed that a planter should manage his enterprise. The government of the Indies tried to establish a stable, Western form of business management. This was also evident in the tone of a memorandum written in 1860 by the resident of Yogyakarta, Carel Pieter Brest van Kempen, which dealt with land-leasing in the area under his jurisdiction. He noted with satisfaction that the cash crop indigo was being grown on almost all the leased lands in his residency (43 out of the 49 estates). The production of indigo was labour intensive and demanded expensive irrigation works.[37] The resident praised the businesses, particularly for their highly effective working methods, and the "correct division of labour, the diligent supervision of all aspects of the work, and above all the painstaking manuring of the soil, which yielded very profitable results".[38]

Business management in Surakarta was quite different. Here, in the 1850s, coffee production dominated. The coffee was not grown on previously cultivated apanage land; thus, there was no tradition of enforcing local residents to do corvée on the plantations. Indeed, labour had to be lured to the high bare lands, with the promise of free seeds and other provisions. Although there were large enterprises in Surakarta, the business of export crops was not so highly organised as in Yogyakarta. The farmlands of these enterprises lay scattered over a large area, and the leaseholders had less control over the labour force; they had to do business with a large number of apanage holders. A final point is that there was so much opportunity in Surakarta to lease land that both the number and the size of individual businesses grew continually, rising from 57 in 1855 to 192 in 1875.[39] It is precisely this growth that explains why government officials drew a picture of a disorganised group of half-breed planters living in Surakarta; ironically enough, the class of leaseholders in this region was less dominated by Mestizos than the one in Yogyakarta. In Surakarta there was a greater turnover among the planters. In 1865, more than 40 per cent of the estates were held by newcomers who were not members of the old, established families. In contrast, only 11 of the 53 enterprises in Yogyakarta were in the hands of "outsiders"; the relatively open nature of the Surakarta planters' community thus offered opportunities to descendants of Europeans living in the residency district, and even more so to newcomers.

The "untidy" nature of the Surakarta planters' community becomes clear in reports from the resident; they regularly refer to the petty gentlemen-farmers who exacted a percentage of the crop from the Javanese peasants working on the lands they leased.[40] They preserved a feudal tradition in the Indies and, together with the village heads, managed to exploit the people. In the words of the resident of Surakarta, these petty landlords would often have "a large following, *wayang* and gamelan players, and sometimes a not too moral lifestyle, in imitation of the native aristocracy" (apparently they also kept a harem). All this, continues the writer "was intended to keep up appearances, but their enterprises were less prosperous than those of orderly Europeans".[41] The majority of these marginal leaseholders, including white newcomers, were considered by the Dutch officials to be lazy people who let their women cultivate the land and sell the produce on the market.[42] It is impossible to say how many European-run plantations and small businesses there were in Surakarta, but the number is undoubtedly greater than that given in the residents' reports. From time to time an official would uncover a leaseholder who was not registered and was thus illegal.[43]

Despite the concerns of the government in Batavia about the planters in Surakarta, and the occasional uprising of a discontented populace —

as in 1855 — things were generally settled and satisfactory for both colonial rulers and landleasers. The lease of land put money in the pockets of the inhabitants of the Principalities, and most of the planters treated the local residents in a less arbitrary manner than did the apanage holders. The European presence became more and more accepted. Indeed, the leaseholders were essential for all parties: for the Dutch officials who thereby increased their influence; for the royal courts, who made money from the system; for the local population, who probably experienced an initial improvement in their living conditions; and, finally, for the business life of Semarang, because the Principalities formed a good market for imported goods.[44] Even Europeans who were not leaseholders profited from the commercial activity in the Principalities. Most of them in Yogyakarta found employment on the plantations, while one-third of the European male population worked in the civil service. A handful of Europeans set up as tradesmen or ran a shop.

There is nothing to support the view that the Javanese and European worlds, like oil and water, refused to mix. Daily life contradicted this notion. Nevertheless, an aspect of colonial ideology chose to emphasise the distinction between the rulers and the ruled. It thus became part of the colonial structure to have translators render speeches into the local language on ceremonial occasions when royalty, colonial civil servants and planters gathered. Translators who were recruited from the local European community were known to be the confidants of both residents and Javanese royalty. Their position was one requiring tact and delicacy. It would seem that many translators saw themselves more as part of the local royal court than as colonial civil servants.[45] This might explain why Johannes Gotlieb Dietrée, interpreter in the residency of Yogyakarta from 1796 to 1825, was Muslim.[46]

In the Principalities, and especially in Surakarta, the study of languages became a family tradition. Best known among these linguistically oriented dynasties are the Winters and the Wilkenses. Carel Friedrich Winter was born in 1788 in Yogyakarta and moved to Surakarta when he was seven years old. There, his father, Johannes Wilhelmus Winter, was appointed a translator for Javanese languages.[47] The young Carel Friedrich did not seem to be learning much at school, so his father taught him at home, and in 1818 the young man became an assistant translator at his father's side. When his father left for Semarang in 1825, Carel Friedrich remained in Surakarta as a translator. Three years later he assumed the extra task of secretary at the newly established Registry of Births, Marriages and Deaths. This was followed in 1829 by his

Illustration 17   Carl Friedrich Winter (1799–1859) drawn by his friend J.A. Wilkens. Winter came from a family of interpreters who secured the position of confidante both at the royal courts of Java and with the Dutch colonial government. [Lithograph by C.W. Mieling in: *Tijdschrift voor Nederlandsch Indië* (1852).]

appointment as the director of the brand-new Institute for the Javanese Languages in Surakarta. This institute had been set up to teach Javanese languages to employees of the Binnenlands Bestuur. When the institute was closed down in 1843, Carel Friedrich lost his position. There had been an inspection of the institute by four residents, who had produced a devastating report on the quality of education there, and on Carel Friedrich as a teacher. His command of Dutch was judged to be very poor, and because he was "a son of the country" (an *inlands kind*) he failed to gain the respect of the students, who all came from the wealthy Netherlands and Indische bourgeoisie.

Despite all this, when a new training college was set up in 1843 in Delft, the Netherlands, for civil servants to be employed in the Binnenlands Bestuur, they could not do without Carel Friedrich Winter and his proficiency in Javanese. The professor of Javanese in Delft, Taco Roorda, was undoubtedly a great linguist, but he taught a language that was not his own as a medium of daily speech.[48] He benefited greatly from the assistance of Carel Friedrich, who made a large number of translations for him. It would seem that despite Carel Friedrich's sporadic elementary schooling, his Dutch was not so bad after all. This also appears in the translations he made of official documents, which have been preserved in the archives. The linguistic scholar Herman Neubronner van der Tuuk remarked somewhat maliciously in 1864 that Roorda was not teaching Javanese, but Winterese.[49] Carel Friedrich earned his place in the history books, however, when the susuhunan granted him permission to bring out the first Javanese-language newspaper, named the *Bromartani*, which was intended for the aristocratic circles of Surakarta. The newspaper contained scientific articles, economic reports, announcements of births and deaths, notices about forthcoming public sales of household effects, and advertisements.[50]

In most cases, translators are seen as go-betweens, but they were go-betweens for the government only in their capacity as translators of official documents and for ceremonial occasions. They were not normally required to act as intermediaries when Europeans and Javanese met. In Yogyakarta, in particular, there were close and warm relations between the leaseholders and the sultan. We read in the correspondence of George Lodewijk Weijnschenk — of which very little survives — what detailed information he had about the comings and goings in the sultan's court.[51] This closeness between court and leaseholder is emphasised by accounts of the regular exchange of gifts, the evenings spent in card-playing, and the sultan's offer to have the Freemasons' lodge Mataram housed in his own palace grounds. Contacts were so warm that members of the royal court also joined the Freemasons' lodge.[52] This was rare in the Indies — seldom did an Indonesian become a Mason — but in Yogyakarta even a Javanese ruler, Paku Alam V, became a member of the Mataram lodge in 1871. The most memorable figure from noble circles to join the Freemasons of Yogyakarta was the famous regent for Paku Alam VII, Notodirojo, who was to play a key role in the early Indonesian nationalist movement at the beginning of the 20th century. It is not unlikely that the Freemasons proved a source of inspiration for the budding nationalism.[53]

The Yogyakartan leaseholders-cum-Freemasons, for their part, cherished a more than superficial interest in Javanese culture. The young Weijnschenk was a member of the Batavian Society for the Arts and

Illustration 18   Georgius Leonardus Dorrepaal (1816–1883) was banker for a large number of firms in the Principalities and elsewhere in Central Java. He was the wealthiest and most influential figure in Central Java.
[Oil painting by J.H. Neuman, n.d., Iconografisch Bureau, The Hague.]

Sciences (*Bataviaasch Genootschap voor Kunsten en Wetenschappen*) and collected Javanese art. In 1886 he presented the Austrian Emperor Francis Joseph with a fine selection of objects, including, it is said, a kris once belonging to the prince rebel Diponegoro.[54] This gift reminds us of the European roots of the Weijnschenk family; their ancestors came from Austria, from the small town of Sankt Pölten, which lies 70 kilometres west of Vienna.[55] Evidently Weijnschenk cherished his European roots.

The economic cycle of Central Java

The Dutch Governor-General Godert Alexander Gerard Philip baron van der Capellen's concern about the land speculation in the Principalities was partly inspired by the fact that British trading houses advanced the capital.[56] By the 1850s, the immediate power and influence of the British trading houses in the Principalities was, however, somewhat diminished. Furthermore, the NHM (Netherlands Trading Company) had virtually pulled out of Central Java after the debacle around the Dezentjé Estate.[57] They were gradually replaced by an independent economic circuit operating between Semarang trading houses and the leaseholders, courtiers and the local population in the Principalities.[58] In the space of a few decades, the economic axis of Semarang and the Principalities grew to be the major economic and political factor outside the government.[59] Almost one-third of all Europeans in Java lived in this region. In 1860 there were 1,544 Europeans living in Surakarta, 870 in Yogyakarta and 3,765 in Semarang, which added up to more than the 5,107 European inhabitants in Batavia, the centre of colonial government.[60]

The leading actor in this economic community of Semarang and the Principalities was Georgius Leonardus Dorrepaal (1816–1883), the son of a Dutch shipowners' family. He settled in Semarang in 1840 and became an associate in a local trading house. In 1842 he opened his own office, Dorrepaal & Co. In 1844 he married Ludovica Manuel (1817–1896), a daughter of the deceased owner of the private property of Peterongan, close to Semarang. It is not known how Dorrepaal acquired his start-up capital. He was well connected, coming from a wealthy family, but it is quite possible, since there were links between the planters in Central Java and Chinese moneylenders in Semarang — and his wife was partly of Chinese descent — that his commercial empire was founded upon Chinese capital. Whatever the precise details, Dorrepaal eventually became the banker for many planters in Central Java. They signed for advance loans from his bank, which gave him the right to the products they delivered, or the value of these products. The goods were exported to the Netherlands, and with the help of bills of exchange, Dorrepaal would receive the capital from the Netherlands importers with which he then made further advance loans to the leaseholders. In this way a financial circulation developed between the Principalities, Semarang and the Netherlands.

Initially, coffee and indigo were the main cash export crops in the Principalities. From about 1860 the cultivation of sugar cane advanced rapidly. With its eight watermills, Surakarta had the lead over Yogyakarta, where only Weijnschenk had built a watermill, in 1860.[61] To begin with, the planters of Yogyakarta had not been so enthusiastic about cultivating sugar cane — after all, indigo was fetching good prices. By 1863, however, the Yogyakartan planters had caught up.[62] By then there were 25 factories in Surakarta, and in the far smaller plantation district of Yogyakarta there were as many as 12 mills.[63] Agricultural production increased at such a rate in these years that it caused considerable logistical headaches. Everything had to be transported overland to Semarang or via the river Solo to Surabaya; this while the shortage of free labour and transport wagons was an acute problem throughout Java.[64] A lobby was created, headed by Dorrepaal, the newborn press and the susuhunan, which managed to push through plans for building a railway track from the Principalities to Semarang harbour.[65] The Surakarta-Semarang line would be the first railway in the Dutch East Indies.

The railway lobby had benefited from the changing political climate in the Netherlands and Batavia. In January 1861 the Minister of the Colonies in the Netherlands, Jan Jacob Rochussen, had to resign. A new minister took over, with liberal policies regarding trade and commerce. This opened the door for developments in the Principalities and Semarang.[66] Shortly after 1860 began what was later to be known as the "liberal" period, in which private business could enter new fields of expansion. The winds of change could already be felt when the new Minister of the Colonies Gerhard Hendrik Uhlenbeck and Governor-General Ludolf A.J.W. baron Sloet van de Beele took office in 1861.[67] In 1863 new financiers arrived on the scene, in the shape of three *cultuurbanken* (agricultural finance corporations): the Koloniale Bank, Internatio and the Nederlandsch-Indische Handelsbank. Their role, however, was not of great significance in the Principalities, where there was already a solid financial infrastructure. What was important here was that at last the long-drawn-out discussions about building the railway track from Semarang to Surakarta could be drawn to a conclusion. The necessary private capital was available, and now there was also the political will.

In August 1862 the new governor-general made a tour of Central Java, ostensibly to inquire about the necessity for a railway track; but the outcome was already decided, for at a banquet given in his honour in Surakarta there was a banner bearing a large painted steam engine, puffing out the words "All honour to the governor-general".[68] Less than a month later, Semarang and the Principalities could prepare themselves to celebrate the granting of the concession. The mighty figures of Dorrepaal and Weijnschenk led the festivities. Processions were planned along the entire trajectory of the future railway line, with imitation steam

Illustration 19   Ludovica Manuel (1817–1896) was the daughter of a family of landholders and entrepreneurs from Central and West Java. In 1844 she married Georgius Leonardus Dorrepaal. Her capital and connections probably accounted in a major way for Dorrepaal's commercial success.
[Oil painting by J.H. Neuman, n.d., Iconografisch Bureau, The Hague.]

engines and a few carriages. Banquets were held, graced by the presence of the sultan and susuhunan. The highlight, however, was the celebrations in Semarang; the entire city, down to the most primitive kampong, was illuminated.[69] According to the newspaper *Samarangsch Advertentieblad*, the Semarangers declared unanimously that this was the most spectacular and grand festival that had ever been seen in the Dutch East Indies. It was indeed a fitting inaugural feast for the new age of economic liberalism, which seemed to promise so much.[70]

As a leading figure in the Central Javanese business world, Dorrepaal had not only had a key share in the implementation of plans to build the railway, he would also profit the most when it was completed.[71] Convinced that once the railway linked them to Semarang, the value of businesses in the Principalities would soar, in the 1860s Dorrepaal made a number of business takeovers, particularly in Surakarta. This was to reach a peak in 1875, at which time he held shares in or owned 24 enterprises in the Principalities.[72] The Dutch East Indies owed a great deal to Dorrepaal, but as he was well aware, he certainly owed much to the Indies. His name is connected with almost every good cause in Semarang and the Principalities: from chairman of the provisional board of the Semarang Theatre to benefactor of the Boys' Orphanage in Surabaya.[73] His wife, too, was a familiar figure in the realm of public charity, organising collections for the Protestant orphanage in Semarang and other worthy causes.[74]

Dorrepaal was the uncrowned king of Central Java, and his social prestige was second only to that of the governor-general. Evidence of his superior status was apparent, for instance, in 1870, when he was awarded a medal, and a spontaneous celebration erupted in Semarang with a torchlight procession, serenades and improvised speeches.[75] The following year when he left for a few months' leave in the Netherlands, after 35 years of unbroken labour in the Indies, a huge crowd, including people from Surakarta and Yogyakarta, accompanied him to the new harbour canal in Semarang. "And when the hour of departure had arrived," reported the local newspaper *De Locomotief*, "the children from the Protestant orphanage performed a special song in honour of their benefactor."[76]

A large number of new enterprises sprang up in the 1860s in the wake of the first Indies railroad. They were established in the Principalities, particularly in Surakarta, where they almost doubled in number between 1860 and 1875, from 100 to 192. Interestingly, this expansion virtually ignored Yogyakarta, where the planters' network was more tight-knit. Smaller entrepreneurs settled mainly in Surakarta, and many of them tried their luck at tobacco growing, because this required far less capital outlay than did sugar production. But tobacco prices fluctuated greatly, and many a tobacco planter went bankrupt when the prices fell at the close of the 1860s and again towards the end of the 1870s. Thus, after the sudden growth in the mid-1860s, the number of companies in Surakarta declined during the next decade.[77]

The powerful planters' families of the Principalities were spared many of the woes of the tobacco growers, since their plantations culti-vated coffee, indigo and, increasingly, sugar cane.[78] Diversification was the watchword. During the 1860s George Lodewijk Weijnschenk began planting coconut groves on his higher land. He also established a soap factory that suffered considerable teething troubles and had still not made any profits in 1871. The newspaper *De Locomotief*, however, complimented the firm for producing soap that was in no way inferior to that from Europe.[79] During those years Weijnschenk's colleagues Raaff and Baumgarten introduced new indigo plants from South and Central America.[80] Meanwhile, it seems there were sensational results from the introduction of a new method for manufacturing indigo — known as the Sayers Method. It was named after the chemist and administrator of the Tempel enterprise on the lands of Jan Samuel Timmerman Thijssen in Yogyakarta. In 1873 a special factory was built where the chemicals could be prepared.[81] In the same year Joseph Paul Henry Sayers won the hand, and presumably also the heart, of Elise Jeanne Antoinette Timmerman Thijssen.[82]

The contrast between well-run businesses, which could make a fortune, and those that were poorly run gradually became clearer. Many newcomers as well as entrepreneurs who failed to modernise lost out; but companies that made large investments in new production methods remained in the hands of their owners during the following decades.[83]

Landholders in the Sunda

Before 1860 the leaseholders in the Principalities and the owners of vast estates in West Java were the only planters in the Dutch East Indies who were not subject to the rules and restrictions of the Cultivation System or the spice monopolies of the Moluccas. In the 1860s others joined them, the best known being the tea planters of the Priangan district in the mountains of western Java. Although business methods evolved and more capital was gradually made available, very little actually changed in the way that family networks controlled business affairs. New entrepreneurs appeared on the scene, but in almost every case they already had connections in the Indies. The laws on immigration and residence, with their strict regulations about a personal guarantee and security for good behaviour, excluded any other possibility.[84] Fortune hunters without capital or connections simply did not get a residence permit for the Dutch East Indies. The agricultural domain stayed in the hands of a few established families, together with the newcomers who managed to ensure connections with these wealthy ruling dynasties.

A good illustration of the importance of the family network is provided by the career of a well-known figure in the history of the Indies: the planter Karel Holle. He began as a clerk in the government of the Indies in 1846, and by 1856 he was banging his head against the glass ceiling, having climbed as high as he could. His problem was that he did not possess the required qualification — a diploma for higher civil service functionaries, or an exemption from these exams. So he left the civil service and went into business. The fact that he was able to set up as a private individual was thanks to his family connection with Guillaume Louis Jacques van der Hucht. This founder of the Van der Hucht-Holle clan started out as a cabin boy and attained the position of captain in the merchant navy; he then settled as a tea planter in Priangan. Once established, he sent for his family in the Netherlands and founded a small colony in the Indies. Among the emigrating relatives was Karel Holle, who, together with his parents, brothers and sisters travelled out with his uncle Van der Hucht. His sisters married prominent planters and businessmen in the Indies.

With such an enterprising family, Holle did not need to sit and gather dust at a government desk. In 1858 he was appointed adminis-trator of the government's tea enterprise at Cikajang, in the hills of West Java, near Garut.[85] Shortly after this, the Netherlands Minister of the Colonies Gerhard Hendrik Uhlenbeck decided to withdraw tea production from the Cultivation System, creating the opportunity for private tea planters, and Holle managed to lease a plot of land.[86] A few years later his brother-in-law Norbert Pieter van den Berg, acting as chief agent for the newly founded Nederlandsch-Indische Handelsbank (Dutch-Indies Trading Bank), assisted him in gaining a bank loan, and in 1865 his business got off the ground. Holle's two brothers and his nephews Eduard and Rudolf Kerkhoven joined the enterprise. Together they would make history as pioneers in the Dutch East Indies tea planta-tions, which really took off in the 20th century and remained centred in Priangan.[87]

The story of the Holles and the Kerkhovens in Priangan would appear to bear little resemblance to that of the aristocratic lifestyle of the landed gentry of West Java or the leaseholders in the Principalities. In Dutch historiography they are described as hard-working Dutch Mennonites who started growing tea in primitive circumstances and were proud of their social involvement. Their style of entrepreneurship, however, was not essentially different from that of the paternalistic rule of the powerful landowners of West Java or the leaseholders of the Principalities. The Holles and the Kerkhovens were, like the first gene-ration of planters in the Principalities, forced to move between various cultures and lifestyles in order to acquire the necessary knowledge, capital and labour force. Just as in the Principalities, contacts with a

British trading house were crucial; in this case it was the firm of John Peet & Co. in Batavia. This firm introduced the Holles and their Kerkhoven nephews to tea cultivation in British India, which was at that time far more highly developed than in the Dutch East Indies.[88]

Holle earned fame as an expert in the Sundanese language and as a promoter of local agriculture. He published many articles on both these subjects, and his brochures were translated into Javanese by the Wilkens and Winter families.[89] In acknowledgment for his ground-breaking recommendations about rice cultivation and his contributions to the reform of government-directed coffee production in Priangan, in 1871 Holle was decorated with the title of Honorary Adviser for Native Affairs.[90] An intriguing aspect of the Holle story is his well-known friendship with Muhammad Musa, chief *penghulu* (Islamic religious leader) of Garut, whose sister he was to marry. More mundane, but equally important, was the fact that without his knowledge of Sundanese, Holle would never have been able to grow a single row of tea bushes. Whereas in the Principalities (unpaid) labour of the Javanese peasantry was generally included, as it were, with the lease of land, in Priangan Holle had to recruit his workers himself. Hence he set up small shops and provided housing for his loyal employees — which included the women tea pickers. Incidentally, other landholders in West Java had already done the same thing.[91] Like the legendary Major Jantji, Holle too created his own image; he was wont to wear a turban and flaunt precious rings on his fingers. In this way he demonstrated that — notwithstanding his simple lifestyle and approachability — he was also the *tuan besar*, the great lord. Although his business collapsed in the great crisis of 1884, the image of him as a benevolent landlord survived after his death, and a monument was unveiled in his memory. This too, fitted into the tradition of the Indies, where similar monuments had been put up for other memorable landlords.

Such monuments suggest the specific manner in which certain landlords wished to be remembered in Sundanese history — that is, as development workers *avant la lettre*. Take, for example, the early 19th-century Andries de Wilde, surgeon-cum-landlord of Sukabumi. Or Pieter (Peter William) Hofland, more of a contemporary of Holle's, who was owner of the Pamanukan and Ciasem lands in West Java, an area the size of Singapore. Hofland and his descendants have gained a lasting place in the history of the East Indies because they inspired the Dutch writers Jan ten Brink and Paul A. Daum, the great chronicler of life in the Indies. Hofland was born in 1802 in the town of Jaggernaikpuram, near Madras in British India, and went to Java together with his brother Thomas Benjamin. Thanks to good connections and marriages, the brothers managed to pocket contracts in the sugar business, and by 1840 they had earned enough to take over the extensive property of the British owner, who saw no profit in developing the land. The Rotterdam magnate Anthony van Hoboken had acted as intermediary at the takeover, as he informed the NHM (Netherlands Trading Company), in order that this vast stretch of land be brought into "more national hands".[92] Hofland turned out to be an exemplary and benevolent landlord. He opened markets where the local residents could buy cheap clothing, and he founded schools where children could learn basic arithmetic and Malay. His most beneficial act was to reduce the level of corvée for the many thousands of peasants living on his lands — in fact he was obliged to do this, in accordance with the ruling regarding private estates. Like Jantji, when he went on a tour of his estates Hofland was accompanied by a guard of honour.[93] His reputation as the *tuan besar* (great lord) Hofland was to endure for generations among the locals, while he too received a monument in front of his country seat, serving to sustain the memory.

Jan ten Brink's work *Oost-Indische dames en heeren* (Ladies and Gentlemen of the East Indies) was published in 1866. The writer stayed with the now elderly Hofland, whom he names "Bokkermans" in his novel, and used this as the basis for a portrayal of life and customs in the Indies, interwoven through the plot of a novel. In true lordly tradition, the Bokkermans family entertained their guests with gamelan music and lodged them in spacious outhouses on their estate. The couple were the epitome of good humour and friendliness: Mrs Bokkermans spoke Dutch with many Malay words thrown in, and the daughters were bashful and modest *nonnas* (maidens). Ten Brink describes Bokkermans (Hofland) with the epithet *sinjo* (boy) — a word, like *nonna*, usually applied to Eurasians — but immediately adds that he had enjoyed a European education and liked to converse with Dutch, and even more so English, visitors about what was happening in the outside world. Meanwhile, his guests lacked for nothing; the household was perfectly managed by the all-efficient Mrs Bokkermans. Strolling through Hofland's extensive and attractively laid-out park, Ten Brink could not help being aware that it was the property of an industrialist: "Here and there a roof could be discerned through the foliage, or the tall chimneys of Mr Bokkermans's sugar factory lifting their heads and peering into the sky."[94]

Bokkermans may have been lord and master on his estate, but the relations between Hofland and the elite of Batavia — and in particular his creditors from the Netherlands Trading Company — were somewhat strained. They had a problem with the fact that he did not speak fluent Dutch, which is hardly surprising in view of his British-Indian background.[95] Ten Brink did not fail to observe the tension between the mercantile elite of newcomers and the landlord with his background in the Indies; in the novel, a veritable conspiracy develops against Bokkermans. Another thread woven into the novel's plot is the jealousy felt by the Totok wives for the (often more beautiful) Mestizo women. As the novel progresses, however, Ten Brink's stereotypes yield before the person of the world citizen, Hofland. His sugar factory is run by an English engineer, and he himself turns out to be a far more cosmopolitan figure than his Dutch antagonists living in Batavia. In portraying the conflict between the global attitude of Sinjo cosmopolitanism and cramped Dutch petty-mindedness, Ten Brink expresses a vision that would become a constant factor in the struggle for Indonesian political emancipation.

Dissolving views

Although after 1860 the Cultivation System gave way to private land cultivation, private enterprises remained centred in the Principalities until the last decades of the 19th century. The introduction of the Agrarian Law of 1870, which made it possible for European entrepreneurs to take out long-term leases of uncultivated land, would ultimately lead to a huge increase in the export cash crops being grown on Java, and on Sumatra in particular; but in the 1870s things had not yet reached this stage. The development of tea cultivation in Priangan moved at a slow pace, and in 1875 there were still only 15 enterprises. In Sumatra, too, plantation agriculture was in its infancy. In 1870 the first limited company for tobacco growing in East Sumatra was established by Jacob Nienhuys. The total issued share capital amounted to only 300,000 guilders, which was less than the value of one sugar mill and less than one-tenth the amount that George Weijnschenk Sr. transferred to his oldest sons in the 1870s. In those years the leaseholders of the Principalities were at the centre of the Indies plantation business. Their enterprises, both sugar cane and indigo production, flourished.[96] The indigo growers of Yogyakarta used their profits to convert to sugar production and to stimulate still further the development of their sugar crops.[97]

Illustration 20 The crown prince of Surakarta and other princes visiting the Dezentjé family at Ampel. The photograph bears evidence to the long-term and warm relations between the planters' families and the susuhunan's court in Surakarta. The words "*Tarima dengen girang*" over the doorway mean "received with happiness". [Photograph, *ca.* 1900, KITLV, Leiden.]

They grew wealthy as never before and built themselves sumptuous villas in the city of Yogyakarta.

Close to the heart of Yogyakarta and the sultan's *keraton*, or palace, lay Fort Vredeburg, surrounded by shady avenues of trees; here could be found the resident's house, the Protestant church and many elegant family homes belonging to Europeans. A road led from here through the Chinese neighbourhood straight to Tugu Station. Nearby lay the beautiful new dwellings of the Weijnschenk family. The wealthy neighbourhood of Surakarta was no less attractive, with wide streets and boulevards shaded by the evergreen tamarind. In this city, too, the European neighbourhood was close to the fortress, whose cannons stood pointing towards the grounds of the susuhunan. The city was famous for its flourishing Javanese skilled crafts — gold and silverwork, weaving and dying batik fabric, and worked leather. Local-born European women played a prominent part in the batik industry, which in those days was centred in small home workshops.[98] The growth of the batik industry in Central Java was comparatively recent. When at the end of the 18th century the Dutch East India Company lost its stations on the Coromandel coast of southeastern India and so could no longer export dyed cotton to Java, the susuhunan and the sultan in the Principalities encouraged domestic production of this type of decorative textile. After the English cotton industry in Lancashire delivered the death-blow to the batik industry in Coromandel in around 1830, batik work developed into a famous craft with distinct artistic codes in Central Java. Even when competition came from the cheaper printed batik known as *cap* (print), the art fabrics managed to hold their own.[99]

Meanwhile, contacts between the leaseholders and Europe intensified; the latest machines appeared in the factories; railways were introduced; and writers, artists and shopkeepers travelled to a city where business was thriving and money could be made. The local newspaper *De Vorstenlanden* (The Principalities) offers a peek into the consumer habits of the area in the 1870s. In 1870 Surakarta had four tokos, or general stores, where you could buy anything from sauerkraut to Parmesan ham, to Edam cheese. There were also two fashion stores and a lone military tailor who also catered to the civilian community. The above-mentioned newspaper was edited and printed, as indeed was the case throughout the Indies, at the local bookstore. There was an apothecary's and a doctor — and the occasional dentist would visit the Principalities. The local photographer would send pictures to Europe and have portraits painted from them. There was an ice factory, and for those who lived too far outside the city, ice-making machines could be purchased.

As the 19th century progressed, the number of shops grew. The shops were run by both Europeans and Chinese — without, incidentally, the Chinese ousting the older European shops.[100] New Europeans arrived bringing their country's specialities: the watchmaker Fritschi was undoubtedly Swiss, and the Italian toko-owner Lobatto used his links with his native land to import Italian products to the East Indies. In contrast, the owner of the large store named the Bazar Soerakarta was a Harloff, an old name in the Principalities. Practically everything was available in his toko: clocks, dinner services and all kinds of European foodstuffs. Meanwhile, the Soerakarta Hotel was busy with the arrival of planters who were regular guests in the city. They came for club meetings or to attend performances of the local theatre company *Utile Dulci*. Theatre companies from abroad also appeared in Surakarta, as for instance in October 1870 the travelling opera company of one Signor

Pompei staged Verdi's *Nabucodonosor* — apparently the new Italian name of the opera, *Nabucco*, was not yet used in Java — as well as performing Donizetti's *Lucia di Lammermoor* and *Lucrezia Borgia*. The audiences were highly enthusiastic, although *De Vorstenlanden* reported that it was a great shame Rossini's *Barber of Seville* was not on the repertoire.[101]

The old tradition of the planters' aristocracy was slowly abandoned — and the fact that the Weijnschenks moved into villas in Yogyakarta in the 1870s is evidence of this. Whereas the founder of the Dezentjé dynasty, like Karel Holle and Pieter Hofland, had moved among his people, rich and resplendent for all to see, by the 1870s the entre-preneurs of the Principalities no longer considered this necessary. They moved their pieds-à-terre to the towns, and even farther afield, to Europe. Contact with Europe had become easier and quicker, thanks to the Suez Canal, opened in 1869. It would seem, if the advertisements for woollen scarves in the Bazar Soerakarta are anything to go by, that after that date a holiday in chilly Europe was nothing exceptional. For instance, Frederik W. Wieseman and his wife, Santje Dom (the Rose of Yogya), took a trip down the River Rhine.[102] And for those who lacked the time or money to travel as far as Europe, there was the *soirée amusante*, the evening's entertainment, offered by the illusionist Professor Calabresini on 26 December 1870 in Surakarta; the highlight of this was the "dissolving views" — a magic-lantern show displaying pictures of Paris, Switzerland and Italy.

Like all well-to-do families living in the Indies, the major planters of the Principalities attached great importance to the education of their children. In the early 1860s Surakarta had a private school run by Miss Claessens. She had 12 young ladies under her supervision, all of them from the wealthiest families.[103] While what mattered for the daughters was the marriage market, the sons would later continue the family business, for which good management training became increasingly necessary. Planters who made a fortune would send their sons to be educated in Europe. Sometimes, parents in the Principalities regretted this decision. Friends or family in Europe with whom the children were sent to lodge would sometimes show scant interest in bringing up other people's children. Boarding schools, too, often failed miserably in their task of educating.[104] So when a *Hogere Burgerschool*, or HBS (a secondary, or grammar, school not offering the classics), was founded in 1877 in Semarang — about a four- to five-hour train ride from Surakarta — many must have been relieved. Elsewhere, many sons of European

Illustration 21   Geertruida Louisa Dom (1833–1909), known in her youth as the Rose of Yogyakarta. She married the successful leaseholder Frederik Wilhelm Wieseman, who became extremely wealthy through his indigo and, later, sugar plantations. In the 1870s the couple moved to The Hague, where this portrait was made. The family business was then taken over by their children.
[Photograph, n.d., KITLV, Leiden.]

families in the Indies, after finishing their HBS, went to study in Delft or Batavia for the higher positions in the Indies civil service. But there seemed little enthusiasm for this in the Principalities. Earlier, between 1845 and 1854, about ten members of families from the Principalities had been granted the *radicaal* certificate, which was required for "Second Class Civil Servant of the Indies"; this was the equivalent of passing the examination that admitted candidates to the higher ranks of the civil service. Among the ten granted this distinction were the translators J.A. Wilkens and Carl Friedrich Winter Jr.[105] The others were sons of well-known leaseholders' families. No simple explanation can be given as to why during the 19th century the names of well-known planters' families in the Principalities almost entirely disappear from the lists of the Binnenlands Bestuur.[106] What is known is that many sons of leaseholders found employment on the estates of their fathers or elsewhere within the planters' network. It is also evident that a job with the Binnenlands Bestuur earned little kudos among planters' circles.

While the planters went to live in Surakarta or Yogyakarta and sent their children to school there — or, if they continued to live on their estates, would send their children to boarding school, sometimes in Europe — for the majority of Europeans living in the Principalities this proved impossible. The Europeans in Surakarta, who at the beginning of the 19th century were people of modest means, had developed into a community with striking class differences. These distinctions would lead to friction. For instance, a dispute broke out within the Harmonie — one of the two clubs in Surakarta, which had about 200 members — over the issue of whether to raise the annual subscription fee in order to pay for the costs of a new building. This would have penalised the poorer members of the club.[107]

There was an even greater social distance, especially in Surakarta, between the leaseholders' elite and the large number of Europeans who had fallen on hard times. When a census was taken by the Dutch colonial government, these people were not included if they were living in the kampong, that is, in Javanese quarters or villages. This is an interesting example of the arbitrary and rigidly class-bound nature of categorisation under the colonial administration. Some of the poor Europeans were the biological sons of planters. They often bore names derived from their fathers, with slight changes. Thus, in the Principalities we find the forms Weijnschenk and Wijnschenk, Dom as well as Zom and Hom, Corli and Carli, and presumably Remij is a corruption of the name Meijer. Most of these descendants would be swallowed up in the ever-expanding class of impecunious Europeans, which was also swollen by the Ambonese (originally from the Moluccas) living in the Principalities who also enjoyed the status of European. In 1862 the Ambonese comprised about 10 per cent of the European population of Yogyakarta.[108] They were probably ex-soldiers from the local garrison. During the 19th century they appear with increasing frequency in the European marriage registries of the residencies.

It was not only European children living in the kampong who were often deprived of elementary education, but also the children of personnel on the plantations, estates and outlying posts, as well as railroad construction workers. In 1875, urged on by the Freemasons' lodge in Surakarta, the leaseholders raised about 87,000 guilders for boarding schools in Surakarta, Klaten and Bojolali. The most generous donor — scarcely a surprise — was Dorrepaal.[109] In 1882 the lodge Mataram in

Yogyakarta set up a fund for school uniforms; in Surakarta, however, no attempt was made to set up something of this sort, although there would in fact have been more call for such a charity in this town than there was in Yogyakarta.[110] It should be added that in 1884 Surakarta gained a privately funded boys' technical school.[111]

Ups and downs of life in the Principalities

The sugar barons of the 19th century have received scant applause from historians. They gained their wealth from exploiting slave labour (as in the Caribbean) or corvée labour (as in the Principalities). Easily won wealth turned them into bloated and reactionary bosses, a picture that continues to persist. Leaseholders are still seen as a curb on the development of modern production methods. But in fact, the Creole sugar planters in both the New World and the Old were usually forward looking and up-to-date with the latest technology of steam and steel. The planters and commercial entrepreneurs in Central Java who built a railroad track to transport goods to the coast had been preceded by the Cuban sugar producers.[112] Both groups understood the political and technological signs of the times. In 1870 the leaseholders of the Principalities went ahead and founded the *Indisch Landbouwgenootschap* (Agricultural Society of the Indies), which had its headquarters in Surakarta and by 1874 already numbered 669 members throughout Java.[113] It published its own newsletter run by Frederik Adriaan Enklaar van Guericke, an indigo planter in Surakarta.[114] We shall meet him later in the role of a propagandist for agricultural colonies for the benefit of impoverished (Indo-)Europeans. The newspaper *De Vorstenlanden*, started in 1870 in Surakarta, advocated the interests of the planters.[115] It was no coincidence that these initiatives appeared at roughly the same time: they evidenced a growing self-awareness and the increasing role of science in agricultural industry.

In 1873 and 1875 Surakarta and Yogyakarta organised the first agricultural conferences, which gave an impetus to systematic experimentation in methods of crop cultivation. The conferences were fore-runners of the sugar research stations built between 1885 and 1887, which the Yogyakartan planters had initially planned as early as 1882.[116] From a social perspective, too, the participants at the conferences could scarcely be called conservative. Karel Holle, Honorary Adviser for Native Affairs, had an appreciative audience when he spoke about general nutrition and improving the rice crop.[117] He put the case for free labour

— which can hardly have met with the approval of his hosts from the Principalities, who relied for most of their labour on corvée. But his utilitarian view that Western entrepreneurial spirit and the people's welfare were essentially congruous met with general agreement.[118] The entire agricultural conference was animated by a sense of carefree optimism concerning the way in which the prosperity introduced by European agricultural entrepreneurs could filter through to the people of Java. The participants had an unshakeable belief that the European estates would stimulate all sorts of economic activity in native society.[119]

Progress and entrepreneurial vigour did not, however, always bring good tidings for the Javanese population. At the beginning of the 1880s the Principalities, with 27 factories, represented about 17 per cent of Java's total sugar production.[120] But the reverse side of this was, apart from environmental waste and woes, an ever-growing work pressure on the population of Yogyakarta and Surakarta.[121] While in the first decades of the 19th century the leaseholders behaved more or less like Javanese aristocracy, as time went by they came increasingly to consider the people living on their land as little more than a labour force. The people had always seen themselves as subjects of the royal court and therefore liable to pay taxes, but they did not consider themselves to be bondsmen. The leaseholders grew to regard those who were responsible for collecting taxes in the villages, the *bekel*, as suppliers of workforce labour — or even as a kind of foremen, whom they could dismiss if they so chose. The government in Batavia tried to remedy this situation by decreeing that the position of bekel was hereditary — but it is doubtful whether this had any effect.[122] The great leaseholders regarded their territory and the population who lived there as part and parcel of their business, and they permitted no interference from the Binnenlands Bestuur. Furthermore, they knew they held the winning hand.[123] In Yogyakarta the two residents Reinier Fillietaz de Bousquet in 1848 and H.F. Buschken in 1858 had had to admit defeat and leave the field after a dispute with the Yogyakartan leaseholders. The next resident, Brest van Kempen, even though he knew he was supported in his struggle by the government in Batavia, found the problems overwhelming and in 1861 suffered a mental breakdown.[124] It was not uncommon for leaseholders to take the law into their own hands; they flogged troublemakers among their labourers, or placed them in the stocks.[125] Not surprisingly, this was not accepted lying down, and the locals would regularly march en masse to the resident's house or even to the sultan, demanding intervention against such treatment.[126] Indeed, a complaint was made against George

Weijnschenk Sr. when, in 1873, he threw a bekel into his own prison
cell in an attempt to quash the disturbance that had broken out among
local residents, who were all refusing corvée. It seems that his good name
as a patriarchal yet kind and friendly leaseholder was considerably
tarnished.[127]

The first signs that the system of land lease was stretched to its
limits appeared towards the end of the 1860s. The Javanese population
deserted the *sawah* (paddy fields) because they found the corvée system
untenable. The peasants moved to more sparsely populated regions in
East Java.[128] Crop failure caused by heavy rains and the severe earthquake of 1867 added fuel to the fire.[129] In 1868 George Weijnschenk's
brother-in-law, Pieter Dom, was killed by a band of robbers in Yogyakarta.
It was suggested that the responsibility for the murder lay with a
gang of hajjis roaming through the Principalities.[130] There were rumours
of a conspiracy between malcontents from the susuhunan's court and
hajjis — whispers that were often conceived by the not-entirely-reliable
police spies.[131] One outcome was that after the murder of Pieter Dom
the Yogyakartan leaseholders were given permission to appoint a police
guard — at their own expense.[132] Not surprisingly, this regulation
failed to deal with the root causes of discontent, and murmurs and
complaints continued to be heard throughout the Weijnschenk family
domains.[133] The Principalities had indeed been nurturing a parasite that
made ever greater demands on the local population, who in turn rose
up in protest, marched to the judges, or went en masse to complain to
the resident.[134] The local newspaper *De Vorstenlanden* admitted that the
peasants had a great deal to complain about, although this paper
(controlled by the leaseholders) laid the blame at the door of the apanage
holders. They, apparently, idled away their time in the palace, while the
local residents slaved on the plantations.[135]

The development of agricultural industry in the Principalities
pushed onwards and upwards towards its ceiling, in economic and
spatial terms. It appears as if the land-greed of the great leaseholders
permitted scant competition from smaller entrepreneurs. It was well
known that the government discouraged small entrepreneurs from setting
up in the Principalities, but in Surakarta they were more numerous —
to the annoyance of the large leaseholders. In 1876 it was the talk of the
town in Surakarta that the large leaseholders wanted to oust the smaller
ones.[136] Scarcity of land is a possible explanation for why the sons of
planters from Yogyakarta took advantage of the new Agrarian Law of
1870 to acquire land on long-term lease elsewhere in Java. Thus in the

final decades of the 19th century we find family names typical of the Principalities — such as Van Prehn, Dom and Van Stralendorff — sprinkled across Java as leaseholders in other residencies.[137] The expansive growth of cash crops for export would henceforth take place elsewhere in Java, in the Eastern Salient (Oosthoek) — and, later, on the island of Sumatra.

The noble landlord

Many nostalgic murmurings would be heard in the 20th century about that mythical figure — the patriarchal and benevolent landlord of yesteryear. Without a doubt, such nabobs had existed, princely patriarchs with a gamelan-playing retinue, generously scattering their riches right and left — but they were not typical for the development of the agricultural industry in the East Indies of the 19th century. After the 1860s the businesses of the established families in the Principalities were just as dynamic as the firms in Pekalongan (north Central Java), centres of innovation in the sugar industry.[138] Indeed, in the Eurocentric way of regarding history, the gentrified lifestyle of the sugar baron in the industrial age appears to be an anachronism. Figures such as Dezentjé and Weijnschenk, however, were pioneers in the industrialisation process. They built their factories in the very cradle of Javanese culture — the Principalities. For those whose imaginations failed them at this point, there were, and still are, the myths about squandermania, prodigality and absurd investments. Thus, there is one story recounting how Dezentjé, wishing to solve his transport problem, which was caused by poor roads and a shortage of carts and water buffalo, proposed digging a 65-kilometre canal from his estate right across the mountainous landscape of Java to the port at Semarang. But it is a legend that is probably based on the exploits of another famous landholder, Andries de Wilde, who in about 1820 had a 20-kilometre canal dug through his estate of Sukabumi.[139]

   In the space of a few decades the landlords in the Principalities and their colleagues along the coastal districts of Cirebon, Pekalongan, Surabaya and elsewhere ensured Java's second place in the world sugarcane market, where only industrialists who continually lowered their production costs could compete. In Dutch literature, their history has been told in a completely different way. The entrepreneurial dynamism of the Dezentjé family and their ilk stands in sharp contrast to the way it is described in Louis Couperus's famous novel *The Hidden Force*.

In this book the author recounts the doings of a family named De Luce, drowning in a stupor of decadence. This novel, by the grandson of the aforementioned Piet Couperus, has become one of the classics of Dutch literature and has greatly contributed to the image of the Dutch East Indies. What actually happened was that the swift growth of industrialised agriculture in the Indies gave rise to a nostalgic pastiche of the aristocratic landlord towards the close of the 19th century. All the stories about benevolent landlords, the statues that were erected, the family vaults, the quests for noble ancestors in distant Europe, betray a deep-seated longing for aristocratic roots. It is no coincidence that such a quest is a major theme in Eddy du Perron's *Het land van herkomst* (The Land of Origin), published in 1935, one of the best-known novels about the Dutch East Indies. Its protagonist, father Du Perron, a landlord from just outside Batavia, but more importantly a slumlord in the city itself, sets off in search of his noble French forefather — in vain.

As the 19th century progressed, mythical figures like Dezentjé faded from the scene or, like Pieter Hofland, they led a lifestyle that harked back to the past. Such, at least, is the picture Paul Daum gives us of the Hofland dynasty. Daum's novel about the Hoflands, first serialised chapter by chapter as a feuilleton in his newspaper *Bataviaasch Nieuwsblad*, doubtlessly contributed to the picture of the landlord in the Indies as a dying breed. His time spent in Semarang had furnished Daum with sufficient insight into the development of agricultural cultivation in Central Java, and he was astonished by what he saw of the great land-owners who lorded it in the vicinity of Batavia. Daum's novel, titled *"Ups" en "downs" in het Indische leven* ("Ups" and "Downs" of Indische Life), appeared in 1890 and deals with the second generation of Hoflands, with whom the downfall commenced. Daum presents one of the sons as a great wastrel who posed as a Javanese prince while on vacation in Europe. To maintain this image, he managed to squander the sum of 200,000 guilders.[140] Even if the story is true, the 200,000 guilders would still have been a pittance compared with the vast sums that had been required to develop the Hoflands' estates in the Indies.[141] A more balanced judgment cannot ignore such seemingly prosaic matters as investments and rentability. Over the years Pieter Hofland had bought out his joint owners (his brother and a Rotterdam merchant), so that by 1858 he was the sole ruler of this estate.[142] To this end he had mortgaged his land heavily, the mortgages being put up by the Batavian Orphan Chamber and the Factory (the Batavia office of the NHM, Netherlands Trading Company).[143]

Hofland's two sons increased the mortgages even more when they bought out their other brother, two sisters and mother.[144] They took a financial blow when around 1880 leaf disease attacked the coffee plants and cattle plague ravaged the herds, seriously affecting the transport of goods. The construction of a 22 kilometre-long canal turned out to be a greater disaster than the one it was intended to solve, since it diverted the irrigation water from the plantations. The vast and unrewarding estates slurped up the money that was continually being pumped into them. In 1885 a limited company was set up in an attempt to repay the debts — but this was only a stay of execution. The NIHB, Dutch-Indies Trading Bank, was transformed from creditor into a large shareholder, finally in 1905 becoming the sole owner. By that time the business was in a miserable state, running the most inefficient sugar factory in Java. Besides this, gangs roamed across the estates, and little remained for the new owner but the taxes he could raise from the people living there.[145] Daum describes in moving detail the downfall of the Hoflands during the year before the family lost all its possessions. For the grandchildren of the mighty Hofland, all that remained was to accept jobs as employees or overseers.[146] The story of the Hofland family reflects the gradual fall from glory of a particular Indische way of life. But it was a lifestyle that lasted as long as it did only because in West Java the land could be used as collateral for bank loans. This could not have happened elsewhere in Java, especially not in the Principalities. Here only the crops growing in the fields could be used as security, and if the harvest was poor, credit was withdrawn.

The leaseholders of the Principalities, far more than the great land-lords of West Java, may thus be seen as part of the pattern that was being continued in the late-19th-century tobacco enterprises of East Java and Sumatra. This development was made possible by the Agrarian Law of 1870. Uncultivated land could be rented on long-term lease, and mortgages could be taken out on the basis of these leases. Thus, large new tracts of land were made available for the expected influx of capital. It was a repetition of what had taken place two generations previously, when the emergence of the leaseholders in the Principalities had been made possible by the British trading houses in Semarang that were looking for somewhere to invest the capital they had made from the opium trade.

The story of the Birnies, also known as the "Kings of the Eastern Salient", follows a similar trajectory. During the 1850s, on the advice of its mother company, A. van Hoboken & Co., the firm of Reynst &

Illustration 22   David Birnie (1862–1931) with his wife and son in their new automobile, 1905. David Birnie was the son of George Birnie, founder of the *Oud-Djember* enterprise. He belonged to the second generation of "Kings of the Eastern Salient". After a brief career in the navy he joined the family business in 1885 and became chief administrator in 1893. In 1918 he was elected a member of the People's Council.
[Photograph, KITLV, Leiden.]

Vinju expanded its activities into new districts east of Surabaya, where they began growing tobacco as well as sugar. In connection with this, in 1858 Reynst & Vinju opened a new office in Surabaya, Anemaet & Co. In George Birnie they found the perfect figure to get the local residents enthused about tobacco cultivation. Birnie was at the time an inspector for the Binnenlands Bestuur in Jember and proved ready to make the changeover to the private sector. Birnie's strength lay in his ability to win the confidence of the local population; he provided them with plants and made agreements with them that they would deliver the tobacco that they had grown according to his instructions. The harvest was then transported, via Anemaet & Co. and the mother company, Reynst & Vinju, to Hoboken in Rotterdam. Photographs and pictures that have been preserved from Birnie's pioneer years in this enterprise reveal the simplicity with which he and his cousin Gerhard David Birnie lived. Like most Javanese planters, in their pioneering years they lived with a Javanese housekeeper, by whom they had children. When success arrived on their doorstep in the early 1870s, they — like George Weijnschenk before them — married the mothers of their children.

The Birnies leased ever-larger tracts of land.[147] This enabled them to construct extensive irrigation works and prevent local residents from selling to competitors the nursery plants that they had been given by the Birnies. Much like his colleagues in the Principalities, George Birnie did not put up with disputes regarding land, labour or sales on the part of smaller planters. In 1893, with a considerable display of his authority — actually accompanied by the resident, who played a passive role in the proceedings — Birnie had a fellow planter's storehouse pulled down. That planter's name was Mr J. Koning. *Koning* is the Dutch word for "king". The ensuing court case attracted a great deal of interest, and the newspaper headlines referred to it as the "King-Birnie" lawsuit.[148] It is probably thanks to this word-play that the Birnie family gained the nickname "Kings of the Eastern Salient".

There is a striking similarity between the history of the development of agricultural industry in the Principalities, East Java and later East Sumatra. One difference was that on the island of Sumatra many of the labourers on the plantations were imported from China and later from Java.[149] But otherwise, in all these places strong trading houses put up the capital and ensured a market; with this support, planters involved the local population in the cultivation of export cash crops. As the businesses expanded and labour grew scarcer, planters became increasingly anxious to control the available labour source. Their next move was to declare that the entire estate, including the people living on it, was private property. When at a later date the inspector J.L.T. Rhemrev drew up a report on the private prisons in Deli, East Sumatra, it appeared that such institutions had long been in existence in the Principalities. Another constant factor is the passive role of the department of Binnenlands Bestuur. The successful late-19th-century planters, such as the Weijnschenks, the Birnies and planters on Sumatra's East Coast, vied with one another in their negligence of the local residents and their lack of respect for the Binnenlands Bestuur.[150] How an entrepreneur behaved seems to have been determined by such things as local circumstances, the type of crop being grown, and a mixture of technological and financial factors. These were the overriding concerns. Of secondary importance were questions about people's backgrounds — whether they were born in Asia or newly arrived in the East Indies.

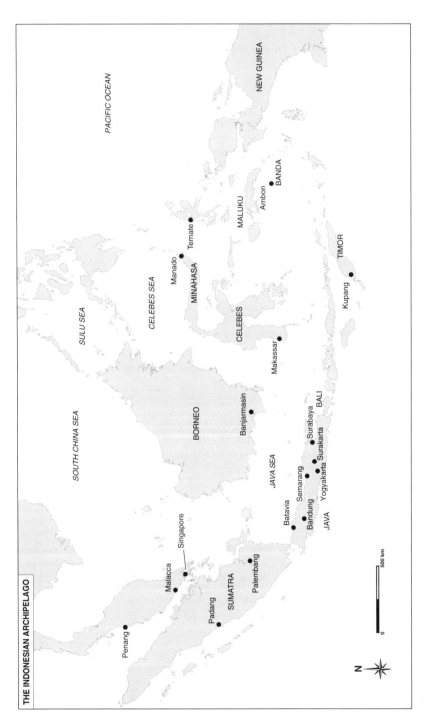

Illustration 23 Map of the Indonesian archipelago

CHAPTER 5

Mixed Worlds in the Eastern Archipelago

The world of the East Indies was nothing if not diverse. The settlements at the eastern end of the archipelago were a far cry from the Indische communities in the Principalities — and, incidentally, far older. The Dutch East India Company (VOC) had established several dozen harbour towns in the eastern isles, connected by proas, schooners or barques, and later by steamship. The influence of the Dutch revealed itself in such things as street planning and house architecture, as well as in municipal regulations concerning rubbish collection, the obligation to keep streets wet to prevent dust from spreading, and to whitewash the houses. These communities were always in touch with European culture via the garrisons and the circulation of civil servants, but newcomers did not dominate the scene. Most of the settlements had their important families stemming from VOC days, forming the nucleus of local activity and government. This was certainly true for Ambon, the oldest European settlement in the Indonesian archipelago, which from the outset was characterised by the coexistence of Portuguese descendants, freed slaves and a large Christian community. A similar situation developed both in Makassar and on the island of Banda, where an established elite of nutmeg growers — known as the *perkeniers*, from the Dutch word *perk*, meaning a plot or allotment — held sway.

In this part of the Indies there was less threat from malaria than in Batavia and other coastal towns of Java, and local European families were better able to survive. The changes in government in the early 19th century, from Dutch to British and back to Dutch, had produced a mere ripple in the deep rhythm of centuries. Each of the islands had its own mixture of Europeans, Burghers and corvée labourers, an idiosyncratic residue of three centuries of colonial intervention. In some cases the civic militia might have been manned by Muslim subjects, considered to be loyal citizens — something that was unthinkable in Java.[1] In other places a settlement of descendants of Europeans was gradually being absorbed into the local population, as was the case in Kisar in the southern Moluccas.[2]

Unlike the large coastal towns of Java, in the 19th century most places in the Moluccas had only a handful of European newcomers. As late as 1885 there were no more than 82 Europeans born outside the Indies living on the island of Ambon.[3] Elsewhere in the Moluccas, for instance on the island of Ternate, their number actually decreased in the 19th century. The consciousness of a particular local history, rather than one belonging to the entity known as the Dutch East Indies, survived here into the 20th century. Even the appearance of daily newspapers in the Indies did not bring about much change in the sense of local orientation, if only because newspapers appeared only in Makassar, with the occasional missionary papers in the Minahasa region (North Sulawesi).[4] Even when people moved away, as happened in the Moluccas when the economy dwindled, little changed with regard to their sense of belonging in the Moluccas. Migration is like a fine thread running through the stories not only of the prominent Moluccan families, but stretching to the farthest corners of the most distant villages.

The years around 1860 formed a watershed in the history of the eastern archipelago. This change was marked by the Moluccan tours of two governor-generals — Albertus Jacobus Duymaer van Twist in 1855 and Charles Ferdinand Pahud in 1860. These tours coincided with the abolition of slavery, introduction of free trade, renewed financial credit for agricultural enterprises, intensification of recruitment for the army and the missions and, finally, improvement and expansion of elementary education. The governors' tours were intended to revive these stagnating provinces and turn them back into useful appendages of the colonial economy. After 1860, people from the Moluccas would become active at all levels in the government of the Indies and in the army. This provides us with the ideal moment to take an imaginary tour of a number of Indische communities and families, with Makassar as the starting point.

Makassar

In 1854, on the eve of a new age in the Moluccas, a 30-year-old British naturalist, Alfred Russel Wallace, stepped ashore in the port of Makassar.

In his pocket he bore two letters of recommendation. One was addressed to a Danish shopkeeper; the other was for Willem Leendert Mesman, who was known to have a good command of the English language. Mesman, at the age of 35, was already a great gentleman, living outside the city in a country residence. It was surrounded by a veritable maze of workplaces, stables and sheds where his numerous servants and slaves lived. After breakfast each day this landlord would change out of his brightly coloured shirt and loose wide trousers and transform himself into a businessman in a spotless white linen suit. Then he would set off in his *bendie*, a two-wheeled horse-drawn carriage, for his office in the city, where the nameplate read: *W.L. Mesman, negotie- en commissiehandel en reders* (W.L. Mesman, merchants, business agents and shipowners).

The old city had scarcely changed since the days of the Dutch East India Company. There were thick-walled houses built in the Dutch Indies style, whose tiny windows and whitewashed exteriors betrayed their tropical setting. Gambling resorts, brothels and bamboo huts alternated with brick houses. From time to time rowdy sailors on shore leave would make the streets unsafe, as did the scuffles initiated by gangs of Buginese. In the 1850s, well-to-do Makassar residents moved out of this part of town and settled along the coastal road just beyond the fort. It was, in fact, a general tendency throughout Asia for Europeans to move out of the old colonial city centres. The city of Makassar, however, cannot have been such a bad place, for Wallace sang its praises, claiming it to be the cleanest and most attractive city in the East.[5] With approximately 800 European inhabitants, Makassar was the fifth-largest European settlement in the Dutch East Indies and was clearly on an upward spiral.[6] Long ago, before the VOC placed the harbour under the yoke of its monopoly in 1668, Makassar had been a free port.[7] In 1847 the tradition was re-established, and within 25 years the total imports and exports had increased fivefold. But it could not rival Singapore, for in the 1870s the turnover of Makassar harbour was less than one-eighth that of the port founded by the Englishman Raffles. Nevertheless, Mesman profited from Makassar's new position as a depot between the eastern islands and the harbour of Singapore.[8] Mesman owned a small proa, which brought mother-of-pearl and tortoiseshell (*karet*) from the islands near New Guinea. Together with his two or three Chinese clerks, he ran a business trading chiefly in coffee and opium. These commodities became increasingly important as the slave trade declined due to diminishing demand for slave labour in Javanese towns and on Moluccan plantations. Eventually, in 1854, the slave trade was made illegal, which brought an

end to Makassar's position as the centre of the slave trade. The emancipation of slaves was to follow, in 1860. In 1854, when Wallace arrived
in Makassar, there were still slaves in the house where he lodged.[9]

The Mesmans of Makassar were an important and widespread
family, with members among the landed gentry and merchants, or
serving in the Binnenlands Bestuur. One constant feature in the lives
of both men and women of the family was the ease with which they
moved in two worlds — that of the Europeans and that of the indigenous
circles. The local European families formed cores of knowledge and
information for Europeans who came from outside; without these families,
newcomers would not be able to gain admittance to indigenous rulers
and officials. Boundaries were notoriously ambiguous. This was also the
case with slaves: although they were merchandise, they were also part
of the family — and not only as servants and child-carers. The great-
grandmother of Willem Leendert Mesman was a slave who was known
as Sara van Buton. One of the Mesman forefathers had come to the
Indies from the Dutch harbour town of Flushing. Within a few generations the family had intermarried with other leading local families such
as the Volls, and with the wealthy shipowners' family the Weijergangs.[10]
The Volls had been declining in importance since the late 18th century,
due to the faux pas of their leading member, the senior merchant and
syahbandar (harbour master) Jan Hendrik. He had abused his good
relations with the Buginese king of Bone, the most important ruler in
South Sulawesi, to gain riches for himself.[11] Despite this setback, the Voll
family continued to supply civil servants for lower government ranks.

Mesman's wealth was comparatively recent. It was his father, Johan
David Mesman, who had laid the basis for the family fortune. He had
kept his position as a civil servant during the British interregnum and
had fought with the British against the Buginese, for which in 1815 and
1816 he was rewarded with the estates of Marana and Atapang, which
had been taken from the conquered enemy.[12] He became more or less
a native nobleman, appointing his own headmen, exacting compulsory
service, and charging taxes on the harvests amounting to one-third of
the produce.[13] Family lore has it that Johan David Mesman's wife, Jacoba
Helena Peters, came from the family of the raja of Sidenreng (South
Sulawesi).[14] Her father, the English paymaster Sir Peters, so the story
goes, abducted her mother from the raja's court, for which at a later date
the lady had to pay with her life: she was lured back to the court under
false pretences and was strangled.[15] It is a most dramatic story, but the
only established fact is that Jacoba Helena Peters's father, Jacob Willem

Illustration 24 Johannes David Mesman (1790–1836) was appointed resident of the district of Maros in southern Sulawesi in 1820. The residency was in the village of Soradjirang. The estate of Maros lay across the river; the British colonial government had presented it to Mesman in 1816 in recognition of his assistance in the struggle against the ruler of Bone.
[Study by Antoine Payen, *ca.* 1824, Rijksmuseum voor Volkenkunde, Leiden (detail).]

Peters, was a simple boy from Makassar who climbed to the position of general receiver and warehouse master, thus gaining a place among the notables of the city. His son-in-law, Johan David Mesman, also belonged to the bureaucratic elite of Makassar, being president of the *landraad* (local court for native affairs) and adjunct-secretary of native affairs. The resident B. Bischoff considered him extremely well qualified for the last-mentioned role because of his knowledge of local languages.[16]

Johan David Mesman's oldest son, Jacob David Matthijs, graduated from the translators college — the Institute for the Javanese Languages — in Surakarta (Solo). On his return to Makassar he became known as Tuan Solo (Lord Solo). The younger son, Willem Leendert — Wallace's host — remained in Makassar, where he took courses in the Buginese and Makassarese languages at the Native Teachers Training College. Although he did not become an interpreter, Willem Leendert's knowledge of these languages would undoubtedly have proved most useful to him as landowner and merchant. For instance, he was able to introduce Wallace to the raja of Goa, whose territories extended almost as far as Makassar. Despite Willem Leendert's rootedness in the Indies, Wallace described his host as "a Dutchman born in Makassar". Willem Leendert accompanied the naturalist on hunting parties on Sunday mornings as well as to receptions hosted by the governor of Makassar, where they enjoyed a game of cards together.[17] Incidentally, Wallace considered such an active Sunday to be typically Dutch — the colonial English tended to pay greater observance to the Lord's Day. Very likely, however, this lack of religious fervour was not typically Dutch, but rather a general feature of society in the Indies. Wallace observed with interest the ease with which Willem Leendert moved in the indigenous circles, but he thought of him primarily as a member of the Makassar elite. Willem Leendert's brother, Tuan Solo, at whose country residence Wallace would later be a guest, led a far more unconventional existence. In Wallace's view, he was a real man of the country.[18] Thanks to the memoirs of Tuan Solo's daughter Emilie, we have a rare and valuable picture of Jacob David Matthijs's adventurous life of constant travel. Like his brother, he owned a proa, named *Le Pirate*, which he used to transport slaves from the islands of Ternate and Ambon. Emilie's childhood recollections describe a family constantly on the move through a vast and boundless world.

The family legends were also of an expansive and exotic nature. One of Emilie's great-grandfathers was said to have been a Huguenot of French noble descent. And her maternal grandmother was the Filipina Paula Saptenno, presumably a slave from Pampanga in the Philippines, a supply area for slaves in the days of the Dutch East India Company. Family tradition, however, has it that the adventurous son of the French count, on one of his lengthy sailing trips, came across a Mestizo beauty in the Philippines and carried her off with him. This, according to Emilie, explained why her mother played the spinet with French grace and punished her slaves and her children with all the ruthlessness of a Spanish duenna. The family estate, governed by Emilie's father, was so vast that he was continually travelling and would often take with him his wife, Emilie, her three younger sisters and a few slaves.[19] Emilie tells how, on one such occasion, they came face to face with pirates, who in the 19th century presented a widespread threat in the waters off the Moluccas. Nor were the little girls spared the sight of a slave market; they realised that the slave women who were part of their family were ultimately no more than goods and chattels to be bought and sold.

The Mesman family were members of the leading European circles in Makassar as well as of the entourage at the courts of the local royals. In 1855 Siti Aisa Tanriollé, a second cousin of Jacob and Willem Leendert Mesman's, was inaugurated as feudal ruler of the Buginese state of Tanete. She was known to be a pro-Netherlands ruler, who, according to the administration in Makassar, governed over her territory with its 13,000 inhabitants in a progressive manner and was an important supporter of the colonial government.[20] The entire Mesman family travelled to Padaëlo, then the major town in Tanete, for the inauguration ceremony, which lasted several weeks. Interestingly, although Emilie's Buginese grandmother's love for Sir Peter apparently had cost her her life, her grandchildren were nevertheless regarded as part of the royal family. "Auntie Netje (Nettie)", as the new queen was called by the Mesman girls, greatly appreciated the attendance of her white cousins (at least, white in the eyes of the Buginese) and presented all four of them with a pair of beautiful thick gold bracelets and a riding horse.[21] This was confirmation of the fact that the Mesman girls had become part of the indigenous political scene, similar to the way in which the landholders in the Principalities were included in the local court protocol.

Emilie and her sisters learned about the local history in great detail from their female slaves, who told them many a story about the legendary figure of Arung Palakka (*ca.* 1635–1696), who, together with the VOC, had ruled over most of South Sulawesi. History was also interwoven into the landscape — supernatural qualities were ascribed to certain geographical features, such as a huge rock close to the Mesman estates. This was said to possess the power to transform people into stone, while a nearby river held protective powers. The Greek myth tells how the baby Achilles was plunged into the river Styx by his mother, Thetis, to make his body invulnerable; similarly, their mother bathed the little Mesman girls in the waters of the local river, in order that later their bones would never break.

When Jacob David Matthijs Mesman and his wife died in rapid succession, in 1855 and 1857, the wandering nomad's life ended abruptly for their daughters. They were taken in by their mother's side of the family, who were considerably less well off than the Mesmans. The girls had to leave school as soon as they reached puberty. The schoolteacher was willing to give them private lessons, but his offer was turned down. The girls were confined to their home, taught to sit with straight backs and learned (European) dances — all as preparation for their coming-out ball.[22] Their aunt was most concerned lest the girls turn into old spinsters, and in her zeal she married off Emilie to the first eligible candidate — an officer in the local garrison. The groom, Lt. Wilhelmus Henricus (Hein) Neijs, came from what initially appeared to be a good family from Surabaya. Father-in-law Neijs, a retired cavalry officer, was the son of the much-lauded resident of Ternate, and his wife was Anna Elisabeth Versteegh, the daughter of a perkenier's family from Banda who ran a batik workshop. Emilie's in-laws had once been wealthy but were now deeply in debt.[23] Hein married Emilie in 1866 on account of her generous dowry, which he could appropriate without any bother, since under the law of the time husband and wife became joint owners of each other's property. Although it would have been possible for Emilie to retain the rights to her property after marriage, her family neglected to make the necessary legal provisions. After the marriage she left for Java accompanied by Mah, formerly her favourite slave, and after the abolition of slavery, her loyal servant. When she arrived in Surabaya, she met with a cool reception from her in-laws; they regarded her not as Indische, like themselves, but as a wealthy Buginese who had been brought up rather too much like a tomboy.

Wide is the sea and Banda small

Emilie's ship sailed westwards towards Surabaya. Many other ships leaving Makassar sailed eastwards to the Moluccas to the island of Ambon and some (about 25 ships a year) to the Banda archipelago, the small but famous volcanic islands that throughout the 19th century and later, too, attracted travellers with their mysterious beauty.[24] The well-known English writer Somerset Maugham waxed lyrical about the vibrant colours and described the green as rich as "a vestment in the treasury of a Spanish cathedral. It was a colour so bizarre and sophisticated that it seemed to belong to art rather than to nature".[25] The first sight of the volcanic mountains rising a sheer 400 metres out of the sea was awe-inspiring. Passing through the Straits of Lonthor the traveller saw on the left the volcano Gunung Api, the Fire Mountain, and on the right Great Banda, or Lonthor. Lining the terraces, shrouded by woodland, stood the homes of the nutmeg and mace growers, the *perkeniers*. Ahead lay the island of Banda Neira, with its town at beach level, dominated by the fortress of Belgica.[26]

But appearances are deceptive — the town was an unhealthy place, veiled under the volcanic smoke of Gunung Api and suffering from frequent volcanic eruptions, earthquakes and tidal waves. In 1778 a

Illustration 25 After the devastating earthquake of 1852 Banda Neira gradually recovered, and by 1868 it presented a prosperous, if somewhat sleepy, picture. The architecture of the houses is an interesting mix: veranda with (Greek) Doric columns, topped by roofs thatched with palm branches, typical of the local homes. In the background can be seen the volcanic mountain Gunung Api.
[Photograph Woodbury & Page, KITLV, Leiden.]

tornado and an earthquake uprooted all the trees, in 1815 the volcano erupted, and another earthquake followed in 1852.[27] Evidently this colony had not chosen a blessed spot; it had begun badly when VOC Governor-General Jan Pieterszoon Coen massacred most of the local population in 1621. Those who escaped death were taken as slaves to Batavia. In 1621 the VOC divided up three islands (Banda, Lonthor and Ai) into 68 plots and donated these to pensioned-off sergeants. They made an agreement that the harvest of nutmeg and mace would be sold to the VOC at a cheap rate. The perkeniers did not, however, hand over the entire crop. They smuggled out the rest, and this, combined with other illicit trafficking, ensured them an easy life until the mid-18th century. But recurring natural disasters combined with commercial competition from Buginese traders brought an end to this period of prosperity.[28] During the 18th century only about five perkeniers managed to keep their heads above water, while the remaining 82 faced never-ending debts.[29]

When Governor-General Duymaer van Twist visited the islands in 1855, he found no more than 500 Europeans, apart from the garrison forces. The capital, Neira, resembled a ghost town; desolate ruins and blackened walls spoke of the earthquake that had struck three years before.[30] But in the 1860s prosperity returned, and Banda Neira regained its reputation as a place of great beauty. Neira was rebuilt according to a geometric street plan, the unpaved roads bordering the front gardens and porches of detached houses. It was a small, ceremonious community; people addressed each other in formal language and would call someone "sir" even if they had known him since childhood. Incidentally, this formality was a general phenomenon in the Moluccas. The two or three oldest inhabitants of Banda were regarded as the local sages and were consulted not only by the locals, but also by traders from other places.[31] Banda's European population was regularly replenished with newcomers employed at the local garrison or the resident's office. These new faces were eagerly welcomed into the community so long as they did not try to impose their ideas on the Bandanese. The resident and his deputy were respected but had little authority. In accordance with the custom among notables throughout the Moluccas, the most prominent perkeniers provided officers for the militia, the members of the Court of Justice, and the board of the Orphans' Chamber. The inhabitants of the Banda Islands, however, were unusual; they perceived their homeland as a tiny state in its own right and had their own national anthem — "Wide is the sea and Banda small".[32]

The homes of the perkeniers could be found both in Neira and on the estates. The town houses were built in a style encountered elsewhere in Asia, for instance in Ceylon.[33] Because of the dangers of earthquakes, these whitewashed homes had only one storey and the roof was made from *atap*, palm branches. The tiles on the floors were shipped from Java and had probably served as ballast on boats sailing from the Netherlands. The perkeniers would receive their guests in the morning in their homes:

> in morning dress, unaffected like himself, which would consist of a white kebaya, a loose kind of jacket, colourful wide breeches, and a pair of red or black leather slippers worn with bare feet. Wife and daughters are equally simply dressed, the heavy jet-black hair contrasting with the white kebaya, which was edged with lace or crochet-work. From under the long skirt or sarong, a pair of white feet would peep, half concealed in delicate gold-embroidered slippers.[34]

That was in the daytime, but if there was an event in the evening, such as a ball or a reception, then the dress code would be linen suits and white gloves, and for the ladies a gown with train. When Governor-General Duymaer van Twist paid his visit to Banda, European evening dress had just come into fashion, while in the early 1850s women still appeared at receptions wearing the traditional sarong and kebaya.

The culture of the perkeniers was a mixture of customs handed down from the days of the VOC, traditions adopted from the slave populations or from other parts of the Moluccas, and — once prosperity arrived — reflections of European colonial habits. There was immense social control, based on a well-greased gossip circuit. Bandanese perkeniers' families would speak Moluccan Malay, richly larded with Dutch expressions.[35] Elementary education should not be blamed for this creolisation

Illustration 26   The families of the perkeniers (nutmeg growers) on Banda lived in grand style, seen, for instance, in the architecture of their houses. Pictured is the home of the Herrebrugh family, on the Matalengko Estate. The family had another estate on the island of Lonthor (Great Banda). Both were later subsumed into the state company of Spanteby and Matelenco.
[Photograph in: V.I. van de Wall, *De Nederlandsche oudheden in de Molukken* (1928).]

since by the 1860s these schools were of an adequate standard. The government schoolmaster, Mr J.L. Bloemhard, one of the few teachers born in the Indies, also organised afternoon and evening school, which provided French, English, mathematics and drawing lessons. And perkeniers' daughters could, if they wished, receive piano tuition out of school hours.

Highlights of the social scene were the parties held on the estates. When such an event was held on the island of Lonthor, the partygoers from Banda Neira would take a sedan chair down to a proa and cross the bay. Having reached the other side of the bay, elderly gentlemen would be helped onto a horse, and the ladies would be carried in a sedan; for them, the wide paved staircase with its 300 steps was considered too daunting a climb to undertake on foot.[36] Music resounded, played by a gamelan orchestra and European string instruments. The young people danced, the older men played cards, and the women amused themselves with European or Chinese card games. At noon the traditional and very rich "rice table" with its innumerable side dishes would be served, followed by a siesta and then a bath. Around seven o'clock people gathered for the evening meal, and after that came the ball.[37]

Grand events of this sort were only for the social elite of the islands: the garrison officers, the top civil servants and the handful of commercial agents living on Banda. Parties and receptions at the resident's home were, in fact, part of the marriage market, and many a union between a perkenier's daughter and a newcomer was arranged at such gatherings. Also included in the guest list might be Arab and Chinese business contacts — but they were seldom accepted as dance partners and very rarely as marriage candidates.[38] As time passed, this list extended to include about a dozen respectable men of similar background. Because social control was so strong on Banda, it would have been unthinkable for a young girl to have been married off in the way that the heiress Emilie Mesman was by her over-hasty aunt. Girls certainly married at a young age there — between 16 and 18 was quite normal — though evidently not every perkenier's daughter was still sweet 17.

Roelandus Nicolaas Rijkschroeff, for instance, married a somewhat older heiress of a nutmeg estate. He came from a good Ambonese family, and through this marriage, despite his rather unimpressive position as civil servant at the warehouse administration, he attained the rank of perkenier. A hard-working and ambitious man, Rijkschroeff had in his role as *commies* (senior clerk) already become a pillar of Bandanese society, although a modest one. He performed his duties in the militia as captain, was a member of the Orphans' and Estates Chamber, clerk for the Court of Justice and deacon in the Dutch Reformed Church. It is clear from marriage certificates that he was welcomed into the clan of perkeniers, since his name appears as a witness at several of their marriages.[39] His first marriage, to the Ambonese Antomina Latoepeirissa, did not make him a rich man. But before long he was a widower, and in 1863 he made an offer for the hand of Adriana Augustina Meijer, a woman who in Bandanese terms could have been a grandmother: she was aged 33. She was, however, the daughter of a woman known as Widow Meijer, who had risen from being a freed slave of a former resident to becoming a "perkenierster", owner of the Keizerstoren Estate on the island of Great Banda. A few years after his marriage, Rijkschroeff inherited the throne, succeeding his mother-in-law.[40]

The perkeniers and the handful of European civil servants and commercial agents stood at the top of the social ladder. On the lower rungs were those of more limited means — descendants of perkeniers, "native Christians" (which often meant freed slaves), and finally Muslims who were self-employed. For simplicity's sake, this highly diverse social group on Banda was labelled "Burghers". Children born from the relationships between perkeniers and slaves were absorbed into the generous group of Bandanese native Christians and generally used the (unadulterated) name of a perkenier's family. The name Leunissen, for instance, belonged in the mid-19th century not only to a perkenier, but also to the first *orang tua* (hereditary head) of a kampong.[41] Impoverished relatives and the natural children of perkeniers were often found labouring on the estates as foresters, in the large sheds where the nuts were handled before shipping, or as overseers. Occasionally one of them would be found working with the Muslim fishermen.

We have few records telling about the relationships between masters and slaves, but we do know that in the mid-19th century one-third of the slaves, that is, about 700, were working as domestics. House slaves were the grandmothers and even mothers of many a perkenier. Until shortly after the emancipation of the slaves, perkeniers would marry their former (baptised) slaves by whom they had children.[42] However, with the abolition of slavery on 1 January 1860, a virtual end came to the contact between perkeniers and the slave population; once freed, the former slaves no longer wished to serve their old masters. Only 73 of the 1,122 slaves on the estates entered paid service. But employment was scarce outside the nut groves on the Banda Islands, and most of the freed slaves passed their days in idleness. They became an impoverished class who merged into one with the exiles from Java who had served a sentence working in the nut groves.[43]

Meanwhile, the emancipation of the slaves did not affect the work in the nutmeg and mace plots. In the 1850s a growing stream of coolies from Java started to arrive in Banda. A contract system was introduced in 1859 whereby "free" labourers bound themselves to work for five to eight years on Bandanese estates. The maximum length of time was stated in order to avoid virtual slavery.[44] The perkeniers were initially not enamoured of the idea of "free labour", but their objections were removed by a sufficient supply of coolies and by a government decree of 2 July 1859 allowing perkeniers to take out interest-free advance loans.[45] These must have been more than welcome. Although after the earthquake of 1852 the nut harvests had soon picked up, and 29 of the 34 plots were yielding profits once more, perkeniers had had to take out large loans to rebuild their businesses. In the 1850s there was an average profit of 2,000 guilders per plot, which sometimes had to be spread over four families as joint owners, as well as paying the interest on their loans. In those years the income for an individual perkenier's family was often little more than what a minor civil servant would be earning.

In the 1860s, however, profits rose to averages between 4,000 and 7,000 guilders.[46] This was partly thanks to improved production methods for nutmeg and mace. One of the leading voices at the time was Pieter Cornelis Lans, shareholder and administrator of the Lautang nut grove. Born on Banda in 1834, Lans had been an army officer and was the son of a former resident of Ternate, in the northern Moluccas. Lans's father was born in Amsterdam and had followed a career in the civil service on Banda. From 1838 until his death in 1840 he held the post of resident. He married the adopted daughter of a perkenier of French descent, Jacob Pinège. Her mother was probably Leonora Schmidhamer, who came from a good Ambonese family.[47]

Lans was a liberal-minded man who abhorred the monopolising policies of the colonial government. As an advocate of free cultivation and trade of spices on Banda, he was one of the seven perkeniers from Banda who in 1860 seized the opportunity of a visit from Governor-General Pahud to put the case for the abolition of the government monopoly on the spice trade.[48] These perkeniers have gone down in history as the Magnificent Seven. Probably the seven were the owners of the most lucrative estates, which in that year made a profit of upwards of 10,000 guilders.[49] In 1866 four of the Magnificent Seven hired a boat from an Arab and shipped nutmeg and mace to Singapore, whence the mace was transported to new markets in southern Asia and the United States.[50] The next 15 years saw a doubling of the nutmeg production on Banda, which found an eager market worldwide.[51] When in 1866 their competitors, the nutmeg growers from Penang, lost their trees, prices for the commodity rose, and profits for the harvest on Banda shot up from 600,000 guilders in 1869 to 1.6 million in 1871.[52] Thus, during the 19th century, the Bandanese perkeniers experienced a period of unprecedented prosperity.[53] The money was not just consumed but also re-invested, as appears from the fact that in 1874 the Lantzius, Versteegh and Mulder families purchased a parcel measuring 287 hectares on one of the Banda islands on long-term lease. There they planned a new nut grove.[54] Lans saw his dream come true by creating a nut grove on the island of Rosengain (today's Pulau Hatta), where the VOC had once destroyed all the nut trees in order to maintain their monopoly. The first nut trees to be harvested there in 250 years yielded their crop in 1878; with this, Lans felt that a wrong committed in the past had been put right. In 1873, one of the perkeniers, A.M.L. Hartog, ordered the construction of a steamship, *Egeron*, in order to shorten travelling time between Banda and the civilised world, and to transport nutmeg and mace to Singapore and Java.[55]

Meanwhile, on Banda in the 1860s, two clubs were founded with a total of 70 members, as well as an amateur dramatic society of 75 members with its own theatre. Undoubtedly, the functionaries at the resident's office and the local garrison officers would have contributed many members to these societies.[56] During those years Banda gained its attractive colonial buildings, for which the most expensive materials were imported. Well-to-do perkeniers, for instance, had costly marble shipped from Italy to pave their floors, replacing the old ceramic tiles.[57] In the town of Neira new dwellings arose, with a strong wall surrounding the grounds. This was not for the sake of appearances — the growth of prosperity did not extend to the freed slaves, former convicts and exiles, and contract labourers. It is quite possible that perkeniers handled their contract coolies far less kindly than they had once treated their slaves. It is known that coolies would cease working in the nut groves and form gangs together with exiles who, after completing their period of forced labour, remained on Banda.

Legal emancipation had arrived with the abolition of slavery, but it had not brought economic advancement. The resulting rise in criminality seems to have been accepted with a shrug — people simply adapted their dwellings, turning them into fortresses. Meanwhile, the pauperised branches of the perkeniers' families did well out of the new prosperity, for many of them found work on the estates. The small group of Banda Islands was home to the largest concentration of agricultural businesses in the Dutch East Indies outside Java. The 132 Europeans who were employed there in 1875 amounted to almost half the total Europeans working that year on agricultural projects in the outlying provinces.[58] The news gradually spread that Banda was again enjoying prosperity. As a result, even girls who were not heiresses of perkeniers received proposals from wealthy newcomers. Banda acquired the nickname of "the island of the rich girls".[59] The knot was only tied, however, if it was established that the bridegroom in question had a promising future; a suitable marriage remained a matter of financial circumstances, religion, upbringing and skin colour.

The *perken*, or "plots", had been in the hands of established perkeniers' families since the days of the Dutch East India Company. The estates had escaped fragmentation, because rights of ownership tended to remain undivided, thanks to frequent family intermarriages. A few families formed a coterie that would have established a ruling oligarchy over the Banda Islands, given half a chance. Without involving any other Bandanese, in 1872 the eight wealthiest perkeniers' families attempted — in vain, as it happened — to persuade the governor-general to set up a municipal council for Banda.[60]

However, the economic prosperity would in the long run sound the death knell for the Bandanese perkeniers' oligarchy. Like their peers in the Principalities, they dreamed of retirement in the mother country. In leaving their nut groves and their homes in Neira, the perkeniers rejected not only life on Banda, but also life in the Moluccas. Perkenier Hartog, who in 1894 had ennobled his name into "Hartog van Banda", had two luxurious villas built in the heart of Amsterdam; he named them *Groot-Banda* and *Neira*. And perkeniers sent their sons to Batavia or even to Europe for their education.[61] In the early 1880s some of these young men followed the training course for higher civil servants in Delft, or in Batavia.[62] Others chose a career with one of the agricultural companies in Java. While on the one hand perkeniers focused their sights increasingly on Europe, on the other hand they made tentative overtures to the occasional Chinese or Arab who had already widened his horizons. In 1886, for instance, Magdalena Claudina Pietersz, granddaughter of the merchant baron Charon de Saint Germain, married Mohammed bin Abdulla Baadella, also known as Sech Abdulrachim Baadilla. This Arab lieutenant of the Muslim civic militia was a splendid match, for he was not only rich but also highly educated. He owned a small fleet of merchant vessels that sailed the waters around Ambon, Ternate and the New Guinea coast. His great wealth came from pearl fishing — in no small measure because he smuggled out most of his catch past the watchful eyes of the Dutch customs.[63]

Variations of mestisation

The first line of Banda's national anthem, "Wide is the sea and Banda small", refers not only to the island's geographical isolation; it speaks above all of a separate identity, based on the unique social structure of these spice islands. In a sense, it is better to compare Banda's community with that of a Caribbean plantation island rather than that of other parts of the Indonesian archipelago.[64] Like Banda, after being conquered by Europeans some of the Caribbean islands were entirely repopulated and the new regime gained complete control of labour and production: initially through slavery and later through using indentured labour. The plantation community was led by a coterie of slave owners who easily absorbed the occasional white merchant or civil servant; one rung down followed the indigent relatives, all lumped together in the category of Burgher; then came the unfranchised workers. A somewhat separate group was formed of entrepreneurs from elsewhere in Asia. In the case of Banda, this latter group consisted of Chinese and Arabs who ran a store; a wealthy shopkeeper could achieve the same status as that of a perkenier. With all its finely regulated status distinctions, Banda, like the Caribbean islands, was populated by an oppressively small, insular community. Two inextricable aspects of this community life were the sexual relations of perkeniers with their female slaves, and hypergamy, which in this situation manifested itself in the efforts made by planters and, above all, their wives, to ensure that their daughters acquired a white husband. Despite their Balinese, Makassarese and Moluccan ancestresses, most of whom were originally slaves, the perkeniers considered themselves to be Dutch.

How can we best understand this discrepancy between a sense of being ethnically white yet brown in complexion? More than 40 years ago, in his study of life on Curaçao, one of the Dutch islands in the Caribbean, Harry Hoetink offered an explanation that in many ways is also applicable to Banda and the Principalities of Java. He observed that on the islands of the Dutch Antilles, "within certain limits of outward characteristics, the groups of whites were more distinguished by features of an economic, social and cultural nature, than by racial purity."[65] Of course, there were limits. In Banda's marriage registers we never come across a perkenier's daughter marrying a baptised slave, just as a perkenier would not marry a woman born in the Netherlands, a Totok, even late in the 19th century, when contact was far more intense between the perkeniers and Europe. White women could be seen on Banda, but in most cases they were already married or had come to marry an officer in the garrison. We find, thus, an economic upper class who considered themselves to be Dutch or European but were not perceived as such by newcomers; beneath this top layer was a group of Mestizo and indigenous Burghers. The term "Burgher" does not imply "bourgeois" but simply those who were "not under the authority of local (indigenous) heads". In other places besides Banda, this category included those descended from Europeans as well as their family members who were not recognised as Europeans, descendants of freed slaves and others who at one time or another had been granted the status of Burgher. The existence of this amalgam explains the high percentage of marriages between Europeans and other defined population groups in the Moluccas. In Java, for instance, from 1850 to 1905 between 10 per cent and 13 per cent of marriages were "mixed"; in the outlying provinces the number lay between 22 per cent and 28 per cent. Most of these mixed marriages took place in the Moluccas.[66]

Far more than in other places, in the Moluccas there were many marriages between local Christian men, and women of European descent; thus, from 1861 a separate ruling was introduced into their marriage acts. It gave the man the opportunity to be bound by Dutch private law. This did not, however, turn anyone into a European in the legal sense — in fact, they remained, constitutionally, in the category of "native" (*Inlands*). Although in 1848 the Dutch government had considered granting equal constitutional rights to Europeans and native Christians, the new colonial legislation of 1854 permitted not a shadow of doubt: there would be no such equality.[67] The Dutch government probably abandoned the idea of equal rights because not all Christians could be labelled "Burgher". If someone were subject to a local head, they were obliged to perform corvée, but anyone categorised as a Burgher was exempt from this.[68] Thus, native Christians who did not enjoy the status of Burgher — and that was by far the majority — remained the subjects of their local overlord and were obliged to perform corvée.[69] But this distinction between those subject to corvée duties and the Burghers was to become watered down during the 19th century, with the abolition of the forced cultivation and delivery of spices in the Moluccas. Moreover, the constitutional position of the native Christians remained unclear and confusing. They were, for instance, allowed to be recorded in the local registry office, but whether or not this conferred the legal status of a European remained an unanswered question.[70]

So it would seem that in practice the distinction between Christian Burgher and European was often no more than a matter of having one's name on a list (that of European inhabitants in the East Indies). People did not always manage to get themselves written into the vital records, as it involved making a long journey by sea to the capital of the residency. The island of Ternate, in the northern Moluccas, is an example of a community where the European population was so poorly registered that it is a historian's nightmare to sort out genealogies and names, written in numerous variations. These variant spellings occur chiefly for the descendants of poorer members of the community. We may safely assume they are not corrupt forms consciously used for the natural children of rich fathers, as could be found on Java.

Ternate: economic stagnation and social mobility

The earthquake of 1840 that ravaged the island had, from a social point of view, a levelling effect on Ternate's European community. At the beginning of the 19th century the cultivation of cocoa was so important that there were as many slaves on Ternate as on Banda. But after the earthquake — which destroyed even the apparently impregnable Fort Oranje — only a few cocoa trees survived.[71] As a result, Ternate never experienced a wealthy elite dreaming that they were Dutchmen, such as occurred on Banda. The economic collapse also left its mark on the town of Ternate, which for many decades bore the scars of the earthquake; not a house was left whole, and only miserable ruins and rubble remained of the once-splendid dwellings.[72]

Ternate provides a good example of the contingent character of colonial registration and classification, as well as of the shifting borders between the different communities. In the mid-19th century the resident of Ternate, Joan Hendrik Tobias, estimated that there were about 2,400 people (on Ternate and its dependent islands) who did not owe formal allegiance to the sultan and were governed directly by the colonial administration. Of this group, about 200 were Christian men from the garrison of Fort Oranje, while 425 were Europeans and 245 indigenous Christian citizens. By the close of the 19th century the latter category had expanded to about 600, while the number of Europeans remained stable at about 445.[73] On examining these figures more closely, it appears that it was difficult to count and classify the population of the various islands in the residency. Until the end of the 19th century there were scarcely any records about the Europeans living on Ternate's dependencies — Halmahera, Bacan, Galela and New Guinea. As far as that goes, it was probably very similar on the island of Kisar, near Timor, where after the garrison was disbanded in 1819, European descendants with names such as Joostenszoon, Visser, Speelman, Hasselt and Bakker lived outside the jurisdiction of the colonial government — although they tried to dress as Europeans and repeatedly made requests for European education, though in vain.[74] On Ternate, too, there were various families whose names betrayed their European origins but who were not registered as Europeans. Since there were probably very few descendants of baptised slaves living on Ternate, it seems likely that all the Christians were descended from soldiers, civil servants or sailors who at some time or other had made Ternate their home. This argument is supported by the fact that there are very few Moluccan names in the registers of marriages and births and baptisms recorded in the Protestant church.[75]

Around 1825 about 60 per cent of the 83 European men — not including soldiers — aged above 16 years had been born on Ternate. A total of 13 men came from the Netherlands, 11 from elsewhere in Europe (mostly from Germany), 1 from Bengal in India, 3 from the Moluccas and 4 from elsewhere in the East Indies. Furthermore, there was the resident, his secretary, and an office housing five clerks, while there were about five retired officers and two soldiers. Several Europeans worked in cocoa production, in the shipping business or in trade. Finally, one-quarter of the European men were described as unemployed, but presumably they made a living as small traders, in agriculture or as sailors.[76]

The military presence had a strong impact on this small community. Many well-known family names on Ternate stem from the local garrison. Between 1830 and 1890 some 10 per cent of the European children born there were registered by fathers who were at the time employed in the local garrison and who had settled as civilians on Ternate after serving out their contracts. But the majority of soldiers left Ternate when their term of service ended, leaving their children behind them on the island, usually without having married the mother.[77] Incidentally, skippers were also often not included in the local registers, even when their boat was registered at Ternate. Of the 166 marriages that took place between 1830 and 1888, in 69 cases the man was not described as a European inhabitant of Ternate or its dependent islands.[78] Most of the 69 were soldiers. Ternate may have had the appearance of a sleepy, forgotten backwater — but there was considerable coming and going, thanks to its garrison and harbour.

Many people left Ternate in search of work. Only in cases when a family could guarantee some kind of decent employment, might one of the sons try his fortune as an entrepreneur. So it was that J.W. Neijs, son of the well-known resident, remained on the island and became the proud owner of the brig *De Hoop*. Another of Neijs's sons, however, who was to become the father-in-law of Emilie Mesman, left Ternate and became an army officer. There is one Ternatan emigrant whom we shall meet again. He was an illegitimate child of Sgt. Johannes Nicolaas Voorneman, who had come to the island in 1816 and established himself as a schoolmaster. However, the chance of a job on Ternate for Frederik Karel, born there in 1824, was less than slim. He ended up in Padang, in Sumatra, where he made a mark as a journalist. His brother, Philippus Franciscus Voorneman, set off for Java, where he ran a bookshop in Surakarta.[79] Other young men headed elsewhere in the Moluccas, and some went to Manado, which lies on the northeast tip of the island of Sulawesi.

Considering the economic decline of Ternate, it should come as no surprise to learn that the number of newcomers declined — not only in comparison with the Ternatan Europeans, but also in absolute terms. When in 1855 Governor-General Duymaer van Twist visited the island, about 80 per cent of the European residents had been born in the Indies, compared with about 60 per cent 30 years previously. Only four of the newcomers were in government employment. The majority were ex-military or people trying to establish a small business. But at least eight of the 15 tradesmen on the island were newcomers. The number of men listed as unemployed had remained the same since the previous census of 1823, and just as in those days, they lived off their sparse savings or from what slaves grew for them in their market gardens. Some were artisans — there were no fewer than eight cobblers — while some were sailors.[80] Apparently the general level of education was poor, as appears from the difficulty that the resident had in finding suitable candidates to sit on the local Court of Justice. There was a shortage of notables, and army officers could not compensate for this lack, so observed the resident C. Bosscher in 1859 when he handed over his post. The officers, he found, were a rather uncivilised bunch, and furthermore many of

them lived in concubinage, which disqualified them. How would such
people be able to pass judgment that held any moral weight when, for
instance, it came to marital questions?[81]

By about 1860 there was only one notable left on Ternate, and that
was Maarten Dick van Renesse van Duivenbode (1805–1878). According
to Alfred Russel Wallace, who termed him the "king of Ternate", he
owned half the town.[82] But more significant than his real estate in town
— where most of the buildings were damaged by earthquakes — was
his small fleet of three schooners and a barque, which placed him in the
elevated category of major shipowner. His position among European
shipowners in the Indies was surpassed only by J.G. Weijergang of
Makassar, and the firm of Cores de Vries in Java.[83] Furthermore, Van
Duivenbode's business had a branch in Manado, where his son had
settled as shipowner.[84] Van Duivenbode enjoyed a luxurious lifestyle
surrounded by male and female slaves in his country residence, whose
grounds were filled with coconut palms and boasted a large fishpond
swarming with saltwater fish. The estate lay 45 minutes by foot from
the town of Ternate. The Dutch quartermaster Jan Baptist Jozef van
Doren, in his memoirs describing his life in the East Indies, recollects
a birthday party held at Van Duivenbode's home sometime in the mid-
19th century. Van Doren took a sedan chair from Ternate town out to
the country house. There the strains of an orchestra greeted him; he
found the music, consisting of dance tunes, quite pleasant. Delicious
food imported from Europe was presented by seductively dressed female
slaves. Dancing continued from nine o'clock until midnight; the more
elderly guests conversed or played cards. At midnight supper appeared,
and once more their host displayed his knowledge of European cuisine.
Finally, from two till four in the morning, everyone was prevailed upon
to join in a quadrille — a dance that was still highly popular in the
Moluccas. This cheerful square dance was enjoyed by all and sundry and
performed with an enthusiasm which, writes Van Doren, was no longer
to be found in the more stiff and formal circles of Batavia.[85]

Just as the upper classes still cherished the dances of the 18th
century, so the less well-to-do retained many customs of a bygone
lifestyle. In the 19th century it was still customary on Ternate to chew
betel, though the teeth were not permitted to become black from it, as
in the days of the Dutch East India Company: now they had to remain
pearly white, conforming to the European ideal of beauty. All the
Christians on the island attended the same Protestant church, where the
Reverend J.E. Höveker preached the Lord's Word alternately in Dutch

Illustration 27   The palace buildings and the customs at the court of the sultan of Ternate (northern Moluccas) reveal the centuries of European influence. In about 1840, Dutch draughtsman Charles William Meredith van de Velde attended a soirée there, to which all "the leading figures in the city were invited". The sultan's military band played Dutch folk songs.
[Lithograph in: C.W.M. van de Velde, *Gezigten uit Neêrlands Indië* (1846).]

and Malay.[86] In the mid-19th century elementary education in the Dutch language was poor, and truancy was rife because many parents kept their children home to work. By the end of the century, however, it seems to have greatly improved and the school had about 100 pupils. The school desks were filled with children from many different backgrounds, including Christian, Muslim and Chinese. The Peranakan (local-born, creolised) Chinese population, numbering between 300 and 400, were culturally connected with the Europeans and indigenous Christians, and many of them spoke quite fluent Dutch, as was also the case in Manado and Ambon. This did not mean, however, that marriages between Chinese and Europeans were common — quite the contrary — although naturally some children must have been born out of their unwed unions.

Ternate had an unusually large population of Muslim Burghers. Throughout the Moluccas there were neighbourhoods consisting of freed slaves and other migrants, most of them coming from Sulawesi and therefore called Makassarese. The Muslim Makassarese district in Ternate had about 1,000 residents who were classified as Burghers, with their own militia armed with lances, which continued to exist until 1896. The militia, incidentally, performed sterling service in 1855 in the battle against pirates.[87] Ternate was a sultanate, though by the 19th century the sultan's court was a mere shadow of what it had been in the glory days of the flourishing spice trade. Built on a hillside, the sultan's palace resembled a dwelling of the VOC, with a wooden veranda resplendent with Greek columns at the front and roofed with braches of *atap* (palm leaves).[88] Although the building's exterior was stylistically eclectic, the interior was filled with European-style furniture, and important guests were entertained by dancers wearing costumes echoing influences of the days when the Spaniards held sway over the island.[89] In many ways, developments on Ternate may be compared with what took place on the sugar islands of the Caribbean when the slave plantations came to an end. There was a process of creolisation, a gradual mixing of material cultures and behavioural patterns of the various ethnic groups; this is the natural process that takes place in communities where a higher authority ceases to draw sharp political or economic distinctions.

Ambon: citizens, civil servants and migrants

The education inspector Jacobus Anne van der Chijs reports that in the 1860s in the town of Ambon, just as in the northern Moluccas, it was almost impossible to see where the "native" category ended and the "European" began. Missionaries and, to a lesser extent, education had left their mark on the Ambonese identity. Although the language mostly spoken among the citizens was Moluccan Malay — a Creole with influences from the various languages of Makassar, Bali and New Guinea that were spoken by the slave population — Van der Chijs observed that the use of Dutch was greatly on the increase.[90]

Starting in the 17th century a large Burgher class had grown up on Ambon, which had rapidly expanded under the British. The latter had encouraged migration to the town in order to expedite the recruitment of soldiers and to have a sufficient supply of labour for working in the town and dockyard.[91] In doing this they broke with VOC policy, which had been to keep the indigenous Ambonese in their villages to facilitate the mobilisation of corvée labour.[92] The result of the trek from the countryside was that in 1854 the residency district had, according to the inspector of public health Everhardus Wijnandus Adrianus Ludeking, 7,433 Burghers out of a total population of 130,000.[93] Some of these people came from the less densely populated Muslim region of Hitu, but the largest group came from Leitimor, the Christian peninsula of Ambon.

The number of Burghers — inhabitants who were exempt from corvée and mostly lived in the town of Ambon — continued to grow. In 1860 came the abolition of slavery, followed on 1 January 1864 by the abolition of compulsory clove cultivation. In its place came taxation; this served to stimulate the monetisation of the economy, whereby the villagers were persuaded to earn money in the town. In the 1860s the local government also made it easier to acquire a pass with which villagers could settle in the town — thereby avoiding both corvée and the authority of the village headmen.[94] In any case, economic necessity — rather than the privilege of being Ambonese Burghers wearing shoes and a top hat like the Europeans — would have induced villagers to migrate to the city and become citizens of Ambon. After all, the coveted shoes would have been an unaffordable luxury. Usually such items as shoes, a high hat and a three-piece suit would be borrowed by bridegrooms for their marriage ceremony. It seems likely that after a time many of the newly freed Ambonese returned to their native villages, having found little work in the town.

Poverty was widespread. This led Governor-General Duymaer van Twist, who also visited Ambon on his Moluccan tour in 1855, to stimulate Ambonese entrepreneurship, as had been done on Banda, by providing interest-free loans. As a result, members of prominent Ambonese families began cultivating cocoa in southwest Seram, the island just north of Ambon.[95] They came from families who had intermarried, whose sons became officers in the militia or sat on the board of the Orphans' Chamber or the Court of Justice. The entrepreneurs did not grow vastly rich from the cocoa beans; in 1874, for instance, the entire harvest of Ambon cocoa fetched no more than 19,748 guilders.[96] What mattered most to these families was building a career in the civil service. They were to be found in all ranks of the civil service — up to the level of secretary to the government of the Moluccas — and thereby formed the backbone of local administration.[97] They married into the families of Bandanese perkeniers, and in the final decades of the 19th century some of their sons were working for the Binnenlands Bestuur in places scattered throughout the Indonesian archipelago.[98]

We have already encountered Roelandus Nicolaas Rijkschroeff, on his way to becoming a perkenier on Banda; his story leads us to the heart

of the group of Ambonese notables. He came from the third generation
of Rijkschroeffs to be born on Ambon. His great-great-grandfather,
Adriaan Rijke Schroeff, had come to the East Indies from the Netherlands
in 1734. Arriving as a simple sailor, he climbed up to the position of
lieutenant captain and bought an estate on Ambon, where generations
of Rijkschroeffs would settle. The father of Nicolaas, Adriaan Hendrik
Rijkschroeff, rose from being *eerste commies* (first senior clerk), then
warehouse master and assistant-resident, to the honourable position of
secretary to the government of the Moluccas (1841–1850). Such a career
was expected in these families. Nicolaas's brother-in-law Dirk Samuel
Hoedt was secretary for the Moluccas from 1854 to 1855. His other
brother-in-law, Frederik J.E. Neumann, held the posts of *commies* on
the Ambonese island Saparua, deputy inspector of spices and secretary
for Timor, and crowned his career, like his brother- and father-in-law,
by becoming secretary for the Moluccas (1878–1887).

The following generation made its appearance in the Binnenlands
Bestuur, thereby becoming part of the official migration circuit. The four
sons of Nicolaas's brother-in-law Frederik Neumann had the most
remarkable careers. They travelled to the farthest corners of the Indonesian archipelago. Neumann was already a widower and had lost three
children, when he married the sister of his deceased wife. This second
marriage produced four sons, all of whom left home at an early age to
be educated outside the Moluccas. On 1 May 1866 the two older sons,
Louis and Gottlieb, still boys, set off for the Netherlands to be educated
at a good boarding school. In 1874, Louis — by this time a student in
Leiden — sent the following letter home:

> How clearly I recall those events of nine years ago […] as if it were only
> yesterday, I see us saying goodbye to our home and habitat and how
> a great crowd of people accompanied us down to the harbour where
> we climbed into the sloop that was to take us out to the ship, and still
> I hear the military music played for us, Ambon's last salute to us.[99]

After having sent his two oldest boys off to the Netherlands, Neumann
decided, during his period as secretary at the residency of Timor, to send
the younger two, Rudolph and Frits, to a boarding school in Batavia,
in distant Java, to prepare themselves for the new training school for civil
servants in the Binnenlands Bestuur that had opened in 1867 at the
Willem III School in the colonial capital. And so the Neumann parents
and children, now separated by thousands of miles, had contact only via
letters; although unfortunately only the correspondence from the boys

has survived, it tells enough to paint a picture of the parents' anxious concern for their children's welfare. The oldest boy, Louis, born in 1856, turned out to be the brightest; in February 1875, after scarcely five month's study, he passed the first part of his law studies at the University of Leiden. In 1882 he was top of his class in the course of study for legal officials. He returned to the East Indies but died young, in 1897, while occupying the post of chairman of the landraad (the local court for native affairs) in Pati, Central Java. His brother Gottlieb, born in 1857, passed the exam for higher civil servants in the Netherlands and began his career with the Binnenlands Bestuur in 1884 in the residency of Kediri (eastern Java), although he spoke not a word of Javanese. He attained the position of assistant-resident and secretary of the district of Banten (West Java) in 1906. Meanwhile, in Batavia, Rudolph, born in 1860, and his one-year-older brother Frits, sat the examination for higher civil servant in 1881 and 1883. Both completed their careers as inspectors for finances.[100] After their early years together, the members of this family hardly saw one another again. Small wonder that when in 1894 Rudolph managed to squeeze out six weeks' leave to visit his home in Ambon for a short time, he wrote to his parents on his return to Batavia: "The dark shadow side of seeing you again, is that I have to leave you. […] I feel as if I need to have you all close to me again, like it was in the past three weeks, in order to stay happy."[101] When his father died in 1897 Rudolph realised with a pang that more than anything else he would miss his father's letters with their elegant, regular handwriting.[102]

From time to time Rudolph saw his brothers when they came to Batavia in expectation of a new government appointment. He was also a key figure for other young relatives who arrived in Batavia from Ambon hoping to find a government job.[103] Rudolph took his two young nephews Frits and Adriaan Rijkschroeff under his wing. He helped them find lodgings with an Ambonese family, though they left almost immediately when they discovered the Risakotta family, who were related to their mother, living in the same kampong near Batavia. Rudolph also attempted, in vain, to get jobs for them with the Post and Telegraph Service and in the department of finances, where he himself worked. In those days it was difficult to get even a voluntary job, "working for the honour of it", as it was euphemistically described. Adriaan certainly had poor prospects, for he had failed the examination for *adjunct-commies* (assistant senior clerk) at the Post Office because his Dutch was so poor. The news must have been a bitter pill for his poverty-stricken family in Ambon.[104] But eventually the two brothers would succeed. Adriaan later became director of a housing agency named *De Combinatie* in Bandung (West Java), and Frits became head of an office in the Department of Justice in Batavia.[105]

The letters of the Neumann family draw our attention yet again to the question of concubinage. Both Rudolph and his oldest brother, Louis, had a child by an Indonesian woman. Rudolph's daughter was evidently regarded as one of the family, for the grandparents in Ambon sent the little girl 25 guilders for her birthday. The mother's name is not mentioned in the correspondence between Rudolph and his parents. As he wanted to avoid being seen in public with his concubine, he tried to have the legitimation procedure take place at his home. He appealed to his old study friend Gerardus Johannes Petrus Valette, who was by this time employed as secretary for the residency of Batavia, to make the necessary arrangements. Rudolph was fully aware of the legal consequences. As soon as he had recognised the child he became the legal father, and the mother consequently lost all her rights. He, the father, was then entirely responsible for the child's upbringing. The only thing that prevented Rudolph from bringing his daughter to live with him was the fact that he was boarding with a landlady. He did, however, turn down a promotion to a position as inspector in Padang (West Sumatra) so that he could remain in Batavia and keep an eye on his child. At last, after she had survived several attacks of malaria, he had her come to live with him. Deeply regretting the position into which his actions had brought the girl's mother, he made certain that mother and daughter were able to maintain contact.[106]

The reason the Neumann brothers kept a concubine does not seem to have been a lack of money. In those years both Rudolph and Louis enjoyed a monthly salary of 600 guilders. But, living far away from their relatives, they had to apply their own resources to finding a partner who came from a suitable background. This was possible only once they had built up a career. To complicate matters, their career growth would be expedited by a good choice of partner. The rich landholders of Makassar or the perkeniers on Banda were free from such complicated pressure. Another consideration is that in Batavia the social opposition to concubinage was stronger than elsewhere in the Indies. This explains why Rudolph never considered for a moment the possibility of living together with the mother of his child. He put on hold his family life in much the same way his colleagues from the Netherlands often did.[107] By repudiating the mother of his illegitimate child, he did not even retain the possibility of marriage at a later date, when he would no longer yearn for a young European bride or retirement in Europe. Novels and stories set in the Dutch East Indies of bygone days, known as *tempo doeloe*, took up the theme of temporary concubinage with considerable relish. Curiously, female European writers showed little concern for the fate of the mothers who lost their children. Even the renowned Dutch feminist-writer Mina Kruseman (1839–1922) apparently considered the bond between a European father and his child to be all-important — which is completely in line with the European upbringing norms of her day.

The growing interest during the 19th century in the question of concubinage — the phenomenon was, in fact, a very old one — coincided with a growing belief in the concept of romantic love, which propagated the mental and spiritual bond between marriage partners. This notion also found its followers in the world of the East Indies. In this respect, the wishes of the Moluccan Rudolph in Batavia were little different from those of the commercial agent from Amsterdam, Dirk Hendrik de Vries, who was stationed in Manado. Living with his concubine, he often longed to be rid of her.[108] It seems that the primary goal of De Vries was to return rich to the Netherlands and lead a comfortable life there. Under no circumstances did he wish to tie himself to the Indies; he thought that he had little in common, spiritually, with the land and its people. The form of late-19th-century concubinage, in which the Indonesian partner was camouflaged as a housekeeper or — as in Rudolph's case — banished from the home, typifies a period in which intrusive social control soon posed a serious threat to one's career. Of course, this also affected attitudes towards marriage. Temporary concubinage fulfilled a need, especially for men far away from the circles in which they had grown up and where they would normally have looked for a marriage partner. The marriage market on the Moluccan islands posed far fewer problems than that in Batavia, where traditionally there were large numbers of male newcomers; and it was also difficult in a remote administrative centre, where there was hardly a European woman to be found. Rudolph's brother Frits was more fortunate than his two other brothers — or maybe he was just more clever — because on a visit to his parents on the island of Timor, he had the good fortune to meet and eventually marry Eugenie Siso, the daughter of an old Makassar family who had engaged in the pearl fishery off Timor.

It is clear from Rudolph's letters that economic opportunities in the Moluccas were extremely limited, even for his relatively prosperous family. Rudolph's uncle, Roelandus Nicolaas Rijkschroeff, had attained the pleasant position of perkenier, but his brother Carel Frederik, a retired clerk, ended up in prison and for a while was forced to trek around Java selling tickets for circus performances as a means of earning a living. When he was unable to pay the doctor's bill for his sick children, he managed to stave off disaster by convincing the doctor that although at the moment he had no ready cash, he was after all a rich perkenier from Banda whose solvency was unquestionable. The elite of Ambon, incidentally, unlike their Bandanese neighbours, had not been able to accumulate much wealth under the liberal economic regime. This makes it all the more surprising that Frederik Neumann could afford to send his children to be educated in the Netherlands and Batavia. It cost easily more than 1,200 guilders a year to send someone to university in Leiden, as the letters of Louis Neumann make all too clear.[109] And evidently, the Neumanns' funds were limited, as can be deduced from one of Frederik Neumann's letters. He tells his son Louis, who was excelling at his studies, that he (Frederik) was already saving up so that he could send his son on a grand tour of Europe as a graduation present. Even after he retired as a civil servant, Frederik retained to the bitter end his post as chairman of the Orphans' and Estates Chamber. He badly needed this extra income to supplement his annual pension of 2,025 guilders, since he did not wish to live off his children.[110]

Families like the Neumanns comprised the top layer of the local community, but they merged seamlessly into the category of native Christian Burghers. The mother of Rudolph's cousins Adriaan and Frits, whose name was Jacoba Dorothea de Fretes, came from a prominent Ambonese family of Christian Burghers who, like the Dias and Soselisa families, had members in the ranks of the civil service in Ambon.[111] As if the picture were not complicated enough, various members of these families were classified before the law as Europeans.[112] One member of the De Fretes family held in succession the positions of clerk, raja and finally the extremely lucrative post of counsel for native residents in lawsuits.[113] In Manado, in the Minahasa district of North Sulawesi, things were no different.[114] There, too, European clerks, civil servants and plantation managers belonged to the same privileged family coterie as rajas or majors and other representatives of the indigenous residents. Until late in the 19th century it was not the newcomers but the local families who pulled the strings, both economically and politically. In this regard, the abolition of the cloves monopoly, the abolition of forced labour and the introduction of free trade around 1860 brought down the curtain on the scene that had evolved during the days of the Dutch

East India Company. From then onwards, a position in the civil service no longer automatically led to economic advantages. It is against this background that we should see the migration of the Neumanns and their poor relations.

Soldiers and teachers

Migration to other territories within the vast Indonesian archipelago was also part of a general pattern in the Moluccas. From the letters of the Neumann family, we gain a unique picture of an Ambonese family that became widely scattered. The letters also offer an occasional glimpse of the poorer relatives who sent their children to study in Batavia in the hope that they would gain an acceptable job as office clerks. Family members who emigrated remained in contact with each other, forming a small colony in the city of Batavia and maintaining their links with Ambon. Relations with home were maintained, and presumably this held true for all the Moluccans who left their native islands and ranged out across the Indonesian archipelago. According to the 1930 census, about 16 per cent of Moluccan Christians lived outside their home islands.[115] Traditionally, the highest status an Ambonese Christian could attain would be Burghership, and a position as clerk or teacher. In contrast, a position in the army was generally spurned. This aversion to military service had already been prevalent in the 18th century when village headmen had to furnish young men for the annual patrols guarding the clove monopoly.[116] For those living on the Ambon islands, upward social mobility came through education, missionary work and Burghership, while the army was traditionally considered to be an instrument of economic oppression.

The bases for missionary work and education, also in the Dutch language, were already laid in the 17th century. However, these became gradually eroded in the 18th century, a period of economic decline in the Moluccas.[117] Things began to pick up when the Reverend Joseph Kam, shortly after his arrival in 1815, installed a small printing press at the back of his home; here he produced religious matter for his local readership.[118] Then in 1834 the missionary Bernhard Roskott founded a teachers' training college, which by 1855 had turned out 82 teachers.[119] Most of them found jobs in the village schools on the Moluccan islands. Although these pupil-teachers in the main received Bible instruction, the missionary background undoubtedly enhanced the status of the elementary schoolteacher. From 1856 on, children of native Christian

Burghers had the opportunity of attending a European elementary
school without having to pay fees. As on the island of Ternate, so too
on Ambon, in most cases a distinction was no longer made between
the descendants of Europeans, and Christian Burghers; admission to
elementary school, and hence the opportunity of gaining a job as a
low-ranking civil servant, became equally possible for them all. However,
this was only in principle; the two elementary schools on Ambon could
not possibly accommodate all the children of the 8,000 Ambonese
Burghers.[120] There were, furthermore, few job opportunities in the
Moluccas for these junior civil servants — unlike the encouraging
outlook for schoolteachers.

It is doubtful whether the missionary teaching made much impact
on Dutch fluency among the Ambonese — the Bible was, after all,
translated into Malay. Nevertheless, in the second part of the 19th
century the Dutch language spread even to the small villages. The
inspector for education, Van der Chijs, reported in about 1860 that the
Ambonese were more inclined to regard Dutch as their language than
were the Indo-Europeans in Java.[121] The affection for the Dutch language
would only grow stronger. After the establishment of the second European
school in 1856, the Ambon Burgher School was founded in 1869; this
was intended for the native Christians of Ambon and had Dutch on its
curriculum. Pupils with the highest marks in their school-leaving exams
received the diploma of junior civil servant.[122] It seems that in the 1860s
there was enormous enthusiasm among the Ambonese Christians to
become teachers. Indeed, they were so keen that it was reported, "If they
are not curbed, half the male population would become a schoolmaster".[123]
Not surprisingly, when the government teacher training college opened
its doors in Ambon in 1874, there were many applicants. Anyone with
a certificate as junior civil servant or schoolteacher who failed to find
work in the Moluccas left for Java, for the towns of Surabaya, Semarang
or Batavia. Some students found their way to the STOVIA (college for
training native medical doctors) in Batavia, which had been founded
in 1852.

Although the army did not enjoy great popularity in the Moluccas,
the colonial administrations found it most important to have a sizeable
contingent of local Christian soldiers in the army, since it was largely
composed of Javanese Muslims. Native Christian soldiers had enjoyed
the status of semi-Europeans ever since, in 1804, Daendels had declared
that the military from the Ambonese islands, Timor and Minahasa were
to be treated as equals of European soldiers.[124] Nevertheless, army
recruitment in the Christianised islands proved a very difficult task

throughout most of the 19th century. In 1854 the local government began a recruitment campaign to increase the numbers in the military, but at the end of two years the army authorities had to concede that all their efforts had yielded no more than a meagre 77 recruits per year for Minahasa and the Ambon islands combined. In 1860, however, the army managed to recruit 1,308 "Ambonese" — this term was used in army statistics to describe soldiers from both Minahasa and the Moluccas. Half this number came from Minahasa. Midway through the Aceh War, in 1875, the numbers from Minahasa had declined to 498, and those from Ambon were merely 398.[125] When the war started in 1873, the residents of Ternate, Manado and Ambon were exhorted to concentrate on recruiting — especially in the Christian villages; but this had little effect, despite a 50-guilder premium to the village headmen for every soldier they provided.[126] At the beginning of the Aceh War, army recruitment moved at a snail's pace. In addition, in 1864 the cloves monopoly was rescinded, which not only led to a growing trek towards the towns but also produced an economic revival in the villages, since during the 1870s and 1880s cloves were fetching a very good price. In Minahasa, too, the numbers of Christians from the Manado district remained meagre, despite a large number of conversions to Christianity during the 1850s.[127] Only at the end of the 1870s, when the early losses in the Aceh War had made enlistment in the military even more unpopular, did the army authorities manage to attract more recruits. In 1879, when a school was opened in Magelang, Java, for army children from the Moluccas, Minahasa and Timor, it proved exactly what was needed.[128] And, besides, training for the military was expanded. Thus, the army became a feasible route to social advancement, all the more since employment as a clerk or teacher proved unattainable for most literate Moluccans.

By 1883 the Ambonese contingent in the Dutch-Indies army had doubled to 801 from Manado and 708 from Ambon.[129] The appeal of the army would increase even more on the Ambon islands in the 1890s, when the prices of cloves fell once again.[130] At last there were sufficient volunteers — and the same was true for Minahasa. Indeed, here the army authorities were even able to select out of the large numbers who applied.[131] Ultimately, the greatest number of soldiers would come from Minahasa; in 1918 there were 6,388 soldiers from Minahasa compared with 3,674 from the Moluccan islands.[132] The increasing majority from Manado can easily be explained: in the 1870s the Christian populations of these two areas were more or less the same size, that is, around 60,000.

The figures for the 1900 census, however, are 72,359 native Christians on the Ambon islands compared with 164,117 in the Minahasa region.[133]

The former military became part of the village notables, along with the raja and other village headmen and the schoolteachers, who were on a slightly lower rung of the social ladder.[134] Both in Minahasa and on the Ambon islands it became part of the local pattern of social mobility to enter military service; it also formed a confirmation of the Christian identity of these communities. The army did not, however, initiate the integration of the Christian communities in the colonial world. The image that has evolved in Dutch colonial history of the Ambonese as a martial race is primarily a colonial picture and does not reflect a predilection for the military life on the part of the Ambonese.

Civil servants of Makassar

From the 1860s on, steadily increasing numbers from the Moluccan communities emigrated to places throughout the Indonesian archipelago, taking up jobs in the army, government administration and commerce. The increasing mobility had a homogenising effect on the culture of the civil service in the Indies. The transfers of sovereignty in the days of Napoleon and the British interregnum caused scarcely a ripple in the smooth waters of local government. Often the resident might have come from abroad, but in the bureaucratic ranks below him it was always the local families that held sway. This continued into the 1860s, but then the patterns changed.[135] Rudolph Neumann's brother Gottlieb ended up as official of the Binnenlands Bestuur in Kediri. Frits Neumann's request in 1890 for the post of secretary to the government of the Moluccas, following in the footsteps of his father, was not granted.[136] Once committed to a career in the East Indies scene, the way back to local employment was closed.

Members of local European families scarcely experienced setbacks in their careers as a result of their background. In the Neumann family, for instance, three of the four brothers apparently suffered little from being born in the Indies. But it was different for Rudolph, who remained in Batavia; it was a good eight years after he had passed the higher civil service examinations that he attained the rank of chief secretary. He complained that in his experience nobody with as high a qualification as his had taken so long to reach this level.[137] But, as mentioned above, he was very ambitious, and he was also honest enough to write to his father that he had been told by his superiors that promotion would certainly come his way if he worked harder. In his own view, his background worked against him, in contrast to the newcomers in the Batavia office; he saw himself as an *Indische jongen* — a son of the Indies. His family, however, enjoyed great respect in high government circles. The personal intervention of Henri Maximiliaan Andrée Wiltens, then vice president of the Council of the Indies, prevented Rudolph's being bypassed for promotion by a newcomer.[138] A combination of factors decided one's position in the government apparatus: diplomas and seniority, individual achievement and good breeding — which is to say, coming from a prominent family with a good reputation.

The local colour may have seeped out of much of the Indies government and business world, but there were exceptions: the frontier districts in the outlying provinces. Here it was essential to know about local connections and the relationships between the descendants of local European families. Indeed, this applied not only to those in government positions, but also as far as economic exploits were concerned. A good example is the story of the exploitation of the Belitung (Billiton) tin deposits. The seams of tin were discovered in 1851 by Johannes F. den Dekker, a "son of the Indies" and clerk at the port of Muntok on nearby Bangka; Den Dekker accompanied the concession-holders Vincent baron van Tuyll van Serooskerken and John F. Loudon on their expedition to the island of Belitung. When the latter two left in 1855, the Dutch owners and supervisors had to accept the fact that Den Dekker pulled the strings on Belitung. After all, he spoke Chinese and was on good terms with the Chinese miners; without him, not an ounce of tin ore would have been extracted from the soil.[139] Interestingly, the Dutch owners never took the step of formally appointing Den Dekker as head of the tin mines. For the first few decades the mighty Belitung concern was typical of the situation in the outlying provinces. The power of the directorate in the Netherlands and the colonial government was balanced out by the influence of the local elites, partly arising from their knowledge of the local languages and familiarity with local circumstances. This equilibrium continued until the early years of the 20th century.

The government of Celebes (Sulawesi) provides several examples of the tensions that arose between the bureaucratic norms for advancement by means of diplomas, and the indispensability of civil servants who had grown up in the district and were familiar with the situation in southern Sulawesi. The contrast between these approaches grew sharper with the development of local newspapers. In 1861 Makassar gained its own newspaper, the *Macassaarsch Weekblad*. It was published by a local bookseller; after two years it was taken over by a rival bookshop and renamed the *Makassaarsch Handels- en Advertentieblad*. The editors considered it their task also to provide news about the Moluccas, for they regarded Makassar as the key to the eastern archipelago.[140] After 1868 two daily newspapers were published in Makassar. But the papers failed to become a flourishing enterprise; they were constantly changing ownership and name, and no illusions should be cherished about either the level of their contents or the number of subscribers. The *Celebes Courant*, for instance, had a circulation of no more than 243 in 1880, which is scarcely surprising considering that in that year Makassar had a tiny European population of around 800.[141] It is, however, thanks to these newspapers that we know something about the life of Makassar's European upper class in those years.

The port was prosperous, profiting from the economic development in the Moluccas and from its shipping connections with Singapore, Europe, China and even the United States.[142] Makassar became more "European", and this was seen not only in the newspapers, whose publication in fact contributed to the process. For Makassar, the days of European slave trade and robber gangs were a thing of the past. The town became a trade centre and came to resemble more and more the ports of the north Java coast. Well-to-do residents of Makassar would no longer put up with theatre productions in the garrison canteen. A society of citizens was founded, named *Tot Nut en Genoegen* (For Benefit and Pleasure), followed a few years later, in 1868, by an amateur orchestra.[143] In 1872 a modest public library appeared in Makassar, initiated by the church council of the Dutch Reformed congregation; once a month they sent around a list to the wealthy middle class asking for a voluntary contribution.[144]

Meanwhile, the Makassar newspapers sharpened the social awareness of the less well-to-do Europeans who had been born and bred in Makassar. This class consciousness found its expression, in 1865, in the founding of a second club in Makassar, named Concordia. To become a member, one had to have a minimum income of 50 guilders a month; it was thus aimed at respectable, middle-class citizens.[145] The founding of the daily newspaper *Dagblad van Celebes* in 1868, by W. Eekhout, was also a sign of the assertion of Indo-European sentiments in Makassar. The journal published letters, for instance, with explicit complaints about discrimination against Indo-Europeans.[146] The *Dagblad van Celebes*, together with the militant paper *Padangsch Handelsblad*, was the first to enter the fray as supporter of the rights of Sinjos (Indo-Europeans).

These rights were perceived as part of a broader agenda of defending the rights of all Europeans born in the Indies. The editor of the *Dagblad van Celebes*, the lawyer W.C.J. van der Moore, also put the case for setting up a course in law studies in the Indies to complement the training for posts in the Binnenlands Bestuur, which had begun in 1867 in Batavia.[147]

The alleged discrimination in cases of civil-service promotion against the *inlandse kinderen*, Europeans born in the Indies, was apparently not a result of increasing competition with newcomers. Nor is there much to indicate that young men from Makassar were ousted from government jobs due to the influx of men from the Netherlands. As the 19th century progressed, the division of jobs among local candidates and newcomers remained roughly the same as in the past. Not until the 1860s, however, do we have the press as an information source.

It is clear that the local press attached great political significance to the career chances for young men from Makassar within the Binnenlands Bestuur. They followed the careers of a number of local civil servants who, without having passed the higher civil service exams, were busily ascending the governmental ladder in Celebes. The successive governors of Celebes Johannes Antonius Bakkers and Charles Christiaan Tromp held key roles in the careers of these local men. The press was most complimentary about them, stating that they treated the local sons with respect — which seems to suggest that elsewhere this was not the case. Governor Bakkers (1864–1876) was not trained as a government civil servant but was an army officer, who in this role had picked up a thorough knowledge of the island. Bakkers's successor as governor was Tromp, born in Batavia in 1830; he held office from 1876 to 1885. Starting out as a clerk, he passed the higher civil service examination in Delft while on leave in 1856. Soon he made a successful career for himself — probably partly thanks to the fact that he came from a prominent family in the Indies.[148]

Particularly striking is the manner in which Bakkers operated. He allowed civil servants to study for the various levels of the Binnenlands Bestuur while remaining within the jurisdiction of his province, whereas normally, people were sent to a new location as they attained each successive level. The governor knew he was better served by people who were familiar with the local situation and spoke the local languages rather than those who had simply studied theories of government. This is illustrated by the career of J.A.G. Brugman, a civil servant from an old Makassar family. From the moment the VOC arrived in South Celebes, at the end of the 17th century, there had been members of the Brugman family, as well as the Volls and Trouerbachs, working for the company as interpreters. In fact, they were more than interpreters; they played an important role in diplomatic negotiations between the local rulers and the VOC government. In the 19th century the families were still providing interpreters.

The professional confidence of Brugman was thus based on almost two centuries of family tradition. Like Willem Leendert Mesman, the wealthy landholder and merchant, he had trained as a translator in Makassar. It was part of Brugman's job as interpreter to accompany numerous expeditions, with only a few dozen soldiers as guards, through hostile terrain. In 1875 Governor Bakkers sent him, on his own authority, to the rebellious Karaeng Bonto-Bonto, a local head, to hold talks with his sons.[149] The latter had been instructed by their father to negotiate only with the assistant-resident or Brugman. Inspector J.W. van Heusden, who felt he had been passed over, took all the credit for leading the expedition, in an announcement in the Semarang newspaper *De Locomotief,* and he tried to put the mere *commies* (senior clerk) Brugman in his place — that of an inferior interpreter.[150] Brugman, it seems, was not to be put down; he wrote a letter to the editor of the newspaper explaining that in his position as government clerk he had not acted as an interpreter, and that it was he, not Van Heusden, who had led the mission. In conclusion, he accused the inspector of putting the governor's reputation in a bad light by airing such jealousies in public.[151] The response to Brugman's letter came from other civil servants in Makassar. They joined Brugman in lauding Governor Bakker. It was Brugman, lower in rank, who had reprimanded Van Heusden by writing to the newspaper. It says much that Brugman's outburst had not the slightest detrimental effect on his career.

Indeed, Brugman's career continued its upward curve under Bakkers's successor, Tromp. In 1881 he was granted exemption from the higher civil service exams by Royal Decree which meant that he could proceed to the corps of the Binnenlands Bestuur.[152] On 12 January 1882 the *Makassaarsch Handelsblad* reported enthusiastically that Brugman had once again accomplished a diplomatic mission with great success, thereby ensuring the smooth succession to the throne of a local prince. The paper suggested it was time this praiseworthy government officer was rewarded with a medal.[153] Meanwhile, in 1883 Brugman made himself even more meritorious by compiling the booklet titled *Nederlandsche en Makassaarsche samenspraken* (Dutch and Makassarese Dialogues).[154]

Subsequently, in a four-year period, he rose from the position of secretary to that of assistant-resident of police, followed shortly by assistant-resident for Native Affairs. The latter position also offered opportunities for spectacular diplomatic triumphs: added to his other successes, Brugman completed a treaty with the kingdom of Wajo. Once again a newspaper, this time the *Celebes Courant*, put the case for his being publicly honoured, in peculiarly lyrical tones: "The breast of Mr B.," pleaded the newspaper, "although he has performed such sterling service for the government in the past, remains like a bush without blossom, like a tree without fruit, pristine and unadorned."[155] This was yet another successful mission by Brugman, in which this time he had been assisted by an interpreter. Finally, in 1892, he was made a knight in the Order of Orange-Nassau. Four years later came an even higher distinction, when he was appointed an officer in the order. Six years after that came the crowning of his career with the appointment to the unique position of "resident for Native Affairs and peripatetic official". The function had apparently been created specially for him, and he would fulfil it for eight years.[156]

With the turn of the century, the bureaucratic norms of Batavia began to make themselves felt more strongly as far afield as Sulawesi. No longer could the scions of prominent Makassar families build themselves a shining career as interpreters, working their way up in the Binnenlands Bestuur. Already during the final years of the 19th century they were no longer admitted into this body if they did not possess the higher civil service diploma. In 1898 and 1899, two other members of the Brugman family were granted the position of civil commander, which was one rung lower than the lowest position in the Binnenlands Bestuur.[157] If someone had the right education — either at the Willem III School in Batavia, or in the Netherlands — the possibilities of a glowing career stretched ahead of them. Willem Leendert Mesman, Alfred Russel Wallace's host, was able to pay for an appropriate education for his oldest son. Johannes Willem, born in 1850, was in one of the first cohorts who sat the higher civil service examination at the Willem III School in Batavia. His classmate was Gerardus Johannes Petrus Valette, brother-in-law of the writer Louis Couperus, and the same man who had helped Rudolph Neumann legitimise his daughter.[158] Johannes Willem finally attained the position of resident of Jepara and Cirebon (northern Java). After a long career spanning 37 years, at his own request he was granted honourable dismissal from the service of his country, in 1908. He was thanked especially for his contributions in the field of

Illustration 28 Johannes Willem Mesman (1850–1932) was one of the first to obtain his higher civil service diploma in Batavia. His career took him to the exalted position of resident of Jepara and Cirebon (Java). He is photographed in the latter place *circa* 1905 with his wife, Rebekka Mathilda van Waasbergen, his daughter Aletta and two sons-in-law.
[Photograph, KITLV, Leiden.]

the People's Credit System (*Volkscredietwezen*). According to the newspaper *Makassaarsche Courant*, his services had not been sufficiently recognised, which the paper thought was due to his extreme modesty. Mesman may well have been a man who never stood on ceremony, but he certainly gained wide recognition for establishing a credit facility for the people of Cirebon.[159] He ended an admirable career as director of the People's Agricultural Credit Bank.[160] His colleagues, too, praised Mesman's modesty and his expertise "in the field of native affairs".[161] The retiring resident was not called a "son of the Indies" in so many words — that was, after all, not entirely appropriate in those years — but the use of adjectives such as "modest" and the reference to his being an expert in native affairs left no doubt about his being a son of the Indies.

We end our journey around the islands of the eastern archipelago by taking one last look at the lives of some of the Mesman children. The daughters of Willem Leendert Mesman and his brother Tuan Solo, with only one exception, married army officers who were stationed in Makassar in the 1860s and 1870s. Emilie made a disastrous marriage with Wilhelmus Henricus (Hein) Neijs, to whom she had been married off hastily. She was lucky to have her uncle Willem Leendert nearby, and she turned to him for protection when she was pregnant; she was mistreated and humiliated by her husband and had her property stolen by her in-laws. She complained bitterly that women lost all their rights when they married, and that they had to surrender their lives and property to their husbands.[162] Her pregnancy ended in a miscarriage, after which she was whisked off by her husband to Fort de Kock on the island of Sumatra, where he was stationed. Here she experienced some respite when her detested husband was sent to Aceh, in northwest Sumatra. Free from his domineering presence, she could go horseback riding and smoke cigars; in the meantime, her in-laws continued to swallow up her capital.[163] When her divorce was finally pronounced, all her money was gone.

Emilie's sister Eugenie, on the other hand, made a love match; she married her cousin Alexander, a younger brother of the worthy resident Mesman. Alexander became administrator for his father's estates and owner of a brick factory. The sons of Eugenie and Alexander were the last generation to pursue fine careers specifically associated with the life of the Indies. The elder son ran a bicycle shop in Makassar.[164] His brother followed in his father's footsteps: he supervised large cattle ranches on the estates of Batu Bassi, Salantang and Aloro near Maros, close to Makassar, an area the size of 1,572 *bouw* (about 1,116 hectares) that he held on long-term lease. He also became the director of the agricultural company named Marana.[165] Furthermore, he could use the title of Raja Laut, a distinction attached to his honorary membership of the Makassar Sailing Club. The proas of his grandfather and great-uncle were no longer used as trading vessels but transformed into pleasure boats for wealthy Europeans. This last Raja Laut of the Mesman family married Emilia Elverina Frederik, who, when Indonesia became independent, chose to acquire Indonesian citizenship and took up fish-farming. The fifth son of Eugenie and Alexander married Lady Jenny Mary Goldman, and this brings us back to the old distinguished European families of Java. Several descendants of the Mesmans, who had once been granted estates in South Sulawesi under the British Raffles, chose to become Indonesian citizens when the country became independent in 1949. Today there are still Mesmans working on the Marana Estate, near Makassar.

CHAPTER 6

Rank and Status

Newcomers

L ocal European families such as the Mesmans, Brugmans, Trouerbachs and Volls occupied the government ranks in Makassar throughout the 19th century. Their histories were far from unique. Throughout the Dutch East Indies, local families supplied men to staff the offices of government. Many civil servants with a background in the Indies became high-ranking members of the Binnenlands Bestuur. As a consequence, this administrative corps, the backbone of colonial authority in the Dutch East Indies, should in no way be seen as a foreign elite; rather, most of the civil servants it employed were born in the Indies.[1] It is far from accurate to assume that the *inlandse kinderen*, as the Europeans born in the East Indies were often called, were excluded from higher posts in the civil service, and that their position could be described as a hereditary caste of mere clerks. This holds not only for the period when the Dutch East India Company held sway, but for the 19th century too.

The tradition of employing men from the Indies predominantly in the civil service began in the 17th century. The directors of the Dutch East India Company did not specify the qualifications that their personnel must possess. Anyone able to read and write was, in theory, qualified for an office job. Of course, it was different for those aiming at higher functions. From the early days of the VOC it was noticeable that Europeans who were local-born — that is, not born in Europe — experienced greater difficulty in attaining the very highest positions, such as councillor of the Indies or governor in one of the local stations spread across Asia. But it was never a hard policy of the VOC to exclude Mestizos, let alone whites born in the Indies, from its ranks. The supply of new personnel from the Netherlands was insufficient, while in the Asian settlements there was a reserve of Europeans to be found among the descendants of

184

company employees. Particularly in the outlying provinces, most of the company employees were *inlandse kinderen*, or "local-born"; many of them rose to high positions in the Dutch East Indies.

The return of Dutch rule in the East Indies in 1816 brought with it a large stream of soldiers from Europe but relatively few civil servants. It is not known exactly how many newcomers arrived in the East Indies during this period. Most of them were part of the expeditionary troops sent from the Netherlands, who in 1815–1817 numbered 5,360 officers and soldiers.[2] But it would be a long time before the number of newcomers in the East Indies reached the level of 1700. In terms of employment, the consequences were not great for the old hands in the Indies, or indeed for those who were born there. Many seasoned employees continued to work for the new government, and some were appointed to significant positions thanks to their knowledge and experience. After 1816, however, new ideas began to spread about how to organise colonial administration. Back in the Netherlands, after the fall of Napoleon, a monarchy had been established under the House of Orange. The VOC had been nationalised in 1796, and the new Dutch government was finally able to shape its own colonial policy for the East Indies. The two most important changes that would have a long-term effect on life in the Indies concerned the strengthening of the national (that is, Dutch) character of colonial government, and the attempt to base its appointments on qualifications rather than on the mechanisms of protection and favouritism. But despite all the rhetoric about professionalisation, the number of newcomers remained small, and protection continued to be the main vehicle for a career in the Indies. It would take many decades before the new developments percolated through to all the provinces and layers of the civil service.

There were huge differences between the administrative centre in Batavia and the smaller posts elsewhere in the Indonesian archipelago. This had already been the case under the VOC. The personnel serving in the outlying posts consisted of a small number of civil servants from Europe and a large number of locally recruited office workers. It was to Batavia that most newcomers initially came, and also where the Totoks (newcomers) dominated. According to the register of adult European males in the Batavian residency in 1819–1820, about two-thirds of the adult men came from Europe, and two-thirds of the group had arrived since 1816.[3] The high percentage of Totoks in the register might well reflect a certain carelessness or bias on the part of the clerk recording the figures. At any rate, it looks as if the poorer classes were not recorded; these included the impoverished Mestizos and the Mardijkers. The numbers are also evidence of the unusual situation in Batavia. Just as in previous centuries, the town was a depot providing soldiers and civil servants for settlements throughout the Indies. Thus, many members of Batavian families left their birthplace and fanned out across the Indonesian archipelago. Incidentally, it is worth noting that the various categories of Europeans — the Indies-born, the old hands from Europe, and the recent newcomers — were spread quite evenly over the various professions. Wealth and high rank were not the preserve of Totoks. There were many newcomers among the higher civil servants, but they are also to be found listed, for instance, in jobs such as caretaker in a hospital, as office clerk or as artisan. On the other hand, many of the men born in Batavia are registered as having "no occupation". This did not mean they were unemployed, but that they had sources of income other than paid employment. Among these were the immensely wealthy landowners such as the six Van Riemsdijk brothers, owners of a vast estate named Campea, who lived off their land, independent of any employer.

In all other places apart from Batavia, the local element was the most important, and many of the top positions in local government were held by Indies-born Europeans. This was very evident in Semarang, on Java's north coast, the largest town in the Dutch East Indies after Batavia.[4] In 1819–1820 there were 609 adult European men there (excluding soldiers on active service). About 40 per cent of this group were newcomers, that is, born in Europe; but, unlike in Batavia, the majority of them had arrived in the Indies before 1816. There was a remarkably high number of retired military personnel in Semarang — no fewer than 70 — while other professional groups also contained retired soldiers and officers. The military veterans were strongly represented among the 171 men registered as Burghers. Since the military was so significant a part of colonial rule, retired soldiers were a common feature of all stations in the Indies; but as we will see, the traces and the troubles of retired soldiers would make their presence felt in Semarang for many years.

The number of newcomers to Semarang after the Dutch regained control of the East Indies was small compared with Batavia: a mere 65. Quite clearly, not all of them were government employees; there were only seven civil servants, one *commies* (senior clerk) and four (junior) clerks. Others found jobs as merchants, and there were a few Burghers. Local-born persons indisputably filled the majority of jobs among the lowest ranks of colonial administration. Among the petty clerks in Semarang, 52 were born in Asia compared with six born in Europe.

But also in higher government ranks there were old hands, both from Europe and from the Indies, who had earned their spurs and occupied prominent posts. One such was the resident of Semarang, Jacobus de Bruyn, who had arrived in Java in 1803. Two out of the four assistant-residents had been born in Asia, although not in Semarang: Jan Claassen was born in Paleacatte (Pulicat), a VOC settlement in India that the Dutch had lost in 1795. He had come to Java in 1804. The other assistant-resident was Johan Arnaud Renoldes Caspersz, born in Colombo and probably returned to the East after a period in the Netherlands. Furthermore, a member of the Court of Justice and the hospital director were also born in the Indies.

The local element was even greater outside the civil service. The only large concentrations of civil servants were in the Batavian departments of the central government. The number of Burghers in places outside Batavia far exceeded the number of clerks and civil servants. Jobs in government posts were strictly limited, especially in local administration. In 1822 in Surabaya, for instance, there were only 18 Europeans, 3 Javanese writers, 1 Chinese clerk and 38 Javanese supervisors, foremen and coolies working in the resident's office.[5] Town councils did not exist. There were many local variations in the composition of the civil service and the distribution of jobs among the different categories of Europeans. In 1826, 64 civil servants were employed in Makassar, the largest settlement outside Java.[6] Only 16 of them had been born in Europe. In contrast to the situation in Javanese towns, most had arrived after 1816. With only one exception, all the newcomers held well-paid functions, earning a monthly salary of more than 100 guilders. Incidentally, there were also 13 men from the Indies who had reached similar high positions; one of them was Johannes David Mcsman, who held the post of deputy secretary to the government of Makassar.

Despite their variations, the statistics from the various towns and cities of the East Indies contradict the widely held picture that the Totoks from Europe slowly supplanted the local-born civil servants after 1816. The modest inflow of newcomers from the Netherlands did little to disturb job opportunities in the civil service for Indies-born men. Those in lower positions, however, encountered a certain amount of competition from newcomers. In 1840 Steven Adriaan Buddingh, one of the directors of the Parapattan Orphanage in Batavia, wrote: "Formerly one only saw 'Portuguese' or native clerks at work here but today you find at every desk either a Netherlander, an Englishman, a Scot or a German".[7] This was an exaggeration, because the number of local-born clerks remained as high as ever. Indeed, a visitor attending a public sale of household effects in Batavia in 1845 remarked that almost all the personnel were Portuguese — both the clerk sitting at the table and the two auctioneers.[8] Although the group termed "Portuguese" gradually fades from the picture, public auction rooms remained a place where many local-born Europeans found employment, just as they did in, for instance, Orphans' Chambers and Courts of Justice. Auctions, too, had become a general pattern before 1800, when Mardijkers would often hold such functions. But the conviction with which Buddingh makes his assertion suggests that migration certainly had some impact on the civil service population and on the general atmosphere in the colony.

As before, and for many years to come, top positions would often be given to Netherlanders, although there were also numerous Indische men to be found in the upper echelons and many more in the lower ranks. There was no question of a huge surge of applicants for the civil service, in the way there would be during the last decades of the century. Indeed, in the 1830s it was difficult to recruit suitable personnel, and offices often had to resort to employing ex-military.[9] Most of the local-born Europeans made a living in some other manner. More than half the European men in Semarang worked as private entrepreneurs, tradesmen or shopkeepers. The urban economies offered opportunities to establish trading offices and shops, despite competition from both Chinese and local artisans and entrepreneurs. There were a large number of tailors among the Europeans, as well as clockmakers, jewellers and people providing coach and cart rental services. Most of the jobs were of a fairly modest nature. The colonial economy did not provide exciting opportunities for Europeans to win fame and fortune outside a career in government. The exceptions to this, as we have seen, were the great landholders of West Java and the entrepreneurs in the Principalities.

Competition

In the 1820s and 1830s there arose an ever-louder and more insistent call to improve the quality of civil servants in the Indies. Notions culled from Napoleonic times regarding the professionalisation of the administrative corps gradually infiltrated the civil service in the Dutch East Indies. The first new regulations date from 1825, when the civil servants of the Indies were divided into three grades, each requiring a further level of qualifications. The lowest grade comprised petty clerks and minor civil servants and extended to the rank of *commies*, or senior clerk;

next came the jobs of higher civil servants, such as those in the Binnenlands Bestuur; at the top, there was a special category of juridical positions requiring a degree in law. The regulations were, in the first place, directed towards rooting out incompetent fortune-hunters coming from the Netherlands; however, the changes turned out to have a spin-off for other civil servants, including those born in the Indies.[10] No longer was the governor-general empowered to grant promotions above the rank of *hoofdcommies* (chief senior clerk); he had to submit candidates to the king of the Netherlands. The governor-general could also recommend persons from the rank of *commies*, or a lower rung, to the minister in the Netherlands, who — "for their exceptional services" — would grant them a *radicaal*, a certificate stating their suitability for appointment into covenanted positions.[11] The *radicaal* was conferred by royal decree and enabled one to stream through to the highest posts.

Initially, things moved slowly: old habits die hard. But gradually, and after some admonitions from The Hague, the specifications assumed a more clearly defined shape. The driving force behind the improvement in the quality of civil servants in the Indies was Jean-Chrétien Baud, interim governor-general (1833–1836) and later minister of the colonies (1839–1848). He also wanted The Hague to have a firmer grip on the appointments policy for the East Indies. It was he who compiled the regulations of 1825 for appointing civil servants, introducing the *radicaal*.[12] He aimed to create a professional and loyal government apparatus. In his vision there was no place for "old-style" civil servants — local officials who had climbed their way up the administrative ladder using connections, family ties and possibly the occasional backhanders. Baud felt particularly strongly that the corps of the Binnenlands Bestuur would be ill served by Indo-European civil servants who could not command the necessary respect from the Javanese. Clearly, Baud had little confidence in the *inlandse kinderen*. Yet this is curious, for on two occasions he married women from the elite of Batavia. His first wife was Wilhelmina Henriëtte Senn van Basel, scion of a prominent Batavian family. She was a daughter from the third marriage of Willem Adriaan Senn van Basel — to Theodora Jacoba van Riemsdijk — and one of his 12 children. In 1833 Baud married again, this time Ursula Susanna van Braam, also from a family prominent among the Batavian elite for several generations. Both Baud's wives were well educated and would certainly not have been labelled *inlandse kinderen*. It was apparently not the colour of one's skin — but one's social milieu and upbringing — that determined one's marriageability.

Things did not stop with the introduction of an elite corps within the civil service. In 1842 a new institute for the training of civil servants in the East Indies opened its doors in Delft. The Netherlands government felt that the Dutch East Indies would be best served by a corps of civil servants trained in the motherland. The new college emphasised linguistic skills (in Malay, Javanese and Dutch), together with ethnology, indigenous law and geometry.[13] The courses did not delve deep; a fairly superficial knowledge was considered sufficient. More important than the details of the curriculum were the possible negative consequences of "Delft" for the careers of Europeans who lived in the Indies. The new regulations appeared to formalise and strengthen the old custom of excluding from the highest government functions Indies-born people who had not enjoyed an education in the Netherlands. But, in fact, the introduction of the "Delft diploma" did not have disastrous results on the career prospects of local-born civil servants. The number of students who completed the Delft course in the first years was so tiny that the civil servants then employed in the Indies scarcely noticed their existence; before 1850, only 27 candidates acquired the Delft diploma.[14]

The new regulation underscored the long-felt need of parents in the Indies to send their children to Europe at an early age to be educated. This had already been the practice for two centuries. There was a heavy price to pay: lengthy separation of parents and children. The problem and the pain for families in the Indies lay not so much in the fact that they ran the risk of being outstripped by newcomers — which was rarely the case — as in the expense, both emotional and financial, of sending their children to be educated in the Netherlands. This is evidenced by the remark of an anonymous author writing on education in the Indies: "One of the most unpleasant and difficult experiences of the Europeans living in the Dutch East Indies is undoubtedly that they are forced to send their children to Europe when they are eight or ten years old, in order that they may receive a reasonable education."[15] The author went on to report that several residents of Batavia had planned to jointly set up a secondary school. Little more was heard of this scheme. It was to be another 26 years before the first secondary school was founded in Java. Until then, and afterwards too, young children — mostly boys, but some girls — were sent to the Netherlands, where they lodged with relatives or acquaintances and attended Dutch schools. With improved travel links, this occurred to an ever-increasing extent. Naturally, such a costly education in the Netherlands was a privilege of the more well-to-do. It was estimated in 1848, for instance, that it cost about 14,200 guilders to send a boy to the Netherlands from the age of eight until his graduation from the Delft Academy.[16]

It is often suggested that Baud's reforms had the effect of excluding Indies-born men from the upper ranks of the civil service.[17] But we may well ask who were most affected by the requirement that civil servants hold the Delft diploma. It was not the less well-to-do Europeans who — even before the introduction of the academy examination — stood little chance of working their way up in the civil service. Nor was it the better-off, who could afford to send their children to the Netherlands. Rather, the effect of Baud's measures was more psychological than an actual impediment for the European citizens of the Indies. Considering that the governor-general, with or without the mediation of the resident or anyone else, was entitled to recommend a civil servant for promotion to a higher rank even if he did not possess the Delft diploma, it would seem that — as before — good connections and patronage remained the prevailing prerequisites for building a career.

What irked people in the Indies most was the tutelage by the government in the motherland. Governor-General Jan Jacob Rochussen (1845–1851), himself a newcomer, saw quite clearly that the pronounced Dutch-centrism of Baud's policy did not go down well in the Dutch colony. He warned the minister about the simmering discontent in Batavia, which he summed up under the heading "Liberal Sentiments". Those born in the Indies could well become estranged from the mother country and, following the example of the former South American colonies, demand greater autonomy for the East Indies.[18] Rochussen was far more accommodating than the inflexible Baud and could sympathise far more readily with the disgruntled citizens.[19]

Rochussen was, in fact, highly concerned about the growing rumbles of discontent among the European citizenry, and especially so when this erupted into protests in May 1848. After this brief explosion he took careful stock of society in the Indies. The European community consisted, as he saw it, of two groups. There were those born in Europe and those born in Asia, who had their roots there and whom he alluded to as "Creoles". The group whom Rochussen terms "old hands" grew more and more to resemble the Creoles: the longer they stayed in the Indies, "the more they become severed from their mother country and grow to see the Indies as their fatherland".[20] Furthermore, there were the "coloureds", who could be subdivided into the Portuguese — Rochussen says they were the descendants of Portuguese men and female slaves from Africa or Alfurs from the Moluccas — and the children of European fathers and native women. Rochussen expressed considerable concern about this group of coloureds; he reported, "the natives hold them in contempt and the Europeans look down on them; they are the veritable outcasts of Javanese society".[21] This harsh judgment reflected the conclusions of Minister Baud. In 1838 — when he was councillor of state — Baud had written to the minister of the colonies saying, "those of Javanese birth despise — either openly or covertly — people of mixed blood and those born out of wedlock".[22] There are no concrete examples to indicate this was indeed the case, but it served Baud's purpose to suggest it was so.

Baud thought that *inlandse kinderen* should not be granted the *radicaal* entitling them to promotion to the upper ranks of the civil service, and Rochussen assured him that he would act in accordance with these wishes.[23] Despite this, many a European born and bred in the Indies gained the *radicaal* during this period. The governor-general made frequent use of his discretionary power in such cases. In the 1830s the number of candidates submitted for the certificate by the governor-general was so large that back in The Hague people grew anxious lest there would not be any need to send out civil servants to the Indies. Between 1834 and 1838 there were 114 nominations for civil servant, only 19 of whom were sent abroad by the king. There were at least 64 nominees from the government of the Indies, while the king made another 21 appointments on his own account. In total, 51 sons of civil servants and officers in the Indies, and 11 ex-military entered the civil service along with 22 "fortune seekers" from Europe who had successfully competed for a post in the Dutch East Indies.[24] The lobbies in the Indies were fully active and managed to turn the recent nominations regulation into a virtually dead letter.

Thus, the image of the Indies-born civil servant being ousted by newcomers is not an accurate one. A survey taken in April 1849 of the personnel in Semarang shows that people born in the Indies were still occupying the middle and higher ranks.[25] However, the route followed by local-born men was often long and tedious. Take, for instance, Henri Léonce van Polanen Petel, born in Batavia in 1815, who started out as a clerk in one of the government offices in Batavia when he was 19 years old. What exactly his work was, we can only guess. Probably he stood for hours at a high desk, his fingers stained with black ink, day in, day out, for four years, copying lists from registries and records. Gradually Van Polanen Petel climbed higher up the ladder, becoming successively "supernumerary civil servant third class" and in 1846 "inspector second class" in Kendal near Semarang. The previous year he had been granted the *radicaal*, which qualified him to apply to the higher ranks of the civil service. He then earned 275 guilders a month, not a fortune, but still not to be sneezed at — and he had as yet no children to support. Van Polanen Petel had grown up in the Indies; this made him, in the eyes of gentlemen of Batavia and The Hague, not so much unacceptable as "less suitable" to perform the duties required in the upper ranks of government. A sojourn in the Netherlands, even if it was not to study for the Delft diploma, would surely provide him with the polish he required. The secretary for the residency of Semarang, for instance, Johan Cornelis de Kock van Leeuwen, who enjoyed the generous salary of 600 guilders a month, had spent 11 years as a young man in the Netherlands. The resident stated this explicitly in the records, adding a note that he considered De Kock qualified to fill a position of higher responsibility.

Clearly, many of the Europeans born in the Indies continued to make a career in the government. The annual list of nominations sent by the governor-general to the king of the Netherlands contained dozens, if not hundreds, of candidates. And so in September 1845, there were 218 civil servants, one of whom was Henri Léonce van Polanen Petel, who in this way were granted the *radicaal*. During the following years there were hundreds more, most of them in the wake of the protest movement of May 1848. In December of that year, 221 men from the Indies were granted the *radicaal* on recommendation. Until 1862, just before the abolition of the diploma in 1864, the king appointed 84 people to the position of civil servant holding the *radicaal* first class, 108 second class and 13 third class. Beside this, the governor-general recommended 16 civil servants for the *radicaal* first class, 360 for the second class and 318 for the third class.[26] The qualification "first class" was used only for functions where an academic degree in law was required, that is, for the highest juridical posts. Those civil servants would be recruited in the Netherlands since there was no university in the Dutch East Indies. But in the other two classes (second and third) there was a predominance of civil servants who had obtained the *radicaal* on recommendation, without having followed the Delft curriculum.

The (theoretical) preference for candidates who had completed their course in Delft for the higher civil service diploma does not necessarily mean that the Dutch government preferred to have its administrative corps composed of Europeans born in the Netherlands and presumably white. In fact, the majority of students at the Delft Academy came from the Indies. Indeed, at the time of the Delft monopoly many children and students born in the East Indies went to the Netherlands to study. Some of them already had experience as civil servants in the Indies. A typical "son of the Indies" was Charles Christiaan Tromp, governor of Celebes, whom we have already encountered in Makassar. Born in Batavia in 1830, he started his career as a clerk in the General Secretariat of the colonial government. Five years later — he was by now a senior clerk second class — he set off for Delft, where he gained the certificate for higher civil service. This meant he could now climb higher in the bureaucratic hierarchy, first becoming a senior clerk first class, then secretary to the residency of Surabaya, then assistant-resident in Batavia and Tangerang, resident in Borneo and Kedu, and finally, in 1876, governor of Celebes. His obituary in the newspaper *Celebes Courant* on 30 December 1884 announced: "It will come as a surprise to many of you to learn that Mr Tromp was an *inlands kind*".[27] Neither his family background, his education, nor his career identified him as Indische, born in the Indies. And there were many like him.

In the second half of the 1840s the regulations regarding the appointment of civil servants became more strict. In 1846 the Dutch government announced that civil servants at third-class level would be excluded from certain functions. An exception might be made for those who had arrived in the Indies before 1 July 1843 or who had been recruited and hired in the Indies. All these civil servants, of course, hoped to be granted the *radicaal* at second-class level, and before long applications for this certificate were pouring in. Many of these requests could not be granted, which produced great bitterness in the offices where applicants worked.[28] Governor-General Rochussen wrote to Baud in March 1847 that when the decision concerning the *radicaal* was made known, he had observed some commotion among the *inlandse kinderen*. He also reported that there had been gatherings of malcontents. Although he viewed the discontent in the first place as a possible cause of public disturbance, at the same time he realised that the colonial government was responsible for the lot of the "sons of the Indies"; he spoke of the government's responsibility to address their needs as a "constitutional necessity".[29]

Anxious fathers and voices of rancour

No one could possibly object to having well-trained bureaucrats. What they could object to was having a place of study situated on the other side of the world, and high barriers to overcome before acquiring a superior rank. Rochussen had rightly observed that government actions regarding the *radicaal*, and the absence of good education in the Indies, touched a raw nerve. Discontent simmered. It exploded in May 1848, when it was made known that King Willem II had dismissed the conservative cabinet in the Netherlands and announced far-reaching constitutional reform. Minister Baud's days in the government were clearly numbered. The power shift in the Netherlands acted as a catalyst for the situation in the Indies. Discontent boiled over. Reports reached the East Indies of the revolutions in Austria, France and Germany in April and infused the critics and malcontents in the towns on Java with a spirit of activism. On 23 April 1848 the Protestant cleric and editor of the journal *Tijdschrift voor Neêrland's Indië* Wolter Robert baron van Hoëvell wrote to the Amsterdam scholar Pieter Johannes Veth that a "general tension and nervous excitement" filled Batavia.[30] The rumours from Europe made the people in the Indies speculate about a possible abolition of the detested *radicaal*. And there were more radical spirits who demanded freedom of the press and a form of people's representation throughout the Dutch East Indies.

Reverend Van Hoëvell, a known critic of the colonial government, was an obvious candidate to act as mouthpiece of the protest movement. He had come in 1837 to be Protestant minister for the Malay congregation in Batavia and belonged to the upper crust of colonial society. His work, however, brought him into close contact with the poorer classes of Batavia's Christian population. He came to consider the East Indies as his second fatherland.[31] During the ten years that he lived in the Indies he made impassioned appeals for liberalisation of the economy and the administration. More than once he had clashes with the government because of the editorial policy of his newspaper *Tijdschrift voor Neêrland's Indië*. With a certain hesitation, Van Hoëvell accepted the invitation from the progressive president of the Board of Property Holders, Johannes Theodorus Canter Visscher, to take on the leadership of the protest movement.[32] Governor-General Rochussen, for his part, thought it would be appropriate to allow "twenty respectable inhabitants and family men" to meet in order to discuss and draw up a petition, which could be presented to the king of the Netherlands.[33] At a later date, Van Hoëvell claimed that Rochussen and the resident of Batavia, Pieter van Rees, were not very much in favour of the *radicaal*, which explained their tolerant attitude towards the events of May 1848.[34] Whatever his opinion about the *radicaal*, Rochussen evidently estimated that tensions could be relieved by allowing a meeting for discussion.

Illustration 29   The city of Batavia had a society named *De Harmonie* (Harmony). It was here that a large gathering was held on 22 May 1848 to protest against the inadequacy of the educational facilities for Europeans in the Indies. Across the way from the Harmonie buildings was the tailor's shop of Oger Frères, established in 1823. Thirty years after the 1848 demonstration, the street scene here was still unchanged.
[Lithograph in: C.Th. Deeleman, *Bataviaasch album, ca.* 1879.]

The idea was to hold a gathering with a small number of concerned citizens on 22 May, in the hall of the Batavian Society for Arts and Sciences, to discuss the plan for a petition to the king. Permission was given for the meeting by Governor-General Rochussen, to whom Van Hoëvell had personally explained the plan, although the former said that no public invitations should be sent out. Van Hoëvell promised to drop, for the time being, questions concerning freedom of the press and popular representation. The points up for discussion would be limited to the *radicaal* system and education in the Indies. The cleric and the governor-general were in agreement — the meeting should be dignified and correct.

Meanwhile, however, the spirit of liberalism had taken possession of the president of the Court of Justice, Pelgrim Charles Ardesch. He announced, also in a letter to the resident, that he would take the opportunity of the meeting to raise the matters not only of the Delft diploma but also of freedom of the press. Copies of his letter circulated through Batavia, raising expectations and stirring up excitement.[35] The atmosphere in the city was restless on the eve of the meeting — at least, in Batavian terms. Police reports state that there were local gatherings "in the old city and in coloured neighbourhoods", where shouts were heard of "*Semuanya radikal*", meaning "The *radicaal* for everyone".[36] Rumours even circulated that there would be a march to the governor's palace to present the request in person to Governor-General Rochussen.[37] A great number of residents wanted to attend the meeting, and it was decided to hold it in a larger hall — in the building of the club named De Harmonie. When the hour of the meeting arrived, about 500 people streamed into the meeting hall. According to a later report from Rochussen, they included about 300 "coloureds". Van Hoëvell reported that there were "many of the most prominent citizens of Batavia as well as large numbers from the poorer classes".[38] For the small city of Batavia, this was an exceptional attendance; at least one-third of all the European men from the city had turned up at the Harmonie.

The meeting attracted far more people than was expected, but one could hardly speak of revolutionary zeal. The moderates, including Van Hoëvell, had not come to wave banners and shout slogans. Van Hoëvell was well aware that his position in the colony was vulnerable, and although he advocated constitutional reform, he kept aloof from the more radical intentions of some of the activists. After all, he had promised Rochussen not to bring up matters of a keenly political nature. Thus, after a short speech in which he explained the general purpose of the meeting and the proposed petition to the king, Van Hoëvell left the Harmonie. But after his departure, more radical elements took over. Among them were two lawyers, a shopkeeper and an ex-military man turned civil servant, all of them outside government service, together with some others who were not named. Chaos reigned; there was no clear statement of aims, and no one emerged as spokesman or leader. Discontent among those present was shushed by Ardesch, who agreed to hold a second meeting. This proved a palliative to the angry voices, which soon died down. Rumours spread that mounted troops were at the ready — the army barracks lay just across the road from the Harmonie — and gradually the movement petered out and the crowds dispersed. By nine in the evening, quiet had returned to the city streets.[39]

The movement of May 1848 would become a *cause célèbre* stamped into the history and memory of the Dutch East Indies. But what, in fact, happened during those few days of agitated expectation? There was certainly no organised movement, and the commotion soon died down. The most tangible result was the petition sent to King Willem of the Netherlands; after the gathering in the Harmonie, it lay there for a few days collecting signatures. Not all those who had attended the meeting signed the petition; there were only 215 signatures when the petition sailed off to the Netherlands on 25 May. In the town of Surabaya there had been a similar meeting, and residents also drew up a petition for the king, requesting, in somewhat pleonastic language, "education for their children and an improved outlook for them in the future".[40]

The major request of the signatories was for improved educational facilities and the abolition of the monopoly of Delft as a training institute for the higher ranks of the civil service. Education in the Indies was indeed below par and was treated by the government there like a sad stepchild. The increasing demands on the training of government personnel caused considerable anxiety among European families in the Indies. It was extremely expensive to send a child to be educated in the Netherlands and it meant years of separation for parents and children. In 1839 the Indies government chief committee for education had pleaded for improvement in the miserable state of education in the colony and had proposed establishing a grammar school in Batavia.[41] The idea came, however, exactly at the time the Dutch government in The Hague made education in Europe conditional for the higher civil service ranks in the colonies. Other complaints and demands did not make it into the Batavian petition. The petition also refrained from mentioning questions concerning popular representation for Indische citizens, or freedom of the press. Another missing complaint concerned the pensions ruling. New regulations had been introduced in 1837 whereby the pension of civil servants who did not hold the *radicaal* for the higher ranks was reduced by half. Nor were they entitled to half-pay. This, of course, directly affected the civil servants in the lower and middle ranks.

Once we understand the background of the signatories, the nature of the movement becomes clear. The binding factor was neither country of birth nor skin colour. Looking at the 215 signatories of the first petition, we find that 91 were born in Europe, 85 in Asia, one elsewhere, and in the case of the remaining 38 the place of birth is unknown.[42] Thus, it would appear that most signatories were born in Europe. Almost all the petitioners held government jobs; the most important group of the private sector were 26 merchants. Most of the signatories had a strong attachment to the Dutch East Indies. Many of them were married to women born in the Indies and were concerned about opportunities for their sons, rather than for themselves. This also appears from the fact that many of the petitioners held high positions. Of the 85 Asia-born signatories who were employed by the government, half held the *radicaal* diploma. It is noteworthy that many of the signatories came from the same departments in the civil service: the legal departments were well represented, as was the department of finances. In contrast, clerks numbered only 32 signatories.[43] In conclusion, the protest meeting had attracted several kinds of discontented citizens, but the petition was by and large a concern of civil servants from the upper echelons. The 1848 demands voiced the concerns of anxious fathers.[44] And it was certainly something typical of the cities of the north coast of Java, with their high numbers of civil servants, where questions concerning *radicaal*, education and state pensions were anxiously debated.

Those May days, however, rumbled with something more than parental concern. There was a second petition, which is generally ignored in the reports about the period. Unlike the first petition, this one was addressed to the governor-general and was almost steaming with bitterness and frustration. The signatories remained anonymous and hid behind a collective name: "Natives of Java".[45] They were particularly incensed against one member of the Council of the Indies, Joan Cornelis Reijnst, who had shown himself to be an outright enemy of the *inlandse kinderen*. The petitioners claimed that he was "greatly opposed to anyone born in the Indies and we consider him to be our chief enemy". But their problems went far deeper than the prejudice of one member of the Council of the Indies and were concerned with the general treatment by the colonial administration. These "Natives of Java" wished to be treated as genuine Europeans, "for those who despise us must also despise every Netherlander, considering that we are their descendants". Not until the conclusion does the petition demand, in two brief sentences, the abolition of the *radicaal* and the "annihilation of the Delft Academy". The petition voiced a sentiment that had never before been aired on so public a scale; it was the burning resentment felt against "Hollanders". Such feelings had certainly been around for some time, but they had seldom appeared in print; there was, after all, neither a free press, nor the right of popular representation, nor the freedom to hold public gatherings.

There was, in fact, a third petition, namely, one from Ardesch and a few of his supporters, made to the Netherlands Lower House of Parliament, in which they requested a general liberalisation of the government of the Indies. They asked for freedom of the press, the end of autocratic forms of government in the Indies, the withdrawal of the monopoly held by the NHM (Netherlands Trading Company), the abolition of slavery and a thorough reform of the makeshift Indies currency system.[46] However, only a few dared or wished to subscribe to these pleas for far-reaching change. They were choked in the dusty alleyways of Batavia, unable to survive in an atmosphere where political debate was absent and the authorities unwilling to consider radical reform.

Even for contemporaries, an assessment of the nature and impact of "May 1848" was a confusing challenge. Was it a protest on behalf of the elite, or the lower classes, of the Indo-European community? In later times, the meeting of 22 May 1848 would often be seen as the first utterance of Indo-European solidarity, a precursor of the political activities that were to develop after 1900, and an instance of Indo-European resistance to official discrimination.[47] The action, however, had received support from all levels of the European community in the Indies, including the whites. The chaotic evening in the Harmonie would seem to have united all the discontents: those who harboured resentment against the diploma system, the appalling state of education in the Indies, or the privileges of the newcomers. At the same time, the May movement revealed to the circumspect observer the chasm that rent colonial society. The events showed with great precision the social fault lines: between those who could reasonably expect advantages from better educational facilities in the Indies and from a just appointments system — and who were thus happy to sign the petition to the king — and those who had little hope of social betterment. The dividing line was not one of skin colour but of class and (civil service) rank. The uprising of 1848 was not — as some have later enthusiastically wished to see it — a movement rejecting discrimination against Indo-Europeans; it opposed discrimination against anyone born in the Indies. It was, in fact, an expression of Indische particularism, not of Indo-European solidarity.

The confusion and misconception is certainly understandable. In his report, Rochussen described the May meeting as having a strongly Indo-European character. He estimated that about 300 of the 500 present were "coloureds". He writes that there were "a few so-called Sinjos and *blaauwtjes*" ("blue-hued", a common invective for Indo-Europeans) who "shouted and heckled a bit" and "did not understand in the slightest what the meeting was about". The government was not very sympathetic towards the bickerings of low-ranking Indo-Europeans. The lower classes were simply not expected to speak up to defend their interests or voice their frustrations. Rochussen considered the "coloureds" as revolutionary troublemakers who had been attracted to the meeting by vague rumours but had no clear policy or plan of their own. The governor-general reported that "a large number of *Liplaps*" (another condescending term for Indo-Europeans) had concealed a kris in their garments or had sword canes and were even plotting to embroil the Chinese — a threat that still caused panic a good century after the Chinese uprising and the pogroms of 1740.[48] Rochussen, who had not attended the conclave, blamed all the radical noises on the "coloureds", while people like Ardesch, a man born on the sandy plains of the central Netherlands, with a wife from the peat lands of the same country, was trumpeting far more revolutionary ideas than some of the dissatisfied "Natives of Java".

A deep-seated bourgeois fear of the rabble had Rochussen in its grip. What is more, he had a personal interest in painting a pessimistic picture of the revolutionary tendencies of the mob. Since the government change in the Netherlands earlier in 1848, he had no political friends there, and he found himself in Batavia confronting almost the entire elite. Rochussen was well aware that internal squabbling and the spirit of revolution would weaken colonial authority. Consequently, in the weeks after the noisy 22 May, the protagonists and those who had voiced the most radical ideas, people such as Canter Visscher and Ardesch, were only reprimanded by Rochussen. He could do no more, "since there were no terms on which to adopt sterner measures".[49] The movement seemed to be no more than a brief outburst, but the Indies government, and Rochussen especially, was deeply affected by the events. He had already pointed out the possible threat from the Europeans in the Indies who felt less loyalty to the motherland in Europe than did the Totoks. Although the protest had not been directed against the colonial government, nevertheless the events around 22 May served to confirm Rochussen's deeper fears.

A distinctly "Indische" voice

May 1848 represents the dawning of a self-awareness among Indies-born Europeans. Despite the different motives of the Batavians who took part, the "May Movement" sounded the first notes of political emancipation of the local-born Europeans. In years to come, when there was open debate about the lower classes in the Indies and the condescending atti-tude of the Netherlands government, there would be repeated references to the brief but significant uprising of May 1848. In the 1870s and

1880s, in particular, among the first voices of Indo-European nationalism, journalists and pamphleteers would hark back to events in the revolutionary year of 1848, in which they preferred to detect chiefly "the voice of the Indo-Europeans". Opponents, too, contributed to this interpretation of events. Arch-conservatives such as the retired naval officer Arnoldus Hermanus Bisschop Grevelink considered the movement "no more nor less than a ridiculous display of political charlatanism" largely supported by Sinjos (Indo-Europeans). This naval officer was so scornful about the Sinjos that it would be insulting to report his words — were it not that his views echoed those often heard in certain circles. He spoke of "degeneration of the blood and a highly defective formation of the skeleton, while [the children] brought up by *baboes* (ayahs) or native mothers learn no other language than the miserable Malay; they thus lack any mental exercise and the Dutch language remains foreign to them so that they never learn to think in it or to express themselves fluently, let alone pronounce it correctly".[50] Apparently both the conservatives and the champions of the Indo-European cause would ascribe a Mestizo character to the May movement. In the 40 years following the 1848 demonstration, opinion-forming in the Indies was to grow more political, while social differences became worded in racial terms.

That, however, still lay in the future. The first reaction of the colonial government to the May action was repressive. Two days after the meeting in the Harmonie club, the resident issued a decree banning further gatherings.[51] And Van Hoëvell, who had long been a thorn in the flesh of the colonial government, left the colony — not on direct government orders, but under pressure from the church council, whose board chairman was a member of the Council of the Indies.[52] The May uprising had certainly jangled some sensitive nerves in the governor-general's offices and in The Hague. In December 1848 Rochussen sent a request that 22 signatories of the petition (born in Asia) be granted the *radicaal*, as well as 199 others who were not signatories.[53] That was no small number and would mean that with a stroke of the pen almost 10 per cent of all the civil servants in the East Indies had been granted the *radicaal*. At the same time, Rochussen put the case for abolition of the pension clause and even that the Delft monopoly be expunged. He thought that a diploma from Delft should still grant preferential treatment but not that it should provide an exclusive privilege. He also voiced his views on the betterment of education in the East Indies.[54] Although his pleas had no immediate effect, at his insistence the ruling of 1837 regarding half-pay was rescinded and a few years later the ordinance (also from 1837) regarding the halving of pensions for civil servants without the *radicaal* was also repealed.

Rochussen's pliant attitude was initially scarcely shared by authorities in The Hague. Indeed, his actions in connection with the May uprising had even cost him the friendship of Baud (who had lost his minister's post as a result of the government reshuffle in favour of the Liberals). Baud's successor, Jules Constantijn Rijk, either did not wish or did not dare to introduce far-reaching policy changes. Nevertheless, change came shortly afterwards, in 1850. The new Minister of the Colonies, Charles Ferdinand Pahud, decided — *nota bene* on the advice of Baud — to abolish any discrimination based on skin colour for appointments to the Binnenlands Bestuur — although in fact the appointments regulations had never stipulated and certainly not enforced the complete exclusion of a candidate on racial grounds. This meant, however, abandoning any formal distinction between Europeans and *inlandse kinderen*.[55] It had little impact on the appointments practice in the Indies. The obligatory Delft diploma continued to exist — but the academy still failed to produce sufficient graduates, and the governor-general continued to grant dispensation to many civil servants on account of "services rendered".

On the other hand, increasingly louder voices were heard — undoubtedly inspired by the May events and the liberal wind blowing from The Hague — demanding better educational facilities and freedom of the press in the colony. During the 1850s, sweeping changes took place in these areas. After the Liberal turnabout in the Netherlands it was widely expected that in the Indies, following developments in the motherland, freedom of the press would soon be introduced. As a result, around 1853 newspapers began to be printed containing more than just advertisements and official news from Europe. Almost immediately, these newspapers and periodicals gave voice to Indische views, although most publishers were cautious about printing articles that might be too critical. Not surprisingly, the grievances felt by the European communities in the Indies were many, and people were eager to express them. The great majority of Europeans were, after all, born in the colony and had to struggle with problems of education and job opportunities. The discrimination against the local-born Europeans was fiercely heckled, and the motherland's indifference to what happened in the Indies was decried in no uncertain terms. The voices of criticism and protest that had marked the May movement could frequently be heard in newspaper articles and letters to the editor. Still echoing were the tones of the high-minded reformers, the anxious and frustrated civil servants, and the embittered men of small means. And a fourth note could now be heard: that of the paternalistic European, pleading the cause of the "children of the Indies".[56] Before long the newspapers became mouthpieces for primarily Indische sentiments; before much longer they voiced an Indo-European consciousness that they would steer onwards with ever-growing vigour through the coming decades.

The developments in the world of the Indies could also be observed in other colonies, and often far earlier. In every colonial society it was the press that formed the driving force behind the growing social and political consciousness of the lower classes and the localised European communities. In Ceylon in the 1830s a press developed in which Burghers and other descendants of Europeans were able to air their grievances. The *Colombo Journal*, a newspaper that first appeared in January 1832, almost immediately published an appeal to all the descendants of Netherlanders and Portuguese, to seek agricultural employment. The article was certainly not written by a Burgher, for an anonymous "writer" promptly replied that the Burghers had little choice left: "Many of us do occasionally writhe under the sway of 'insolence of office', but must admit to having no alternative." These Burghers, we read, were declared to be synonymous with "junior clerks". Lacking both capital and educational facilities, their only recourse was to take up office work.[57] Similar situations could be observed in other British colonies. In British India, where people were denied access to both higher and lower colonial ranks, the growth of the press stimulated an increasing group consciousness and led to the combined action of local civilians in Calcutta.[58] In 1830 between 600 and 700 "respectable East Indians" signed a petition that was sent to the British Parliament, in which they emphasised the fact that they were British, demanding the rights that belonged with this status. The petition had a history of ten years' struggle for improvement of educational facilities. Interestingly, similar complaints were also heard from the British colonies in the Caribbean, where the "free coloureds" had begun to take part in political activities in the 1830s.[59]

Contact between the various colonies scattered around the globe was minimal. Newspapers tended to be local — they wrote about events in their own colony or motherland and Europe, and they scarcely paid attention to other European communities in Asia or elsewhere. Not until the beginning of the 20th century would events in British India or the Philippines resonate in the Dutch East Indies. The painfully slow birth of the free press here was to blame for the fact that the "awakening" of the Dutch Indies came so late. In the first half of the 19th century there had been only a few newspapers, such as the "official" daily, the *Javasche Courant*, which represented government views. Then in 1836 came the *Soerabaijasch Advertentieblad*, followed in the 1840s by the *Samarangsch Advertentieblad* and the *Samarangsche Courant*, both of them chiefly vehicles for innocent advertisements and "mail news", reports of events in Europe. Not until 1850 did a few private individuals gain permission to distribute papers printed on their own press. That year the book-printer Wernard Bruining began the *Bataviaasch Handelsblad*, which two years later was renamed the *Java-Bode*.[60] The paper *De Oostpost* had a more boisterous start, its first issue appearing on 1 January 1853, printed by the publisher Eduard Johannes Lourens Fuhri in Surabaya. In this first issue the editor made it clear that this paper would take up the cause of the "descendants of Europeans" and support "both their intellectual and material interests". The editorials did not beat about the bush and wrote that "the vast majority of the Christian population in this colony is still lingering in a state of grievous deprivation and it is high time that adequate measures be taken to improve their welfare".[61] It cannot be denied that the tone of the editorial was strongly paternalistic; the *inlandse kinderen* were at a lower level of development than the Javanese. Although such politically tinted editorials ceased after about a year, the precedent had been set.

In 1854 a government statute was issued defining the general outlines for the administration of the Dutch East Indies and guaranteeing freedom of the press — albeit with certain limitations, which were later to be defined. These rules were specified two years later in the Indies Press Act, which gave the government in Batavia the right to exercise strict control over the press; it required that printers have a licence and that everything printed be open for inspection.[62] Despite the short leash on the press, the very fact that the printing presses were now regulated seems to have inspired many to produce their own newspaper. In the years following 1856 there came an ever-swelling flow of newspapers and journals. Most were simply innocent advertisers; others, however, developed into widely read papers with news articles that were closely followed throughout the Dutch East Indies. They varied from the critical *De Oostpost* or the *Padangsch Handelsblad* to the *Java-Bode*, which propounded government views. Various newspapers expressed their concern about the poor situation for the *inlandse kinderen* — a term they invariably used to mean local-born Europeans of the lower classes. This concern was coupled with criticism of the motherland, which sucked enormous wealth out of the Indies and gave too little in return.

Opinions of this nature were not restricted to the towns and cities of northern Java. Indeed, we have only to look at the newspapers published in the 1860s in such towns as Makassar and Padang. The newspaper *Makassaarsch Handels- en Advertentieblad*, first published in early 1861, contains a fair number of articles about local Europeans. In September and October 1864, for instance, a debate arose concerning the desirability for *inlandse kinderen* to learn a trade rather than to yearn for a low-ranking job as office clerk. Just as had happened a good 30 years before in Ceylon, this too created passionate reactions. One letter, signed by someone with the nom de plume of *Bruintje* (Brownie), well describes the sense of pride, mingled with a certain resignation, of a local-born Indo-European: "People call me by the nickname 'Brownie' and I'm very happy with it". And, a little further: "Possibly the education that I received as native-born, was somewhat limited. I did not have the honour to have been born in a colder climate and to have been educated there; nor were my parents wealthy enough to provide higher education for me; don't worry, I do not disappoint my teacher and I remain eternally grateful to him for what he gave me."[63] These are the words of an Indo-European who evidently appreciated the disadvantages of his ancestry but who felt a bond with the land of his birth. What he objected to was being stigmatised by newcomers.

Schooling

The most often-heard complaint in European circles concerned the inadequacy of local schooling. Indeed, this problem lay at the heart of the cultural and social divisions in the society of the Indies. Education provided the key to advancement and equal opportunity for the European middle classes living in the Indies. Improved education was not only a means towards emancipation, it also strengthened the ties of the European community in the Indies with the Dutch metropolitan culture. But to create an extensive infrastructure of good schools was a costly undertaking; nor was it ever the intention that the *inlandse kinderen* should have equal opportunities or gain equal social status with the white European elite.

Thus, until well into the 19th century the educational opportunities in the Dutch East Indies were few and inadequate. Elementary education did, in fact, improve fairly rapidly after the return of Dutch government to the Indies in 1816. The first government school was opened in November 1816 in Batavia. Its stated aim was to teach children to become "virtuous, decent and useful members of society". There was a striking difference with the school system under VOC rule: now the same rules were enforced as for schools in the Netherlands, and school books were sent from the Netherlands.[64] But school attendance was not compulsory, and the building was primitive. Initially, the school was housed in a warehouse made of bamboo, with room for 200 pupils. In 1819 it moved into a brick-built structure, which also accommodated about 25 boarders.[65]

Gradually, the government extended the school network. The number of state elementary schools in 1826 was 13, while seven years later it was 19. In 1833 a total of 1,801 pupils were attending both government and private schools; this figure includes the 289 pupils at orphanages, poorhouses and military schools.[66] From then onwards many children living in the larger towns and cities experienced, at least for a few years, some kind of Dutch schooling. But the statistics paint too rosy a picture of school attendance. The chief inspector of education admitted that there was large-scale truancy, which he blamed on the children's upbringing.[67] For those children who persisted for several years, the schools did provide a rudimentary training. All government schools taught reading, writing, arithmetic, Dutch, geography, history and singing. Even an unpretentious private school like that of J.A. Paulus in Batavia taught the approximately 50 pupils it had in 1833 the basics of reading, writing and "a little arithmetic". This provided the pupils with sufficient skills so that "they could be employed as reasonably efficient junior clerks". In downtown Batavia, the now impoverished former centre of the VOC, the children only learned the basic skills of "reading, writing and arithmetic, the rudiments of Dutch, and singing" — just sufficient to qualify them for a job as petty clerk. With a few exceptions, the 47 pupils at this school — and probably also the teacher, Mr A.J. Thomas — would have been Portuguese and Asian Christians. They were the descendants of the former Mardijker community, still living in the run-down inner city; almost all the Europeans had moved out.[68]

The chief aim of education in the Indies, according to the 1833 report, was "to provide for the moral improvement and civilisation of large numbers of children, most of them born here in this country". Without state intervention in their education, these children would be "utterly neglected and of no use whatever to society, indeed, they would become a financial burden upon hard-working members of the community and ultimately upon the government itself".[69] In practice, what this implied was that Indies-born children should be brought up to become diligent office clerks and respectable spouses. Many of the pupils left school early in order to work in a government office — or, in more fortunate circumstances, to follow higher (and better) education in the Netherlands.[70] So although education was intended to "civilise" the children of the Indies to a certain extent, it did not aim to introduce social equality. This did not, however, impede the upward thrust of education after 1848. School attendance increased considerably with the expanded number of schools, in both absolute and relative terms. In 1848 there were 1,921 pupils at government schools and 750 at private schools.[71] By the end of 1882 the 122 government schools in the Dutch East Indies had 9,201 students.[72] The total number of European residents in the Indies was then estimated to be approximately 45,000 — which means that most of these children attended school for some time at least.

A typical Indische community on the north coast of Java was Salatiga, in the residency of Semarang. Most of the members of the European circles here had been born in the Indies. They were employed chiefly in agricultural enterprises and in government. Writing his political report in 1864, the resident stated that most of these Europeans were able to send their children to school and — he added optimistically — the desire to attend school had been increasing remarkably "so that this class of people will indubitably improve".[73] The resident was clearly looking on the bright side and presumably had good reason to congratulate himself on the improved state of education. But the effects of this educational upsurge were slow to be felt throughout the length and breadth of the European community in the Dutch East Indies. One result was certainly that the local-born Europeans began to feel more drawn towards European culture. Teaching the children Dutch was an important element here; it meant people could read Dutch newspapers and increasingly perceive themselves as distinct from the Indonesian population, which received its education — if it did so at all — in Malay. It was, after all, essential to have a command of Dutch in order to make a career in government or the commercial world.

Those who chiefly benefited from government education were the children from poorer classes. The following citation describes the children attending government schools in the early days: "The vast majority of pupils are local-born, wholly or partially of European descent. They are completely unfamiliar with the Dutch language [...] The children must first be given an adequate grounding in Dutch before anything serious can be attempted in the way of education."[74] This is a stereotypical picture, and the general tone of the report is pedantic, but the observation is probably accurate. The pupils at government schools tended not to come from the best circles. General education was provided for those families who could not afford tutors or governors for their children at home. There are also many instances from later in the century indicating the poor level of Dutch in the Indies. Apparently most local-born European children arrived at school not speaking a word of Dutch.[75] Although by the time they left school they had a fair smattering of Dutch, the languages most widely used in Indische circles until after 1900 continued to be Malay and Petjo — the latter a mixture of Malay, Dutch and other languages.[76] The language used at school could not replace that spoken in the playground, the street and the home.[77] At best, a kind of bilingualism developed, generally consisting of a halting Dutch and a fluent Petjo.

Education in the Dutch East Indies was — as everywhere around the world — strictly determined by social class; this did not change with the expansion of schooling in the second half of the 19th century. Schools could, at most, strengthen or confirm the differences between those with a strong European orientation, and those from poorer backgrounds. And if this were true of elementary schooling, it was all the more so in secondary education. Initially, there was no secondary schooling, apart from a handful of private institutions. The first secondary school was the Young Ladies' Seminary, founded in Batavia in 1824 but closed not long after, in 1832.[78] There were a few other private institutions, mostly run by widows who earned their living in this way, and attended by young ladies who received "a polite education" in the necessary social graces.[79] Presumably such seminaries were attended chiefly by girls from better circles, from the families who sent their sons back to the Netherlands for their secondary education. Although requests were addressed to the government education committee as early as the 1830s asking for secondary education, it was not until after 1850 that this really started to take off. The first government *Hogere Burger School* (HBS, a secondary school somewhat comparable with an English grammar school) was founded in 1864; this was the Willem III *Gymnasium* (Willem III School) in Batavia. It was followed by secondary schools in Surabaya (1875) and Semarang (1878). Without a doubt, these secondary schools filled a gap: in the academic year 1880–1881 there were 191 pupils registered at the Willem III School in Batavia, 92 in Semarang and 104 in Surabaya (in addition to 65 students at the evening school in Surabaya). These are, however, very small numbers in comparison with the 8,223 pupils registered for government elementary schooling.[80]

Illustration 30 In 1864 the first HBS (secondary school, comparable to a grammar school) of the Indies opened its doors in Batavia. The Willem III School, named after the Dutch king, offered "European" children living in the Indies a good Dutch secondary education. Despite this, children from families who could afford it continued to go to the Netherlands for their studies.
[Photograph, *ca.* 1890, KITLV, Leiden.]

The introduction of secondary schools tended to perpetuate class differences — indeed, this often reinforced them. A fee of 180 guilders a year (in 1879) was charged for each pupil at the school; this was a lot of money, especially for families who had to survive on the salary of a junior clerk. Occasionally there were school funds available for the needy, but it was a very small number of pupils who could benefit from these. For instance, in the school year 1880–1881 only four out of the 104 pupils at the secondary school in Surabaya could be subsidised by the Surabaya School Fund.[81] Not surprisingly, a cleft developed between children who had completed only elementary school education and thus were eligible for only the lowest jobs, and those who had gained a diploma from the secondary schools.

The educational reforms and expansion did not necessarily mean an improvement for the lower classes. Indeed, the head of the Willem III

School observed in 1874 that the secondary schools were irrelevant "for that colourful group of full-blood and half-blood European children who swarm into the government offices like bees to a honeycomb".[82] Until well into the 20th century, education would be extolled as the means whereby the poorer Indische could rise in society. However, until the modernisation of the economy in the 1890s there were too few suitable jobs. Systematic support for the *inlandse kinderen* in their efforts to climb the social ladder turned out, furthermore, to be not only impossible but also apparently undesirable.

Opportunities

The government of the Dutch East Indies depended upon a body of civil servants that was thoroughly Indische. Despite every attempt at regulation, and opinions about excluding local-born civil servants, throughout the 19th century we encounter many Indies-born men in high-ranking positions. Initially these men had gained their posts before the introduction of the *radicaal*; but as time went on, more and more people holding government posts had to apply for, and gained, dispensation from this Delft diploma. The certificate system had not lived up to Minister Baud's expectations; it had floundered on the sandbanks of nepotism in the Indies.

The situation began to change only in 1864, when the first secondary school was founded in Batavia and the certificate system was abolished. Those wishing to enter the civil service could still study in Delft, but courses also sprang up in the Dutch city of Leiden and, in 1867, in the Indies — at the Willem III School in Batavia. This school created a special section called Department B, officially the *Inrichting voor de Indische Taal-, Land- en Volkenkunde* (College for Languages, Geography and Ethnography of the Indies). It meant the next step in the formalisation of the bureaucracy of the Dutch East Indies. The age of protectionism, which had lasted so long, came to an end. More than ever before, the government could demand formal qualifications as a sine qua non for appointments. In fact, after 1864 most of the civil servants appointed did indeed have the requisite diploma, acquired either in the Netherlands or in the East Indies. It was now almost impossible to climb to the top of the bureaucratic tree simply by having the right connections and recommendations; it became essential to complete the higher civil service course. Only in rare exceptions might someone be exempted from the higher civil servants' examination, as happened in the case of J.A.G.

Brugman, *commies* (senior clerk) in the department of Native Affairs in Makassar; he was granted exemption from the higher civil service exam in 1881 and finally, as recounted above, attained the eminent position of resident.

Despite schooling being more widely available, it remained difficult for children from poor homes to reach a high rank in the civil service. Once a man was caught up in the system as an office clerk, it was difficult for him to work his way up the ladder — and his children would face the same problem. Civil servants or employees who enjoyed a reasonable salary could, with a little penny-pinching, afford to send their children to Batavia or even to the Netherlands, as Frederik Neumann had done for his sons. Another such man was Johan Jacob Coert, who after humble beginnings rose to be resident of Kediri in eastern Java. On his father's side he was the fourth generation to be born in the Indies: his great-great-grandfather, Jan Johannes Coert, was a soldier from Westphalia in Germany and arrived in Java in 1756. His two daughters married members of the upper circles in Indies society: one, the resident Gerardus van den Berg, and the other, vice president of the Council of the Indies, Johan Christiaan Goldman. But then things began to go downhill for the family. One of the daughters of the latter marriage, Maria Elisabeth Goldman, married Nicolaas Wilhelmus Coert, a *commies* in the Orphans' Chamber, someone far beneath her. This same Nicolaas Wilhelmus, it is suggested in family tradition, was possibly also a grandchild of Jan Johannes, from a premarital relationship. Already at that time, it was virtually impossible for a *commies* (senior clerk) to obtain the certificate for the higher civil service unless he had exceptionally good connections. The son of this union, Johan Willem Christiaan Coert, was born in 1843. He too got stuck halfway up the bureaucratic ladder; he worked in the office of the General Secretariat of the colonial government, became secretary to various residents and ended up as auctioneer in Batavia — all of these typical jobs for Indies-born men lacking a higher civil service diploma. Initially, Johan Willem lived with a Chinese concubine, Oey Toa Nio, with whom he had a son. He later repudiated his companion to marry Marie Warnars from the Netherlands. Apparently she accepted the premarital activities of her husband.

Johan Willem's son from his extramarital relationship with Oey Toa Nio, named Johan Jacob, was — unlike his father — able to study in Delft for the higher civil service diploma; thereafter, he pursued an extremely successful career in the department of Binnenlands Bestuur. He died in harness, as resident of Kediri. "The corps of the B.B. loses

Illustration 31 In 1864 a special stream was started in the Willem III School known as the *Afdeling B* (B-department). This provided many men in the Indies with the opportunity of preparing for the Dutch civil service exams without having to incur the expense of travelling to Europe for schooling. Gottlieb Neumann (1857–1933) was one of the four Neumann brothers who passed the higher civil service exams. He is seen here in Surabaya.
[Photograph Charls & Van Es, *ca.* 1890, KITLV, Leiden.]

in him one of its most eminent figures," wrote the weekly *Indië* at his death in 1922. He married — incidentally, without a trace of previous sorties into concubinage — a Totok woman, Anna Aleida Volten. When Johan Jacob was appointed resident in Kediri, he wrote to his son that "the question of colour is no longer relevant in this type of appointment to a higher post in the civil service" — which suggests that he was thoroughly conscious of his Mestizo heritage and the colour of his skin. It is not clear what exactly prompted this remark — was it his Indonesian-Chinese mother or his awareness that his family were minor civil servants? But whatever lay behind it, he was highly conscious of his own "emancipation" from his family's lowly status.[83]

Neither before nor after 1865 was the Binnenlands Bestuur a corps composed of Totoks, that is, of Dutch newcomers.[84] The number of (aspirant) civil servants who gained their diplomas for the higher civil service ranks between 1865 and 1900 in the Netherlands was certainly far larger than that in Batavia: 1,119 compared with 370. Each cohort of students in the Netherlands delivered about 35 candidates with the higher civil service diploma, in contrast to about ten in Batavia.[85] It became usual for about one-third of the Binnenlands Bestuur appointed annually to have obtained the higher diploma in Batavia.[86] And indeed, a study carried out in 1906 showed that one-third of civil servants holding a higher diploma had obtained it in Batavia.[87] The distinction between Batavian and Netherlands-trained candidates was, however, artificial as far as background is concerned, for about one-third to a half of the Delft Academy students were from the Dutch East Indies. Nor were all the candidates in Batavia Indies-born young men. Some of them were low-ranking civil servants from the Indies who wanted to improve their career prospects.[88]

The introduction of the civil service examinations was a triumph for the citizens of the Indies. Together with the establishment of a training institute for higher positions in the civil service in Batavia, this opened the door to a career in government. The ideas of minister Baud had introduced an intermezzo lasting no more than two decades, which had become bogged down in nepotism and protest. With the new examination, standards of quality could be applied for the first time — which is not to say that connections and patronage disappeared entirely from the world of bureaucracy; they remained powerful forces. Indeed, the pressure to ensure a good position in the civil service became ever greater. Although before 1864 there were never enough applicants to fill the available posts in the civil service, there was soon to be a considerable surplus. With the improved education in the Dutch East Indies and the demographic growth of the Europeans living there, the number of young men in search of a good job increased dramatically. But there was little on offer. In 1850 there were only 158 officials in the Binnenlands Bestuur, and in 1890, 277.[89] Equally limited was the number of jobs available in the higher and middle ranks of the residencies and government departments. Nor did this keep pace with the population growth. The economic structure of the world of the East Indies had a depressing effect on job prospects and career opportunities for local-born young men. The expansion of schooling and the higher demands placed on qualifications of civil servants underline the social differences between the well-to-do citizens and those from poorer backgrounds. An inspection of the genealogies of Indische families generally produces a powerful image of downward social progression.

Race and status in the world of the East Indies

With education being offered to growing numbers, life changed radically
in the society of the Indies. Those planning a career in the civil service
found themselves eased into the European world, largely through their
education. In other ways, too, European culture exerted an ever-growing
influence on the world of the East Indies. The gently swelling rivulet
of newcomers arriving in the East Indies also added to the European
element. Furthermore, growing numbers of Indies-born Europeans now
travelled to the Netherlands. Throughout the 19th century the central
government in Batavia expanded its scope and influence. Improved
connections with Europe, the growth of the press and the interweaving
of enterprises from the Indies and Europe after 1860, all affected Indische
culture. With the telegraph service, a direct link was established between the Netherlands and the Dutch East Indies, appreciably reducing
the colony's sense of isolation. In the newspapers of the time we find
evidence of these changes and a growing orientation towards Europe.
According to the advertisements, more and more European luxury items
were exported to the Indies — and apparently there were more and
more people who could afford them. Whereas in the 1810s tradesmen
had advertised sauerkraut and Spanish wine, later in the century these
items were found in the company of pianos, Parisian toilet water and
machinery.[90] The most significant changes were to take place after 1900,
when bicycles, automobiles, Western clothing and the gramophone
made their appearance.

At the same time, daily newspapers bear witness to the openness and
continuing diversity of Indische culture and consumption patterns. For
instance, in an advertisement on 16 December 1889 in the *Pemberita
Betawi*, Batavia's Malay-language newspaper, right beside a notice for a
"most attractive piano made by the Lipp firm" we find the following
goods for sale: a Japanese gas lamp, rattan matting, an electric doorbell
and an ice-making machine.[91] It has been suggested that the Indische
culture came under pressure from European influences.[92] This notion,
however, assumes such a thing as a fixed, unchanging Indische culture,
which, under attack from a Dutch cultural offensive, grew weak and
feeble. The reality could be viewed in a different light. The Indische
lifestyle continued as before — distinct and recognisable, while at the
same time being flexible and multiform. It could be observed in such
things as language, clothing, eating habits and housing. Indische culture
altered in form and content, just as it had continuously been transformed

Illustration 32 Jan Abraham Ament (1843–1911) was the son of the powerful West Javanese landholder (and resident of Cirebon) Tjalling Ament, who, through his marriage with Dina Cornelia van Riemsdijk, inherited the enormous estate of East Tanjung. Jan Abraham's brothers became sugar barons, but he himself had a distinguished career in the civil service, becoming resident of Yogyakarta, where this photograph was taken. He is seen here in 1898 with his wife (who came from Semarang), Carolina Justina van Beusechem, and their daughter.
[Photograph, *ca.* 1898, KITLV, Leiden.]

over the centuries, subject to outside influences but still undeniably "Indische". Certainly, the Totok norm grew stronger and the lure of the metropolis increased, but it was never so that a carbon copy of life in the Netherlands was stamped upon the Dutch East Indies. The European community in the Indies adapted to the changes and the new openings offered by education, material culture and work opportunity.

In Europe, meanwhile, change was occurring at a rapid pace; mass production of goods and the development of new technologies introduced fresh social divisions. There was worldwide interest in the products of the new European industries, but perhaps nowhere more so than in a colonial society like that of the East Indies. The imported European goods bought kudos to their owners. But the effects were not the same for everyone. Easier access to education, along with increased migration and the modernisation of colonial society, only highlighted the contrasts between the domain of high-ranking colonial officials and indigenous circles. Within the European community, too, social differences that already existed were reinforced through an increasing European orientation. To balance this, social boundaries shifted considerably. Whereas in the 18th century only the very rich could afford to send their children to be educated in Europe, now both school and university were open to a far wider circle. Time spent in the Netherlands — for schooling or on leave — increased one's status in colonial circles. But of course the poorer Europeans living in the Indies could still not afford such journeys; furthermore, European articles were often too expensive, and good education usually cost too much. This new world was not for them — just as it was not for the poorer classes of the Western countries.

There was a marked tendency among the higher classes of Totoks, who controlled most of the channels of information, to play down the contrasts between white and coloured. Thus, writing in the newspaper *Mataram*, the editor-in-chief could ask, "Are there actual grievances that might cause the Indo-Europeans to be discontented with their treatment by the Government? Is there truly a difference in the legal rights of a full-blood and a Netherlander born in this country?"[93] He cites as an example the famous general Karel van der Heijden — nicknamed Karel One-Eye — and enquires, "Is there the smallest hint of a suggestion that the Government slighted this worthy General because he was not a full-blood Netherlander?" This provides a good example of how the newspaper *Mataram* approached the subject of labelling; it thought in terms of race as well as class. Those who wished to, and had the opportunity, could aspire to climb the social ladder in the Dutch East Indies. In formal terms, there were no restrictions just because someone was Indo-European. Indeed, successful Indo-Europeans such as General Van der Heijden, who had attended school in the Netherlands, had extricated themselves from any stigmas attached to being "Indo". His success merely underscores the characteristics typically attributed to the Indo-European: they were generally considered to be mentally disadvantaged and culturally degenerate. The fact that Indo-Europeans had managed to rise out of this milieu — indeed, had in many cases never belonged there — says nothing about the mechanisms that excluded large numbers of Indies-born Europeans from being considered of the same ilk.

Distinctions between white and coloured Europeans see-sawed and were subject to change. There was a period — particularly the years around the 1830s and 1840s — when the language heard in government circles, and without doubt in many other circles too, was unashamedly discriminatory. Nevertheless, the argument of racism does not provide an adequate explanation for the divisions that developed. Behind the façade of colonial rhetoric there were clearly other forces at play. There was no question of systematic or institutionalised exclusion of people on grounds of race. Whatever the current considerations may have been, formal prejudice on the government's part applied in the first place to those born in the Indies, not to the Mestizos. The "Indo" problem was primarily one of class, exacerbated by the distinction made between newcomers and those born locally.

It is as well to realise that the social order in the Indies could not be dictated by a colonial elite of newcomers. The simple fact that at least 80 per cent of the Europeans living in the Dutch East Indies were born there and that the majority of them had at least one Asian parent or ancestor, together with the information that quite a number of these local-born Europeans held high government posts and positions in the community, and that there were communities where the white newcomers quickly integrated into the Indische setting — all this should make the historian cautious about viewing the society of the Dutch East Indies in terms of a racist colonial culture.

The situation may have been different in other colonies. In the regions under British rule in India and the Malay Peninsula, racial boundaries were drawn more rigidly and Eurasians were formally excluded from higher administrative ranks.[94] However, we would do well to ask whether the almost exclusive emphasis on racial boundary lines is justified, also when considering British colonies.[95] Here, too, colonial rhetoric has produced so dense a fog that the reality — far more subtle and refined — has disappeared from view. There were, of course, "internal boundaries", as in most societies that possess a heterogeneous mixture of cultures, languages, religions and races. The society of the Dutch East Indies did not have a simplistic racial structure with whites (Totoks) at the top, mixed-blooded Indo-Europeans in between, and native Indonesians at the bottom. Apart from certain exceptions, such as the interpreters in the offices of residents, there is little reason to argue that people of mixed blood provided a link between East and West.[96] Nor, as is sometimes suggested, were the Mestizos, or Indos, the chief means whereby the West gained a foothold in the East.[97] It is out of place to produce generalisations about the nature and function of the Indo-European. After all, most such generalisations are rooted in a world-view that is basically white, or Totok, an outlook that disregards multiform reality and the fact that reading the word "race" instead of "class" fails to account for local variations and subtle social ties.

CHAPTER **7**

The Underclass

Upstairs, downstairs

Only the middle classes who were oriented towards making a career in government were concerned about educational opportunities and examinations for the civil service. For most Europeans born in the Indies, such questions were irrelevant. Their unassuming lives were centred around their jobs — perhaps as the proverbial clerk in an administrative department, or running a shop, or as an artisan or gardener. They neither dreamed of, nor were they ever likely to attain, a high-ranking position in the civil service; nor was visiting Europe on leave and eventually retiring to the Netherlands ever likely to be an option.

To a certain extent, the office clerks belonged to the circle of Europeans and formed part of colonial society; but there were a large number who were Europeans in the legal sense of the word but had scarcely any contact with the social layer that fed the civil service. These people inhabited a different world from that of the well-to-do. Their homes were in poor neighbourhoods; they formed part of the urban proletariat, a richly diverse crowd from many different countries and backgrounds. It was often difficult to draw precise cultural boundaries in these poorer urban milieus. Nevertheless, during the 19th century an individual's ethnic and cultural background was to become increasingly important as an indication of whether or not they could be (legally) labelled European.

In the 17th and 18th centuries, the government of the Dutch East India Company had not shown much interest in questions concerning poor Europeans or Mestizos. Although repeated efforts were made to rescue Mestizo children from towns and villages and place them in (Christian) orphanages, little more was done on their behalf. Then, in the 19th century, a new concept emerged: the (Indo-)European pauper.

This was to have a far-reaching impact on the world of the East Indies. The term "pauper" was typical for the late 19th century. Curiously, it was not used in the East Indies to apply to the large numbers of Indonesians; it was reserved for those of European ancestry. The concept of a pauper implied both a sense of distance and of closeness, although the discovery of pauperism took place against a background of increasing government intervention and the struggle for social and political emancipation of the lower classes.[1] The poor Europeans in the Dutch East Indies would witness a similar growth in class consciousness.

In the 19th century the phrase "assimilated into the kampong" was used to refer to the descendants of Europeans whose social and cultural links with the European elite had grown weak and who lived or grew up in an Indonesian milieu. Often these children had a European father who had not adopted them or legally acknowledged them; they grew up with the family of their Indonesian mother or became vagrants in the villages and urban kampongs. There were also retired soldiers who — often out of economic necessity — lived among the Javanese and other Indonesians. Another group was the (Indo-)Europeans who had married or lived with an Indonesian Muslim woman and had integrated into the Muslim community. It is not possible to estimate their number since they are not recorded: they lived outside the scope of European record books and religious registers. Nevertheless, during the 19th century the Dutch authorities became increasingly concerned about Europeans who ended up in Indonesian environments. In the Dutch-language newspapers of the time we read emotional reports about Europeans who had "gone native". In the *Bataviaasch Nieuwsblad*, the newspaper edited by Paul A. Daum, generally known for his liberal views, the following article appeared in 1885 under the headline "Incredible": "We learn that in the town of Buitenzorg, in the kampong of Ciwaringin, there are large numbers of Europeans who have adopted the Mohammedan faith, driven by poverty, and who, it is reported, are fed and housed by the council of Muslim priests, the Kaum."[2]

What was so intensely threatening in the idea of Europeans becoming absorbed into the Indonesian community? Was it simply the fear that they might convert to Islam, and so be lost for Christianity? Undeniably, in the 19th century, as in earlier times, the notion of Christian unity was important for keeping stray sheep within the fold; but other sentiments were now becoming increasingly powerful. The colonial authorities were far more concerned about the lot of white or Indo-European Christians than about the children of "native Christians". In other words, it was not just a question of religious belief but also of skin colour. There was a strong racial tang to the notion of "solidarity within one's own circle". The colonial army's quartermaster, Jan Baptist Jozef van Doren, reported that during a tour of inspection in 1827 he came across a 19-year-old girl of European descent in one of the kampongs; as he put it, "her skin colour and hair betrayed her origins". She was the daughter of a Javanese woman and a Dutch gunner who had returned to the Netherlands. People living in the kampong had been looking after the girl. Van Doren asked a friend of his to provide her board and keep. He left no room for doubt as to what prompted this action, asking rhetorically: "Is it not a crying shame that such creatures, whose parentage can be discerned at the first glance, soil the reputation of Europeans in the eyes of the Javanese population?"[3] There was no question of religious principles here, but rather a colonial discourse regarding the maintenance of European honour and status in front of the Indonesians.

As the Dutch government and high-ranking newcomers viewed matters, the fact that some (Indo-)Europeans had sunk into the lower circles of Indonesian society tarnished the image of the Netherlands' colonial authority in the eyes of the natives. With a view to maintaining the image of colonial authority, Indo-Europeans were included in the category of Europeans. A further consideration was that this inclusion would forestall the growth of a group of grumbling discontents. This can be deduced from a letter written by the head of the technical school in Surabaya, in 1855: "Generally mocked and scorned by us Hollanders; oft-time treated rudely and with derision, it seems highly unlikely that they will grow to form a large group that is well-disposed towards us. Quite the reverse — they have every reason to hate us."[4]

The inclusion of the Mestizos and the poor whites in the category "European" was a legal and, to some extent, a cultural question; but despite this incorporation, a vast social gulf remained between rich and poor. Newcomers expressed their discomfort (caused by the lower-class Europeans) by mocking those born in the Indies, particularly Indo-Europeans. Interestingly, just as it had been a century earlier, it was not the Mestizo men but the women who came in for criticism. Johannes Olivier, who travelled in the East between 1817 and 1826, referred — like his 17th- and 18th-century predecessors — to the "loose manners of the female *Liplaps* [half-breeds]". At the same time he admitted that "there are some exceptions, and indeed certain of the Creole girls are truly beautiful, with souls as pure as their skin is white".[5] Skin colour would frequently be related to inner purity. This same Olivier, who was expelled from the colony in 1826 on account of drunken and unseemly behaviour, returned to the Netherlands and became head of a boarding school in Kampen. He saw fit to air his prejudiced views in his own periodical *De Oosterling*, the oldest journal about the East Indies to be published in the Netherlands. In it he made fun of the garbled Dutch spoken by the "coloureds".[6]

Olivier was, of course, a colonial snob, horrified (at least, on paper) by racial mixing and contact between European men and Indo-European or Indonesian women. But he was one of many. Feelings arising out of racial prejudice would often be expressed in moral terms, cloaked in arguments of public decency and educational standards. Thus, in 1835 the commander-in-chief of the Dutch Indies' army Hubert J.J.L. Ridder de Stuers wrote of Indo-Europeans: "They possess the bad characteristics of the European, combined with those of the Indonesians. They take after their fathers in their excessively lascivious ways, and by their mothers they are brought up in idleness. How could they possibly turn out good?"[7] What De Stuers was describing here was the notion of the hybrid, a concept that took firm root in the later 19th century. It had its origins in biology, where it was used to refer to the crossing of two breeds of animal, implying the combining of two pure strains. As used here, it seems to mean the combination of two "pure" racial types. It is striking that the hybrid apparently combines most remarkably all the bad qualities of the two parent races from which it is composed.[8] Although the term "hybrid" never became part of everyday speech, it was certainly widely used in the Indies and contributed to the racial stereotyping associated with the European underclass.[9] Many expressions came into everyday use to refer to the poor (Indo-)Europeans, for instance, *Liplap, blauwtje* (blue-hued), *sinjo* (for men), *nonna* (for girls), *petjoek* (a cormorant), *Indo* and the accepted "correct" term *inlandse kinderen*, which means literally, "native children".[10]

Besides the ever-present prejudices, there also developed a social vision in which the various offshoots of the European clan were deliberately drawn closer to the European community. In this process, the long history of the Dutch presence in the East Indies and the fact that most government jobs were filled by Indies-born Europeans were both highly significant. Indeed, the Indische element in colonial society was so overwhelming that it would have been impossible to exclude on explicit grounds the Europeans born in the Indies. After all, upper-class society in the Indies consisted of families with innumerable connections, through marriage or otherwise, to local European families — most of whom had several poor relations in the neighbourhood. Although the number of newcomers to the East Indies gradually rose, at the same time the number of Europeans born in the Indies also increased, and the balance altered only very slowly. From 1849 on there are excellent records telling us the number of European (civilian) residents, although the information about their place of origin is not always entirely trustworthy. Between 1855 and 1900 those born in Europe increased from 13.4 per cent to 19.6 per cent, a relatively gradual rise. It also meant that within the European community in the Indies the expatriates remained in the minority.

In one segment of the European community, newcomers dominated: the military. For a long time they formed the largest group of Europeans, and their impact left deep imprints on society in the Indies. In 1860 they numbered 13,576, and in 1900 they had increased to 15,309. More than 90 per cent came from Europe.[11] As late as 1900 half the newcomers to the East Indies were soldiers, while among the European civilians there were many retired and former military personnel to be found.

Civic registry

Historians have often claimed that in the 17th and 18th centuries religion was the most important touchstone for measuring the social and legal status of those in colonial society. In the 19th century religion made way for racial criteria.[12] Most authors base their arguments on the juridical status of the various population groups, which do show an assertion of racial criteria in the 19th century. But reality was far more complicated. There had always been judgments based on racial factors, even before 1800. Nor did the religious element disappear in the 19th century; indeed, religion remained a determining factor in the definition of Europeanness and in people's day-to-day social intercourse. The legal-constitutional dividing lines between population groups became more firmly defined during the colonial period and more firmly anchored in the constitution. Similar developments could be observed worldwide.[13] An important moment — if perhaps largely a symbolic one — in the constitutional construction of separate population groups was the introduction of local civic registry offices in 1828. Christians and Jews were obliged to register births, marriages and deaths, thereby determining their legal status. The registry offices introduced a paper building-block into the gradually expanding edifice of classification and separation.

The Government Regulation of 1854 divided the population into two groups: natives (*Inlanders*) and Europeans, to which a third group, Foreign Orientals, was later added. This tripartite division was not entirely new, for a similar system of legal communities had already developed under the Dutch East India Company in Batavia, although then having the categories of Muslim, Dutch and Chinese. Family law and inheritance law of both Chinese and Muslims had been acknowledged and codified as distinct from the laws governing the Europeans and other Christians. Although in the categorisation according to the Government Regulation of 1854 the constitutional categories seemed, for the first time, to avoid a religious element, religion certainly remained an important touchstone when determining a person's legal status. According to the codes regulating the equalisation of persons from other groups with the Europeans, it was easier for a Christian to claim European status than it was for a Muslim or the follower of another religion. In terms of law, the Christian faith was an important criterion for acquiring the status of European. Thus, even after the implementation of the new code, the position of the native Christians remained ambiguous.[14] Not surprisingly, mixed marriages, that is, between two people from different constitutionally defined groups, were far more common in Christian parts than in islands where Islam was the dominant faith. In the Moluccas, as we have seen, social distinctions were far less pronounced than in Java. Indeed, it became possible after 1828 for native Christian Burghers in the Moluccas to register their marriages and children in the public civic registries. This meant that boundaries between groups were not so sharp as in non-Christian regions.

The precise effect of this legal and administrative categorisation on the lives of individuals remains unclear. In some cases the classification had far-reaching consequences. It would often happen that people applying for a widow's pension or orphan's allowance could not provide a certificate of birth, baptism or marriage. If the local authority could not solve the problem, then the request for a pension or benefit-payment would be rejected.[15] Clearly, people had a financial interest in registration, although this did not mean that everybody met their obligations.

It was in the upper classes that the demarcation lines showed most clearly, in the government circles of the cities of northern Java. At the bottom of the scale, distinctions were less important; where there was reduced social opportunity, the attraction of colonial regulations was less strongly felt. The civil servants working in the registry offices had a considerable struggle with the people who failed to register on time (if at all) or could not produce the required documents. But despite governmental attempts to submit all the Europeans to registration, the effects of the official classifications should not be exaggerated. The European population register had not the slightest effect on, for instance, patterns of marriage among the Europeans, or the number of illegitimate births. Presumably no one batted an eyelid when a father came to register a baby whose mother was his concubine. Indeed, the number of marriages in Batavia actually declined slightly after 1828, the year in which the Registry of Births, Marriages and Deaths was officially established. And the number of children born out of wedlock remained high. About 29 per cent of the (registered) births in Batavia between 1829 and 1836 were illegitimate — that is, not born to wedded parents — although many children were legitimised afterwards by the father through adoption or legal acknowledgement. By comparison, in the Netherlands during the same period the figure was just over 5 per cent. During the 1840s the number of children who were acknowledged in the East Indies rose slightly — to one in three.[16] In Semarang the number of legitimate and illegitimate births was about even.[17] The number of acknowledged children (that is, children born out of wedlock) continued to rise even further until the close of the 19th century.[18]

Social practices did not change simply because a registry office was established; concubinage and the adoption or legal acknowledgement of illegitimate children all continued much as before. The only difference was that now European fathers started to register the births of their children with the civil authorities. The practice of concubinage only declined very slowly. In the upper circles of the Batavian civil servants, concubinage was gradually banished to the back rooms, as for instance happened in the case of Rudolph Neumann; but old patterns persisted on Java's north coast. One man with respect for the past was Frederik Willem Pinket van Haak, the resident of Pekalongan, which lies 100 kilometres west of Semarang. He was born in 1779 in Batavia, son of the secretary to the High Government of Batavia. Educated in the Netherlands, he returned to Java in 1798 and began a flourishing career. In 1811 he was local administrator in the small town of Jepara on Java's north coast. When the Dutch returned after the British interregnum he became the resident in Surakarta and later in Jepara and Surabaya. Pinket van Haak was not married but kept, as one Dutch traveller described it in 1817, "several of those half-breed women". His household, moreover, "was very extensive and truly Oriental". He was a worthy follower — if somewhat more modest — of Van Reede tot de Parkeler, the harem-holder who 20 years earlier had kept court on Java's north coast.

Pinket van Haak persisted in his own peculiar lifestyle.[19] In 1829, when he was resident of Surabaya, he wrote a formal request to Governor-General Leonard Pierre Joseph Du Bus de Gisignies, asking if he could have several of his children legitimised. He wanted to marry their mother, chiefly to make the children legitimate, but the official at the registry office objected because the woman was Muslim. Pinket van Haak claimed that a decision regarding matters of marriage no longer fell under the jurisdiction of the church and that, moreover, the Netherlands constitution had declared all religions equal. He therefore sought permission to marry the mother of his children. Both Governor-General Du Bus de Gisignies and the attorney general felt inclined to permit the marriage, but some members of the Council of the Indies made vehement protests. For them, Pinket van Haak's way of life revealed "immorality and a deeply sunken character", and they declared that the constitution of the Netherlands did not apply to the Dutch East Indies. Based on the Statutes (Law Code) of Batavia of 1642, which had never been repealed, these councillors maintained that there was still a ban on marriages between Christians and non-Christians. What ruffled these councillors even more about Pinket van Haak's behaviour was, as they claimed, that "he has often boasted of being a Javanese, and looks upon the Javanese as his brothers and his family", and to cap it all, not only had he kept a concubine, but he had chosen one who came from the very lowest class. After all, continued the councillors, "almost every unmarried European has a concubine, some more openly than others, depending on his sense of shame", and public opinion in the Indies was much more lenient in this respect than in Europe. The problem with Pinket van Haak was not that he lived in concubinage or had illegitimate children, but that his concubine was lowly born. If they were to marry, she would be entitled to mix with ladies of upper-class Javanese society. This was beyond the pale; it would taint the prestige of the Netherlands. According to Governor-General Du Bus de Gisignies, a firm line had to be drawn between the rulers and the ruled; too much mixing of cultures and classes would undermine colonial authority. The Javanese woman was obliged to accept her position as mistress or concubine.[20]

Pinket van Haak was a "son of the Indies", held a top position in the colonial government and maintained a lifestyle typical of the north

Javanese coast. He came up against certain Dutch rules that perceived a mixed marriage as a greater evil than concubinage. In daily practice, there was little objection to concubinage — indeed, it was sometimes encouraged. But a mixed marriage aroused objections of a legal, political and emotional nature. This was the situation until 1854, when a ruling was introduced obliging a local woman to be baptised before she could marry a European — a reiteration of laws dating from the VOC period. Still, in the upper classes of European society, marriage with an Asian woman was far less accepted than in poorer classes. The story of Resident Pinket van Haak amply illustrates this. But as a resident, Pinket van Haak was perhaps a special case. In practice, with the institutionalisation of legal distinctions between population groups, the government also established procedures to grant dispensation for mixed marriages (of partners from different categories). Between 1856 and 1878, 8 per cent to 10 per cent of marriages in Java registered in the public registry office were mixed marriages. Outside Java it was two to three times as many, since in regions like the Moluccas and Manado (Sulawesi) there was a large local Christian community providing wives for European men in the area.[21]

Despite the changes introduced, concubinage continued in all its variations, not only among the military but also in civilian circles. This was only partly the result of the imbalance of the sexes in the European community. The proportion of men to women among the Europeans born in the Indies was more or less equal, while among the newcomers, women were in the minority.[22] Very often, concubinage is presented as if it were a cultural phenomenon in the first place, whereas it was actually the outcome of practical restrictions. Soldiers and young officers were not allowed to marry, and marriage was also sometimes forbidden for employees in many businesses. Concubinage, or sexual exploitation of local women by unmarried civil servants, entrepreneurs and employees, remained a common practice — particularly in the outlying regions — until the 20th century. It aroused not the slightest opposition.[23] But there was another type of concubinage of a very different nature. This could be found in poorer circles and was born primarily out of financial need. For newcomers, a concubine was a temporary solution; for the less well-to-do Europeans, a concubine was virtually the same as a wife. A large inquiry into pauperism on Java launched by the government in 1901 makes it very clear that concubinage was particularly common among those with minimum incomes. Throughout Java, 35 per cent of the poorest segment who had children lived in concubinage. The number of unmarried men living with a concubine decreased as their incomes rose.[24]

Couples often married after living some time together. Here again, practical reasons weighed heavy. In many cases the man was an ex-military man from the Netherlands who had lived together with his housekeeper when he was in the army in the Indies — since as a soldier he was not allowed to marry. When his contract expired he was faced with the choice of returning to the Netherlands or remaining in the Indies with his concubine and their children. Marriage provided his companion and their family with pension rights on his death. However, marriage could be a costly or complicated affair, so many men and women preferred to remain without the legal documents. Concubinage was widespread throughout the East Indies and began to decrease slowly after 1900 and more rapidly after 1920.[25] This was connected with the fact that more women (and married men) came to the Indies from Europe, so that the ratio of men to women among the newcomers in the Indies became more balanced. Other reasons were growing prosperity, the ending of the marriage ban for employees in enterprises, and pressure from both Dutch and Indonesian circles.

The discovery of pauperism

The gradual expansion of the European population in the Indies led to a growing awareness and greater visibility of the poor and destitute. The 19th century witnessed a paradoxical development — the community of Europeans, which included those born in the Indies, became more clearly defined, not only juridically but also culturally. At the same time, the internal dividing lines became more sharply drawn. This phenomenon revealed itself chiefly in urban centres, where differences in culture and prosperity could be most plainly seen.

The vast majority of Europeans (army personnel excepted) could be found in the towns and cities. In 1870 half the number of Europeans in Java occupied the three large cities of Batavia, Semarang and Surabaya, which had expanded noticeably after 1850. But while in the latter two cities the newcomers and local-born Europeans stayed proportionately more or less the same, in Batavia the Totok group grew ever larger. Official records tell us that in 1855 there were 4,145 Europeans living in Batavia. These were subdivided into various categories. There were 2,099 "Mestizos and other coloureds", 1,206 white Europeans born in the Indies (Creoles) and 840 Totoks (whites born in Europe).[26] The European military were not included in these figures. Thus, we see that 80 per cent of the Europeans in Batavia were born in the East Indies. In the category "other coloureds" there were also 196 native Christians. Since then, the number of Europeans increased. Although those born in the Indies remained in the majority, Batavia became an increasingly white city. In 1870 Europeans born in the Indies formed a good 63 per cent of the European population there. The figure was almost 87 per cent in Semarang, while even in Surabaya, which expanded dramatically in these decades, it was 84 per cent.[27]

With the growth in urban population, the physical distance between the colonial elite and the lower classes also increased. New suburbs appeared in the towns, where the European elite could withdraw into their comfortable bourgeois homes. Under the VOC, the towns and cities had long preserved their vivid patchwork appearance, with people of different ethnic groups and income levels living, if not exactly on the same street, still in close proximity. The move to outlying suburbs had begun in Batavia as early as the 18th century and was to continue into the 19th century. The neighbourhood of Weltevreden, numbering no more than a few hundred houses in the first decades of the 19th century, grew into a new town, where the government officers and top brass inhabited luxurious houses lining airy avenues.

The separation of various population groups was made even more visible by the different tempos in which urban quarters were modernised. For instance, gas-lit streetlamps were introduced at first only in the European suburbs. In 1862 Batavia had its first gas lamps, but not until 1895 did these appear in the Chinese quarters — and after this date other neighbourhoods still continued in the shade.[28] It was the same story for installing piped water and, at a later date, paved roads. The luxuries of life reached the rich far sooner than they did the poor. The contrasts between the different neighbourhoods became only more marked with time, and the residents came to bear the tag of the neighbourhood in which they lived — with all its accompanying implications of class and style of housing and living. The spacious avenues around Koningsplein, the central square in Weltevreden, became the exclusive territory of high-ranking civil servants. Their world was illuminated by the glowing gleams of street lamps; in the surrounding suburbs the people still walked in darkness.

Batavia had neighbourhoods — such as Djambatan, Besie, Pasar Baroe, Gang Petjangan, Noordwijk and Gang Chaulan — that were

Illustration 33   One of the main streets of Vlaardingen, the urban district in Makassar beside the fort. This district was populated by a large number of local European families, as well as Chinese and Malays. On the left is the Makassar Orphanage, which was shut down in 1858. The children were transferred to the orphanages in Semarang (Java).
[Oil painting by Antoine Payen, 1846, Rijksmuseum voor Volkenkunde, Leiden.]

known to be densely populated districts inhabited by many poor Indo-Europeans.[29] They were not the old neighbourhoods from the days of the VOC but had developed as suburbs around the new town centre of Weltevreden. Large numbers of poor Europeans, who were described as living "in the kampong", in fact often lived on the edge of the kampong, along the roadside. It was hard to tell the difference between their houses and those of the local Indonesians. The buildings were made of woven bamboo, wood planks and (partially) brick. There was a definite advantage in having such simple buildings, for houses with a rental value of less than 15 guilders were not taxed.[30]

Batavia was an early and extreme example of the separation of poor and rich neighbourhoods, because at the beginning of the 19th century the European centre of the city had been moved. In such cities as Semarang, Surabaya and Makassar, however, for a long time the urban pattern continued to be modelled on the structure of the 17th- and

18th-century VOC settlements. The old urban pattern still dominated there, a mixture of races and classes living in the shadow of the VOC fort, surrounded by Javanese neighbourhoods. The old city of Semarang consisted largely of small, cramped dwellings in narrow streets within the city wall, as they had developed in the 18th century. Probably life was not so different in the mid-19th century from what it had been 100 years earlier. A visitor from the Netherlands, recording his impressions, spoke of the *nonna-nonnas*, the Indo-European girls who could be seen at the close of day, ambling with their parents along the unpaved streets that were being sprayed with water to keep the dust down.[31]

Yet in Semarang, too, a split gradually developed between the poorer residents who lived in the old neighbourhoods, and the more well-to-do, many of them newcomers, who settled outside the city. In the unhealthy inner city, notorious for its unwholesome atmosphere, lived the Chinese, Javanese and Europeans who "could not afford to have a house in the newer districts of the city".[32] Most of the poor lived in the old inner city, on the streets located on the eastern side of Semarang, such as Karang Bidara, and on Zeestrand (today Jalan Mpu Tantular), the road leading northwards from the city to the sea. Writing in 1891, the journalist Otto Knaap described this as "a desolate district, where only a few Europeans live", and he called the sea road, Zeestrand, "Semarang's hell".[33] It was where the handicapped and the drop-outs lived, managing somehow to survive by begging and hawking. High-ranking officials who were posted to Semarang would not for a moment consider living in the old city. Almost without exception they found a place along the road leading to Bodjong (Jalan Pemuda), which ran east out of the city towards the dwelling of the resident.[34] This shady avenue was flanked by large villas, the homes of wealthy European officials and entrepreneurs. The Hogere Burger School (secondary school), which was founded in 1877, also stood on the road to Bodjong. Another district for the more wealthy Semarangers was later built a few kilometres south of the city. Called Candi, it lay atop a hill and had a far more salubrious setting than the old city on the plain, where the houses were packed close together and in the rainy season the streets constantly flooded.[35]

At the same time as the (physical) separation of rich and poor increased, came the "discovery" of the problem of poverty. Naturally, there had always been poverty. From the earliest days of the VOC in Java there had been handicapped and destitute Europeans begging for assistance. But sometime in the mid-19th century influential voices began to be heard, expressing concern about the class of poverty-stricken

Europeans in the colonies. It was essentially an urban concern, not because there was no poverty outside the urban centres, but because the poor in the cities presented a contrast to what the local administrations considered to be a decent lifestyle. Thus the "social question", which around this time emerged on a global scale, was given a peculiarly colonial tinge. It was not to do with starvation; it was a matter of European prestige. In British colonies the terms "poor white" and "white trash" had been coined to label the impoverished; in the Dutch East Indies the word "pauper" was used.

While no one would deny there was poverty in the East Indies, it could not be called extreme. In the case of the 4,145 Europeans registered as living in Batavia in 1855, their professions were also recorded. Around 63 per cent of those in the category "Mestizos" were employed by the government. Of the government civil servants, 54 per cent were Mestizos, while 18 per cent were born in the Indies and had two white European parents. In this city of bureaucrats the government was by far the largest employer for the European community, especially Europeans born in the Indies. The report states that the majority of Mestizos held inferior positions such as office clerk or "minor posts in private companies dealing in agriculture, trade and commerce, as well as shipping".[36] Trade and industry were dominated by newcomers. Those in the category "industrials" were employees in the couple of factories that Batavia boasted; there were a few forges, a sugar factory, and some brickyards and tile works.[37] In the statistics we find not the slightest indication that there was a poverty problem, certainly not among the Mestizos. The number of them that is categorised "without profession" (the rentier class and those who had retired with a pension also fell under this heading) is remarkably low: only 31. Statistics do not, of course, reveal the whole truth. Impoverished Europeans may well have been living in neighbourhoods where they escaped the pen of the professional recorders. Furthermore, of the 662 Mestizo men, the profession is given only for 612, leaving the source of income of 50 men unclear.

All in all, therefore, the employment situation in Batavia appears not to have been problematic, at least at this time. Nevertheless, civil servants and journalists became increasingly preoccupied with the question of lower-class Europeans. Various factors encouraged this discussion, among them a growing awareness of government responsibility and the progressive expansion of cultural and legal spheres. The government, however, was extremely cautious about becoming involved in the care of the poor, orphans and vagabonds. The same story could be told for the Netherlands.

The Netherlands Poor Law of 1854 even stipulated that the benefits provided by the civil authorities should be only of a supplementary nature.[38] The discussion around "factory children" and what was called the social question was taken up by several parties. There were those who favoured state intervention, and there was also the group of anti-interventionists, who found support with the religious groups who wanted to keep control of poor relief in the hands of the church — with the result that the civil government remained reticent about taking full responsibility for poor relief. Not until World War I would government expenditure on social benefits (including poor relief) together with a general social policy increase in any real measure.[39]

Thus, poor relief in the East Indies remained a matter for the churches, although this did not mean that temporal authorities eschewed the problem entirely. Indeed, in the days of the VOC, the High Government of Batavia had regulated the financing of poor relief, and in the 19th century the government became increasingly involved in discussions about poverty among the Europeans in the Indies. The colonial government's sense of responsibility for its poor advanced tentatively — though, it must be said, the forward march was largely rhetorical. In government circles, there was not yet a whisper of social and political emancipation of the lower classes. Neither in the Dutch East Indies nor in the Netherlands did egalitarian ideas suggest the notion of increased responsibility of the state for its poorer classes. Christian concepts of charity were wedded to notions about the place of the underclass: they should become useful but undemanding members of society.

The problems concerning poverty were primarily a matter of perception. The turbulent events of May 1848, the growth of the press and increasing social awareness all served to underscore questions about the poor and coloured Europeans for the administrative and intellectual upper circles in the Indies. The first voices calling for action on behalf of poor Europeans were heard in the 1840s. Initially, such murmurs were quenched inside a bureaucratic drawer; but the voices kept on calling. In 1864 the resident of Batavia noted that many Mestizos working as office clerks in government departments earned no more than 100 guilders per month, with which they had to support their large families. They were living on the breadline. In his annual political reports the resident mentions repeatedly the "unenviable circumstances" of these people, adding, "the Government has so far done little to remedy this situation".[40] The resident observed quite correctly that the gap between lower and higher civil servants was increased by the demands of training (such as the Delft diploma for the higher civil servants). "Those who have been abroad [that is, have been in Europe] are regarded in every way as if they were Europeans, while those who have only lived in Java form, for the most part, a separate community, which is also enhanced by their low level of intellectual training."[41]

Reports of a growing European underclass in the Indies finally prompted a small research study in the residency of Batavia, to place the question of poverty in perspective. The government set up a committee in April 1872, charged with investigating poverty in Batavia.[42] Those on the committee included a member of the Council of the Indies, religious leaders from four different congregations, the resident of Batavia, the president of the Orphans' Chamber, the city surgeon, several lawyers, merchants and a teacher. All of them were newcomers (Totoks). It was their task to investigate whether or not Europeans born in the Indies encountered difficulties in finding a source of income. The committee was also instructed to investigate whether people born in Europe met with similar difficulties. The next step was to find out whether these Totoks mixed with the *inlandse kinderen*, for apparently such intercourse was considered one of the causes of poverty among Totoks. And finally, the committee was required to throw some light on the question of "whether peace and order in society is in any way threatened by these classes of inhabitants".[43] Thus, the aim appeared to be not only the improvement of the lot of the less-educated class of (Indo-)Europeans, but also to keep them from threatening the stability of the colony.

The committee worked diligently. Many meetings were held, minutes were taken, all the members produced memoranda. The astonishing conclusion was that in Batavia only 39 of those "born in Europe" (that is, Totoks) had "insufficient" incomes. Of this number, 22 were ex-military. The chief problem, according to the report, was not that social standards were deteriorating, but rather that colonial government might be losing prestige. The committee felt that the state of Europeans born in the Indies was far more worrisome — although there was no attempt to quantify this problem. It emerges from the minutes of the discussions that the committee had a fairly rigid concept of what the *inlandse kinderen* were like. They were poor, ill-educated, lived in kampongs, became excessively sensual at a young age, and developed a great fondness for gambling, dicing and cockfighting. Most of them were the offspring of concubinage and grew up "stained by their illegitimate birth".[44] The committee was more concerned with the level of morality among the paupers than with their material state. Much discussion was expended on the educational role of mothers, and in this the committee members were treading a well-worn path. It was said that Indo-Europeans received a poor upbringing, which was all the fault of their mothers, who had little understanding of the responsibilities of motherhood.[45]

The committee could scarcely be described as having an empirical approach; it hardly collected any concrete facts about the nature or causes of poverty, and it wallowed in imaginative speculations. One committee member, A.J.W. van Delden, director of the firm of Reynst & Vinju, acknowledged the existence of a split in the European community. On one side were the newcomers who arrived and swiftly departed, and on the other were the *inlandse kinderen*. Was there really a split, and if so, was what separated the two groups a matter of birthplace and skin colour, as suggested by the distinction between newcomers and *inlandse kinderen*? The study made by the committee could neither confirm nor refute this; there was simply not enough information. We do know that in this very period it became easier for Indies-born Europeans to gain government appointments. And there were many newcomers who had fallen on hard times, especially ex-military in the towns and villages, so that, in fact, the split between rich and poor was not according to land of birth and skin colour.

The committee proposed a solution, sketched in very general terms. It placed the emphasis on moral education, which would be implemented by expanding elementary schooling and setting up a network of kindergartens. Since the government could not provide sufficient jobs, there would have to be agricultural and artisanal colleges to train the young men. It was the government's job to extract the children at the earliest possible age from the influences of their parents, offering them a programme of elementary and secondary education, trade apprenticeships and training in agricultural practices, so that they could become useful and worthy citizens. The committee expressed a view widely held by the colonial elite: the goal of government was to shape the local-born *inlandse kinderen* into "useful members of the community". This did not imply emancipation in the sense of raising their social status to that of mainstream European citizenry in the colony; rather, it suggested preventing the impoverished Europeans from becoming a burden on the community and bringing the colonial government into disrepute. For the Minister of the Colonies, Isaäc Dignus Fransen van de Putte, the proposed solutions were many bridges too far. He would not budge from the conviction that the government should intervene only if private charitable organisations appeared inadequate.[46]

The committee's report met the same fate as many another diligently compiled government paper: it was ignored. In view of this, it would seem superfluous to discuss it any further, were it not for the fact that the report illustrates so vividly how the notables of Batavia looked upon the situation. Furthermore, the very fact that a committee of enquiry was set up signals a changing attitude on the part of the government. Slowly but surely, the group of impoverished Europeans were entering the colonial government's field of vision — although the committee's recommendations concerning improvements were considered far too innovative and costly. In fact, only one of the committee's recommendations was adopted: that was the proposal to give free medical care to every member of the household of a civil servant, including the illegal concubines and children; so far it had only been the men in government employment who enjoyed this privilege. The treatment of venereal diseases was explicitly excluded from the free medical package.[47]

Living on charity

The 1872 study dealt only with the city of Batavia. This was far and away the largest metropolis in the Indonesian archipelago, home to the most populous European community and having the highest number of newcomers, and it was a typical settlement of civil servants. Five hundred kilometres to the east lay Semarang, with a population only slightly smaller than Batavia's but with a very different feel to it. Here the Indische element was far more prominent. Semarang had become a crossroads for Central Java; here the straggling remnants from garrisons in Magelang, Ambarawa, the Principalities and elsewhere found their way. They streamed into Semarang, many of them down-at-heel, crippled and disabled, alcoholic and altogether pitiful old soldiers, with their families. There were also a large number of orphaned and abandoned children. Semarang had two orphanages that offered shelter to homeless children, especially offspring of the Dutch military, coming from the length and breadth of the archipelago.

The committee of 1872 had suggested that it was chiefly the army that was the source of poverty among the Europeans in the Indies. The 1901 large-scale government inquiry into poverty on Java and the adjacent island of Madura only confirmed this finding. The report drawn up for the residency of Semarang in 1901 recorded 652 "indigent" heads of family. "Indigent" was the categorisation for families who had a monthly income of 100 guilders, and single persons who earned less than

50 guilders per month. Of the indigents, 35 per cent were on a pension, 26 per cent had no occupation, and 17 per cent were self-employed, running a small business or trade. These percentages were more or less the same throughout Java.[48] It is striking how many small tradesmen and artisans there were among the less well-off. The report lists, for instance, musicians, guardsmen, carters, photographers, one cobbler, one stonemason, smiths, dairy supervisors, a puppeteer (for wayang shadow plays) and people running gambling joints for the Chinese. All these were modest jobs, but they were generally considered quite respectable. The largest group of indigents in Semarang were ex-military (often unmarried) and made up 40 per cent — a total of 263 men. This number included most of the paupers, that is, families who, according to the questionnaire, had to live off less than 75 guilders a month. More than half the military paupers had once been newcomers from Europe. The ex-military were a heavy drain on Semarang's poor relief, and elsewhere too they were a major source of pauperism. Throughout Java and Madura they formed about 30 per cent of all paupers.[49] Then there were large numbers of destitute children, fathered by soldiers.[50] Poverty and lack of scope to improve one's social status were passed on from generation to generation.

Most of the so-called paupers managed somehow to eke out a living. After all, financial assistance was only meant for the most extreme cases, chiefly the disabled, widows and orphans. Batavia, Surabaya and Semarang each had a Committee for the Support of Needy Christians, set up in 1829 in order to distribute the money collected from the Poor Tax. It was intended to fill the gaps left by the churches' charitable system. The benefits issued by the committee were only a supplement to the churches' poor relief and intended for those who were not physically capable of work. Those who wished to apply for poor relief from the committee had to acquire a paper signed by the district head where they lived, attesting to their infirmity.[51] There is a record from February 1838 of the head of district S in Semarang, together with the chief district head of that city, visiting the impoverished family of Jan George Masius, who was suffering from an eye complaint and was almost blind. Each month the family received seven guilders from the church's poor fund — which was far from adequate. Masius had seven children, described as running around "almost naked". Four of them had not been baptised, because the family could not afford it. The furniture in the house consisted of "a broken table & two wobbly old chairs and a *balie balie* [*balai-balai*, a kind of couch]". One of the daughters, having lost her husband, had

Illustration 34   One of Semarang's charitable homes provided shelter for destitute ex-soldiers from the Dutch Indies army. There were many Ambonese and African soldiers among them. Quite a few of the African soldiers, like the Dutch, kept a housekeeper with whom they had a family. This print shows an African soldier with his children.
[Lithograph by Auguste van Pers in: *Nederlandsch Oost-Indische typen* (1851).]

returned to her father's home; she was pregnant. It was also stated that because Masius, being a Christian himself, "wished to bring up his children in the knowledge and understanding of the Christian faith", his case was submitted to the committee.[52]

It is remarkable that although there was a gradual growth in the population of Europeans in the East Indies, there was not an increase in the number of people claiming poor relief. The only place where such an increase can be noted in these years is Semarang. Here, in 1858, 81 people were granted poor relief by the Committee for the Support of Needy Christians. The numbers on poor relief only increased after 1870: in 1880 there were 134.[53] Almost half this number were men, mostly ex-military. The outbreak of war in Aceh (North Sumatra) drew large numbers of Dutch soldiers from the Netherlands to the Indonesian archipelago and also produced a stream of men who had left the army but still had to earn a living somehow. Meanwhile, the ex soldiers who were crippled or somehow incapable of working turned to the poor relief provided by the church and the poor committees.

Old soldiers made heavy demands on the churches' poor relief funds; and many of them lived in the poorhouses or old people's homes. Around 1845 the old men's home in Semarang sheltered around 57 people, most of them ex-military and their families.[54] In 1868 there were 134 people living there, 71 of whom were adult men. Seven of these men were described as indigent; all the others were pensioned soldiers, corporals or sergeants.[55] Among them were a few soldiers who had been recruited on the African Gold Coast, where the Netherlands had some colonial stations until 1872, and soldiers from Minahasa and Ambon. We can see, therefore, that in comparison with Batavia and Surabaya, Semarang was exceptional because of its large military presence. With the flood of soldiers arriving in the years after 1870, the small band of impoverished ex-military in the city also grew appreciably, as did the number of destitute orphans.

But on the whole, there is no notable increase in the numbers of Europeans dependent on poor relief in this period. Even the crisis in sugar production in 1884 did not drain the coffers of the charitable bodies.[56] Those who were not pensioned off by the army, or widowed, orphaned or chronically invalid, were forced to scrape a living somehow. But few actually died of starvation. The study of poverty in the Dutch East Indies carried out in 1901 provides a similar picture: "a mere" 17.5 per cent of all European civilians in the East Indies were classified as indigent (the city of Batavia and its suburbs were not included in this count because the officials in question failed to produce a usable report). Almost everyone had a roof over their head, if only one of palm branches or reed, and even the poorest families kept a servant.[57] Thus, it would seem that the problem of pauperism should not be considered a matter of dire necessity; it arose in the first instance out of government concern that the prestige and reputation of the Europeans might be jeopardised. A European should, under all circumstances, maintain a certain distance from the indigenous population.

On the other hand, the chief complaint from many Indies-born Europeans was not poverty but the fact that they were being discriminated against. The committee investigating pauperism in 1901 in the residency of Batavia wrote: "The Indo-European [...] is not by nature dissatisfied with his lot. He feels at home here in the Indies and has no reason to have a sense of discomfort or discontent, knowing as he does that his life here is better — or at least as good as — that of the vast majority of indigenes around him." The report goes on to say that feelings of discontent were aroused by a few troublemakers.[58] In a way, the committee was right, certainly in its perception that there were Indies-born Europeans who experienced their lifestyle as natural and satisfying. But it ignored the fact that the government itself was a source of discontent for these Europeans, because of the way it created special regulations for them, thereby making them into a separate group with their distinct rights and obligations. One committee member from Batavia observed, with some justification, that the strict juridical distinctions drawn between the various population groups was what lay at the root of all the problems.[59]

There were many people in the Indies who disliked intensely the stigmatisation of Indo-Europeans implicit in the investigation into pauperism. In 1903, for instance, a man who had grown up in an orphanage in the Indies, writing under the pseudonym *Si Miskin* (The Poor Man), protested against the cultural arrogance of the colonial authorities. As he wrote, "where it concerns combating pauperism there is too much emphasis on introducing European standards and ways of thought into the situation in the Indies and too little attention paid to what the people are actually like, to whom one wishes to be "charitable".[60] He asserted, quite rightly, that down-and-out "pure-blood" Europeans who ended up in the kampongs created more trouble than the Sinjos who on the whole complained very little, only cherishing "an inborn distrust" of the "pure-blooded" Europeans, because of their arrogant attitude. Most of the destitute Europeans, after all, were pensioned-off or worn-out soldiers who had chosen to remain in the Indies. And it was many of these ex-military men who formed a social problem and were a public nuisance.

But besides the problem of ex-army men was the problem of the many hundreds of children they fathered and abandoned. Whereas the problem of pauperism hardly aroused very heated feelings and scarcely stirred the government to charitable motions, the question of the many orphan children was recognised as a far more serious matter. Rather than pauperism and concubinage, these children incited in the colonial government deep feelings of responsibility for the fate of the Dutch race. Nor was it a small problem: in 1860 there were about 900 children in the orphanages and the *Pupillenkorps* (Army Training School) out of a total of almost 11,000 European children in Java.[61] Forty years on, in 1900, there were no fewer than 2,673 orphans living in the various orphanage homes in the Indies. Of the approximately 30,000 European children in the Indies, this represented a rise in both absolute numbers and percentages.[62]

The first orphanages were built in the early days of the Dutch East India Company, first in Batavia and later in Semarang and other places. The orphans were brought up to be good Christians and received a basic education. Initially, the Dutch Protestant Church managed poor relief and care for orphans. The first non-church orphans' home was Parapattan, established in 1832 on the southeast outskirts of Batavia by Walter Henry Medhurst, a missionary from the London Missionary Society; several years later, in 1846, they moved into a spacious villa in the Batavia district of Rijswijk. To begin with, the home looked after orphan children with an English background. The departure of the British from the East Indies in 1816 had an unexpected result. Even as late as 1840, almost half the orphans in the Parapattan Institute had an English

Illustration 35 The first privately run orphanage in the East Indies was that of Parapattan, in Batavia. It was set up in 1832 by the London Missionary Society and for many years retained its British character. Initially, children were accepted only if they were acknowledged by their father, but the rule was relaxed somewhat after 1857.
[Anonymous lithograph in: *Het leeskabinet* (1881).]

name.[63] The number of English children only began to decline in the 1840s, and lessons were no longer given in English.[64] The number of orphans in the school gradually increased, from 37 in 1838 to 65 in 1879 and 73 in 1900.[65] Although initially only legitimate children were accepted, this regulation was abandoned in 1857.[66]

The Parapattan Orphanage acquired a good reputation. Pupils became proficient in Dutch, and many of them found employment with the Dutch government when they left school at 18. Others joined the army, became sailors, or took jobs in the agricultural business or the printing trade and, after the 1860s, as engineers. Girls leaving the orphanage took up positions such as children's nanny, maidservant, dressmaker, lady's companion, or domestic help in a European family; many of them married straight away upon quitting school.[67] The aim of the school was to assist children in becoming members of the "well-educated middle class"; the result fell hopelessly short of this.[68]

Besides the Parapattan Orphanage, Batavia had the Djati Institute, a home for orphans that aimed to "care for and educate destitute and needy children". It was founded in 1854 by Emanuel Francis, who was later to become director of the Javasche Bank. Francis was born in Cochin in South India and arrived in Java at the beginning of the 19th century. Djati was small, providing shelter for 40 to 50 children.[69] It was intended for children who had nowhere else to go. Throughout the Indonesian archipelago, "agents" — who were generally local notables — would keep an eye out for needy children; it was a method commonly used by institutes such as orphanages and private schools. The agents formed a network helping to source needy children and collect money.[70]

All things considered, the number of children in the Batavia orphanage remained quite small. Some children were brought up in other families, but many were shipped off to the big orphanages in Semarang. Here the number of orphans exceeded that in any other place, and it continued to rise steadily. The city had two orphanages, one Protestant (founded in 1769) and the other Roman Catholic (founded in 1809). In 1835 the Protestant orphanage housed 42 girls and 27 boys, compared with 36 and 44 in the Roman Catholic home.[71] In 1868 these numbers had jumped to 141 and 69, and 203 and 56, respectively.[72] In a space of 30 years the number of orphans in the homes had increased threefold. What is striking is the relative drop in the number of boys living in the orphanages. Many boys found an alternative form of shelter — most of them in the army school, the Pupillenkorps, founded in 1848 in Gombong (Central Java). During the 1860s the numbers in the Semarang orphanages ceased to rise — doubtless because the homes had reached their maximum capacity and training schools were being built in other places.

The education offered by the orphanages was, at best, minimal; and the home comforts were few. They cannot have been joyful places. In 1846 the Protestant orphanage was severely over-crowded, the children were squashed into dormitories like the proverbial sardines in a can, sleeping on pallets with thin mattresses filled with cotton and bristling with bedbugs. A visitor in the 1840s exclaimed aghast, "It is almost impossible to believe that the children can get a wink's sleep at night." The diet was basic, consisting of rice, vegetables, chillies, fish and meat. The children left the grounds only to go to church or for a group walk; otherwise they remained in the building or in the — reportedly dismal — inner courtyard. The Roman Catholic orphans had a better deal. They lived in a new building close to the former city walls, on the east side; the rooms were large and airy, and the beds were moderately comfortable. Surprisingly, the children here were less healthy than those in the Protestant home; out of 250 children, 40 died each year — a figure that seems shockingly high, even for those days.[73]

Clearly, the orphan children could not spend the whole day plastered to their school benches, and in the afternoons there was a considerable amount of idling and lazing. The boys and girls were offered little by way of preparation for life "in the outside world". In fact, most of the boys ended up in the army. Already when the Protestant orphanage was founded in 1769, it was stated that the boys would be sent to join the army at a certain age.[74] Of the 27 boys who left the orphanage between July 1851 and April 1853, 19 went into the army, six entered private service, and one went to live with his brother.[75] In 1857 no fewer than 37 boys left the Roman Catholic orphanage to join the army, most of them going to the Army Training School in Gombong; another large group joined the artillery. There was little choice when youths quit the orphanage.

Girls tended to be older than boys when they left the orphanage. They would take up posts as maidservants or nannies to families, but most of them went straight into marriage. In such cases the girl would be given a "certificate" from the head of the orphanage, declaring to her future husband that she was a chaste and upright maiden.[76] Bearing this precious document, the husband-to-be would go to the registry office and ask for the marriage announcement to be made public. Most girls would marry someone who lived locally, or an ex-military man from a neighbouring garrison or wanting to settle in the district. Girls often married young, some as young as 15 years old.[77] How exactly the girls met their future partners is not recorded, but presumably there were occasions when unmarried men and orphan girls were introduced and could look each other over. The authorities were only too happy if the girls "remained true to the principles of honourable and virtuous behaviour". However, this was often far from the case, as is apparent from complaints that there were always girls who "couldn't resist temptation" and strayed from the straight and narrow path.[78]

Life in the barracks

The 1901 government report on pauperism concluded there was one chief culprit responsible for the poverty among Indies-born Europeans: army concubinage, unions between European soldiers and local women not sanctioned by the law. Indeed, soldiers were neither permitted to bring a wife with them from the Netherlands, nor allowed to marry once in the Indies — so it is hardly surprising that the soldiers resorted to prostitutes. An alternative was officially accepted by the army in 1836: Dutch soldiers were allowed to live together with Asian women. Seen in terms of 19th-century Dutch morality, this was shocking, but it was generally tolerated "in order to further the good health, comfort and few pleasures that the poorer soldiers enjoyed in these districts".[79] The choice was simple: prostitute or concubine. The presence of women in the barracks had a certain restraining influence upon the soldiers and prevented the unbridled growth of prostitution, with the inevitable concurrent spread of venereal disease — which, incidentally, was rife in the 19th century. Many soldiers became very attached to their concubines, or *njai*, and when their army contract expired they would marry them and legitimise their children. Abhorrent as the system was to contemporaries, it worked well and was therefore tolerated by both soldiers and civil authorities. Garrison life was no salacious Sodom, although the women had few rights and abuse was common. In true Dutch manner, authorities turned a blind eye to the somewhat illegal aspects of life and even created new regulations to address the situation. The army commanders of the barracks kept registers of the women and children living there. A concubine was not admitted into the barracks without first showing some proof of good behaviour from her village head.[80]

Inside the barracks, domestic arrangements left a lot to be desired. The soldiers' quarters consisted of large rooms within which each soldier and his concubine had to curtain off their "bed table" — a raised platform of wooden planks serving as a bed. The soldiers who were single had a separate section from the men living with a woman. Children also lived in these improvised rooms, usually sleeping on top of, or underneath, the bed table. In 1888, of the 13,000 European military personnel in the Dutch East Indies, almost 3,000 — chiefly sergeants and corporals — had a woman housekeeper.[81] Thus, on average, almost a quarter of the soldiers lived with a concubine; in some places the figure was a little higher.

The number of children living in barracks fluctuated considerably, but some couples had large families. In 1904, from a total of 12,593 European soldiers in the barracks throughout the Dutch East Indies, there were 410 legitimate and recognised children, and 827 illegitimate. Of these, 90 per cent were below the age of nine, and most were considerably younger. There were 563 children aged below four. This suggests that at the turn of the 19th century around 150 children were being born in the barracks each year — the actual figure was probably higher, since some babies would not remain in the barracks and some would die as infants. We have no information on which of these barracks-born children were later classified as European; what is evident is that they formed a slowly swelling stream of needy and destitute children who were sent to orphanages, and that they grew up and joined the army in a seemingly never-ending cycle. Curiously, the phenomenon of barracks children seems to have existed mainly in Java. The number of children was far smaller in the garrison settlements outside Java and in the regiments on active service. In Fort de Kock in West Sumatra, for instance, in 1904 there were only 15 children to 366 European soldiers, while Magelang had 107 children to 1,015 soldiers; Yogyakarta (Central Java) had 35 children to 225 military men.[82]

The formalisation of concubinage in the army barracks was typical for the Dutch East Indies. In British India the problem posed by soldiers' sexual needs was resolved by creating clear regulations for prostitution.[83] Only after 1913 did the political opposition to army concubines in the Dutch East Indies become so intense that the nyai of the European military gradually disappeared from the picture and prostitution won the day from concubinage.[84] There was another problem connected with concubinage: that of the children. Many soldiers were either unwilling, or too poor, to provide for their offspring. Soldiers often wanted to return to the Netherlands when their period of service was finished. In some cases the children were cared for by other soldiers at the garrison, or they would be taken in by their mother's family. The latter practice, however, was a thorn in the flesh of the colonial government. "How many soldiers there must be in our ranks, who are unable to support their children, who hand them over entirely into the mother's care, so that they grow up among natives in the local kampongs!" wrote the commander-in-chief of the army Hubert J.J.L. de Stuers in 1835.[85] Just as in the days of the VOC, the colonial authorities did not wish to see soldiers' children raised in indigenous circles; they wanted to preserve them for the European way of life.

Throughout the 19th century the position of the barracks children became an increasing headache for the colonial authorities. A few attempts were made to build schools — where soldiers were also welcome — beside the barracks, and in 1828 Maj. Gen. Willem Schenck founded a school for soldiers' children in Batavia.[86] It was run on a shoestring, since few of the children could pay fees. They were taught reading, writing, geography, Dutch and Malay; the girls also learned needlework. The teachers were non-commissioned officers and soldiers.[87] In 1832 the government decided to give financial support to the struggling school, so that the 100 or so pupils then attending could remain.[88] Despite this, the school went downhill, and it closed a few years later. Most of the pupils transferred to the newly founded elementary school in Weltevreden (central Batavia). The supervisory committee for the soldiers' school voiced some opposition to the move. The soldiers' children were poorly clothed and had rough manners, which would arouse the derision and contempt of the children of civilians already attending this school.[89] Despite this, the school for soldiers' children was not resuscitated. So, apart from this brief attempt, scant education was offered to the Mestizos of the barracks. The most they could hope for was some improvised teaching from well-disposed soldiers. Only later in the 19th century did it become customary to send children to a nearby elementary school, or even to a Fröbel school (nursery school) if there was one in the neighbourhood.[90] Clearly, there was a need to educate the barracks children, just as there was a need for army recruits; these two require-ments complemented each other and motivated the plans to found a military school. Here the children would receive a solid education, and the army gained a welcome source of recruits. De Stuers put the case for establishing an army training school where the children would have ex-soldiers as their masters and enjoy a "completely military and strict education". Education, discipline and employment joined and marched together hand in hand.[91]

In the 1840s the first steps were taken to set up an army school in Kedung Kebo, which lay in the residency of Bagelen in Central Java. The initiative came from the commandant of the Fourth Battalion, which had been stationed in Purworejo since 1836. Scarcely had the troops been established in the garrison than children were running around in the army camp; so a school was set up for them. Initially, the children lived outside the camp, "in the kampong" — that is, with their mother or her family — and in the daytime they went to school, where they held military exercises with wooden rifles. But very soon the children became boarders, and school uniforms were created for them from second-hand soldiers' garments. A former sergeant-major was the teacher.[92] In 1847 the government decided to intervene, and the Pupillenkorps (Army Training School) was founded. There were then 23 children attending the school in Kedung Kebo, and their numbers were supplemented with all the boys between the ages of seven and 14 living in the orphanages of Semarang.[93]

The school moved in 1854, after the buildings had collapsed during a heavy rainstorm; the new location was Fort Cochius, near Gombong, also in the residency of Bagelen. Here the school was housed in a low, octagonal bombardment-proof building — a far more sturdy home than the wobbly walls in Kedung Kebo. Gombong consisted of a kampong and an encampment where the officers and their families had their houses. There was also a fort with its outhouses, a military hospital, and homes of other staff. The school stated that its aim was: "To raise the standards of children of European stock who had been brought up like natives, and draw them up out of the neglected circumstances into which they had sunk."[94] High-minded as this may sound, what the government really hoped was to turn the problem of the deserted children of soldiers to its own advantage and create a new source of army recruits.[95] In order to be accepted at the school, candidates had to be Christian and of European ancestry. According to the rules, a birth certificate had to be produced — which only Christians, Jews and others with the same civil rights as these groups actually possessed.[96] Formally speaking, it did not matter what the mother's origin was. In practice, most of the children had an Indonesian, often Javanese, mother.[97] Children whose father was a soldier were admitted free; if the parents were civilians they had to pay school fees according to their means.

The Army Training School was a world in itself. The children of Gombong had their own jargon, "pupil-speak", which was a variation of army slang, or *Tangsi* Malay, the language spoken in the barracks. This

Illustration 36. The Army Training School, Pupillenkorps, was founded in 1855 in Gombong. Most of the pupils were the sons of soldiers and did not have to pay school fees. The curriculum was dominated by military drill, and there were lessons in language, arithmetic and ethics, as well as shooting practice.
[Lithograph after a painting by Justus Pieter de Veer, 1898, KITLV, Leiden.]

feisty dialect withstood every attempt to introduce respectable, civilised Dutch.[98] Regular elementary schooling was introduced only in the 1880s, and this helped spread the use of Dutch, although dialect still abounded. Boys would be aged between seven and ten when they started school, and when they were 18 they were given a ten-year contract with the army. The curriculum was varied, with regular subjects as well as singing, dancing, administration, physical training — which included fencing and sword fighting with sticks — and general ethics.[99] It was thought that Indies-born children possessed a great flair for drawing and copying, and consequently there were frequent lessons devoted to these subjects. The school produced many topographical draughtsmen, just as in the days of the VOC many Mestizos were employed as surveyors and mapmakers. Another highly regarded subject was gymnastics, for it was observed that "Indische children were by nature lean and agile". When the boys reached their 13th year they began military education.[100]

It would be hard to tell whether the lessons in general ethics bore fruit. When they started school the boys were already seven years old, by which age a child's character has largely been formed. It is clear that the school was far from pleasant. Many of the children suffered from eye infections; the cane was frequently used to punish unruly pupils. Strict discipline was maintained along military lines, and even though most of the boys had been born in an army camp, the harshness — especially for younger children — was hard to bear.[101] Not surprisingly, many pupils ran away. At the beginning of 1879 a group of 85 pupils escaped from the barracks in Gombong. When the boys were found, they explained that they had saved up their pocket money and planned to go to the seaport towns of Cilacap or Tegal, where they would sign up as cabin boys or join the army. Some of them reported that "it was most unpleasant at the Army School, they weren't given much opportunity to go out for walks and they were often dressed down by the commanding officer". This large-scale breakout did not suggest to the army authorities that they might possibly examine school policy. The "deserters" were punished; they were given extra work and punishment drill and put into prison.[102]

A few hundred children from the army barracks were thus able to be educated at the Army Training School. The authorities were fighting a losing battle, because as the army gradually increased, the number of children born in the barracks followed suit. There was plenty of work for the Seventh-Day Adventist and one-time city missionary in the slums of Amsterdam Johannes van der Steur, who arrived in Java in 1892 and founded an ex-soldiers' home in Magelang, not far from Semarang. Before long, the first four soldiers' children were also living there, and by 1895 the number had risen to 40.[103] With the major military operations in Lombok and Aceh in the 1890s, large numbers of children ended up homeless. The home for army children gradually expanded. Van der Steur regularly came across European-looking children living in the kampongs, and he would try, with their mothers' permission, to "adopt" them for his home. He also had children who came to his school only for lessons but continued to live at home. In 1896 Van der Steur founded the Society for the Spread of Christian Standards and Mutual Benefit. The orphanage gained a cobbler's and a tailor's. With limited means and strict discipline, Van der Steur, who continued working until his death shortly after the Japanese capitulation in 1945, managed to bring up and educate hundreds of children in his school-cum-home.[104]

The school in Gombong provided only a partial solution to the educational question in the Indies, but as a source of recruits for the Dutch colonial army the Army Training School was most successful. In 1852 there were 198 pupils, and by 1876 there were already 371.[105] By this date most of the boys are recorded as being the sons of soldiers (244). There were also 72 sons of civilians, 39 orphans and 16 abandoned children. Almost all the children were Indo-European (357).[106] It became very common for soldiers leaving Indonesia to send their sons to Gombong, and the school also received a constant stream of pupils from the orphanages. At the end of 1860 there were 1,119 army children registered by the government, and 326 of them were at the Army Training School.[107] Between 1848 and the end of 1870 the school in Gombong saw 1,074 children pass through its doors.[108] Most of the boys who attended the Army Training School went straight into the army. In fact, they did not have much choice; there were scant job opportunities for boys with a poor education. There was also an exorbitant fine imposed should parents or guardians have the temerity to remove boys from school before they joined the army. Most of the lads joined the infantry. From the above-mentioned 1,074 pupils in the first decades of the school's existence, only 35 became artisans, 96 entered the topographical department, and 34 became army musicians. At the beginning of 1884 there were 590 old boys from Gombong in the army, forming the majority of the Indo-European troops. But among the officers' ranks, there was scarcely an old boy from Gombong to be found.[109] In all, the Indo-Europeans in the Dutch colonial army formed a small group — about 10 per cent of the officers and 5 per cent of the soldiers.

Propagating the artisan

The principal sources of army recruits were the orphanages and army school; few soldiers joined up from other sections of society in the Indies. The army did not provide adequate means to rescue local-born Europeans from a life of poverty. It did not enjoy high social prestige, and the

Illustration 37. A large stream of soldiers' children eddied around the army barracks. In 1892 Johannes van der Steur (1865–1945), a missionary from Haarlem in the Netherlands, arrived in Java. He founded a home for these army children in Magelang. This housed not only orphans but also children who were evidently partly European, found with their Javanese mothers or families and removed in order to receive a Christian education.
[Photograph, *ca.* 1897, KITLV, Leiden.]

colonial authorities were well aware of this. Plans to improve the lot of the pauper class, which were frequently discussed in the papers and in government memoranda, considered such things as agricultural education and teaching skilled crafts to *inlandse kinderen*. The importance of providing work was often justified with a double argument: there was a shortage of office jobs, and also the young (men) needed to be encouraged to combat their inborn laziness. Thus we hear the Batavian clergyman Rev. Steven Adriaan Buddingh as early as 1840 lamenting the fact that job opportunities — especially the chance of building a career as an office employee — were drastically declining, because so many newcomers were arriving from Europe, and the government had introduced the requirement that civil servants held the *radicaal*. Buddingh admitted, at the same time, that "most of the children born here of native mothers [...] have a very limited intelligence, and added to the cloud of murky mist which overshadows their abilities they frequently seem to add the blemish of being bone idle". As Buddingh saw it, the orphan boy scarcely rejoiced in the prospect of a glorious future: "He can become a clerk, [...] or a printer's mate, or a sailor." Buddingh was very much in favour of giving the orphan boys an adequate training in a craft; this would avoid the problem of teaching them useless subjects like geography, natural history or history until they were 17: "There is no better nor more honourable career for them today, than that of artisan!"[110]

The idea of training *inlandse kinderen* — and especially orphan children — in a skilled craft was popular in Indonesia for a long time. In 1849 the resident of Batavia, Pieter van Rees, proposed setting up an industrial school, but his suggestion met with no response.[111] However, from the 1850s there were many attempts to found specialised schools for boys to enhance their career opportunities in the civil sector. The Freemasons, with their tradition of charitable works, were strongly attached to the ideals of the Enlightenment with its emphasis on education, and from 1850 they championed the cause of improving education and in some cases even founded schools themselves. Not surprisingly, the Freemason lodges also concentrated on the Indies-born children. The Semarang lodge in particular, which was named *La Constante et Fidèle* (Constant and Faithful), was extremely active. Under the enthusiastic leadership of Carel Eliza van Kesteren, editor-in-chief of the newspaper *De Locomotief*, the Masons founded a Fröbel school in 1875 and advocated the establishment of a secondary school (Dutch HBS) and handwork training for girls. In 1865, on the initiative of the Masons, a technical school was founded in Batavia, later called Queen Wilhelmina School, which concentrated on training students to work in the Java sugar industry.[112]

The greatest achievement in the attempts to make artisans out of the orphan boys came with the opening of the Jongens-Weezeninrichting (Orphan Boys' Institution) in Surabaya in 1860. Surabaya was a most suitable location for a school like this because it had a navy workshop, a department of civil engineering, a factory producing artillery, and a shipbuilding yard — all of which could offer the boys a period of practical training and, later on, employment.

People in Surabaya had been imploring the government for years to build a technical school. The main obstacle was, of course, financial — and the government proved unwilling to commit. Governor-General

Albertus Jacobus Duymaer van Twist denied that "the Government had any moral obligation to provide for the future of children who are begotten upon native women by European fathers, who upon their father's death, and sometimes also through the death of their mothers, are left entirely without parents, roaming in the kampongs or elsewhere, and only cared for by the native people".[113] As he saw it, the upbringing and education of children was the responsibility of their parents, not the state. The argument went farther: were the state to intervene in providing for such children, parents would become lazy and irresponsible. The government would finance a school for technical training only if this seemed in its own interest, according to the governor-general. In contrast to this attitude, a member of the Council of the Indies, C. Visscher, felt strongly that it was the government's duty to care for "the orphaned and destitute children of Europeans" as a preventative measure, lest they should grow "into natural enemies".[114]

Events in Surabaya made it very clear how great was the need for a technical school. In 1853 a kind of training school for skilled crafts was established. The stated aim of the school was to train orphan boys in a skilled craft so they could then find jobs as artisans and foremen.[115] Despite his disobliging and utilitarian attitude towards the neglected children, Governor-General Duymaer van Twist promised 300 guilders a year and permitted himself to be elected the school's patron. It was not a school in the true sense of the word, for it provided lessons only three evenings a week, to 66 pupils, whose ages varied from 13 to 22. Most of the students who enrolled already had a job, as artisans or foremen with the navy or, more often, as transcribers or clerks.[116] Students enthusiastically subscribed for the courses — clear evidence that such technical training was in high demand, and that many young men were glad of any chance to improve their lot. Before long, however, the school came to grief — the teaching was too theoretical, and the financial basis was insecure. In 1856 the course was discontinued.[117]

Finally, in 1860, Surabaya gained an Orphan Boys' Institution, a combined orphanage and technical school. Most of the orphans came from the city, which gave the boarding school strong local links, more so than the orphanages in Semarang, which took in children from all over Java.[118] The level of teaching was not exactly overwhelming. Apparently the main aim of the school was to instil discipline. It would seem that the most difficult children ended up in the Boys' Institution. In accordance with 19th-century notions, discipline was extremely severe. In 1878, one of the orphan boys described his experiences in the newspaper *De Locomotief,* in which he recounted how he had been abused in a "barbaric fashion". In some cases the boys would be manacled like criminals with iron chains on their right hand and left foot, and thrown into a small shed.[119] Punishment was constantly being meted out for so-called indecent behaviour and for running away from school. Indeed, the boys ran away so often that in 1872 the local police were given a bonus of five guilders for every escaped orphan whom they managed to pick up. The impertinence of some of the boys was imaginative and unabashed. In 1882, for instance, a boy was caught pretending that he had found work in a sugar factory in Malang; in reality he was running a brothel in Surabaya.[120] According to the school board, such behaviour was explained by the "nature" of Indo-European boys, who had an inborn tendency towards a life of idle pleasure. Interestingly, problems encountered in the Netherlands with bringing up orphan boys were no less severe. There was not, of course, a problem of inborn "immorality" such as the authorities in the Indies so often complained about; the children in question usually came from a lower social milieu. Their inferior position and maladjusted behaviour was largely a class problem, but it was interpreted in racial terms.

The boys who grew up in the Orphan Boys' Institution sometimes acquired such a bad record that it was difficult for them to find a job. If we examine the (presumably, positively adjusted) statistics, however, most of them landed on their feet. Between 1880 and 1897 there were even two pupils from the school who passed the entrance exam for the higher secondary school (Dutch HBS). One of them went on to do the course for higher civil servants in Batavia and ended up being assistant-resident with the Binnenlands Bestuur. Of the remaining 100 pupils who "graduated" from the Orphan Boys' Institution between 1880 and 1897, most found employment in navy workshops, the railways, the artillery factory, tramway companies, petrol companies and agricultural enterprises.[121] They took up jobs such as engine drivers, station masters, tram conductors, instrument makers, smiths, day labourers, site foremen and gunners. A number found a post in the administrative sector, as lower civil servants or clerk with a company, and a few with the civil service, though these were in the minority. Twenty-two of the boys are recorded as being transcribers, clerks or accountants. Although the number who actually worked as artisans was very small, the cliché that assumed Indo-European young men aimed only at being clerks or civil servants was contradicted by the reality. The statistics on this matter, incidentally, date from 1897. That was a time when all sorts of new functions were being created that required people with technical training, especially in the railways and telegraph services, in enterprises and workplaces where mechanisation was surging ahead.

At the same time as debates were being held about setting up technical schools, the first plans were being developed to found agricultural colonies and teach boys agricultural techniques. The inspiration for such an enterprise was born in France. There, in 1840, Frédéric de Metz had founded a kind of school for the re-education of delinquent and orphaned boys in the village of Mettray, near Tours; the owner of a private estate had offered his land for this use. The boys lived in small groups supervised by a guardian and were given physical training, taught a craft and had lessons in ethics.[122] Mettray soon had its followers in the Netherlands, where in 1851 an agricultural colony was founded in Gorssel, near Zutphen, in the east of the country. For several decades the Netherlands had known agricultural institutions as a form of punishment, or re-education, but an institute existing solely for the benefit of young people was something new.[123] The reactions in Gorssel to the "Netherlands Mettray" were positive, and enthusiastic noises wafted across to the East Indies. There, the notion of an agricultural educational establishment slotted extremely well into the debate around children from poorer social milieus. In the Dutch East Indies, where the large number of orphans led to social problems and a feeling of unease in the upper classes, it was not long before the call was heard for such an establishment to care for the destitute *inlandse kinderen*.

The committee that in 1872 studied the question of poverty among Europeans in the city of Batavia sounded alarm bells regarding pauperism. The alarm bells were to go on ringing throughout the last quarter of the 19th century. The committee's report drew attention to the presence of a group of impoverished Europeans and aroused a feeling of responsibility for the indigent people of European descent. This sense would only increase as the century moved on. Rather than pleading for a technical school to train the poorly off Indies-born children, the committee suggested establishing an agricultural colony.[124] The aim of this would be "to raise the above-mentioned class out of its destitute circumstances"; it would provide a good education and offer a means of existence through agricultural employment. The director of the Binnenlands Bestuur, Fitz Verploegh, suggested in 1876 that such a colony be founded on the uninhabited island of (Great) Obi, near Ternate, in the Moluccas. What he intended, above all, was to turn the pupils into "perfected natives". His colleague in the department of education, religion and industry enquired cynically whether the Binnenlands Bestuur was envisaging a detention colony on the island. Governor-General Johan Wilhelm van Lansberge was equally unimpressed by the plan — and the idea fizzled out like a damp squib. The discussion, however, shows clearly how people in the upper echelons of government thought about *inlandse kinderen*. The director of education predicted that the agricultural colony was doomed to failure: "The girls will become the concubines of Europeans and Chinese, and the boys will become the dependents of the community, that is if they do not end up in prison on account of their illegal practices." Clearly, the plan was overambitious: the institute aimed at no more nor less than the "improvement of a race", and in order for it to succeed, as many needy children as possible were required to be gathered together in such a colony.[125]

The language used in the discussions is often so cliché ridden, the tone so patronising, and the suggestions so naive that it is hard to take them seriously. Nevertheless, setting up the committee was one of the first signals that the government was willing to intervene in the lot of the pauperised classes in the Indies, or that it was in any way concerned with the effect such a group had upon the rest of society. It is remarkable how stubbornly the agricultural colonies were advocated, in combination with an equally persistent and ridiculous stereotype of Indo-Europeans as bone-idle, lacking the slightest interest in craftwork and skilled labour. It appears, however, from various government and residents' reports, and not least from the results of the 1901 enquiry into pauperism, that in reality many Europeans living in the Indies did practise some kind of skilled craft. But the plans for an agricultural colony were slow to materialise. Not until the final decades of the 19th century were a few colonies set up, and they were hardly a blazing success.

Of the three possible scenarios to relieve the situation of the indigent Europeans in the Indies — they could become soldiers, artisans or farmers — the first option was usually the most successful. Not only was there a supply of prospective soldiers from the orphanages, there was also a guaranteed job in the army. Garrisons, orphanages and the Army Training School formed a firm circle; it was difficult to break out of its grip. Many orphans or abandoned children had an army father; their lives repeated a similar pattern. There was also a demand for artisans in the Indies world, which prompted the establishment of technical training schools. But the financial and economic structure of society in the East Indies, together with the reticence of the colonial government to consider education as a means to social advancement, left little room to manoeuvre. The government was extremely cautious, so that most social initiatives began as private undertakings, which meant they had only a fragile basis; consequently, they usually faded into extinction. Meanwhile, the pauper in the European community was in most cases a white soldier or his child. The colonial upper classes and the often arrogant authorities could scarcely imagine, let alone deal with, a life of struggling impecuniousness. A huge social divide separated rich from poor.

CHAPTER 8

Crisis and Change in the Indische World

The agricultural crisis of 1884 is usually thought of as a watershed in the history of the Indies. The year 1884 was one of calamities, disaster following hard upon the heels of disaster: coffee-leaf disease, sugar-cane disease and, to cap it all, the collapse of sugar prices on the world market. It would be hard to compare this crisis, however, with the Great Depression of the 1930s, when vast sections of the population had no job. Although in the East Indies not every European could find work with the government, a private firm or an agricultural enterprise, it is important to remember that the employment problem was merely exacerbated, and certainly not caused, by the agricultural crisis. The number of Europeans competing for office jobs had always been high, and the numbers continued to increase. During the 19th century, work in the European segment of the colonial economy gradually came to be seen as the norm for being properly employed, and this partly instigated the discussions on pauperism that began in the 1850s. It was not that the year 1884 witnessed a sudden explosion in the number of paupers — but rather that the norm for what European colonial society understood by "a decent and respectable way of making a living" became more sharply defined.

The suggestion that there was growing poverty among the Europeans in the Indies following a reorganisation of the plantation economy is far from accurate — but this does not make it less relevant. It forms part of the mythical stereotype that contrasts "Indische wastefulness" with "Western efficiency". According to this stereotype, companies in the Indies, with their inefficient production methods, could not cope with the agricultural crisis of 1884. The crisis, it is said, paved the way for intervention from banks in the Netherlands. A similar picture can be found in other colonies worldwide. It was, for instance, assumed that the traditional Creole sugar-plantation owners of Cuba, Puerto Rico and the Philippines would have to acknowledge the superiority of foreign capitalism. These notions have, in the meantime, gained more nuance.[1] We know that in Java the local business world was far more modern than the stereotypes would have us believe. Here the industrialisation of sugar production had already got under way in the early 19th century, and by 1884 it was certainly not hopelessly out-of-date. Historians have tended to confuse the opulent lifestyle of successful sugar planters with notions of inefficiency and certain failure. Another point to consider is that the end of the 19th century coincided with the heyday of imperialism. The Netherlands, too, was part of the process in which the "mother country" tightened control over its colonies. The marginalisation of 19th-century economic elites in the Indies was, following a similar line of reasoning, an inevitable result of this stricter control. Furthermore, it is said that these elites had to relinquish their businesses to Netherlands banks and trading houses, which immediately turned them into an NV (*Naamloze Venootschap*), that is, Public Limited Company, or PLC. Certainly, the number of PLCs began to increase in Java in the 1880s. But what is plausible is not necessarily true.

The fact is, there was no question of a rapid takeover by Netherlands financial backers. Technical and financial innovations came to the Java sugar industry in fits and starts but, in general, fairly evenly. Traditionally, each planter needed a financier to provide cash in advance and a regular buyer who would supervise selling the products in Europe. From the early 19th century, overseas bankers and trading houses had played an active part in the business. There was the NHM, the *Nederlandsche Handel-Maatschappij* (Netherlands Trading Company), as well as British trading houses in the coastal towns of Java, and in the 1840s and 1850s there were branches of Reynst & Vinju, and Anemaet, daughter companies of Dorrepaal and Van Hoboken. In the 1860s the *cultuurbanken* (agricultural finance corporations) appeared. This banking system threatened to collapse as a result of the agricultural crisis of 1884. On the eve of an unexpectedly sharp drop in prices on the world market, the exporters had bought up sugar at too high a price and consequently suffered huge losses.[2] To make matters worse, the sale of the next sugar crop stagnated, because the world market was swamped with sugar. Two Dutch banks set up in 1863, the Koloniale Bank and the NIHB (*Nederlandsch-Indische Handelsbank*, Netherlands-Indies Trading Bank), fell short by millions of guilders and had to be saved by the swift issue of new shares and bonds.[3] The Dorrepaalsche Bank, which financed

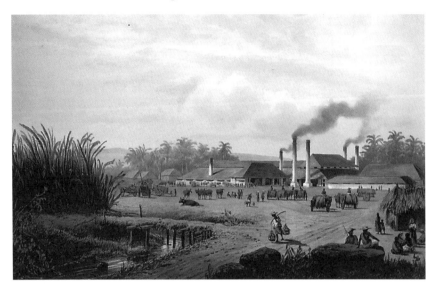

Illustration 38   Pekalongan-Tegal, on Java's north coast, was already a major sugar-producing region in the early 19th century. One of the largest factories was Pangka. [Lithograph after a painting by Abraham Salm, 1872, KITLV, Leiden.]

45 per cent of the sugar production in Java's Principalities, was forced to buy sugar from its clients using money that it should have reserved for advance payments on the following crop.[4] On 1 December 1884, one day after nine million guilders worth of bonds had been scraped together — with extreme difficulty — in an attempt to save the NIHB, the Dorrepaalsche Bank had to ask the NHM and the Bank of Java to bale them out.[5]

It is, however, an exaggeration to conclude — as many have done, in agreement with the British historian John S. Furnivall — that in 1884 between 30 million and 35 million guilders of new capital from the Netherlands was pumped into the agricultural enterprises, amounting to a takeover by Dutch banks.[6] In fact, what happened was that capital from the Netherlands, which had become worthless, was replaced. Furthermore, not all the replacement millions came from the Netherlands — a considerable quantity came from the East Indies themselves. Normally speaking, far more money streamed out of the Indies into the Netherlands than vice versa. Even in the final decades of the 19th century, most investments were financed by profits made in the Indies, with the exception of the new agricultural areas in Sumatra.[7] The only remaining verifiable fact in the story alleging a Dutch coup in its colonies is that the sole bank to be taken over by a Netherlands company was the Dorrepaalsche Bank.

It appeared with hindsight that the difficulties of the Dorrepaalsche Bank had been underestimated, and that half measures had finally pushed the bank into the arms of a consortium of Amsterdam trading houses and banks in which the NHM played a leading role. This whole process was not the result of a bid for power by a bank in the Netherlands. It was because too little new capital was acquired to finance the restructuring, so that the Dorrepaalsche Bank could not survive the renewed blows of 1885, which in that year mainly struck the coffee sector.[8] So far this bank had always been able to show clemency when a client was in need. Now, however, the successors to Georgius Leonardus Dorrepaal, C. van Lennep and H.J.P. van den Berg, were forced to make a long, sad journey through the Principalities. Many a coffee planter and the occasional indigo planter, people whom the bank had managed to keep going up until then, were told that their credit had expired. However, the blow was not equally hard for everyone concerned. This emerges, for instance, in a letter from Wolter Broese van Groenou written in June 1885 to his mother-in-law, Santje Dom, once known in the Indies as the Rose of Yogya, now living in The Hague. It seems that with the exception of the newcomer H. Eekhout, all the landholders of Yogyakarta were managing to keep their heads above water.

> Possibly it has not yet come to your knowledge that Eekhout had had his credit discontinued by the Dorrepaalsche Bank. That was the end of his enterprise, for he found himself paying more in rent than the indigo brought in. We feel very sorry for him, but what can you do? Now he is thinking of selling some of his land, but who wants or can afford to buy land at the present time? Apart from that, Yogya has survived unscathed. Van Lennep and Van den Berg are shortly off to Solo, and there things will probably turn out very differently. All the coffee plantations that are no longer worth a cent will have their credit withdrawn, and many will be the sorrier for it.[9]

The journey of inspection, however, came too late to restore the people's confidence in the Dorrepaalsche Bank. The Weijnschenk, Raaff and Dezentjé families moved their business dealings to the Factorij, the local office of the NHM in Batavia.[10] The prospect of gaining these important clients seems to have made the NHM somewhat deaf to the pleas of the minister of the colonies about trying to rescue the

Dorrepaalsche Bank.[11] In August 1886 the bank's death knell was tolled, when it went into a process of liquidation. The bank's assets and properties were transferred to a new company, and on 30 March 1888 the Dorrepaalsche Bank was liquidated — which was more or less a formality. Its property passed to a new society under Amsterdam management. This society, the Cultuurmaatschappij der Vorstenlanden (Estate Company of the Principalities), was exceeded in size only by the NHM and the Nederlandsch-Indische Landbouwmaatschappij (Netherlands-Indies Agricultural Company), which was the estate company that had broken off from the NIHB. Meanwhile, in 1887 Dorrepaal's heirs had subsumed their factories under the NV Klattensche Cultuurmaatschappij (an estate company), which in 1890 still held an interest in 16 businesses in the Principalities.[12]

Family firms in an age of economic consolidation

Prominent Dutch families in the Principalities had deserted the sinking ship of the Dorrepaalsche Bank and in doing so sealed its fate. But there must have been few who in 1885 perceived the death throes of this bank as a struggle between the interests of the Netherlands and those of the business community in the Indies. It is true, however, that in the end the NHM, like other cultuurbanken, strengthened its hold on the business management of its clients and increasingly often appointed its own administrators. The aim was not so much to take over a company as to provide better protection in cases of outstanding capital. In those instances when factories fell completely, or partly, into the hands of a cultuurbank, it was often the end of a long process. This was the case with the Ament sugar factory in Cirebon, West Java. In 1884 and 1888 their banker, the NHM, had successfully helped the Ament brothers to overcome the disease attacking the sugar cane. In 1893 the brothers restructured their firm into a PLC in order to make new investments, probably just in time to avoid a new crisis the following year, when sugar prices once again reached rock bottom. Not until 1903, when the outlook for the sugar crop improved substantially, did the Aments decide to transfer a considerable number of their shares to the NHM in order to buy new machinery for their factory.[13] The transfer of shares gave the NHM a controlling interest in the business, although this did not mean the end of the Ament sugar factories. In fact, the Aments remained on the board of their company. In Yogyakarta, too, most of the sales of businesses and conversions into PLCs took place after the 1902 sugar convention in Brussels. It was thus not the crisis, but the golden years of the sugar industry, that heralded the expansion of sugar production and the concentration of factories, since now investment held the promise of sizeable gains.

The events in Banda underscore the fact that a restructuring of a banking system did not in itself mean that family property was being transferred to a bank in the Netherlands. In the Banda islands, from 1886, the *Crediet- en Handelsvereeniging Banda* (Credit and Trading Society of Banda), or CHV, would gradually take over the role of the *Nederlandsch-Indische Handelsbank* (NIHB).[14] In 1890 the CHV, as the largest creditor, controlled eight of the 34 estates, although it owned only two. Almost all the other estates were registered in the name of old perkeniers' families from Banda, or members who had married into these families. It is, of course, quite possible that these families had taken out heavy mortgages — but large debts were nothing new to Banda.[15] And it appears that the most wealthy perkeniers' families of Banda had sufficient capital even after the turn of the century to set up new enterprises on the islands of Ambon and Ceram.[16] After the turn of the 19th century the Banda islands were no longer significant producers of nutmeg and mace — but this was because new nutmeg plantations were developed in the Malay peninsula as well as elsewhere in the Indonesian archipelago.

In the Principalities of Java, business also continued as usual. In Yogyakarta indigo and sugar remained of equal importance until the late 1890s, when sugar took the lead as the major product. Businesses became increasingly interlinked. This was a characteristic of the sugar industry in the 20th century, and in Yogyakarta it had already begun before the 1884 crisis. Indeed, the share of the Principalities' sugar factories in the production of Java sugar actually increased slightly in the years following the crisis, from 17 per cent in 1885 to 17.5 per cent in 1908. Although the total number of factories in Java rose from 116 to 177, the number in the Principalities remained more or less steady: 27 in 1885 and 28 in 1908. In that year the production of the sugar factories in the Principalities was often above the factory average for the whole of Java, that is, almost 7,000 tons.[17]

The sugar industry in the Principalities remained to a large extent in the hands of the old families, even though the appearance of PLCs might suggest the contrary. This setup was most suitable for preserving family capital in the family business. As early as 1883, Eduard Kerkhoven and Albert Holle had converted their tea plantation, in the Priangan district of Java, into the estate company of Sinagar Tjirohani.[18] Never-theless, it would be about another 25 years before most of the old family firms had been converted into PLCs. The location of a PLC says little about the nature of an enterprise or whom exactly it employed. In 1893 the Birnie family, for instance, converted its business into the *NV Landbouwmaatschappij Oud Djember* (Estate Company of Oud Djember, PLC), registered in the Dutch town of Deventer, in the Netherlands. But the directors of the estates all lived in the Indies.[19] This, too, was a continuation of the existing practice in the Indies. For many decades the owners of companies in the Indies had been accus-tomed, after a life of hard work in the Tropics, to retire somewhere in the Netherlands, such as The Hague, while handing over the daily running of their estate to a junior member of the family or an adminis-trator. Many old families from the Principalities converted the family business into a PLC after 1900, while continuing to occupy the key positions. For instance, Carel van Stralendorff (*circa* 1838–1902), son

Illustration 39   After 1900 many of the families in the Principalities turned their enterprises into limited companies while continuing to hold the chief positions. Carel van Stralendorff (*ca.* 1838–1902), son of Johan Caspar and Ambrosina Weijnschenk, administered the indigo and coffee plantations of Krajan Jatimalang, near Sukoarjo. He was descended from a German soldier who had settled in Surakarta in the mid-18th century.
[Photograph, *ca.* 1900, KITLV, Leiden.]

of Johan Caspar and Ambrosina Weijnschenk, was administrator of the indigo and coffee enterprise Krajan Jatimalang, near Sukoarjo. He was descended from a German soldier who had settled in Surakarta in the mid-18th century.

We should not, therefore, draw conclusions about possible Netherlands ownership merely from looking at the rising number of PLCs. All that is certain is that in 1910 the large enterprises based in the Netherlands owned no more than 37 of the 177 sugar factories in the Indies.[20] This was undeniably an increase since 1879, when they had owned only six, five of which were Van Hoboken's — as it had established its business in the east of Java early on.[21] Of far greater significance was the fact that in 1910 the family names of a company's founders (or the names of sons-in-law) were linked to the companies as director or head of the board of commissioners in 82 of the 177 sugar factories. There were also 22 other enterprises where the commissioners — who even after 1910 remained deeply involved in the sugar industry and sugar trade — had Chinese names.[22] In the Principalities the names of the families Weijnschenk, Dezentjé, Wieseman and his sons-in-law Pijnacker Hordijk and Broese van Groenou, not forgetting the daughters and sons-in-law of Dorrepaal, continued to be linked with sugar production. From a source dating to about 1910, for instance, we hear that Jacobus Marinus Pijnacker Hordijk was on the board of directors of not only four companies in Yogyakarta, but also one in Surakarta and another three in the residency of Banyumas, which borders on Yogyakarta.

The founding fathers of the agricultural enterprises have become legendary figures. They bequeathed to their children family businesses that their grandchildren inherited as shares in the property. Things were different in the sugar business in, for instance, Cuba and Puerto Rico. There, a clear (and geographic) division existed between the Creole-owned factories and the more modern ones financed by Americans. In Java, however, the distinction between home capital and foreign (from the Netherlands) capital did not arise. Traditionally there was a strong intertwining of the economic interests of families and financiers. This family network manifested itself in the shape of a close-knit "colonial lobby" in Dutch politics. In his classic study *Imperialism* (published in 1902), John A. Hobson has outlined this very process, pointing to the fact that imperialistic politics was born abroad — that is, "abroad" from the Netherlands' perspective. In this scenario, it was the colonial rentier class who managed to extend their colonial interests into the general interests and concerns of the Netherlands.[23] The agglomeration of the

Illustration 40   For many generations the descendants of Johannes Augustinus Dezentjé were coffee planters in Surakarta. At the turn of the 19th century his descendant and namesake Johannes Augustinus Dezentjé was administrator of the coffee enterprise Sukabumi, near Ampel. It was customary in the Indies to place a small photo on one's visiting card.
[Photograph, *ca.* 1900, KITLV, Leiden.]

Java sugar industry was no more than the continuation of a rationalising process that had started far earlier. That was the only way in which the sugar industry could survive the crisis of 1884 and the 15 difficult years that followed.[24] The heyday of late colonialism, which fell somewhere between the turn of the century and the Depression of the 1930s, rested on sugar as the major export crop of the Indies. During those years the sugar industry managed to develop into a powerful and formidable factor in colonial politics.[25]

Aftermath of the agricultural crisis

Despite the agricultural crisis of 1884, the economic power of the old planters' families remained unbroken. The only change was that they turned their family businesses into PLCs, becoming absorbed into larger economic conglomerates. This was a gradual process, and the 1884 crisis only partly contributed to an ongoing process of selection, elimination and consolidation. In fact, the 1884 crisis made a far deeper impression on people at the time than the immediate economic effects would seem to justify. The shock created by the collapse of the cultuurbanken must have contributed to this. The 1884 crisis appears to have had little impact on the number of unemployed Europeans in the Indies, although the government statistics are not entirely reliable. After 1885 private businesses flourished, and even the impoverished government experienced a considerable growth in the number of jobs it could offer. Between 1885 and 1900 the number of Europeans in government employment increased by 37 per cent (from 4,930 to 6,749). In the sphere of private business, the number of jobs increased by as much as 54 per cent (from 5,468 to 8,437). Competition from newcomers from Europe did not increase during this period, the percentage of male newcomers remaining at 40 per cent of the adult European male population. The influx into civilian life of large numbers of retired soldiers peaked in the early 1880s; the numbers declined rapidly after that.[26] Information gained from the *Koloniale verslagen* (Colonial Reports) would suggest a slight rise after 1884 in the number of Europeans without either a job or pension. In 1885 about 12 per cent of those recorded (1,667 people) appeared to be jobless, while the Colonial Report of 1900 calculates this as being 16 per cent, which is almost as high as the figure for 1870. The main cause for the increase in unemployment was the rising birth rate of Europeans born in the Indies. Thus, at the end of the 19th century, job openings were growing too slowly to cope with the population increase. Too many young people were banging on the gates of firms, factories and government offices.[27] By this time there were so many young men who had completed secondary education that even the better educated had difficulty finding a job.[28]

The agricultural crisis of 1884 did not, therefore, have any noticeable effect on the problem of unemployment and poverty among Europeans in the Indies. Indeed, well before the crisis, newspapers had been full of jeremiads about unemployed Europeans clamouring in their hundreds for a few scant office jobs, or who were found guilty of poaching and racketeering.[29] At the time of the tobacco crisis in 1880, the press in Surabaya complained:

> It is truly remarkable, the number of people without means who are presently living in this city; among them we find ship's captains, engineers, helmsmen, tobacco inspectors, shop assistants, commercial employees, even government officials — all of them recently made redundant and longing for re-employment.[30]

Towards the end of the 1870s, inhabitants of Batavia, too, received
begging letters from fellow European citizens who had fallen upon hard
times and who, with no means of support, had settled in the city's poorer
neighbourhoods.[31]

Naturally, there were other reasons apart from poverty causing the
Europeans to move "into the kampong". Some staff in the lower ranks
of the civil service had not had a salary rise since the 1850s.[32] But the
price of housing had risen rapidly since the 1860s, and indeed, builders
could not work quickly enough to satisfy the demand for brick houses.[33]
This applied not only to Batavia, where it seems that 220 guilders a
month was scarcely sufficient to maintain a family in a decent European
standard of living. It was equally true of such places as Makassar and
Semarang, where there was also a shortage of good, affordable housing.[34]
In 1879, on top of rising housing costs came the hated tax on the
property's rentable value (house and its contents).[35] The cost of living
rose steadily, but the salaries of civil servants did not keep pace. Even
commiezen (senior clerks) in some parts were forced to look for lodgings
outside the European neighbourhoods. Incidentally, these were not necessarily slum dwellings.

One clear result of the 1884 crisis was an increased sense of social
insecurity, especially since it followed hard on the heels of the tobacco
crisis. The feeling of malaise in the East Indies would last until the
beginning of the 1890s. The children of Europeans, in particular, faced
an uncertain future, particularly if they did not have the means to study
in Europe. The sense of anxiety was exacerbated by the press, which lost
no opportunity to air social problems. During those years the press
landscape had been entirely restructured, and a number of new, cheaper
papers were now available. For many years there had been newspapers
in such places as Padang and Makassar voicing the sentiments of the
Indos or Sinjos, but in the coastal towns of Java this democratisation of
the press took place only around 1885.[36] In the 1880s the discussion on
pauperism took a new turn, and the issue found new spokespersons in
the press. In the columns written by these new champions of the Indo-
European in Java, three points recur time and again: the threat of
unemployment; criticism of the fact that Europeans born in the Indies
were treated as second-class citizens; and the axiom that "European"
status brought with it greater obligations regarding comportment and
conferred more material rights than did a "native" status. The newspapers did not fail to impress upon their readers the importance of
this distinction, whereby they underscored once more the connection

between "European work" and "European status". Poverty in the kampong and the slums, previously a problem left to the care of preachers, pastors and police, had by then made it into newspapers. These reports form a unique source from which to reconstruct the picture of poverty and social deprivation suffered by the European have-nots in the East Indies at the close of the 19th century. Poverty among the European community was nothing new; what *was* new was that poverty and the social shame associated with it began to function as a reference point for defining who could rightly be called Europeans in the Dutch East Indies community, and then to decide what rights they were entitled to. In a way, the debate on pauperism in the East Indies newspapers formed the start of a process of political emancipation for the lower European classes.

Survival strategies

Poverty and lack of propriety were considered more or less synonymous in European society in the Dutch East Indies. A lack of money meant a lack of status. If an employee lost his job with the government or a business, experienced a marked drop in income, or had to make ends meet on a meagre pension, he would look for cheaper housing and gradually sell his belongings. Some such impoverished unfortunates would go from door to door, or through the kampong, with a list of their furnishings and clothes, for which people could buy lottery tickets. This must often have been little more than a form of begging — but without completely losing face. In colonial society, such begging by Europeans was taboo, and authorities even took measures to eliminate it. European beggars tramping from place to place would be arrested and returned to their domicile.[37] During the 1880s the press signalled with great indignation the fact that Indo-European children were seen out collecting kindling wood, or even begging in the streets of Semarang and Surabaya.[38] When in 1885 Cirebon, West Java, was plagued by the *sereh* disease, which affected the sugar cane plants, the local newspaper *Tjerimai* had the following to say: "How many Indo-Europeans do we not see walking round the kampong here, in rags and tatters, neglected, indeed almost naked."[39] Hunger banished the last vestiges of decorum. In one report, the *Tjerimai* tells of starving Indo-Europeans who plundered a street stall, and the journalist adds sententiously: "Great indeed must have been the need, that people would stoop to such behaviour!"[40]

The voice of the press tended to be judgmental and condemning, rather than compassionate, about Europeans who tried to make a living outside the European community. Journalists only appeared to see things from their public's point of view. This public shuddered at the thought of losing European status. Although newspapers criticised the colonial taboo against manual labour (by Europeans, that is), they considered that for Europeans to perform unskilled tasks was utterly beyond the pale. The social stigma connected with unskilled labour, implying that it was demeaning and diminished European prestige, caused many young men with a lower civil service certificate to hammer at the doors of government offices seeking employment. They would rather work for a pittance at an "honourable job" than be rejected by their community. Of course, not everyone had relatives who could provide board and keep while they waited, hoping and praying for the longed-for office appointment. Besides all the European-educated young people living in Java's major cities, migrants came from the other islands, where jobs of any sort were extremely thin upon the ground. For those who were unemployed, the slim chance of a paid job lay in the informal sector, where the distinctions between European, Javanese and Chinese became watered down and diffuse. It was tempting to try to make money out of one's European status or privileges. A European who was a drug addict might well barter his certificate entitling him to free medical assistance — which was issued to civil servants as well as the poor and needy — to Javanese or Chinese, who would supply him with opium.[41] Incidentally, the opium trade, although largely in the hands of the Chinese, offered work to Europeans — if not as independent dealers then at least as runners employed by Chinese opium sellers.[42] Widows, in particular, figured as opium dealers in newspaper reports. As for young women, they always had recourse to prostitution, and — to add to the horror of the decent European bourgeoisie — their clients also included Chinese, Arabs and Javanese. There was possibly even more disapproval of the prostitutes' parents, who permitted their daughters to make a living in so unseemly a fashion, than of the girls themselves.[43]

Young men who had no work often joined one of the gangs that were making their presence increasingly felt. The name for these gang members was *buaya*, which means, literally, "crocodile". They can best be described as fringe figures, or gangsters.[44] In Padang, the honest middle class prepared themselves for attacks from these gangs by setting up a vigilante patrol in 1883. In other places people only watched as the gangs grew bolder and more threatening. In Surabaya the press reported that Indo-gangs were plaguing the kampong and were particularly targeting the Chinese quarter, where the police seldom patrolled.[45]

On one occasion, a gang even disrupted a Chinese wedding, driving away the bridegroom and his family. Then they carried off the bride, who was never heard of again. Although the newspapers refer to "Indo-gangs", it seems more likely that Indo-Europeans joined up with existing criminal groups with a Javanese or other Indonesian background. Incidentally, cockfighting was also controlled by gangs, giving rise to another term besides buaya — the word *jago* ("cock"), which implied someone was a hooligan. That Indo-Europeans should be involved with cockfighting was considered most reprehensible by other Europeans. To involve oneself in such activities was to bring European prestige into utter disrepute.[46] The phenomenon of Europeans taking up "native" pastimes was a very old one. What was new was that the press gave it such wide publicity.

The press expanded and was read by increasing numbers and various sectors of the European community; it spread the notion that European prestige was permanently under threat and must be defended. The boundaries of decent comportment were drawn ever tighter. The *Celebes Courant* reported in 1890 on an article from a paper in Semarang about the European wife of a Javanese teacher who "introduced" his colleagues to her European lady friends. The reporter, scandalised by such behaviour, demanded that the authorities intervene: "This kind of pairing-off should, in our opinion, be most adamantly discouraged. It would seem, to make matters worse, that the lady in question is making a financial profit from her doings."[47] Her work, apparently, was that of a salaried matchmaker. But the problem went farther. In all probability the Javanese teacher in question was Muslim, and the bride had converted to the religion of her husband without further ado.[48] The fact that Islam was considered the religion of the "subject race" was why many Europeans condemned mixed marriage. By making such a marriage, a European woman placed herself outside her community. The law of 1898 regarding mixed marriages confirmed prevailing social attitudes when it stated that upon marriage not only native women but also European women were considered to acquire the legally defined population category of the husband.[49]

Another ground for violent disapproval was the adoption of a child from a different religious faith. It had long been the custom for poorer families to hand over their children to more wealthy relatives or friends when the financial going got too tough. European families in the East Indies sometimes had wealthy Indonesian or Chinese relatives who were Muslim. Thus, it was not uncommon for the family safety net to include a variety of religions. Whereas in former times the Church had cared for the poor and needy, thus protecting indigent Europeans from the need to convert to Islam, now the press had joined in as watchdog over white morality and gave an added political content to religious denomination. During the 1880s Islam was very active, and this undoubtedly coloured the perceptions of the press. Although Muslim friends and relations might care for a Christian relative purely out of family feelings, among upper-class Europeans living in the East Indies this pious act of charity could easily be dismissed as detrimental to colonial prestige.[50]

From the end of the 1870s, newspapers regularly noted European men converting to Islam — which was deemed equivalent to selling one's birthright, and certainly to selling European (white) prestige.[51] In some cases it was motivated by material prospects — there might be a better job opportunity if someone were Muslim, possibly in a religious capacity, in which case the local villagers were obliged to feed and support them.[52] The Malay-language newspapers also scornfully dismissed such religious conversions. Presumably, they wrote, the lazy Indos imagined that they could live off the charity of their new brothers.[53] Not that it was always so: a European converting to Islam could also be considered an indication of the power of the Muslim faith, and this often radiated from the new convert. Take the story of Sinjo Frederik, alias Pangeran Timoer. Born in Surabaya to Indo-European parents, after their death he became a devout Muslim and deeply impressed the local Indonesians. They were in awe of him and would kiss his hand. In Islam, Frederik found a new identity, new certainty and, somewhat unexpectedly, new respect.[54] Frederik was an orphan, and his position was similar to that of children who were brought up as Europeans only to discover that their natural fathers had never acknowledged them, which made them — according to the letter of the law — "native".

It would be almost impossible to imagine real live people behind the bland newspaper reports recording conversions to Islam, or individuals who in some way lost their European status, were it not for Paul A. Daum's remarkable novel *Aboe Bakar*. It recounts, in meticulous detail, the life of a man who converted to Islam in order to regain his sense of self-respect. Daum paid numerous visits to a kampong in Batavia, researching the life story of an unknown man who was to become the novel's protagonist, Adam Silver, or Abu Bakar, as he called himself after performing the hajj. Adam's mother was the concubine of the Bandanese perkenier John Silver, and his (unacknowledged) father was an Arab merchant. The perkenier knew the child was not his but treated Adam as if he were his own son, and indeed favoured him above his biological children. He even sent Adam to study in the Netherlands, despite the boy's somewhat limited intellectual capacities. Not until after John Silver's death, when his will was read out, did his cruel revenge become apparent. Adam was cut out of the inheritance. This was not as dire as it might have been, since his "brothers" insisted on sharing it equally with him. What was far worse was that he was not acknowledged as the perkenier's son and thus fell into the category of native. Deprived of his European status — Daum does not hesitate to make this quite clear — it was inevitable that Adam should manifest the inborn depravity of the Malay-Arab. In the account of Aboe Bakar, Daum points out that the legal status of European was a birthright. Indeed, that is the message permeating Daum's novel.

Even in exceptional cases, however, it is difficult to see a person's conversion to Islam simply as a reaction to loss of employment and a concomitant loss of European identity. People do not convert and change their identity as if they were changing clothes. By far the majority of youngsters remained within the European sphere of influence, while introducing their own Indische cultural accents. There were groups of young people who made a living by playing Krontjong (*Keroncong*) music. Krontjong was born out of a mixture of Portuguese and Indonesian musical styles and sounds like a distant relative of the Portuguese fado folk songs. Youth culture always manifests itself through characteristic clothing and group behaviour. In the Indies, youth groups cultivated a rough-and-ready manner, exuding social nonconformity and adorning themselves with those outlawed titles, the rebel names of buaya or jago. The buaya wore batik trousers with the legs rolled up to just below the knee, a neckerchief knotted nonchalantly at the throat, and a cap perched upon the head. As with today's rappers, there was considerable internal rivalry. The musicians challenged each other to improvise tunes and songs, or *pantun*, accompanying themselves on the guitar, violin and flute.

Art forms such as Krontjong, or the *Komedie Stamboel* (Stamboel Comedy Theatre), an Indische type of commedia dell'arte, are difficult to ascribe to any one ethnic group or class. Various traditions exist explaining how the highly successful Stamboel Comedy Theatre was born. Success always has many parents, and both Indische and Chinese writers claim the discovery of the theatre for their tribe. Undeniably, its origins are diffuse. It is also clear that there is an early connection with the Parsi Theatre, which arose in Bombay (today's Mumbai, in India)

Illustration 41   At the turn of the 19th century, Krontjong music became extremely popular. The successful Stamboel Comedy Theatre partly contributed to this. The songs were accompanied by flute and guitar, and the latter instrument became much loved in the Indies.
[Photograph, *ca.* 1915, KITLV, Leiden.]

in the 1840s and reached audiences in Southeast Asia by way of touring companies. In 1888 one of the groups, calling itself Bombay Comedy — although it was actually from Hyderabad — performed for several successive weeks in Surabaya and went on to draw delighted crowds in Batavia.[55] Another source of inspiration of the Stamboel Comedy Theatre was Krontjong music, which enjoyed immense popularity. This persuaded the rich Chinese businessman, firework-maker and restaurant-owner Yap Guan Thay to found his own theatre. So in 1891 the Stamboel Comedy Theatre was born. With the help of an Italian salon orchestra and an Indo-European group of performers, he presented the public with a mixture of Western music and instrumentation, Krontjong melodies, and stories taken from *The Thousand and One Nights* or the plays of Shakespeare.

The star of the company was Auguste Mahieu (1865–1903). If we are to believe the obituary notice of his friend, the well-known journalist Otto Knaap, Mahieu was not employed by Yap, but the latter had simply lent him a few thousand guilders. Presumably Knaap had played down the relationship between the star Mahieu and his producer Yap, so that he could claim the triumph for the Indo-Europeans. Here too, reality was more diffuse than the story that was handed down. Throughout their shared colonial history, Chinese and Europeans were business partners. As often as not, the European was the junior partner, because it was the Chinese who put up the capital.

Yap continued as theatre producer until 1894, but from the close of 1891 Mahieu was the figurehead of the Stamboel Comedy Theatre. The performances were inspired by the actors' talent for improvisation. They presented a kind of cabaret — addressing political events with a mixture of mockery and melancholy. According to Knaap, the dyed-in-the-wool socialist Mahieu aimed to present a people's theatre for all classes.[56] The critics writing in the European papers were almost unanimous in their disapproval: the Stamboel Comedy Theatre was too native and too sentimental. They failed to report the sheer delight engendered by the breathlessly swift pace, the variety and the interaction between actor and audience.

The critics might have carped, but the European audiences simply ignored them. They loved the Stamboel and looked forward to a theatre performance in the same way as they would the horse races.[57] Mahieu's Stamboel was enormously popular, and his songs were sung and whistled in the streets of Batavia like those of Gilbert and Sullivan in London. Incidentally, inside the theatre the seating was arranged in such a way that everyone could retain the position they occupied in the ranks of the colonial hierarchy.[58] The sharp barbs referring to the "native nature" of Stamboel simply missed their goal. Equally ineffectual was the criticism about the lifestyle of the players. Although the Makassar newspaper *Makassaarsch Handelsblad* encouraged jobless Indo-Europeans to join the army rather than be lured into the loose and depraved life of the Stamboel Comedy Theatre, working conditions in the army could not compare with what Mahieu offered.[59] His employees earned 30 to 75 guilders a month. The army could not match this, and office workers earned as much only after several years as a clerk. On top of this, Mahieu's workers shared in the profits, and their bonuses could be as much as 500 guilders.[60]

Mahieu travelled far and wide throughout the Indonesian archipelago with his theatre company. In 1893 the group had become a business company, with a capital of 40,000 guilders and a sizeable repertoire. Mahieu then split his troupe into two groups of roughly the same size, both of which became touring companies. The actors and actresses had a train wagon filled with stage sets and theatre props, which accompanied them on their journeys. From the very outset, the newspaper *Soerabaiasch Handelsblad*, which often criticised the government for its lukewarm concern for the position of Indo-Europeans, applauded wholeheartedly both the Stamboel Comedy Theatre and Mahieu's "theatrical entrepreneurship".[61] Mahieu brightened the lives of thousands and provided jobs for dozens of Indo-Europeans. He employed at least 60 people who would otherwise have been begging on the streets, leading an aimless life. "For years the government has been asked to provide work; in vain. Now the Stamboel Theatre has answered these pleas."[62]

Cris de coeur of early nationalism

The success of the Stamboel Comedy Theatre suggests that a good deal of the journalistic complaints about violation of European standards of decency should be taken with a sizeable pinch of salt. After all, the press itself was forced to take sides. As the morally outraged voice airing views on petty scandals, it had one eye on its commercial interests (and the other on its ideals). Life unrolling on the kampong's edges or in Chinese neighbourhoods eluded the watchful eye of authority but would often provide juicy copy for the growing regiments of journalists who had to fill their daily paper.[63] Interestingly, reporters who did not hesitate to name themselves Sinjo bemoaned the loss of European prestige with wails as loud as those of their colleagues fresh from the Netherlands.

Until the mid-1880s the voice of the press in Java was, to say the least, petty bourgeois in tone. The mood of crisis and the sense of social uncertainty that overcame European society in the mid-1880s promoted social conservatism. If we are looking for a voice that suggests more than simply the fear of losing European status, we should examine the daily papers published in the regions outside Java. This world consisted of small communities, where people knew each other and newcomers were easily detected. In Makassar and Padang there was still a strong sense of local identity, something that was already fading in Java, where people more frequently moved from place to place, and also where the European population was constantly growing. The newspaper *Padangsch Handelsblad* was an excellent mouthpiece for feelings of local chauvinism. Padang lay in a region that held few attractions for white fortune-hunters. Indeed, newcomers were far from welcome there, if we are to credit a story that wafted across to Java in 1878. It was said that *inlandse kinderen* had incited the locals to pester white soldiers. Apparently leaflets were distributed advocating Malay as the national language and propagating a combined resistance from the *inlandse kinderen* and Indonesians. Similar ideas were also to be read in the paper *Padangsch Handelsblad*, which the local government viewed as the platform of a bunch of "arch revolutionaries".[64] It was the *Padangsch Handelsblad* that in 1877 published a programme titled *Jong Indië* ("Young Indies"), appealing to all progressive elements throughout the Indonesian archipelago as well as those in the Netherlands. The remarkable thing about the article was that it did not address concrete social problems but was basically a manifesto about civil rights and duties: it discussed independent administration of justice, the influence of the Dutch East Indies on the legislative power in the Netherlands, and general conscription. The only demand that could be seen as having a more social content was the right to receive good and inexpensive education.[65]

A powerful feeling of Indische patriotism, combined with deep loyalty to the Dutch royal House of Orange, filled the columns of the *Padangsch Handelsblad* and set the tone for many other dailies in the Indies. A good comparison for the Padang *Jong Indië* Movement was the Young Ceylon Movement, which had arisen 27 years previously, also set up by descendants of VOC employees. The Sinjos writing for the *Padangsch Handelsblad* were opposed in principle to white domination by the Netherlands and its misappropriation of the country's wealth — something the Mestizos and Creoles of Latin America had successfully rebelled against earlier in the century.[66] More recently, in 1871, Cuba had seen an uprising against Spanish colonial rule. Not, of course, that the journalists of the *Padangsch Handelsblad* wished to see the Dutch East Indies go the same way as Cuba. The comparison was rhetorical and served to arouse the conscience of readers. Other papers used the comparison too. In 1871 even a respectable paper such as *De Locomotief* could not resist letting the government know just where the passion for exploitation could lead: to an uprising.[67] But for the *Padangsch Handelsblad* the comparison with the Mestizo and Creole revolutionaries in Latin

Illustration 42   With the growth of local newspapers, the Europeans in the Indies gained a forum and a platform for discussion. Most of the newspapers were started by bookshops. From 1885 on, the newspaper *Bataviaasch Nieuwsblad* was printed in the bookstore of G. Kolff & Co. in Batavia.
[Photograph, *ca.* 1870, KITLV, Leiden.]

America was very close to home, for "we too are Mestizos"; the caveat was clear.

In 1884 a book was published compiling the early nationalistic political philosophy of the *Padangsch Handelsblad*: it was titled *Het jonge Indië* (The Young Indies). The book contained articles written by Frederik Karel Voorneman, the illegitimate son, born in 1824, of an ex-sergeant who had ended up as a school teacher on Ternate, in the Moluccas. Voorneman worked in the civil service in Java and on the island of Banda, finally becoming *commies* to the assistant-resident of the Padang police.[68] He frequently contributed articles to the *Padangsch Handelsblad*. In order to avoid press censorship he sometimes wrote pieces in the form of a fable, with the characters as animals.[69] In one such allegorical exercise, he presented the Netherlands and its representatives as beasts of prey, land scavengers, whose victims — and therein lay the moral warning — finally rose up and destroyed them.[70] Voorneman died in 1881, but his son Adolph Martinus Voorneman continued his work, becoming a journalist in Java and publishing his father's newspaper articles. Another former staff member of the *Padangsch Handelsblad*, the journalist Arnold Snackey, also left Padang to settle in Batavia. Thus the voice of Jong Indië was exported to Java, where it was to resound for many a decade.

In 1881 A.M. Voorneman returned to settle in his birthplace, Rembang, on the north coast of Java, probably together with his mother, who was also born there.[71] He became editor of the *Bintang Timor*, a Malay-language newspaper published in Surabaya, but continued to write for the *Padangsch Handelsblad* and also began to contribute to *De Nieuwe Vorstenlanden*. He pleaded the cause of the Indo-Europeans and soon found an ally in Frederik Adriaan Enklaar van Guericke, with whom he corresponded. Enklaar van Guericke, who had organised the successful agricultural conferences in Surakarta and Yogyakarta, had in the early 1880s temporarily exchanged his planter's life for that of manager and editor-in-chief of the paper *Het Indisch Vaderland*. In 1881 A.M. Voorneman published three articles in this newspaper, on the topic of a Society for the Prevention of Pauperism; he wished to introduce such a society in the Indies, modelled on similar organisations in the Netherlands. What he did not want was a poorhouse. He envisaged a body that would assist Europeans who, through no fault of their own, had fallen upon hard times.[72] Enklaar van Guericke, as editor, was encouraged by these articles to take up his old plan to establish an agricultural colony for impoverished Europeans. Six years previously, he had put forward the plan at the Yogyakartan agricultural conference.[73] Positive reactions from his readers then suggested to him the idea of holding a lottery so that he could obtain enough money to pay for the freehold lease of the property. He had conceived an area of 500 *bouw* (355 hectares) and planned to train about 25 young people as coffee planters who would immediately start earning a living.[74]

Enklaar van Guericke's optimism met with a cold shoulder. The government refused permission for the lottery. He managed, nevertheless, to get a sustained discussion going on the subject of pauperism among the Indo-Europeans — a discussion that re-echoed as far as Padang and Makassar. It even reached the palace of Buitenzorg, where Governor-General Frederik s'Jacob instructed his director of education, religion and industry to consider how to address the problem of pauperism.[75] For the time being, the government got no farther than encouraging those in charge in the residencies and government departments to comply with the 1862 instruction requiring that jobs of office clerks be reserved for Indies-born Europeans. It was, nevertheless, of historic significance that an Indo-European journalist had been heard by the government when he pointed out that Sinjos had a right, by birth, to a decent existence in their own land.[76] A.M. Voorneman's and Arnold Snackey's arrival in Java brought a new dynamic impulse to discussions about European pauperism. They championed the right of decently educated Indo-Europeans to maintain a European lifestyle.

The Jong Indië Movement, also known as the Padang Movement, spread rapidly partly because it soon found sympathisers across Java. In 1883, for instance, A.M. Voorneman spent some time with the new editor of *De Nieuwe Vorstenlanden*, Theodorus Roeland Landouw, who had taken over the publisher's, printer's and bookstore in Surakarta from A.M. Voorneman's uncle, Philippus Franciscus Voorneman.[77] Landouw was to remain editor of the *Nieuwe Vorstenlanden* until his death in 1926 and was also, for a period, editor of the Javanese-language *Bromartani*. As an Indische patriot he became a passionate supporter in 1912 of Ernest F.E. Douwes Dekker's *Indische Partij*.[78] Undoubtedly inspired by A.M. Voorneman, Landouw presented his cautious social criticism addressing the subject of pauperism and supporting the rights of Jong Indië. His newspaper, *De Nieuwe Vorstenlanden*, had hoisted the flag of the Padang Movement on Java's soil.

Recognition for Jong Indië

To set the record straight: the debate in the press about pauperism was not sparked off by the agricultural crisis of 1884, but by the Padang Movement. Clearly, it was not a debate about the depths of poverty; rather, it was a discussion about civil rights. It concerned the interests of the Europeans born in the Dutch East Indies who were being forced to play second fiddle to the newcomers. That was the complaint heard loud and clear in the press. Apart from the daily papers, there was no sounding board for the voices of the Indische community. The absence of structure for a civil society remained concealed by the semblance of order presented by the European communities across the archipelago. A planter from Ceylon, visiting the Dutch East Indies in 1880, was pleasantly surprised by the clean and orderly appearance of the towns, the charming sight of the locals sauntering beneath the shady trees, and the illuminated front verandas. The people, he felt, were more friendly and easy-going than in British India, and what is more, he considered that the Hollanders survived extremely well in a tropical climate — not least because the Dutch had managed to convey their love of hygiene to their native servants.[79] East Indies society was bourgeois, in the sense that it attempted to maintain respectability. This reflected the fact that the government never aimed to create a European community in the Dutch East Indies; it merely attempted to preserve Dutch colonial authority. Laws regarding migration to the Indies were strict: newcomers who could not provide for themselves were likely to be sent back to Europe.[80]

This explains why the Padang Movement kept pushing for civil rights. It helped underscore the fact that social exclusion of Europeans born in the Indies was a denial of political rights. Of course, this was an old cry, because the government, legal system and financial bodies had been set up to turn the colony into a profit-making enterprise. That had been the case in the days of the VOC and the Cultivation System and continued even after the Agrarian Law was passed in 1870. European citizens came at the bottom of the list on the colonial budget. Pioneers who lacked the backing of a bank or trading house were few and far between. Estate employees who, after the introduction of the Agrarian Law, had themselves gone to the hills to try out small-scale coffee cultivation, were the exception. A few journalists sought the causes for this lack of pioneering spirit in the fact that less than a generation before, they had been a community dependent on slaves. This, they argued, had resulted in the Mestizos' complacency and lack of initiative.[81] Others pointed to the discrimination against less well-off Indo-Europeans: neither the Binnenlands Bestuur nor the banks would assist them in any way. Then there was a third voice — the most calm and reasonable. This said that the whole problem boiled down to a lack of expertise and capital. This message, proclaimed by Enklaar van Guericke and A.M. Voorneman, was the one most clearly heard.

Such debates made it clear to readers from poorer circles — if they did not know it already — that they belonged to a social class whose interests were not high on the priority list of the colonial government and the financial elite of the East Indies. Looking at examples elsewhere, too, the "insignificant" Europeans in the Indies realised that they must break out of the vicious circle that confined them to a subsidiary position in their society. It is no coincidence that it was a disciple of the great Dutch politician Abraham Kuyper — champion of the Dutch Reformed petty bourgeois — who was to lead the Indo-Europeans into the Promised Land of agricultural entrepreneurship. His name was Teun Ottolander,

and he was the son of a tree-nurseryman from the Netherlands. With
the fiery enthusiasm of an Old Testament prophet, he had established
coffee plantations in Banyuwangi in East Java.[82] In the respite of the
evening hours he edited a newsletter for planters, *De Indische Opmerker*,
and even found time to contribute to the colonial programme devised
by Kuyper's Protestant *Anti-Revolutionaire Partij*, the ARP. Ottolander
was a staunch supporter of Enklaar van Guericke's plan to acquire a piece
of land on a long lease, where some European boys could cultivate coffee,
following the example of the Eurasians in British India who had set up
a colony in Madras.[83] Just as at home in the Netherlands the ordinary
members of the Dutch Reformed Church were saving up their pennies
to pay for their own university, so in the East Indies poor people could
offer financial support to an agricultural colony. Unfortunately, Ottolander
was appealing to an Indische sense of solidarity, or group feeling, that
was far less developed than that of either the Anglo-Indians in the British
colony or the Dutch Reformed in the Netherlands. In the world of the
Dutch East Indies, he was ahead of his time.

A.M. Voorneman and Ottolander were, each in their own way,
ideologically inspired — the one by a vision of respectable bourgeois
society, the other by religion. In contrast, Enklaar van Guericke's way
of thinking was down-to-earth: he saw the agricultural colony as an
educational experiment. He took his plans very seriously, and in 1883
he was actively involved in marshalling volunteers to set up an agricultural
society for impoverished Indo-Europeans. On 11 March 1883 he
organised a meeting in Semarang that was attended by many bigwigs —
presumably they came out of respect for Enklaar van Guericke. It had
been largely due to his enthusiastic input that the 1875 agricultural
conference held in Yogyakarta had been such an overwhelming success.
But his new plan smacked too much of a charitable institution. An
agent of the Dorrepaalsche Bank and chairman of the Semarang Chamber
of Commerce, H.J.P. van den Berg, summed up the feelings of those
present when he said that the Indies did not appear to need a beggars'
colony.[84] He could not have pronounced a more concise or deadly
conclusion.

In the first half of the 1880s much ink was spilt on such topics as
pauperism, agriculture and artisanal work. The more that was written,
the more opinions diverged. A.M. Voorneman and like-minded journalists
wanted to discuss the situation of people in the Indies who had grown
up as Europeans only to find there were no suitable jobs available for
them. Other journalists devoted themselves to what they saw as the

overarching problem of social injustice. The contrasting views revealed themselves most clearly in newspaper discussions about whether the army was a suitable employer for Indo-Europeans. Initially, A.M. Voorneman was against promoting a military career, but journalists fresh from the Netherlands felt strongly that Sinjos who whiled away their time idly lounging on their *balai-balai* could best be enlisted.[85] There was, in fact, a chronic shortage of soldiers, so this seemed an admirable way to kill two birds with one stone. But this line of reasoning merely underscored the existing image of the army in European society, as a rubbish dump for tramps and ne'er-do-wells. This image was not too inaccurate, if we are to believe a newspaper report recounting that one of the bailiffs of Surabaya had arrested three young Indos caught in the act of stealing, and he had then relieved his city of their unwelcome presence by conscripting them into the army.

As one critic of the plan to conscript Indo-Europeans into the army put it: "Nothing could be expected from luring these young men from their positions as clerks or transcribers — for once they had joined the army, and were attired in their smart uniforms, with meticulously ironed shirt, spotless white trousers and short jacket, their hair neatly combed, with perfumed handkerchief and cigarette-holder — why, they felt themselves to be such perfect gentlemen and imagined they were far superior to the mere private."[86] Clearly this was a caricature, for many young men failed to gain positions as office clerks. The aversion to joining up had little to do with a preference for an office job — and everything to do with the possibility of being killed, and also with discrimination. In the army, bullying by white soldiers and officers was rife.[87] That was already the case in the 1850s and brought the Indies government to the idea of establishing a separate army corps for Indo-Europeans. But they realised in time that this would only serve to confirm discrimination, and they backtracked.[88]

But the idea was revived in the 1880s. The plan to set up a separate "Indo-corps" became a hot topic in the debates about European paupers. The *Sumatra Courant* suggested providing an Indo-battalion with attractive uniforms "since the Indos very much like to be finely dressed".[89] The *Soerabaiasch Handelsblad* proposed recruiting young Indo-European men for the rifle corps because "our calm and moderate, courageous Indo-European brothers" were very fond of hunting.[90] Reactions to such proposals were predictable: "We native children, we born in the Indies, thank you most humbly for such honorary positions. [...] We are offered a few hundred guilders up front, for which we are to spend years marching through the jungle for the cause of the Netherlands, rifle in hand, knapsack on our back, and lose an arm or a leg fighting the Acehnese."[91] People in the Indies were well aware that in 1875 two-thirds of the troops stationed in Aceh had lost their lives. Although the numbers killed in fighting would very soon diminish, the damage had been done — people connected the army with suffering and death. On top of all this, ex-soldiers — and the country was flooded with them at the end of the 1870s and early 1880s — were no recommendation for the military life. Some of them had served only a short while or had managed to be dismissed as "unfit for service". Those who had some skill or training tried to get out of the army as quickly as possible and find a job in civilian society. Some would set up shop as taverners or run a bordello within easy distance of an army barracks.[92] Other army rejects were those who, after years at the front, wore out their final years in the Indies as opium addicts or alcoholics.[93] Only when living and working standards in the army improved towards the turn of the century would the number of Indies-born soldiers in the European contingent increase.[94] In the 1880s, however, the army suffered from a very bad reputation, and the topic of military service soon disappeared from the agenda of Jong Indië. The rift between military service as part of citizenship, in the way the Padang Movement would have liked to see it, and the status of a mercenary soldier working for colonial interests could not be bridged.

Two newspapers: *De Oosterling* and *De Telefoon*

The press was full of the debate about Jong Indië, but this did not mean that Europeans born in the Dutch East Indies suddenly became conscious of their previously slumbering Indische identity. The sense of being a Sinjo went back much farther. The word "Sinjo" (of Portuguese origin) was used in the early 19th century as a more or less derogatory name for Indo-Europeans coming from the lower class, with little education and consequently a poor command of the Dutch language. As early as the 1860s, the nickname Sinjo was used in the press as a badge of honour by those who wanted to contest white condescension.[95] In the 1870s, contributors to the paper *Padangsch Handelsblad* would call themselves Sinjos to emphasise the point that they wished to be seen as equals of the newcomers while stating their difference. As the Sinjo journalists perceived it, the government should not be overgenerous in doling out European status. When people of European birth were absorbed into the

Indonesian population, there was no cause for lamentation. Their future was far better than that of a European in the Indies on the margins of society.[96] The articles by A.M. Voorneman or Landouw show no compassion for vagrants — after all, their existence harmed the claim made by Indo-Europeans for equality with the European newcomers. The two journalists only wanted to support people who, having gained their civil service diploma, discovered that there was not enough room at the government's table to offer a place to everyone who had a European education and training. This explains why it was journalists labelling themselves Sinjo who complained that the government had not taken sufficient steps to define the status of European and to keep a strict control over those entitled to it.[97] It had been the case, for instance, that descendants of slaves and African soldiers were regularly included in the registers of European residents. Christian Ambonese were still eligible to be included, and since 1871 non-Europeans could request the granting of equal rights. This had never been a bone of contention, since the people concerned were almost always Christian, and furthermore, there were very few of them.[98] The champions of Jong Indië nonetheless felt it was time to define more strictly who exactly could claim European status. Religion, of course, played an important part here, but there were also the major considerations of education and language — and especially one's birthright of belonging to the European group, which would be indicated by a European family name.

The almost jealous protection of the European constitutional position and the insistence on European standards of decency did not mean that the journalists associated with Jong Indië wished to identify themselves with the newcomers. Quite the contrary — and they defended their own Indische cultural domain with equal ferocity. According to the Indian historian Partha Chatterjee, in his observations on early nationalism in India, this belongs to the early phases on the path of national awareness.[99] The introduction of the word "Sinjo" by members of the Padang Movement is closely connected with delimiting a cultural domain and with the realisation that the Indies was their motherland. The journalist Snackey put it thus: "We Sinjos from Sumatra are like the so-called *Geuzen* [Sea Beggars during the Dutch Revolt against Spain in the 16th century], who transformed the invective into a badge of honour."[100] Writing in 1882, the *Padangsch Handelsblad* observed that *inlands kind* was the polite term and Sinjo was actually a term of abuse. What this suggested was that the two terms in fact applied to the same group of impoverished descendants of Europeans with a culturally mixed ancestry.[101] It should be added that members of wealthy Indische families did not think of themselves as *inlandse kinderen,* however culturally mixed their ancestry. The development of the word "Sinjo" as a complimentary rather than derogatory name may thus be seen to be partly connected with a growing class awareness, and partly with a developing notion of "the Indies as motherland" — and *not* with a possible growth of discrimination. This is clearly different from the situation in the British colonies, where a sharper distinction was drawn between Mestizo and white European and the former had become embedded in official jargon with expressions such as "half-caste". In the Dutch East Indies there would always be a stronger emphasis on the combination of class consciousness and patriotism, rather than the racial distinctions within the wider European community.[102]

The rise of "Sinjo-consciousness" established an Indische identity in contrast to that of the Totoks, and this was a first step in the long history that would lead to the Indo-European emancipation movement and Indonesian nationalism. Journalists such as Snackey and A.M. Voorneman understood only too well that to picture *inlandse kinderen* as the neglected offspring of Europeans left them with no alternative but to perceive themselves as second-class Europeans. This prompted A.M. Voorneman to remark in 1884 that however much the Sinjo prospered and climbed the social ladder, he would always remain a Sinjo and never become a pure-blooded white: "He is and will *always* be a Sinjo with the stamp of *Jonge Indië* upon his features."[103] A.M. Voorneman's comment contained far more than a complaint against social discrimination based on the colour of one's skin. The Sinjo, he implied, is essentially different, whatever his social position. He is a European, but not the same as the newcomers. He is certainly not inferior; indeed, he is possibly superior. Snackey had earlier spoken of the benefits of cross-breeding, praising the gene mix that united the best of the Indo-Germanic worlds. In contrast to the pathetic picture of the *inlandse kind* as a creature lurking in the margins of the European community, Snackey and A.M. Voorneman proudly introduced the "Sinjo": a cosmopolitan, a citizen of the world.[104]

A.M. Voorneman and Snackey can be credited with demonstrating that the cultural territory of the Indo-European was worth defending. The Totok was the outsider, and his role was that of spoilsport. Thus, for instance, we read in the newspaper *De Telefoon* in 1886 an entertaining article from a witty writer who had decided that the word "Totok" had been coined in the distant past by the local people, on discovering that the money-grubbing employees of the VOC were little more than empty-headed jackals on the prowl. Totok, the anonymous author continues, appears to be Malay for "empty shell". The reference to the days of the VOC was simply a device to avoid press censorship and in no way diminished the message addressed to the white newcomers who arrived in the East Indies with the sole purpose of getting rich quick.[105] One writer complained in the Makassar press that the actions of parvenus polluted the atmosphere.[106] Similar sounds could be heard elsewhere. Formerly, so wrote a reader in the Batavian newspaper *Bataviaasch Nieuwsblad*, people were more religious. Then, the resident and notables still showed an interest in the citizens, office clerks did not deck themselves out in clothes unsuitable for their position or their purse, nor were there any boozers and gamblers.[107] Those were the good old days, when everything was better — and what is more, it was more Indische and thus more modest and unassuming. Thus, the contours of an Indische identity were defined.

The Totoks failed to understand the Indische identity, and nowhere is their lack of comprehension better worded than in an article by Snackey. Who knows what feelings of homesickness poured out in the nostalgic unburdening of this writer far from home, who had left his birthplace on Sumatra and now lived in the city of Batavia. He had been highly respected in Padang for his knowledge of local languages and literature and as editor — although he was that for only a brief period — of the newspaper *Bintara Melajoe*.[108] Arriving in Java, Snackey addressed loving words to his native island, where retired civil servants felt so *senang* (relaxed and comfortable) that they had not the slightest wish to return to Europe.[109] Newcomers to Java had a pretty low opinion of the language spoken in the Padang district, a form of Sinjo-Malay, but Snackey explained that it was still spoken in the old, established Sinjo families. There, people would recall stories about the stirring deeds of the past, of how in 1785 the courageous Padang citizens had joined with Malays and valiantly defended the country against attacks from thousands of highlanders (the Padris) and how they had defeated a pirate fleet in a sea battle off Sauh Island. Snackey dreamed of that "dear old friendly Padang, with its gaiety, unpretentious piety, hospitality, firmness and chivalry of feelings and conduct", murmuring the names of old faces and distant places. Put simply — the Sinjo-Malay language belonged to a world that was lost, that had existed before the Indische communities were defiled by "Hollanders with their parvenu manners and stench of gin".[110]

Indische communities had a local identity, or formed part of a family network, until well into the 19th century. These were not large groups, and it was possible to know everyone's family tree. In Java's cities of Batavia, Surabaya and Semarang, it was quite different. The journalists who in their daily papers contributed so much to developing a sense of group consciousness among the Indo-Europeans did not come from these big cities but from much smaller places. Although the majority of Indies-born Europeans lived in Java's coastal towns, until the mid-1880s these towns were dominated by the established newspapers whose writers almost without exception came from Europe and who had little understanding of the world of the Indies.[111]

The new newspapers advocating the cause of the Indo, which began to appear around 1885, tended to polarise issues. This not only reflected the social divide between the Indo-Europeans and the European elite but also introduced the new brand of journalists making their debut on the European press podium of the Indies. This new phenomenon arrived just at the moment when the landscape of journalism was in a state of turmoil because the press was being harshly hamstrung. This censorship was the direct result of outspoken press criticism of the government — which, the papers said, had simply sat by and done nothing during the agricultural crisis of 1884. Two journalists in Semarang had been forced to resign — Scheltema, editor-in-chief of *De Locomotief,* and his colleague Paul A. Daum of the *Indisch Vaderland.* On an earlier occasion, in 1882, the editor of the *Padangsch Handelsblad* had been forced to resign after the court had found him guilty of infringing the Press Act. Feelings were running high: the press and government were at loggerheads. It was in such an atmosphere that the newspapers were wooing lower-paid Europeans. Particularly successful in this respect was Daum's daily, the *Bataviaasch Nieuwsblad,* an inexpensive paper with a handy format. Daum aimed to woo and win the potentially large market of Indo-European clerks. It did not mean, however, that Daum was just profit-seeking and had no ideals. Indeed, his great contribution is that he incorporated discussions dealing with the interests of the Indo-Europeans into the public debate about the self-interested colonial politics of the Netherlands. The editor-in-chief of the capital city's daily, the *Bataviaasch Nieuwsblad,* could see no justification for repeated expatiations upon the rift between the Indo-Europeans and the newcomers. This explains why Daum opposed the approach of a newly established paper called *De Oosterling.* The founder of this paper distributed a leaflet in which he claimed that "pure-blooded" whites regarded the (European) people born in the Indies as pariahs, social outcasts.[112]

When Daum and other colleagues reacted with considerable irritation, the publisher of the new paper, P. Abraham Jansz, informed them that he had anticipated such criticism since the Indo was about to find his own voice, whereas he had previously been gagged due to his inferior social position.[113] This had made it easy in the past to bluntly deny the second-class treatment of the poorer Europeans and to dismiss what was now finally being written on the subject as inflammatory articles intended to set the Indos against the white Europeans. The resident of Semarang did not hesitate to make use of the Press Act and put a stop to the publication of *De Oosterling*, which only served to bolster the paper's arguments. For the resident, it was a bad business when Indo-Europeans started to protest via their own newspaper; it smacked of revolution. He therefore imposed the maximum security deposit of 5,000 guilders on the publisher of *De Oosterling*. This was an impossibly large sum and meant, in fact, a ban on the publication of the paper.[114] Finally, however, Jansz took the case to the high court and gained a more favourable arrangement. The newspaper was required to change its name to *De Telefoon*, but as far as content was concerned it was not required to mince words. *De Telefoon* advertised itself as the first "Voice of the Indo-European". Censorship of the press had proven to be counterproductive.

The eruption of such expressions as "Indo-hater" and "full-blood pariahs" appeared short-lived and died down during 1886. But the rift between Indos and Totoks remained. The newspaper *De Telefoon* made such a powerful appeal to the sense of Indische identity that Enklaar van Guericke was moved to state that although he sometimes contributed to the paper, he in no way supported the line taken by Jansz.[115] He was, therefore, shortly to go his own way, pursuing plans to establish an agricultural community. He refused to join the movement that *De Telefoon* was trying to get going. Interestingly, even in the circles of *De Telefoon* the prevailing atmosphere was petty-bourgeois, and this characterised the early Indo-European activism in the coastal towns of northern Java. Thus, Jansz made no bones about the fact that the mainspring for his action was the urgent necessity to stem the tide of Indo-Europeans converting to Islam.[116]

It was Snackey who ultimately managed to combine the two elements — the awareness of an Indische identity, and the struggle to become fully accepted within the European community. He did so by referring to examples elsewhere in Asia: organisations of Eurasians in British India and Singapore.[117] His model was the Mutual Improvement Society, established in 1876 in Singapore. He realised, of course, that Singapore had an entirely different social structure from the Dutch East Indies. There, people spoke of "prominent members of the Eurasian community" who could represent their community, acting as role models.[118] Despite the differences, the Singapore society was precisely what Snackey had in mind, to wit: an organisation to provide social education for the Sinjos. Self-help had priority, but it was also, Snackey felt, essential to have expert guidance from outside. Taking the Mutual Improvement Society as a model, he also saw an ancillary role for the Church in the Dutch East Indies. He believed that the Church would be only too glad to support him, since they could scarcely have been clapping their hands for joy as they watched Indo-Europeans converting to Islam.[119]

Without a doubt, Snackey had struck just the right chord. *De Telefoon* distributed free copies of his article, and A.M. Voorneman's newspaper *Batara Indra* gave the project its unqualified blessing.[120] Indeed, *De Telefoon* succeeded in mobilising local representatives of the churches and several notables, after the Binnenlands Bestuur in Semarang had carried out its own investigations and decided that the state of poverty among Indo-Europeans was not too drastic. Thus, the action *Hulp in Nood* (Help in Need) was launched.[121] The existence of acute poverty was undeniable — but the appeal tried to make clear that it was not asking for charity. As suggested in many letters on this topic published in *De Telefoon*, it was widely believed that benefits would only encourage laziness. Indeed, it was thought they would discourage those people who were just managing to keep their heads above water from continuing to work.[122] Such arguments sound all too familiar to today's reader.

A.M. Voorneman also joined the critics arguing that while the Javanese received charity only when they were old or sick, the Indo-Europeans were having charity doled out without even asking for it.[123] And charity cheapened the workers. Not to be daunted, on 10 January 1887 *De Telefoon* proclaimed the birth of the society Help in Need, which was to be a fund for the support of the needy.[124] It was somewhat comparable to announcing the imminent birth of an elephant, only to be followed by glad tidings of the safe arrival of a flea. Angry readers accused the editorial board of surrendering the struggle for the Indo-Europeans now that they had achieved their goal of publishing a newspaper.[125] The reporter and distributor for *De Telefoon*, G.F. van Blommestein, did not take this accusation of betrayal lying down. Until such time as Snackey implemented his Society for Indo-European Welfare, he initiated a temporary association called the First Rays of Sunlight, or *Soeria Soemirat* as it was known in Javanese. Almost immediately, the new society had 70 members and Van Blommestein himself became chairman until a more notable figure could be found to fill the post. In the Dutch East Indies it was a truism that a society without a prestigious board of directors would be short-lived.[126] For the time being, however, such considerations were not important. The board of Soeria Soemirat was formed within a few days, and the society's statutes followed a couple of days later.[127]

So a union between churchly charity and Indische self-awareness gave birth to the society Soeria Soemirat. And, once awakened, the consciousness of the Indische world was not to be smothered. Soon there was a competition for a Netherlands-Indies national anthem.[128] Critical readers of *De Telefoon* at last got their money's worth when the young association announced that they wanted a regulation stating that the government would in future appoint a newcomer from Europe for a job only if there were no suitable candidate from the Indies. The suggestion to cut the pensions of Netherlands-Indies civil servants who returned to the Netherlands was a populist expression of the often-heard complaint that Totoks only came to the East Indies in order to get rich quick or ensure themselves a plump pension. Due to tragic circumstances, this movement lost its political steam within a couple of years. On 24 October 1888 Van Blommestein succumbed to cholera, and hardly a year later Jansz died of malaria. The revolutionary voice of *De Telefoon* was silenced.[129] And an attempt made in the meantime to found a branch of Soeria Soemirat in Surakarta had also failed.[130] The other newspaper issuing a call to combat for the Indo-Europeans, A.M. Voorneman's *De Morgenpost* in Surabaya, met its demise on 31 December 1888.

Soeria Soemirat would have disappeared without a trace had not the Dutch Reformed Church pointed out to certain notables of Semarang that they had responsibilities towards the Indische community.[131] It was Soeria Soemirat's fate to be a mixture of church welfare work and emancipation, which caused it eventually to fall under the supervision of a Protestant minister. Under the autocratic rule of the Reverend W. van Lingen, the long-drawn-out discussions concerning artisanal enterprises and small-scale agriculture for Europeans finally bore fruit. In 1889 the government cooperated by providing land in the Malang district of East Java for the use of needy Europeans.[132] They also, in 1896, released Van Lingen for a year from his duties as clergyman in order to set up an agricultural colony, although it would appear that he shouldered this task with considerable reluctance.[133] Van Lingen's lack of faith in the agricultural colony is shown by the fact that he contemplated inviting farmers from Europe to get the project up and running.[134]

As it turned out, every nervous prediction would come true. In 1897 Soeria Soemirat acquired a fertile expanse of land at a height of 1,200 metres, in Cibogo (West Java).[135] The labourers promptly turned into gentlemen-farmers, arranging for others to work the land. And the shops that had been set up in Semarang with aid from Soeria Soemirat were soon running at a loss.[136] However, it was a more cheerful story with regard to the workplaces also set up in Semarang by Soeria Soemirat. They developed into a thriving complex with a shoemaker, smithy, saddler and tinner. They had a turnover of 4,051 guilders per year, and wages were between 1.20 and 9 guilders a week. The highest wage was paid only to smiths who would have been able to earn at least as much working somewhere else. At the Soeria Soemirat workplace there were 76 Europeans and about a dozen Javanese.[137]

And so it was curtains for the optimistic notion that Indo-Europeans in their "own land" — as the newspaper *De Telefoon* printed in capitals — could create a Mutual Improvement Society. Such entities could not put down roots in the Dutch East Indies, where the European upper class was forever shifting and changing. The only instance of self-organisation by the Indo classes in that period was the society *De Voorzorg* (Precaution), set up by employees of the State Railways, who formed a body of civil servants with an outspoken group identity. Their society had been founded on order that when a member died, it could offer financial assistance to the widows, orphans, legally acknowledged children and other interested parties.[138] It was a remarkable step, even if far removed from the introduction of improvements in the living conditions of workers, such as were being introduced in Europe at the time. Socialist ideas had not yet wafted over to the Dutch East Indies, and there was certainly no suggestion that the charitable organisations established in the early 19th century to assist needy Christians were perhaps becoming redundant.[139] But despite the changes that were to come, the Sinjo intellectuals from Sumatra's Padang and journalists like Van Blommestein would not be forgotten. They played a pioneering role in the Indo-European movement. Newspapers such as *De Telefoon* had not yet managed to fulfil their plans to establish a dynamic Indo-European movement. But before the century was over, the promise would be kept, and a young journalist would again take up the cause of the emancipation of the Indo-Europeans in the Dutch East Indies.

CHAPTER 9

"Indische": Defined and Identified

The 20th century arrived in the Dutch East Indies accompanied by a chorus bewailing the growing number of children who had concubines as mothers. The prevailing tone was that many of these children did not merit the status of European. A commonly heard anecdote was that of the down-and-out soldier who, in exchange for a bottle of Dutch gin, acknowledged that he was the legitimate father of a child who had not a drop of Dutch blood.[1] The newspaper *Java-Bode* reported the growing number of "degenerate Indos and complete hybrids" who were in fact natives but were entitled to call themselves European: "Without a doubt, such people must feel deeply dissatisfied with their lot."[2] These gloomy musings were, however, seldom based on more than anecdotal accounts and were certainly not founded upon systematic research. It was nothing new to hear of "immoral" goings-on in the army barracks, while concubinage and large families of pauperised (Indo-)Europeans were a familiar phenomenon. What *was* new were the growing complaints about the situation and the sombreness of their tone. Such attitudes became widespread at the end of the 19th century, when interest grew in matters such as genetic inheritance, Malthusian ideas about population control and the theme of ennobling the lower classes.

The fin de siècle Zeitgeist encouraged the notion of a moral decline of European society in the Indies. Colonial policy in the Indies had always tried to draw a clear distinction between European society and the natives. Until the close of the 19th century the emphasis had continually lain on reclaiming the stray sheep of the European flock and returning them to the fold of European culture and values. But now the idea arose that it might be better for them to remain in their native environment. This notion, born largely out of discussions on inheritance, race and degeneration, now buzzed on every side. The *Java-Bode*, which represented the conservative opinions of the more wealthy Batavian

civil servants, used the word "hybrid" to highlight the problematic
aspects of racial mixing. Understandably, this newspaper did not dispute
the fact that there were large numbers of decent Indo-European families
bringing up their children in a correct and seemly manner. But once the
journalists got the bit between their teeth, they became carried away by
polemics regarding degeneracy and childhood neglect. It only needed a
tiny slip of the pen before they were fulminating about the stereotypical
Indische family where the eternal ne'er-do-wells lazed around and never
lifted a finger, convinced as they were from birth that to do manual work
would debase them forever.[3]

This caricature was not something new. A hundred years earlier, at
the beginning of the 19th century, newcomers to the East Indies had
written with shocked amazement about the lack of parental care, about
the frequent beatings that children received, and about how their mothers
carried on their peddling trades and spent their time playing cards
instead of looking after their children.[4] Around 1900 such commentaries
became imbued with pseudo-scientific arguments on the topic of racial
inferiority. Articles and reviews with scientific pretensions were published
claiming to substantiate the stereotypical pictures of Indo-Europeans as
people who were underhand, easily suspicious and quickly roused to
anger.[5] The widely held opinion in British colonies that when European
populations became mixed with a native race they dissolved into native
society also crept insidiously into Dutch (Indies) publications. Some
suggested that several generations of mixed marriage resulted in infertility
— although such an opinion would appear to be firmly disproved by
the many large and flourishing Indo-European families. However, a
conservative newspaper like the *Java-Bode* could not be shaken from its
conviction that social improvement — with all its biological connotations
of crop or cattle improvement — was the same thing as opposing mixed
marriages. In the Netherlands, newspapers were quite unabashed in
stating that pauperism was the result of racial mixing.[6] The word *volbloed*
(pure-blood) began to appear in advertisements for domestic staff and
personnel. Cynical remarks were heard to the effect that the elite corps
of the Binnenlands Bestuur, in Dutch *keurkorps*, was turning into a
coloured corps, Dutch *kleurkorps*. In short, with the arrival of the 20th
century, the colonial discourse became strongly racialised.

It is tempting to think — although inaccurately — that Darwinism,
then a fashionable ideology, was responsible for this racist thinking.
Social Darwinism was widely accepted in Europe, but in the Indies it
was the Spencerian theory of evolution that predominated. Herbert

Spencer saw human ability as the product of social evolution, and not of biological selection. It proved a difficult task, however, to distinguish between inherited propensities and the effects of upbringing. The journalist Paul Daum, for instance, was a fervent Spencerian, yet in his novel published in 1890, titled *"Ups" en "downs" in het Indische leven* ("Ups" and "Downs" of Indische Life) — which recounts the downfall of the aristocratic planters' family the Hoflands — he invokes heredity as a major element in the family's decline. In his journalistic writing, however, he pleaded the cause of education as the driving force behind social advancement and the best possible cure for the ills assailing the European community in the Indies. City gardens, public parks, theatrical performances and concerts were surely more attractive ways of passing the time than cockfighting, *tandakken* (Javanese dancing) or Javanese wayang puppet theatres. Cultural paternalism of this nature encountered little opposition; indeed, it was applauded by the newspaper *De Telefoon*, which wrote in this context of "the improvement of destitute Europeans".[7]

All the complaints about the effects of mixing and the negative influences of an Indische lifestyle might almost make one forget that ever-growing numbers of Europeans in the Indies were now speaking Dutch, reading the paper, and writing letters to the editor on touchy topics. It was a recent development, for until well into the 19th century — even in wealthy families in the Indies — the lingua franca was not necessarily Dutch, but Malay. This appears, for instance, from a complaint made in 1887 by the education inspector about the poor level of Dutch among students at the HBS School, which was intended for children from the better circles.[8] It was only in the closing years of the 19th century that Dutch began to be more widely used among Europeans. It first became the standard language at work and then moved into informal areas. In contrast to the much-quoted opinion of the education inspectors that in 1900 the majority of Indies-born European children at elementary school had a very poor command of Dutch, we find that at that time already 40 per cent of Europeans used Dutch in their everyday affairs.[9]

The early 20th century also witnessed an alternative wave against the assumption that "Indische" meant "inferior". While the terms "hybridity" and "Indische" when used in the colonial context both had negative overtones, the cultural avant-garde in the Netherlands and elsewhere in the Western world embraced the exotic. The artistic style of *Jugendstil* (art nouveau) made use of exotic shapes and designs. The

artist Jan Toorop, born in Java in 1858, who was greatly celebrated in
the Netherlands, exploited heavy symbolism borrowed from Javanese
art and even transported this into his painted posters advertising salad
dressing. For the colonial newcomers, belief in animism was superstitious,
possibly even dangerous, nonsense, but in the Netherlands it was all the
fashion to hold séances and make contact with the spirits of the dead.
What might be described as an organic way of thinking, most powerfully
expressed through the eclectic and unrestrained images of Jugendstil,
flourished among the elite of the Netherlands. The urge to reconcile
opposites also reached the colonies and was to have an influential role
in the rejection of conventional European tastes and values. One
manifestation was the growth of the Theosophical Society (founded in
1875), which acquired a considerable following in the first decades of
the 20th century. Before this, the Freemasons had been the chief instigators
of dialogue between the various cultures and faiths in the colony. In
about 1908 the Theosophists took over. In the Indies their champion
was Dirk van Hinloopen Labberton, who taught Javanese at the training
institute for the Binnenlands Bestuur in Batavia, the Willem III School.
This eloquent, indeed loquacious, man was inspired by the great British
Theosophist Annie Besant (1847–1938), who had left England for
British India in 1893, declared the Indians to be her brothers and sisters,
and become a tireless advocate of home rule for India.[10] Theosophy also
appealed to nationalist intellectuals in the East Indies, who applauded
its approach of an Eastern counter-current against the materialism of
the West.

Thus, the world of the East Indies became aware of two contrasting,
indeed opposing, voices. Since the rise of the Soeria Soemirat movement,
the Indo-Europeans had spoken out as a separate group, although their
plea was to be accepted as Europeans. In contrast, the notion of an
Indische domain as a space where European and Asian cultural influences
were equally valid steadily gained ground. The politically tense period
linked with the growth of nationalism served to reveal the tensions
between the concept of "Indo-Europeans" — people who constituted a
category of class and race within the wider group of "Europeans" — and
"Indische", a term that could be applied to everything connected with
the Dutch East Indies. On the one hand, the expression "Indo-European"
(or Indo) was used to apply to Europeans who had a part-Asian ancestry
as opposed to pure-blood white. At the same time, the word "Indische"
was used in contrast to *Hollands* (Netherlandish) but never to demarcate
Europeans from Indonesian, Chinese or other population groups living

in the East Indies. The "closed" character of the term "Indo-European" and its opposite, the boundless connotations of the word "Indische", have dominated the political evolution of the Indies. During those years of budding nationalism the political pendulum swung continually between the struggle to establish a movement representing the more general Indische interests, and a Union of Indo-Europeans. Two Dutch words crystallised the differences: *beweging* (movement) stood for new and open, while *bond* (union) implied the formation of a group to defend one's own interests. Everything born out of the Indische movement was to be absorbed almost unnoticed into Indonesian nationalism, while the notion of a union or brotherhood gained definitive form in 1919 in the Indo-Europeesch Verbond (IEV) — the Indo-European Union.

Indische grievances and the prejudices of the motherland

A mood of transitoriness and decline pervaded society in the Indies during the fin de siècle. Literary works describing the period, such as Daum's novel about the Hoflands in West Java, or Louis Couperus's *The Hidden Force*, set in Surakarta, sketch a picture of the planters' aristocracy sinking beneath a stupor of indolence and genteel poverty. The Sumatra-born writer Augusta de Wit (1864–1939) in her popular work *Natuur en menschen in Indië* (Nature and People in the East Indies, 1914) draws a picture in Darwinian terms of the planters in the Principalities of Central Java. She too believed that most of the descendants of the Yogyakartan leaseholders had sunk into poverty and were disappearing into the local population. She did not deny that there were also triumphant survivors, but in her view these had lost their Indische identity and had become "Hollanders". They were the major shareholders of factories running high-powered machines, which, to use her words, produced the gleaming white sugar crystals, scintillating like snow.[11]

From all this Yogyakartan sugar, about half the dividends went to the children and grandchildren of the 19th-century leaseholders. In 1865 there were 43 enterprises run by old Yogyakartan families, of which 17 were still owned by these established dynasties in 1916. Some families had sold their factories when, after 1903, they could obtain such a good price for them that they were able to write off their debts. Other families continued simply running a sugar-cane plantation and delivered the crop to a nearby factory. In around 1910 the sugar plantations had concentrated their refinery capacity in a few major plants. Railway lines ran many miles from the fields to the plants, connecting up with the

Illustration 43   Even after many of the major families in the Principalities had converted their enterprises into limited companies, members of those families retained their influential position in society. In this group portrait of staff at the Bantool sugar factory near Yogyakarta, owned by the Wieseman-Pijnacker Hordijk family, surnames recur: at the extreme rear is seated Pieter Melior Dom; in front of him, from left, C.M.E. Petersdorf, J.C. van Stralendorff, H. van der Brugghen, J.G. Dom, F. Jager and J. van Stralendorff.
[Photograph Céphas, *ca.* 1898, KITLV, Leiden.]

main line to Semarang. Of the 15 Yogyakartan sugar factories, six were still run by old planters' dynasties — such as the Weijnschenks and the brothers-in-law Broese van Groenou and Pijnacker Hordijk. These families had reinvested their profits and thereby expanded their businesses. The shares, and thus the dividends too, stayed in the family. The book recording the history of the Broese van Groenou family firm of Tandjong Tirto shows that this enterprise was, and continued to be, a family affair in which brothers and sisters together took the important decisions.[12]

What happened to all the relatives of Broese van Groenou who — to use the terminology of De Wit — had not become "Hollanders"? The question probes far beyond the boundaries of Yogyakarta, for this region was only one part of the wider area of the expanding sugar industry. Although increasing numbers of personnel were now coming from the Netherlands, the majority of the European employees were born in the Indies. The expatriate platoon, incidentally, was not a new phenomenon, for, from the early 1800s on, sugar enterprises in the East Indies had been attracting engineers from England, France and Germany to manage their factories. There was a huge growth in the number of jobs in the sugar factories in the 20th century. This growth in turn led to a great deal of construction and maintenance work on the many canals, bridges and channels for irrigating and transporting the sugar cane. This created new jobs in the railway sector, involving sugar transport. A contemporary estimate calculates that in 1905 about 5,000 Europeans were employed by both the privately owned and the state railways.[13] Thus, notwithstanding all the sombre stories about becoming submerged, the group of lower middle class Europeans flourished apace and became part of the colonial economy.

In this class struggle for social recognition, the press was to play a crucial role. By now, the newspapers were occupying the moral high ground, a position formerly held by the churches. Also, daily papers had grown cheaper and people on low incomes would often share a subscription. Newspapers were now freely available in tram and railway waiting rooms, where they could be leafed through by all and sundry. It was in the commercial interests of the press not to offend the lower classes in the Indies. There were undeniable prejudices and discrimination based on colour, but these did not dominate public opinion. The contrast between Indo-Europeans and "full-blood whites", which had been stirred up when the Soeria Soemirat society was being established, faded from the pages of the newspapers. But the columns continued a vigorous discussion on the differences between motherland and colony, between the East Indies and the Netherlands. The sharp criticisms against the government in the Indies grew milder, however, making room for a general lamentation about the Netherlands.

But racial prejudices were alive in the Netherlands. There, colonial correspondents felt a growing need to protest against the dilution of European culture in the East Indies. Colonial experts in the Netherlands and the Dutch daily paper *Algemeen Handelsblad*, which was the mouth-piece of Amsterdam commercial interests in the colonies, strongly opposed the presence of many Indies-born civil servants in government depart-ments. What the East Indies constantly needed, it was argued, was "fresh Dutch blood" in government office. According to the newspaper, older civil servants became affected by the "Indische" atmosphere. As a result, their efficiency was gradually undermined by slackness, a fear of making a fuss and dislike of change.[14] Not surprisingly, Dutch parliament considered concentrating the professional training for civil servants for the Indies in the Dutch university city of Leiden. For the European citizenry in the Indies it was clear that the politicians of the Netherlands wished to ease the *inlandse kinderen* out of the Indies government. Although the Dutch government was fully aware of this resentment, it wanted to close down the training college at the Willem III School in Batavia. The military academy in Meester Cornelis (south of Batavia) had already been discontinued. The Dutch government did, however, have sufficient sensitivity towards public sentiment in the Indies not to axe these institutions outright. First came more demanding selection and examination procedures, which, reported observers in the Indies, reached a standard higher than that expected of Dutch students in equivalent conditions. As a result, the number of students fell. The high fees and the preference of parents to send their children back to Europe for education provided the final arguments for closing down the two languishing training colleges.

The discussion about whether or not to close down the training college for higher civil servants dragged on from 1896 to 1912 and came to occupy a prominent place in the political consciousness of the Indies. The critical articles and reports that sealed the fate of the college drove the rich and poor of the Indies into each other's arms. Things had been very different before this, when it was chiefly the wealthy notables who complained about how little they received as parents in return for the high taxes that were squeezed out of them.

Until the early 1890s, the wealthy and the poorer Europeans had little in common as far as educational interests were concerned. Secondary education in the Indies was so expensive that only those with considerable incomes felt the urge to fight for it. Some individuals had established scholarship funds and educational trusts for the benefit of gifted children whose parents could not afford to pay school fees, but in both Semarang and Batavia these funds led a limping existence.[15] And so it was that the government in The Hague was able to maintain that wealthy residents in the Indies preferred to send their offspring to the Netherlands, and that to provide higher education in the East Indies for a miniscule elite was simply a waste of money. However, the derisive attitude expressed in post-1890s colonial education policy towards Indies society encouraged a sense of unity hitherto unknown among all ranks of the European population. The announcement in 1893 that the military academy in Meester Cornelis was to be closed down evoked widespread protest. To replace the academy there would be a few scholarships made available for candidates from the Indies to follow the officers' training in the Netherlands. This was a hard blow for the European families in the Indies.[16] Captain F.A. Kleian — probably born in the Indies — took the lead and submitted a petition to the queen regent in the Netherlands begging that the military academy be saved from closure. Support came from all sides: from Makassar to Padang and from high government officials to lowly clerks. Indeed, there would have been far more signatures had not many a civil servant, fearing for his position and career, refrained from signing.[17]

Kleian's campaign could not save the Military Academy, but it did serve to show that the voices of protest that sounded in May 1848 had now become a far louder chorus. In fact, the protests then had been largely about ensuring job security in the higher echelons of the civil service, for the children of the elite. Now the debate was played out on a far greater stage, and far more classes were involved. Once again the Semarang newspaper *De Telefoon* took the bit between the teeth. This time the lead voice was that of George Albertus Andriesse, a failed planter who had spent some time in Surabaya as journalist and joined the editorial board of *De Telefoon* in about 1895.[18] He was born in 1837, the son of a *commies* (senior clerk) who worked in the resident's office in Pekalongan and came from an old and prominent family in the Indies. His grandfather, J. Andriesse, a naval commander, was one of the leaders in 1795 of the Patriots' movement in the Indies. His uncle had attained the rank of resident of the island of Ambon.[19] In all probability Andriesse's failure as a planter helped to make him into a passionate socialist and ally of the no-less-ruby-tinged director of the Semarang technical school, J.F.L. Stroo Westerman. Together they were to compose the historic call published in 1896 in *De Telefoon* urging the formation of an *Indische Bond*, or Indische Union.[20]

It all began with a series of articles titled *Indische grieven contra Nederlandse belangen* (Indische grievances vs. the interests of the Netherlands), which Andriesse wrote during 1895. Most of his complaints were familiar: the theme of the pauperisation of the East Indies had already been extensively — and far better — dealt with in the respected Semarang paper *De Locomotief* under its editors in chief, Van Kesteren and Pieter Brooshooft. What Andriesse wrote about education had already been treated by the journalist Paul Daum. Nor was there anything new in his complaints about the preferential treatment given to Hollanders when it came to jobs — be they in the civil service, in the army, or as skilled craftsmen.[21] Activists in the early days of the Soeria Soemirat movement had already demanded that the government give precedence to Indo-European candidates for jobs. What was new was that Andriesse delivered his no-confidence vote to the address of ex-colonials and colonial experts back home in the Netherlands. He had no faith in their support for the cause of the Indies when it came up for discussion in parliament. He described them as "sojourners" (*trekkers*) who, after they had lined their pockets in the Indies for 15 or 20 years, returned to the motherland to live off their savings or the pension they had built up. How could such people represent the "stayers" (*blijvers*), those who looked upon the Indies as their motherland? The introduction of the terms "stayers" and "sojourners" was a brilliant stroke. It spoke to the dozens, and sometimes hundreds, of unemployed who queued up for the scanty jobs in the Indies while the wealthy upper class could afford to send their children to study in the Netherlands and, after passing their working days milking the colony, retired contentedly to live off their savings back home in The Hague.

Andriesse attacked the financial extortionists of the East Indies. In many ways he spoke a language similar to that of the British-Indian nationalists, who protested against the financial drainage of British India.[22] Andriesse's economic nationalism was something new, as was the slogan he developed, *Indië voor de Indiërs*.[23] Nevertheless, his battle charge came a cropper when up against the desirability of creating a society of "stayers" rather than viewing the Indies as an overseas territory where people could get rich quick. Andriesse was not, however, planning a political ideology. Rather, he assumed — probably quite correctly — that the vast majority of the descendants of the Dutch in the East Indies were not upwardly, but downwardly, mobile. They would be rejected as candidates for the Binnenlands Bestuur, driven off plantations and homesteads, and expelled from small businesses. Andriesse laid the blame fairly and squarely on the shoulders of the government in the Netherlands, the "sojourners" and the "dishonest" Chinese, in competition with whom the Indo-Europeans would always be worsted. Indeed, it was just at this time that anti-Chinese feelings were enflamed by newspaper reports describing how the Chinese were involved in many cases of fraud. Added to this, wealthy Chinese considered themselves the equals of Totok Europeans, and this gave both Indonesians and Indo-Europeans a sense of inferiority.

In short, the "socialist" Andriesse skilfully put into words the feelings of a lower-middle-class group that felt pushed with its back against the wall. The enemy they faced was the growing force of the outsiders, the newcomers and the "foreigners" as he called them, including the Peranakan Chinese, who were born in the Indies. These figures deprived the impoverished "stayers" of their legitimate birthright in their land of origin. In order to resist these enemy forces they must form an Indische Bond, an Indische Union. Although at first Andriesse's strident tones made many feel somewhat apprehensive, once the government had accepted the statutes of the Indische Bond in 1898, members flooded in, from Java as well as the other islands.[24]

Even before 1898 the lower-middle-class Indo-Europeans had resented the more well-to-do who could afford to bid farewell to the Tropics and retire to a life of ease in the Netherlands. The Soeria Soemirat movement had already made this clear, but the populism that characterised the Indische Bond introduced a new unifying element. Contemporaries, and indeed historians, have suggested that the birth of this organisation, with its economic nationalist rhetoric, may have been inspired by the rebellion in the Philippines.[25] However, Andriesse's propaganda had already started in 1895, a good year before the revolution broke out in the Philippines. The man who inspired this revolution, the ophthalmologist José Rizal, a descendant of a Chinese-Mestizo planter's family from the sugar-growing district of Laguna, near Manila, was virtually unknown in the Dutch East Indies. Although the news of his execution on 30 December 1896 was printed on the front page of the newspaper *Bataviaasch Nieuwsblad*, this was probably the only paper to have a correspondent in Manila.[26] Other papers, with their frequently meagre foreign news commentary, spared scarcely a word for the event.

Indeed, the struggle of the Filipinos under Emilio Aguinaldo against the Americans in 1898 was completely overshadowed in the Indies press by the Boer War in South Africa. In 1899, for instance, the *Bataviaasch Nieuwsblad* published for some time an extra Sunday edition of the paper dedicated entirely to the desperate struggle of the South African Boers against the superior might of imperialist Britain. Travelling fairs in the Indies would present tableaux vivants showing the tragic fate of the Boers, and at masked balls some of the employees from sugar factories appeared in costumes representing their heroic brothers in South Africa.[27] Indeed, a small group of Europeans from the Indies went to South Africa to fight against the British on the side of the Boers. The feeling of sympathetic brotherhood stemmed from a common ancestry in the Netherlands. It was certainly not based on ideological anti-imperialism, for the Europeans in the Indies were enthusiastic about military expeditions to subdue obstreperous rulers in the Outlying Provinces, as for instance in 1894 when the "traitorous" island of Lombok was brought under Dutch rule.

Andriesse's account of European descendants in the East Indies, describing them as the victims of imperialistic policies, was a mirror image of the stigmatising theme of decline and decay so popular at the fin de siècle. His story is as lacking in subtlety as the one telling of the decline of Indische society. Every member of the lower middle class experiences the dread of social drowning — this sentiment was clearly something Andriesse played on — but the growth of employment in the railway sector reveals how inaccurate is the suggestion that lower-class Europeans in the Indies were severing ties with the European world. The railway employees were a major element in the Indische Bond. They were also the most socially aware. In Batavia, Th.K.J. van Kuyk, an active member of the Indische Bond, had attempted just before the turn of the century to set up a section of the *Nederlandse Vereeniging van Spoor- en Tramwegpersoneel* (Netherlands Association of Railway and Tram Employees) in the Indies.[28] The attempt failed, as it proved impossible to set up such a union for the whole of Java. Besides Van Kuyk there was A. Bijvoet, senior clerk in the department of education, religion and industry, the major spokesman for this trade-union-oriented section within the Indische Bond.[29] In 1897, on behalf of the Indische Bond, he had contacted the leaders in the Netherlands of the then still small *Sociaal-Democratische Arbeiders Partij* (SDAP), the Dutch Labour Party. The press reacted nervously to the contacts between active members of the Indische Bond and Dutch Social Democrats, warning against "red sympathisers".[30] In the end, nothing came of this contact, and cooperation between the Indische Bond and the SDAP never materialised. Bijvoet, after a conflict with the board, soon left the Bond.[31]

The Indische Bond did not develop into a trade union, nor into a branch of the Dutch Labour Party. The same thing happened as had earlier with Soeria Soemirat — a number of socially prominent people took the Indische Bond under their wing. After the statutes had been accepted by the government in 1898, people thronged to join. Andriesse faded into the background, and the Assistant-Resident C. Beynon became the chairman.[32] Carping and spiteful tongues claimed that the appointment was manipulated by the government in order to place in charge of the Indische Bond someone who would keep it loyal to the colonial authorities. For the time being, however, such grumbles and complaints did not affect the Indische Bond — it had something else on which to vent its wrath. The Groeneveldt Commission, set up by the government, made the recommendation in 1899 to close down the training college for higher civil servants at the Willem III School in Batavia. The commission remarked dryly that prospective high-ranking civil servants needed to develop a "broad perspective" in Europe before taking up a post in the Indies. Even in the Netherlands this comment raised some eyebrows. In 1906 the Minister of the Colonies, Dirk Fock, wryly observed that he found it hard to believe that studying in Leiden, a small town in the province of South Holland, or its environs, could substantially contribute to the broadening of one's European perspective. Furthermore, a student who had spent all his early years in the Indies would not, in the minister's opinion, later be able to change his attitude to life.[33]

Understandably, the commission's report infuriated many in the Indies. The reference to the "broad perspective" was to echo through the press for many decades. It was seized upon as exemplary of colonial arrogance and scarcely veiled racism. The Indische Bond drew up a petition against the closure of the special training course for civil servants. The pro-government newspaper *Java-Bode* informed civil servants and officials that they need not be afraid of losing their jobs if they signed the petition.[34] This letter of protest — just like that against the closure of the military academy — gained support from as far away as Makassar. Not only the geographic, but also the social, basis of the petition was extremely wide reaching.[35] It appeared that the differences between the upper class and those lower down the social ladder — which had been measured in detail in the 1880s by, for instance, the paper *De Telefoon* — had now been resolved thanks to a shared sense of injury caused by the Dutch condescension.

The Indische Bond, the union for Indo-Europeans

After a few initial wobbly steps, the Indische Bond found its feet. It gained sympathy among Europeans of all ranks who felt themselves at home in the Indies. Well-known figures such as the journalist Otto Knaap and Auguste Mahieu, the founding father of the travelling theatre Komedie Stamboel, made efforts to attract the less-educated Indo-Europeans from poor neighbourhoods and involve them in the union. Special shops and meeting halls were set up, where parties were held and — on a more serious note — lectures were delivered. In 1900 the union had 3,500 members, and within a year the figure had risen to almost 4,500.[36] Although Andriesse was politically sidelined, he managed to return in 1900 as editor of *Het Bondsblad*, the union's newspaper and mouthpiece. On one point Andriesse could feel satisfied: in 1901 the union's new board of directors declared that the motherland was deliberately depriving the Indies of educational services. Andriesse could not have voiced it more pungently. Despite this, the board members all came from the upper classes in the Indies and were socially far removed from their supporters.[37] The directors refused to consider the Indische Bond as primarily an organisation to further the cause of the Indo-Europeans. They proposed that the Indische Bond should primarily concern itself with such matters as education and civil rights. It should certainly not concentrate solely on the cause of the Indo-Europeans. The board of directors even suggested that well-bred and educated Indonesians also be allowed to have membership.

This suggestion showed a failure to understand how the Indische Bond had emerged from a mix of class and ethnic consciousness. Little is actually known of the social composition of the Indische Bond because the administration concerning its membership has been lost. Nevertheless, we can be almost certain that the main body of support came from the railway workers and the civil service milieu of the northern Javanese coastal towns and cities. Here, European workers grumbled increasingly about long working hours, low wages and authoritarian bosses — most of whom were born in the Netherlands. From time to time the situation exploded, as when in 1901 a wildcat strike broke out in the railway company of the Nederlandsch-Indische Spoorwegmaatschappij. This strike was, however, soon extinguished and the strike leaders were fired.[38] In the Post Office and Customs and Excise departments there was not a whisper of a wildcat strike — still less an organised one. But this did not mean the sense of frustration was any less. The discontent caused by long working hours and condescending superiors not only found a voice in the press but also began to sow seeds of disruption in the Indische Bond. As editor of the Indische Bond's newspaper, *Het Bondsblad*, Andriesse gave support to the feelings of discontent among members of the autocratic board — which led to his dismissal. This caused another storm of letters to the editors of Batavian newspapers, the general tenor of which was to accuse the leaders of the Indische Bond of being Totoks who wanted to keep the Indo-Europeans in the role of underdog.[39]

The conflict within the Indische Bond reveals how deeply class differences were experienced as a struggle between the Totoks and the

Indos. Just as in the days when Soeria Soemirat was created, the press underscored the dividing lines. One of the vociferous journalists involved was Karel Wybrands, born in Amsterdam. He had arrived in Batavia from Medan in East Sumatra at exactly the moment when the arguments broke out within the Indische Bond. He came to take over the organisation of a newspaper, the *Nieuws van den Dag voor Nederlandsch-Indië*, and was to transform this nondescript daily into one of the most successful papers of the Indies. Arriving in his new office, he immediately put pen to paper, composing an article supporting Andriesse and those within the Indische Bond who were opposed to the Totoks in general and the notables leading the Indische Bond, in particular. Although Wybrands was to go down in history as a colonial journalist who made no bones about a situation, a ruthless writer with a trenchant conservatism, during his early years in Batavia he revealed himself as radical and progressive. At that time, socialism and the trade unions were perceived in the East Indies — possibly more so even than in the Netherlands — as threats to the established order. Wybrands found such an outlook narrow and limited and was delighted that Indo-Europeans were finally speaking out for themselves. This would help them, he thought, to find their true place in society: in a European liberal civilised milieu, not in the despotic Javanese world.

Wybrands created such fury among the mass of supporters of the Indische Bond against the leaders, that the ruling figures were forced to quit the scene. The Indische Bond never recovered from this blow. With hindsight, we can understand that the swift demise of the Indische Bond was no more than a consequence of resistance to paternalistic social attitudes, which manifested themselves in the behaviour of the Indische Bond's running committee. This patronising approach was the product of a small colonial society in which, on the one hand, it was thought necessary to show European solidarity, while on the other hand class differences were too great to be simply brushed under the mat. When, a few years after the Indische Bond was set up, the first Railway Union in the Indies was created, the same pattern of paternalism and resistance emerged. The long-hoped-for State Railway Union was established in 1906, once the managers had stepped forward to take the lead. Within a year the Union had 1,300 members, which meant that 65 per cent of the railway workers had joined the organisation. In 1908 its membership was opened up to Indonesian railway employees, and the trade union circular was published in both Dutch and Malay. However, unlike their "European" colleagues, the Indonesian members of the union did not have the right to vote, although in 1909 they formed the majority of the union's members. They did gain voting rights in the more radical *Vereeniging van Spoor- en Tramwegpersoneel* (Association of Railway and Tram Employees) set up in 1909 in Semarang, which registered 1,877 members in that same year, of whom 1,200 were Indonesian.[40]

The Indo-Europeans working for the railways may have involved their Javanese colleagues in their trade union, but this was by no means the general tendency. In the sugar industry, for instance, things were quite different. Although the majority of the members of the Sugar Union, the professional body established in 1907 for the sugar industry, were Indo-European employees, the union was strongly influenced by newcomers in the East Indies. Each factory or business in the sugar industry had a fairly limited number of European employees with a large number of Indonesian workers under them. The Europeans definitely felt superior and identified themselves with their employers. The idea of admitting Indonesians into this union was out of the question. The contrasts between the conservative sugar-producing regions and the city of Semarang, popularly considered a red bastion in the 1920s, only serve to underscore the differences in attitude towards labour in the sugar industry, on the one hand, and the ports and railways on the other.

During this period the press and the trade unions played a major part in the growing self-awareness of Indo-Europeans, and the Indische Bond faded into insignificance. In the Outlying Provinces, where the government was not a big employer of Indo-Europeans, a different pattern emerged. The trade unions had not been able to gain a foothold there. Although one came across the occasional branch of the Indische Bond, there was scant contact between head office and distant branches in outlying parts of the archipelago, and what there was sometimes broke down. The Padang Union in Sumatra, for instance, had broken off from the Indische Bond as early as 1899.[41] Europeans from Manado never even joined — although in Sulawesi the distinction between "stayers" and "sojourners" was certainly as strongly felt as in Java. In Manado, however, this contrast was not primarily one of class, but instead served to stimulate feelings of local nationalism. The juridical distinction between "European" and "native" had in fact remained secondary here. Far more important was the feeling of belonging to an extended Christian population.[42]

The Indische Bond — which was succeeded in 1919 by the *Indo-Europeesch Verbond*, the IEV — born in the cities of Semarang and Batavia, seemed somehow irrelevant outside Java, where in the 19th century the descendants of Europeans had experienced an entirely different history. The combination of ethnic and class consciousness was typical for Java's northern coastal centres, where the colonial economy as well as the all-important press were furthest developed.

The Indo-pauper revisited

The government of the Indies viewed the emergence of the Indische Bond as a dangerous symptom of social unrest. Unemployment among the European residents and the downhill effect this had on wages for those not highly educated would, they feared, almost certainly lead to radicalism of the Indische Bond.[43] In this context what they most feared — remarkably enough — was not so much the influence of the Dutch Labour Party, the SDAP, as the flames of revolution that might wing their way from the Philippines. This was why the governor-general of the time, Willem Rooseboom, set up the already mentioned study into pauperism among the Europeans, in June 1900.[44] About 20 years after the journalists Landouw and A.M. Voorneman had appealed for a systematic enquiry into pauperism, few saw the need now for any such investigation. Paternalistic research studies into the lifestyle of certain social groups had become an anachronism in a society where the lower classes were busy organising themselves. After the turn of the century such studies were only set up in colonies where those in control saw "poor whites" and their descendants as a threat to colonial (read white) prestige.[45]

In the Dutch East Indies many protested against the breach of personal privacy in the families being studied. This was especially so since the study included those in the lower ranks of the civil service who, naturally, did not wish to find themselves associated with pauperism. Large numbers from this class were members of the Indische Bond, and newspaper readers. The official government explanation — that these "less well-to-do" were included in the research study because it was considering not only unemployment but also family size as possible causes of poverty — failed to mollify. This Malthusian twist, linking poverty with progeny, made it look as if the guilty parties were those who engendered large (and consequently poor) families — and not their employers. The *Bataviaasch Nieuwsblad*, which was publishing almost weekly articles attacking the exploitation of civil servants in the lower ranks, reacted with the headline "Inquisition!"[46] How could the government insult its own employees by subjecting them to a study that was so stigmatising? Those investigating the question of pauperism got nowhere in Batavia; indeed, in some kampongs they received a very hostile reception. Even the resident of Batavia supported his office clerks fairly and squarely when they refused to cooperate with the investigation.[47]

But the fear of finding disturbing results from the questionnaires was soon laid to rest. There were 3,711 "indigent" European family heads living in Java and Madura (the other islands were unfortunately not included in the study). Together with their families, this accounted for 9,381 persons, that is, 17.5 per cent of the European population. Out of this 9,381, the number classified as "pauper" was 64 per cent, which was less than 11 per cent of the entire European population. And of these, almost one-third were ex-soldiers, the vast majority of whom had been born in the Netherlands. The problem of pauperism among the Europeans in the East Indies thus concerned no more than the 8 per cent who were sick, were victims of the economic crisis of 1885, or for some other reason had become indigent.[48] Once more it was made clear — presumably unnecessarily so — that the army barracks were a major supplier of paupers. At the most, the research study provided a legitimation for banning concubinage among the military and civil servants. In 1904 military officers and in 1911 junior officers were refused advancement if they were found to be living in concubinage. For ordinary privates, concubinage was outlawed in 1914.[49] The Europeans living in the Dutch East Indies — at least, those enjoying good health — felt the research study into pauperism to be an unnecessary afterthought. Thanks to the flourishing sugar industry and the increasing number of government jobs, those who had a reasonable education did not need to fear unemployment. The problem of pauperism among these Europeans was limited — until there was a short but severe economic crisis in 1922 — to the sick and the socially maladapted. They had to rely on the charities that had developed over the centuries, a hotchpotch of orphanages, religious establishments for the poor, funds and charities, income earned from auction taxes and the right to free medical help. This lack of organisation was not something the government of the Indies could do much about without coming into conflict with the churches, who considered care for the poor to be one of their tasks. The government proposed the centralisation of poor relief, but this met defeat in The Hague because of disagreement from the successive (Dutch Reformed Church) Ministers of the Colonies Alexander Willem Frederik Idenburg and Jan Hendrik de Waal Malefijt.[50]

Not surprisingly, there was also a rural variation on urban pauperism. The European rural poor consisted of small landholders who often owned a plot of land illegally and rented it out to be worked by local Javanese. This illegal form of agricultural enterprise was a result of the government policy that allocated only large parcels to Europeans, on short- or long-term lease. The government gradually came to realise that regulation was preferable to prohibition. After 1901, Europeans were also allowed to rent small parcels, up to 25 *bouw* (17 hectares) in size, on long-term lease and could even become owners of parcels measuring more than 10 *bouw* (7 hectares).[51] But one problem was not resolved: the small landholders did not possess the financial means to invest in the production of crops either for urban consumption or for export, and they continued to behave like gentlemen-farmers. This prompted the government of the Indies in 1904 to introduce an arrangement for credit, known as the ordinance regarding small-scale farming. This made small-scale farming (especially market gardening) now possible (at least, in theory) for those with little capital. Also, after 1904, agricultural colonies, of the kind proposed as early as 1881 by Enklaar van Guericke, were assured of government credit.[52] And in the same year the Indische Bond was granted a parcel of land in West Java's mountainous Priangan region. This agricultural colony, however, prospered no better than its antecedents.

The measures to facilitate European smallholdership were only partially successful. In 1916, on the basis of this ruling, there were 156 parcels measuring between one-quarter and 25 *bouw*, granted to farmers in Java, Madura, Manado and Sumatra.[53] But the ordinance contributed little to the development of small-scale market gardening directed towards the European consumer. At least, this is what we assume, since the information over what exactly was produced is missing for many of the parcels. Only a very few cultivated — in the spirit of the ordinance — products such as vanilla, rubber, banana, pineapple, potatoes or vegetables. The ordinance was chiefly intended to remedy the situation in Java, where the illegal occupation of land caused the government grave concern. The situation was less worrying in the other islands because due to the abundance of land there was little reason to restrict the issue of small parcels of land on long-term lease.[54] But even in Java the ordinance produced little or no reduction in illegal land occupation by Europeans. Thus, in the 1920s, this question was to become a hot number for the Indo-Europeesch Verbond.

The Report on Pauperism arose from an out-of-date social picture. It had a backward-looking tone, seen also in its detailed retrospective consideration of government policy to prevent the displacement of Indo-European clerks by newcomers. In the longer term, competition from Javanese candidates was a much more serious threat. In 1902 there was open competition between Indonesian (Javanese) and European candidates for the lower posts.[55] Henceforth, the Europeans no longer held a monopoly over these positions.

Nevertheless, the report certainly identified the cause of the problem of poverty, namely, the lack of adequate education in the Indies. Incidentally, this had been said for at least the past 50 years by many journalists and more recently by the unfortunate board of the Indische Bond. But nothing resulted from the recommendations in the report to expand educational opportunities in the East Indies. And it was the same story for other criticisms made in the report: for instance, government abuse of the fact that large numbers applied for the posts of office clerk, and the consequently very low wages. Indeed, the government even wanted to cut the wages of clerks. This plan had the support of those in favour of the new approach in colonial policy, the "ethical politics". They acknowledged that in the past Dutch colonial policies had been exploitative and that Dutch efforts should be geared towards the social development of the Indonesians (then still called "natives") and greater autonomy for the administration.

The ethical policy was promulgated by the Dutch queen at the opening session of Dutch parliament in 1901 and was endorsed by all the main political parties. In the context of the ethical policy, Europeans who had been educated in the Netherlands would restrict themselves to teaching and supervision, while the Indonesian population would be involved in all other tasks of government. In this respect the colonial government was inclined to assume that all Europeans without some kind of higher certificate or diploma — which constituted the majority of those born in the Indies — fell within the category of "native". A directive from the colonial government (a government circular) drawn up in 1905 at the instigation of the Minister of the Colonies, Alexander Idenburg, who was the major "ethical" statesman of the day, wasted no words formulating the consequences of the new ethical principles for the lower-ranking civil servants. Many jobs in the East Indies could well be given to natives for a lower wage. Such positions remained available for Indo-Europeans, but for the same low wage.[56] It is remarkable — and it did not escape notice — that this is the only one of the many thousands of government circulars to contain the term "Indo-European", thereby acknowledging the distinction between expatriates and indigenous Europeans.

This circular — which was rapidly withdrawn — sounded the closing chords on 30 years of discussion about European pauperism. It formed, at the same time, a provisional conclusion to the debate on the position in colonial society of descendants of Europeans. The thread running through this debate was the effort to establish a boundary line around a group of Indo-Europeans and to retain this group within the European community of the East Indies; but with the proviso that they be categorised as "indigenous Europeans". This was apparent from the 1905 wages and salaries circular, which was to overshadow the Report on Pauperism. Indeed, it formed the basis of a new salary policy, which entailed a Tropics Supplement for those who had received a training in the Netherlands. But most of the Indies-born Europeans lacked the means to send their children to the Netherlands to be educated.

Discrimination and education

There can be absolutely no doubt, in light of how the discussions on pauperism were concluded, that the Dutch colonial authorities — and with them, the upper echelons in the Indies — considered the Indo-Europeans as a class of local-born Europeans. But the authorities did not want to give Indo-Europeans preferential treatment. Due to their limited financial means and — consequently — scant education, most Indo-Europeans could not attain high government posts. It should be noted, however, that this exclusion from high government posts was not, strictly speaking, based on skin colour but was the outcome of social milieu. A growing minority of fairly well-to-do Indies-born families sent their children to the Netherlands to be educated.

Meanwhile, in the business world there was open discrimination based on skin colour; advertisements would appear explicitly asking for "pure-blooded" employees.[57] Of course, not every business practised racial discrimination. In practice things were endlessly more complex than could be suggested by a schematic plan showing the Indo-European sandwiched in between the whites (on top) and the natives (underneath). A finely woven texture had developed, which enclosed notions about status, determining who were to be considered social equals. It was regulated by such issues as income, education, family, position within private business or rank in the civil service. Only one of the issues was skin colour. Nevertheless, with the rise and decline of the Indische Bond, the press, economic expansion and not least a constant influx of Totoks, a stereotypical image of Indo-Europeans arose: of a group who had always been Indo-European and who would always remain so. At more or less the same time a turnabout took place within Indo-European circles, from paternalistic self-help to an emancipation movement that strove for social advancement whereby they might escape from their own Indo-European class. It was this very struggle for emancipation that strengthened the self-awareness of the Indo-Europeans.

It appears from the available immigration statistics that in the first decade of the 20th century the annual figure for male emigrants from the Netherlands was between 3,000 and 4,000 — double that of the previous decade. The figures for women immigrants rose from 500 in the 1890s to 1,749 in 1912. Many of these Dutch immigrants should not be seen as newcomers. Some of them were, for instance, returning from leave, and there were those born in the Indies who had spent some time studying in the Netherlands before returning to their native land. What is clear, however, is that for the first time since the beginning of the 19th century the number of newcomers increased more rapidly than did the number of Europeans born in the Indies.[58] Although the picture of thousands of newcomers flooding the job market is somewhat exaggerated, there was a gradual influx of well-educated newcomers, while there was a drop in the numbers of (mostly) poorly educated soldiers arriving from Europe.[59] The skilled immigrants filled an obvious gap in the labour market of the Indies. In 1906, for instance, the State Railways had almost immediately plucked the bitter fruits of their decision to improve terms of employment for drivers and technical personnel, at the cost of office staff — who would in future have to put up with lower wages. The result was that office workers quit their jobs, looking for better-paid positions elsewhere, and the directors of the railways had to recruit staff in the Netherlands.[60] After 1905 the small number of Indonesians who had attended elementary school were easily absorbed by the job market without presenting any great threat to (Indo-)European employees.

We do not have any statistics to help us determine whether the inequality in salaries increased among the Europeans of the Indies during the first decades of the 20th century. We may assume, however, that the increased prosperity was not evenly distributed, since among the lower classes there was still considerable competition for jobs, while at the same time there was a shortage of highly trained and skilled personnel.

The public owning substantial capital increased. The Indies newspapers carried advertisements for car makes such as Fiat, Ford and Mercedes, and the number of vehicles on the roads grew every year. On average, the Europeans of the East Indies were wealthier than their counterparts in the Netherlands. They shopped in the most upmarket department stores in Batavia, Semarang, Surabaya and Bandung. All the latest products could be bought in the Indies — provided people had the money, for everything was expensive and there were huge income differences. A car could easily cost 4,000 guilders, and a Steinway piano made of teak would fetch 450 guilders. Compare this with the incomes: a "pure-blood" newcomer fresh to the job might earn 150 guilders a month working on a cultivation enterprise, while such an income would be attained by an office clerk only towards the close of his career.

During these years it was said that quite a few Indo-Europeans cherished feelings of resentment, stemming largely from their realisation that they were not sharing in the new prosperity.[61] Indo-Europeans frequently missed the boat, especially during these times when the number of government posts was visibly growing. For instance, there were employees with the State Railways in 1904 who had worked for more than 20 years without being given tenure. This could make a great difference: as "temporary" employees, they were unable to build a pension.[62] When the economic situation improved, they observed that personnel were being invited from the Netherlands to fill the better positions that they had hoped for.[63] Of course, neither discrimination nor lack of opportunity was anything new. The term *presentkaasje*, meaning "a fresh young cheese-head sent uninvited from Holland", had been coined in the 19th century, and already at that time the Indo-Europeans resented these newcomers and felt elbowed out by them. But in those days there was not so outspoken a preference for "pure-bloods", and furthermore, neither public opinion nor social organisations were very developed.

As time went by, however, attitudes became more sharply defined and the Indo-Europeans became more vocal, which explains the rise of the association "Insulinde" established in 1907 in Bandung. It was a reaction to the spineless and sluggish nature of the Indische Bond. Insulinde was led by the journalist Henri Carel Zentgraaff (who, like the above-mentioned Karel Wybrands, would later make his name as an aggressive journalist who pulled no punches); the new organisation devoted itself to publicising cases of discrimination by employers. There was also the *Bataviaasch Nieuwsblad*, the daily with the largest circulation

Illustration 44   The newspaper *Bataviaasch Nieuwsblad* was started in 1885 by the journalist and novelist Paul A. Daum. Pictured are the editorial staff *circa* 1909, from left: Karel Zaalberg, Ernest Douwes Dekker, Marius Nieuwenhuysen and Bart Daum. Douwes Dekker's foot is resting on the pro-government newspaper *Java-Bode*.
[Photograph in: *Vijftig jaar 1885 1 Dec. 1935.*]

in the Indies, helmed by Karel Zaalberg — a man who was vocal about the fact that he was an Indo and identified himself with lower-class Indos. During those years he reported dozens of cases of discrimination against Indos and exposed the indifference of the Totoks. The theme was taken up in novels and plays of the time. Possibly the best-known example is the novel published in 1915 by Hans van de Wall (pseudonym for Victor Ido) titled *De paupers*. It provides a realistic and authentic picture of the problems and frustrations of the Indo-Europeans.

Between 1906 and 1910 the discussions in the Indische Bond — which carried on more or less in the 19th-century tradition, concerning itself with funding, workplaces and agricultural colonies — evolved into a struggle against discrimination and the patronising attitude of the Netherlands government. This alteration was arguably more than a reaction to the growing number of newcomers from Europe. The Indische movement formed part of a broader Asian political revival that affected almost all the large countries of Asia. In India, Japan, China and the Philippines, nationalist movements had already challenged the European colonial hegemony, and in about 1906 Java too became part of the "Awakening East". Under Governor-General Joannes Benedictus van Heutsz, the subjugator of Aceh, the government began to show a serious interest in the emancipation of the Javanese elites. Van Heutsz's adviser was none other than the famous Islam expert Christiaan Snouck Hurgronje, who urged the appointment of educated Javanese in the colonial government. Van Heutsz himself encouraged the Javanese journalist Tirtoadhisoerjo, the physician Wahidin Soediro Hoesodo and the regent of the Paku Alam, Notodirojo, to propagate the idea of a Javanese educational fund, following the example of the Chinese in Java. The latter had, as early as 1901, set up a schools' association named *Tiong Hoa Hwee Koan*. The three Javanese notables toured the country, and press reports soon granted them the status of a "Young Java" revival. Repercussions were also felt in discussions among European groups, where, since the demise of the Indische Bond in 1901, there had been no movement propagating better education.[64]

It was, above all, the newspaper *Bataviaasch Nieuwsblad* that attempted to link the emancipation of Indo-Europeans and the struggle against patronising and discrimination, with the dominant themes in the Young Java revival. An added impetus arrived when Ernest Douwes Dekker, great-nephew of the famous Dutch writer Multatuli and one of the fathers of Indonesian nationalism, joined the board of editors in 1908. He already had an eventful career behind him. Having spent his childhood in Semeru, he attended the HBS (secondary school) in Batavia. He went on to work as a chemist in a sugar factory but had to leave after — according to his account — he stood up for the local people against the factory boss. Douwes Dekker and his two brothers then set off for South Africa to fight against the British on the side of the Boers. Returning from the Boer War, Douwes Dekker worked for various newspapers, including *De Locomotief*. In 1907 Zaalberg persuaded him to write for his paper, and the two became firm friends.

In 1908 Douwes Dekker became Zaalberg's deputy, and in the same year his merciless cartoons were published in the paper. The two editors excelled in unmasking the absurdity of Totok arrogance in assuming that the Netherlands was performing mighty deeds in the Tropics. Douwes Dekker's iconoclastic style, his outspoken sympathy with the Asian revival and his "love of Javanese" elicited reprimands from the government — addressed to the newspaper publisher.[65] The *Bataviaasch Nieuwsblad* shrugged these off. After all, the paper was increasingly popular with Dutch-reading Indonesians.

Douwes Dekker, meanwhile, had regular contact with the students of the Indies medical school, the STOVIA, who spent much of their time in the library of his home, which lay only a stone's throw away from their institute. It was this group of students who on 20 May 1908 formed the society *Boedi Oetomo* (Glorious Endeavour). This date was later pronounced the birthdate of Indonesian nationalism. The students, who advertised themselves as *Jong Javanen* (Young Javanese) undoubtedly wanted political change. However, the movement had its teeth drawn by the government and was redirected from political oceans into safe shallows: it became a Javanese cultural society. The students faded into the sidelines. So Douwes Dekker lost his allies in the society. His friends, among them the physician Tjipto Mangoenkoesoemo and the STOVIA student Soewardi Soerjaningrat, quit Boedi Oetomo. It was to be several years before they returned to their original political plan.

The mood of the times, however, seemed unfriendly towards those who supported emancipation of native peoples under guidance from the West. Equally under pressure — for the time being — was the notion of a strict division between what was European and what was native. Patronising colonial policies were, however, losing popularity and being increasingly criticised by the 1910s. The belle époque, the period leading up to World War I, witnessed a fine flourishing of holistic philosophies of life, the most important one in the Indies being Theosophy. The Theosophists claimed to derive their ideas from the sacred writings of Buddhism and Brahmanism but wanted to rise above the world religions, and they argued that Christianity was neither ethically nor culturally superior. There were also other spurs to resistance in the Indies against Dutch racism and the Western sense of superiority. The editors of the *Bataviaasch Nieuwsblad* were influenced by the ideas of the famous German biologist and Darwinist Ernst Haeckel. His philosophy of identity assumed that human thought was a unity, which explained why different cultures and religions could be traced back to the same fundamental truths.[66] The work of Max Müller was also extremely popular at this time. Basing his philosophy on 19th-century European metaphysics and Hindu philosophy (including Brahmanism), Müller propounded the shared origins of Indo-Germanic mythology. Intellectuals in India, Mexico and the Dutch East Indies devoured his writings, which proffered one common source of all religious consciousness.[67]

In his newspaper articles and later in his political propaganda, Ernest Douwes Dekker attacked the establishment with a mixture of romanticism and provocative irony. It is interesting to observe that even with his liberal attitude, Douwes Dekker could not rid himself entirely of racial notions. He struggled with the relationship between the Indo-Europeans — whom he considered to be a separate racial category, namely, Mestizo — and a broader, non-racial concept of the *Indiër*. He published a series of articles in 1912 in his own newspaper, *De Expres*, under the heading "Racial-psychological notions about the *Indiër*". In these, he first examines the Indo-European as a product of racial mixture and continues to state that this hybridity has nothing to do with race, but with environment and upbringing. He concludes, almost as an incidental correction, that *Indiërs* are more than simply Indo-European.[68] We may well wonder how Douwes Dekker perceived the relationship between Indo-Europeans and *Indiërs*, between the Indische Europeans and the far larger population of Javanese. His ideas here strongly resemble those of José Vasconcelos (1882–1959), the Mexican revolutionary, minister of education and perpetual world traveller. Vasconcelos is famous for his 1925 book *La Raza Cósmica* (The Cosmic Race), a manifesto in praise of the spiritual strength of the "Mestizo race", which he saw as the future "race" of Latin America. Indeed, not only in Mexico, but also in Brazil, mestisation, the mixing of races, came to be seen as the basis of a new nation-forming.[69] For Douwes Dekker there could be no doubt that Indo-Europeans, those of mixed race, formed the essential nature of the "Indische identity". In this conviction he resumed the old theme that perceived the Indo as a cosmopolitan citizen of the world. But he went a step farther, presenting himself as an intellectual Indo-European and demanding an assured role as leader in a national movement for the Indies, which would ultimately include every different group and race.

The first sign of this ambition was the campaign of the editors of the *Bataviaasch Nieuwsblad* to set up a university in the Indies. They suggested combining the already existing law school with the STOVIA (medical school) and a technical college that the Dutch government had agreed to set up in 1901. Their efforts were crowned with success. In March 1910 Douwes Dekker managed to assemble several eminent personalities to form the board of the new *Indische Universiteits-Vereeniging* (University Association of the Indies): Snouck Hurgronje's former pupil, the regent of Serang, Achmad Djajadiningrat, the directors of the Javanese medical school and law school, the director of the *Nederlandsch-Indische Escompto Maatschappij*, Jan Dinger, Phoa Keng Hek, chairman of the group of Chinese schools Tiong Hoa Hwee Koan, and of course Douwes Dekker himself. In 1912 this board managed to acquire 150,000 guilders in gifts from business circles in the Indies in order to found a technical college in Batavia.[70] However, the government's reaction to this proposal was cool. The University Association was presumably too much of a protest against the monopoly held in the colony by Netherlanders from overseas. But it was a triumph for the political manipulations of Douwes Dekker.

Noticeable absentees from the board of the University Association of the Indies were representatives of the Ambonese and Manadonese, who, in fact, were steeped in Dutch education. About six months previously, in September 1909, Wim K. Tehupeiory had set up the *Ambonsch Studiefonds* (Ambonese Educational Trust) in Batavia. He, like the editorial board of the *Bataviaasch Nieuwsblad*, was inspired by the founding of Boedi Oetomo. When studying in the Netherlands, Tehupeiory had got to know some members of Young Java. He planned, after his studies in the Netherlands, to qualify as a doctor at STOVIA. Once back in the Indies he had been granted equal civic status with "Europeans" and proceeded to work holding the status of European surgeon in Bangka, the tin-rich island off Sumatra.[71] The statutes for the Ambonese Educational Trust were not accepted until 1911, and then civil servants and soldiers thronged to join this society, which was open only to Christians. Thus, at the time of the founding of the University Association, the Ambonese Educational Trust was still only in an embryonic form and its founder was on his way to the island of Bangka. It would seem that Douwes Dekker and Tehupeiory did not cross paths.

The Indische Party

After the days of A.M. Voorneman and Andriesse, the struggle for education in the Indies and the resistance to the curtailing of civil rights were no longer the exclusive concern of a group of European notables. This had certainly been the case during the protests of May 1848. But since the 1880s the lower classes had also been mobilised. Furthermore, the Freemasons and the ever-expanding local press — with the *Bataviaasch Nieuwsblad* in the vanguard — had acquainted Javanese elites with the programme. In Javanese circles there was support for certain aspects of the programme, such as the proposal for a university in the Indies. But when Douwes Dekker and his friends withdrew from Boedi Oetomo, it became clear how difficult it was for this essentially European political tradition to take root in the growing Javanese national movement. Douwes Dekker had, incidentally, soured his own credit. He had managed to make an enemy of Tirtoadhisoerjo, editor-in-chief of the Indonesian paper with the largest circulation, the *Medan Prijaji*, a publication dedicated to publishing the voice of the common man.[72]

Thus, the University Association, set up with the ideal of uniting all the population groups in the Dutch East Indies, remained an isolated phenomenon. The fact that it succeeded to a certain extent — the technical college in Bandung did materialise — was chiefly due to the happy circumstance that Snouck Hurgronje's ideas were well received at the time. The nucleus of his philosophy of "association" was that the leadership of the colony should be given to Indonesian elites with a Western education, and to European civil servants. The ties with the Netherlands should evolve from that of ruler and ruled to that of friendly cooperation. The notion that various population groups and two countries — geographically so far apart — could be bound by a bond of loyalty to a royal house was a deeply held conviction at that time. The jubilant celebrations following the birth of Princess Juliana in 1909, in which all sections of the population shared, were an impressive demonstration of solidarity and loyalty to Queen Wilhelmina of the Netherlands. Even Tirtoadhisoerjo's newspaper, the caustic *Medan Prijaji*, joined in with the chorus of devoted supporters and well-wishers.[73]

Discussions about a more rigid distinction between "European" and "indigenous" gradually gave way to a climate in which the "Indische" could be perceived not as a problem, but rather as playing an essential part in maintaining the links between motherland and colony. This shift in the debate also produced a change of tack in the organisations that existed to promote the interests of the Indo-Europeans. It applied in particular to the Insulinde society in Semarang, which in 1910 opened its doors to Indonesian members. The Indische Bond had not yet made this step, although the question of more open membership was up for discussion. In 1911 both the periodicals published by Insulinde and those of the Indische Bond spoke out in favour of an "Indische" movement — in the sense of not exclusively "European" — for improved educational and civil rights. There was a great deal of talk about fusing Insulinde and the Indische Bond, and there were some suggestions from within these organisations about looking for ways of cooperation with Boedi Oetomo and perhaps other organisations too. Together they would then form a cohesive front, a large party ready for a parliament of the Indies.[74]

Yet no one, not even Douwes Dekker, could conceive of a mass movement of Indonesians with many thousands of followers. The horizon was narrow — enclosing a few thousand Europeans, the few thousand members of Boedi Oetomo and possibly the Chinese schools association Tiong Hoa Hwee Koan. These organisations in combination could produce at most 50 politically experienced intellectuals. Of all the Indo-European leaders, Douwes Dekker was on the best terms with the Javanese elite who had been educated in the Western tradition. Among his friends were the Theosophists Tjipto Mangoenkoesoemo and Soewardi Soerjaningrat. He had known both of them since their student days at the medical school in Batavia.

Douwes Dekker unfolded the ground plan for a parliamentary movement in November 1911 at a meeting of the Indische Bond. He had been invited by his friend Karel Zaalberg to give a lecture. Titled "*Aansluiting tussen Blank en Bruin*" ("White and Brown Alignment"), the lecture urged the necessity of forming a strictly secular movement with its agenda free from social, religious and racial arguments. His new vision was inspired by a recent journey through Europe.[75] There he had met nationalists from (then British) India and learned about the Indian National Congress, a conglomeration of organisations that aimed to supersede differences of a religious, ethnic or social nature. For Douwes Dekker there was only one contradistinction that mattered: that between the ruler and the ruled. The Indo-European was a product of colonialism, and the *Indiër* was a member of a yet-to-be-created free political community. Douwes Dekker thought that everyone, irrespective of race, religion or riches, who devoted their "best powers to the development of the country and felt that it was their own land" deserved to be called an "Indiër".[76] Not only because he held this key concept, but also because of the way he tried to put it into practice, Douwes Dekker earned himself the title of father of secular Indonesian nationalism.

In the spring of 1912 Douwes Dekker started publishing a newspaper of his own in Bandung, called *De Expres*, to be a mouthpiece for a parliamentary movement for the Indies. It is hard to estimate the effect of his propaganda. The same holds for the articles published earlier by Douwes Dekker and Zaalberg in the *Bataviaasch Nieuwsblad*. Fellow journalists had sometimes observed wryly that although he might write till his fingers were black with ink he would never get the Indo-Europeans interested in the movement.[77] One thing is certain: neither Douwes Dekker's newspaper *De Expres* nor his pretentious monthly *Het Tijdschrift* had many subscribers. Despite this, in the autumn of 1912 he managed

to assemble thousands of supporters for his political movement, the
Indische Partÿ (Indische Party). He contrived to turn to his advantage a
mass political movement that appeared at just that time in Java, in the
form of an Islamic revival. The movement, called Sarekat Islam, was
started in 1911 by Hadji Samanhoedi, a batik producer from Surakarta,
with the support of Tirtoadhisoerjo, and began to grow rapidly in the
autumn of 1912. During the same years the Chinese in the Indies also
became more aware of themselves as a group. At Chinese New Year they
raised the republican flag with its five colours and demanded civic
equality with the Europeans, which the Japanese had been granted more
than ten years previously.[78] Many Javanese and Indo-Europeans viewed
the emancipation of the Chinese as a form of "pure arrogance", and the
reaction was often physical intimidation.

Another revival during this period was that of the slumbering Boedi
Oetomo, roused from its soporific state by the energetic Notodirojo,
a highly respected aristocrat from the Principalities. To the delight of
Douwes Dekker, in August 1912 Notodirojo took Boedi Oetomo under
his wing. Even if Douwes Dekker did not deal with Boedi Oetomo in
consultation with his Javanese friends, at least he adjusted his actions to
their deeds. In the closing days of August 1912, together with his trusty
friends from Bandung, he put the leadership of the Indische Bond in
Batavia out of action, and his friends in Semarang manoeuvred the board
of the Insulinde society onto the sidelines. Then on 6 September 1912,
at a meeting in Bandung, they announced the merger of the Indische
Bond and Insulinde — to become the Indische Party.

The founding of the Indische Party was far more than another
expression of the Indo-European struggle for emancipation. Yet from the
very start, that is how it was perceived, possibly because there was an
unexpectedly large influx of Indo-Europeans. This was the result of an
article from the *Bond van Geneesheren* (Medical Association) that was
discussed in several newspapers on 7 September. In their article the
medical doctors expressed their vehement reaction to the decision by the
government to allow candidates of all backgrounds to attend the second
medical school in Surabaya (a decision that the University Association
had most forcefully urged earlier). The remarks of the doctors were
extremely offensive and painful. They wrote that well-to-do Europeans
and Chinese would not even consider having their children study in the
Indies and that the medical school in Surabaya would merely attract a
few students from less-wealthy European families, who would go on to

practice as doctors, earning their money from "performing abortions and whiling away their time in adultery".

With an almost unanimous voice the press condemned the article by the doctors. But it was too late. The impression was created that the Totoks had let slip their mask of amiability and political correctness and had shown themselves in their true colours. They had revealed their undisguised contempt for the Indo-Europeans. Douwes Dekker realised that he must strike while the iron was hot. Together with some loyal supporters, he boarded the train for a propaganda tour of Java. He went first to Yogyakarta, then to Semarang, Surabaya, Pekalongan, Tegal and Cirebon, finishing on 3 October in the Zoological Gardens of Batavia. He and his band spoke of the sores that suppurated: abolition of the training college for higher civil servants in Batavia, the way the government was dragging its feet over a university in the Indies, how there was no representative parliament in the Indies.[79] Cheered on by enthusiastic crowds, Douwes Dekker challenged the government to issue criminal proceedings against the Medical Association for their scandalous remarks; without such a prosecution neither he nor his supporters could guarantee peace and order in the colony.[80]

The reactions from the European press were as divided as they were predictable. The *Soerabaiasch Handelsblad*, a newspaper representing the relatively new economic power base of East Java, voiced sharp criticism of Douwes Dekker. On the other hand, the *De Nieuwe Vorstenlanden*, a paper supported by the old European community in Surakarta and Yogyakarta, gave him its wholehearted endorsement. There was firm rejection from the "ethically" inclined and strongly Totok daily *De Locomotief*, while the respected *Java-Bode*, widely read by Batavian civil servants, voiced a muted judgement. Both *De Locomotief*, which presented itself as a progressive paper, and the conservative *Soerabaiasch Handelsblad* were in agreement that Douwes Dekker and his followers culled their support from the "lower-class" Indo-Europeans and condemned them for stirring up racial hatred. This accusation was enough to make many an Indo-European's blood boil — and in fact had the opposite effect from what was intended. Even the dramatic break-up between the close friends Douwes Dekker and Zaalberg — the latter produced five long emotional editorials condemning the hastiness and overconfidence of his former disciple — failed to stem the tide.[81] New branches of the Indische Party burgeoned on all sides, and within a few months the movement had several thousand members. The organisation was restricted to Java, but it was followed closely and carefully elsewhere.

All the Indische newspapers revelled in the juicy copy provided by passages, sometimes whole pages, from the polemics between the erstwhile friends Zaalberg and Douwes Dekker.[82]

Because of all this commotion the image of the Indische Party as a parliamentary movement became diluted. Even today, there is no consensus among historians about its true significance. Was it a movement of Indo-Europeans swept along on the current of a Javanese political revival, or was it a crucial stage in the growth of Indonesian nationalism? In the first place, Douwes Dekker's relations with leading Javanese intellectuals were too good (in contrast to those of his friend and mentor Karel Zaalberg) to consider him merely as an Indo-European leader. Both from newspaper reports and letters to the editor it can be deduced that the chief concerns of the Indische Party, namely, a parliament and a university for the Indies, were widely felt needs extending well beyond the Indo-European communities. Although these concerns arose out of 19th-century political demands by Europeans in the Indies, it took Douwes Dekker little effort to find important Javanese supporters. Nevertheless, his opponents were right when they claimed that the Indo-European would never identify with the Javanese. Furthermore, there was something ironical in having a journalist from a Dutch-language newspaper using the rulers' language to encourage "Indiërs" to become conscious of their Indonesian roots and look upon the Indonesians as their brothers and sisters. This call for fraternisation sounded less absurd, however, when Tjipto Mangoenkoesoemo took up the post of co-editor of *De Expres* in October 1912 and promulgated the political programme of the Indische Party. Towards the close of 1912 around 20 per cent of the Indische Party were Javanese.[83] At that time the Indische Party was just beginning to make inroads among the Javanese intelligentsia. Meanwhile, Sarekat Islam, under a new leader, Tjokroaminoto, was becoming the first Indonesian mass movement. The leaders of this movement were well disposed towards the Indische Party. At the festive opening meeting of the Indische Party in Bandung on 25 December, Tjokroaminoto himself was guest of honour. Progressive civil servants from the religious parties were gaining influence, and they convinced the governor-general to pacify the Javanese intellectuals by spending more on the then abysmal educational facilities for the Javanese people and not to increase military expenditure.

The Indische Party was soon banned and its leaders exiled, since it threatened to become a local variation on the Indian National Congress in British India. Governor-General Idenburg and his advisers wished to prevent this, because they saw the Indische Party as an alien element in the process of Javanese emancipation. The Japanese historian Takashi Shiraishi has demonstrated that the Indische Party's image as something of an odd one out in the Indonesian nationalist story has clung to it ever since.[84] As things turned out, the government did not have much difficulty in producing formal reasons for banning the Indische Party. At the meeting setting up the party, on 25 December 1912, Douwes Dekker had quite unexpectedly suggested the goal of an "independent people's existence in the years to come". This was greeted with loud cheers of approval by a public that was both enthusiastic and politically naive. Douwes Dekker wished to see this goal explicitly included in the statutes of the Indische Party in order to force the government to show its hand. But for a few months the government made no move, hoping that the movement would die down of its own accord. Then in March 1913 the government decided to ban the Indische Party because of the "revolutionary spirit" it manifested.[85] By then the danger had grown too great that the revolutionary spirit would blow across to the Sarekat Islam movement. The government was well aware how diffuse were the connections between the Indische Party and Sarekat Islam. No less a person than Soewardi Soerjaningrat, board member of the Indische Party and editor of the newspaper *De Expres*, was on the running committee of the Sarekat Islam branch in Bandung.

In the months following the ban on the Indische Party, the common ground shared by the Indische Party, Sarekat Islam and Boedi Oetomo would become more apparent. Tjipto and Soewardi took over the running of the movement — this had meanwhile found itself temporary shelter under the wings of the Insulinde organisation, which was still legal — while Douwes Dekker made for the Netherlands to win support among the Dutch parliamentary Social Democrats against the ban on the Indische Party. During his absence, Soewardi, Tjipto and Abdoel Moeis formed the *Boemi Poetra* Committee (meaning "Children of the Soil"). Celebrating the centenary of the regaining of Dutch independence (after the Napoleonic Wars) in 1813, they appealed to the magnanimity of the Netherlanders to take a step in the right direction — of freedom for the people of the Indies. The Boemi Poetra Committee requested that a parliament be established, and that Article 111 of the Government Regulations be rescinded; this article included the ban on political associations and meetings. Not only did the Sarekat Islam branch in Bandung propagate the ideals of the Indische Party, there was also a sizeable minority within Boedi Oetomo who sympathised with the

Illustration 45 After the fall of the Indische Party, its exiled leaders toured the Netherlands. This photograph was probably taken in The Hague in 1913. Seated, from left: Tjipto Mangoenkoesoemo, Ernest F.E. Douwes Dekker and Soewardi Soerjaningrat. Standing, from left: Frans Berding, G.L. Topée and J. Vermaesen. [Photograph, KITLV, Leiden.]

Boemi Poetra Committee. Under pressure from the somewhat hysterical reports in the European press about the Sarekat Islam movement, the governor-general was forced to take a hard line against Boemi Poetra. In August 1913 Tjipto, Soewardi, Abdoel Moeis and one of the other board members of the Bandung branch of Sarekat Islam were arrested, with a great show of military strength. When, shortly after this, Douwes Dekker returned from the Netherlands, he too was put in prison. There he wrote a furious article for *De Expres*, honouring his two friends and describing them as "proud-spirited martyrs" and warning the government that abuse of power had led to the downfall of the Spanish colonial government in the Philippines.[86] Such wisdom was, however, as pearls before the proverbial swine (in this case the governor-general). Although Douwes Dekker had played no part in the Boemi Poetra melodrama, he was banished together with his two friends.

On 8 September 1913 Douwes Dekker, Soewardi and Tjipto set sail for the Netherlands. The three cheerfully expected that in the coming Dutch elections the then-ruling coalition of conservative Christian parties would fall; they hoped for more input from the Social Democrats in a new cabinet. They looked forward to a speedy political comeback. Full of high hopes, friends waved them off from the quayside of Tanjung Priok, Batavia's harbour, as if the three were going on leave. But — partly because of the intervening World War I — it was to be ten years before they were reunited on East Indies soil.

The Dutch East Indies: old and new

The Indische Party, which emerged as an independence movement, was not only a culmination of the already 60-year-old demands for civil rights and freedom of the press, it was also the obvious consequence of these pleas. The historic meeting of 25 December 1912, when the dream of independence was voiced at the large gathering in Bandung, was the moment linking this tradition with Indonesian nationalism. The joint role of Zaalberg and Douwes Dekker as pioneers of the Indische Party is overshadowed by the picture we have of Douwes Dekker as a political agitator who wished to mobilise the Indonesians for something that was essentially an Indo-European question, and the image of Zaalberg as trusty paladin for the colonial court. It is only when we consider their political agenda that we realise such unsubtle sketches diminish the historic role they played. During World War I the ever-growing nationalist movement and, in fact, the government took over the programme of the Indische Party. This change of tack was also inspired by the fact that the East Indies became isolated during the war and by international rhetoric, primarily voiced by the victorious Allies, about the self-determination of peoples. Nevertheless, the new policy of the government in the Indies was primarily a response to the growth of nationalism, of which the demand for political representation formed an inextricable facet — thanks to the Indische Party.

The Indische Party may have been defunct, but its ideas lived on and indeed sometimes became reality. In 1916 Dutch parliament decided to give the Indies a representative body, a People's Council (*Volksraad*), and although this only had advisory powers, it was conceived as a big step forward towards self-government. The previous year had seen the rescinding of the ban on associations and gatherings of political organisations, contained in Article 111 of the Government Statute. The complete legitimisation of the right to gather and form associations followed in December 1918.[87] The government of the Indies announced that it was in favour of rescinding all constitutional inequalities between the various population groups within the space of a few years.[88] In 1914 Idenburg had commissioned the drawing up of a new educational plan that would meet the requirements of the people of the East Indies and was in line with the principle of constitutional equality for all colonial subjects. The colonial government even gave up its resistance to the idea of a university in the Indies and welcomed a generous donation to the University Association of the Indies from Dutch entrepreneurs. The Technical University in Bandung was opened in 1920.

The threat of war also proved a direct stimulation for the growth of political parties, since it kindled a widespread debate about the need to strengthen the military defences of the Netherlands Indies. The discussion became concentrated on the necessity of military service for all (male) inhabitants. The first organisation to call for such a people's militia was the Indische Party, which saw this as part of its nationalist agenda. Looking at the question from an entirely different point of view, Governor-General Idenburg then raised the issue of military service in circles of Boedi Oetomo. He saw it as a financial problem if the naval fleet were to be expanded, and he was therefore ready to examine the possibility of forming a militia. Both Idenburg's ideas and those of the Indische Party finally found a voice in the 1916 campaign *Indië Weerbaar* ("Defending the Indies"), in which thousands from different population groups took part, expressing their dissatisfaction with the measures being taken by the Dutch government to defend the Indies. The idea of a people's militia was linked with the demand for political representation and thus gave both Sarekat Islam and Boedi Oetomo a means of manifesting themselves as political organisations. *Indië Weerbaar* formed a climax in the "association politics" and was a symbol of the solidarity of the different population groups in the Indies.

The first People's Council met in 1918 and immediately gained a far greater political significance than had been foreseen. Among the earliest members of the People's Council were the Theosophist Dirk van Hinloopen Labberton; the Indies-born lawyer W.M.G. Schumann; the tea planter Karel Bosscha (a member of the Holle-Kerkhoven family); the tobacco planter David Birnie; leading figures from the Sarekat Islam movement, Tjokroaminoto and Abdoel Moeis; the former mayor of Manado, A.L. Waworuntu; the chairman of the Ambon Educational Trust, J.A. Soselisa; and the regent of Serang, Achmad Djajadiningrat.[89]

Illustration 46 Huge political gatherings gradually became a familiar sight in the Indies after about 1910. In August 1916 in Batavia's Decca Park thousands demonstrated in favour of the *Indië Weerbaar* (Defending the Indies) movement. The magazine *De Reflector* made a report of this.
[Photograph in: *De Reflector* (1916).]

The flag that united the members of the Indische Party was now Insulinde, which was represented by four members: Tjipto Mangoenkoesoemo, who had returned from exile in 1914, and his fellow party members; Abdoel Rivai, a doctor from Sumatra; and G.L. Topée and J.J.E. Teeuwen, employees of the Nederlandsch-Indische Spoorwegmaatschappÿ.

The highlight of the first People's Council was the *novemberbeloften* ("November Promises") made by Governor-General Johan Paul, Count of Limburg Stirum (1916–1921). In 1918 he declared that within the foreseeable future the Indies would to a large extent be granted the right to govern its own affairs. These November Promises were more or less a duplicate of the declaration made in the British parliament by British Secretary of State Edwin Montagu the previous year, promising British India home rule in the near future. In many ways the disturbing events of World War I had sped up the process towards autonomy in the Indies. For instance, the to-and-from between the motherland and its colony had almost come to a standstill, greatly reducing the number of newcomers to the Indies.[90] On the economic front, too, there was a noticeable shift. During World War I the economy of the Indies began to interact increasingly with other Pacific countries. With the economic growth of both the United States and Japan, this shift of interests would become permanent.

In those years, too, American culture was having an increasing impact on patterns of consumption and leisure. In a short space of time newspapers became full of English expressions and lists of the latest films to be seen at the cinema; the news journal in cinemas brought viewers into direct contact with the most recent world events.[91] The first two decades of the 20th century witnessed spectacular changes in people's way of life, with the introduction of telephones, automobiles, the cinema and electricity, and also saw the growth of mass movements and representative bodies, such as the People's Council. For Europeans born in the Indies it felt as if an epoch were drawing to a close. While the archivist Frederik de Haan was busy working on his account of *Oud Batavia*, with the approach of the third centenary celebrations marking the founding of Batavia, the Indische publicist Victor Ido van de Wall began tracing the history of some of the buildings in the Indies — old country homes and the splendid dwellings of patrician residents. In keeping with the spirit of the time, in 1916 an exquisitely illustrated magazine titled *Indië Oud en Nieuw* (The Indies — Old and New) was published. The same year saw the inauguration of another magazine, *De Reflector*. Almost all its contributors were Indies-born, tracking and applauding the vibrant changes in the world of the East Indies. A sense of pride in the past and optimism about the future formed a sharp contrast with the mood at the start of the century. Then, the influence of the Indische culture had been feared as a threat to the future of the Netherlands in the East Indies. But in the years leading up to the 1920s a new perspective generated animated interest in, for instance, Krontjong music, as the voice of an authentic Indische culture. A search for a truly Indische identity had begun: it developed out of the huge political changes that had made their mark over the past few years, but it was also made possible by a fresh new outlook that had sprung up during World War I.

Clearly, there was a great sense of confidence at this time. Nevertheless, there were also signs of the first cracks in a smooth surface: nationalist aspirations and colonial conservatism started to collide. In the Indies, as in other countries, the processes of democratisation served to sharpen rather than soften racial and religious differences. The growth

of the Sarekat Islam mass movement to include a following of around
800,000 was viewed as a serious threat by the European press in the
Indies. Also, the more conservative section of the Indies-born Europeans
felt that the People's Council did not represent them, and they certainly
did not consider that the radical Insulinde association could act as their
mouthpiece.

The feeling of being politically excluded and socially threatened
increased at an equal rate. What was gradually happening was that with
increasing ease Indonesians were filling the jobs that had traditionally
been the preserve of (Indo-)European clerks and *commiezen*. Between
1910 and 1920 the number of Indonesian and Chinese children attending
school increased fourfold, from 13,000 to 56,000.[92] In the midst of
many others who had also had the benefit of a Western elementary
education, it became practically impossible to discern the Indo-Europeans.
Here we find the explanation for why in 1916 the ageing journalist
Landouw — still editor-in-chief of the paper *De Nieuwe Vorstenlanden*
— introduced the concept of "Indische Nederlander". For many a
decade he had pleaded the cause of emancipation of the Indies, and he
supported with heart and soul Douwes Dekker's calls for a parliament,
until the latter suddenly came up with his plea for independence. Now,
Landouw felt, the Indische Netherlanders should pay due attention to
their own needs.[93]

Towards the end of World War I there was no longer a shortage of
unskilled personnel in the Indies; there was a consequent drop in wages
for labourers and the not-so-highly qualified. Soon, in the lower government jobs Europeans and Indonesians would earn equal pay for equal
work.[94] In addition, because of the sharp monetary inflation during
World War I, many felt the ground slipping under their feet — in an
economic sense. This was particularly true for civil servants whose salary
increases during those years lagged far behind the price increases. It was
against such a backdrop that Karel Zaalberg took his stand. He had
always championed the cause of the Indo-Europeans, in an effort to
prevent their "descent into the kampong". Now he took up his old battle
cry once more: only through education could the Indo-Europeans compete with Indonesians on the job market.

But the time was not yet ripe for Zaalberg. Supported by Douwes
Dekker and his allies, Insulinde managed to mobilise the people in the
Indies. In 1917 Insulinde had sailed into more politically tranquil waters
and gained a great deal of support, especially for its active role in local
politics. The Indo-Europeans, struggling with the housing shortage and

rising cost of living, greatly appreciated Insulinde's work. The organisation was active on the municipal council and in other areas too, such as housing associations and cooperative shops. Not surprisingly, in the local council elections of 1917 in Batavia, Insulinde gained a large majority, after the reigning municipal council had become involved in a scandal involving land speculation. That same year, a group of Ambonese political activists in Semarang joined Insulinde. The chairman of the *Vereeniging Ambonsch Studiefonds* (Ambonese Educational Trust) in Semarang, Alexander J. Patty, decided to give his support to Insulinde and brought along his own branch, as well as that on Ambon, thus giving Insulinde a foothold in the Moluccas. There was a noticeable influx of members in the Principalities and on Ambon, where during a long period the colonial presence had made itself strongly felt. Dockers from the town of Ambon who originally came from Pelauw (on the island of Ambon) persuaded the local leaders of Insulinde to support their relatives in their fight against corvée labour obligations and against unpopular local rulers.[95] Up to that time neither the Indische Bond nor the Indische Party had gained a foothold in the Moluccas. Insulinde continued to grow so swiftly that by June 1919 it had a membership of 17,000, of whom 13,000 were Javanese, Malays and Manadonese; the remaining 4,000 were probably Europeans and Ambonese.[96] Insulinde was well represented on the People's Council, where it had joined the "radical concentration" and formed close ties with Sarekat Islam, Boedi Oetomo and the Social Democrats. With the support it received from the "ethical" newspapers, it would have been possible for it to consolidate its position.[97] However, Insulinde did not do so. In 1918 Douwes Dekker returned to the East Indies, and Soewardi Soerjaningrat followed shortly after, in 1919. The moment had now arrived for them to rekindle the nationalist flames of the Indische Party. To this end, Insulinde was renamed the *Nationaal Indische Partij* (NIP) or, in Malay, *Sarekat Hindia*.

It looked as if the history of 1913 was repeating itself, as once again the government thwarted the NIP's ambition to become a mass movement. When in December 1919 a delegation of 350 NIP members from Pelauw took part in a large demonstration in the town of Saparua, the local government seized the opportunity to arrest the local NIP leaders and imprison them in Java and Sumatra. In 1920, when the NIP was involved in activities in the Principalities, working closely with Sarekat Islam, its three leaders — Douwes Dekker, Soewardi and Tjipto — had charges brought against them. This was a heavy blow for the NIP. The activities had certainly gained them members, but at the same time they had broken the basic rules formulated by Douwes Dekker in 1911, namely, that social, religious and racial considerations should never interfere with the Indies people's struggle for freedom. According to him, demonstrations and actions in support of human rights might well be in line with the NIP's ideal of freedom, but they could be a hurdle on the road to political emancipation of the Indies.[98]

When in 1921 the NIP attempted to direct its policies towards more parliamentary paths, its Indo-European supporters began turning towards the *Indo-Europeesch Verbond* (IEV; Indo-European Union), which had been established in 1919. Despite a successful inaugural meeting led by Karel Zaalberg, it had initially looked as if the IEV would fail to become an organisation of any weight or importance; but in 1921 it gained 1,000 new members. This growth was a reaction to the government policy to unify education and standardise the wages of civil servants. In 1921 it became clear that less-highly-trained European civil servants could in the long term expect only the same salary as Indonesians — lower than they hoped. Their children could only expect to attend the general elementary school, which was short of both cash and teachers. At the same time the government announced that it was inevitable that there should be a Tropics Supplement, paid out to those who had gained a higher diploma from studying in the Netherlands, to be granted because of the dire shortage of doctors and teachers. Although during World War I there had apparently been a consensus on the educational system in the Indies — that Dutch and Malay would be the two main languages taught — there was now violent opposition to this proposal. The resistance was led by IEV front man Karel Zaalberg, who explained in minute detail to his readers of the *Bataviaasch Nieuwsblad* that newcomers who were being paid a Tropics Supplement could afford to send their children to elite schools and were in no way interested in maintaining or supporting good education for Indo-Europeans with a lower income. Indeed, his concern proved well founded. A veritable ravine was revealed between those Europeans who formed part of the colonial migratory circuit, that is, the "sojourners", and those who were destined to remain in the Indies, the "stayers".[99] After 1921 the Indo-Europeans joined ranks in the IEV.

A fork in the road

And so the paths divided — in 1922 the political river diverged irreversibly into two: one stream became part of the wider Indonesian nationalist movement, and in the other direction flowed the IEV. Little remained of the optimism that had coloured politics during World War I. After 1920 the government in the Netherlands was actively concerned with considerably watering down the terms of the November Promises made in 1918 by Governor-General Van Limburg Stirum. The colonial lobby in the Netherlands strongly opposed the governor-general for apparently supporting the government in the Indies in its desire to impose taxes on the enormous profits the sugar industry was enjoying shortly after World War I. The government had to cut its budget in order to keep the corporate taxes low, which would in turn keep up profitability of the estates.[100] Van Limburg Stirum himself had given his full support and appointed a commission to enquire into the revision of the constitution of the Indies. With J.H. Carpentier Alting as chairman, the commission handed over its report in June 1920 to the government. A sizeable majority of the commission proposed introducing suffrage based on literacy, a suggestion that was warmly supported by the People's Council of 1918, which had been assembled in the spirit of association politics. But Simon de Graaff, then minister of the colonies, was firmly opposed to the democratic tendencies smouldering in the commission's report and presented the parliament of the Netherlands with his own proposals — which already in 1914 had been labelled purely administrative and largely passé — for the reform of the constitution.

It was the Theosophists who sounded the alarm bell, warning against the tendency to set back the clock emanating from the Netherlands. Their idealistic expectations of cooperation between East and West had set the tone for the association politics and also given momentum to the Indische Party and the Boemi Poetra Committee. The *Vrijzinnig Theosofisch Comité* (Liberal Theosophist Committee) — represented by Van Hinloopen Labberton — and the three progressive Javanese regents Achmad Djajadiningrat, Koesoemo Oetoyo and Wiranata Koesoemo initiated the movement *Autonomie voor Indië* (Autonomy for the Indies). In the Netherlands this movement was supported by none less than Snouck Hurgronje and the chairman of the commission for revision of the constitution, Carpentier Alting. Here too we may see a connection with the Theosophist movement, for it was said that Snouck Hurgronje was sympathetic towards the Theosophists.[101] One thing is certain: the initiators of the *Autonomie voor Indië* movement were fired by the ideal of friendly coexistence between the Netherlands and the East Indies as one united kingdom.

Almost every Indonesian organisation of any significance declared support for the autonomy movement, although, not surprisingly, they often had very diverse agendas. Take, for instance, the Perserikatan Minahasa (Minahasa Association) from Sulawesi with its 12,000 members, many of whom were in the military. Explaining the campaign to the military members of this organisation, the prominent Minahasa politician Sam Ratulangie declared that the plan was to maintain links with the Netherlands; on the other hand, the People's Council member and Perserikatan Minahasa chairman A.L. Waworuntu, addressing his local followers, emphasised that autonomy necessarily implied an independent role for the Minahasa region.[102] Even the NIP joined in. Once they had been released from prison, the NIP leaders — now popularly known as the "three-leaf clover" — were soon busily involved in political activities. It should be mentioned that Tjipto could not refrain from expressing his true feelings and declared that if he had his way the movement would not have been named "Autonomy for the Indies" but "Free from the Netherlands".

All the participating organisations expected that the IEV, which had grown to be an organisation of considerable importance, would also support the movement for autonomy. Indeed, in his newspaper *Bataviaasch Nieuwsblad* Karel Zaalberg had been writing vituperative articles for the past one and a half years about the manner in which Minister of the Colonies De Graaff was trying to undo the work of the commission for the revision of the constitution. Despite this, the IEV withheld its support. The IEV felt dependent on the interests of the colonial government and felt obliged to consider the fundamental shifts in colonial economy and social structure, which presented a considerable threat to many of their supporters. These changes implied at the same time a justification for the IEV and also the end of the old world of the Dutch East Indies.

The centre of gravity, economically speaking, and thus also the power centre of the business world in the Indies shifted from the sugar industry in Java to the oil production in the Outlying Provinces. After 1918 there was a further stream of newcomers: thousands arrived to work in private companies and, to a lesser extent, in education. In the Outlying Provinces, especially Sumatra, the newcomers now formed the majority of the adult male population. In 1930 there were twice as many newcomers as there were Indies-born working in oil production or "cultivations", while in contrast Java, both on its sugar plantations and in government employment, still had twice as many Indies-born as newcomers. The demographic balance in Java also remained the same as it had been since the 1880s, that is, six out of ten adult European males were Indies-born. But it was in the sugar business and the government, traditionally Java's two chief employers for Indies-born, that things began to decline after the first two decades of the 20th century. Both government and sugar industry economised on their Indies-born employees. The number of civil servants in government employment dropped by 5 per cent between 1923 and 1926. Whereas the sugar industry had previously been an industrial branch deeply rooted in the world of the Indies, after 1918 it changed into an almost closed front represented by the *Suikersyndicaat* (Sugar Syndicate) and the *Java Suiker Werkgevers Bond* (Java Sugar Employers Union), an organisation headed by Netherlands professionals.[103] In the face of such competition even the powerful *Suikerbond* (Sugar Union), which in 1922 had half a million guilders sitting in the strike fund and numbered 3,861 members, eventually had to relinquish its resistance.[104] The IEV appreciated that Indische Netherlanders were in a very weak position.

The professional lobbyists promoting the cause of export agriculture and oil production saw nothing in association politics, nor had they the slightest interest in the concerns of the Indies-born Europeans in Java. Their attitude was underscored by the newcomers who arrived during the 1920s in the Indies and enjoyed a life of luxury, revelling in the climate and the range of products available to them. In 1923, for instance, there were more than 23,000 cars on the roads in the Indies, twice the number in the Netherlands.[105] Every Dutch department store boasting its bon ton had branches in the large cities of Java and Medan (in Sumatra). The street scene in the 1920s gave the impression of extreme European opulence. But the riches were not evenly distributed. During the 1920s there was again increasing unemployment among Europeans and others born in the Indies. Indonesian organisations lost their confidence in the political institutions that had grown up during the twilight years of the old world of the East Indies. In the space of five years the fundaments of association politics had crumbled.

While the IEV was completely absorbed in dealing with its rank and file's concerns about the future, Douwes Dekker's party, the Nationaal Indische Partij (NIP), was quietly quitting the stage. Economic polarisation brought an end to its role as pioneer of "democratic nationalism". The party was banned in 1923. The NIP had aimed to forge the final link in the long chain running from the protesting Batavian notables of 1848 to the Indonesian national movement. But it was not to be. Its leaders declared in their closing manifesto:

> It appeared to be that part of the [party's] task was to assist in creating
> the parliamentary forms for a future political state. After ten years of
> toil it has become manifestly clear that this work was not to be granted
> to us. Colonial relations deny the development of an opposition party,
> even be it a parliamentary opposition.[106]

The nationalist struggle had for the time being withdrawn from
parliamentary action, but it was far from extinct. When in 1922 the
supporters of the movement for autonomy perceived that political activities were floundering under repression, education became a central
issue. The *Al-Indië* (All Indies) Congress held in Bandung on 2, 4 and
5 June 1922, organised by Douwes Dekker, marked a decisive moment
of change in Indonesian nationalism. Those gathered there represented,
according to their calculations, two million members of various organisations. An eyewitness reported, "Representatives from all corners of
the Indies were present; the mood was bursting with enthusiasm, such
as has seldom or never previously been known."[107] Although the ideal
of autonomy was not forsaken, the real significance of the congress lay
in the fact that literacy stood at the top of the agenda: it was the essential
prerequisite for political emancipation.

Douwes Dekker and Soewardi Soerjaningrat turned their activities
to educational concerns. The former founded his Ksatrian Institute in
Bandung, while the latter became the driving force behind the Taman
Siswa schools. Douwes Dekker was convinced that the notion of an
independent "Indonesia" could best develop within an educational
framework. Indeed, the motto of his handbook, published in 1921 and
titled *Handboek voor den Indischen nationalist*, was *Onhoorbaar groeit
de padi*, which can be translated as "The paddy fields sprout and
grow noiseless and unheard".[108] The other section of the Indo-European
movement for emancipation, which had formed itself into the IEV, had
very similar ideas. The Freemasons, who dominated the board of the
IEV, initially concerned themselves with only education, much like their
19th-century forebears. The IEV was, after all, the product of a long
history of struggle for equality between the Europeans born in the Indies
and the newcomers from Europe. And from that process a strong Indische
identity had emerged.

End of an Old World

The old world of the Indies ended with a brief but brilliant finale. The doctrine of "association politics", resounding triumphantly if briefly, was at the same time both the product and the negation of the idea (professed by the colonial government) that people should be categorised into ethnic groups. Those who supported the doctrine almost succeeded in abolishing the formal racially based labels and distinctions — but they failed. This left the field wide open for a more absolute contradistinction and separation between what were considered to be the "Dutch" and "native" spheres.

Meanwhile, in the space of a few years the world of the Indies had witnessed the turbulent arrival of mass politics. It had developed nationalist organisations, trade unions, political parties and a People's Council, all vying for public approval. At the same time, public life was becoming increasingly organised, and these regulating forces determined a person's status in society far more than had formerly been the case. Political parties, religious movements, workers' and employers' organisations all attracted thousands of followers and could rally huge crowds. In the face of this, the colonial state could do little more than enact repressive measures.

These years of political polarisation were accompanied by a veritable inundation of Western influences. For the first time, large numbers of people living in the Indies encountered the culture of the West — and were eager to embrace it. In demographic terms, the world of the Indies became more "Netherlandish". In the 1920s the Indies witnessed for the first time a steady influx of thousands of newcomers from Europe. By 1930 about 7 per cent of the population of the coastal cities of Java was European, while in comparison the Europeans in the cities of British India never exceeded 2 per cent.[1] Dutch-language education expanded rapidly, and Indonesian students began to attend universities in the

Illustration 47   After about 1910 the street scene in the cities of the East Indies altered radically. The automobile made its presence felt, along with many other influences from the United States, such as women's hairdressing salons offering a "permanent wave". The famous shopping street Braga Street in Bandung changed within the space of a few years from an unpaved track to an asphalt road teeming with traffic.
[Photograph, *ca.* 1920, KITLV, Leiden.]

Netherlands. Ever-growing numbers of Indonesians understood and spoke Dutch. In 1930 about 4 per cent of the non-European urban population had some command of Dutch, and these percentages reached 10 in Manado and as much as 13 on the Moluccan island of Ambon. This upward curve continued until 1939, by when the number of Indonesians who understood some Dutch had quadrupled. This was largely thanks to the *wilde scholen* — a movement of private schools in which Soewardi Soerjaningrat played a major role, and which flourished greatly in the 1930s. Indeed, it would seem that some members of the IEV, the Indo-European Union, began noticing in 1939 that even the street urchins were beginning to speak Dutch.[2]

It would be far from accurate to speak of a "Dutchification" of the Indies; rather, it was a "Westernisation" or "internationalisation", with American culture playing an increasingly dominant role. The Indies became part of a world equipped with telephones, automobiles, radios and then aeroplanes. Many residents of the Dutch East Indies adopted modern pastimes, enjoying bicycle tours, football matches, outings in the automobile, watching films in the cinema, listening to the radio, and following the latest sartorial fashions. The changes were most apparent to those who had been away from the Indies for some time. Returning to Java in 1921 after 20 years' absence, the writer Louis Couperus was astonished to see how much things had altered. The street scene was considerably changed — no more horse-drawn carriages, but cars; no more open-air concerts, but cinemas where both Indonesians and Netherlanders sat glued to their seats watching American films.[3] The urban landscape was dramatically reshaped. Nothing bears witness to this metamorphosis as much as the films made in the first decades of the 20th century showing the street scene in Indonesian cities. The unpaved roads and the villas with their classical architecture made room for asphalt streets buzzing with automobiles and lined with New Realism buildings, peppered with Javanese elements appearing like an architectural echo from the glory days of the "association-politics" dream.[4]

The notion of globalisation was not new to Southeast Asia. Down the centuries this part of the world had known cosmopolitanism, world religions and international commerce. Undeniably, the early 20th century with its rapid methods of communication introduced a new phase in this globalisation, if for no other reason than that it brought enormous changes to the economy of the Indies. The age of the automobile had arrived, and in the Indies this meant that the Dutch-Indies economy shifted its chief concern to oil and rubber produced outside Java. The Outlying Provinces had already awakened to their renaissance towards the end of the 19th century with vast land reclamation in Deli (North Sumatra) and the discovery of oil in North Sumatra and Borneo. Then, in the early decades of the 20th century, the rubber plantations developed. The scale of business expanded with the opportunities for investment. Enormous financial trusts were set up, amidst which the sugar syndicate came to resemble a little fish in a big pond, now far smaller and less renowned than, for instance, Koninklijke Olie (Royal Oil). After World War I the colonial economy was no longer dominated by the NHM (Netherlands Trading Company), the old Javanese family networks and the wealthy nutmeg growers on the island of Banda. International capitalism increasingly pulled the strings.

The Western way of life turned out to be a more effective means of extinguishing the old world of the Indies than did colonial snobbery, which, after all, had always existed. The writer Couperus, undertaking his nostalgic journey through the Indies he had not seen for many years, noted, for instance, that the Europeans had abolished the traditional meal known as a "rice table" on the pretext that it was "too Indische". And the wardrobes of European women discarded the sarong and kebaya in favour of clothes based on designs produced for Hollywood film stars. No longer were European products exclusively to be found adorning the homes of the European or Javanese elites; with the introduction of mass production, together with the mass media, the Western lifestyle was within far more people's reach.[5] But because the time-honoured traditions of colonial stratification were being threatened with extinction, the European elite in the Indies felt it essential to reinforce the demarcation lines. For instance, whereas in the 19th century the three-piece suit would have been worn only occasionally by Javanese aristocrats, by the early 20th century it had become a familiar sight on city streets. Schools offering education in Dutch, and the opening up of jobs in "Western" offices and enterprises, brought Indonesians and Chinese into closer touch with the European community. This in turn created a backlash — the tennis clubs, swimming pools and restaurants became "whites only" territory. The European newcomers, who until well into the 19th century had been expected to adapt to the mores of the Indies world, were now able to distance themselves — and they did.[6] For Indonesians, too, the seductive lure of the Western world with its many ready-mades introduced new tensions. In increasing numbers, Indonesians were buying Western garments and adopting Western habits and ideas. Yet, at precisely this time, Western dress was becoming a source of passionate dispute; dress and lifestyle acquired political connotations and thus became a source of contention.[7]

The slogan "*Indië voor de Indiërs*" had had its day, but the Indische political tradition pursued a path that circumvented the exclusivity of the Indo-European Union (IEV). Although after his *Al-Indië* Congress in 1922 Douwes Dekker no longer played a politically significant role, he was still an influential figure. His connection with Soekarno, who grew up in a Theosophical environment, is well known, as is also his friendship with Hoesni Thamrin, who was commissioner for the school that Douwes Dekker founded, the Ksatrian Institute.[8] Thamrin, grandson of the English hotel-owner Ort, became a member of the Batavian municipal council shortly after Governor-General Van Limburg Stirum made the so-called November Promises. Seven years on and Thamrin had attained the position of alderman of Batavia. He was to enjoy an impressive political career as leader of the nationalist party in the People's Council from 1927 to 1941. He was perhaps the most prominent Indonesian nationalist whose political frame of reference was that of the old world of the Indies: a world dominated in its final phase by the doctrine of association politics. Those years were something of a belle époque in the Indies and are vividly described by Pramoedya Ananta Toer in his books about the journalist Tirtoadhisoerjo. The same years also witnessed the political debuts of those who would later be seen as the grand old men of Indonesian nationalism, Tjipto Mangoenkoesoemo and Thamrin.[9]

This old world culminated in a scene of contradictory extremes. It seems far removed from the many-faceted and pluralistic nature of the old cities and settlements in the Indies. Gradually, the colonial system of racial categorisation was being eroded. Indeed, the late colonial period experienced a peak in the patterns of ethnic rapprochement and mixing. There were more marriages between members of different population groups, flying in the face of the passionately maintained legal-constitutional distinctions. In 1930 in the capital city of Batavia about 18 per cent of the marriages with a European partner were mixed; elsewhere in West Java the figure was as high as 28.5 per cent. Even considering that many of these marriages replaced what formerly would have been a life of concubinage, these percentages stoutly oppose the picture of a pluralistic society split into diverse population groups.[10] In that sense, the old world of the Indies had changed very little during four centuries — or perhaps the wheel had come full circle. In many ways, the doctrine of association politics and the patterns of the old world of the Indies were irreversible, just as cosmopolitanism and miscegenation were not to be curbed. The old world of the Indies was drawing to an end, and the newcomers, more and more assuming the lifestyle of expatriates, burrowed back into their enclaves from which they had emerged centuries before. They were now economically more powerful and more arrogant than they had ever been. Paradoxically, they were filled with a growing terror of the mighty Asian world, a world whose forces they were powerless to withstand, a world whose many languages they had not yet learnt to comprehend.

Glossary

assistant-resident	official of the Binnenlands Bestuur one rank below the resident
balai balai	wooden or bamboo couch
baljuw	bailiff
ban	village or district
bekel	village official
Betawi	Batavia, term for the local culture of Asian inhabitants of the city
Binnenlands Bestuur	Interior Administration; the Dutch administrative corps for the provinces
blijver	a European who "stays" *(blijven)* in the Indies as a long-term resident
bouw	area measure (1 bouw = 0.71 hectare, 7,100 square metres)
Burgher	citizen, European not in employment of the VOC
bupati	see "regent"
cap	block-print (batik)
casados brancos	white colonists in Portuguese colonies
casados pretos	black colonists in Portuguese colonies
commies	senior clerk; civil servant of middle rank
Cultivation System	system of forced delivery of cash crops by Javanese peasants
Cultuurbank	agricultural finance corporation
dalem	palace of a Javanese nobleman
desa	village
diakonie	church welfare board
Dutch Burghers	residents of Ceylon of Dutch descent under British rule
Estado da India	Portuguese colonies in Asias

European	person classified under colonial law as belonging to the European legal community
gamelan	(Javanese) Indonesian percussion orchestra
hajji, hadji	Muslim who has made a pilgrimage to Mecca; also used as a title of respect
HBS (Hogere Burgerschool)	secondary, grammar school (without classics)
IEV (Indo-Europeesch Verbond)	Indo-European Union
Indische	belonging to the Indies
Indische Bond	Indische Union
Indo	shortened (or derogatory) form for Indo-European
Indo-European	child of Indonesian and European parents
inlands kind	person born in the Indies of a "European" father
Jongens-Weezeninrichting	Orphan Boys' Institution (Surabaya)
juffrouw	Miss (Mistress, as title)
kampong	administrative ward, village
kebaya (kabaya)	light cotton blouse worn over a sarong or wraparound skirt
keraton	palace
Koninklijke Paketvaart Maatschappij (KPM)	Royal Shipping Company
koopman	merchant (rank within the VOC)
Krontjong (keroncong)	"Indische" popular music style with European (Portuguese) and Indonesian influences
landraad	local court for "native" affairs
liplap	derogatory term for Indo-European
Mardijker	Christian free man or woman of slave descent
Mechanics	see Tupass
Mestiços	Portuguese for "Mestizos"
Mestizo	term used for lower-class people of Asian-European ancestry

Nederlandsche Handel-Maatschappij (NHM)	Netherlands Trading Company
Nederlandsch-Indische Handelsbank	Netherlands-Indies Trading Bank
negorijlieden	villagers, usually to perform corvée
NIP	Nationaal Indische Party
nonna	maiden
novemberbeloften	November Promises, promising autonomy for the Indies (1918)
nyai	concubine
onderkoopman	junior merchant (rank within the VOC)
opperkoopman	senior merchant (rank within the VOC)
Outlying Provinces	colonial districts outside Java
pacinan	Chinese neighbourhood
pandeling	debt-bondsman or debt-bondswoman
penghulu	Islamic religious leader
Peranakan	Chinese born in the East Indies/Indonesia
perkenier	owner of a nutmeg grove on one of the Banda islands
petak	hut
Petjo	creolised language of Dutch, Malay and Javanese
petjoek (pecuk)	small cormorant (black seabird)
phrakhlang	Siamese minister of trade and foreign affairs
pikol	measure of weight (1 pikol = approximately 61.8 kg)
prajurit	soldier
Pupillenkorps	Army Training School (in Gombong)
radicaal	certificate entitling a civil servant to enter the higher ranks of government office
raja	ruler, king
regent (bupati)	Javanese head of a regency district
reinols	Portuguese coming from Europe
resident	chief colonial administrator of a residency
rix-dollar	48 stivers or 2.4 guilders
sarong	wraparound skirt
saya	wide cotton skirt
sawah	paddy fields
schepenen	bailiffs

SDAP (Sociaal-Democratische Arbeiders Partij)	Social-Democrat Labour Party
senang	comfortable
Sinjo	Indo-European man
sirih	betel
STOVIA (School tot Opleiding van Inlandsche Artsen)	College for Training Native Medical Doctors
susuhunan	emperor of Surakarta
syahbandar	harbour master
tangsi	barracks
tempo doeloe	bygone days
toko	general store
Totok	European (or Chinese) newcomer
Tupass	inhabitants of Ceylon, usually of slave descent, with Portuguese names
Verenigde Oostindische Compagnie (VOC)	Dutch East India Company
Volksraad	People's Council (representative body with primarily advisory task)
vrijburger	free European citizen not employed by the VOC
wayang	puppet theatre
weeskamer	orphans' chamber

Notes

Prologue

1. Gruzinski, *The Mestizo Mind*.
2. Amselle, *Mestizo Logics*, p. 161; Vergès, *Monsters and revolutionaries*.
3. Gist and Wright, *Marginality and Identity*.
4. Bonacich, "A Theory of Middlemen Minorities".

Chapter 1

1. [Ibn Battuta], *The Rehla of Ibn Battuta*, pp. 172, 188.
2. O'Kane, ed., *The Ship of Sulaiman*, pp. 51, 94–103; Aubin, "Les Persans au Siam", pp. 96–102.
3. Kaempfer, *A Description of the Kingdom of Siam*, pp. 43–44, 51; see also the map in De la Loubère, *Du Royaume de Siam*, vol. I, map following p. 24.
4. Kaempfer, *A Description of the Kingdom of Siam*, p. 51.
5. Kuløy, "Introduction to the 1981 Edition" in: [Tachard], *A Relation of the Voyage to Siam*.
6. Wyatt, "A Persian Mission to Siam"; Wyatt, "Family Politics in Seventeenth- and Eighteenth-Century Siam"; Wyatt, "King Borommakot, His Court, and Their World", p. 56.
7. [Pires], *The Suma Oriental of Tomé Pires*, vol. II, p. 265.
8. Reid, *Southeast Asia in the Age of Commerce*, vol. II, pp. 71–72, uncritically uses the travellers' guesses; for a critical assessment see Talens, *Een feodale samenleving in koloniaal vaarwater*, pp. 46–51; Nagtegaal, "The Premodern City in Indonesia".
9. Bougas, "Patani in the Beginning of the XVIIth Century".
10. Barendse, *The Arabian Seas*, pp. 62–66.
11. Reid, "Economic and Social Change", pp. 482–83.
12. Morgan, "Persian Perceptions of Mongols and Europeans", pp. 201–17.
13. This source is the *Hai Yü* of 1537, covering the situation before the Portuguese conquest; quoted in Purcell, "Chinese Settlement in Malacca", p. 117.
14. Barendse, *The Arabian Seas*, p. 64.
15. Thomaz, "The Malay Sultanate of Melaka".
16. Nordin Hussin, "Melaka and Penang 1780–1830", pp. 205–11, 234–35.

17. Reid, "The Rise and Fall of Sino-Javanese Shipping".

18. De Graaf and Pigeaud, *Chinese Muslims in Java*, p. 173.

19. Reid, "The Rise and Fall of Sino-Javanese Shipping".

20. Carey, "Changing Javanese Perceptions", pp. 3, 14; Hoadley, "Javanese, Peranakan, and Chinese Elites in Cirebon", pp. 507–9.

21. Carey, "Changing Javanese Perceptions", pp. 3–8.

22. Medhurst, ed., *Ong Tae Hae*, p. 33.

23. Skinner, "Creolized Chinese Societies in Southeast Asia", pp. 52–53.

24. Reid, "Early Southeast Asian Categorizations of Europeans", p. 159.

25. Alexandrowicz, *An Introduction to the History of the Law of Nations in the East Indies*, pp. 98–100.

26. [Heecq], "De derde voyagie van Gijsbert Heecq", p. 442.

27. Dhiravat na Pombejra, "VOC Employees and Their Relationships", pp. 198–99, 210–11.

28. Van Goor, "Koopman in koninklijke dienst".

29. Dhiravat na Pombejra, "Ayutthaya as a Cosmopolitan Society"; regarding the treatment of King Thaisa's throat cancer see Raben and Dhiravat, "Tipping Balances", pp. 66–67.

30. Nationaal Archief (National Archives), The Hague (hereafter NA), Archives of the Verenigde Oostindische Compagnie (hereafter VOC), inv. no. 5785, f. 28, Ship's pay-ledger Lugtenburg, 1722; NA, VOC, inv. no. 6850, Testament no. 1081 (11 Sept. 1749).

31. Ten Brummelhuis, *Merchant, Courtier and Diplomat*, p. 54.

32. Ten Brummelhuis, *Merchant, Courtier and Diplomat*, p. 58.

33. NA, VOC, inv. no. 5640, f. 147, Ship's pay-ledger Beverwijk 1713, attestatie van Willem de Ghij (25 July 1739).

34. See also Van Opstall, "From Alkmaar to Ayudhya and Back", pp. 111–12.

35. [Heecq], "De derde voyagie van Gijsbert Heecq", p. 442.

36. In 1737, when the VOC trade in Ayutthaya was already on the ebb, there were 33 people living in the company lodge. Only two of them were born in Siam. NA, VOC, inv. no. 5185, Muster rolls (30 June 1737), 2nd series, Siam, f. 299v–300r.

37. Kolff, "La 'nation' chrétienne à Surate au début du XVIIe siècle".

38. Canter Visscher, *Mallabaarse brieven*, pp. 242–43.

39. Lequin, *Het personeel van de Verenigde Oost-Indische Compagnie in Azië*, vol. I, p. 174.

40. Scammell, "European Exiles, Renegades and Outlaws", p. 125.

41. Winius, "The 'Shadow Empire' of Goa in the Bay of Bengal".

42. Thomaz, "Malaka et ses communautés marchandes".

43. See the map in Cardon, "Portuguese Malacca".

44. Magalhães Godinho, "Portuguese Emigration", p. 17; Subrahmanyam uses an average of 1700, reaching a peak at 2700 in the period 1571–1610: Subrahmanyam, *The Portuguese Empire in Asia*, pp. 218–19.

45. Subrahmanyam, *The Portuguese Empire in Asia*, pp. 217–23.
46. Da Fonseca, *An Historical and Archaeological Sketch of the City of Goa*, p. 8.
47. NA, VOC, inv. no. 1105, f. 332, Survey of the population of Batavia (1 Nov. 1632).
48. NA, VOC, inv. no. 1614, f. 891, f. 1078 (Population census Batavia 1699); NA, VOC, inv. no. 11534, Muster roll Batavia 1699.
49. Raffles, *The History of Java*, vol. I, table I, following p. 62; *Koloniaal Verslag* (Annual report on the state of the colonies) (hereafter KV) 1871, Appendix A, p. 6.
50. NA, VOC, inv. no. 1544, f. 820–47, List of all Europeans, Mestizos and Tupasses in the fort and town of Colombo, 1694; Raben, "Batavia and Colombo", pp. 104–6.
51. NA, VOC, inv. no. 1332, f. 561–63 (Inhabitants of Malacca 1678); Knaap, "A City of Migrants", p. 120.
52. Lequin, *Het personeel van de Verenigde Oost-Indische Compagnie in Azië*, vol. II, p. 349.
53. Hill, *List of Europeans and Others in the English Factories in Bengal*.
54. Ghosh, *The Social Condition of the British Community in Bengal*, p. 61.
55. Lequin, *Het personeel van de Verenigde Oost-Indische Compagnie in Azië*, vol. II, p. 416; KV 1860, 31 and Appendix A, pp. 4, 14.
56. Van Marle, "De groep der Europeanen", p. 485.
57. Marshall, "British Immigration into India in the Nineteenth Century", p. 183.
58. Blussé, *Strange Company*, p. 81.
59. Van Kan, "Uit de Ceilonsche rechtsgeschiedenis"; *Nederlandsch-Indisch plakaatboek*, vol. VII, pp. 476–90 and vol. X, pp. 417–31.
60. Hovy, *Ceylonees plakkaatboek*, vol. I, p. cxxvi.
61. For the differences between the Portuguese and Dutch styles of colonial settlement see Raben, "Colombo. Mirror of the Colonial Mind".
62. Knaap, *Kruidnagelen en christenen*, pp. 34–37, 159.
63. Anderson, *Imagined Communities*, pp. 164–70; Appadurai, "Number in the Colonial Imagination".
64. Goldberg, *The Racial State*; Comaroff, "Reflections on the Colonial State".
65. De Graaf and Pigeaud, *Chinese Muslims in Java*, pp. 183–84.
66. See, for example, Dirks, *Castes of Mind*; Roberts, *Caste Conflict and Elite Formation*.
67. Daus, *Portuguese Eurasian Communities in Southeast Asia*, p. 8.
68. NA, VOC, inv. no. 1175 contains advice from high-ranking company officials in Batavia about the organisation of the colonies; see, for example, the advice of Councillor of the Indies Gerard Demmer (20 Jan. 1651), f. 193–210, esp. f. 202ff.
69. See, for example, Bitterli, *Cultures in Conflict*, p. 45.

70. Knaap, "Europeans, Mestizos and Slaves"; Raben, "Batavia and Colombo", pp. 104–5.
71. Marshall, "British Immigration into India in the Nineteenth Century", p. 192.
72. Ballhatchet, *Race, Sex and Class under the Raj*, pp. 96–97, 144–54.
73. NA, VOC, inv. no. 1175, Advice of Gerard Demmer (20 Jan. 1651), f. 200r-v.
74. Boxer, *Race Relations in the Portuguese Colonial Empire*, pp. 64–65; Jack-Hinton, "Malacca and Goa and the Question of Race Relations".
75. Penny, *The Church in Madras*, p. 26.
76. The image of Portuguese Burghers as actual Portuguese descendants has become a fixed idea in literature: Roberts, Raheem and Colin-Thomé, *People Inbetween*, pp. 43, 140–47; McGilvray, "Dutch Burghers and Portuguese Mechanics", pp. 238–40; Colin-Thomé, "The Portuguese Burghers and the Dutch Burghers of Sri Lanka", p. 172.
77. Similar categories also emerged in India; see Gaikwad, *The Anglo-Indians*.
78. See, for example, Hannaford, *Race*, Ch. 7; Poliakov, "Racism from the Enlightenment to the Age of Imperialism", p. 53.
79. Radermaker, "Proeve nopens de verschillende gedaante en koleur der menschen"; Sens, *"Mensaap, heiden, slaaf"*, pp. 53–55.
80. Jordan, *White over Black*, pp. 35–36.
81. Stoler and Cooper, "Between Metropole and Colony", p. 6.

Chapter 2

1. Schutte, "De gereformeerde kerk onder de Verenigde Oostindische Compagnie", pp. 66–67.
2. Koks, *De Indo*, pp. 7–9.
3. Rietbergen, *De eerste landvoogd Pieter Both*, vol. I, pp. 39–44.
4. *Nederlandsch-Indisch plakaatboek*, vol. I, p. 82 (11 Dec. 1620); also in Mooij, ed., *Bouwstoffen voor de geschiedenis der protestantsche kerk*, vol. I, pp. 88–89.
5. *Nederlandsch-Indisch plakaatboek*, vol. I, pp. 99–102 (20 July 1622).
6. Hovy, *Ceylonees plakkaatboek*, vol. I, p. 3 (30 May/3 June 1641).
7. Hovy, *Ceylonees plakkaatboek*, vol. I, pp. 14–15 (1 Aug. 1647).
8. Sri Lanka National Archives, Colombo (hereafter SLNA), inv. no. 1/9, Resolutions Governor and Council Colombo, f. 138 (27 June 1659); Hovy, *Ceylonees plakkaatboek*, vol. I, pp. 34–35 (19 Nov. 1658).
9. SLNA, inv. no. 1/14, Resolutions Governor and Council Colombo, f. 7, n.d. [*ca.* Sept. 1668].
10. Jacobs, "Ambon as a Portuguese and Catholic Town", p. 4; Tiele, ed., "Documenten voor de geschiedenis der Nederlanders in het Oosten", pp. 285, 289; Jacobs, ed., *Documenta Malucensia*, pp. 681, 690.

11. NA, VOC, inv. no. 1227, f. 254, Governor A. van der Meijden and Council to Governor-General and Council (30 Apr. 1658).
12. Arsip Nasional Republik Indonesia, Jakarta (hereafter ANRI), Archive Schepenen, inv. no. 515, Criminal court records 1651–1652 (8 Dec. 1651).
13. Barchewitz, *Allerneueste und Wahrhafte Ost-Indianische Reise-Beschreibung*, p. 583.
14. [Heydt], *Heydt's Ceylon*, p. 46.
15. Niemeijer, "Calvinisme en koloniale stadscultuur", p. 213.
16. ANRI, Archive Schepenen, inv. no. 689, Attestations 1632–1633.
17. ANRI, Archive Schepenen, inv. no. 516, Criminal court records 1653–1654, Baljuw vs. Josua and Annetje van Batavia (9 July 1653); NA, Archive Schepenbank in Batavia, inv. no. 11960, Criminal court records 1647, 1664–1667, pp. 37–38, Baljuw Casembroot vs. Matthijs Pietersen van Paleacatte and Annetje van Batavia (26 Sept. 1664); Idem, p. 47, Baljuw Ferment vs. Pieter Claessen and Susanna van Malaca (6 Feb. 1665).
18. Niemeijer, "Calvinisme en koloniale stadscultuur", p. 307.
19. NA, VOC, inv. no. 1078, f. 53–57v, List of marriages in the church of Batavia (3 Oct. 1621–29 Jan. 1623); also in Raben, "Batavia and Colombo", pp. 283–84.
20. NA, VOC, inv. no. 1078, f. 59–64, List of baptisms in the church of Batavia (23 Jan. 1622 – 22 Jan. 1623).
21. NA, VOC, inv. no. 1104, f. 14, Governor-General and Council to Heeren XVII (1 Dec. 1632).
22. De Jonge and Van Deventer, ed., *De opkomst*, vol. V, p. 183 (5 June 1631); Blussé, *Strange Company*, p. 163.
23. Niemeijer, "Calvinisme en koloniale stadscultuur", pp. 40–41.
24. *Nederlandsch-Indisch plakaatboek*, vol. I, pp. 279–81 (22 Sept. 1632).
25. NA, VOC, inv. no. 1105, f. 332, Survey of the population of Batavia (1 Nov. 1632); Coolhaas and Van Goor, ed., *Generale missiven*, vol. I, p. 594 (28 Dec. 1636).
26. De Jonge and Van Deventer, ed., *De opkomst*, vol. VI, pp. vi–xxiv.
27. Van den Berg, "Een smeekschrift van de Bataviasche burgerij".
28. *Dagh-register gehouden int casteel Batavia [...] 1674*, p. 30.
29. "Beschryving van de stad Batavia", p. 62.
30. De Jonge and Van Deventer, ed., *De opkomst*, vol. V, p. 86 (Resolution of Governor-General and Council, 1 Feb. 1627).
31. Openbare Bibliotheek (Public Library) Rotterdam, Manuscript 86 n 11, Description of the inhabitants of Batavia, n.d. [*ca.* 1650].
32. Centraal Bureau voor Genealogie (hereafter CBG), The Hague, microfiches marriage registers, Batavia, Dutch marriage register 1616–1652, marriages 1650.
33. Bruijn, Gaastra and Schöffer, *Dutch-Asiatic Shipping*, vol. II.
34. Wijnaendts van Resandt, "Huwelijken te Batavia in den Compagniestijd".

35. Raben, "Batavia and Colombo", p. 111.
36. Christiaans and Van Duijn, "De 'jet-set' van Batavia anno 1763".
37. Raben, "Batavia and Colombo", pp. 99, 109.
38. NA, VOC, inv. no. 5197, Land muster roll Ceylon 1749; NA, VOC, inv. no. 5237, Land muster roll Ceylon 1789.
39. NA, VOC, inv. no. 5236, Land muster roll Malabar 1788.
40. NA, VOC, inv. no. 1396, unpag., Survey of inhabitants of Colombo, n.d. [1684]; Raben, "Batavia and Colombo", pp. 284, 303; Knaap, "Europeans, Mestizos and Slaves", p. 91.
41. NA, VOC, inv. no. 1396, unpag., Summary of children, n.d. [1684].
42. See, for example, NA, VOC, inv. no. 3324, Resolutions Governor and Council Colombo (20 May 1771).
43. See, for example, SLNA, inv. no. 1/572, Annexes resolutions Governor and Council Colombo (19 May 1779), Survey of arrears of rent.
44. SLNA, inv. no. 1/2511, Register of donations (*Gifteboek*) 1712–1745, pp. 177–79, Request of Simon de Mello and Nella Tambij (21 Jan. 1739).
45. Hovy, *Ceylonees plakkaatboek*, vol. I, p. 46 (10/17 June 1659).
46. SLNA, inv. no. 1/24, Resolutions Governor and Council Colombo, f. 61v–64, Petition of citizens (21 Nov. 1678).
47. SLNA, inv. no. 1/2509, Register of donations (*Gifteboek*) 1679–1685.
48. NA, VOC, inv. no. 1396, unpag., Survey of inhabitants of Colombo, n.d. [1684]; NA, VOC, inv. no. 1544, f. 820–47, Survey of the city quarters of Colombo (4 May and 23 Aug. 1694) (corrected by comparison with a second copy in NA, VOC, inv. no. 9743, unpag.).
49. CBG, Archives Wolvendaal Church, Colombo (microfiches), Marriage register of the fort and marriage register of natives, 1736–1796.
50. NA, VOC, inv. no. 1359, f. 501–21.
51. CBG, Archives Wolvendaal Church, Colombo (microfiches), Marriage registers. The partners were: one minister, two senior merchants, five junior merchants, two bookkeepers, two secretaries, one assistant, one commander, one ship's captain, one lieutenant-colonel, one major, two lieutenants, one sergeant, one junior gunner, one soldier and one citizen.
52. NA, Collection Cnoll, inv. no. 119, List of Dutch freeburghers in Semarang, n.d. [*ca.* 1700–1710].
53. Nagtegaal, *Riding the Dutch Tiger*, p. 95; NA, VOC, inv. no. 3214, Resolutions Semarang (27 May 1767), Report of the chief wardmasters to Governor Johannes Vos and Council (28 Feb. 1767) (our calculations).
54. Knaap, *Shallow Waters*, pp. 202–3.
55. Knaap, *Shallow Waters*, p. 208.
56. Lombard, "Une description de la ville de Semarang", p. 264, following an account of Johan Knops, *ca.* 1812.
57. Nagtegaal, "Halzenkussers en hermafrodieten", p. 5.
58. Niemeijer, "Calvinisme en koloniale stadscultuur", p. 317.

59. Coolhaas and Van Goor, ed., *Generale missiven*, vol. VII, p. 256 (30 Nov. 1716).
60. See also Lutter, "Landmonsterrol van Java's Noordoostkust 1798".
61. ANRI, Archive Kerk/diakonie, inv. no. 315, Annexes resolutions church council 1724–1733, p. 81.
62. ANRI, Archive Residentie Surakarta, inv. no. 35, Notarial documents 1779–1794.
63. "Naam rolle van alle sodanige Christenen". The number of registered married men is 31, but the list also includes the name of the spouse of citizen Keijser, who was mistakenly registered as unmarried. Regarding *onderkoopman* (junior merchant) Domis, "no spouse" was registered, although he was married.
64. Groneman, *Vorstenlandsche toestanden*.
65. Ricklefs, *Jogjakarta under Sultan Mangkubumi*, p. 366; Christiaans, "Van Stralendorff", pp. 126–27.
66. Abeyasekere, *Jakarta. A History*, p. 73.
67. Knaap, "Europeans, Mestizos and Slaves", p. 94; Knaap, "A City of Migrants", p. 124.
68. Raben, "Batavia and Colombo", p. 96.
69. Niemeijer, "The Free Asian Christian Community", p. 75.
70. See for an example of a will: Niemeijer, "The Free Asian Christian Community", p. 82.
71. *Dagh-register gehouden int casteel Batavia […] 1653–1682*; Raben, "Batavia and Colombo", pp. 122–24.
72. ANRI, Archive Kerk/diakonie, inv. no. 110, Resolutions church council 1700–1710 (30 Apr. 1708), Considerations of ministers of the Portuguese church, p. 534.
73. ANRI, Archive Kerk/diakonie, inv. no. 121, Resolutions church council 1781–1788.
74. Raben, "Batavia and Colombo", pp. 96, 112.
75. De Bruijn, "Journey to Batavia" in: De Bruijn and Raben, ed., *The World of Jan Brandes*, pp. 28–45, esp. p. 35.
76. Roberts, Raheem and Colin-Thomé, *People Inbetween*, pp. 140–47. See also McGilvray, "Dutch Burghers and Portuguese Mechanics".
77. Caplan, *Children of Colonialism*, p. 15.
78. ANRI, Archive Kerk/diakonie, inv. no. 269, Orphanage and poorhouse 1724–1728, p. 599.
79. ANRI, Archive Kerk/diakonie, inv. no. 269, Orphanage and poorhouse 1724–1728, p. 364.
80. Niemeijer, "The Free Asian Christian Community", p. 87.
81. Dorren, *Eenheid en verscheidenheid*, p. 36.
82. ANRI, Archive Kerk/diakonie, inv. no. 271, Register of charities 1700–1711; Idem, inv. no. 325, Annexes resolutions 1739–1744; Idem, inv. no. 277, Register of charities of the poorhouse 1758–1779.

83. ANRI, Archive Kerk/diakonie, inv. no. 277, Register of charities of the poorhouse 1758–1779.

84. Van Till, "Social Care in Eighteenth-Century Batavia", p. 27.

85. Niemeijer, "Calvinisme en koloniale stadscultuur", p. 315.

86. ANRI, Archive Kerk/diakonie, inv. no. 315, Annexes resolutions church council 1724–1733, p. 341.

87. De Graaf, ed., *De expeditie van Anthonio Hurdt*, pp. 35–36.

88. NA, Archive Schepenbank Batavia, inv. no. 11999d, fourth volume. This paragraph is based on Raben, "Batavia and Colombo", pp. 280–83.

89. Barchewitz, *Allerneueste und Wahrhafte Ost-Indianische Reise-Beschreibung*, p. 90; "Beschryving van de Stad Batavia", p. 61.

90. NA, VOC, inv. no. 9347, Criminal court records, Council of Justice Batavia vs. Michiel Aernout van Leijsich and Matthijs Lubeecq vander Luchstad, 1655.

91. See, for example, Hoynck van Papendrecht, "Some Old Private Letters", pp. 14–15.

92. Taylor, *The Social World of Batavia*.

93. Hoynck van Papendrecht, "Some Old Private Letters", p. 23.

94. *Nederlandsch-Indisch plakaatboek*, vol. IV (28 Aug. 1727), p. 199.

95. See, for example, De Bruijn and Raben, "Return to Europe" in: idem, ed., *The World of Jan Brandes*, pp. 46–54, esp. p. 46.

96. NA, Collection Fagel, inv. no. 2429, P. Sluijsken to Hendrik Fagel (30 Jan. 1773).

97. Christiaans and Van Duijn, "Genealogie van de Indische tak van de familie Van Angelbeek".

98. Taylor, *The Social World of Batavia*.

99. NA, VOC, inv. no. 5180, Land muster roll Colombo 1732; Wijnaendts van Resandt, *De gezaghebbers*, pp. 227–28.

100. Hoynck van Papendrecht, "Some Old Private Letters", p. 22.

101. Christiaans and Van Duijn, "De 'jet-set' van Batavia anno 1763".

102. A review of the not-always-thorough or complete study of Wijnaendts van Resandt, *De gezaghebbers*, generates a list of 22 — out of more than 400 — Indies-born governors and directors of company establishments outside the Indonesian Archipelago; ten of them followed a career without previous travels to Europe.

103. Wijnaendts van Resandt, *De gezaghebbers*.

104. De Haan, *Oud Batavia*, vol. I, pp. 547–48.

105. De Neve, "De Bataviasche adresbeweging van december 1795", p. 87.

106. De Haan, *Priangan*, vol. III, p. 852.

107. De Neve, "De Bataviasche adresbeweging van december 1795", p. 87.

108. Taylor, *The Social World of Batavia*, p. 96.

109. Rijksmuseum Amsterdam, Collection Jan Brandes, Draft letters, Brandes to his sister Maria Brouwer (25 Oct. 1784).

110. Rijksmuseum Amsterdam, Collection Jan Brandes, Draft letters, Brandes to Jan Nieuwenhuis (10 March 1784).
111. Wijnaendts van Resandt, *De gezaghebbers*, pp. 97–98, 103–4.
112. Lennon, "Journal of a Voyage through the Straits of Malacca".
113. Bulley, ed., *Free Mariner*, pp. 101–3.
114. Quoted in Roeper and Van Gelder, ed., *In dienst van de Compagnie*, p. 149.
115. Rijksmuseum Amsterdam, Collection Jan Brandes, inv. no. NG-1985-7-2-15.

Chapter 3

1. Van der Brug, *Malaria en malaise*, pp. 57, 234; Dillo, *De nadagen van de Verenigde Oostindische Compagnie*, pp. 279–80.
2. Van der Brug, *Malaria en malaise*, p. 79.
3. NA, Collection Radermacher, inv. no. 409.
4. ANRI, Archive Schepenen, inv. no. 1027, Census Batavia 1797.
5. NA, VOC, inv. no. 1614, f. 891, List of families in the city and southern suburb (Dec. 1699).
6. Lequin, ed., *The Private Correspondence of Isaac Titsingh*, pp. 245–46, Titsingh to P. H. van de Wall (24 March 1793).
7. Van den Berg, "De Bataviasche decemberbeweging van 1795".
8. Schutte, *De Nederlandse patriotten en de koloniën*, p. 159.
9. De Neve, "De Bataviasche adresbeweging van december 1795".
10. De Neve, "Personalia en historisch-genealogische bronnen".
11. Wijnaendts van Resandt, "Huwelijken te Batavia in den Compagniestijd".
12. Lequin, ed., *The Private Correspondence of Isaac Titsingh*, vol. I, p. 442, Titsingh to Captain De Jongh (17 Apr. 1797).
13. Lequin, ed., *The Private Correspondence of Isaac Titsingh*, vol. I, p. 244, Titsingh to Jan Titsingh (28 Oct. 1792). See also Lequin, *Isaac Titsingh*, pp. 140, 239.
14. *Nederlandsch-Indisch plakaatboek*, vol. XV, pp. 145–46 (25 Aug. 1808).
15. Du Perron-de Roos, "Correspondentie van Dirk van Hogendorp".
16. De Haan, *Priangan*, vol. IV, p. 246.
17. Brummel, "Achttiende-eeuws kolonialisme in brieven", p. 200.
18. See also Wijnaendts van Resandt, "Oude Indische families II. Het geslacht Senn van Basel", pp. 262–63.
19. Wijnaendts van Resandt, "Oude Indische families VI. Het geslacht Couperus".
20. CBG, Archive Suringar, Abraham Couperus to Petrus Couperus, n.d. [*ca.* 1788].
21. Idem; Meyer Timmerman Thijssen, *Twee gouverneurs en een equipagemeester*, pp. 57–58.

22. CBG, Archive Suringar, Johan M. Meijer to Hendrina E. Meijer (4 Aug. 1801).

23. CBG, Archive Suringar, Johan H. Meijer to Jan S. Timmerman Thijssen and Hendrina F. Meijer (23 March 1805).

24. CBG, Archive Suringar, Johan H. Meijer to Jan S. Timmerman Thijssen and Hendrina E. Meijer (23 March 1805).

25. CBG, Archive Suringar, J.S. and G. Timmerman Thijssen to S.E. Suringar-Thijssen (26 Oct. 1810 and 25 Sept. 1813).

26. De Haan, "Personalia der periode van het Engelsch bestuur over Java", p. 652; CBG, Archive Suringar, J.S. and G. Timmerman Thijssen to S.E. Suringar-Thijssen (25 Sept. 1813 and 19 Oct. 1813).

27. CBG, Archive Suringar, P. Couperus to S.E. Suringar-Thijssen (12 Sept. 1814); Idem, J.S. and G. Timmerman Thijssen to S.E. Suringar-Thijssen (19 Sept. 1814).

28. CBG, Archive Suringar, P. Couperus to S.E. Suringar-Thijssen (4 Aug. 1815).

29. CBG, Archive Suringar, P. Couperus to S.E. Suringar-Thijssen (12 Feb. 1815).

30. CBG, Archive Suringar, J.S. and G. Timmerman Thijssen to S.E. Suringar-Thijssen (19 Oct. 1813).

31. CBG, Archive Suringar, Abraham Couperus to Petrus Couperus, n.d.

32. CBG, Archive Suringar, J.S. and G. Timmerman Thijssen to S.E. Suringar-Thijssen (26 Oct. 1810).

33. CBG, Archive Suringar, J.S. and G. Timmerman Thijssen to S.E. Suringar-Thijssen (25 Sept. 1813).

34. Nordin Hussin, "Melaka and Penang", p. 318.

35. Christiaans, "De Europese bevolking van Malakka", p. 272.

36. NA, Archive Hoge Regering van Batavia, p. 527, Secret documents received from Ceylon in 1808, R. Prediger to Daendels (1 Feb. 1808).

37. Christiaans, "Ondaatje"; Ondaatje, "Peter Ondaatje, of Ceylon", pp. 22–23; "The Only Asiatic to Figure in European History"; Davies, *Memorials and Times of Peter Philip Juriaan Quint Ondaatje*.

38. See for the Colombo Chetty Family Genealogy the Sri Lanka Genweb: http://www.rootsweb.com/~lkawgw/gen7000.html.

39. SLNA, inv. no. 1/2510, Register of donations (*Gifteboek*) 1685–1712, pp. 68–70 (23 Apr. 1686); NA, VOC, inv. no. 1754, Resolutions Governor and Council Colombo, f. 423ff (27 Feb. 1708).

40. Van Goor, *Jan Kompenie as Schoolmaster*, pp. 38–61.

41. Van Goor, *Jan Kompenie as Schoolmaster*, pp. 151–58.

42. Roberts, Raheem and Colin-Thomé, *People Inbetween*, pp. 226, 229.

43. Van Goor, *Jan Kompenie as Schoolmaster*, p. 99.

44. Davies, *Memorials and Times of Peter Philip Juriaan Quint Ondaatje*, pp. 271–76.

45. Christiaans, "Ondaatje", p. 148.
46. "Pieter Philip Christiaan Oortman Ondaatje".
47. Christiaans, "Ondaatje", pp. 148–49.
48. Bertolacci, *A View of the Agricultural, Commercial, and Financial Interests of Ceylon*, p. 55.
49. Cordiner, *A Description of Ceylon*, p. 51.
50. Raben, "Batavia and Colombo", pp. 131, 282.
51. Cordiner, *A Description of Ceylon*, pp. 44–45.
52. CBG, Archives Wolvendaal Church, Colombo (microfiches), Marriage register of the fort; "Penny" is spelled as "Jems Pennij".
53. Cordiner, *A Description of Ceylon*, pp. 51–52.
54. Roberts, Raheem and Colin-Thomé, *People Inbetween*, pp. 59–61.
55. Braga-Blake and Ebert-Oehlers, ed., *Singapore Eurasians*, pp. 26–30, 43.
56. Engelhard, *Overzigt van den staat der Nederlandsche Oost-Indische bezittingen*, p. 157.
57. Raffles, *The History of Java*, vol. II, p. 270; NA, Family archive Couperus, inv. no. 44, Treatise of P. Th. Couperus on the situation in Batavia, 1815, Appendix.
58. Taylor, *The Social World of Batavia*, pp. 100–101.
59. [Addison], *Original Familiar Correspondence between Residents in India*, p. 373 (Letter from Buitenzorg, Apr. 1814).
60. Thorn, *Memoir of the Conquest of Java*, p. 18.
61. For example, *Java Government Gazette* (12 Aug. 1815, 9 Dec. 1815).
62. *Java Government Gazette* (6 Jan. 1816).
63. *Java Government Gazette* (3 Apr. 1813).
64. *Java Government Gazette* (20 Feb. 1813).
65. *Java Government Gazette* (6 March 1813).
66. *Java Government Gazette* (3 Apr. 1813).
67. NA, Family archive Couperus, inv. no. 44, Treatise of P. Th. Couperus on the situation in Batavia, 1815, unpag.
68. NA, Family archive Couperus, inv. no. 44, Treatise of P. Th. Couperus on the situation in Batavia, 1815, unpag.
69. Quoted in Van de Wall, *The Influence of Olivia Mariamne Raffles*, p. 5.
70. *Java Government Gazette* (14 June 1814).
71. [Arnold], *The Java Journal of Dr. Joseph Arnold*, pp. 34–35.
72. Wurtzburg, *Raffles of the Eastern Isles*, pp. 354–56.
73. [Arnold], *The Java Journal of Dr. Joseph Arnold*, p. 33.
74. De Haan, "Personalia der periode van het Engelsch bestuur", p. 493.
75. *Java Government Gazette* (12 June 1813).
76. *Java Government Gazette* (27 Aug. 1814).
77. Van de Wall, *The Influence of Olivia Mariamne Raffles*, p. 5.
78. De Haan, "Personalia der periode van het Engelsch bestuur", p. 525.
79. [Arnold], *The Java Journal of Dr. Joseph Arnold*, pp. 69–70 note 366.

80. The boy died two years later. *Java Government Gazette* (26 Nov. 1814).
81. Van de Wall, *The Influence of Olivia Mariamne Raffles*, p. 6.
82. CBG, Archive Suringar, J.S. and G. Timmerman Thijssen to S.E. Suringar-Thijssen (25 Sept. 1813).
83. Veth, *Het eiland Timor*, pp. 83–95.
84. Van der Kemp, ed., *Oost-Indië's herstel in 1816*, p. 317; Kniphorst, "Een terugblik op Timor en onderhoorigheden", pp. 416–18.
85. Scalliet, *Antoine Payen*, pp. 635–36; Van der Kemp, ed., *Brieven van en aan Mr. H.J. van de Graaff*, vol. I, pp. 46–47 and vol. II, p. 175.
86. Van der Capellen, "Het Journaal van den baron Van der Capellen", p. 309.
87. Scalliet, *Antoine Payen*, p. 402.
88. *Java Government Gazette* (4 June 1814, 14 June 1814).
89. *Java Government Gazette* (23 July 1814).
90. *Java Government Gazette* (6 Aug. 1814, 1 Oct. 1814).
91. Van Doren, *Reis naar Nederlands Oost-Indië*, vol. II, pp. 41–43.
92. *Bataviasche Courant* (22 Nov. 1817).
93. *Java Government Gazette* (6 Feb. 1813).
94. NA, VOC, inv. no. 3824, f. 2583–2584; Bleeker, "Bijdragen tot de geneeskundige topographie van Batavia IV", p. 448.
95. *Java Government Gazette* (16 March 1816, 23 March 1816); *Bataviasche Courant* (1 March 1817).
96. Van der Kemp, ed., *Brieven van en aan Mr. H.J. van de Graaff*, vol. I, pp. 24–25.
97. Openbare Bibliotheek Rotterdam, Manuscript 86 N 11, Description of the inhabitants of Batavia, n.d. [*ca.* 1650]; also in Brommer and De Vries, *Batavia*, pp. 75–80.
98. NA, Archive Schepenbank Batavia, inv. no. 11.937, Property register 1753.
99. Hageman, "Geschied- en aardrijkskundig overzigt van Java".
100. *Nederlandsch-Indisch plakaatboek*, vol. VI, p. 182 (7 Feb. 1752).
101. Tromp, "Het partikulier landbezit in de Bataviasche ommelanden", p. 338.
102. [Arnold], *The Java Journal of Dr. Joseph Arnold*, p. 70 note 366.
103. NA, Family collection Couperus, inv. no. 44, Treatise of P. Th. Couperus on the situation in Batavia, 1815, unpag.; NA, Collection Du Bus de Gisignies, inv. no. 231, Report of Du Bus' tour of inspection over Java, n.d., eighth sheet, 1.
104. Ver Huell, *Herinneringen van eene reis naar de Oost-Indiën*, vol. II, p. 116.
105. Bastin, *The Development of Raffles' Ideas*, p. 28.
106. Van Enk, "Britse kooplieden en de cultures op Java", p. 103; Bastin, *The Development of Raffles' Ideas*, p. 84.
107. Raffles purchased the lands of Pegadungan, Ciheulang, Cimahi and Gunung Parang. Wurtzburg, *Raffles of the Eastern Isles*, p. 273.

108. De Haan, "Personalia der periode van het Engelsch bestuur", p. 606.

109. De Haan, *Priangan*, vol. I, pp. 284–309; Westland, *De levensroman van Andries de Wilde*.

110. Van Delden, *De particuliere landerijen op Java*, p. 5.

111. Bastin, *The Development of Raffles' Ideas*, pp. 86–88.

112. Van Dissel, *De particuliere landerijen in het gewest Celebes*, pp. 65–70.

113. NA, Collection G.J.C. Schneither, inv. no. 109, Vorstenlanden, Resident Nahuijs to Governor-General, secret (2 Dec. 1821).

114. NA, MvK I, inv. no. 4262, Geheim verbaal 300 (28 Aug. 1840), Survey of leased-out lands in the Residency Surakarta in November 1837.

115. The Dutch Indies government sent him to Aja in late 1809 to make sure that the rebellious Ingebey of Dalimas, Djaeng Patti, was hanged: *Bataviasche Koloniale Courant* (9 Sprokkelmaand [Feb.] 1810).

116. Meyer Timmerman Thijssen, *Twee gouverneurs en een equipagemeester*, pp. 174–79.

117. *Bataviasche Koloniale Courant* (25 Louwmaand [Jan.] 1811, 31 Bloeimaand [May] 1811).

118. *Java Government Gazette* (23 Jan. 1813).

119. See, for example, CBG, Archive Suringar, J.S. and G. Timmerman Thijssen to S.E. Suringar-Thijssen (19 Sept. 1814); De Haan, "Personalia der periode van het Engelsch bestuur over Java", 652.

120. Van Enk, "Britse kooplieden en de cultures op Java", pp. 108–12.

121. *Almanak van Nederlandsch-Indië 1817* and *1827*; Mansvelt, *De eerste Indische handelshuizen*, p. 5.

122. Mansvelt, *De eerste Indische handelshuizen*, p. 3.

123. Mansvelt, *De eerste Indische handelshuizen*, p. 8.

Chapter 4

1. Ottow, *De oorsprong der conservatieve richting*, p. 238.

2. During the period 1837–1863 the NHM took care of 86 per cent of the export. Mansvelt, *De eerste Indische handelshuizen*, p. 10.

3. Fasseur, *Kultuurstelsel*, pp. 66, 68.

4. Fasseur, *Kultuurstelsel*, pp. 65–66 and 223.

5. Knight, "The Contractor as *Suiker*lord", pp. 194–95.

6. Knight, "The Contractor as *Suiker*lord", p. 197; Leidelmeijer, *Van suikermolen tot grootbedrijf*, p. 151.

7. Fasseur, *Kultuurstelsel*, pp. 65–66; Leidelmeijer, *Van suikermolen tot grootbedrijf*, p. 226; Knight, "The Visible Hand in *Tempo Doeloe*", p. 74; Dye, *Cuban Sugar*, p. 27.

8. *The Java Half-Yearly Almanac 1815*.

9. Louw, *De Java-oorlog*, vol. I, p. 79; "Kronijk van Nederlandsch Indië", pp. 218–19.

10. NA, MvK I, Resolution Governor-General and Council (14 Jan. 1823). The British Indian government also discouraged Eurasians from working for Indian princes. See: Hawes, *Poor Relations*, pp. 101–105.
11. NA, MvK I, inv. no. 2778, Resolution Governor-General and Council (6 May 1823), no. 7.
12. Louw, *De Java-oorlog*, vol. I, p. 82.
13. Europeans who did not possess Dutch nationality could appear only as an associate of a Dutch leaseholder.
14. Louw, *De Java-oorlog*, vol. IV, p. 420. The lands concerned were Ampel, Brajan, Enden, Plaor, Getessan, Mojosongo. See NA, MvK I, inv. no. 650, Verbaal 11 Dec. 1828, no. 89.
15. *Almanak van Nederlandsch-Indië 1836*. In 1828 he was married to Henrietta van den Bergen. Louw, *De Java-oorlog*, vol. IV, pp. 488–89.
16. Buddingh, *Neêrlands-Oost-Indië*, vol. I, p. 227.
17. NA, Archive Nederlandsche Handel-Maatschappij (hereafter NHM), inv. no. 4397, Minutes of the board of the Factorij (30 Sept. 1837).
18. Adtornisch Papers, Gillian Maclaine to Angus Maclaine (19 Dec. 1837).
19. NA, Archive NHM, inv. no. 4398, Minutes of the board of the Factorij (12 Nov. 1839).
20. *Gedenkboek der Nederlandsche Handel-Maatschappij*, p. 61; De Bree, *Gedenkboek van de Javasche Bank*, p. 414.
21. NA, Archive NHM, inv. no. 2399, President Factorij to president of the NHM (10 May 1841), no. 7, and (25 May 1841), no. 8 secret.
22. Houben, *Kraton and Kumpeni*, p. 286.
23. "Reglement betreffende de huur en verhuur van gronden voor den landbouw in de rijken van Soerakarta en Djocjakarta", Gouvernementsbesluit (governmental decree) (hereafter GB) 21 Dec. 1857, *Staatsblad van Nederlandsch-Indië*, no. 116. For the considerations leading to the Provisional Regulation, see KV 1857, Handelingen der Tweede Kamer (Proceedings of the Lower House of the Dutch parliament) (hereafter HTK) (1859–1860), p. 477.
24. Article 23 of the regulation concerning the lease and rent of lands of 1857, GB 21 Dec. 1857, *Staatsblad van Nederlandsch-Indië*, no. 116.
25. Lach de Bère, *Genealogie van het Nederlandsch-Indische geslacht Weijnschenk*, pp. 3–4.
26. Christiaans, "Naamlijst van de oprichters van de loge 'Mataram' te Jogjakarta", p. 64.
27. Koninklijk Instituut voor Taal-, Land- en Volkenkunde (Royal Netherlands Institute of Southeast Asian and Caribbean Studies), Leiden (hereafter KITLV), Department of Historical Documentation (hereafter Hisdoc), Photo 12064.
28. KITLV, Hisdoc, Western manuscripts H 928, Essay by F.C. van Vreede-Broese van Groenou, p. 2.

29.   KITLV, Hisdoc, Western manuscripts H 579, Engelbert van Bevervoorde, "Eigenaardigheden en bezienswaardigheden", p. 142; KITLV, Hisdoc, Western manuscripts H 928, Essay by F.C. van Vreede-Broese van Groenou, p. 4. Similar card evenings were also known to have been held at the Surakarta court. See Stark, *Uit Indië*, p. 96.

30.   ANRI, Archive Residentie Djocjakarta, inv. no. 1, Political report 1869 and 1871.

31.   Van Marle, "De groep der Europeanen", p. 317.

32.   This concerns George Weijnschenk, Johan Cornelis Baumgarten, Andreas Emanuel Kläring, Frederik Andreas Emanuel Kläring, Karel Emanuel Kläring, George Lodewijk Weijnschenk, Arend Nicolaas Dom, Henning Joachim van Prehn, Pieter Bernardus Lammers, Pieter Melior Dom, Cherrie Weijnschenk, Frans Hendrik Kraag. See Christiaans, *Het gereconstrueerde huwelijksregister van Djokjakarta*, pp. 22, 24, 55, 56, 62, 68, 78, 138, 157, 172.

33.   Taylor, *Smeltkroes Batavia*, p. 180.

34.   Private collection Sonja Weijnschenk, Testament George Weijnschenk; Lach de Bère, *Genealogie van het Nederlandsch Indische geslacht Weijnschenk*, pp. 16–17.

35.   Private collection Sonja Weijnschenk, Testament George Weijnschenk.

36.   ANRI, Archive Residentie Djocjakarta, inv. no. 1, Political report 1859, p. 29; ANRI, Archive Residentie Surakarta, inv. no. 111, Political report 1855, p. 8.

37.   KV 1857, HTK (1859–1860), p. 478.

38.   KV 1860, Attachment IJ, HTK (1862–1863), C.P. Brest van Kempen, "Nota betrekkelijk de landverhuur in de residentie Djokdjokarta", p. 735.

39.   ANRI, Archive Residentie Surakarta, inv. no. 111, Political report 1855, p. 15; Idem, inv. no. 129, Political report 1873; Houben, *Kraton and Kumpeni*, p. 283.

40.   ANRI, Archive Residentie Surakarta, inv. no. 112, Political report 1856 and 1857, p. 8; Idem, inv. no. 113, Political report 1858.

41.   ANRI, Archive Residentie Surakarta, inv. no. 111, Political report 1855, p. 10.

42.   ANRI, Archive Residentie Surakarta, inv. no. 111, Political report 1855, p. 15.

43.   ANRI, Archive Residentie Surakarta, inv. no. 125, Political report 1869, p. 17.

44.   KV 1863, HTK (1865–1866), p. 1016.

45.   Houben, *Kraton and Kumpeni*, pp. 121–26, 136.

46.   Payen, *Journal de mon voyage*, p. 88 note 13.

47.   "Twee Indische kinderen in Indië opgevoed", pp. 215–21.

48.   Fasseur, *De Indologen*, p. 66.

49.   Fasseur, *De Indologen*, p. 147; Houben, *Kraton and Kumpeni*, pp. 124–25.

50. Adam, *The Vernacular Press*, pp. 16–18.
51. NA, Family collection Van Beresteyn, inv. no. 184, G. Weijnschenk to H.P. van Beresteyn (11 Jan. 1864); Idem, inv. no. 227 (21 March 1864).
52. Groneman, *Bladen uit het dagboek van een Indisch geneesheer*, pp. 319, 324.
53. Stevens, *Vrijmetselarij*, pp. 39, 184, 215.
54. Oesterreichisches Staatsarchiv, Haus-, Hof- und Staatsarchiv, Vienna, dvr: 056006, Archiv Omea rub *50/7s12* zl 977 ex 1866.
55. According to the Roman Catholic register of baptisms of Semarang, Leopold Weijnschenk was born in "Sanpalten in Austria". See Christiaans, *Het rooms-katholieke doopregister van Semarang*, p. 2.
56. NA, MvK I, Resolution Governor-General and Council (14 Jan. 1823).
57. Furthermore, the NHM found a new field of activity in 1847, when the Dutch East Indies government gave up granting credit to sugar contractors. See Fasseur, *Kultuurstelsel*, p. 69.
58. Houben, *Kraton and Kumpeni*, p. 263.
59. De Bree, *Gedenkboek van de Javasche Bank*, vol. II, pp. 9, 23, 88.
60. KV 1860, HTK (1862–1863), Appendix A, "Algemeene staat der bevolking van Java en Madoera" no. 3.
61. KV 1860, Attachment Z, HTK (1862–1863), F.N. Nieuwenhuijzen, "Nota betrekkelijk de landverhuur in de residentie Soerakarta", p. 737.
62. ANRI, Archive Residentie Djocjakarta, inv. no. 1, Political report 1857.
63. In Surakarta three of the mills were steam driven, 11 water driven and the others buffalo driven. In Yogyakarta ten sugar mills were water driven, one buffalo driven and one steam driven. KV 1863, HTK (1865–1866), p. 1129.
64. *Samarangsch Advertentieblad* (2 Aug. 1861); ANRI, Archive Residentie Djocjakarta, Political report 1864; KV 1863, HTK (1865–1866), p. 1129.
65. *Samarangsch Advertentieblad* (10 Oct. 1862, 7 Nov. 1862).
66. Fasseur, *Kultuurstelsel*, pp. 185–90, 193.
67. *Samarangsch Advertentieblad* (28 Feb. 1862).
68. *Samarangsch Advertentieblad* (20 June 1862).
69. The programme of the party is printed in the *Samarangsch Advertentieblad* (26 Sept. 1862).
70. *Samarangsch Advertentieblad* (3 Oct. 1862).
71. *De Locomotief* remarked that Dorrepaal was the man who made the Principalities a "most important economic factor" in the Netherlands Indies. *De Locomotief* (19 June 1871).
72. *Regeerings-almanak 1875*, pp. 289–94.
73. *Samarangsch Advertentieblad* (7 Feb. 1862).
74. *De Vorstenlanden* (6 Feb. 1874).
75. *De Locomotief* (10 Oct. 1870).
76. *De Locomotief* (19 June 1871).

77. ANRI, Archive Residentie Surakarta, inv. no. 116, Political report 1860; Idem, inv. no. 117, Political report 1861, p. 9; ANRI, Archive Residentie Djocjakarta, inv. no. 1, Political report 1864; *De Locomotief* (21 Feb. 1870): De Bree, *Gedenkboek van de Javasche Bank*, vol. II, pp. 172, 174.
78. *De Locomotief* (28 May 1870).
79. ANRI, Archive Residentie Djocjakarta, inv. no. 1, Political report 1871; *De Locomotief* (9 Sept. 1870).
80. De Bree, *Nederlandsch-Indië in de twintigste eeuw*, p. 179.
81. ANRI, Archive Residentie Djocjakarta, inv. no. 1, Political report 1873.
82. Christiaans, *Het gereconstrueerde huwelijksregister van Djokjakarta*, p. 66.
83. ANRI, Archive Residentie Surakarta, inv. no. 125, Political report 1869, p. 12; *De Vorstenlanden* of 6 Nov. 1874 identified half of the 190 enterprises in Surakarta as impoverished.
84. Koninklijk Besluit (royal decree) (hereafter KB) 29 Oct. 1860, no. 68, *Staatsblad van Nederlandsch-Indië* (1861), no. 40 and 41.
85. Wormser, *Ontginners van Java*, p. 8.
86. Van der Chijs, *Geschiedenis van de gouvernements thee-cultuur*, pp. 559–95.
87. Cohen Stuart, *Gedenkboek der Nederlandsch-Indische theecultuur*, pp. 149–56.
88. Cohen Stuart, *Gedenkboek der Nederlandsch-Indische theecultuur*, pp. 181–83.
89. Van den Berge, *Karel Frederik Holle*, 96; *De Locomotief* (30 March 1875).
90. Van den Berge, *Karel Frederik Holle*, p. 48.
91. Van den Berge, *Karel Frederik Holle*, p. 38.
92. NA, Archive NHM, inv. no. 2395, confidential (25 Nov. 1837), NHM Rotterdam to the Secretarie, no. 164, confidential.
93. Broersma, *De Pamanoekan- en Tjiassem-landen*, p. 19; Ten Brink, *Oost-Indische dames en heeren*, p. 147.
94. Ten Brink, *Oost-Indische dames en heeren*, pp. 109, 112.
95. NA, Archive NHM, inv. no. 7334, Factorij to NHM Amsterdam (11 July 1840), no. 1505.
96. *De Locomotief* (27 Apr. 1875).
97. *De Vorstenlanden* (3 Dec. 1875, 28 July 1876, 25 May 1877).
98. Veldhuizen, *Batik Belanda*, pp. 12–13; De Raadt Apell, *De batikkerijen Van Zuylen*.
99. Rouffaer and Juynboll, *De batik-kunst in Nederlandsch-Indië*, vol. I, ix, pp. 441, 446, 448.
100. KITLV, Hisdoc, Western manuscripts H 579, Engelbert van Bevervoorde, "Eigenaardigheden en bezienswaardigheden", p. 25.
101. *De Vorstenlanden* (29 Oct. 1870).
102. KITLV, Hisdoc, Western manuscripts H 928, Essay by F.C. van Vreede-Broese van Groenou, p. 2.
103. KV 1859, HTK (1861–1862), p. 70.

104. ANRI, Archive Residentie Surakarta, inv. no. 127, Political report 1871.

105. KB 29 Aug. 1853.

106. The *Regeerings-almanak* of 1898 mentions J.P. Dom (1888, Dutch East Indies) and L.E. Dom (1890, The Netherlands) as holding the "diploma for higher civil servants".

107. *De Vorstenlanden* (19 March 1875, 23 Feb. 1875, 23 March 1875).

108. ANRI, Archive Residentie Djocjakarta, inv. no. 1, Political report 1862.

109. *De Locomotief* (16 Nov. 1874, 18 Feb. 1875); *De Vorstenlanden* (23 Feb. 1875).

110. *Soerakarta's Nieuws- en Advertentieblad* (13 June 1882).

111. *De Nieuwe Vorstenlanden* (13 Aug. 1884).

112. Allahar, *Class, Politics, and Sugar in Colonial Cuba*, pp. 37, 56.

113. *De Locomotief* (31 May 1870, 26 May 1874).

114. Between 1865 and 1870 Enklaar van Guericke was active as an indigo planter, and between 1880 and 1885 he was the administrator of the indigo enterprise of widow A.M. Engel, née Baumgarten.

115. Publisher was Ph.F. Voorneman, who had previously been a leaseholder in Ambarawa: *Regeerings-almanak 1870*, p. 231; *De Locomotief* (12 Jan. 1870).

116. *De Indische Opmerker* (16 March 1882); that same year, however, an association of sugar manufacturers was established in Surakarta. *Soerakarta's Nieuws- en Advertentieblad* (13 Jan. 1882, 25 Aug. 1882).

117. *De Locomotief* (29 Apr. 1875).

118. Van den Berge, *Karel Frederik Holle*, p. 38.

119. *De Locomotief* (26 Apr. 1875).

120. Van den Berg, *Over de productiekosten van de Java-suiker*, p. 1.

121. *De Locomotief* (27 Nov. 1878) reported water pollution in southern Yogyakarta.

122. ANRI, Archive Residentie Surakarta, inv. no. 124, Political report 1868; *De Vorstenlanden* (23 Jan. 1877). According to Van den Haspel, the position of the *bekel* was already more or less that of a *mandur* (overseer, foreman): Van den Haspel, *Overwicht in overleg*, p. 14.

123. Haspel, *Overwicht in overleg*, p. 15; *De Vorstenlanden* (23 Nov. 1875).

124. See Houben, *Kraton and Kumpeni*, pp. 274–75, 277; NA, Collection R. Filliettaz Bousquet, inv. no. 5.

125. Van Kol, *Reisbrieven*, p. 44; Houben, *Kraton and Kumpeni*, p. 277.

126. *De Locomotief* (4 Dec. 1875).

127. *De Vorstenlanden* (17 May 1873, 8 July 1873).

128. Fernando, "In the Eyes of the Beholder", p. 276.

129. *Javasche Courant* (11, 14, 15 June 1867).

130. *De Vorstenlanden* (7 Nov. 1873).

131. KV 1865, HTK (1867–1868), p. 630.

132. Van Kol, *Reisbrieven*; KV 1868, HTK (1869–1870), p. 269.

133. *De Locomotief* (3 Dec. 1875).

134. Margana, "Agrarian Dispute".

135. *De Vorstenlanden* (3 Apr. 1877).

136. *De Vorstenlanden* (6 Feb. 1877, 8 June 1877).

137. *Particuliere landbouwnijverheid. Lijst van ondernemingen*, vol. I, pp. 76, 160, 166, 212.

138. See Knight, "The Visible Hand in *Tempo Doeloe*".

139. Van Bruggen, Wassink a.o., *Jogja en Solo*, p. 23; De Haan, *Priangan*, vol. I, pp. 292–93.

140. Daum, *Verzamelde romans*, vol. III, p. 568.

141. The property fell into the hands of the Nederlandsch-Indische Landbouw-maatschappij and later of the Anglo-Dutch Java United Planters Ltd. See: Broersma, *De Pamanoekan- en Tjiassem-landen*, p. 26.

142. NA, Archive NHM, inv. no. 3193, pp. 89, 114 (referring to Verbaal 29 Jan. 1835, no. 11), 120 (referring to Verbaal 26 May 1838, no. 13), 137 (referring to Verbaal 25 Oct. 1839, no. 11).

143. Broersma, *De Pamanoekan- en Tjiassem-landen*, p. 15.

144. G.H. Hofland, who had gained a degree in law, retired from the company. Johannes Theodorus and Egbert Charles bought out their brother, sisters and mother.

145. Broersma, *De Pamanoekan- en Tjiassem-landen*, pp. 23–24.

146. Termorshuizen, *P.A. Daum*, p. 434, following Broersma, *Pamanoekan- en Tjiassem-landen*, p. 24.

147. "Kort overzicht van oprichting, bestaan en bedrijf van de onderneming 'Oud Djember'".

148. *Soerabaiasch Handelsblad* (20 Jan. 1893, 25 Jan. 1893).

149. On the pioneering times of J. Nienhuys on Sumatra: Breman, *Koelies, planters en koloniale politiek*, pp. 44–46.

150. Wertheim, "Conditions on Sugar Estates in Colonial Java", p. 274.

Chapter 5

1. Van der Crab, *De Moluksche eilanden*, pp. 284–85.

2. Rodenwaldt, *Die Mestizen auf Kisar*; Van der Crab, *De Moluksche eilanden*, p. 99.

3. KV 1885 HTK (1885–1886), Appendix C. [5.3], Statistics of the population of the Netherlands Indies.

4. The mission paper *Tjehaja Siang* appeared monthly in Minahasa after 1868. See Adam, *The Vernacular Press*, pp. 27–29.

5. Sutherland, "Mestizos as Middlemen?", p. 258; Wallace, *Het Maleise eilandenrijk*, pp. 231–32.

6. The 800 inhabitants already lived there at the beginning of the 19th century. Van Hogendorp, *Beschouwingen der Nederlandsche bezittingen*, p. 527.

7. Sutherland, "The Makassar Malays", p. 403.

8. GB 6 Sept. 1846, no. 27. The import and export from the harbour of Makassar rose from 4,261,911 guilders in 1847 to 21,512,887 in 1873, and in Singapore from 58,680,000 in 1846 to 173,880,000 in 1873. *De Locomotief* (26 Feb. 1879).

9. Wallace, *Het Maleise eilandenrijk*, p. 246.

10. They were not related to the Volls. After his grandfather (on his father's side) had died, Willem Leendert's grandmother remarried Jan Adriaan Voll in 1792. Jacoba Margaretha Mesman (1822–1843) married Antonie Martin Weijergang in 1842. See Christiaans, "Makassaarse families I. De familie Weijergang I", p. 79.

11. Sutherland, "Mestizos as Middlemen?" p. 263.

12. Like Alexander de Siso, Captain of the Malays, Peranakan-Chinese and others. Van Dissel, *De particuliere landen in het gewest Celebes*, Appendices (letters).

13. Van Dissel, *De particuliere landen in het gewest Celebes*, pp. 19, 25, 58.

14. Christiaans, "Genealogie familie Mesman".

15. KITLV, Hisdoc, Western manuscripts H 1007, Houtman-Mesman, "Uit tempo doeloe", pp. 3–4.

16. NA, Collection Du Bus de Gisignies, inv. no. 26, Survey of civil servants of the government in Makassar, n.d.

17. Wallace, *Het Maleise eilandenrijk*, p. 247.

18. Wallace, *Het Maleise eilandenrijk*, p. 250.

19. KITLV, Hisdoc, Western manuscripts H 1007, Houtman-Mesman, "Uit tempo doeloe", pp. 1, 42.

20. See regarding Tante Netje, Siti Tanriollé or We Tanriollé: Sutherland, "Power and Politics", p. 166.

21. KITLV, Hisdoc, Western manuscripts H 1007, Houtman-Mesman, "Uit tempo doeloe", p. 11.

22. KITLV, Hisdoc, Western manuscripts H 1007, Houtman-Mesman, "Uit tempo doeloe", p. 29.

23. Etmans, *De bevolking van Banda*, p. 102; KITLV, Hisdoc, Western manuscripts H 1007, Houtman-Mesman, "Uit tempo doeloe", p. 33; Etmans, *Huwelijksregister van Banda*, p. 17.

24. In 1854, 25 ships with "European" rigging and 206 ships with "indigenous" rigging anchored in the roadstead of Banda Neira. See Bleeker, *Reis door de Minahasa*, vol. II, p. 263.

25. Somerset Maugham, *The Narrow Corner*, p. 100.

26. Olivier, *Reizen in den Molukschen archipel*, vol. I, pp. 149 ff.

27. Van Vliet, *Belangrijk verslag over den staat Banda*, p. 95.

28. According to Van der Crab, *De Moluksche eilanden*, p. 19; Pino, "Banda en de perkeniers", p. 541.
29. Van Vliet, *Belangrijk verslag over den staat Banda*, pp. 94–95.
30. Quarles van Ufford, *Aanteekeningen betreffende eene reis door de Molukken*, p. 131.
31. Van der Linden, *Banda en zijne bewoners*, p. 54.
32. This text is printed in Van den Berg, *Het verloren volk*, p. 38.
33. Van de Wall, *De Nederlandsche oudheden*, p. 15.
34. Van der Linden, *Banda en zijne bewoners*, pp. 32–33.
35. Van der Linden, *Banda en zijne bewoners*, p. 33.
36. Van der Crab, *De Moluksche eilanden*, p. 14; Quarles van Ufford, *Aantekeningen betreffende eene reis door de Molukken*, p. 151.
37. Van der Linden, *Banda en zijne bewoners*, p. 38.
38. Etmans, *Huwelijksregister van Banda*, pp. 26, 31, 50, 64, 93.
39. *Almanak en naamregister van Nederlandsch-Indië 1862*, pp. 17, 72, 294, 411.
40. Etmans, *Huwelijksregister van Banda*, pp. 39, 51, 59.
41. Etmans, *Huwelijksregister van Banda*, p. 67.
42. In 1866 the *perkenier* Johannes Adrianus Delmaar married the "Christian native woman" Selfisina Francisca, who had been baptised two years before her marriage and had been a Muslim before. That same year Adrianus Andries Leunissen married Mariana Sarah Saul, who had been baptised three years earlier and had also been a Muslim. See Etmans, *Huwelijksregister van Banda*, pp. 66–67.
43. Van der Crab, *De Moluksche eilanden*, pp. 37, 44; Quarles van Ufford, *Aantekeningen betreffende eene reis door de Molukken*, pp. 134–35.
44. Van der Crab, *De Moluksche eilanden*, p. 36.
45. NA, MvK I, inv. no. 7263, GB 2 July 1859, no. 6.
46. The total profit for 1860 was 213,470.08 guilders, for 1861 it was 183,118.49, for 1862 it was 190,793.66, and for 1863 it was 161,880. For 18 *perken* the profit was between 1,000 and 3,000 guilders; one had a profit of more than 12,000 guilders. KV 1863, HTK (1864–1865), p. 1140.
47. Etmans, *De bevolking van Banda*, pp. 35, 75, 92, 166.
48. Van Vliet, *Belangrijk verslag over den staat Banda*, p. 115.
49. NA, MvK II, inv. no. 1367, Verbaal 12 Aug. 1863, no. 22; Idem, inv. no. 1379, Verbaal 18 Aug. 1863, no. 8; Idem, inv. no. 1348 (16 June 1863), Letter of Governor-General with appendices, 16 April 1863, no. 321. In this letter only J.A. Delmaar is mentioned as one of the seven petitioners.
50. Ponder, *In Javanese Waters*, pp. 116, 135.
51. From 1,800 *pikol* mace and 7,200 *pikol* nutmeg in 1864 to 3,250 *pikol* mace and 13,500 *pikol* nutmeg in 1880. See Lans, *Causeriën*, p. 41.
52. Van der Wolk, "Tropenromantiek", pp. 79–80.

53. De Wit, *Natuur en menschen in Indië*, p. 418.

54. *Particuliere landbouw-nijverheid. Lijst van ondernemingen*, vol. I, p. 388.

55. Feenstra, *Beschouwingen over de ontwikkeling van handel, cultuur en nijverheid*, p. 12; Van der Linden, *Banda en zijne bewoners*, p. 62.

56. *De Locomotief* (27 Dec. 1870).

57. Ponder, *In Javanese Waters*, p. 116.

58. KV 1875, HTK (1876–1877), pp. 8–9, Appendix no. III. Beroepen en Bedrijven.

59. *Makassaarsch Handelsblad* (26 July 1872).

60. Van de Wall, *De Nederlandsche oudheden*, p. 82.

61. *De Locomotief* (27 Dec. 1870).

62. M.J.H. Lantzius (1871, Delft), H.W. Hoeke (1879, Delft) and L.F. Hoeke (1882, Batavia). W.H. Versteegh died during his studies in Delft in 1879. Etmans, *De bevolking van Banda*, pp. 107, 247, 251.

63. Van den Berg, *Het verloren volk*, p. 92.

64. Dealing with the origins of the Banda plantation society, Vincent Loth calls the economic system that the VOC created on Banda a "Caribbean Cuckoo in an Asian Nest". This qualification can also be applied to the society of Banda. Loth, "Pioneers and Perkeniers".

65. Hoetink, *Het patroon van de oude Curaçaose samenleving*, p. 107.

66. *De Morgenpost* (24 Apr. 1888); Van Marle, "De groep der Europeanen", pp. 317–18.

67. Fasseur, "Hoeksteen en struikelblok", p. 146.

68. This applies at least to Ambon. See Leirissa, "The Bugis-Makassarese in the Port Towns", p. 251.

69. Clause 4 of article 109 of the Government Regulation of 1854 stated: "The native Christians are to remain subject to the native headmen and as regards their rights and duties and obligations will continue to obey the same general provincial and municipal decrees and ruling bodies as do the natives who are not Christian". Thus, Olivier, who visited the island of Amboina and Ceram in 1824 in the company of Governor-General Van der Capellen, observed that the vast majority of the Christian village population (from a native village or kampong) was living in serfdom. See Olivier, *Reizen in den Molukschen archipel*, vol. I, p. 37.

70. See "Reglement op het houden van Registers der burgerlijke stand van europeesche en daarmede gelijkgestelde bevolking in Nederlandsch-Indië" (regulations on the keeping of registers of births, marriages and deaths), GB 10 May, no. 4, *Staatsblad van Nederlandsch-Indië* (1849), no. 25. Regarding marriages in the Moluccas, see: GB 1 Dec. 1851, *Staatsblad van Nederlandsch-Indië* (1851), no. 70 and GB 28 May 1861, *Staatsblad van Nederlandsch-Indië* (1861), no. 38. This regulation was extended to Timor in 1874 (GB 20 Feb. 1874, *Staatsblad van Nederlandsch-Indië* (1874), no. 83) but was eventually withdrawn on 1 Dec. 1898 (*Staatsblad van Nederlandsch-Indië* (1898), no. 160).

71. Van Coeverden, "Beknopt overzigt", p. 203; Van der Crab, *De Moluksche eilanden*, p. 274. The number of slaves decreased from 1,844 in 1828 to 550 in 1840. Most of the 200 to 300 slaves who remained on Ternate over the next 20 years were probably household slaves.
72. KITLV, Hisdoc, Western manuscripts, Memorie van overgave (memorandum of transfer) J.H. Tobias (1857), p. 78.
73. Van Doren, *Herinneringen en schetsen*, vol. II, p. 266; De Clercq, *Bijdragen tot de kennis der residentie Ternate*, p. 20.
74. Van Hoëvell, "Leti-eilanden", pp. 215–17.
75. Christiaans, "Europese bevolking van Ternate".
76. Christiaans, "Europese bevolking van Ternate"; De Clercq, *Bijdragen tot de kennis der residentie Ternate*, p. 20.
77. Christiaans, "Europese bevolking van Ternate".
78. Ibid.
79. Kal, "Een aanzet voor het opstellen van een genealogie van het Indische geslacht Voorneman", p. 50.
80. Bleeker, *Reis door de Minahassa*, vol. I, p. 196.
81. KITLV, Hisdoc, Western manuscripts, Memorie van overgave (memorandum of transfer) C. Bosscher, p. 238.
82. Wallace, *Het Maleise eilandenrijk*, pp. 328–29.
83. *Regeerings-almanak 1862*, p. 508.
84. *Regeerings-almanak 1862*, pp. 134–35. Regarding the son who settled in Manado, see Wallace, *Het Maleise eilandenrijk*, p. 261. L.D.W.A. van Renesse van Duivenbode, born in Ternate (5 March 1828), died in Manado (14 Jan. 1879). Regarding the Duivenbodes from Manado, see De Vries, *Een Amsterdamse koopman in de Molukken*, p. 194.
85. Van Doren, *Herinneringen en schetsen*, vol. II, pp. 264–65.
86. KITLV, Hisdoc, Western manuscripts, Memorie van overgave (memorandum of transfer) J.H. Tobias (1857), p. 78.
87. De Clercq, *Bijdragen tot de kennis der residentie Ternate*, p. 19; KITLV, Hisdoc, Western manuscripts, Memorie van overgave (memorandum of transfer) J.H. Tobias (1857), pp. 80, 85; Leirissa, "The Bugis-Makassarese in the Port Towns", pp. 243, 247.
88. Van de Wall, *De Nederlandsche oudheden*, p. 248.
89. Van Doren, *Herinneringen en schetsen*, vol. II, p. 225; Van der Crab, *De Moluksche eilanden*, p. 266.
90. Groeneboer, *Gateway to the West*, pp. 103–104; Van Mastenbroek, *De historische ontwikkeling van de staatsrechtelijke indeeling*, p. 36.
91. Leirissa, "Social Developments", p. 3.
92. Knaap, "Tjengkeh, Kompeni, Agama", p. 23.
93. Ludeking, *Schets van de residentie Amboina*, pp. 127–28; Leirissa, "The Bugis-Makassarese in the Port Towns", p. 247.
94. [Bakhuizen van den Brink], "De inlandsche burgers in de Molukken", p. 597.

95. Leirissa, "Social Developments", p. 7.
96. KV 1875, HTK (1876–1877), p. 201.
97. For example, in the *Almanak en naamregister van Nederlandsch-Indië* of 1862 M.J. Guttig, K.R. Moorrees, H.E. Hoedt and D.F. Moorrees are recorded as officers of the Ambonese citizen's militia. D.F. Pietersz, H.E. Hoedt and A.G. Schmidhamer are recorded as members of the *weeskamer* (on the board that governed the Orphans' Chamber). F.J. Hoedt is *commies* (holding the position of officer) for the postal services on Banda.
98. Willem Joseph Hoedt married Christina Elisabeth Keijser, and his son Pieter Johannes Hoedt married Alexandrina Helena De Bouville — daughter of a landowner of the Banda islands — in 1883. His cousin Carel Hendrik Hoedt, son of George Alexander Hoedt, married Jeanetta Antoinetta Louise van Bloemen Waanders — assistant teacher at the Openbare Lagere Meisjesschool (Public Elementary Girls' School) in Banda — in 1893. Willem Jacobus Fredrik Bernard, son of Willem Hendrik Bernard, also married to a woman from Banda, married Frederika Anthoinetta Meijer in 1870. Etmans, *Huwelijksregister van Banda*, pp. 98, 111, 112.
99. Koninklijke Bibliotheek (Royal Library), The Hague (hereafter KoBib), Collection Neumann, Louis Neumann to his parents, no. 39 (2 May 1875).
100. NA, Stamboeken burgerlijke ambtenaren Oost-Indië, Ludwig Adolph Wilhelm Georg Neumann, A1 22, Gottlieb Christian Diederich Neumann, A1 366, F.H.R. Neumann, A1 539, Rudolph Johann Heinrich, II rom 23.
101. KoBib, Collection Neumann, Rudolph Neumann to his parents, no. 218 (2 Feb. 1894).
102. KoBib, Collection Neumann, Rudolph Neumann to his mother and his sister Mina, no. 279 (18 May 1897).
103. KoBib, Collection Neumann, Rudolph Neumann to his parents, no. 222 (26 May 1894), no. 226 (20 Oct. 1894).
104. KoBib, Collection Neumann, Rudolph Neumann to his parents, no. 206 (15 May 1893); Idem, no. 246 (22 June 1895).
105. Christiaans, "Gegevens voor de samenstelling van de genealogie van de familie Rijkschroeff", pp. 181–82.
106. KoBib, Collection Neumann, Rudolph Neumann to his parents, no. 228 (15 Dec. 1894); Idem, no. 278 (8 Nov. 1897); Idem, no. 265 (9 Dec. 1896).
107. Van Marle, "De groep der Europeanen", p. 491.
108. De Vries, *Een Amsterdamse koopman in de Molukken*, p. 239.
109. KoBib, Collection Neumann, Louis Neumann to his parents, no. 30 (1 Aug. 1875).
110. KoBib, Collection Neumann, Rudolph Neumann to his parents, no. 269 (29 March 1897).

111. E.R. Soselisa, *eerste commies* and *raad van justitie* (member of the Court of Justice), see: Leirissa, "Social Developments", p. 6. Andreas Dias is mentioned in the *Almanak en naamregister van Nederlandsch-Indië* of 1843 as *commies* on Larike. *Almanak en naamregister van Nederlandsch-Indië 1843*, p. 58.

112. *Almanak en naamregister van Nederlandsch-Indië 1862*, pp. 129, 130.

113. Leirissa, "Social Developments", p. 5.

114. See the marriage of Joost Weijdemuller to Wilhelmina Wawoeroentoe, 1861, *Almanak en naamregister van Nederlandsch-Indië 1862*, p. 21.

115. Chauvel, *Nationalists, Soldiers and Separatists*, pp. 32–33.

116. Riedel, "Hoe denken de Amboneezen over indiensttreding bij het Indische leger?", p. 321.

117. Groeneboer, *Gateway to the West*, pp. 30–34.

118. Olivier, *Reizen in den Molukschen archipel*, vol. I, p. 48.

119. Groeneboer, *Gateway to the West*, p. 127.

120. Chauvel, *Nationalists, Soldiers and Separatists*, p. 31; Groeneboer, *Gateway to the West*, pp. 116–17, 121.

121. J.A. van der Chijs quoted in Groeneboer, *Gateway to the West*, pp. 103–104.

122. See also: [Bakhuizen van den Brink], "De inlandsche burgers in de Molukken", pp. 595–649; Leirissa, "Social Developments", p. 5.

123. Van der Crab, *De Moluksche eilanden*, p. 115.

124. Van Mastenbroek, *De historische ontwikkeling van de staatsrechtelijke indeeling*, p. 48.

125. KV 1856, HTK (1857–1858), p. 41; KV 1875, HTK (1875–1876) [5.4], p. 36; KV 1860, HTK (1861–1862), p. 30; Schouten, *Leadership and Social Mobility*, p. 123.

126. GB 5 Sept. 1873, no. 24, and GB 13 Apr. 1875, no. 30; *Encyclopaedie van Nederlandsch-Indië*, vol. I, pp. 38–40.

127. In 1854, 30,618 out of the 91,561 inhabitants of Minahasa were Christian; in 1860 the figures were 56,660 out of 99,036. The percentage of Christians rose from 33 per cent in 1854 to 57 per cent in 1860. Van der Crab, *De Moluksche eilanden*, p. 353.

128. Groeneboer, *Gateway to the West*, p. 104; Chauvel, *Nationalists, Soldiers and Separatists*, p. 44.

129. KV 1918, HTK (1918–1919), Appendix B, p. 5.

130. KV 1865, HTK (1866–1867), 131st sheet, p. 519; KV 1876, HTK (1876–1877), Appendix E, Recapitulatie van de sterfte en ziektecijfers bij het leger.

131. NA, MvK II, Mailrapport 1904, no. 1, Acting army commander Van der Wyck to Governor-General (9 March 1903).

132. KV 1885, HTK (1886–1887), Appendix C, [5.4], p. 5.

133. KV 1902, HTK (1902–1903), Appendix P. I, Christelijke godsdienst, pp. 4–5.

134. Schouten, *Leadership and Social Mobility*, p. 124.

135. Regarding the example of J.A. Hazaart, see Veth, *Het eiland Timor*, pp. 83–95.

136. KoBib, Collection Neumann, Rudolph Neumann to his parents, no. 170 (17 Oct. 1890).

137. KoBib, Collection Neumann, Rudolph Neumann to his parents, no. 169 (17 Sept. 1890).

138. KoBib, Collection Neumann, Rudolph Neumann to his parents, no. 123 (15 March 1884); Idem, no. 223 (21 July 1894).

139. Loudon, *De eerste jaren der Billiton-onderneming*, p. 115.

140. *Makassaarsch Handelsblad* (24 Jan. 1863).

141. *Celebes Courant* (6 Apr. 1880); Termorshuizen, *Journalisten en heethoofden*, pp. 672–73.

142. Feenstra, *Beschouwingen over de ontwikkeling van handel, cultuur en nijverheid*, p. 11.

143. Termorshuizen "De oudste krant van Celebes", p. 103.

144. *Nieuws- en Advertentieblad van Celebes en Onderhoorigheden* (31 Oct. 1879).

145. Termorshuizen, "De oudste krant van Celebes", p. 113.

146. *Dagblad van Celebes* (17 June 1868).

147. *Dagblad van Celebes* (3 June 1868).

148. Obituary of C.C. Tromp in *Celebes Courant* (30 Dec. 1884).

149. Sutherland, "Power and Politics", p. 180.

150. *De Locomotief* (10 Aug. 1875).

151. *De Locomotief* (4 Sept. 1875).

152. KB 27 April 1881, no. 8.

153. *Celebes Courant* (6 March 1883).

154. Van den Berge, *Karel Frederik Holle*, p. 165.

155. *Celebes Courant* (20 Nov. 1888).

156. NA, Stamboeken burgerlijke ambtenaren Oost-Indië, r. 475.

157. W.H. Brugman became civil commander of Bima in 1898 and L.A. Brugman civil commander of Tontoli in 1899; see *Makassaarsche Courant* (17 Aug. 1898, 18 Sept. 1899).

158. *De Locomotief* (21 June 1871).

159. *Tjerimai* (18 Jan. 1908).

160. *Makassaarsche Courant* (25 Feb. 1908).

161. *Makassaarsche Courant* (27 Apr. 1908).

162. KITLV, Hisdoc, Western manuscripts H 1007, Houtman-Mesman, "Uit tempo doeloe", pp. 44–46.

163. KITLV, Hisdoc, Western manuscripts H 1007, Houtman-Mesman, "Uit tempo doeloe", p. 68.

164. See advertisement F. Mesman & Co. in *Makassaarsche Courant* (7 July 1908).

165. *Particuliere landbouwnijverheid. Lijst van ondernemingen*, vol. I, p. 378.

Chapter 6

1.   Van den Doel, *De stille macht*, pp. 345, 348.
2.   Bossenbroek, *Van Holland naar Indië*, p. 49.
3.   NA, MvK I, inv. no. 3106, Register of European personnel and their male descendants in Batavia, 1819. A sample is taken of the men with family names starting with A, H, M and R, a total of 223 persons.
4.   NA, MvK I, inv. no. 3114, Register of European personnel and their male descendants in Semarang, 1819.
5.   ANRI, Archive Residentie Surabaya, Box 74 no. 130 d, List of payments of the general administration, 1822.
6.   NA, Collection Du Bus de Gisignies, inv. no. 252, no. 26, Survey of civil servants and employees in the government of Makassar, unpag.
7.   Buddingh, "Weeshuis te Parapattan", p. 254.
8.   "Venduties te Batavia".
9.   NA, MvK I, inv. no. 1167, Verbaal 28 June 1838, no. 3/319, Considerations and advice of J.C. Baud (2 May 1838), unpag.
10. NA, MvK I, inv. no. 1167, Verbaal 28 June 1838, no. 3/319, Considerations and advice of J.C. Baud (2 May 1838), unpag.
11. *Historische nota over het vraagstuk van de opleiding*, pp. 2–3.
12. Fasseur, "De 'adeldom' van de huid", pp. 16–17.
13. Fasseur, *De Indologen*, pp. 105–6.
14. Fasseur, *De Indologen*, p. 109.
15. "De opvoeding van jongelingen in Indië", p. 77.
16. *Historische nota over het vraagstuk van de opleiding*, p. 40.
17. Taylor, *The Social World of Batavia*, p. 118.
18. Rochussen to Baud (31 March 1847), in: Baud, ed., *Semi-officiële en particuliere briefwisseling*, vol. II, p. 225; NA, MvK I, inv. no. 4345, Verbaal 10 Aug. 1848, no. 327, Rochussen to Minister of the Colonies (26 May 1848), p. 9.
19. Van Hoëvell, *Beschuldiging en veroordeeling*, p. 10.
20. NA, MvK I, inv. no. 4345, Verbaal 10 Aug. 1848, no. 327, Rochussen to Minister of the Colonies (26 May 1848), p. 9.
21. NA, MvK I, inv. no. 4345, Verbaal 10 Aug. 1848, no. 327, Rochussen to Minister of the Colonies (26 May 1848), p. 10.
22. NA, MvK I, inv. no. 1167, Verbaal 28 June 1838, no. 3/319, Considerations and advice of J.C. Baud (2 May 1838), unpag. See also Fasseur, "De 'adeldom' van de huid".
23. Rochussen to Baud (25 Aug. 1847), in: Baud, ed., *Semi-officiële en particuliere briefwisseling*, vol. II, p. 278.
24. NA, MvK I, inv. no. 1167, Verbaal 28 June 1838, no. 3/319, Considerations and advice of J.C. Baud (2 May 1838), unpag.
25. ANRI, Archive Residentie Semarang, inv. no. 2322, Records of service of European personnel 1849–1869, as of 1 April 1849.

26. *Almanak en naamregister van Nederlandsch-Indië 1862*, pp. 167–271, 272–88.

27. *Celebes Courant* (30 Dec. 1884).

28. *Historische nota over het vraagstuk van de opleiding*, p. 37.

29. Rochussen to Baud (31 March 1847), in: Baud, ed., *Semi-officiële en particuliere briefwisseling*, vol. II, p. 225.

30. Universiteitsbibliotheek Leiden (hereafter UBL), Collection P. J. Veth, Van Hoëvell to Veth (23 Apr. 1848).

31. UBL, Collection P. J. Veth, Van Hoëvell to Veth (26 May 1846).

32. UBL, Collection P. J. Veth, Van Hoëvell to Veth (26 May 1848).

33. Rochussen, *Toelichting en verdediging van eenige daden van mijn bestuur*, p. 108.

34. Van Hoëvell, *De beschuldiging en veroordeeling*, pp. 14–15.

35. Van Hoëvell, *De beschuldiging en veroordeeling*, pp. 18–19, 21, 71–72, Appendix V.

36. NA, MvK I, inv. no. 4345, Geheim verbaal 10 Aug. 1848, no. 327, Report of Governor-General Rochussen to Minister Rijk (26 May 1848), p. 20.

37. Rochussen, *Toelichting en verdediging van eenige daden van mijn bestuur*, p. 111.

38. Van Hoëvell, *De beschuldiging en veroordeeling*, p. 23.

39. NA, MvK I, inv. no. 4345, Geheim verbaal 10 Aug. 1848, no. 327, Report of Governor-General Rochussen to Minister Rijk (26 May 1848), pp. 21–23; also UBL, Collection P. J. Veth, Van Hoëvell to Veth (26 May 1848); Canter Visscher, "De waarheid over 22 Mei 1848", pp. 408–10.

40. NA, MvK I, inv. no. 4345, Geheim verbaal 10 Aug. 1848, no. 327.

41. Van Hoëvell, *De beschuldiging en veroordeeling*, p. 5.

42. De Neve, "De Bataviase meibeweging", pp. 537–38.

43. De Neve, "De Bataviase meibeweging", p. 535.

44. NA, MvK I, inv. no. 4345, Geheim verbaal 10 Aug. 1848, no. 327.

45. NA, MvK I, inv. no. 4345, Geheim verbaal 10 Aug. 1848, no. 327.

46. Veth, *Bijdragen tot de kennis van den politieken toestand van Nederlandsch Indië*, vol. I.

47. Petrus Blumberger, *De Indo-Europeesche beweging in Nederlandsch-Indië*, p. 13.

48. Rochussen to Baud (27 May 1848), in: Baud, ed., *Semi-officiële en particuliere briefwisseling*, vol. II, p. 364.

49. Rochussen, *Toelichting en verdediging van eenige daden van mijn bestuur*, p. 112.

50. Bisschop Grevelink, *De Bataviasche mei-beweging van 1848*, pp. 8, 11–12.

51. *Javasche Courant* (24 May 1848).

52. UBL, Collection P. J. Veth, Van Hoëvell to his parents (26 July 1848).

53. De Neve, "De Bataviase meibeweging", p. 536.

54. Rochussen, *Toelichting en verdediging van eenige daden van mijn bestuur*, pp. 103–17.

55.   Fasseur, "De 'adeldom' van de huid", p. 19.

56.   Termorshuizen, *Journalisten en heethoofden*, p. 171.

57.   *Colombo Journal* (8 Feb. 1832, 14 March 1832, 24 Nov. 1832) supplement.

58.   Hawes, *Poor Relations*, p. 133.

59.   Heuman, *Between Black and White*.

60.   Fasseur, "Een martelaar voor het vrije woord", pp. 86–87.

61.   *De Oostpost* (1 Jan. 1853).

62.   Fasseur, "Een martelaar voor het vrije woord", pp. 95–97.

63.   Termorshuizen, "De oudste krant van Celebes", p. 111.

64.   *Bataviasche Courant* (8 Feb. 1817).

65.   *Algemeen verslag van den staat van het schoolwezen [...] 1833*, pp. 17–18.

66.   *Algemeen verslag van den staat van het schoolwezen [...] 1833*, p. 5.

67.   *Algemeen verslag van den staat van het schoolwezen [...] 1845*, pp. 27–28.

68.   *Algemeen verslag van den staat van het schoolwezen [...] 1833*, pp. 8, 23, 49.

69.   *Algemeen verslag van den staat van het schoolwezen [...] 1833*, p. 55.

70.   *Algemeen verslag van den staat van het schoolwezen [...] 1833*, pp. 19–20.

71.   *Algemeen verslag van den staat van het schoolwezen [...] 1849*, Appendices G and H.

72.   *Het pauperisme onder de Europeanen*, vol. IV. *Onderwijs*, pp. 15–16.

73.   ANRI, Archive Residentie Semarang, inv. no. 2169, Political report 1864, Section Salatiga, unpag., par. 7.

74.   "Algemeene en bijzondere narigten omtrent het schoolwezen", pp. 578–79.

75.   Groeneboer, *Weg tot het westen*, p. 137.

76.   Groeneboer, *Weg tot het westen*, p. 143.

77.   Prick Van Wely, *Neerlands taal in 't Verre Oosten*, p. 56.

78.   *Algemeen verslag van den staat van het schoolwezen [...] 1833*, pp. 12–14.

79.   *Algemeen verslag van den staat van het schoolwezen [...] 1833*, pp. 14–16.

80.   KV 1881, pp. 92–93.

81.   KV 1881, p. 93.

82.   NA, MvK II, inv. no. 2668, Verbaal 28 March 1874, no. 47, Minister to Governor-General.

83.   KITLV, Hisdoc, Western manuscripts H 873, W.H. Coert, "Geschiedenis van de familie Coert 1756–1963".

84.   Bosma and Raben, "De macht van de pen", p. 91.

85.   *Regeerings-almanak voor Nederlandsch-Indië 1868–1901*.

86.   Fasseur, *De Indologen*, p. 212.

87.   Hasselman, "De practische resultaten van de recruteering van civiele ambtenaren"; see also: Walbeehm, "Iets over cijfers en percentages in verband met de afdeeling B".

88.   Fasseur, *De Indologen*, pp. 232–33; Fasseur, "De 'adeldom' van de huid", p. 20.

89.   Van den Doel, *De stille macht*, pp. 74, 132.

90. Bedjo Riyanto, *Iklan Surat Kabar*, pp. 180–91, illustrations pp. 226–366.
91. Bedjo Riyanto, *Iklan Surat Kabar*, p. 299.
92. Taylor, *The Social World of Batavia*.
93. *Mataram* (19 Feb. 1880).
94. Shennan, *Out in the Midday Sun*, pp. 69–70; Butcher, *The British in Malaya*; Ballhatchet, *Race, Sex and Class under the Raj*.
95. Cannadine, *Ornamentalism*.
96. Van Doorn, *A Divided Society*, p. 27; Van der Veur, "Introduction to a Socio-Political Study of the Eurasians", p. 427.
97. Van der Veur, "Introduction to a Socio-Political Study of the Eurasians", p. 428; see also: Houben, "De Indo-aristocratie van Midden Java", p. 47.

Chapter 7

1. Himmelfarb, *Poverty and Compassion*, pp. 3–18.
2. *Bataviaasch Nieuwsblad* (14 Dec. 1885).
3. Van Doren, *Reis naar Nederlands Oost-Indië*, vol. II, pp. 154–55.
4. NA, Collection I.D. Fransen van de Putte, inv. no. 38, A short history of the technical school in Surabaya, Letter of 28 Feb. 1855.
5. Olivier, *Land- en zeetogten in Nederland's Indië*, vol. I, p. 38 and vol. II, p. 26.
6. F., ["Rekest van eenen kleurling"].
7. De Stuers in his plan for the defence of Java, 1835, quoted in: Veth, "Iets over de opvoeding", p. 90.
8. Young, *Colonial Desire*, pp. 5–6.
9. One of the first articles to use this term was: H., "De hybriden in de Indische samenleving".
10. Prick van Wely, "De Indische kleurlingen en hun benamingen".
11. Groeneboer, *Weg tot het westen*, 476; KV 1860, pp. 29–31.
12. Van Mastenbroek, *De historische ontwikkeling van de staatsrechtelijke indeeling*; Van der Wal, "Het rascriterium en het overheidsbeleid", p. 833; Fasseur, "Hoeksteen en struikelblok", p. 141; Van Goor, *De Nederlandse koloniën*, p. 157.
13. Anderson, *Imagined Communities*.
14. Fasseur, "Hoeksteen en struikelblok", p. 145.
15. See, for example, ANRI, Archive Residentie Semarang, inv. no. 4035, Register of outgoing letters of the chief wardmaster, unpag., Copy of letter to resident, n.d., no. 206, regarding a request by Louisa Debora van Spall.
16. B., "Statistieke opgave der residentie Batavia", pp. 552–54. In 1847 this ratio was 30 per cent: *Javasche Courant* (1 Apr. 1848).
17. Muller, "Geneeskundige topographie van Samarang", Appendix F.

18. Van Marle, "De groep der Europeanen in Nederlands-Indië", p. 491.

19. Van Doren, *Fragmenten*, vol. I, p. 32.

20. NA, Collection Du Bus de Gisignies, inv. no. 493, Letter Lieutenant-Governor-General (23 Oct. 1829), no. 16 secret, regarding the request of Pinket van Haak.

21. Van Marle, "De groep der Europeanen in Nederlands-Indië", pp. 319–20.

22. Van Marle, "De groep der Europeanen in Nederlands-Indië", p. 321.

23. Adelante, "Concubinaat bij de ambtenaren van het Binnenlandsch Bestuur", pp. 312–13; Van Marle, "De groep der Europeanen in Nederlands-Indië", p. 486.

24. *Uitkomsten der pauperisme-enquête. Gewestelijke verslagen* I. *Semarang*, p. 2; Idem, *Algemeen verslag*, pp. 10–11.

25. Van Marle, "De groep der Europeanen in Nederlands-Indië", p. 491.

26. ANRI, Archive Residentie Batavia, inv. no. 18, Political report 1855, Population survey.

27. KV 1871, Appendix A, pp. 6–7; Van Hoëvell, *Reis over Java*; Van Doren, *De Javaan in het ware daglicht*, pp. 227–66.

28. Boele, *De jaren van de Javaanse gasfabrieken*, pp. 25, 63.

29. NA, MvK II, inv. no. 2668, Verbaal 24 March 1874, no. 47, Memorandum A.J.W. van Delden (7 Aug. 1872), unpag.

30. Boelen, "Vrijwillige sinjokorpsen", p. 211.

31. See, for example, Gerdessen, *Vijf jaar gedetacheerd*, pp. 36–37.

32. Knaap, "Samarang in vogelvlucht", p. 325.

33. Knaap, "Samarang in vogelvlucht", p. 361.

34. See, for example, Naber, ed., "Nicolette Peronneau van Leyden's herinneringen", p. 64.

35. Knaap, "Samarang in vogelvlucht", pp. 360–61.

36. ANRI, Archive Residentie Batavia, inv. no. 18, Political report 1855, p. 19.

37. ANRI, Archive Residentie Batavia, inv. no. 18, Political report 1863, p. 22.

38. Gouda, *Poverty and Political Culture*, pp. 191–92.

39. Roebroek and Hertogh, *"De beschavende invloed des tijds"*, p. 254.

40. ANRI, Archive Residentie Batavia, inv. no. 18, Political report 1859, p. 36.

41. ANRI, Archive Residentie Batavia, inv. no. 18, Political report 1862, p. 25.

42. NA, MvK II, inv. no. 6026, Kabinet geheim 18 July 1872, r11/ no. 27.

43. NA, MvK II, inv. no. 6026, Kabinet geheim 18 July 1872, r11/ no. 27.

44. NA, MvK II, inv. no. 2668, Verbaal 28 March 1874, no. 47, Report of the committee (30 Dec. 1872).

45. See, for example, also Groneman, *Vorstenlandsche toestanden*, p. 14.

46. NA, MvK II, inv. no. 2668, Verbaal 28 March 1874, no. 47, Minister to Governor-General.

47. *Het pauperisme onder de Europeanen*, vol. I. *Algemeen overzicht*, p. 27. See also GB 19 oktober 1882, no. 5, *Staatsblad van Nederlandsch-Indië*, p. 257.

48. *Uitkomsten der pauperisme-enquête. Algemeen verslag*, p. 12.

49. *Rapport der pauperisme-commissie*, La c, p. 2.

50. *Uitkomsten der pauperisme-enquête. Algemeen verslag*, p. 19; Idem, *Gewestelijke verslagen* I. *Semarang*, pp. 3–5.

51. ANRI, Archive Residentie Semarang, inv. no. 4031, Correspondence chief wardmaster of Semarang, 1862, unpag., Wardmaster of ward D to chief wardmaster, n.d.

52. ANRI, Archive Residentie Semarang, inv. no. 4433, Incoming letters of the Commissie van Weldadigheid in Semarang, 1838–1846, Chief wardmaster to Committee (7 Feb. 1838); Idem, Wardmaster of ward S to chief wardmaster (7 Feb. 1838).

53. ANRI, Archive Residentie Semarang, inv. no. 4460, Documents concerning allowances: survey of indigent Christians (Jan. 1858); ANRI, Archive Residentie Semarang, inv. no. 4465, List of recipients of allowances from the fund of assistance for indigent Christians (1 Jan. 1870).

54. Muller, "Geneeskundige topographie van Samarang", p. 510.

55. ANRI, Archive Residentie Semarang, inv. no. 4427, Survey of the population of the old men's home in Semarang (15 Dec. 1868).

56. *Regeerings-almanak voor Nederlandsch-Indië* 1865–1868 and 1883–1887.

57. *Uitkomsten der pauperisme-enquête. Gewestelijke verslagen* I. *Semarang*, p. 7.

58. *Uitkomsten der pauperisme-enquête. Gewestelijke verslagen* I. *Batavia*, p. 6.

59. This appeared to be the case in Ceylon, for example, where the "Dutch Burghers", descendants of VOC employees and native women, started a successful cultural and social emancipation movement in the 19th century. See: Roberts, Raheem and Colin-Thomé, *People Inbetween*.

60. Si Miskin, "Een onderdeel van het paupervraagstuk", p. 298.

61. KV 1860, pp. 35, 60, Appendix A, p. 18.

62. KV 1902–1903.

63. *Achtste jaarlijksch verslag van de directie van het weeshuis te Parapattan*, pp. 11–12.

64. *Tiende jaarlijksch verslag van de directie van het gesticht te Parapattan*, p. 14.

65. *Zesde jaarlijksch verslag van de directie van het gesticht te Parapattan*, p. 7; Mandor, "Het Parapattan weezen-gesticht te Batavia", pp. 35–36; *De staatsarmenzorg voor Europeanen*, vol. IV. *De door den staat gesubsidieerde particuliere weesinrichtingen*, p. 4.

66. *De staatsarmenzorg voor Europeanen*, vol. IV. *De door den staat gesubsidieerde particuliere weesinrichtingen*, pp. 1–2.

67. Mandor, "Het Parapattan weezen-gesticht te Batavia", p. 36; *Achtste jaarlijksch verslag van de directie van het gesticht te Parapattan*, pp. 7–9; *Tiende jaarlijksch verslag van de directie van het gesticht te Parapattan*, pp. 11–12.

68. *Verslag der feestviering*, pp. 22–23.
69. KV 1871, p. 104.
70. *Tweede verslag der directie van het gesticht [...] te Djattie.*
71. Muller, "Geneeskundige topographie van Samarang", Appendix G, Extract from the registers of the orphanages in Samarang.
72. ANRI, Archive Residentie Semarang, inv. no. 4427, Survey of children in the Roman Catholic orphanage (14 Dec. 1868); Idem, inv. no. 4429, Survey of the population in the Protestant orphanage, 1868.
73. Muller, "Geneeskundige topographie van Samarang", pp. 511–13.
74. *De staatsarmenzorg voor Europeanen*, vol. III. *De armenverpleging van staatswege*, p. 6.
75. NA, MvK II, inv. no. 265, Verbaal 23 June 1853, no. 7, Monthly report of Governor-General to Minister of the Colonies over April 1853 (24 Apr. 1853), unpag.
76. See, for example, ANRI, Archive Residentie Semarang, inv. no. 4404, Certificate of good conduct for Sophia Engels by the *binnenregent* of the Protestant orphanage D.C. de Bruin (30 Nov. 1857).
77. ANRI, Archive Residentie Semarang, inv. no. 4205, Correspondence concerning the regulations of the Registry of Births, Marriages and Deaths, 1828.
78. NA, MvK II, inv. no. 265, Verbaal 23 June 1853, no. 7, Monthly report of Governor-General to Minister of the Colonies over April 1853 (24 Apr. 1853), unpag.
79. Campen, *Het Korps Pupillen*, pp. 1–2.
80. NA, MvK II, inv. no. 6480, Mailrapport 1890, no. 500; see also Matthijs, *Het verboden huwelijk.*
81. *Het pauperisme onder de Europeanen*, vol. V, p. 37.
82. NA, MvK II, Mailrapport 1904, no. 91; Ming, "Barracks-Concubinage in the Indies".
83. Ballhatchet, *Race, Sex and Class under the Raj.*
84. Van Marle, "De groep der Europeanen in Nederlands-Indië", p. 486.
85. De Stuers in his plan for the defence of Java, 1835, quoted in: Veth, "Iets over de opvoeding", p. 90.
86. Regarding the attempts to provide education for soldiers' children, see Veth, "Iets over de opvoeding", pp. 89–99. GB 15 June 1818, no. 6, *Staatsblad van Nederlandsch-Indië* 39.
87. *Het pauperisme onder de Europeanen*, vol. II, p. 29.
88. *Algemeen verslag van den staat van het schoolwezen [...] 1833.*
89. *Het pauperisme onder de Europeanen*, vol. II, p. 30.
90. NA, MvK II, inv. no. 6480, Mailrapport 1890, no. 500.
91. Veth, "Iets over de opvoeding", p. 93.
92. Campen, *Het Korps Pupillen*, pp. 2–3.
93. Campen, *Het Korps Pupillen*, p. 4.

94. Herman, "Het onderwijs in Nederlandsch-Indië", p. 268.
95. Ruitenbach, "De opleiding der Pupillen te Gombong", pp. 613–17.
96. Campen, *Het Korps Pupillen*, Appendix.
97. Alexander, "Het Korps Pupillen te Gombong", p. 365.
98. Groeneboer, *Weg naar het westen*, p. 147.
99. Campen, *Het Korps Pupillen*, pp. 2–3.
100. Campen, *Het Korps Pupillen*, pp. 11, 16–19, 24.
101. "Het Pupillen-Korps op Java", p. 343; De Moor, "Van reveille tot taptoe", p. 76.
102. NA, MvK II, Mailrapport 1879, no. 183+, unpag.
103. Brakkee, *Pa van der Steur vader van 7000 kinderen*, pp. 25, 30–31.
104. Carlos, *Johannes van der Steur*, pp. 236–37.
105. Buddingh, *Neêrlands-Oost-Indië*, vol. I, p. 188.
106. Alexander, "Het Korps Pupillen te Gombong", 368 note.
107. KV 1860, Appendices, p. 18. 376 boys and 417 girls were elsewhere.
108. KV 1871, p. 24.
109. Campen, *Het Korps Pupillen*, pp. 34–36.
110. Buddingh, "Weeshuis te Parapattan".
111. ANRI, Archive Residentie Batavia, inv. no. 18, Political report 1859, p. 36.
112. M., "Fröbelscholen in Indië", p. 7; Stevens, *Vrijmetselarij*, pp. 118, 189, 205.
113. NA, MvK II, inv. no. 508, Verbaal 16 April 1856, no. 3/351, Duymaer van Twist to Council of the Indies (9 Sept. 1854).
114. NA, MvK II, inv. no. 508, Verbaal 16 April 1856, no. 3/351, Advice of C. Visscher (22 Aug. 1854).
115. NA, MvK II, inv. no. 1022, Verbaal 16 Jan. 1861, no. 2, Extract-decree of Governor-General (20 Nov. 1860).
116. "Verslag van den staat der ambachtsschool te Soerabaja", pp. 146–48.
117. *Het pauperisme onder de Europeanen*, vol. II, pp. 57–61.
118. Morren, *De Jongens-Weezen-Inrichting*, p. 55.
119. *De Locomotief* (9 Feb. 18/8).
120. Morren, *De Jongens-Weezen-Inrichting*, pp. 104–9.
121. Morren, *De Jongens-Weezen-Inrichting*, pp. 72–74.
122. Gouda, *Poverty and Political Culture*, p. 242.
123. Dekker, *Straffen, redden en opvoeden*, pp. 175–79, 205.
124. NA, MvK II, inv. no. 2668, Verbaal 28 March 1874, no. 47.
125. NA, MvK II, inv. no. 2893, Verbaal 20 June 1876, no. 51.

Chapter 8

1. Larkin, *Sugar and the Origins of Modern Philippine Society*, pp. 100, 167.
2. De Bree, *Gedenkboek van de Javasche Bank*, vol. II, p. 260.
3. De Bree, *Gedenkboek van de Javasche Bank*, vol. II, p. 233; *Gedenkboek der Nederlandsche Handel-Maatschappij*, p. 78.

4.   NA, NHM, inv. no. 7939, Survey of the advance loan made to the Dorrepaalsche Bank der Vorstenlanden 1885.

5.   De Bree, *Gedenkboek van de Javasche Bank*, vol. II, pp. 242–43.

6.   Furnivall, *Netherlands India*, pp. 196–97.

7.   Bosch, *De Nederlandse beleggingen in de Verenigde Staten*, p. 77.

8.   NA, NHM, inv. no. 2443, Memorandum concerning Dorrepaal and Factorij to the Secretarie/geheim, pp. 392, 1885; De Bree, *Gedenkboek van de Javasche Bank*, vol. II, pp. 249–50, 252–53, 258; NA, NHM, inv. no. 2444, Factorij to the board of directors NHM (4 Sept. 1886), no. 455.

9.   KITLV, Hisdoc, Western manuscripts H 928, Letters Wieseman-Broese van Groenou, W. Broese van Groenou to G.L. Wieseman-Dom (8 June 1885).

10.   *Gedenkboek der Nederlandsche Handel-Maatschappij*, p. 78; NA, NHM, inv. no. 2444, Factorij to the Board of Directors (4 Sept. 1886); inv. no. 471, Secretarie/geheim (23 Nov. 1886).

11.   NA, NHM, inv. no. 2829, Secretarie/geheim both to the Minister for the Colonies and in encoded copy to the Factorij (3 Sept. 1886), no. 61, Secretarie/geheim, to the Factorij (2 Sept. 1886), no. 59/383, Factorij to the NHM, Secretarie/geheim (17 Nov. 1886), no. 93. Secretarie NHM to the Factorij (10 Sept. 1886), no. 64/384; NA, NHM, inv. no. 2444, Factorij to the Secretarie/geheim (12 Oct. 1886), no. 461 and Minister of the Colonies, J.P. Sprenger van Eyk, to the board of NHM (7 Sept. 1886).

12.   *Jaarverslag Klattensche Cultuurmaatschappij* 1888. The assets of the PLC amount to 1.6 million guilders.

13.   *Tjerimai* (15 Aug. 1888, 15 Sept. 1888); *De Telefoon* (18 Feb. 1888); NA, NHM, inv. no. 7966, vol. 35, D. Ament, H.M. Ament and J.L. Ament to the creditors of the factories Ament (3 Oct. 1889).

14.   *De Morgenpost* (14 Apr. 1888); *Jaarverslag Nederlandsch-Indische Handelsbank* 1886.

15.   In 1895, of the 34 orchard groves (*perken*) in Banda, one belonged to an Arab, one to a Chinese, one to the Weeskamer (Orphans' Chamber) of Batavia and only two to the Crediet- en Handelsvereeniging Banda. See *Regeerings-almanak* 1895, Appendix UU, pp. 510–13.

16.   Large coconut and nutmeg plantations on the islands of Ceram and Amboina continued to be associated — into the 20th century — with the names of J.A. Delmaar, A. Versteegh, Gebr. Baadilla and Ph.G. Schmidhamer. *Particuliere landbouwnijverheid. Lijst van ondernemingen*, vol. I, pp. 388–89.

17.   *Handboek voor cultuur- en handelsondernemingen* 1910. According to KV 1885, HTK (1885–1886) and Mansvelt, the share of the Principalities in the production of Java sugar was about 17 per cent in 1885. Mansvelt, *Export cultures*, p. 30.

18.   Both of them participated with two-fifths, and Albert's brother-in-law N.P. van den Berg with one-fifth. See Wormser, *Ontginners van Java*, p. 16.

19. "Kort overzicht van oprichting, bestaan en bedrijf van de onderneming 'Oud Djember'".

20. Six companies belonged to the NHM, six to the NILM, eight to the HVA, seven to the Koloniale Bank, four to the Cultuurmaatschappij der Vorstenlanden and six to Van Hoboken. *Handboek voor cultuur- en handelsondernemingen 1910*.

21. The data derive from *Handboek voor cultuur- en handelsondernemingen 1910*; *Regeerings-almanak 1880*; Van den Berg, "Over de productiekosten van de Java-suiker", p. 1.

22. Post, "The Kwik Hoo Tong Trading Society", p. 295.

23. Hobson, *Imperialism*, p. 132.

24. Knight, "The Visible Hand in *Tempo Doeloe*".

25. Maddison, "Dutch Income in and from Indonesia", p. 36.

26. Several sources refer to problems that emerged due to soldiers who had fulfilled their military service and could not make a living, causing trouble in the interior and kampongs. See *Celebes Courant* (13 Jan. 1882); Bossenbroek, *Volk voor Indië*, pp. 357, 364.

27. KV 1870, HTK (1870–1871), Appendix 5766, Tables 4 and 5. The *Koloniaal Verslag* of 1870 reports 22 per cent without a profession, but if we deduct all men above 60 years of age, only 17 per cent remain. For 1885 we estimated 12 per cent unemployment. KV 1870, HTK (1870–1871), Appendix 5766, Tables 4 and 5; KV 1885, HTK (1885–1886), [5.3] pp. 10–11; KV 1902, HTK (1902–1903), Appendix A, IV, pp. 14–15. During those years the number of male adult newcomers outside the army increased 40 per cent (from 6,403 to 9,003), while the number of adult men born in the Indies increased 44 per cent (from 10,080 to 14,906).

28. *Padangsch Handelsblad* (27 Oct. 1881).

29. *Makassaarsch Handelsblad* (7 July 1876); *Celebes Courant* (20 May 1880, 3 Dec. 1880).

30. *Celebes Courant* (4 May 1880).

31. *De Locomotief* (10 Jan. 1878).

32. *Soerabaiasch Handelsblad* (27 Apr. 1887).

33. *De Locomotief* (4 March 1878).

34. *Nieuws- en Advertentieblad van Celebes en Onderhoorigheden* (31 Oct. 1879).

35. *Celebes Courant* (16 March 1883); *De Locomotief* (25 Feb. 1878).

36. Termorshuizen, *P.A. Daum*, pp. 277–87.

37. *De Vorstenlanden* (20 Aug. 1878, 27 Aug. 1878); *De Nieuwe Vorstenlanden* (19 Sept. 1884).

38. *De Telefoon* (21 Aug. 1889); *Tjerimai* (25 Jan. 1888).

39. *Tjerimai* (11 June 1887).

40. *Tjerimai* (21 Aug. 1886).

41. *De Telefoon* (30 May 1890).
42. *De Nieuwe Vorstenlanden* (18 Aug. 1886); *De Telefoon* (17 Jan. 1888, 27 March 1890, 17 Sept. 1890).
43. *De Telefoon* (22 May 1886).
44. Schulte Nordholt and Van Till, "Colonial Criminals in Java", pp. 51, 68–69.
45. *Padangsch Handelsblad* (18 Apr. 1882); *De Nieuwe Vorstenlanden* (18 Feb. 1887).
46. *De Nieuwe Vorstenlanden* (20 Oct. 1884).
47. From *De Telefoon* quoted in the *Celebes Courant* (30 Oct. 1890).
48. *De Telefoon* (20 Aug. 1890).
49. Van Marle, "De groep der Europeanen", p. 319; *Staatsblad van Nederlandsch-Indië* (1898), no. 160, Ordonnantie 1 Dec. 1898.
50. *De Telefoon* (21 Aug. 1890).
51. *De Locomotief* (24 May 1875).
52. *De Telefoon* (6 March 1886, 13 Feb. 1888).
53. *De Telefoon* (30 Jan. 1888, 6 Feb. 1888).
54. *Celebes Courant* (24 Dec. 1881, 14 Jan. 1882); *De Telefoon* (6 March 1886).
55. Cohen, "On the Origin of the Komedie Stamboel"; Cohen, *Komedie Stamboel*.
56. *Het Bondsblad* (18 July 1903, 25 July 1903).
57. *De Oostkust* (8 Sept. 1896), quoted in *Het Nieuw Bataviaasch Handelsblad*.
58. *De Telefoon* (9 Jan. 1897).
59. *Makassaarsche Courant* (22 Jan. 1897).
60. *Soerabaiasch Handelsblad* (31 Dec. 1892).
61. Termorshuizen, *Journalisten en heethoofden*, pp. 264–65.
62. *Soerabaiasch Handelsblad* (26 Jan. 1893).
63. *Celebes Courant* (3 Dec. 1880); *De Telefoon* (4 Sept. 1890, 23 Aug. 1890).
64. *De Locomotief* (27 Sept. 1878, 10 Dec. 1878, 12 Dec. 1878); *Soerabaiasch Handelsblad* (24 Apr. 1880); Termorshuizen, *Journalisten en heethoofden*, pp. 174–77.
65. The programme of "Jong Indië" is printed in Termorshuizen, *Journalisten en heethoofden*, p. 176.
66. *Padangsch Handelsblad* (30 Jan. 1878, 11 May 1878).
67. *De Locomotief* (10 July 1871).
68. Kal, "Een aanzet voor het opstellen van een genealogie van het Indische geslacht Voorneman", p. 50.
69. Bosma, *Karel Zaalberg*, p. 70.
70. Voorneman, *Het Jonge Indië*, pp. 86–87.
71. Kal, "Een aanzet voor het opstellen van een genealogie van het Indische geslacht Voorneman", p. 59.

72. The relevant editions of *Het Indisch Vaderland* were not available for inspection in the Koninklijke Bibliotheek. See also *Soerakarta's Nieuws- en Advertentieblad* (12 Apr. 1881).

73. *De Locomotief* (3 May 1875); *Soerakarta's Nieuws- en Advertentieblad* (21 June 1881, 26 July 1881).

74. *Padangsch Handelsblad* (9 Aug. 1881).

75. The *Padangsch Handelsblad* concluded, to its delight, that the Indies government had by means of this challenged the opinion of several daily newspapers in Java (namely, the *Soerabaiasch Handelsblad*, the *Java-Bode* and the *Bataviaasch Handelsblad*). *Padangsch Handelsblad* (27 Sept. 1881).

76. Bosma, *Karel Zaalberg*, pp. 31–32.

77. Philippus Franciscus Voorneman (Ternate 7 Jan. 1821–Salatiga 8 March 1892); Kal, "Een aanzet voor het opstellen van een genealogie van het Indische geslacht Voorneman", p. 50.

78. *De Preanger-Bode* (2 Feb. 1926).

79. *De Locomotief* (30 Sept. 1879).

80. KB 19 Feb. 1882, no. 12, *Staatsblad van Nederlandsch-Indië*, no. 25, Nieuw reglement op de toekenning van overtogt van Nederland naar Nederlandsch-Indië en omgekeerd. By GB 6 Sept. 1882, no. 5, residents were authorised to send indigent Europeans and soldiers who had fulfilled their service back to Europe.

81. *Celebes Courant* (7 Dec. 1880); *De Telefoon* (29 May 1886, 23 June 1886).

82. Wormser, *Ontginners van Java*, 33; Koch, *Batig slot*, pp. 70–79.

83. *De Indische Opmerker* (20 July 1882). In the *Soerakarta's Nieuws- en Advertentieblad* of 14 July 1882 there was a small report on the Eurasian agricultural colony in Mysore, for which money was collected by a lottery.

84. Bosma, *Karel Zaalberg*, p. 35.

85. *De Nieuwe Vorstenlanden* (6 March 1885, 11 March 1885).

86. Boelen, "Vrijwillige sinjokorpsen", p. 50.

87. *Padangsch Handelsblad* (9 March 1882, 28 March 1882).

88. *De Nieuwe Vorstenlanden* (18 Oct. 1886); *Soerabaiasch Handelsblad* (1 March 1889).

89. *Soerakarta's Nieuws- en Advertentieblad* (3 Feb. 1882).

90. *Soerabaiasch Handelsblad* (28 Feb. 1889).

91. *De Locomotief* (24 Sept. 1878).

92. "Het algemeen voorschrift. Bijblad nr. 3428", pp. 493–516.

93. Curtin, *Death by Migration*, pp. 8, 83; *De Locomotief* (29 May 1875); *Celebes Courant (*13 Jan. 1882).

94. The number of Europeans recruited in the Dutch East Indies increased from 182 in the years 1891–1893 to 256 in 1895. KV 1896, HTK (1896–1897), Appendix C [5.2], p. 42.

95. *Insulinde* (3 Dec. 1869).

96. *Celebes Courant* (29 Oct. 1880).

97. *De Telefoon* (21 Sept. 1889); *De Nieuwe Vorstenlanden* (18 May 1887).
98. Fasseur, "Hoeksteen en struikelblok", p. 147.
99. Chatterjee, *The Nation and Its Fragments*, p. 6.
100. *Padangsch Handelsblad* (22 Feb. 1880).
101. *Padangsch Handelsblad* (9 March 1882).
102. See, for example, the 1850 Singapore census, as published in *The Singapore Free Press* (1 Feb. 1850).
103. *De Nieuwe Vorstenlanden* (7 Jan. 1884).
104. *Padangsch Handelsblad* (28 Feb. 1880).
105. *De Telefoon* (9 June 1886).
106. *Celebes Courant* (15 Feb. 1881).
107. *Celebes Courant* (6 Nov. 1888).
108. Adam, *The Vernacular Press*, pp. 39–40; *De Vorstenlanden* (30 Jan. 1877).
109. Netscher, *Padang in het laatst der* XVIIIe *eeuw*; Van Hogendorp, *Beschouwingen der Nederlandsche bezittingen*, p. 541.
110. *Padangsch Handelsblad* (22 Apr. 1882).
111. W. Halkema, as well as A.M. Voorneman, editor of the *Bintang Timor*, could be added. He did not start his own Dutch paper but contributed to several daily papers, such as *De Telefoon*. See also: Adam, *The Vernacular Press*, p. 44.
112. *Bataviaasch Nieuwsblad* (17 Dec. 1885).
113. *De Telefoon* (17 Feb. 1886).
114. *De Nieuwe Vorstenlanden* (5 Jan. 1886).
115. *De Telefoon* (17 Apr. 1886).
116. *De Telefoon* (13 March 1886, 1 May 1886).
117. *De Telefoon* (22 May 1886).
118. *The Straits Times* (15 Jan. 1876, 5 Jan. 1892).
119. *De Telefoon* (22 May 1886).
120. *De Telefoon* (22 May 1886, 2 June 1886).
121. The idea of an enquiry into pauperism among Europeans had already been put forward by Th.R. Landouw, who saw an important role for the clergy in such a survey. *De Vorstenlanden* (11 Nov. 1885); *De Telefoon* (2 Oct. 1886, 6 Oct. 1886).
122. *De Locomotief* (7 Oct. 1886).
123. *De Locomotief* (11 Oct. 1886).
124. *De Telefoon* (10 Jan. 1887, 14 Jan. 1887).
125. *De Telefoon* (22 Dec. 1886).
126. *De Locomotief* (31 Jan. 1887).
127. The recognition as a legal entity occurred by the GB of 12 July 1887, *Staatsblad van Nederlandsch-Indië* (1887), no. 126.
128. *De Telefoon* (26 Feb. 1887).
129. *De Telefoon* (24 Oct. 1888); *De Nieuwe Vorstenlanden* (23 Sept. 1889). The new editor, H. Pissuise, firmly put an end to the opinion-forming

character of the newspaper and changed its name to *De Telefoon. Dagblad voor Indië*. See: *De Telefoon* (21 Nov. 1889).

130. *De Nieuwe Vorstenlanden* (9 Feb. 1887).
131. The Semarang dignitaries' lawyer, C. Voûte, and notary J.G.L. Houthuysen Sr. rescued the association from decline. *De Telefoon* (17 March 1888, 29 March 1888, 16 Apr. 1888, 26 June 1888).
132. *De Telefoon* (23 July 1889).
133. Bosma, *Karel Zaalberg*, pp. 36–37.
134. *De Telefoon* (23 Sept. 1896).
135. *De Telefoon* (25 March 1897).
136. *Tjerimai* (28 Jan. 1893).
137. *De Telefoon* (25 March 1897).
138. *De Telefoon* (27 March 1888).
139. *Staatsblad van Nederlandsch-Indië* (1864), no. 46.

Chapter 9

1. *Algemeen Handelsblad* quoted in *Makassaarsche Courant* (26 Feb. 1900); *Insulinde* (1 March 1911), pp. 7–8.
2. *Java-Bode* quoted in *De Telefoon* (9 Jan. 1897).
3. Ibid.
4. Van Eyk, *Het openbaar lager onderwijs voor Europeanen*, pp. 29–30, 58.
5. *De Telefoon* (22 Feb. 1890, 19 Feb. 1897); Kohlbrugge, *Blikken in het zieleleven*, pp. 109–53; Boissevain, *Tropisch Nederland*, pp. 263–76.
6. *De Telefoon* (8 Sept. 1896, 9 Jan. 1897).
7. *De Telefoon* (18 Sept. 1889); Termorshuizen, *P.A. Daum*, p. 295.
8. *Soerakarta's Nieuws- en Advertentieblad* (29 March 1881); Bosma, *Karel Zaalberg*, p. 38.
9. Groeneboer, *Gateway to the West*, p. 159.
10. Taylor, *Annie Besant*.
11. De Wit, *Natuur en menschen*, pp. 78, 100.
12. De Jong, *Gedenkboek ter herinnering aan het 25-jarig bestaan der NV Suikerfabriek Tandjong Tirto*, pp. 10, 17.
13. Dye, *Cuban Sugar*, p. 27; *Voorwaarts* (21 Apr. 1904).
14. *Algemeen Handelsblad* quoted in *De Telefoon* (19 Feb. 1897).
15. *De Telefoon* (5 Apr. 1890); *Soerakarta's Nieuws- en Advertentieblad* (13 June 1882).
16. *De Telefoon* (2 Jan. 1895); Bosma, *Karel Zaalberg*, pp. 40–41; *Makassaarsche Courant* (18 July 1898, 25 July 1898).
17. *De Telefoon* (19 Sept. 1894, 13 Oct. 1894, 9 Nov. 1894).
18. *De Locomotief* (7 July 1874); Termorshuizen, *Journalisten en heethoofden*, p. 231.

19. Bosma, *Karel Zaalberg*, p. 41. *Almanak en naamregister 1838*, p. 236 and *Almanak en naamregister 1835*, p. 173.
20. *De Telefoon* (26 Nov. 1895, 9 Dec. 1895, 18 Jan. 1896).
21. *De Telefoon* (6 Nov. 1895).
22. Naoroji, *Poverty and Un-British Rule*.
23. *De Telefoon* (24 Dec. 1895, 22 Sept. 1896).
24. *De Telefoon* (25 Jan. 1896).
25. Kuitenbrouwer, *Nederland en de opkomst van het moderne imperialisme*, p. 156.
26. *Bataviaasch Nieuwsblad* (16 Jan. 1897).
27. De Jong, "Lotgevallen van de drie broers Douwes Dekker", p. 32.
28. Tichelman, *Socialisme in Indonesië*, p. 118.
29. The brochure of Andriesse and Stroo Westerman has been lost. See in addition *Soerabaija Courant* (2 July 1898), *Sumatra Courant* (23 May 1898).
30. *De Locomotief* (15 March 1898).
31. *Bataviaasch Nieuwsblad* (9 June 1898, 26 Apr. 1899); *Makassaarsche Courant* (3 May 1899).
32. *Java-Bode* (13 Dec. 1898).
33. HTK (1905–1906), p. 469.
34. Bosma, *Karel Zaalberg*, pp. 122–23; Fasseur, *De Indologen*, pp. 334–35.
35. *Makassaarsche Courant* (25 Sept. 1899).
36. *Bataviaasch Nieuwsblad* (13 Oct. 1902, 18 June 1901).
37. Bosma, *Karel Zaalberg*, p. 128.
38. Bosma, *Karel Zaalberg*, p. 147.
39. Bosma, *Karel Zaalberg*, pp. 126–27.
40. In 1909, 650 out of 2,000 European and 861 out of 6,000 Indonesian railway employees were members of the *Staatsspoorbond* (State Railway Union). *Bataviaasch Nieuwsblad* (6 Sept. 1910, 21 June 1911); Ingleson, *In Search of Justice*, p. 74.
41. *Nieuw Padangsch Handelsblad* (2 June 1899).
42. Henley, *Nationalism and Regionalism*, pp. 72–73, 76.
43. Bosma, *Karel Zaalberg*, p. 83.
44. NA, MvK II, Verbaal 23 Dec. 1901, Advice of the Council of the Indies (10 May 1901).
45. Lis Lange, *White, Poor and Angry*.
46. *Bataviaasch Nieuwsblad* (4 Jan. 1902).
47. *Uitkomsten der pauperisme-enquête. Algemeen verslag*, p. 4.
48. Bosma, *Karel Zaalberg*, p. 86.
49. Ming, "Barracks-Concubinage in the Indies", pp. 82–83.
50. Bosma, *Karel Zaalberg*, p. 89.
51. GB 20 June 1901, no. 10, *Staatsblad van Nederlandsch-Indië*, Bijblad 5611.

52. De Graaff, *Nota over het verleenen van landbouwcrediet*, pp. 13–14, 28; *Staatsblad van Nederlandsch-Indië* (10 Aug. 1904), no. 326.

53. In 1916, in addition to the 156 allotments according to *Staatsblad van Nederlandsch-Indië* (10 Aug. 1904), no. 326, another 100 allotments were registered as intended for small-scale agriculture and horticulture. See *Particuliere landbouwnijverheid. Lijst van ondernemingen*, vol. I, pp. 400–409.

54. *Particuliere landbouwnijverheid. Lijst van ondernemingen*, vol. II.

55. GB 4 Sept. 1900, no. 30, *Staatsblad van Nederlandsch-Indië*, Bijblad 5523.

56. Circulaire van de Gouvernementssecretaris (7 Jan. 1905), no. 91, *Staatsblad van Nederlandsch-Indië*, Bijblad 6193.

57. Those advertisements even appeared in the *Bataviaasch Nieuwsblad*, led by the Indo-European journalist Karel Zaalberg. *Bataviaasch Nieuwsblad* (1 Sept. 1910).

58. *Volkstelling 1930*, p. 19; *Jaarcijfers voor het Koninkrijk der Nederlanden 1912*, p. 17.

59. Swierenga, "The Delayed Transition", p. 423.

60. *Orgaan der Ned. Vereeniging van Spoor- en Tramwegpersoneel* (19 Oct. 1907).

61. Steengracht, "Het Indo-vraagstuk en de rassenhaat".

62. *Voorwaarts* (1 Sept. 1904), p. 73.

63. *Bataviaasch Nieuwsblad* (21 Jan. 1907, 24 Aug. 1921); *Bataviaasch Handelsblad* (31 Oct. 1913).

64. Bosma, *Karel Zaalberg*, p. 188.

65. Van der Wal, *De opkomst van de nationalistische beweging*, p. 63.

66. Douwes Dekker, *Een sociogenetische grondwet*, p. 7.

67. Chatterjee, *The Nation and Its Fragments*, p. 53.

68. *De Expres* (6 July 1912).

69. Vasconcelos, *A Mexican Ulysses*; Freyre, *The Masters and the Slaves*.

70. *Java-Bode* (16 Oct. 1912).

71. Chauvel, *Nationalists, Soldiers and Separatists*, pp. 72–73.

72. Bosma, *Karel Zaalberg*, p. 169.

73. Adam, *The Vernacular Press*, p. 115.

74. *Jong-Indië* (6 Aug. 1910), pp. 70–72; *Bondsblad* (18 Feb. 1911), p. 54; *Insulinde* (1 Dec. 1910), pp. 9–10.

75. *Insulinde* (16 June 1910), pp. 4–6.

76. [Douwes Dekker], *Aansluiting tusschen blank en bruin*.

77. *Soerabaiasch Handelsblad* (14 March 1908).

78. *Het Tijdschrift* (1 March 1912), 433.

79. Bosma, *Karel Zaalberg*, pp. 217–23.

80. *Het Tijdschrift* (1 Oct. 1912), p. 99.

81. Bosma, *Karel Zaalberg*, pp. 224–27.

82. *De Padanger* (13 Oct. 1912, 8 Nov. 1912).

83. Koch, "Dr. E.F.E. Douwes Dekker", p. 59.
84. Shiraishi, *An Age in Motion*, pp. xii–xiii; Bosma, *Karel Zaalberg*, p. 5.
85. Van der Wal, *De opkomst van de nationalistische beweging*, p. 156.
86. *Het Tijdschrift* (15 May 1913), p. 571.
87. Bosma, *Karel Zaalberg*, p. 73.
88. See Fasseur, "Hoeksteen en struikelblok", pp. 155–57.
89. The Ambonese political leaders W.K. Tehupeyorie and R.P. de Queljoe were not elected but were appointed by the governor-general.
90. In 1913, 4,527 men and 1,972 women migrated to the colonies; in 1917 the figures were 1,603 men and 727 women; and it was not until 1920 that these numbers returned to prewar levels. See *Statistiek van den loop der bevolking in Nederland over 1921*, pp. 92–93.
91. *Bataviaasch Nieuwsblad* (3 July 1917).
92. Groeneboer, *Gateway to the West*, p. 245.
93. *De Nieuwe Vorstenlanden* (30 June 1916).
94. In the Post Office and Telegraph Services, equal pay for Indonesian and European staff was implemented on 20 July 1917. See GB 20 July 1917, no. 69.
95. In 1917 Insulinde was able to start a branch on Ambon that obtained the support of the local branch of the "Vereeniging Ambonsch Studiefonds". Chauvel, *Nationalists, Soldiers and Separatists*, pp. 74, 90–92. For the Principalities see Shiriashi, *An Age in Motion*, pp. 157–74 and Larson, *Prelude to Revolution*, pp. 108–10.
96. *De Beweging* (24 May 1919), p. 553. This number increased later that year to 23,000 members. See Bosma, *Karel Zaalberg*, p. 300.
97. Namely, the *Bataviaasch Handelsblad*, the *Bataviaasch Nieuwsblad* and *De Reflector*.
98. *De Beweging* (3 July 1920), p. 416.
99. *Bataviaasch Nieuwsblad* (12 March 1921).
100. Taselaar, *De Nederlandse koloniale lobby*, pp. 220–21.
101. Idenburg in HTK 1919, p. 635; De Bruijn and Puchinger, *Briefwisseling*, pp. 292–94, 307.
102. *Vrijzinnig Weekblad* (26 May 1922), pp. 241–43; Henley, *Nationalism and Regionalism*, pp. 41, 59; *Handelingen van de Volksraad*, 1918, Eerste zitting, pp. 207–209.
103. Taselaar, *De Nederlandse koloniale lobby*, p. 50.
104. *De Suikerbond* (15 Dec. 1922).
105. Bosma, *Karel Zaalberg*, p. 388.
106. *De Taak* (11 Aug. 1923), p. 1629.
107. Koch, *Verantwoording*, p. 124.
108. Douwes Dekker, *Indië. Handboek voor den Indischen nationalist*, title page.

Epilogue

1.   *Volkstelling 1930*, p. 135.
2.   Groeneboer, *Gateway to the West*, p. 246; Doeve, *Een Indisch-burgerschap*, p. 14.
3.   Couperus, *Oostwaarts*, pp. 124–26.
4.   Compare, for example, the movies of J.C. Lamster, such as *Autotocht door Bandoeng* (1913), Willy Mullens's *Soerabaia* (1929), or the movies made by the film studio Umbgrove — an old family from the Indies — in Surabaya in 1929. Filmmuseum, Amsterdam, Collection of films from the Netherlands Indies.
5.   Mrázek, *Engineers of Happy Land*.
6.   Locher-Scholten, "Summer Dresses and Canned Food".
7.   Van Dijk, "Sarong, Jubbah, and Trousers", pp. 58–71.
8.   Hering, *Soekarno*, pp. 12–13.
9.   Hering, *Thamrin*, pp. 18–45.
10. Van Marle, "De groep der Europeanen", p. 319; Coppel, "Revisiting Furnivall's 'Plural Society'".

Bibliography

Unpublished records

Arsip Nasional Republik Indonesia, Jakarta (ANRI)
Archive Heemraden
Archive Kerk/diakonie
Archive Residentie Batavia
Archive Residentie Djocjakarta
Archive Residentie Makassar
Archive Residentie Semarang
Archive Residentie Surabaya
Archive Residentie Surakarta
Archive Schepenen

Centraal Bureau voor Genealogie, 's-Gravenhage (CBG)
Archive Suringar
Microfiches Trouwboeken (register of marriages), Batavia
Microfiches Archive Wolvendaalse Kerk, Colombo

Filmmuseum, Amsterdam
Collection of films from the Netherlands East Indies

Koninklijk Instituut voor Taal-, Land- en Volkenkunde (*Royal Netherlands Institute
    of Southeast Asian and Caribbean Studies*), *Leiden* (KITLV)
Afdeling Historische Documentatie (Department of Historical Documentation)
    (Hisdoc)
Collection Westerse handschriften (Western manuscripts)
* H 579, Engelbert van Bevervoorde, "Eigenaardigheden en
    bezienswaardigheden van Jogjakarta", 1903
* H 873, W.H. Coert, "Geschiedenis van de familie Coert 1756–
    1963"
* H 928, Brieven en foto's van de Jogjase families Wieseman en
    Broese van Groenau, 1833–1908
* H 1007, E. Houtman-Mesman en A. Bouman-Houtman, "Uit
    tempo doeloe. Herinneringen aan de jaren 1850–1880 in Zuid-
    Celebes"
    Memorie van overgave J.H. Tobias (1857)
    Memorie van overgave C. Bosscher (1859)

Koninklijke Bibliotheek (Royal Library), 's-Gravenhage (KoBib)
Afdeling Handschriften (Manuscripts Department)
Collection Neumann

Maritiem Museum Prins Hendrik, Rotterdam
Dossier D. van Lennep

Nationaal Archief, 's-Gravenhage (NA)
Archive Hoge Regering van Batavia
Archive Ministerie van Koloniën 1814–1849 (MvK I)
Archive Ministerie van Koloniën 1850–1900 (MvK II)
Archive Nederlandsche Handel-Maatschappij (NHM)
Archive Schepenbank te Batavia
Archive Verenigde Oostindische Compagnie (VOC)
Archive Wolvendaalse Kerk, Colombo (microfilm)
Collection Du Bus de Gisignies
Collection Cnoll
Collection Fagel
Collection R. Filliettaz Bousquet
Collection I.D. Fransen van de Putte
Collection Radermacher
Collection G.J.C. Schneither
Family collection Van Beresteyn
Family collection Couperus
Stamboeken burgerlijke ambtenaren Oost-Indië

Oesterreichisches Staatsarchiv, Vienna
Haus-, Hof und Staatsarchiv

Openbare Bibliotheek (Public Library), Rotterdam
Manuscript 86 N 11, Beschryving van de inwoond van Batavia, n.d. [*ca.* 1650]

Rijksmuseum Amsterdam
Collection Jan Brandes

Sri Lanka National Archives, Colombo
Dutch records

Universiteitsbibliotheek (University Library), Leiden (UBL)
Collection P.J. Veth

Private Collections
Adtornisch Papers (Gillian Maclaine, thanks to Roger Knight)
Sonja Weijnschenk, Testament George Weijnschenk

Newspapers

Bataviaasch Handelsblad (1858–1895)
Bataviaasch Nieuwsblad (1885–1942)
Bataviasche Koloniale Courant (1810–1811)
Bataviasche Courant (1816–1828)
Celebes-Courant. Nieuws-, handels- en advertentieblad (1880–1894)
Colombo Journal (1832–1833)
Dagblad van Celebes (1868–1869)
De Expres (1912–1914)
De Indische Opmerker (1882–1888)
Insulinde. Nieuws- en advertentieblad voor Java's Oosthoek (1869–1871)
Java-Bode. Nieuws-, handels- en advertentieblad voor Nederlandsch-Indië (1852–1942)
Java Government Gazette (1812–1816)
Javasche Courant (1828–1949)
De Locomotief. Samarangsch handels- en advertentieblad (1863–1942)
Makassaarsch Handelsblad (1868–1883)
Makassaarsche Courant. Nieuws-, handels- en advertentieblad (1894–1942)
Makassaarsch Weekblad (1891–1893)
De Morgenpost. Algemeen nieuws- en advertentieblad (1888)
De Nieuwe Vorstenlanden. Nieuws- en advertentieblad voor Midden Java (1883–1930)
Het Nieuw Bataviaasch Handelsblad (1895–1897)
Nieuw Padangsch Handelsblad (1882–1900)
Nieuws- en Advertentieblad voor Celebes en Onderhoorigheden (1879–1880)
De Oostpost. Letterkundig, wetenschappelijk en commercieel nieuws- en advertentieblad (1853–1858)
De Padanger. Dagblad voor Sumatra's Westkust, Atjeh en Benkoelen (1900–1925)
Padangsch Handelsblad. Nieuws-, handels- en advertentieblad (1872–1882)
De Preanger-Bode. Nieuws- en advertentieblad voor de Preangerregentschappen. Tevens mailcourant (1896–1923)
Samarangsch Advertentieblad (1845–1863)
The Singapore Free Press and Mercantile Advertiser (1835–1962)
Soerabaiasch Handelsblad (1865–1942)
Soerabaija Courant (1861–1905)
Soerakarta's Nieuws- en Advertentieblad (1879–1883)
Staatsblad van Nederlandsch-Indië (1816–1948)
The Straits Times (1845–)
Sumatra Courant (1862–1900)
De Telefoon. Weekblad voor Indië (1886–1897). From 3 Feb. 1886 until 30 Oct. 1886 with the addition *Orgaan voor den Indo-Europeaan*
Tjerimai. Nieuws- en advertentieblad voor Cheribon en Omstreken (1885–1915)
De Vorstenlanden. Nieuws- en advertentieblad (1870–1879)

Periodicals

De Beweging. Algemeen politiek weekblad tevens officiëel orgaan der Nationaal Indische Partij (1919–1921)

Het Bondsblad. Het orgaan van de Indische Bond (1898–1905). Continued as *Stem van Indië. Sociaal-oeconomisch weekblad. Orgaan van de vereeniging "De Indische Bond"* (Batavia 1905–1911)

Indische Kroniek. Weekblad voor Nederlandsch-Indië (1911–1912)

Insulinde. Orgaan van de vereeniging "Insulinde" (1910–1913)

Jong-Indië. Een algemeen weekblad (1908–1911)

Orgaan der Ned. Vereeniging van Spoor- en Tramwegpersoneel (1890–1915)

Soerja Soemirat. Weekblad gewijd aan de belangen van maatschappij, huisgezin, onderwijs en opvoeding in Nederlandsch-Indië (1892–1903)

De Suikerbond. Orgaan van den bond van geëmployeerden in de suikerindustrie en aanverwante bedrijven in Nederlandsch-Indië (1917–1940)

De Taak. Algemeen Indisch weekblad (1917–1925)

Het Tijdschrift (1911–1913)

Voorwaarts. Vakblad voor spoor- en tramwezen, post- telegraafdienst (Jogjakarta 1899–1905?)

Vrijzinnig Weekblad. Orgaan van den Nederlandsch-Indischen Vrijzinnigen Bond (1917–1928)

Published works

Abeyasekere, Susan, *Jakarta. A History.* Oxford: Oxford University Press, 1987.

Adam, Ahmat B., *The Vernacular Press and the Emergence of Modern Indonesian Consciousness (1855–1913).* Studies on Southeast Asia 17. Ithaca: Cornell University Southeast Asia Program, 1995.

[Addison, G.A.], *Original Familiar Correspondence between Residents in India. Including Sketches of Java.* Edinburgh: W. Blackwood & Sons, 1846.

Adelante, "Concubinaat bij de ambtenaren van het Binnenlandsch Bestuur in Nederlandsch-Indië", *Tijdschrift voor Nederlandsch-Indië* 2de nieuwe serie 2 (1898): 304–14.

Alexander, "Het Korps Pupillen te Gombong", *Indisch Militair Tijdschrift* 10, 2 (1879): 365–77, 516–27.

Alexandrowicz, C.H., *An Introduction to the History of the Law of Nations in the East Indies (16th, 17th and 18th Centuries).* Oxford: Clarendon Press, 1967.

"De Alfoeren in het Nederlandsch-Indische leger", *Indisch Militair Tijdschrift* 10, 1 (1879): 99–108.

Algemeen verslag van den staat van het schoolwezen in Nederlandsch-Indië, onder ultimo december 1833. N.p. [Batavia]: Landsdrukkerij, n.d. [1834].

Algemeen verslag van den staat van het schoolwezen in Nederlandsch-Indie, onder ultimo december 1845. Batavia: Landsdrukkerij, 1849.

Algemeen verslag van den staat van het schoolwezen in Nederlandsch-Indie, onder ultimo december 1849. Batavia: Landsdrukkerij, 1849.

"Het algemeen voorschrift. Bijblad no. 3428", *Indisch Militair Tijdschrift* 15, 1 (1884): 493–516.

"Algemeene en bijzondere narigten omtrent het schoolwezen in Nederlandsch Indie", *Bijdragen over het Schoolwezen* 2 (1831): 572–90.

Allahar, Anton L., *Class, Politics, and Sugar in Colonial Cuba*. Caribbean Studies 2. Lewiston: Edwin Mellon Press, 1990.

Almanak en naamregister van Nederlandsch-Indië voor het jaar [...]. Batavia: Landsdrukkerij, 1827–1864.

Almanak van Nederlandsch-Indië voor het jaar [...]. Batavia: Landsdrukkerij, 1817–1826.

Amselle, Jean-Loup, *Mestizo Logics. Anthropology of Identity in Africa and Elsewhere.* Stanford: Stanford University Press, 1998.

Anderson, Benedict, *Imagined Communities. Reflections on the Origin and Spread of Nationalism.* London: Verso, 1991 (1st ed. London: Verso, 1983).

Appadurai, Arjun, "Number in the Colonial Imagination", in: Carol A. Breckenridge and Peter van der Veer, ed., *Orientalism and the Postcolonial Predicament. Perspectives on South Asia.* Philadelphia: University of Pennsylvania Press, 1993, pp. 314–29.

[Arnold, Joseph], *The Java Journal of Dr. Joseph Arnold, 3 September–17 December 1815.* John Bastin, ed. Wassenaar: n.n., 1973. Also published as: John Bastin, ed., "The Java Journal of Dr. Joseph Arnold", *Journal of the Malaysian Branch of the Royal Asiatic Society* 46, 1 (1973): 1–92.

Aubin, Jean, "Les Persans au Siam sous le règne de Narai (1656–1688)", *Mare Luso-Indicum* 4 (1980), pp. 95–126.

[Bakhuizen van den Brink, Ch.R.], "De inlandsche burgers in de Molukken", *Bijdragen tot de Taal-, Land- en Volkenkunde* 70 (1915): 595–649.

Ballhatchet, Kenneth, *Race, Sex and Class under the Raj. Imperial Attitudes and Policies and Their Critics, 1793–1905.* London: Weidenfeld and Nicolson, 1980.

Barchewitz, Ernst Christoph, *Allerneueste und Wahrhafte Ost-Indianische Reise-Beschreibung [...].* Chemnitz: Stözeln, 1730.

Barendse, R.J., *The Arabian Seas 1640–1700.* Leiden: Research School CNWS, 1998.

Bartholo, *De ambtenaar bij het Binnenlandsch Bestuur in Oost-Indie, meer bijzonder de kontroleur bij de landelijke inkomsten en kultures. Eenige losse schetsen en opmerkingen.* 's-Gravenhage: M. Nijhoff, 1861.

Bastiaans, W.Ch.J., *Figuren uit de Indische journalistiek.* Groningen: [the author], 1975.

Bastin, John Sturgus, *The Development of Raffles' Ideas on the Land Rent System in Java and the Work of the Mackenzie Land Tenure Commission.* 's-Gravenhage: H.L. Smits, 1954.

Basu, Dilip K., ed., *The Rise and Growth of the Colonial Port Cities in Asia*. Center for South and Southeast Asia Studies, University of California, Monograph Series 25. Lanham: University Press of America, 1985.

Baud, W.A., ed., *De semi-officiële en particuliere briefwisseling tussen J.C. Baud en J.J. Rochussen 1845–1851 en enige daarop betrekking hebbende andere stukken* (3 volumes). Assen: Van Gorcum, 1983.

Beknopte geschiedenis van het R.K. weeshuis te Semarang 1809–1909. Semarang: Van Dorp, 1909.

Berg, Joop van den, *Het verloren volk. Een geschiedenis van de Banda-eilanden*. 's-Gravenhage: BZZTôH, 1995.

Berg, N.P. van den, *Over de productiekosten van de Java-suiker*. N.p.: n.n, 1886 (reprinted from *Algemeen Dagblad van Nederlandsch-Indië*, 23 and 24 Sept. 1886).

Berg, N.P. van den, "Een smeekschrift van de Bataviasche burgerij", *Tijdschrift voor Indische Taal-, Land- en Volkenkunde. Uitgegeven door het Bataviaasch Genootschap voor Kunsten en Wetenschappen* 22 (1875): 532–67.

Berg, N.P. van den, "De Bataviasche decemberbeweging van 1795", in: Idem, *Uit de dagen der Compagnie. Geschiedkundige schetsen*. Haarlem: Tjeenk Willink, 1904, pp. 256–304.

Berge, Tom van den, *Karel Frederik Holle. Theeplanter in Indië 1829–1896*. Amsterdam: Bert Bakker, 1998.

Bertolacci, Anthony, *A View of the Agricultural, Commercial, and Financial Interests of Ceylon*. The Ceylon Historical Journal, Monograph Series 8. 2nd ed. Dehiwala: Tisara Prakasakayo, 1983 (1st ed. London: Black, Parbury and Allen, 1817).

"Beschryving van de stad Batavia", *Verhandelingen van het Bataviaasch Genootschap van Kunsten en Wetenschappen* 1 (1779): 42–70.

Bisschop Grevelink, A.H., *De Bataviasche mei-beweging van 1848 in haren oorsprong en gevolgen herdacht*. 's-Gravenhage: Susan, 1881.

Bitterli, Urs, *Cultures in Conflict. Encounters between European and Non-European Cultures, 1492–1800*. Cambridge: Polity Press, 1993.

Bleeker, P., *Reis door de Minahassa en den Molukschen archipel gedaan in de maanden september en oktober 1855 in het gevolg van den gouverneur generaal mr. A.J. Duymaer van Twist* (2 volumes). Batavia: Lange & Co, 1856.

Bleeker, [P.], "Bijdragen tot de geneeskundige topographie van Batavia IV. Bevolking", *Tijdschrift voor Neêrland's Indië* 8, 2 (1846): 445–506.

Blussé, Leonard, *Strange Company. Chinese Settlers, Mestizo Women and the Dutch in VOC Batavia*. Verhandelingen van het Koninklijk Instituut voor Taal-, Land- en Volkenkunde 122. Dordrecht and Riverton: Foris, 1986.

Boele, Cora, *De jaren van de Javaanse gasfabrieken 1863–1905. Een episode uit de geschiedenis van het OGEM-concern*. Rotterdam: Waterstad, 1990.

Boelen, Anton, "Vrijwillige sinjokorpsen. Ernst of kortswijl?", *Indisch Militair Tijdschrift* 15, 1 (1884): 50–55, 203–18.

B[oer], W.R., "Statistieke opgave der residentie Batavia", *Bijdragen tot de kennis der Nederlandsche en vreemde koloniën, bijzonder betrekkelijk de vrijlating der slaven* 4 (1847): 550–58.

Bonacich, E., "A Theory of Middlemen Minorities", *American Sociological Review* 38 (1973): 583–94.

Boissevain, Charles, *Tropisch Nederland. Indrukken eener reis door Nederlandsch-Indië*. Haarlem: Tjeenk Willink, 1909.

Bosch, K.D., *De Nederlandse beleggingen in de Verenigde Staten*. Amsterdam: Elsevier, 1948.

Bosma, Ulbe, *Karel Zaalberg. Journalist en strijder voor de Indo*. Verhandelingen van het Koninklijk Instituut voor Taal-, Land- en Volkenkunde 175. Leiden: KITLV Press, 1997.

Bosma, Ulbe, and Remco Raben, "De macht van de pen. Indo-Europeanen en het gouvernement", in: Wim Willems a.o., ed., *Uit Indië geboren. Vier eeuwen familiegeschiedenis*. Zwolle: Waanders, 1997, pp. 83–96.

Bossenbroek, M.P., *Van Holland naar Indië. Het transport van koloniale troepen voor het Oost-Indische leger 1815–1909*. Amsterdam and Dieren: De Bataafsche Leeuw, 1986.

Bossenbroek, M.P., *Volk voor Indië. De werving van Europese militairen voor de Nederlandse koloniale dienst 1814–1909*. Amsterdam: Van Soeren, 1992.

Bougas, Wayne A., "Patani in the Beginning of the XVIIth Century", *Archipel* 39 (1990): 113–38.

Boxer, C.R., *Race Relations in the Portuguese Colonial Empire 1415–1825*. Oxford: Clarendon Press, 1963.

Braga-Blake, Myrna, and Ann Ebert-Oehlers, ed., *Singapore Eurasians. Memories and Hopes*. Singapore: The Eurasian Association, 1992.

Brakkee, C.H.G.H., *Pa van der Steur vader van 7000 kinderen*. N.p.: n.n., n.d. [1981].

Bree, L. de, *Gedenkboek van de Javasche Bank, 1828–24 januari–1928*. (2 volumes) Weltevreden: n.n., 1928.

Bree, L. de, *Nederlandsch-Indië in de twintigste eeuw. Schets van den vooruitgang en de beteekenis van Ned.-Indië in de jaren 1900–1913*. Batavia: Kolff, 1916.

Breman, J.C., *Koelies, planters en koloniale politiek. Het arbeidsregime op de grootlandbouwondernemingen aan Sumatra's Oostkust in het begin van de twintigste eeuw*. Verhandelingen van het Koninklijk Instituut voor Taal-, Land- en Volkenkunde 123. Leiden: KITLV Press, 1992 (1st ed. Dordrecht: Foris, 1987).

Brink, Jan ten, *Oost-Indische dames en heeren. Vier bijdragen tot de kennis van de zeden en gebruiken der Europeesche maatschappij in Nederlandsch-Indië*. Leiden: Sijthoff, 1885 (1st ed. Arnhem: Thieme, 1866).

Broersma, R., *De Pamanoekan- en Tjiassem-landen. Bijdrage tot de kennis van het particulier landbezit op Java*. Batavia: Papyrus, n.d. [1912].

Brommer, Bea, and Dirk de Vries, *Batavia*. Historische plattegronden van Nederlandse steden 4. Alphen aan den Rijn: Canaletto, 1992.

Brug, Peter Harmen van der, *Malaria en malaise. De VOC in Batavia in de achttiende eeuw*. Amsterdam: De Bataafsche Leeuw, 1994.

Bruggen M.P. van, R.S. Wassink a.o., *Jogja en Solo. Beeld van de Vorstensteden*. Purmerend: Asia Maior, 1998.

Bruijn, J. de, and G. Puchinger, ed., *Briefwisseling Kuyper-Idenburg*. Franeker: Wever, 1985.

Bruijn, J.R., F.S. Gaastra and I. Schöffer, *Dutch-Asiatic Shipping in the 17th and 18th Centuries*. Rijks Geschiedkundige Publicatiën grote serie 165–167 (3 volumes). 's-Gravenhage: Nijhoff, 1979–1987.

Bruijn, Max de, and Remco Raben, ed., *The World of Jan Brandes. Painter in Asia, Africa and Europe, 1743–1808*. Amsterdam and Zwolle: Waanders, 2003.

Brummel, L., "Achttiende-eeuws kolonialisme in brieven", *Bijdragen en Mededelingen betreffende de Geschiedenis der Nederlanden* 87 (1972): 171–204.

Brummelhuis, Han ten, *Merchant, Courtier and Diplomat. A History of the Contacts between the Netherlands and Thailand*. Lochem and Gent: De tijdstroom, 1987.

Buddingh, S.A., *Neêrlands-Oost-Indië. Reizen over Java, Madura, Makasser, Saleijer, Bima, Menado, Sangier-eilanden [...] gedaan gedurende het tijdvak van 1852–1857* (3 volumes). Rotterdam: Wijt, 1859–1861.

Buddingh, S.A., "Weeshuis te Parapattan", *Tijdschrift voor Neêrland's Indië* 3, 2 (1840): 253–59.

Bulley, Anne, ed., *Free Mariner. John Adolphus Pope in the East Indies 1786–1821*. London: British Association for Cemeteries in South Asia, 1992.

Butcher, John G., *The British in Malaya 1880–1941. The Social History of a European Community in Colonial South-East Asia*. Kuala Lumpur: Oxford University Press, 1979.

Campen, C.F.H., *Het Korps Pupillen te Gombong. Gids voor belanghebbenden en belangstellenden*. Batavia: Landsdrukkerij, 1886.

Cannadine, David, *Ornamentalism. How the British Saw Their Empire*. New York: Oxford University Press, 2001.

Canter Visscher, J., *Mallabaarse brieven, behelzende eene naukeurige beschrijving van de kust van Mallabaar [...]*. Leeuwarden: Ferwerda, 1743.

Canter Visscher, J.Th., "De waarheid over 22 Mei 1848", *Tijdschrift voor Nederlandsch-Indië* nieuwe serie 10, 2 (1881): 401–34.

Capellen, G.A.G.Ph. van der, "Het journaal van den baron Van der Capellen op zijne reis door de Molukko's", *Tijdschrift voor Nederlandsch Indië* 17, 2 (1855): 281–315, 357–96.

Caplan, Lionel, *Children of Colonialism. Anglo-Indians in a Postcolonial World*. Oxford and New York: Berg, 2001.

Cardon, R., "Portuguese Malacca", *Journal of the Malaysian Branch of the Royal Asiatic Society* 12, 2 (1934): 1–23.

Carey, Peter, "Changing Javanese Perceptions of the Chinese Communities in Central Java, 1755–1825", *Indonesia* 37 (Apr. 1984): 1–47.

Carlos, Poldi, *Johannes van der Steur. Een Haarlemse diamant in de Gordel van Smaragd.* Gouda: Saueressig, n.d. [1998].

Chatterjee, Partha, *The Nation and Its Fragments. Colonial and Postcolonial Histories.* Princeton: Princeton University Press, 1993.

Chauvel, Richard, *Nationalists, Soldiers and Separatists. The Ambonese Islands from Colonialism to Revolt 1880–1950.* Verhandelingen van het Koninklijk Instituut voor Taal-, Land- en Volkenkunde 143. Leiden: KITLV Press, 1990.

Chijs, J.A. van der, *Geschiedenis van de gouvernements thee-cultuur op Java. Zamengesteld voornamelijk uit officiëele bronnen.* Batavia: Landsdrukkerij, 1903.

Christiaans, P.A., *Het gereconstrueerde huwelijksregister van Djokjakarta 1817–1905.* Bronnenpublikaties van de Indische Genealogische Vereniging 3. 's-Gravenhage: Indische Genealogische Vereniging, 1994.

Christiaans, P.A., *Het rooms-katholieke doopregister van Semarang 1809–1829.* Bronnenpublikaties van de Indische Genealogische Vereniging 15. 's-Gravenhage: Indische Genealogische Vereniging, 2002.

Christiaans, P.A., "Van Stralendorff", in: *Jaarboek van het Centraal Bureau voor Genealogie en het Iconographisch Bureau* 34. 's-Gravenhage: Centraal Bureau voor Genealogie, 1980, pp. 125–41.

Christiaans, P.A., "De Europese bevolking van Malakka onder het laatste Nederlandse bestuur, 1818–1825", *Jaarboek van het Centraal Bureau voor Genealogie en het Iconographisch Bureau* 40. 's-Gravenhage, Centraal Bureau voor Genealogie, 1986, pp. 257–87.

Christiaans, P.A., "Ondaatje", *De Indische Navorscher* 2, 4 (1989): 145–51.

Christiaans, P.A. "Gegevens voor de samenstelling van de genealogie van de familie Rijkschroeff", *De Indische Navorscher* 5, 4 (1992): 173–84.

Christiaans, P.A., "Naamlijst van de oprichters van de loge "Mataram" te Jogjakarta", *De Indische Navorscher* 8, 1 (1995): 64–82.

Christiaans, P.A., "Makassaarse families I. De familie Weijergang I", *De Indische Navorscher* 9, 2 (1996): 76–80.

Christiaans, P.A., "Europese bevolking van Ternate". Unpublished manuscript, 's-Gravenhage, 1987.

Christiaans, P.A., "Genealogie familie Mesman". Unpublished manuscript, 's-Gravenhage, n.d.

Christiaans, P.A., and D. van Duijn, "De 'jet-set' van Batavia anno 1763", *De Indische Navorscher* 3, 2 (1990): 65–88; Idem 3, 3 (1990): 132–35; Idem 3, 4 (1990): 164–78; Idem 4, 1 (1991): 33–40.

Christiaans, P.A., and D. van Duijn, "Genealogie van de Indische tak van de familie Van Angelbeek", *De Indische Navorscher* 8, 1 (1995): 1–8.

Clercq, F.S.A. de, *Bijdragen tot de kennis der residentie Ternate*. Leiden: Brill, 1890.

Coeverden, J.S. van, "Beknopt overzigt van het eiland Ternate", *Tijdschrift voor Neêrland's Indië* 2 (1844): 195–221.

Cohen, Matthew Isaac, "On the Origin of the Komedie Stamboel. Popular Culture, Colonial Society, and Parsi Theatre Movement", *Bijdragen tot de Taal-, Land- en Volkenkunde* 157, 2 (2001): 313–57.

Cohen, Matthew Isaac, *The Komedie Stamboel. Popular Theatre in Colonial Indonesia, 1891–1903*. Leiden: KITLV Press, 2006.

Cohen Stuart, C.P., *Gedenkboek der Nederlandsch-Indische theecultuur 1824–1924*. Bandoeng and Weltevreden: Proefstation voor Thee, 1924.

Colin-Thomé, Percy, "The Portuguese Burghers and the Dutch Burghers of Sri Lanka", *Journal of the Dutch Burgher Union of Ceylon* 62 (1985): 169–217.

Comaroff, John, "Reflections on the Colonial State, in South Africa and Elsewhere. Factions, Fragments, Facts and Fictions", *Social Identities. Journal for the Study of Race, Nation and Culture* 4, 3 (1998): 317–25.

Coolhaas, W.Ph., and J. van Goor, ed., *Generale missiven van gouverneurs-generaal en raden aan Heren XVII der Verenigde Oostindische Compagnie*. Rijks Geschiedkundige Publicatiën grote serie 104, 112, 125, 134, 150, 159, 164, 193, 205, 232 and 250 (11 volumes). 's-Gravenhage: Nijhoff, 1960–2004.

Coppel, Charles A., "Revisiting Furnivall's 'Plural Society'. Colonial Java as a Mestizo Society?" *Ethnic and Racial Studies* 20, 3 (1997): 562–79.

Cordiner, James A., *A Description of Ceylon*. The Ceylon Historical Journal, Monograph Series 4. New Delhi: Navrang, 1983 (1st ed. London: Longman, Hurst, Rees and Orme, 1807).

Couperus, Louis, *Oostwaarts*. Volledige werken Louis Couperus 45. Amsterdam and Antwerpen: Veen, 1992 (1st ed. 's-Gravenhage: Leopold, 1924).

Crab, P. van der, *De Moluksche eilanden. Reis van Z.E. den Gouverneur-Generaal Charles Ferdinand Pahud, door den Molukschen archipel*. Batavia: Lange, 1862.

Curtin, Philip D., *Death by Migration. Europe's Encounter with the Tropical World in the Nineteenth Century*. Cambridge: Cambridge University Press, 1989.

Dagh-register gehouden int casteel Batavia vant passerende daer ter plaetse als over geheel Nederlandts-India. Anno 1624–1629 [...]–1682 (36 volumes). Batavia and 's-Gravenhage: Nijhoff, 1887–1931.

Daum, P.A., *Verzamelde romans* (3 volumes). Amsterdam: Nijgh & Van Ditmar, 1997–1998.

Daus, Ronald, *Portuguese Eurasian Communities in Southeast Asia*. Singapore: Institute of Southeast Asian Studies, 1989.

Davies, C.M., *Memorials and Times of Peter Philip Juriaan Quint Ondaatje*. Werken uitgegeven door het Historisch Genootschap, nieuwe reeks 13. Utrecht: Kemink, 1870.

Dekker, Jeroen Johannes Hubertus, "Straffen, redden en opvoeden. Het ontstaan en de ontwikkeling van de residentiële heropvoeding in West-Europa, 1814–1914, met bijzondere aandacht voor 'Nederlandsch Mettray'". Ph.D. dissertation, Utrecht University, 1985.

Delden, Emile van, *De particuliere landerijen op Java.* Leiden: Doesburgh, 1911.

Dhiravat na Pombejra, "Ayutthaya as a Cosmopolitan Society: a Case Study of Daniel Brochebourde and His Descendants", in: Idem, *Court, Company, and Campong. Essays on the VOC Presence in Ayutthaya.* Phra Nakhon Sri Ayutthaya: Ayutthaya Historical Study Centre, 1992, pp. 25–42.

Dhiravat na Pombejra, "VOC Employees and Their Relationships with Mon and Siamese Women. A Case Study of Osoet Pegua", in: Barbara Watson Andaya, ed., *Other Pasts. Women, Gender and History in Early Modern Southeast Asia.* Honolulu: Center for Southeast Asian Studies, 2000, pp. 195–214.

Dijk, Kees van, "Sarong, Jubbah, and Trousers. Appearance as a Means of Distinction and Discrimination", in: Henk Schulte Nordholt, ed., *Outward Appearances. Dressing State and Society in Indonesia.* Koninklijk Instituut voor Taal-, Land- en Volkenkunde Proceedings 4. Leiden: KITLV Press, 1997, pp. 39–83.

Dillo, Ingrid G., *De nadagen van de Verenigde Oostindische Compagnie 1783–1795. Schepen en zeevarenden.* Amsterdam: De Bataafsche Leeuw, 1992.

Dirks, Nicholas B., *Castes of Mind. Colonialism and the Making of Modern India.* Princeton and Oxford: Princeton University Press, 2001.

Dissel Szn., H. van, *De particuliere landerijen in het gewest Celebes en onderhoorigheden.* Batavia: Landsdrukkerij, 1885.

Doel, H.W. van den, *De stille macht. Het Europese Binnenlands Bestuur op Java en Madoera, 1808–1942.* Amsterdam: Bert Bakker, 1994.

Doeve, W.Ch.A., *Een Indisch-burgerschap. Voordracht gehouden voor de afdeeling Meester Cornelis van het Indo-Europeesch Verbond op 19 januari 1937.* N.p. [Batavia]: Visser & Co., 1939.

Doorn, Jacques van, *A Divided Society. Segmentation and Mediation in Late-Colonial Indonesia.* Comparative Asian Studies Program 7. Rotterdam: Erasmus University, Faculty of Social Sciences, 1983.

Doren, J.B.J. van, *De Javaan in het ware daglicht geschetst. Benevens eenige inlichtingen over het Binnenlandsch Bestuur op Java.* 's-Gravenhage: Van Langenhuysen, 1851.

Doren, J.B.J. van, *Reis naar Nederlands Oost-Indië of land- en zeetogten gedurende de twee eerste jaren mijns verblijfs op Java* (2 volumes). 's-Gravenhage: Van Langenhuysen, 1851.

Doren, J.B.J. van, *Fragmenten uit de reizen in den Indischen archipel [...]* (2 volumes). Amsterdam: J.D. Sybrandi, 1854–1856.

Doren, J.B.J. van, *Herinneringen en schetsen van Nederlands Oost-Indië. Vervolg op de fragmenten uit de reizen in die gewesten* (2 volumes). Amsterdam: J.D. Sybrandi, 1857–1860.

Dorren, Gabriëlle, *Eenheid en verscheidenheid. De burgers van Haarlem in de Gouden Eeuw.* Amsterdam: Prometheus/Bert Bakker, 2001.

[Douwes Dekker, E.F.E.], *Aansluiting tusschen blank en bruin. Rede uitgesproken in een openbare bijeenkomst, gehouden te Batavia op 17 december 1911.* Batavia: Vereeniging de Indische Bond, 1912.

Douwes Dekker, E.F.E., *Een sociogenetische grondwet. Eén der hoeksteenen voor het gebouw onzer revolutionaire maatschappij beschouwing. Populair-wetenschappelijke vingerwijzing aan onze nationalisten.* Semarang: De Indonesische Boek- en Brochurehandel, 1920.

Douwes Dekker, E.F.E., *Indië. Handboek voor den Indischen nationalist*, vol. I. N.p.[Semarang]: Hoofdbestuur Nationaal Indische Partij, 1921.

Dye, Alan, *Cuban Sugar in the Age of Mass Production. Technology and the Economics of the Sugar Central, 1899–1929.* Stanford: Stanford University Press, 1998.

Encyclopaedie van Nederlandsch-Indië (9 volumes). 's-Gravenhage and Leiden: Nijhoff, 1917–1939.

Engelhard, Nicolaus, *Overzigt van den staat der Nederlandsche Oost-Indische bezittingen onder het bestuur van den gouverneur-generaal Herman Willem Daendels [...].* 's-Gravenhage and Amsterdam: Van Cleef, 1816.

Enk, E.M.C. van, "Britse kooplieden en de cultures op Java. Harvey Thomson (1790–1837) en zijn financiers". Ph.D. dissertation, Free University Amsterdam, 1999.

Etmans, M.D., *Huwelijksregister van Banda [1813] 1818–1820 [1938], akten en reconstructies.* Bronnenpublikaties van de Indische Genealogische Vereniging 9. 's-Gravenhage: Indische Genealogische Vereniging, 1998.

Etmans, M.D., *De bevolking van Banda van 1818 tot 1920. Europeanen en inlandse christenen uit registers van kerk en burgerlijke stand en andere bronnen gerangschikt in familieverband, met veel vermeldingen van buiten Banda wonende ouders en nazaten, en van vorige en volgende woonplaatsen* (2 volumes). Ferwerd: [the author], 1998.

Eyk, W.B.J. van, *Het openbaar lager onderwijs voor Europeanen in Nederlandsch Indië.* Deventer: Hulscher, 1870.

F., G.J., ["Rekest van eenen kleurling"], *De Oosterling. Tijdschrift bij uitsluiting toegewijd aan de verbreiding der kennis van Oost-Indië* 2 (1836): 51–54.

Fasseur, C., *Kultuurstelsel en koloniale baten. De Nederlandse exploitatie van Java, 1840–1860.* Leiden: Universitaire Pers, 1975.

Fasseur, C., *De Indologen. Ambtenaren voor de Oost 1825–1950.* Amsterdam: Bert Bakker, 1994 (1st ed. Amsterdam: Bert Bakker, 1993).

Fasseur, C., "De 'adeldom' van de huid. De rol van de Indische Nederlander in het Nederlands-Indisch bestuur", in: Wim Willems, ed., *Sporen van een Indisch verleden (1600–1942).* Centrum voor Onderzoek van Maatschappelijke Tegenstellingen (COMT) 44. Leiden: COMT, 1992, pp. 13–22.

Fasseur, C., "Hoeksteen en struikelblok. Rassenonderscheid en overheidsbeleid in Nederlands-Indië", in: Idem, *De weg naar het paradijs en andere Indische geschiedenissen*. Amsterdam: Bert Bakker, 1995, pp. 139–71.

Fasseur, C., "Een martelaar voor het vrije woord", in: Idem, *Indischgasten*. Amsterdam: Bert Bakker, 1997, pp. 86–112.

Feenstra, Y., *Beschouwingen over de ontwikkeling van handel, cultuur en nijverheid onzer Oost-Indische buiten-bezittingen en in het bijzonder van de Molukken*. Amsterdam: Joh. G. Stemler Czn., 1880.

Fernando, Radin, "In the Eyes of the Beholder. Discourses of a Peasant Riot in Java", *Journal of Southeast Asian Studies* 30, 2 (1999): 263–85.

Fonseca, José Nicolau Da, *An Historical and Archaeological Sketch of the City of Goa, Preceded by a Short Statistical Account of the Territory of Goa*. Bombay: Thacker, 1878.

Freyre, Gilberto, *The Masters and the Slaves (Casa-Grande & Senzala). A Study in the Development of Brazilian Civilization*. New York: Weidenfeld & Nicolson, 1970 (1st ed. New York: Alfred A. Knopf, 1946).

Furnivall, J.S., *Netherlands India. A Study of Plural Economy*. Cambridge and New York: Cambridge University Press, 1944.

Gaikwad, V.R., *The Anglo-Indians. A Study in the Problems and Processes Involved in Emotional and Cultural Integration*. London: Asia Publishing House, 1967.

Gedenkboek der Nederlandsche Handel-Maatschappij 1824–1924. Amsterdam: De Maatschappij, 1924.

Gerdessen, L.E., *Vijf jaar gedetacheerd. Indische schetsen*. Amsterdam: Van Kampen en Zoon, 1873.

Ghosh, Suresh Chandra, *The Social Condition of the British Community in Bengal 1757–1800*. Leiden: Brill, 1970.

Gist, Noel P., and Roy Dean Wright, *Marginality and Identity. Anglo-Indians as a Racially-Mixed Minority in India*. Leiden: Brill, 1973.

Goldberg, David Theo, *The Racial State*. Malden and Oxford: Blackwell, 2002.

Goor, J. van, *Jan Kompenie as Schoolmaster. Dutch Education in Ceylon 1690–1795*. Historische Studies uitgegeven vanwege het Instituut voor Geschiedenis der Rijksuniversiteit te Utrecht 34. Groningen: Wolters-Noordhoff, 1978.

Goor, J. van, *De Nederlandse koloniën. Geschiedenis van de Nederlandse expansie 1600–1975*. N.p. ['s-Gravenhage]: Sdu, n.d. [1994].

Goor, J. van, "Koopman in koninklijke dienst", in: Idem, *Indische avonturen. Opmerkelijke ontmoetingen met een andere wereld*. Den Haag: Sdu, 2000, pp. 35–62.

Gouda, Frances, *Poverty and Political Culture. The Rhetoric of Social Welfare in the Netherlands and France, 1815–1854*. Amsterdam: Amsterdam University Press, 1995.

Graaf, H.J. de, ed., *De expeditie van Anthonio Hurdt, raad van Indië, als admiraal en superintendent naar de binnenlanden van Java, sept.–dec. 1678, volgens het journaal van Johan Jurgen Briel, secretaris.* Werken van de Linschoten-Vereeniging 72. 's-Gravenhage: Nijhoff, 1971.

Graaf, H.J. de, and Th.G.Th. Pigeaud, *Chinese Muslims in Java in the 15th and 16th Centuries. The Malay Annals of Semarang and Cerbon.* M.C. Ricklefs, ed. N.p. [Melbourne]: Ruskin Press, 1984.

Graaff, S. de, *Bijlage, behoorende bij het eerste gedeelte van "Het pauperisme onder Europeanen in Nederlandsch-Indië". Nota over het verleenen van landbouwcrediet van staatswege ten behoeve van den Europeeschen kleinen land- of tuinbouw.* Batavia: Landsdrukkerij, 1902.

Groeneboer, Kees, *Weg tot het westen. Het Nederlands voor Indië 1600–1950. Een taal-politieke geschiedenis.* Verhandelingen van het Koninklijk Instituut voor Taal-, Land- en Volkenkunde 158. Leiden: KITLV Press, 1993. Translated as *Gateway to the West. The Dutch Language in Colonial Indonesia 1600–1950. A History of Language Policy.* Amsterdam: Amsterdam University Press, 1998.

Groneman, J., *Bladen uit het dagboek van een Indisch geneesheer.* Groningen: J.B. Wolters, 1874.

Groneman, J., *Vorstenlandsche toestanden*, vol. I. Dordrecht: Revers, 1883.

Gruzinski, Serge, *The Mestizo Mind. The Intellectual Dynamics of Colonization and Globalization.* New York: Routledge, 2002.

H., "De hybriden in de Indische samenleving", *Tijdschrift voor Nederlandsch-Indië* nieuwe serie 5, 2 (1876): 225–40.

Haan, F. de, *Priangan. De Preanger-regentschappen onder het Nederlandsch bestuur tot 1811* (4 volumes). N.p. [Batavia]: Kolff & Co., 1910–1912.

Haan, F. de, *Oud Batavia. Gedenkboek uitgegeven door het Bataviaasch Genootschap voor Kunsten en Wetenschappen naar aanleiding van het driehonderdjarig bestaan der stad in 1919* (3 volumes). Batavia: Kolff & Co., 1922–1923.

Haan, F. de, "Personalia der periode van het Engelsch bestuur over Java 1811–1816", *Bijdragen van het Koninklijk Instituut voor Taal-, Land- en Volkenkunde* 92 (1935): 477–681.

Hageman Jcz, J., "Geschied- en aardrijkskundig overzigt van Java, op het einde der achttiende eeuw", *Tijdschrift voor Indische Taal-, Land- en Volkenkunde. Uitgegeven door het Bataviaasch Genootschap voor Kunsten en Wetenschappen* 9 (1860): 261–419.

Handboek voor cultuur- en handelsondernemingen. Amsterdam: De Bussy, 1888–1940.

Handelingen van de Tweede Kamer der Staten-Generaal. 's-Gravenhage: Algemeene Landsdrukkerij, 1847–.

Hannaford, Ivan, *Race. The History of an Idea in the West.* Washington: Woodrow Wilson Center Press, 1996.

Haspel, C.Ch. van den, *Overwicht in overleg. Hervormingen van justitie, grondgebruik en bestuur in de Vorstenlanden op Java 1880–1930.* Verhandelingen van het Koninklijk Instituut voor Taal-, Land- en Volkenkunde 111. Dordrecht: Foris, 1985.

Hasselman, C.J., "De practische resultaten van de recruteering van civiele ambtenaren uit Indië", *Tijdschrift voor het Binnenlandsch Bestuur* 31 (1906): 155–66.

Hawes, C.J., *Poor Relations. The Making of a Eurasian Community in British India 1773–1833*. Richmond: Curzon, 1996.

[Heecq, Gijsbert], "De derde voyagie van Gijsbert Heecq naar Oost Indijen". S.P. l'Honoré Naber, ed., *Marineblad. Bijblad op de Verslagen der Marine-Vereeniging* 25 (1910–1911): 193–231, 289–317, 422–52, 533–63.

Henley, David, *Nationalism and Regionalism in a Colonial Context. Minahasa in the Dutch East Indies*. Verhandelingen van het Koninklijk Instituut voor Taal-, Land- en Volkenkunde 168. Leiden: KITLV Press, 1996.

Hering, Bob, *Mohammad Hoesni Thamrin and His Quest for Indonesian Nation-hood 1917–1941*. N.p. [Stein]: Edisi Khusus Kabar Sebarang, 1996.

Hering, Bob, *Soekarno. Founding Father of Indonesia 1901–1945*. Verhandelingen van het Koninklijk Instituut voor Taal-, Land- en Volkenkunde 192. Leiden: KITLV Press, 2002.

Heuman, Gad J., *Between Black and White. Race, Politics, and the Free Coloreds in Jamaica, 1792–1865*. Oxford: Clio, 1981.

[Heydt, Johann Wolfgang], *Heydt's Ceylon Being the Relevant Sections of the "Allerneuester Geographisch- und Topographischer Schau-Platz on Africa und Ost-Indien"*, R. Raven-Hart, ed. Colombo: Ceylon Government Information Department, 1952.

Hill, Samuel Charles, *List of Europeans and Others in the English Factories in Bengal at the Time of the Siege of Calcutta in the Year 1756*. Calcutta: Office of the Superintendent of Government Printing, 1902.

Himmelfarb, Gertrude, *Poverty and Compassion. The Moral Imagination of the Late Victorians*. New York: Knopf, 1992.

Historische nota over het vraagstuk van de opleiding en benoembaarheid voor den administratieven dienst in Nederlandsch-Indië. Batavia: Landsdrukkerij, 1900.

Hoadley, Mason C., "Javanese, Peranakan, and Chinese Elites in Cirebon. Changing Ethnic Boundaries", *The Journal of Asian Studies* 47, 3 (1988): 503–18.

Hobson, J.A., *Imperialism. A Study*. London: Constable, 1905 (1st ed. London: Nisbet, 1902).

Hoetink, H., *Het patroon van de oude Curaçaose samenleving. Een sociologische studie*. Assen: Van Gennep, 1958.

Hoëvell, W.R. van, *Reis over Java, Madura en Bali in het midden van 1847* (3 volumes). Amsterdam: Van Kampen, 1849–1854.

Hoëvell, W.R. van, *De beschuldiging en veroordeeling in Indië, en de regtvaardiging in Nederland*. Zaltbommel: Noman, 1850.

Hoëvell, G.W.W.C. baron van, "Leti-eilanden", *Tijdschrift voor Indische Taal-, Land- en Volkenkunde. Uitgegeven door het Bataviaasch Genootschap voor Kunsten en Wetenschappen* 33 (1890): 200–32.

Hogendorp, C.S.W. van, *Beschouwing der Nederlandsche bezittingen in Oost-Indië*. Amsterdam: C.G. Sulpke, 1833.

Houben, Vincent J.H., *Kraton and Kumpeni. Surakarta and Yogyakarta 1830–1870*. Verhandelingen van het Koninklijk Instituut voor Taal-, Land- en Volkenkunde 164. Leiden: KITLV Press, 1994.

Houben, V.J.H., "De Indo-aristocratie van Midden Java: de familie Dezentjé", in: Wim Willems, ed., *Sporen van een Indisch verleden (1600–1942)*. Centrum voor Onderzoek van Maatschappelijke Tegenstellingen (COMT) 44. Leiden: COMT, 1992, pp. 39–50.

Hovy, L., ed., *Ceylonees plakkaatboek. Plakkaten en andere wetten uitgevaardigd door het Nederlandse bestuur op Ceylon, 1638–1796* (2 volumes). Hilversum: Verloren, 1991.

Hoynck van Papendrecht, P.C., "Some Old Private Letters from the Cape, Batavia and Malacca (1778–1788)", *Journal of the Malaysian Branch of the Royal Asiatic Society* 2, 1 (1924): 9–24.

[Ibn Battuta], *The Rehla of Ibn Battuta (India, Maldive Islands and Ceylon)*. Mahdi Husain, ed. Gaekwad's Oriental Series 122. Baroda: Oriental Institute, 1953.

Ingleson, John, *In Search of Justice. Workers and Unions in Colonial Java, 1908–1926*. Southeast Asia Publications Series 12. Oxford: Oxford University Press, 1986.

Jaarcijfers voor het koninkrijk der Nederlanden. Rijk in Europa. Centraal Bureau voor de Statistiek. 's-Gravenhage: Belinfante, 1898–1923.

Jaarlijksch verslag van de directie van het gesticht te Parapattan [...], Zesde -. Batavia: Landsdrukkerij, 1839.

Jaarlijksch verslag van de directie van het weeshuis te Parapattan, Achtste -. Batavia: Landsdrukkerij, 1841.

Jaarlijksch verslag van de directie van het weeshuis te Parapattan, Tiende -. Batavia: Landsdrukkerij, 1843.

Jaarverslag van de Klattensche Cultuurmaatschappij. 's-Gravenhage: Klattensche Cultuurmaatschappij, 1888–1968.

Jaarverslag van de Nederlandsch-Indische Handelsbank. 's-Gravenhage: Nederlandsch-Indische Handelsbank, 1864–1964.

Jack-Hinton, Colin, "Malacca and Goa and the Question of Race Relations in the Portuguese Overseas Provinces", *Journal of Southeast Asian History* 10, 2/3 (1969): 513–39.

Jacobs, Hubert, ed., *Documenta Malucensia*, vol. II. Momenta Historica Societas Jesu. Rome: Institutum Historicum Societatis Jesu, 1980.

Jacobs, Hubert, "Ambon as a Portuguese and Catholic Town, 1576–1605", *Neue Zeitschrift für Missionswissenschaft* 41, 1 (1985): 1–17.

The Java Half-Yearly Almanac and Directory. Batavia: Hubbard, 1815–1816.

Jong, C. de, "Lotgevallen van de drie broers Douwes Dekker in de Anglo-Boerenoorlog 1899–1902 I. Ernest Francois Eugène Douwes Dekker",

Historia. Amptelike orgaan van die historiese genootskap van Suid-Afrika 24, 2 (1979): 32–43.

Jong, W.M. de, *1905–1930. Gedenkboek ter herinnering aan het 25-jarig bestaan der NV Suikerfabriek "Tandjong Tirto"*. 's-Gravenhage: n.n., 1931.

Jonge, J.K.J. de, and M.L. van Deventer, ed., *De opkomst van het Nederlandsch gezag in Oost-Indië. Verzameling van onuitgegeven stukken uit het oud-koloniaal archief* (13 volumes). 's-Gravenhage and Amsterdam: Nijhoff, 1862–1909.

Jordan, Winthrop D., *White over Black. American Attitudes toward the Negro, 1550–1812*. Chapel Hill: University of North Carolina Press, 1968.

Kaempfer, Engelbert, *A Description of the Kingdom of Siam 1690*. Bangkok: White Orchid Press, 1998.

Kal, P., "Een aanzet voor het opstellen van een genealogie van het Indische geslacht Voorneman", *De Indische Navorscher* 10, 2 (1997): 49–65.

Kan, J. van, "Uit de Ceilonsche rechtsgeschiedenis", *Bijdragen van het Koninklijk Instituut voor Taal-, Land- en Volkenkunde* 102 (1943): 441–59.

Kemp, P.H. van der, ed., *Brieven van en aan mr. H.J. van de Graaff 1816–1826. Eene bijdrage tot de kennis der Oost-Indische bestuurstoestanden onder de regeering van G.A.G.P. baron van der Capellen*. Verhandelingen van het Bataviaasch Genootschap van Kunsten en Wetenschappen 52. Batavia and 's-Gravenhage: Albrecht, 1901.

Kemp, P.H. van der, ed., *Oost-Indië's herstel in 1816 naar oorspronkelijke stukken*. 's-Gravenhage: Nijhoff, 1911.

Knaap, G.J., *Kruidnagelen en christenen. De Verenigde Oost-Indische Compagnie en de bevolking van Ambon 1656–1696*. Verhandelingen van het Koninklijk Instituut voor Taal-, Land- en Volkenkunde 125. Dordrecht and Providence: Foris, 1987.

Knaap, Gerrit J., *Shallow Waters, Rising Tide. Shipping and Trade in Java around 1775*. Verhandelingen van het Koninklijk Instituut voor Taal-, Land- en Volkenkunde 172. Leiden: KITLV Press, 1996.

Knaap, G.J., "Europeans, Mestizos and Slaves. The Population of Colombo at the End of the Seventeenth Century", *Itinerario* 5, 2 (1981): 84–101.

Knaap, G.J., "A City of Migrants. Kota Ambon at the End of the Seventeenth Century", *Indonesia* 51 (Apr. 1991): 105–32.

Knaap, G.J., "Tjengkeh, kompeni, agama. Hoofdlijnen uit de geschiedenis van de Ambonse eilanden 1500–1800", in: G.J. Knaap, W. Manuhutu and H. Smeets, ed., *Sedjarah Maluku. Molukse geschiedenis in Nederlandse bronnen*. Amsterdam: Van Soeren, 1992.

Knaap, O., "Samarang in vogelvlucht", *Eigen Haard* (1902): 360–64.

Knight, Roger, "The Visible Hand in *Tempo Doeloe*. The Culture of Management and the Organization of Business in Java's Colonial Sugar Industry", *Journal of Southeast Asian Studies* 30, 1 (1999): 74–98.

Knight, Roger, "The Contractor as *Suiker*lord and Entrepreneur. Otto Carel Holmberg de Beckfelt (1794–1857)", in: J. Thomas Lindblad and Willem van der Molen, ed., *Macht en majesteit. Opstellen voor Cees Fasseur bij zijn afscheid als hoogleraar in de geschiedenis van Indonesië aan de universiteit Leiden*. Semaian 22. Leiden: Vakgroep Talen en Culturen van Zuidoost-Azië en Oceanië, 2002, pp. 190–205.

Kniphorst, J.H.P.E., "Een terugblik op Timor en onderhoorigheden", *Tijdschrift voor Nederlandsch-Indië* nieuwe serie 14, 2 (1885): 401–83.

Koch, D.M.G., *Verantwoording. Een halve eeuw in Indonesië*. 's-Gravenhage: Van Hoeve, 1956.

Koch, D.M.G., *Batig slot. Figuren uit het oude Indië*. Amsterdam: De Brug-Djambattan, 1960.

Koch, D.M.G., "Dr. E.F.E. Douwes Dekker", *Oriëntatie. Cultureel Maandblad* 34, 5 (1950): 56–64.

Kohlbrugge, J.H.F., *Blikken in het zieleleven van den Javaan en zijner overheerschers*. Leiden: Brill, 1907.

Koks, J.Th., *De Indo*. Amsterdam: H.J. Paris, 1931.

Kol, H. van, *Reisbrieven. De reorganisatie der Vorstenlanden en Vorstenlandsche toestanden naar aanleiding van reisbrieven der heeren van Kol door J.J.S.*. Djocja: n.n., 1911.

Kolff, D.H.A., "La 'Nation' chrétienne à Surate au début du XVIIe siècle", in: *La Femme dans les sociétés coloniales*. Institut d'Histoire des Pays d'Outre-Mer, Université de Provence. Études et Documents 19. Aix: Institut d'Histoire des Pays d'Outre-Mer, 1984, pp. 7–16.

Koloniaal verslag. 's-Gravenhage: Landsdrukkerij, 1849–.

"Kort overzicht van oprichting, bestaan en bedrijf van de onderneming "Oud Djember", in: *NV Landbouwmaatschappij Oud-Djember, 1859–1909*. N.p. [Deventer]: Oud Djember, 1909.

"Kronijk van Nederlandsch Indië, loopende van af het jaar 1816. De jaren 1822 en 1823", *Tijdschrift voor Neêrland's Indië* 4, 1 (1842): 129–228.

Kuitenbrouwer, Maarten, *Nederland en de opkomst van het moderne imperialisme. Koloniën en buitenlandse politiek 1870–1942*. Amsterdam: De Bataafsche Leeuw, 1985.

Lach de Bère, Ph., *Genealogie van het Nederlandsch Indische geslacht Weijnschenk*. 's-Gravenhage: n.n., n.d. [1908].

Lans, P.C., *Causeriën over urgente onderwerpen op koloniaal gebied, ter overweging en betrachting het Nederlandsche volk, zijne vertegenwoordiging en zijne regeering aangeboden*. Rotterdam: n.n., 1881.

Larkin, John A., *Sugar and the Origins of Modern Philippine Society*. Berkeley: University of California Press, 1993.

Larson, George D., *Prelude to Revolution. Palaces and Politics in Surakarta, 1912–1942*. Verhandelingen van het Koninklijk Instituut voor Taal-, Land- en Volkenkunde 124. Dordrecht: Foris, 1987.

Leidelmeijer, Margaret, *Van suikermolen tot grootbedrijf. Technische vernieuwing in de Java-suikerindustrie in de negentiende eeuw.* Amsterdam: NEHA, 1997.

Leirissa, R.Z., "The Bugis-Makassarese in the Port Towns. Ambon and Ternate through the Nineteenth Century", *Bijdragen tot de Taal-, Land- en Volkenkunde* 156, 2 (2000): 619–33.

Leirissa, R.Z., "Social Developments in Ambon during the 19th Century. Ambonese Burger", *Cakalele. Maluku Research Journal* 6 (1995): 1–11.

Lennon, Walter Caulfield, "Journal of a Voyage through the Straits of Malacca on an Expedition to the Molucca Islands under the Command of Admiral Rainier", *Journal of the Straits Branch of the Royal Asiatic Society* 7 (1881): 51–74.

Lequin, Frank, *Het personeel van de Verenigde Oost-Indische Compagnie in Azië in de achttiende eeuw, meer in het bijzonder in de vestiging Bengalen* (2 volumes). Leiden: [the author], 1982.

Lequin, Frank, ed., *The Private Correspondence of Isaac Titsingh, vol. 1 (1785–1811)*. Amsterdam: Gieben, 1990.

Lequin, Frank, *Isaac Titsingh (1745–1812). Een passie voor Japan. Leven en werk van de grondlegger van de Europese Japanologie.* Alphen aan den Rijn: Canaletto/Repro-Holland, 2002.

Linden, Herman Otto van der, *Banda en zijne bewoners.* Dordrecht: Blussé en Van Braam, 1873.

Lis Lange, Maria, *White, Poor and Angry. White Working Class Families in Johannesburg.* Aldershot: Ashgate, 2003.

Locher-Scholten, Elsbeth, "Summer Dresses and Canned Food: European Women and Western Lifestyles" in: Idem, *Women and the Colonial State. Essays on Gender and Modernity in the Netherlands Indies 1900–1942.* Amsterdam: Amsterdam University Press, 2000, pp. 121–50.

Lombard, Denys, "Une description de la ville de Semarang vers 1812 (D'après un manuscrit de l'India Office)", *Archipel* 37 (1989): 263–77.

Loth, Vincent C., "Pioneers and Perkeniers. The Banda Islands in the 17th Century", *Cakalele. Maluku Research Journal* 6 (1995): 13–35.

Loubère, Simon de la, *Du Royaume de Siam [Par Mons.r De la Loubère, envoyé extraordinaire du roy auprès du roy de Siam en 1687 & 1688]* (2 volumes). Amsterdam: Abraham Wolfgang, 1691.

Loudon, John F., *De eerste jaren der Billiton-onderneming.* Amsterdam: De Bussy, 1883 (reprinted from *De Indische Gids. Staat- en Letterkundig Maandschrift,* Nov. 1883).

Louw, P.J.F., *De Java-oorlog van 1825–1830* (6 volumes). Batavia: Bataviaasch Genootschap van Kunsten en Wetenschappen, 1894.

Ludeking, E.W.A., *Schets van de residentie Amboina.* 's-Gravenhage: Nijhoff, 1868.

Lutter, A.A., "Landmonsterrol van Java's noordoostkust 1798", *De Indische Navorscher* 10, 1 (1997): 22–40.

M., V. v., "Fröbelscholen in Indië", *De Indische Gids. Staat- en Letterkundig Maandschrift* 2, 1 (1880): 1–12.

Maddison, Angus, "Dutch Income in and from Indonesia, 1700–1936", in: Angus Maddison and Gé Prince, ed., *Economic Growth in Indonesia 1820–1940*. Verhandelingen van het Koninklijk Instituut voor Taal-, Land- en Volkenkunde 137. Dordrecht: Foris, 1989, pp. 15–42.

Magalhães Godinho, Vitorino, "Portuguese Emigration from the Fifteenth to the Twentieth Century. Constants and Changes", in: P.C. Emmer and M. Mörner, ed., *European Expansion and Migration. Essays on the Intercontinental Migration from Africa, Asia, and Europe*. New York and Oxford: Berg, 1992, pp. 13–48.

Mandor, "Het Parapattan weezen-gesticht te Batavia", *Het Leeskabinet* 2 (1881): 33–38.

Mansvelt, W.M.F., *De eerste Indische handelshuizen. Mededeelingen over de resultaten van een onderzoek naar de nationaliteit van het Nederlandsch-Indisch handelsapparaat in de eerste helft van de 19ᵉ eeuw*. Batavia: Centraal Kantoor voor de Statistiek, 1937.

Mansvelt, W.M.F., *Exportcultures van Ned.-Indië 1830–1937*. N.p. [Batavia]: Centraal Kantoor voor de Statistiek, 1939.

Margana, S., "Agrarian Dispute and the Social Basis of a Colonial Plantation in a Javanese Principality", in: Ulbe Bosma, Juan Giusti and G. Roger Knight, ed., *Sugarlandia revisited. Sugar and Colonialism in Asia and the America's 1800–1940*. New York and Oxford: Berghahn, forthcoming.

Marle, A. van, "De groep der Europeanen in Nederlands-Indië, iets over ontstaan en groei", *Indonesië* 5 (1951–1952): 97–121, 314–41, 481–507.

Marshall, P.J., "British Immigration into India in the Nineteenth Century", in: P.C. Emmer and M. Mörner, ed., *European Expansion and Migration. Essays on the Intercontinental Migration from Africa, Asia, and Europe*. New York and Oxford: Berg, 1992, pp. 179–96.

Mastenbroek, William Edward van, *De historische ontwikkeling van de staatsrechtelijke indeeling der bevolking van Nederlandsch-Indië*. Wageningen: Veenman, 1934.

Matthijs, Hein, *Het verboden huwelijk*. Schoorl: Conserve, 2001.

Medhurst, W.H., ed., *Ong Tae Hae. The Chinaman Abroad. A Desultory Account of the Malayan Archipelago Particularly of Java*. Shanghai: n.n., 1849.

Meyer Timmerman Thijssen, D., *Twee gouverneurs en een equipagemeester. In en om Malakka 1778–1823*. Bilthoven: Knuf, 1991.

Ming, Hanneke, "Barracks-Concubinage in the Indies, 1887–1920", *Indonesia* 35 (Apr. 1983): 65–93.

Mooij, J., ed., *Bouwstoffen voor de geschiedenis der protestantsche kerk in Nederlandsch-Indië* (3 volumes). Weltevreden: Landsdrukkerij, 1927–1931.

Moor, Jaap de, "Van reveille tot taptoe. Het Indische leger", in: Wim Willems a.o., ed., *Uit Indië geboren. Vier eeuwen familiegeschiedenis*. Zwolle: Waanders, 1997, pp. 65–81.

Morgan, David, "Persian Perceptions of Mongols and Europeans", in: Stuart B. Schwartz, ed., *Implicit Understandings. Observing, Reporting, and Reflecting on the Encounters between Europeans and Other Peoples in the Early Modern Era*. Cambridge: Cambridge University Press, 1994, pp. 201–17.

Morren, Th., *De Jongens-Weezen-Inrichting te Soerabaia 1858–1918*. N.p. [Soerabaia]: n.n., n.d. [*ca.* 1918].

Mrázek, Rudolf, *Engineers of Happy Land. Technology and Nationalism in a Colony*. Princeton and Oxford: Princeton University Press, 2002.

Muller, M.J.E., "Geneeskundige topographie van Samarang", *Tijdschrift voor Neêrland's Indië* 7, 3 (1845): 314–80; Idem 8, 1 (1846): 327–47; Idem 8, 2 (1846): 507–33.

"Naam rolle van alle sodanige christenen als zig ten deesen comptoire bevinden met aanwijsing welken godsdienst dezelve belijden als meede het getal der getrouwden en kinderen", *De Indische Navorscher* 4, 1 (1991): 26–32.

Naber, Johanna W.A., "Nicolette Peronneau van Leyden's herinneringen uit Indië 1817–1820", in: Idem, ed., *Onbetreden paden van ons koloniaal verleden 1816–1873. Naar nog onuitgegeven familiepapieren*. Amsterdam: P.N. van Kampen & Zoon, 1938, pp.17–88.

Nagtegaal, Luc, *Riding the Dutch Tiger. The Dutch East Indies Company and the Northeast Coast of Java 1680–1743*. Verhandelingen van het Koninklijk Instituut voor Taal-, Land- en Volkenkunde 171. Leiden: KITLV Press, 1996.

Nagtegaal, Luc, "Halzenkussers en hermafrodieten. Nederlands-Javaans cultuurcontact voor 1900", *Jambatan* 2, 3 (1983–1984): 3–20.

Nagtegaal, Luc, "The Pre-Modern City in Indonesia and Its Fall from Grace with the Gods", *Economic and Social History in the Netherlands* 5 (1993): 39–59.

Naoroji, Dadabhai, *Poverty and Un-British Rule in India*. London: G. Sonnenschein & Co., 1901.

Nederlandsch-Indisch plakaatboek, 1602–1811. J.A. van der Chijs, ed. (17 volumes). Batavia and 's-Gravenhage: Landsdrukkerij, 1885–1900.

Netscher, E., *Padang in het laatst der XVIIIe eeuw*. Verhandelingen van het Bataviaasch Genootschap van Kunsten en Wetenschappen 41, 2. Batavia and 's-Gravenhage: Bruining and Nijhoff, n.d. [1881].

Neve, R.G. de, "De Bataviasche adresbeweging van december 1795", in: L.A.F. Barjesteh van Waalwijk van Doorn and F.J. van Rooijen, ed., *Tussen vrijheidsboom en oranjewimpel. Bijdragen tot de geschiedenis van de periode 1795–1813*. Rotterdam: Historische Uitgeverij, 1995, pp. 53–149.

Neve, R.G. de, "Personalia en historisch-genealogische bronnen betreffende in Azië dienend personeel gedurende de Bataafs-Franse tijd", *De Indische Navorscher* 8, 3/4 (1995): 97–178.

Neve, R.G. de, "De Bataviase meibeweging van 1848", *De Nederlandsche Leeuw* 116, 11/12 (1999): 484–538.

Niemeijer, H.E., "Calvinisme en koloniale stadscultuur. Batavia 1619–1725". Ph.D. dissertation, Free University Amsterdam, 1996.

Niemeijer, H.E., "The Free Asian Christian Community and Poverty in Pre-Modern Batavia", in: Kees Grijns and Peter J.M. Nas, ed., *Jakarta-Batavia. Socio-Cultural Essays*. Verhandelingen van het Koninklijk Instituut voor Taal-, Land- en Volkenkunde 187. Leiden: KITLV Press, 2000, pp. 75–92.

Nordin Hussin, "Melaka and Penang 1780–1830. A Study of Two Port Towns in the Straits of Melaka". Ph.D. dissertation, Free University Amsterdam, 2002.

O'Kane, John, ed., *The Ship of Sulaiman*. New York: Columbia University Press, 1972.

Olivier, Johannes, *Land- en zeetogten in Nederland's Indië en eenige Britsche etablissementen, gedaan in de jaren 1817 tot 1826* (3 volumes). Amsterdam: Sulpke, 1827–1830.

Olivier, J. Jz., *Reizen in den Molukschen archipel naar Makassar [...] in het gevolg van den gouverneur-generaal van Nederland's Indië in 1824 gedaan en volgens dagboeken en aanteekeningen van ondersch. reisgenooten beschreven* (2 volumes). Amsterdam: Beijerinck, 1834–1837.

Ondaatje, Mathew, "Peter Ondaatje, of Ceylon", *Ceylon Antiquary and Literary Register* 9, 1 (July 1923): 22–30.

"The Only Asiatic to Figure in European History. Pieter Philip Juriaan Quint Ondaatje 1758–1818", *Ceylon Literary Register* third series 3, 8 (Aug. 1934): 337–45.

Opstall, M.E. van, "From Alkmaar to Ayudhya and Back", *Itinerario* 9, 2 (1985): 108–20.

"De opvoeding van jongelingen in Indië", *Tijdschrift voor Neêrland's Indië* 1, 2 (1838): 77–80.

Ottow, S.J., *De oorsprong der conservatieve richting. Het kolonisatierapport van der Capellen, uitgegeven en toegelicht door S.J. Ottow*. Utrecht: Oosthoek, 1937.

Particuliere landbouwnijverheid. Lijst van ondernemingen. Departement van Binnenlandsch Bestuur. Batavia: Landsdrukkerij, 1915–1922.

Het pauperisme onder de Europeanen in Nederlandsch-Indië (5 volumes). Batavia: Landsdrukkerij, 1901.

Payen, A.A.J., *Journal de mon voyage à Jogja Karta en 1825. The Outbreak of the Java War (1825–1830) as Seen by a Painter*. Peter Carey, ed. Cahier d'Archipel 17. Paris: Association Archipel, 1988.

Penny, Frank, *The Church in Madras. Being the History of the Ecclesiastical and Missionary Action in the East India Company in the Presidency of Madras in the Seventeenth and Eighteenth Centuries*. N.p.: Smith Elder & Co., 1904.

Perron-de Roos, E.G. du, "Correspondentie van Dirk van Hogendorp met zijn broeder Gijsbert Karel", *Bijdragen van het Koninklijk Instituut voor Taal-, Land- en Volkenkunde* 102 (1943): 125–273.

Petrus Blumberger, J.Th., *De Indo-Europeesche beweging in Nederlandsch-Indië.* Haarlem: H.D. Tjeenk Willink, 1939.

"Pieter Philip Christiaan Oortman Ondaatje, majoor der genie bij het Nederlandsch Indische leger", *Handelingen en geschriften van het Indisch Genootschap* 5 (1858): 247–52.

[Pires, Tomé], *The Suma Oriental of Tomé Pires. An Account of the East, from the Red Sea to Japan, Written in Malacca and India in 1512–1515 [...].* Armando Cortesão, ed. The Hakluyt Society Second Series 89 and 90 (2 volumes). London: Hakluyt Society, 1944.

Poliakov, Léon, "Racism from the Enlightenment to the Age of Imperialism", in: Robert Ross, ed., *Racism and Colonialism.* 's-Gravenhage: Nijhoff, 1982, pp. 53–64.

Ponder, H.W., *In Javanese Waters. Some Sidelights on a Few of the Countless, Loveley, Little Known Islands Scattered over the Banda Sea & Some Glimpses of Their Strange & Stormy History.* London: Seeley, 1944.

Post, Peter, "The Kwik Hoo Tong Trading Society of Semarang, Java. A Chinese Business Network in Late Colonial Asia", *Journal of Southeast Asian Studies* 33, 2 (2002): 279–96.

Prick van Wely, F.P.H., *Neerlands taal in 't verre oosten. Een bijdrage tot de kennis en de historie van het Hollandsch in Indië.* Semarang and Soerabaja: Van Dorp & Co., 1906.

Prick van Wely, F.P.H., "De Indische kleurlingen en hun benamingen", *Taal en Letteren* 15 (1905): 515–22.

"Het Pupillen-korps op Java", *Tijdschrift voor Nederlandsch Indië* 17, 2 (1855): 334–44.

Purcell, Victor, "Chinese Settlement in Malacca", *Journal of the Malayan Branch of the Royal Asiatic Society* 20, 1 (1947): 115–25.

Quarles van Ufford, H., *Aanteekeningen betreffende eene reis door de Molukken van zijne excellentie den gouverneur-generaal mr. A.J. Duymaer van Twist in de maanden september en oktober 1855.* 's-Gravenhage: Nijhoff, 1856.

Raadt Apell, M.J. de, *De batikkerijen van Zuylen te Pekalongan. Midden-Java 1890–1946.* Zutphen: Terra, 1981.

Raben, Remco, "Batavia and Colombo. The Ethnic and Spatial Order of Two Colonial Cities 1600–1800". Ph.D. dissertation, Leiden University, 1996.

Raben, Remco, "Colombo. Mirror of the Colonial Mind", *Mare Liberum* 13 (June 1997): 95–117.

Raben, Remco, and Dhiravat na Pombejra, "Tipping Balances. King Borommakot and the Dutch East India Company", in: Idem, ed., *In the King's Trail. An 18th Century Dutch Journey to the Buddha's Footprint. Theodorus Jacobus van den Heuvel's Account of His Voyage to Phra Phutthabat in 1737.* Bangkok: The Royal Netherlands Embassy, 1997, pp. 63–79.

Radermaker, J.C.M., "Proeve nopens de verschillende gedaante en koleur der menschen", *Verhandelingen van het Bataviaasch Genootschap der Konsten en Wetenschappen* 2 (1780): 213–28.

Raffles, Thomas Stamford, *The History of Java* (2 volumes). Kuala Lumpur: Oxford University Press, 1978 (1st ed. London: Black, Parbury and Allen, 1817).

Rapport der pauperisme-commissie. Batavia: Landsdrukkerij, 1903.

Regeerings-almanak voor Nederlandsch-Indië. Batavia: Landsdrukkerij, 1865–1942.

Reid, Anthony, *Southeast Asia in the Age of Commerce 1450–1680*, vol. II. *Expansion and Crisis.* New Haven and London: Yale University Press, 1993.

Reid, Anthony, "Economic and Social Change, *ca.* 1400–1800", in: Nicholas Tarling, ed., *The Cambridge History of Southeast Asia*, vol. I. *From Early Times to c. 1800.* Cambridge: Cambridge University Press, 1992, pp. 460–507.

Reid, Anthony, "The Rise and Fall of Sino-Javanese Shipping", in: Idem, *Charting the Shape of Early Modern Southeast Asia.* Chiang Mai: Silkworm Books, 1999, pp. 56–84.

Reid, Anthony, "Early Southeast Asian Categorizations of Europeans", in: Idem, *Charting the Shape of Early Modern Southeast Asia.* Chiang Mai: Silkworm Books, 1999, pp. 155–80.

Ricklefs, M.C., *Jogjakarta under Sultan Mangkubumi 1749–1792. A History of the Division of Java.* London: Oxford University Press, 1974.

Riedel, J.G.F., "Hoe denken de Amboneezen over de indiensttreding bij het Indische leger?", *De Indische Gids. Staat- en Letterkundig Maandschrift* 7 (1885): 321–24.

Rietbergen, P.J.A.N., *De eerste landvoogd Pieter Both (1568–1615), gouverneur-generaal van Nederlands-Indië (1609–1614)* (2 volumes). Zutphen: De Walburg Pers, 1987.

Riyanto, Bedjo, *Iklan Surat Kabar dan Perubahan Masyarakat di Jawa Masa Kolonial (1870–1915).* Yogyakarta: Tarawang, 2000.

Roberts, Michael, *Caste Conflict and Elite Formation. The Rise of a Karava Elite in Sri Lanka 1500–1931.* Cambridge South Asian Studies 24. Cambridge: Cambridge University Press, 1982.

Roberts, Michael, Ismeth Raheem and Percy Colin-Thomé, *People Inbetween. The Burghers and the Middle Class in the Transformations within Sri Lanka, 1790s–1960s*, vol. I. Ratmalana: Sarvodaya Book Publishing Services, 1989.

Rochussen, J.J., *Toelichting en verdediging van eenige daden van mijn bestuur in Indië, in antwoord op sommige vragen van jhr. J.P. Cornets de Groot van Kraaijenburg, oud-raad van Indië.* 's-Gravenhage: Gebroeders van Cleef, 1853.

Rodenwaldt, Ernst, *Die Mestizen auf Kisar. Mit einem Beitrag von K. Saller ueber "Mikroskopische Beobachtungen an den Haaren der Kisaresen und Kisarbastarde".* Hrsg. durch die "Mededeelingen van den Dienst der Volksgezondheid in Nederlansch-Indië" (2 volumes). Batavia: Kolff & Co., 1927.

Roebroek, Joop M., and Mirjam Hertogh, *"De beschavende invloed des tijds".* *Twee eeuwen sociale politiek, verzorgingsstaat en sociale zekerheid in Nederland.* 's-Gravenhage: VUGA, 1998.

Roeper, Vibeke, and Roelof van Gelder, ed., *In dienst van de Compagnie. Leven bij de VOC in honderd getuigenissen [1602–1799].* Amsterdam: Atheneum-Polak & Van Gennep, 2002.

Rouffaer, G.P., and H.H. Juynboll, *De batik-kunst in Nederlandsch-Indië en haar geschiedenis op grond van materiaal aanwezig in 's Rijks Etnographisch Museum en andere openbare en particuliere verzamelingen in Nederland bewerkt* (2 volumes). Haarlem: Kleinmann, 1899–1914.

Ruitenbach, D.J., "De opleiding der pupillen te Gombong", *De Indische Gids. Staat- en Letterkundig Maandschrift* 24, 1 (1902): 613–30.

Scalliet, Marie-Odette, *Antoine Payen. Peintre des Indes Orientales. Vie et écrits d'un artiste du XIXe siècle (1792–1853).* Leiden: Research School CNWS, 1995.

Scammell, G.V., "European Exiles, Renegades and Outlaws and the Maritime Economy of Asia c. 1500–1750", in: K.S. Mathew, ed., *Mariners, Merchants and Oceans. Studies in Maritime History.* New Delhi: Manohar, 1995, pp. 121–42.

Schouten, M.J.C., *Leadership and Social Mobility in a Southeast Asian Society. Minahassa, 1677–1983.* Verhandelingen van het Koninklijk Instituut voor Taal-, Land- en Volkenkunde 179. Leiden: KITLV Press, 1998.

Schulte Nordholt, Henk, and Margreet van Till, "Colonial Criminals in Java, 1870–1905", in: Vicente L. Rafael, ed., *Figures of Criminality in Indonesia, the Philippines and Colonial Vietnam.* Ithaca: Cornell University Press, 1999, pp. 47–69.

Schutte, G.J., "De gereformeerde kerk onder de Verenigde Oostindische Compagnie", in: Idem, *Het calvinistische Nederland. Mythe en werkelijkheid.* Hilversum: Verloren, 2000, pp. 46–75.

Schutte, G.J., *De Nederlandse patriotten en de koloniën. Een onderzoek naar hun denkbeelden en optreden, 1770–1800.* Historische Studies 29. Groningen: Wolters, 1974.

Sens, Angelie, *"Mensaap, heiden, slaaf". Nederlandse visies op de wereld rond 1800.* Den Haag: Sdu, 2001.

Shennan, Margaret, *Out in the Midday Sun. The British in Malaya 1880–1960.* London: John Murray, 2000.

Shiraishi, Takashi, *An Age in Motion. Popular Radicalism in Java, 1912–1926.* Ithaca: Cornell University Press, 1990.

Si Miskin, "Een onderdeel van het paupervraagstuk", *Tijdschrift voor het Binnenlandsch Bestuur* 24 (1903): 298–306.

Skinner, G. William, "Creolized Chinese Societies in Southeast Asia", in: Anthony Reid, ed., *Sojourners and Settlers. Histories of Southeast Asia and the Chinese.* St. Leonards: University of Hawaii Press, 1996, pp. 51–93.

Somerset Maugham, W., *The Narrow Corner*. London: Penguin, 1993 (1st ed. London: William Heineman, 1932).

De staatsarmenzorg voor Europeanen in Nederlandsch-Indië (5 volumes). Batavia: Landsdrukkerij, 1901–1902.

Stark, E., *Uit Indië, Egypte en het Heilige Land. Brieven aan zijne vrienden.* Amersfoort: Veen, 1910.

Statistiek van den loop der bevolking in Nederland over [...]. Centraal Bureau voor de Statistiek. 's-Gravenhage: Van Weelden en Mingelen, 1876–1947.

Steengracht, Hans [A.D. van der Gon Netscher], "Het Indo-vraagstuk en de rassenhaat", *Indische Kroniek. Tijdschrift voor Nederlandsch-Indië* 1, 28 (1911): 351–53.

Stevens, Th., *Vrijmetselarij en samenleving in Nederlands-Indië en Indonesië 1764–1962.* Hilversum: Verloren, 1994.

Stoler, Ann Laura, and Frederick Cooper, "Between Metropole and Colony. Rethinking a Research Agenda", in: Idem, ed., *Tensions of Empire. Colonial Cultures in a Bourgeois World.* Berkeley: University of California Press, 1997, pp. 1–56.

Subrahmanyam, Sanjay, *The Portuguese Empire in Asia, 1500–1700. A Political and Economic History.* London and New York: Longman, 1993.

Sutherland, H., "Mestizos as Middlemen? Ethnicity and Access in Colonial Macassar", in: *Papers of the Dutch-Indonesian Historical Conference Held at Lage Vuursche, the Netherlands, 23–27 June 1980.* Leiden and Jakarta: Bureau of Indonesian Studies, 1982, pp. 250–77.

Sutherland, Heather, "Power and Politics in South Sulawesi, 1860–1880", *Review of Indonesian and Malaysian Affairs* 17 (1983): 161–207.

Sutherland, Heather, "The Makassar Malays. Adaptation and Identity, c. 1660–1790", *Journal of Southeast Asian Studies* 32, 3 (2001): 397–421.

Swierenga, Robert P., "The Delayed Transition from Folk to Labor Migration. The Netherlands 1880–1920", *The International Migration Review* 27, 2 (1993): 406–24.

[Tachard, Guy], *A Relation of the Voyage to Siam Performed by Six Jesuits Sent by the French King, to the Indies and China, in the Year, 1685 [...].* Bangkok: White Orchid Press, 1981 (1st ed. Amsterdam: Chez Pierre Mortier, 1688).

Talens, Johan, *Een feodale samenleving in koloniaal vaarwater. Staatsvorming, koloniale expansie en economische onderontwikkeling in Banten, West-Java (1600–1750).* Hilversum: Verloren, 1999.

Taselaar, Arjen, *De Nederlandse koloniale lobby. Ondernemers en de Indische politiek, 1914–1940.* Leiden: Research School CNWS, 1998.

Taylor, Anne, *Annie Besant. A Biography.* Oxford: Oxford University Press, 1992.

Taylor, Jean Gelman, *The Social World of Batavia. European and Eurasian in Dutch Asia* (Madison: University of Wisconsin Press, 1983). Translated as *Smeltkroes Batavia. Europeanen en Euraziaten in de Nederlandse vestigingen in Azië.* Groningen: Wolters, 1988.

Termorshuizen, Gerard, *P.A. Daum. Journalist en romancier van tempo doeloe.* Amsterdam: Nijgh & Van Ditmar, 1988.

Termorshuizen, Gerard, with Anneke Scholte, *Journalisten en heethoofden. Een geschiedenis van de Indisch-Nederlandse dagbladpers 1744–1905.* Amsterdam: Nijgh & Van Ditmar, 2001.

Termorshuizen, Gerard, "De oudste krant van Celebes: het Makassaarsch Handels- en Advertentieblad", in: Harry A. Poeze and Pim Schoorl, ed., *Excursies in Celebes.* Verhandelingen van het Koninklijk Instituut voor Taal-, Land- en Volkenkunde 147. Leiden: KITLV Press, 1991, pp. 95–114.

Thomaz, Luis Filipe F.R., "Malaka et ses communautés marchandes au tournant du 16e siècle", in: Denys Lombard and Jean Aubin, ed., *Marchands et hommes d'affaires asiatiques dans l'Océan Indien et la Mer de Chine 13e-20e siècles.* Paris: EHESS, 1988, pp. 31–48.

Thomaz, Luis Filipe F.R., "The Malay Sultanate of Melaka", in: Anthony Reid, ed., *Southeast Asia in the Early Modern Era. Trade, Power, and Belief.* Ithaca and London: Cornell University Press, 1993, pp. 69–90.

Thorn, William, *Memoir of the Conquest of Java. With the Subsequent Operations of the British Forces in the Oriental Archipelago.* Singapore: Periplus, 1993 (1st ed. London: Egerton, 1815).

Tichelman, F., *Socialisme in Indonesië. De Indische Sociaal-Democratische Vereeniging 1897–1917*, vol. I. *Een bronnenpublikatie.* Dordrecht: Foris, 1985.

Tiele, P.A., ed., "Documenten voor de geschiedenis der Nederlanders in het Oosten", *Bijdragen en Mededeelingen van het Historisch Genootschap* 6 (1883): 222–376.

Till, Margreet van, "Social Care in Eighteenth-Century Batavia. The Poorhouse, 1725–1750", *Itinerario* 19, 1 (1995): 18–31.

Tromp, J., "Het partikulier landbezit in de Bataviasche ommelanden tot 1857", *Tijdschrift voor Nederlandsch-Indië* nieuwe serie 3, 1 (1865): 329–47.

"Twee Indische kinderen in Indië opgevoed", *Tijdschrift voor Nederlandsch Indië* 14, 2 (1852): 215–21.

Tweede verslag der directie van het gesticht voor verwaarloosde en hulpbehoevende kinderen te Djattie (Batavia). Onder ultimo december 1856. N.p. [Batavia], n.n., n.d. [1856].

Uitkomsten der pauperisme-enquête, ingesteld ingevolge de circulaire van den directeur van Onderwijs, Eeredienst en Nijverheid van 26 juni 1901, no. 7771A (3 volumes). Batavia: Landsdrukkerij, 1902.

Vasconcelos, José, *A Mexican Ulysses. An Autobiography.* W. Rex Crawford, transl. Bloomington: Indiana University Press, 1963.

Veldhuizen, Harmen C., *Batik Belanda 1840–1940. Dutch Influence in Batik from Java. History and Stories.* Jakarta: Gaya Favorit Press, 1993.

"Venduties te Batavia", *Tijdschrift voor Neêrland's Indië* 7, 1 (1845): 402–20.

Ver Huell, Q.M.R., *Herinneringen van eene reis naar de Oost-Indiën* (2 volumes). Haarlem: Vincent Loosjes, 1835–1836.

Vergès, Françoise, *Monsters and Revolutionaries. Colonial Family Romance and Métissage*. Durham: Duke University Press, 1999.

Verslag der feestviering, bij gelegenheid van het vijf-en-twintig-jarig bestaan van het Parapattan weezengesticht, op zaturdag, 17 october 1857. Batavia: Lange & Co., 1857.

"Verslag van den staat der ambachtsschool te Soerabaja", *Tijdschrift voor Nijverheid in Nederlandsch Indië* 1 (1854): 145–50.

Veth, P.J., *Bijdragen tot de kennis van den politieken toestand van Nederlandsch Indië*, vol. I. *De openbaarheid in koloniale aangelegenheden*. Amsterdam: Van Kampen, 1848.

Veth, P.J., *Het eiland Timor*. N.p.: n.n., 1855 (reprinted from *De Gids*).

Veth, P.J., "Iets over de opvoeding der kinderen van Europesche militairen in N. Indië", *Tijdschrift voor Nederlandsch Indië* 13, 1 (1851): 89–99.

Veur, Paul Willem Johan van der, "Introduction to a Socio-Political Study of the Eurasians of Indonesia". Ph.D. dissertation, Cornell University, Ithaca, 1955.

Vliet, C.A.M. van, *Belangrijk verslag over den staat Banda en omliggende eilanden aan zijne excellentie den gouverneur-generaal van Ned.-Indië Jacob Mossel door Reinier de Klerk. Met eene korte beschrijving van Banda in het bijzonder en de Molukken in het algemeen van 1795 tot 1894 door C.A.M. van Vliet*. Den Haag: n.n., n.d. [1894].

Volkstelling 1930, vol. VI. *Europeanen in Nederlandsch-Indië*. Departement van Landbouw, Nijverheid en Handel. Batavia: Landsdrukkerij, 1933.

Voorneman, A.M., *Het jonge Indië. Verspreide stukken van A.M. Voorneman en wijlen F.K. Voorneman*. Soerabaja: n.n., 1884.

Vries, D.H. de, *Een Amsterdamse koopman in de Molukken 1883–1901. Ingeleid en samengesteld door Ruard Wallis de Vries*. Baarn: Ambo, 1996.

Wal, S.L. van der, *De opkomst van de nationalistische beweging in Nederlandsch-Indië. Een bronnenpublikatie*. Groningen: Wolters, 1967.

Wal, S.L. van der, "Het rascriterium en het overheidsbeleid in Nederlands-Indië", *Internationale Spectator. Tijdschrift voor Internationale Politiek* 20 (1966): 832–53.

Walbeehm, A.H.J.G., "Iets over cijfers en percentages in verband met de Afdeeling B", *Tijdschrift voor het Binnenlandsch Bestuur* 31 (1906): 281–85.

Wall, V.I. van de, *The Influence of Olivia Mariamne Raffles on European Society in Java (1812–1814)*. N.p. [Batavia]: n.n., n.d. [1930].

Wall, V.I. van de, *De Nederlandsche oudheden in de Molukken*. 's-Gravenhage: Nijhoff, 1928.

Wallace, Alfred Russel, *Het Maleise eilandenrijk*. Amsterdam: Atlas, 1998. Translation of *The Malay Archipelago*. London: Macmillan, 1869.

Wertheim, W.F., "Conditions on Sugar Estates in Colonial Java. Comparisons with Deli", *Journal of Southeast Asian Studies* 24, 2 (Sept. 1993): 268–84.

Westland, Cora, *De levensroman van Andries de Wilde*. Wageningen: Veenman, n.d.

Wijnaendts van Resandt, W., *De gezaghebbers der Oost-Indische Compagnie op hare buiten-comptoiren in Azië*. Centrale Dienst voor Sibbekunde, Genealogische Bibliotheek 2. Amsterdam: Liebaert, 1944.

Wijnaendts van Resandt, W., "Huwelijken te Batavia in den Compagniestijd", *Maandblad van het Genealogisch-Heraldiek Genootschap "De Nederlandsche Leeuw"* 22 (1904): 209–18, 245–51, 279–83, 311–16; Idem 23 (1905): 15–21, 55–63, 96–100, 129–39, 192–201, 232–36, 253–58, 283–92; Idem 24 (1906): 19–26, 55–62.

Wijnaendts van Resandt, W., "Oude Indische families II. Het geslacht Senn van Basel", *Maandblad van het Genealogisch-Heraldiek Genootschap "De Nederlandsche Leeuw"* 23 (1905): 182–90, 217–25, 258–67, 292–97; Idem 24 (1906): 10–18.

Wijnaendts van Resandt, W., "Oude Indische families VI. Het geslacht Couperus", *Maandblad van het Genealogisch-Heraldiek Genootschap "De Nederlandsche Leeuw"* 26 (1908): 208–14, 239–43, 271–75, 303–6.

Winius, George, "The 'Shadow Empire' of Goa in the Bay of Bengal", *Itinerario* 7, 2 (1983): 83–101.

Wit, Augusta de, *Natuur en menschen in Indië*. Amsterdam: Maatschappij voor Goede en Goedkoope Lectuur, 1914.

Wolk, P.J. van der, "Tropenromantiek. (Geschiedenis van onze nootmuskaat-cultuur)", *Cultura. Orgaan van het Ned. Genootschap voor Landbouwwetenschap* 32 (1920): 100–13, 157–68, 259–69, 307–14, 344–54; Idem 33 (1921): 60–68.

Wormser, C.W., *Ontginners van Java*. Deventer: Van Hoeve, n.d. [*ca.* 1925].

Wurtzburg, C.E., *Raffles of the Eastern Isles*. Singapore: Oxford University Press, 1986 (orig. publ. London: Hodder & Stoughton, 1954).

Wyatt, David K., "A Persian Mission to Siam in the Reign of King Narai", in: Idem, *Studies in Thai History. Collected Articles*. Chiang Mai: Silkworm Books, 1994, pp. 90–97.

Wyatt, David K., "Family Politics in Seventeenth- and Eighteenth-Century Siam", in: Idem, *Studies in Thai History. Collected Articles*. Chiang Mai: Silkworm Books, 1994, pp. 98–106.

Wyatt, David K., "King Borommakot, His Court, and Their World", in: Remco Raben and Dhiravat na Pombejra, ed., *In the King's Trail. An 18th Century Dutch Journey to the Buddha's Footprint. Theodorus Jacobus van den Heuvel's Account of His Voyage to Phra Phutthabat in 1737*. Bangkok: The Royal Netherlands Embassy, 1997, pp. 53–60.

Young, Robert J.C., *Colonial Desire. Hybridity in Theory, Culture and Race*. London and New York: Routledge, 1995.

Index

Abrahams, Margaretha Juliana 46
Aceh 3, 183, 239, 249, 284, 317
Aceh War 175
adoption 32, 33, 38, 44, 46, 225, 271
Africa 1, 3, 4, 191, 239
African soldiers ix, 238, 239, 285
Agra 14
Agrarian Law (1870) 128, 136, 139, 281
agricultural colonies 134, 255, 256, 311, 316
agricultural conference 134, 135, 279, 282
agricultural crisis (1884) 258, 259, 262, 266, 267, 280, 288
agricultural education 235, 251, 252, 255
agriculture 41, 47, 51, 53, 95, 96, 99, 104, 110, 121, 124, 126, 128, 136–38, 162, 208, 232, 260, 282, 291, 337, 388
Aguinaldo, Emilio 303
Albuquerque, Afonso de 22
All Indies Congress 338, 342
Alting, Pieternella Gerhardina 73
Alting, Willem Arnold 74, 88
Amaril 69
Ambarawa 236, 365
Ambon (Amboina)/Ambonese 16, 19, 27–29, 46, 67, 72, 75, 89, 91, 133, 143, 144, 148, 150, 154–56, 159, 165–70, 172–76, 238, 239, 263, 285, 301, 320, 329, 333, 340, 369, 371, 389, 390

Ambon Burgher School 174
Ambonese Educational Trust (Vereeniging Ambonsch Studiefonds) 320, 333, 390
Ament 262
Ament, D. 382
Ament, H.M. 382
Ament, J.L. 382
Ament, Jan Abraham 216
Ament, Tjalling 216
America (see also United States) 16, 57, 71, 124, 191, 265, 277, 278, 303, 319, 331, 340, 341
Amiens, Peace of 75
Amsterdam 11, 77, 78, 98, 156, 158, 171, 195, 249, 261, 262, 299, 307
Anderson, Benedict 20
Andrée Wiltens, Henri Maximiliaan 177
Andriesse, George Albertus 301–307, 320, 387
Andriesse, J. 301
Anemaet & Co. 140, 259
Angelbeek, Van 56, 57, 355
Angelbeek, Christiaan van 56, 57
Angelbeek, Johan Gerard van 57
Angelbeek, Johann Gerhard van 56
Anglo-Dutch Java United Planters Ltd 366
Anglo-Dutch War, Fourth 67, 69
Anglo-Indians (see also Eurasians) 49, 262, 282
Antilles 159
Anti-Revolutionaire Partij 282

Arabia 3, 66
Arabs 3, 7, 14, 154, 156, 158,
    159, 270, 272, 273
Arcot 76
Ardesch, Pelgrim Charles 196,
    197, 199, 201
Armenians 3, 9, 13
army *passim*
Army Training School (Pupillenkorps)
    241–43, 246–50, 256, 346
Arnold, Joseph 88, 98
artisans 25, 26, 36, 37, 42, 51–53,
    163, 186, 188, 219, 235, 237,
    250, 252–54, 256, 282
Aserappa 77
association politics 329, 335, 337,
    339, 341, 343
Austria 119, 195
A. van Hoboken & Co. 139, 140,
    259, 265
Ayutthaya 3–5, 8–12, 14, 349

Baadilla 382
Baadella, Mohammed bin Abdulla
    (Sech Abdulrachim Baadilla)
    158, 159
Bacan 162
Bagelen 247
Bake, Adriana Johanna 61
Bake, Ida Wilhelmina 70
Bakker 162
Bakkers, Johannes Antonius 179,
    180
Bali 47, 51, 159, 166
Baljé, Jacobus Martinus 59
Banda xvi, 5, 61, 72, 110, 143,
    150–61, 167, 170, 172, 263,
    272, 278, 341, 346, 369, 371,
    382
Banda Neira 150–52, 154, 158, 367
Bandung 97, 98, 170, 315, 321–23,
    325–29, 338, 340

Bang, Michiel 12
Bang, Nicolaas 11
Bangka 177, 320
Banjarmasin 78
banks 258–61, 281
Banten 36, 84, 169
Banyumas 265
Banyuwangi 282
Barrett, William 88
Batavian Society for the Arts and
    Sciences (Bataviaasch
    Genootschap voor Kunsten en
    Wetenschappen) 118, 119, 196
batik 129, 130, 150, 273, 323,
    344
Baud, Jean-Chrétien 189, 191,
    192, 194, 195, 203, 211, 214
Baumgarten 111, 365
Baumgarten, Christoffel Willem
    113, 124
Baumgarten, Johan Cornelis 362
Baumgarten, Maria Dorothea 113
Belitung (Billiton) 177
Bengal 3, 5, 10, 13, 16, 35, 40,
    61, 67, 69, 72, 97, 162
Bengalis 3, 69
Berding, Frans 327
Berg, Gerardus van den 212
Berg, H.J.P. van den 261, 282
Berg, Norbert Pieter van den 125,
    352, 356, 382
Bergen, Henrietta van den 361
Bernard, Willem Hendrik 371
Bernard, Willem Jacobus Fredrik
    371
Berretty, Louis Frederik 110
Besant, Annie 296
Besuki 106
Beusechem, Carolina Justina van
    216
Beynon, C. 304
Bijvoet, A. 304
Billiton-Maatschappij 177

Binnenlands Bestuur (the Interior Administration) 114, 117, 132, 133, 135, 140, 141, 146, 167–69, 176, 179–81, 184, 189, 203, 212–14, 254–56, 281, 290, 294, 296, 302, 344
Birnie 139, 141, 264
Birnie, David 140, 329
Birnie, George 140, 141
Birnie, Gerhard David 140
Bisschop Grevelink, Arnoldus Hermanus 202
Bitter, Rijckloff de 61
Bloemen Waanders, Jeanetta Antoinetta Louise van 371
Bloemhard, J.L. 154
Blommestein, G.F. van 290–92
Bocarro, António 15, 23
Boedi Oetomo 318, 320–23, 326, 329, 333
Boemi Poetra 326, 327, 335
Boer War 303, 317
Bombay 98, 273, 274
Bond van Geneesheren (Medical Association) 323, 324
Bone 99, 146, 147
Bonto-Bonto, Karaeng 180
Borneo 5, 78, 194, 341
Bosscha, Karel 329
Bosscher, C. 163
Boursse, Esaias 30
Bouville, Alexandrina Helena de 371
Boxer, Charles 23
Braam, J.A. van 90
Braam, Ursula Susanna van 189
Brandes, Jan 48, 54, 60, 61, 65
Brazil 109, 319
Brest van Kempen, Carel Pieter 114, 135
Brink, Jan ten 126–28
British *passim*
British rule 84, 104, 218, 344

Brochebourde, Daniel de 10, 11
Brochebourde, Jeremias de 11
Brochebourde, Moses de 11, 12
Brochebourde, Paulus de 11
Brochebourde, Pieter de 12
Broese van Groenou, Wolter 112, 261, 265, 298
Bronsveld, Siebert Abrahamszen 77
Brooshooft, Pieter 301
Brugghen, H. van der 298
Brugman 180, 184
Brugman, J.A.G. 179–81, 212
Bruining, Wernard 205
Bruyn, Jacobus de 187
Bruyn, Pieter Gerardus de 57
Buddhism 318
Buddingh, Steven Adriaan 187, 188, 251, 252
Buginese 145–47, 149–51
Buitenzorg (Bogor) 74, 84, 95, 97, 98, 220, 279
Burgemeestre 46
Burghers (Ceylon) 39–41, 63, 64, 77, 80–82, 204, 344
Burghers (Moluccas) 75, 155, 160, 165–67, 174, 224
Burghers (*vrijburgers*, VOC) 24, 29, 34–44, 49, 51, 58, 68, 75, 81, 82, 95, 143, 160, 172, 186, 187, 344, 351
Burn (resident) 91
Bus de Gisignies, Leonard Pierre Joseph du 226
Buschken, H.F. 135

Calabresini 131
Calcutta (Kolkota) 16, 74, 97, 102, 103, 204
Calicut (Kozhikode) 3
Cambay 3
Canter Visscher, Jacobus 13

Canter Visscher, Johannes
    Theodorus 195, 201
Cape of Good Hope 75, 80
Capellen, Godert Alexander Gerard
    Philip baron van der 92, 98,
    105, 107, 119, 369
Caribbean 134, 159, 166, 204,
    369
Cardoso, Anna 51
Carels, Geertruida Carolina Frederica
    78
Carels, Jan Frederik 79
Carli 133
Carpentier Alting, J.H. 335
Caspersz, Johan Arnaud Renoldes
    187
Celebes *see* Sulawesi
Ceram 263, 369, 382
Ceylon (Sri Lanka) 3, 16, 18, 19,
    22, 24, 28, 30, 31, 38–40, 42,
    43, 52, 54, 56–58, 61, 67, 72,
    75–80, 82, 152, 204, 206,
    277, 280, 344, 347, 379
Charon de Saint Germain, baron
    158
Chatterjee, Partha 285
Chêne de Vienne, Maria Clara du
    59
Chettiyar 40, 77, 357
Chijs, Jacobus Anne van der 166,
    174
China 1, 3, 4, 6, 8, 35–37, 58,
    94, 141, 178, 317
Chinese *passim*
Chinsura 69
Christianity 13, 23, 24, 28, 42,
    76, 77, 175, 220, 318
Christians xiv, 11, 26, 27, 32, 33,
    37, 44, 48, 50, 52, 80, 81, 84,
    93, 94, 155, 160–62, 164,
    165, 173–76, 207, 220, 223,
    224, 226, 229, 237, 238, 241,
    247, 292, 320, 369, 372

church 26–28, 31, 32, 34, 43, 45,
    47–53, 59, 63, 64, 67, 70, 77,
    93, 129, 155, 162, 164, 178,
    202, 226, 233, 237, 239, 241,
    243, 272, 282, 290, 291, 299,
    310, 344
Cianjur 97, 98
Cibogo 292
Cilacap 249
Cirebon 98, 106, 137, 181, 182,
    216, 262, 269, 324
civil servants *passim*
civil servants' examination 132,
    169, 176, 179, 181, 191, 211,
    214, 219, 300
Claassen, Jan 187
Claessens 131
cloves 19, 172, 173, 175
club (*sociëteit*) xi, 130, 133, 157,
    178, 183, 197, 202
Cochin (South India) 13, 23, 39,
    40, 76, 242
Cochin-China 4, 35
cocoa 161, 162, 167
Coen, Jan Pieterszoon 27, 28, 151
Coert, Jan Johannes 212
Coert, Johan Jacob 212, 213
Coert, Johan Willem Christiaan
    212
Coert, Nicolaas Wilhelmus 212
coffee 98, 99, 101, 108, 109, 114,
    120, 123, 126, 139, 145, 258,
    261, 264–66, 279, 281, 282
Colombo 16, 19, 23, 28–30, 39–41,
    46, 49, 54, 56–58, 76, 77, 81,
    83, 187
Committee for East Indies Affairs
    78
Committee for the Support of
    Needy Christians 237, 238
concubinage 9, 10, 12, 13, 16, 21,
    27, 28, 32–34, 38, 42, 45, 46,
    50, 69, 70, 87, 94, 113, 164,

170, 171, 212, 213, 225–28, 234, 236, 240, 244, 245, 256, 272, 293, 310, 343, 346
Condro Kusumo, Raden Ayu 108
Confucian 7
coolies 25, 30, 156, 157, 187
Cores de Vries 164
Corli 133
Cornelius 83
Coromandel 4, 5, 61, 67, 72, 130
corvée labour 19, 95, 96, 110, 115, 127, 134–36, 143, 160, 166, 167, 333, 346
Council of Justice 78
Couperus, Abraham 63, 64, 73, 75
Couperus, Anna Gerhardina (Antje) 75
Couperus, Catharina Elisabeth (Elise) 63, 74
Couperus, Gesina 73, 75, 91, 102
Couperus, Jacobina Maria 74, 91
Couperus, Louis 137, 181, 297, 341, 342
Couperus, Petrus Theodorus (Piet) 74, 75, 84, 86–90, 94, 138
Couperus, Willem Jacob Thomas Raffles 90
Court of Justice 54, 152, 155, 163, 167, 187, 188, 196
Cranssen, Catharina Rica 86, 89
Cranssen, Willem Jacob 75, 88–90, 92, 96
Crediet- en Handelsvereeniging Banda (CHV, Credit and Trading Society of Banda) 263, 382
creolisation xiii, 14, 17, 21, 69, 153, 165, 166
Croos, Magdalene de 76
Cuba 106, 134, 259, 265, 277
Cultivation System 103, 105, 106, 124, 125, 128, 281, 344

Cultuurmaatschappij der Vorstenlanden (Estate Company of the Principalities) 262, 382
Curaçao 159
Cuylenburg, Van 82

Daendels, Herman Willem 69, 83, 84, 89–91, 94, 96–98, 174
Damsi, Helena 58
Darwinism 294, 297, 318
Datangh 31
Daum, Bart 316
Daum, P.A. (Paul) 126, 138, 139, 220, 272, 273, 288, 289, 295, 297, 301, 316
Deans, Scott & Co. 102
Debt-bondsman or debt-bondswoman (*pandeling*) 42, 43, 346
Dekker, Johannes F. den 177
Delden, A.J.W. van 235
Delft (Academy) 100, 117, 118, 132, 158, 179, 190, 191, 193, 194, 197–99, 202, 203, 211, 212, 214, 234, 369
Delhi 14
Deli 141, 341
Delmaar, Johannes Adrianus 368, 382
Demmer, Gerard 22
Deshima 69
Desker 83
Deux 46
Deventer 264
Dezentjé 46, 108, 111, 112, 120, 129, 131, 137, 261, 265
Dezentjé, Johannes Augustinus 100, 107–11, 137, 138, 266
Dezentjé, Sara Helena 108
Dias 172
Dias, Andreas 372
Dietrée, Johannes Gottlieb 116

Dinger, Jan 319
Diponegoro 107, 119
Djaeng Patti 360
Djajadiningrat, Achmad 319, 329, 335
Djati Institute 242
Dom 111, 113, 133, 137
Dom, Arend Nicolaas 362
Dom, Geertruida Louisa (Santje) 112, 131, 132, 261
Dom, J.G. 298
Dom, J.P. 365
Dom, L.E. 365
Dom, Pieter 113, 136
Dom, Pieter Melior 298, 362
Doren, Jan Baptist Jozef van 93, 164, 221
Dorrepaal, Georgius Leonardus 119–23, 133, 261–63, 265, 363
Dorrepaalsche Bank (Dorrepaal & Co.) 120, 121, 259–62, 282
Douwes Dekker, Ernest F.E. 280, 316–28, 332–34, 337, 338, 342
Duivenbode 370
Duivenbode, L.D.W.A. van Renesse van 370
Duivenbode, Maarten Dick van Renesse van 164
Duymaer van Twist, Albertus Jacobus 144, 152, 153, 163, 167, 253
Dutch Reformed Church 26, 32, 43, 45, 47, 155, 178, 281, 282, 291, 310

Eberts 82
education *passim*
educational trust 300, 320, 329, 333
Eekhout, H. 261
Eekhout, W. 178
Engelhard 96
Engelhard, Nicolaus 88, 90, 97, 98

Enklaar van Guericke, Frederik Adriaan 134, 279, 281, 282, 289, 311, 365
England 84, 88–90, 296, 299
Eurasians 9, 12, 22, 37, 64, 107, 127, 218, 282, 289, 290, 361, 385

Falck, Iman Willem 58, 77
Fillietaz de Bousquet, Reinier 135
Fock, Dirk 305
Forbes, Charles 98
Fort de Kock 183, 245
France 4, 10, 68, 84, 106, 195, 255, 299
Francis, Emanuel (E.M.) 242
Francisca, Selfisina 368
Fransen van de Putte, Isaäc Dignus 235
Francis Joseph, Emperor 119
Frederik, Emilia Elverina 183
Freemasonry 63, 111, 118, 133, 252, 296, 320, 338
free trade 144, 172
French 58, 67, 68, 72, 90, 94, 100, 138, 148, 154, 156
Fretes, De 172
Fretes, Jacoba Dorothea de 172
Fritschi 130
Fuhri, Eduard Johannes Lourens 205
Furnivall, John S. 260

Galela 162
Galle 28, 31, 39, 40, 54, 77
Gamelan 108, 115, 127, 137, 154, 345
Garut 125, 126
George III, King 89, 90, 92
German 31, 54, 61, 64, 73, 187, 264, 265, 286, 318

Germany 56, 162, 195, 212, 299
Geyzel, Van 82
Ghij, Willem de 12
Ginkel, Charlotte Elizabeth 79
Goa (Sulawesi) 47, 148
Goa (India) 15, 22
Gobius, Adriana 58
Goldberg, Theo 20
Goldman, Jacoba Maria 89
Goldman, Jenny Mary 183
Goldman, Johan Christiaan 89, 212
Goldman, Maria Elisabeth 212
Gombong 242, 243, 247–50, 346
Gorssel 255
Government Regulation (1854)
    224, 326, 369
Graaff, Simon de 335, 336
Graaff, Willem Jacob van de 56, 57
Great Obi 255
Greek 5, 10, 78, 149, 151, 166
Gujarat 3–6, 9, 14, 15
Guttig, M.J. 371

Haan, Frederik de 331
Haarlem 50, 251
Haeckel, Ernst 318
Hague, The 132, 189, 192, 193,
    198, 202, 203, 261, 264, 300,
    302, 310, 327
hajji 136, 272, 345
Halkema, W. 386
Halmahera 162
harbour masters (*syahbandar*) 5, 8,
    57, 146, 347
Harloff 130
Hartog, A.M.L. 157, 158
Hartsinck, Willem 61
Hasselt 162
Hazaart, Jacobus Arnoldus 91, 373
HBS (Hogere Burgerschool) 131,
    132, 209, 210, 252, 254, 295,
    317, 345

Heijden, Karel van der 217
Heijden, Maria Simons van der 51
Hendricks 83
Hendriks, B.L. 108
Herrebrugh 153
Heusden, J.W. van 180
Heutsz, Joannes Benedictus van
    317
Heydt, Johann Wolfgang 31
Hinloopen Labberton, Dirk J. van
    296, 329, 335
Hitu 167
Hoboken, Anthony van 103, 127
Hobson, John A. 265
Hoedt, Carel Hendrik 371
Hoedt, Dirk Samuel 168
Hoedt, F.J. 371
Hoedt, George Alexander 371
Hoedt, H.E. 371
Hoedt, Pieter Johannes 371
Hoedt, Willem Joseph 371
Hoeke, H.W. 369
Hoeke, L.F. 369
Hoetink, Harry 159
Hoëvell, Wolter Robert baron van
    195–97, 202
Hoevenaar, Christina 78
Hofland 138, 139, 295, 297
Hofland, Egbert Charles 366
Hofland, G.H. 366
Hofland, Johannes Theodorus 366
Hofland, Peter William (Pieter)
    98, 99, 126–28, 131, 138, 139
Hofland, Thomas Benjamin 127
Hogendorp, Dirk van 70
Holle 125, 126, 329
Holle, Albert 263
Holle, Karel 124–26, 131, 134,
    135
Holmberg de Beckfelt, Otto Carel
    105, 106
Hom 133
Houthuysen, J.G.L., sr. 386

Höveker, J.E. 164
Hoynck van Papendrecht, Reynier
    Bernardus 55–57, 60
Hucht, Guillaume Louis Jacques
    van der 125
Hustaert, Maria 61
Hyderabad 274

Ibn Battuta, Abu Abdullah 3
Idenburg, Alexander Willem Frederik
    310, 312, 325, 326, 329
IJsseldijk, Wouter Hendrik van 90
Indië Weerbaar movement
    (Defending the Indies) 329, 330
India 1, 3, 5, 13, 16, 17, 22–24,
    35, 36, 39, 40, 47–49, 52, 61,
    64, 66, 67, 72, 73, 76, 77,
    79–81, 103, 126–28, 130,
    162, 187, 204, 218, 242, 245,
    273, 281, 282, 285, 289, 296,
    302, 317, 318, 322, 325, 330,
    339, 344, 351, 361
Indian National Congress 322, 325
indigo 97, 100, 102, 114, 120,
    121, 123, 124, 128, 132, 134,
    261, 263–65, 365
Indisch Landbouwgenootschap
    (Agricultural Society of the
    Indies) 134
Indische Bond 301, 303–308, 311,
    312, 314–17, 321–23, 333, 345
Indische Party 280, 320, 323–30,
    333, 335, 337, 346
Indische Universiteits-Vereeniging
    (University Association of the
    Indies) 319
Indo-Europeesch Verbond (Indo-
    European Union) or IEV 297,
    308, 311, 334, 336–38, 340,
    342, 345
Institute for the Javanese Languages
    117, 147

Insulinde 315, 321, 323, 326,
    330, 332, 333, 390
Internatio 121
interpreter 11, 76, 100, 116–18,
    132, 147, 180, 181, 218
Islam (Muslims) 3, 6, 7, 18, 20,
    40, 92, 116, 144, 155, 158,
    165–67, 174, 126, 220, 224,
    226, 271–73, 289, 290, 317,
    323, 345, 346, 368

Jacob, Frederik 's 279
Jaffnapatnam 76, 77
Jaggernaikpuram 126
Jansz, Isaac 51–53
Jansz, P. Abraham 289, 291
Jan van Batavia 50
Japan 1, 4, 6, 36, 69, 102, 317,
    331
Japanese 1, 9, 69, 102, 215, 250,
    323, 326
Java Benevolent Society (Javaansch
    Menschlievend Genootschap)
    92
Java Bible Fellowship (Javaansch
    Medewerkend
    Bijbelgenootschap) 92
Javasche Bank 242
Java Suiker Werkgevers Bond (Java
    Sugar Employers Union) 337
Java War 107, 110, 112
Jember 140
John Peet & Co. 126
Jongens-Weezeninrichting (Orphan
    Boys' Institution) 252, 253,
    254, 345
Jong Indië (Young Indies) 277,
    279–81, 284, 285
Joostenszoon 162
Juliana, Princess 321
justice, administration of 5, 18,
    32, 170, 277

Kal, Jacob van 73
Kalenberg van Dort, John Leonard 83
Kam, Joseph 173
Kartasura 44
Kediri 169, 176, 212, 213
Kedung Kebo 247
Kedu 194
Keijser, Christina Elisabeth 371
Kendal 193
Kerkhoven 125, 126, 329
Kerkhoven, Eduard 263
Kerkhoven, Rudolf 125
keroncong *see* Krontjong
Kesteren, Carel Eliza van 252, 301
Kisar 144, 162
Kittelman, Christiaan 49
Kläring, Andreas Emanuel 362
Kläring, Frederik Andreas Emanuel 362
Kläring, Karel Emanuel 362
Klaten 133
Klattensche Cultuurmaatschappij (Klattensche Estate Company) 262
Kleian, F.A. 301
kleinelandbouwordonnantie (Decree regarding small-scale farming) 311
Knaap, Otto 231, 275, 305
Kock van Leeuwen, Johan Cornelis de 193
Koek, Catharina Johanna 63, 73
Koesoemo Oetoyo 335
Koloniale Bank 121, 259, 382
Komedie Stamboel (*Comedy Stamboel*) 273–76, 305
Koning, J. 141
Koninklijke Olie 341
Kraag, Frans Hendrik 362
Krämer, Wilhelmina 113
Karawang 98

Krontjong (keroncong) 273–75, 331, 345
Kruseman, Mina 171
Ksatrian Institute 338, 342
Kupang 91
Kuyk, Th.K.J. van 304
Kuyper, Abraham 281, 282

labour union *see* trade union
Lancashire 130
Lammers, Pieter Bernardus 362
Landbouwmaatschappij Oud Djember NV (Estate Company of Oud Djember, PLC) 140, 264
Landouw, Theodorus Roeland 280, 285, 309, 332, 386
landowners 41, 58, 59, 75, 94–100, 103, 104, 125, 138, 148, 186, 371
language 3, 6, 7, 9, 13, 19, 47, 49, 53, 85, 92, 104, 108, 116–18, 126, 145, 147, 152, 165, 166, 173, 174, 177, 179, 198, 202, 208, 209, 211, 215, 217, 218, 220, 247, 248, 256, 272, 279, 280, 284, 285, 287, 295, 302, 325, 334, 339, 343, 346
Lans, Pieter Cornelis 156, 157
Lansberge, Johan Wilhelm van 256
Lantzius 157
Lantzius, M.J.H. 369
Lao 10
Latin America 277, 319
Latoepeirissa, Antomina 155
lease holders 100, 104, 106, 107, 110–16, 118, 120, 124, 125, 130, 132–37, 139, 297
Leembruggen 82
Leiden 78, 168, 169, 172, 211, 300, 305

Leitimor 167
Lennep, C. van 261
Lennon, Walter Caulfield 63, 64
Lequin, Frank 13
Leunissen 155
Leunissen, Adrianus Andries 368
Ligor (Nakhon Si Thammasat)
   10, 58
Limburg Stirum, Johan Paul Count
   of 330, 335, 342
Lingen, W. van 291
Lobatto 130
local council elections 333
Lombok 249, 304
London 74, 94, 241, 275
Lonthor (Great Banda) 150, 151,
   153–55
Lorenz, Charles Ambrose 82
Loudon, John F. 177
Lucassen, Theodoor 105, 106
Ludeking, Everhardus Wijnandus
   Adrianus 167
Luzon 3, 5

Macau 36
mace (*see also* nutmeg) 150, 151,
   156, 157, 263, 368
Maclaine, Gillian 109
Maclaine, Watson & Co. 109
Macquoid, Thomas 97, 98
Madras (Chennai) 49, 127, 282
Madura 91, 236, 237, 310, 311
Magelang 175, 236, 245, 249,
   251
Mahieu, Auguste 275, 276, 305
Makassar xi, 4, 7, 36, 47, 61, 67,
   99, 100, 102, 143–50, 159,
   164, 166, 170, 171, 176–81,
   183, 184, 187, 194, 206, 212,
   230, 268, 275, 276, 279, 287,
   301, 305, 367
Makassarese xii, 70, 147, 166, 180

Malacca 4, 5, 7, 14, 16, 19, 23,
   29, 41, 42, 55, 57, 58, 63–65,
   67, 72–75, 80, 83, 86, 110
Malang 254, 291
malaria 38, 43, 66, 67, 76, 143,
   170, 291
Malay 3–8, 14, 47, 52, 63, 64,
   69, 83, 85, 99, 127, 153, 165,
   166, 174, 190, 195, 202, 208,
   209, 215, 218, 230, 246, 247,
   263, 272, 273, 277, 279, 287,
   295, 307, 333, 334, 346, 367
Maldives 1, 3
Manado 91, 163–65, 171, 172,
   175, 227, 308, 311, 320, 329,
   340, 370
Manadonese 320, 333
Mangkubumi 107
Mangoenkoesoemo, Tjipto 318,
   322, 325–27, 330, 333, 336,
   343
Manila 303
Manuel, Ludovica 120, 122
Marana estate 146, 183
Mardijkers 31, 32, 34, 37, 42,
   46–53, 60, 84, 93, 95, 104,
   185, 188, 207, 345
Maros 147, 183
Masius, Jan George 237, 238
May movement (1848) 191, 193,
   195–203, 233, 301, 320
Mazzini, Giuseppe 82
Mecca 3, 345
Medan 307, 337
Medhurst, Walter Henry 241
Meijer 133
Meijer, Adriana Augustina 155
Meijer, Frederika Anthoinetta 371
Meijer, Hendrina 73
Meijer, Johan Hendrik 73, 74
Meijer, Johannes Jacobus 77
Meijer (Timmerman Thijssen),
   Pieter Henry 100

Meijer & Co. 101

Melho, Philip de 77

Mesman xii, 146, 149, 182–84

Mesman, Aletta 182

Mesman, Alexander 183

Mesman, Emilie xi, xvii, 154, 163, 183

Mesman, Eugenie 183

Mesman, Jacob David Matthijs 147, 149

Mesman, Jacoba Margaretha 367

Mesman, Johannes 100

Mesman, Johan David 146, 147, 187

Mesman, Johannes Willem 181, 182

Mesman, Willem Leendert 145, 146, 149, 180, 181, 183

Mettray 255

Metz, Frédéric de 255

Meuka 12

Meu Nooy 12

Meutha 12

Mexico 318, 319

Michiels 96

Michielsz, Augustijn (Major Jantji) 104, 109, 126, 127

Michielsz, Pieter 95

Mieling, C.W. 117

migration xii, xvi, xvii, 15–17, 25, 26, 35, 41, 57, 76, 124, 144, 166, 168, 173, 188, 216, 281, 314

Military Academy 300, 301, 305

military *passim*

militia 40, 49, 52, 144, 152, 154, 158, 166, 167, 329, 371

Minahasa 144, 172, 174–76, 239, 336, 366, 372

Minto, Lord Gilbert Elliot 97, 102

mission/missionary 1, 87, 144, 166, 173, 174, 241, 249, 251, 366

mixed marriage xiii, 8, 17, 21–23, 34, 37, 62, 160, 224, 227, 271, 294, 343

Mocca 7

Moeis, Abdoel 326, 327, 329

Moergappa, Manuel 77

Moluccas xvi, 5, 36, 46, 61, 72, 90–92, 110, 124, 133, 144, 148, 150, 152, 153, 156, 158, 160–68, 171, 173–76, 178, 191, 224, 227, 255, 278, 333, 369

Mon 5, 10–12

Moore, W.C.J. van der 179

Moorrees, D.F. 371

Moorrees, K.R. 371

Moors 4, 40

Morgenstern, Heinrich Ludwig 64

Mulder 157

Müller, Max 318

Muller Kruseman, J.C. 108

Multatuli 317

Muntok 177

Mutual Improvement Society 289, 290, 292

Musa, Muhammad 126

music 127, 154, 164, 168, 273–75, 331, 345

Muslims *see* Islam

Mysore 385

naamloze vennootschap see Public Limited Company

Nagapattinam 40

Nahuys van Burgst, Huibert Gerard 106, 107

Nallur 76

Napoleon 66, 84, 88, 102, 176, 185, 188, 326

Narai, King 10

Nationaal Indische Partij (NIP) 333, 334, 336, 337, 346

nationalism xvii, 82, 118, 202, 276, 278, 285, 286, 296, 297, 302, 303, 308, 317, 318, 322, 325, 326, 328, 329, 337–40, 343

Nederlandsche Handel-Maatschappij (Netherlands Trading Company) or NHM 101, 103, 105, 109, 120, 127, 138, 200, 259, 260–62, 341, 346, 360, 363, 382

Nederlandsch-Indische Escompto Maatschappij 319

Nederlandsch-Indische Handelsbank (NIHB) 121, 125, 139, 259, 260, 262, 263, 346, 382

Nederlandsch-Indische Landbouwmaatschappij (Netherlands-Indies Agricultural Company) 262, 366

Nederlandse Vereeniging van Spoor- en Tramweg Personeel (Netherlands Association of Railway and Tram Employees) 304

Neijs xii, 150, 163

Neijs, Johannes Alexander 91, 92

Neijs, J.W. 163

Neijs, Wilhelmus Henricus (Hein) xi, xvii, 150, 183

Nell, Frederick 82

Nell, Louis 82

Neubronner van der Tuuk, Herman 118

Neuman, J.H. 119, 122

Neumann 170, 172, 173, 176, 213

Neumann, Frederik J.E. 168, 172, 212

Neumann, Frits 168, 169, 171, 176

Neumann, Gottlieb Chr. D. 168, 169, 176, 213

Neumann, Louis 168–70, 172

Neumann, Rudolph 168–72, 176, 177, 181, 225

New Guinea xi, 145, 159, 162, 166

newspapers 82, 85, 87, 93, 118, 134, 144, 177, 178, 203–206, 208, 215, 220, 267–72, 278, 284, 288–92, 294, 299, 306, 315, 323, 325, 331, 333, 384

Nienhuys, Jacob 128, 366

Nieuwenhuysen, Marius 316

Notodirojo 118, 317, 323

nutmeg xvi, 110, 143, 150, 151, 153, 154, 156, 157, 263, 341, 346, 368, 382

Oey Toa Nio 212

Olivier, Johannes 221, 222, 369

Ondaatchi, Michael Jurie (Ondaatie, Michiel Jurjansz) 76

Ondaatje 76, 77, 80

Ondaatje, Adriaan Marius Elaarst 76, 78, 79, 80

Ondaatje, Pieter Philip Christiaan 78, 79, 80

Ondaatje, Pieter Philip Juriaan (Quint) 78, 79

Ondaatje, Willem Juriaan 77, 78

Ong Tae Hae (Wang Dahai) 8

Onrust 55

opium 107, 139, 145, 270, 284

orphans/orphanage 12, 33–35, 43, 50, 51, 123, 187, 207, 219, 224, 230, 232, 236, 237, 239–45, 247, 250–56, 272, 292, 310, 345

Orphans' Chamber 80, 138, 152, 155, 167, 172, 188, 212, 234, 347, 371, 382

Ort 342

Ottolander, Teun 281, 282
Oud Djember *see*
    Landbouwmaatschappij Oud
    Djember
Outhoorn, Cornelis van 52

Padang 163, 170, 206, 268, 270,
    276–79, 287, 292, 301
Padang Movement *see* Jong Indië
Padang Union (Padangsche Bond)
    308
Padris 287
Pahud, Charles Ferdinand 144,
    156, 203
Paku Alam V 118
Paku Alam VII 118, 317
Palakka, Arung 149
Paleacatte (Pulicat) 187
Palembang 5, 42, 78
Palmer & Co. 74
Pamanukan and Ciasem lands 98,
    126
Pampanga 148
Parapattan Orphanage 187, 241,
    242
Parra, Petrus Albertus van der 38,
    57, 61
Pasai 5, 6
Pasuruan 42, 106
Pattani 6
Patty, Alexander J. 333
Paulus, J.A. 207
pauperism 12, 17, 219, 220, 227,
    228, 234–37, 239, 240, 244,
    251, 255–58, 268, 269, 279,
    280, 282, 283, 293, 294, 301,
    309–313
pauperism enquiry 227, 236, 237,
    239, 240, 244, 255, 256, 309,
    310, 312, 313, 386
Payen, Antoine 92, 96, 147, 230
Pegu 4, 5, 10, 47

Pekalongan 97, 106, 137, 225,
    260, 301, 324
Pelauw 333
Penang 7, 98, 102, 157
People's Agricultural Credit Bank
    182
People's Council (*Volksraad*) 140,
    328–33, 335, 336, 339, 343,
    347
pepper 59
perkeniers (owners of Banda nutmeg
    groves) 110, 143, 150–60, 167,
    170, 172, 263, 272, 273, 346
Perron, E. du 138
Pers, Auguste van 238
Perserikatan Minahasa 336
Persia 1, 3, 6
Persians 1, 3, 5–7
Petel, Louis 97
Peters, Jacob Willem 146, 147
Peters, Jacoba Helena 146
Petersdorf, C.M.E. 298
petition xvi, 36, 40, 49, 68,
    195–200, 202, 204, 301, 305,
    368
Petjo 209, 346
Phaulkon, Constantine 10, 14
Philippines 8, 29, 148, 204, 259,
    303, 309, 317, 327
Philipsz, Gerardus 77
Philipsz, Hendrik 77
Phoa Keng Hek 319
Pietersz, D.F. 371
Pietersz, Magdalena Claudina 158
Pijl, Laurens 52
Pijnacker Hordijk 298
Pijnacker Hordijk, Jacob Marinus
    112, 265
Pinège, Jacob 156
Pinket van Haak, Frederik Willem
    225–27
Piquerie, Vincent 44
Pires, Tomé 5

Pissuise, H. 386
Pit, Elisabeth 61
Pit, Johan 61
Pit, Laurens 61
Pit, Laurens, Jr. 61
Pit, Maarten 61
Pit, Maria 61
Polanen Petel, Henri Léonce van
    192, 193
Pompei 131
poor relief 49, 50, 51, 53, 67, 207,
    232, 233, 237–39, 241, 310
Pope, John 64
Portugal 4, 15, 23
Portuguese (descendants of) 3, 4–6,
    9, 11, 14–16, 19, 22–24, 28–30,
    39, 42, 47–49, 52–54, 63, 64,
    76, 77, 80–82, 143, 187, 188,
    191, 204, 207, 273, 284,
    344–48, 350, 351
poverty (*see also* pauperism) 26,
    31, 49, 50, 53, 60, 167, 170,
    219–23, 228–40, 242, 244,
    245, 250, 253, 255, 258,
    267–72, 279, 280, 282, 290,
    295, 297, 309, 310, 312
Pramudya Ananta Toer 343
Preanger *see* Priangan
Prehn, Van 137
Prehn, Henning Joachim van 362
Prehn, Rijck van 88
press *see* newspapers
Priangan 95, 97–99, 124–26, 128,
    263, 311
Principalities xvi, xvii, 44–46, 100,
    102, 103, 106–108, 110, 111,
    113, 116, 119–26, 128,
    130–37, 139, 141, 143, 149,
    158, 159, 188, 236, 260–65,
    297, 298, 323, 333, 363, 382,
    390
prostitution 16, 27, 29, 30–32,
    244, 245, 270

Public Limited Company (PLC)
    128, 139, 259, 262–66, 298
Puerto Rico 259, 265
Pupillenkorps *see* Army Training
    School
Purworejo 247

Queen Wilhelmina School 252
Queljoe, R.P. de 389
Quint, Hermina 77

Raaff 111, 124, 261
race 8, 21, 23–25, 32, 54, 82,
    215, 217, 218, 222, 231, 240,
    256, 271, 293, 294, 296, 319,
    322
Rach, Johannes 48
radicaal 132, 189, 192–99, 202,
    203, 211, 212, 251, 270, 346
Raffles, Marianne Olivia 87, 91
Raffles, Thomas Stamford 74, 85,
    88, 90–93, 96–98, 102, 145,
    183, 359
railways 121, 122, 130, 254, 255,
    292, 297, 299, 304, 306–308,
    314, 315, 388
Ramag (Busug) 113
Rappard, J.C. 101
Ratulangie, Sam (G.S.S.J.) 336
Reede tot de Parkeler, Johan
    Frederik van 70, 226
Rees, Pieter van 195, 252
regeringsreglement *see* Government
    Regulation
Registry of Births, Marriages and
    Deaths 116, 225
Registry Office xi, 161, 223–27,
    243
Reguleth, David 52
Reijnst 90
Reijnst, Joan Cornelis 199

Reinwardt, Caspar Georg Carl 92
Rembang 42, 279
Remij 133
residence permit 124
Reynst & Vinju 103, 139, 140, 235, 259
Rhemrev, J.L.T. 141
Ribalt, François 58
Ribalt, Frederik 58
Riebeeck, Elisabeth van 61
Riemsdijk, Van 96, 97, 186
Riemsdijk, Dina Cornelia van 216
Riemsdijk, Theodora Jacoba van 189
Rijk, Jules Constantijn 203
Rijke Schroeff, Adriaan 168, 170, 172
Rijkschroeff, Adriaan 169
Rijkschroeff, Adriaan Hendrik 168, 169
Rijkschroeff, Frits 169, 170, 172
Rijkschroeff, Roelandus Nicolaas 154, 155, 167, 168, 171
Risakotta 169
Rivai, Abdoel 330
Rizal, José 303
Rochussen, Jan Jacob 121, 191, 192, 194–97, 200–203
Rodrigo, Daniel 77
Roorda, Taco 118
Rooseboom, Willem 309
Rosie van Bima 78
Rosengain (Pulau Hatta) 157
Ryukyu 3

Salatiga 208
Salm, Abraham 260
Samanhoedi, Hadji 323
Santiap 44
Saparua 168, 333
Saptenno, Paula 148
Sara van Buton 146

Sarekat Islam 323, 325–27, 329, 332, 333
Sauh 287
Saul, Mariana Sarah 368
Sayers, Joseph Paul Henry 124
Schagen, Johan Paul 58
Scheltema, J.F. 288
Schenck, Willem 246
Schmidhamer, A.G. 371
Schmidhamer, Leonora 156
Schmidhamer, Ph.G. 382
Schulz, H. 71
Schumann, W.M.G. 329
Scott, Robert 102
Semarang 42, 43, 58, 70, 93, 97, 99, 102, 103, 107, 116, 120–23, 131, 137–39, 174, 180, 186–88, 192, 193, 208, 209, 216, 225, 228–31, 236–39, 241–43, 247, 249, 252, 253, 268, 269, 271, 282, 288–92, 298, 300, 301, 308, 315, 321, 323, 324, 333, 363, 386
Semeru 317
Senn van Basel, Huibrecht 71
Senn van Basel, Wilhelmina Henriëtte 189
Senn van Basel, Willem Adriaan 189
Serang 319, 329
shipowner 7, 9, 75, 103, 120, 145, 146, 164
shipping (private) 7, 15, 34–36, 55, 58, 67, 155, 162, 178, 232
Shiraishi Takashi 326
shopkeepers 25, 26, 36, 42, 71, 72, 102, 106, 116, 126, 130, 145, 150, 159, 163, 183, 188, 197, 219, 292
Shrapnell, James 98
Siam (Thailand) 3–5, 9–13, 58, 346, 349
Siberg, Johannes 73, 87, 88

Sidenreng 146
Silva, Petrus de 77
Sinagar Tjirohani estate company
    264
Singapore 82, 126, 145, 156, 157,
    178, 289, 290, 367, 385
Sinjo Frederik (Pangeran Timoer)
    272
Sintes 46
Siso, Alexander de 367
Siso, Eugenie 171
Siti Aisa Tanriollé 149
Skelton, Philip 98
slaves xi, xv, 4, 7, 12, 13, 24, 26,
    29–34, 37, 40, 42, 43, 46–54,
    63–65, 69–71, 74, 77, 78,
    80–82, 85, 87, 92–95, 134,
    143–46, 148–51, 153, 155–57,
    159–64, 166, 167, 191, 200,
    281, 285, 345, 347, 370
Sloet van de Beele, Ludolf A.J.W.
    121
Sluijsken, Pieter 56
Snackey, Arnold 279, 280, 285–87,
    289, 290
Snouck Hurgronje, Christiaan
    317, 319, 321, 335
Sociaal-Democratische Arbeiders
    Partij (SDAP) 304, 309, 347
Society for the Spread of Christian
    Standards and Mutual Benefit
    250
sociëteit (*see* club) 130, 133, 157,
    178, 183, 197, 202, 342
Soekarno 342
Soeria Soemirat 291, 292, 296,
    299, 302–304, 307
Soewardi Soerjaningrat 318, 322,
    326–28, 333, 338, 340
Solo *see* Surakarta
Solor 36
Somerset Maugham, W. 150
Soradjirang 147

Soselisa 172
Soselisa, E.R. 372
Soselisa, J.A. 329
South Africa 303, 317
Spain 285
Spanier, E. 71
Speelman 162
Sri Lanka *see* Ceylon
Staatsspoorbond (State Railway
    Union) 307, 388
Steijn Parvé, Jan Adriaan 75
Stel, Hendrik van der 58
Steur, Johannes van der 249–51
STOVIA (school for training native
    doctors) 174, 318–20, 347
Stralendorff, Van 46, 111, 137
Stralendorff, Carel van 264, 265
Stralendorff, Friedrich Christoph
    van 45, 46
Stralendorff, J. van 298
Stralendorff, J.C. van 298
Stralendorff, Johan Caspar van
    264
Stroo Westerman, J.F.L. 301, 387
Stuers, Hubert J.J.L. de 45, 222,
    246, 377, 380
Suez Canal 131
sugar 46, 58, 59, 105, 106, 109,
    120, 121, 123, 127, 128, 132,
    134, 135, 137, 139, 140, 166,
    216, 232, 239, 252, 254,
    258–60, 262, 263, 265, 266,
    269, 297–99, 303, 308, 310,
    317, 335–37, 341, 363, 365, 382
Suikerbond (Sugar Union) 337
Suikersyndicaat (Sugar Syndicate)
    337
Sukabumi 97, 98, 126, 137, 266
Sukoarjo 264, 265
Sulawesi xi, 36, 47, 61, 91, 99,
    100, 144, 146, 147, 149, 163,
    164, 166, 172, 177, 179–81,
    183, 194, 271, 308, 336

Sumatra 3, 5, 42, 78, 128, 137, 139, 141, 163, 170, 183, 239, 245, 260, 285, 287, 292, 297, 307, 308, 311, 320, 330, 333, 336, 337, 341, 366

Sumenep 91

Surabaya xi, 42, 43, 70, 79, 91, 97, 99, 102, 103, 106, 121, 123, 137, 140, 150, 174, 187, 194, 198, 205, 209, 210, 213, 221, 225, 226, 228–30, 237, 239, 252–54, 267, 269, 270, 272, 274, 279, 283, 288, 291, 301, 315, 323, 324, 345, 390

Surakarta (Solo) 44, 45, 100–102, 106, 107, 111–18, 120, 121, 123, 129–31, 133–36, 147, 163, 225, 261, 264–66, 279, 280, 291, 297, 323, 324, 347, 362, 363, 364

Surat 13, 67, 72

Taman Siswa schools 338

Tamils 3, 9, 14, 15, 18, 20, 40, 76, 77, 82

Tanete xi, xvii, 149

Tangerang 59, 194

Tanjung 97, 216, 328

Taylor, Jean Gelman 55, 60, 84

tea 105, 124–26, 128, 263, 329

technical school 134, 221, 252, 253, 255, 256, 301

Technical University 319–21, 329

Teeuwen, J.J.E. 330

Tegal 249, 260, 324

Tehupeiory, Wim K. 320, 389

Teisseire, Andries 58, 59

Teisseire, Guillaume 58

Teisseire, Guillaume Elie 59

tempo doeloe xviii, 171

Ternate 61, 75, 91, 92, 144, 148, 150, 156, 159, 161–66, 174, 175, 255, 278, 370, 384

Thaisa, K 11, 349

Thamrin, Hoesni 342, 343

Thanjavur 76

theatre 92, 93, 111, 123, 130, 157, 178, 273–76, 295, 305, 347

Theosophy 296, 318, 322, 329, 335, 342

Thomas, A.J. 207

Thomaszoon, Jan 51

Thomson, Harvey 102

Timmerman Thijssen 73, 75, 94, 110

Timmerman Thijssen, Elise Jeanne Antoinette 124

Timmerman Thijssen, Gesina (*see also* Couperus, Gesina) 74, 75, 91, 102

Timmerman Thijssen, Jan Samuel 73–75, 90, 100, 102, 124

Timmerman Thijssen, Olivia 74, 91

Timmerman Thijssen, Pieter Henry Meijer 100, 101

Timor 91, 162, 168, 171, 174, 175, 369

Tiong Hoa Hwee Koan 317, 320, 322

Titsingh, Isaac 67, 69

Titsingh, William 69

Tjokroaminoto 325, 329

tobacco 123, 128, 139, 140, 267, 268, 329

Tobias, Joan Hendrik 161, 370

Tomas de Fransman 12

Toorop, Jan 296

Topée, G.L. 327, 330

trade union xvii, 297, 304, 307, 308, 337, 339, 388

trading houses 101–103, 107, 109, 120, 126, 139, 141, 259, 261, 281

Tranquebar 73, 75

Tromp, Charles Christiaan 179, 180, 194
Trouerbach 180, 184
Trouerbach, Jacob 100
Tulloch, John 91
Tulloch, Stamford William Raffles 91
Tupass 24, 345, 347
Turkey 3
Tuyll van Serooskerken, Vincent G. baron 177

Uhlenbeck, Gerhard Hendrik 121, 125
Ukine 69
unemployment 162, 163, 186, 267, 268, 270, 275, 302, 309, 310, 337, 383
United States (*see also* America) 157, 178, 331, 340
Utrecht 56, 57, 77–79, 98

Valette, Gerardus Johannes Petrus 170, 181
Vasconcelos, José 319
Veer, Justus Pieter de 248
Velde, Charles William Meredith van de 165
Vereeniging van Spoor- en Tramwegpersoneel (Association of Railway and Tram Employees) 308
Vermaesen, J. 327
Verploegh, Fitz 255
Versteegh 157
Versteegh, A. 382
Versteegh, Anna Elisabeth 150
Versteegh, W.H. 369
Veth, Pieter Johannes 195
Visscher, C. 253
Visser 162

Vogels, Elisabeth 61
Volksraad see People's Council
Voll 146, 180, 184, 367
Voll, Jan Adriaan 367
Voll, Jan Hendrik 146
Volten, Anna Aleida 213
Voorneman, Adolph Martinus 279–83, 285, 286, 290, 291, 309, 320, 386
Voorneman, Frederik Karel 163, 278, 279
Voorneman, Johannes Nicolaas 163
Voorneman, Philippus Franciscus 163, 280, 365, 384
Vos, Ida Petronella Jacoba 70
Vos, Johannes 70
Voûte, C. 386
Vries, Dirk Hendrik de 171
Vuyst, Pieter 58

Waal Malefijt, Jan Hendrik de 310
Waasbergen, Rebekka Mathilda van 182
Wahidin Soediro Hoesoedo 317
Wajo 181
Wall, Hans van de (Victor Ido) 316
Wall, Victor Ido van de 153, 331
Wallace, Alfred Russell 144–48, 164, 181
Warnars, Marie 212
Waterloo, Battle of 94
Wawoeroentoe, Wilhelmina 372
Waworuntu, A.L. 329, 336
Weijdemuller, Joost 372
Weijergang 146, 367
Weijergang, Antonie Martin 367
Weijergang, J.G. 164
Weijnschenk 113, 119, 129, 131, 133, 136, 137, 141, 261, 265, 298
Weijnschenk, Ambrosina 264, 265

Weijnschenk, Cherrie 362
Weijnschenk, George 110, 111, 113, 114, 120, 121, 128, 136, 141, 362
Weijnschenk, George Lodewijk 110, 111, 113, 118–20, 123, 124, 362
Weijnschenk, Leopold 363
Westerhout 83
Westermann, Bernt Wilhelm 74, 102
Wieseman 265, 298
Wieseman, Frederik Wilhelm 112, 131, 132
Wijnschenk 133
Wilde, Andries de 97–99, 126, 137
Wilhelmina, Queen 321
Wilkens 116, 126
Wilkens, J.A. 117, 132
Willem I, King 94
Willem II, King 195, 198
Willem III Gymnasium 168, 181, 209–211, 213, 296, 300, 305
Winter 116, 126
Winter, Carel Friedrich 116–18, 132
Winter, Johannes Wilhelmus 116

Wiranata Koesoemo 335
Wit, Augusta de 297, 298
World War I 233, 318, 328, 330–32, 334, 335, 341
Wybrands, Karel 307, 315

Yap Guan Thay 274, 275
Yemen 3, 7
Yogyakarta 44–46, 70, 100, 102, 106, 107, 110–16, 118, 120, 121, 123, 124, 128, 129, 131–36, 216, 245, 261–63, 265, 279, 282, 297–99, 324, 363, 365
Young Ceylon 82, 277
youth culture 273

Zaalberg, Karel 316, 317, 322, 324, 325, 328, 332, 334, 336, 388
Zentgraaff, Henri Carel 315
Zom 133
Zoza, Anna de 49
Zutphen 255